IMPORTANT MACROECONOMIC DATA FOR THE U.S. ECONOMY: I

Year	GNP	C	I	G	NX	$GNP	CPI	M1	M2
1955	1,494.9	873.8	259.8	361.3	−0.0	406.0	80.3		
1956	1,525.7	899.8	257.8	363.7	4.3	428.2	81.5		
1957	1,551.1	919.7	243.4	381.1	7.0	451.0	84.2		
1958	1,539.3	932.9	221.4	395.3	−10.3	456.8	86.5		
1959	1,629.1	979.3	270.3	397.6	−18.2	495.8	87.3	141.4	293.3
1960	1,665.2	1,005.1	260.5	403.7	−4.0	515.3	88.6	141.4	304.3
1961	1,708.7	1,025.1	259.1	427.1	−2.7	533.8	89.6	144.3	324.9
1962	1,799.4	1,069.0	288.6	449.4	−7.5	574.7	90.6	147.9	350.2
1963	1,873.3	1,108.3	307.1	459.8	−1.9	606.9	91.8	152.4	379.7
1964	1,973.3	1,170.6	325.9	470.8	5.9	649.8	93.0	158.3	409.4
1965	2,087.6	1,236.3	367.0	486.9	−2.8	705.1	94.4	165.1	442.5
1966	2,208.4	1,298.9	390.5	532.6	−13.7	772.0	97.3	172.7	471.4
1967	2,271.3	1,337.7	374.4	576.1	−16.9	816.4	100.0	179.5	503.7
1968	2,365.6	1,405.8	391.8	597.7	−29.7	892.7	104.2	192.1	545.4
1969	2,423.3	1,456.6	410.3	591.2	−34.9	964.0	109.8	203.5	579.1
1970	2,416.2	1,492.0	381.6	572.6	−30.0	1,015.5	116.3	211.2	603.2
1971	2,484.8	1,538.7	419.3	566.5	−39.7	1,102.7	121.3	225.5	676.4
1972	2,608.5	1,621.8	465.4	570.7	−49.4	1,212.8	125.3	241.6	760.9
1973	2,744.0	1,689.6	520.8	565.3	−31.6	1,359.3	133.1	259.2	836.3
1974	2,729.3	1,674.0	481.3	573.1	0.8	1,472.8	147.7	272.2	887.2
1975	2,695.0	1,711.9	383.3	580.9	18.9	1,598.4	161.3	285.0	970.1
1976	2,826.7	1,803.9	453.6	580.3	−11.0	1,782.8	170.5	301.0	1,095.7
1977	2,958.7	1,883.7	521.3	589.1	−35.5	1,990.5	181.6	324.0	1,234.4
1978	3,115.2	1,960.9	576.9	604.1	−26.8	2,249.7	195.4	350.5	1,339.6
1979	3,192.3	2,004.4	575.2	609.2	3.5	2,508.2	217.5	377.6	1,450.2
1980	3,187.2	2,000.4	509.3	620.5	57.1	2,732.0	246.8	401.1	1,566.7
1981	3,248.7	2,024.2	545.5	629.7	49.3	3,052.6	272.4	429.4	1,714.6
1982	3,166.0	2,050.7	447.3	641.7	26.4	3,166.0	289.1	457.6	1,874.5
1983	3,277.6	2,145.9	503.4	647.8	−19.4	3,401.6	298.4	508.9	2,109.3
1984	3,492.0	2,239.9	661.3	675.9	−85.0	3,774.7	311.1	544.5	2,277.9
1985	3,570.0	2,313.0	645.0	716.4	−108.4	3,988.6	322.1	593.9	2,484.4

Note: GNP, C, I, G, and NX are in billions of 1982 dollars, and $GNP is in billions of current dollars. The CPI has a base year 1967 = 100; M1 and M2 are in billions of dollars.

IMPORTANT MACROECONOMIC DATA FOR THE U.S. ECONOMY: II

Year	Potential output	GNP gap	Unemployment rate	Inflation	T-Bill rate	Long-term rate
1955	1,485.6	−0.6	4.2	−0.3	1.7	2.8
1956	1,535.4	0.6	4.0	1.5	2.6	3.2
1957	1,586.5	2.3	4.1	3.4	3.2	3.6
1958	1,634.8	6.2	6.6	2.7	1.8	3.3
1959	1,689.6	3.7	5.3	0.9	3.4	4.3
1960	1,749.3	5.1	5.4	1.5	2.9	4.1
1961	1,809.2	5.9	6.5	1.1	2.4	3.9
1962	1,863.7	3.6	5.4	1.2	2.8	3.9
1963	1,934.7	3.3	5.5	1.3	3.2	4.0
1964	1,895.8	−3.9	5.0	1.3	3.5	4.1
1965	1,966.1	−5.8	4.4	1.6	3.9	4.3
1966	2,103.7	−4.7	3.4	3.0	4.9	4.9
1967	2,144.7	−5.6	3.7	2.8	4.3	5.1
1968	2,251.0	−4.8	3.5	4.2	5.3	5.6
1969	2,393.1	−1.2	3.4	5.4	6.7	6.7
1970	2,390.4	−1.1	4.9	5.9	6.4	7.3
1971	2,410.2	−3.0	5.8	4.2	4.3	6.2
1972	2,478.1	−5.0	5.5	3.3	4.1	6.2
1973	2,717.7	−1.0	4.8	6.2	7.0	6.8
1974	2,747.4	0.7	5.5	11.0	7.8	7.6
1975	2,830.9	5.0	8.3	9.2	5.8	8.0
1976	2,914.4	3.1	7.6	5.7	5.0	7.6
1977	3,000.4	1.4	7.0	6.5	5.3	7.4
1978	3,088.9	−0.8	6.0	7.6	7.2	8.4
1979	3,180.0	−0.4	5.8	11.3	10.1	9.4
1980	3,273.7	2.7	7.1	13.5	11.4	11.6
1981	3,353.4	3.2	7.5	10.4	14.0	13.9
1982	3,424.7	8.1	9.6	6.2	10.6	13.0
1983	3,497.5	6.7	9.4	3.2	8.6	11.1
1984	3,571.9	2.3	7.4	4.3	9.5	12.4
1985	3,647.9	2.1	7.1	3.5	7.5	10.6

Note: Potential output is in billions of 1982 dollars; all other series are percentages. The GNP gap and potential output are based for the period following 1973 on the 6 percent unemployment benchmark. The inflation rate is for the CPI.

MACRO-
ECONOMICS

McGRAW-HILL BOOK COMPANY

New York   St. Louis   San Francisco   Auckland
Bogotá   Hamburg   London
Madrid   Mexico   Milan   Montreal   New Delhi
Panama   Paris   São Paulo   Singapore
Sydney   Tokyo   Toronto

MACRO- FOURTH EDITION
ECONOMICS

RUDIGER DORNBUSCH
STANLEY FISCHER

Department of Economics
Massachusetts Institute of Technology

MACRO-ECONOMICS

34567890   DODO   89098

ISBN 0-07-017776-7

This book was set in Caledonia by Progressive Typographers, Inc.
The editor was Paul V. Short;
the designer was Jo Jones;
the production supervisor was Diane Renda.
The cover was designed by Joseph Gillians.
New drawings were done by J & R Services, Inc.
R. R. Donnelley & Sons Company was printer and binder.

Library of Congress Cataloging-in-Publication Data

Dornbusch, Rudiger.
   Macroeconomics.

   Includes bibliographical references and index.
   1. Macroeconomics.   I. Fischer, Stanley.   II. Title.
HB172.5.D67   1987   339   86-21114
ISBN 0-07-017776-7

ABOUT THE AUTHORS

Rudiger Dornbusch did his undergraduate work in Switzerland, and holds a Ph.D. from the University of Chicago. He has taught at Chicago, Rochester, and since 1975 at MIT. His research is primarily in international economics, with a major macroeconomic component. His special research interests are the behavior of exchange rates and, more recently, high inflation and hyperinflation. He visits and lectures extensively in Europe and in Latin America, where he takes an active interest in problems of stabilization policy, and has held visiting appointments in Brazil and Argentina. His writing includes *Open Economy Macroeconomics* and, with Stanley Fischer, *Economics*. His interests in public policy take him frequently to testify before Congress and to participate in international conferences. He regularly contributes newspaper editorials on current policy issues here and abroad.

Stanley Fischer was an undergraduate at the London School of Economics and has a Ph.D. from MIT. He taught at the University of Chicago while Rudi Dornbusch was a student there, starting a long friendship and collaboration. Since 1973 he has taught at MIT, and spent several leaves at the Hebrew University in Jerusalem. His main research interests are in monetary theory and macroeconomic policy. He has published widely in these areas and participates regularly in scholarly meetings. He is the editor of the *NBER Macroeconomics Annual*, initiated by the National Bureau of Economic Research to bridge the gap between theory and policy in the macroeconomic area. He frequently testifies before Congress, and has served as a consultant to the World Bank.

TO
RHODA

CONTENTS

Preface   xi

PART ONE

1   Introduction   3
2   National Income Accounting   29
3   Aggregate Demand and Equilibrium Income and Output   63
4   Money, Interest, and Income   111
5   Fiscal Policy, Crowding Out, and the Policy Mix   153
6   International Linkages   179
7   Aggregate Supply and Demand: An Introduction   219

PART TWO

8   Consumption and Saving   253
9   Investment Spending   289
10 The Demand for Money   333
11 The Money Supply, the Fed, and Monetary Policy   369
12 Stabilization Policy: Prospects and Problems   415

PART THREE

13 Aggregate Supply: Wages, Prices, and Employment   461
14 Inflation and Unemployment   499
15 The Tradeoffs between Inflation and Unemployment   537
16 Budget Deficits and the Public Debt   581
17 Money, Deficits, and Inflation   623
18 Macroeconomics: The Interaction of Events and Ideas   659
19 Long-term Growth and Productivity   697
20 Money, Prices, and Exchange Rates   733

Index   775

PREFACE

This fourth edition started out to be a modest revision, and ended as the most radical of our three revisions of *Macroeconomics*. There are three major organizational changes:

- Chapter 6, "International Linkages," brings the introduction to open economy macroeconomics up front, where it belongs, as the United States becomes an increasingly open economy — in both the goods and the capital markets.

- We have moved "Aggregate Supply and Demand: An Introduction" to Chapter 7, so that instructors can present a complete aggregate supply-demand model earlier in the course. Students can now discuss inflation using a simple model well before the midterm. Those instructors who prefer the arrangement of the first three editions, in which the detailed material developing the aggregate demand side of the economy (contained now in Chapters 8 to 12) precedes aggregate supply, may choose to defer Chapter 7 for later.

- We have added a new Chapter, 17, "Money, Deficits, and Inflation," that both presents new material and brings together material on these topics previously spread through the book. Our experience has shown that students are fascinated by the topics treated in this chapter.

As to our general approach, we repeat here what we said in the preface to the third edition. We have remained faithful to our basic approach — presenting the relevant theory and at the same time showing both its empirical relevance and policy applications. We have, of course, stayed with our general eclectic outlook on macroeconomics. But there have been changes in details of the presentation and the weight given various topics, to meet the changing emphasis of macroeconomic issues and theory over the last few years.

In this edition we have added material on the microfoundations of macroeconomics, and substantially increased the space devoted to the rational expectations-equilibrium approach to macroeconomics. Chapter 18, "Macroeconomics: The Interaction of Events and Ideas," presents the ideas underlying frontier developments in the field at a level appropriate for an intermediate text. The instructor who makes a detailed comparison with the third edition will find changes throughout — for instance, in the addition of material on the share economy in Chapter 18, on base drift in Chapter 11, on the sacrifice ratio and disinflation in Chapter 14, on debt and adjustment in developing countries in Chapter 20.

By popular request we have restored to this edition the dynamic model of aggregate supply and demand (originally Chapter 13), whose removal from the third edition caused far more dismay than we had anticipated. That now appears in Chapter 14, and is used also in Chapter 17. The simplest aggregate supply-demand model (now Chapter 7) has also been revised after suggestions by users (including ourselves) and reviewers.

Although there are major changes from earlier editions, the book remains recognizably the same in that it develops, and teaches students to use, a broad-based, critical, and useful macroeconomics. Our overriding objective is to explain how modern macroeconomics is used in understanding important economic issues, and to help the reader analyze macroeconomic issues for herself or himself. The book provides full coverage of all major topics in macroeconomics. No important topic has been omitted because it is too difficult, but we have taken great pains to make nothing more difficult than it need be.

TEACHING AIDS

An *Instructor's Manual*, prepared by Professor Patricia Pando of Houston Baptist University, is available to accompany this edition. Professor Pando has updated and improved the *Instructor's Manual* that she prepared for the third edition. The *Study Guide* by Professor Richard Startz of the University of Washington, Seattle, has also been updated.

Professor Ben Bernanke of Princeton, one of the profession's best teachers, has prepared a book of case studies and readings to accompany *Macroeconomics*. Further assistance comes from a data diskette, from Data Resources Inc., which includes data series, numerical problems, and answers to some of the questions in this book. A major benefit of the diskette is that it will be updated annually.

For this fourth edition, as for the first and third, we shall be preparing a yearly *Update* to the book, which will be made available to instructors by McGraw-Hill. Instructors who have adopted the text may obtain copies of the *Instructor's Manual*, and, in due course, the *Update*, from their local McGraw-Hill sales representative.

ACKNOWLEDGMENTS

In writing this book in its various editions we have had much help from friends, present and former students, and colleagues who advised us on how to improve the book. We wish to thank especially Andrew Abel, Richard Anderson, Yves Balcer, Robert Bishop, Olivier Blanchard, Cary Brown, Eliana Cardoso, Jacques Cremer, Allen Drazen, Robert Feldman, Jeffrey Frankel, Jacob Frenkel, Ronald Jones, Paul Joskow, Edi Karni, Tim Kehoe, Robert Pindyck, Donald Richter, David Romer, Michael Rothschild, Paul Samuelson, Steven Sheffrin, Robert Solow, Richard Startz, Larry Summers, Peter Temin, Michael Schmid, Charles Steindel, Hal Varian, and Michael Veall.

Many readers and users of our book have given us the benefit of their teaching experience and particular suggestions. We would like to thank especially Eskarder Alvi, Joseph Aubareda, Alan Auerbach, Francis Bator, Thomas Bonsor, Carl Christ, David Colander, Giacomo Costa, Kevin Davis, Jim Devine, Clifford B. Donn, Gerald Egerer, Robert Eisner, Liang Shing Fan, George Feiwel, Rendigs Fels, Benjamin Friedman, Joanna Froyden, James Gale, Charles C. Gillete, Micha Gisser, Kalmon Goldberg, Robert J. Gordon, Joseph Guerin, John Haltiwanger, Raundi Halvorson, Dennis J. Hanseman, Brian Horrigan, Mike Jacobson, James Johannes, O. Honkalehto, Yoshiaki Kaoru, S. W. Kardasz, John Kareken, M. P. Kidd, David Laidler, Kathleen Langley, David Levhari, Michael Lopez, Barry A. Love, Jaime Marquez, David McClain, Erwin Miller, Richard Miller, Douglas W. Mitchell, Masanori Morita, Robert Murphy, John Naylor, Norman Obst, Edward Akova Offenbacher, Patricia Pando, Lochlan H. Rose, Thomas Russell, Walter Salant, Robert Schenk, Edward Shapiro, Masaki Shinbo, Richard Startz, Kirker Stevens, Houston Stokes, Earl Thompson, Hal Varian, David H. Vrooman, Shinichi Watanabe, Ken West and Randy Williams.

We owe a special debt to reviewers of various editions who prepared very detailed comments and suggestions. We would like to mention especially Lloyd Atkinson, Alan Deardorff, Don Heckerman, Thomas Mayer, William Poole, Steven Shapiro, Michael Babcock, Arnold Collery, William Hosek, Timothy Kersten, Charles Knapp, Charles Lieberman, Andrew Policano, James Duga, Michael Edgmand, Hajime Miyazaki, Aris Protopapadakis, Stephen Van der Ploeg, Ben Bernanke, Shirley Browning, and Roland Artle. McGraw-Hill and the authors would like to thank the following reviewers for their useful suggestions: Ian Bain, University of Minnesota; John Burkett, University of Rhode Island; Dale Henderson, Georgetown University; David McClain, Boston University; Walter W. McMahon, University of Illinois; and Michael J. Sattinger, SUNY at Albany.

Over the years we have enjoyed and benefitted from the most competent and dedicated research assistance. We would like to thank particularly Carl Shapiro and David Modest who helped us with the first two editions and Michael Gavin and Patricia Mosser who did the work for the third edition. Carol McIntire, Liz Walb, Barbara Ventresco, Nancy Johnson, and Carolyn Dedutis have at different times performed valiant and cheerful feats in handling drafts of chapters. For this edition we are grateful for assistance by Takeo Hoshi and Pat Petraccia.

TO THE STUDENT

Macroeconomics is not cut and dried. There are disputes over basic issues — for instance, over whether the government should try actively to fight unemployment. That makes macroeconomics unsatisfying if you are looking for clearcut, definite answers to all the economy's problems. But it should also make it more interesting because you have to think hard and critically about the material being presented.

Despite the disagreements, there is a substantial basic core of macroeconomics that we present in this book, and that will continue to be useful in understanding the behavior of the economy. We have not hesitated to say where we think theories are incomplete, or where the evidence on a question is not yet decisive. But we have not hesitated, either, to describe the many areas in which macroeconomic theory does a good job of explaining the real world.

Because we have not shied away from important topics even if they are difficult, parts of the book require careful reading. There is no mathematics except simple algebra. Some of the analysis, however, involves sustained reasoning. Careful reading should therefore pay off in enhanced understanding. Chapter 1 gives you suggestions on how to learn from this book. The single most important suggestion is that you learn actively. Some of the chapters (such as Chapter 12) are suitable for bedtime reading, but most are not. Use pencil and paper to be sure you are following the argument. See if you can find reasons to disagree with arguments we make. Work the problem sets! Be sure you understand the points contained in the summaries to each chapter. Follow the economic news in the press, and see how that relates to what you are learning. Try to follow the logic of the budget or any economic packages the administration may present. Occasionally, the chairpersons of the Federal Reserve Board or the Council of Economic Advisers testify before the Congress. Read what they have to say, and see if it makes sense to you.

A *Study Guide*, prepared and updated by Richard Startz of the University of Washington, Seattle, is available to accompany this edition. The *Study Guide* contains a wide range of questions, starting from the very easy and progressing in each chapter to material that will challenge the more advanced student. It is a great help in studying, particularly since active learning is so important.

Rudiger Dornbusch
Stanley Fischer

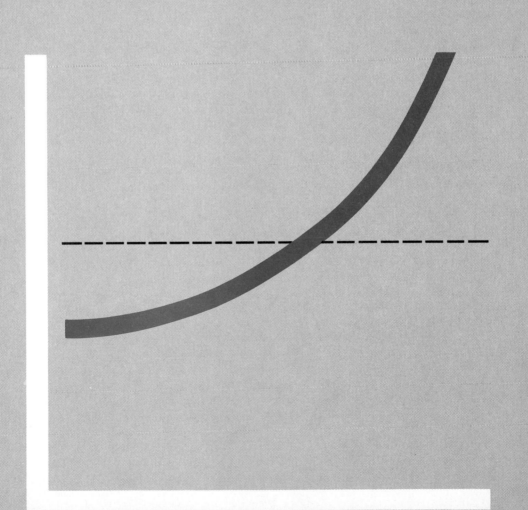

1

INTRODUCTION

Macroeconomics is concerned with the behavior of the economy as a whole — with booms and recessions, the economy's total output of goods and services and the growth of output, the rates of inflation and unemployment, the balance of payments, and exchange rates. To study the overall performance of the economy, macroeconomics focuses on the economic behavior and policies that affect that performance — on consumption and investment, the determinants of changes in wages and prices, monetary and fiscal policies, the money stock, the federal budget, interest rates, the national debt. In brief, macroeconomics deals with the major economic issues and problems of the day.

Macroeconomics is interesting because it deals with important issues. But it is fascinating and challenging too, because it reduces complicated details of the economy to manageable essentials. *Those essentials lie in the interactions among the goods, labor, and assets markets of the economy.*

In dealing with the essentials, we have to disregard details of the behavior of individual economic units, such as households and firms, or the determination of prices in particular markets, or the effects of monopoly on individual markets. These are the subject matter of microeconomics. In macroeconomics we deal with the market for goods as a whole, treating all the markets for different goods — such as the markets for agricultural products and for medical services — as a single market. Similarly, we deal with the labor market as a whole, abstracting from differences between the markets for, say, migrant labor and doctors. We deal with the assets markets as a whole, abstracting from the differences between the markets for IBM shares and Rembrandt paintings. The cost of the abstraction is that omitted details sometimes matter. The benefit of the abstraction is increased understanding of the vital interactions among the goods, labor, and assets markets.

Despite the contrast between macroeconomics and microeconomics, there is no basic conflict between them. After all, the economy in the aggregate is nothing but the sum of its submarkets. The difference between microeconomics and macroeconomics is therefore primarily one of emphasis and exposition. In studying price determination in a single industry, it is convenient for microeconomists to assume that prices in other industries are given. In macroeconomics, where we study the price level, it is for the most part sensible to ignore changes in relative prices of goods among different industries. In microeconomics, it is convenient to assume the total income of all consumers is given and to ask how consumers divide their spending out of that income among different goods. In macroeconomics, by contrast, the aggregate level of income or spending is among the key variables to be studied.

The great macroeconomists, including Keynes, and modern American leaders in the field — the older Nobel Prize–winning generation such as Milton Friedman of the University of Chicago and the Hoover Institution, Franco Modigliani of the Massachusetts Institute of Technology, and James Tobin of Yale University, and the younger generation such as Martin Feldstein of Harvard University, Robert Lucas of the University of Chicago, and Thomas Sargent of the University of Minnesota — have all had a keen interest in the applications of macrotheory to problems of policy making. Indeed, developments in macrotheory are closely related to the economic problems of the day. Keynesian economics developed during the great depression of the 1930s and showed the way out of such depressions. Monetarism developed during the 1960s, promising a way of solving the inflation problem. *Supply-side economics* became the fad of the early 1980s, promising an easy way out of the economic mess of the time, by cutting taxes. But supply-side economics overpromised, and there was no easy way out.

Because macroeconomics is closely related to the economic problems of the day, it does not yield its greatest rewards to those whose primary interest is theoretical. The need for compromise between the comprehensiveness of the theory and its manageability inevitably makes macrotheory a little untidy at the edges. And the emphasis in macroeconomics is on the manageability of the theory and on its applications. To demonstrate that emphasis, this book uses the theories we present to illuminate economic events from the great depression to the 1980s. We also refer continually to real world events to elucidate the meaning and the relevance of the theoretical material.

Schools of Thought

There have for long been two intellectual traditions in macroeconomics. One school of thought believes that markets work best if left to themselves; another believes that government intervention can significantly improve the operation of the economy. In the 1960s the debate on these questions involved *monetarists*, led by Milton Friedman, on one side and *Keynesians*, including Franco Modigliani and James Tobin, on the other side. In the 1970s the debate on much the same issues brought to the fore a new group — the *new classical macroeconomists* — including among the leaders Robert Lucas and Thomas Sargent. That group remains influential in the macroeconomics of the 1980s.

The new classical macroeconomics shares many policy views with Friedman. It sees the world as one where individuals act rationally in their self-interest in markets that adjust rapidly to changing conditions. The government, it is claimed, is likely only to make things worse by intervening. That model is a challenge to traditional macroeconomics, which sees a role for useful government action in an economy which is viewed as adjusting sluggishly, with rigidities, poor information, and social customs impeding the rapid clearing of markets.

Macroeconomics is often presented as the battleground between implacably opposed schools of thought. There is no denying that there are conflicts of opinion and even theory between different camps. And because macroeconomics is about the real world, the differences that exist are sure to be highlighted in political and media discussions of economic policy. But it is also the case that there are significant areas of agreement and that the different groups, through discussion and research, continually evolve new areas of consensus and a sharper idea of where precisely the differences lie. In this book we do not emphasize the debate, preferring to discuss the substantive matters while indicating alternative views of an issue whenever relevant.

We shall now in Section 1-1 present an overview of the key concepts with which macroeconomics deals. Section 1-2 examines relationships among the main macroeconomic variables, while Section 1-3 discusses stabilization policy. Section 1-4 presents a diagrammatic introduction to aggregate demand and supply and their interaction; it gives a very general perspective on the fundamentals of macroeconomics and the organization of this book. Then, in Section 1-5, we outline the approach of the book to the study of macroeconomics and macropolicy making, and present a preview of the order in which topics are taken up. Section 1-6 contains brief remarks on how to use the book.

1-1 KEY CONCEPTS

Gross National Product

Gross National Product (GNP) is the value of all goods and services produced in the economy in a given time period (quarter or year). **GNP is the basic measure of economic activity.**

Figure 1-1 shows two measures of **GNP** — *nominal,* or *current dollar,*

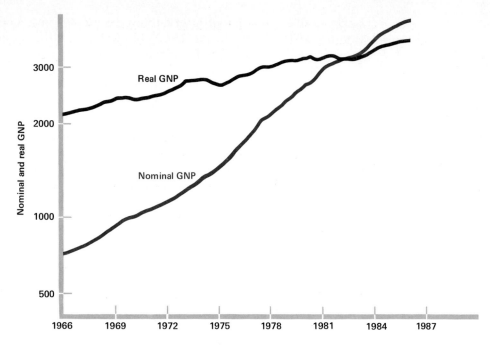

FIGURE 1-1   REAL AND NOMINAL GNP, 1966–1986. (*Source:* Data Resources, Inc.) Nominal GNP measures the output of final goods and services produced in the economy in a given period, using the prices of that period. Real GNP measures the value of the output using the prices of a *given* year, in this case 1982. Nominal GNP has risen more rapidly than real GNP because prices have been rising.

GNP and *real*, or *constant dollar*, GNP.[1] Nominal GNP measures the value of output at the prices prevailing in the period the output is produced, while real GNP measures the output produced in any one period at the prices of some base year. At present, 1982 serves as the base year for real output measurement. GNP statistics become available quarterly.

In Figure 1-1 nominal GNP is equal to $3,989 billion in 1985 and $1,598 billion in 1975. Thus nominal GNP grew at an average rate of 9.6 percent during that period. If we divide total GNP by population, we obtain per capita nominal GNP, which was $16,700 in 1985. Accordingly, the average value of output produced in the U.S. economy in 1985 was $16,700 per

---

[1] Notice that the scale for GNP in Fig. 1-1 is not linear. The scale is logarithmic, which means that equal ratios are represented by equal distances. For instance, the distance from 900 to 1,800 is the same as the distance from 1,200 to 2,400 since GNP doubles in both cases. On a logarithmic scale, a variable growing at a constant rate (e.g., 4 percent per annum) is represented by a straight line.

member of the population. Real GNP was \$3,570 billion in 1985 and \$2,695 billion in 1975, implying an average annual growth rate of real GNP of only 2.9 percent over the period.

Inflation and Nominal GNP

Figure 1-1 shows that nominal GNP has risen much more rapidly than real GNP. The difference between the growth rates of real and nominal GNP occurs because the prices of goods have been rising, or there has been *inflation*. The inflation rate is the percentage rate of increase of the level of prices during a given period.

Real GNP grew at an average rate of 2.9 percent over the 10 years from 1975 to 1985, while nominal GNP grew at an average annual rate of 9.6 percent per year. Because real GNP is calculated holding the prices of goods constant, the difference is entirely due to inflation, or rising prices. Over the 10-year period, prices were on average rising at 6.7 percent per year. In other words, the average rate of inflation over that period was 6.7 percent per year.

With 1982 as the base year for the prices at which output is valued, we observe in Figure 1-1 two implications of the distinction between nominal and real GNP. First, in 1982 the two are equal, because in the base year, current and constant dollars are the same dollars. Second, with inflation, nominal GNP rises faster than real GNP, and therefore, after 1982, nominal GNP exceeds real GNP. The converse is, of course, true before 1982.

Growth and Real GNP

We turn next to the reasons for the growth of real GNP. The *growth rate* of the economy is the rate at which real GNP is increasing. Anytime we refer to growth or the growth rate without any other qualifying word, we mean the growth rate of GNP. On average, most economies grow by a few percent per year over long periods. For instance, U.S. real GNP grew at an average rate of 3.1 percent per year from 1960 to 1985. But this growth has certainly not been smooth, as Figure 1-1 confirms.

What causes GNP to grow? The first reason real GNP changes is that the available amount of resources in the economy changes. The resources are conveniently split into capital and labor. The labor force, consisting of people either working or looking for work, grows over time and thus provides one source of increased production. The capital stock, including buildings and machines, likewise has been rising over time, providing another source of increased output. Increases in the availability of factors of production — the labor and capital used in the production of goods and services — thus account for part of the increase in real GNP.

The second reason for real GNP to change is that the efficiency with which factors of production work may change.[2] Over time, the same factors of production can produce more output. These increases in the efficiency of production result from changes in knowledge, including learning by doing, as people learn through experience to perform familiar tasks better.

Employment and Unemployment

The third source of change in real GNP is a change in the employment of the given resources available for production. Not all the capital and labor available to the economy are actually used at all times.

The *unemployment rate* is the fraction of the labor force that cannot find jobs. For example, in 1982, a reduction in the employment of labor, or a rise in unemployment, shows up in Figure 1-1 as a fall in real GNP. Indeed, in that year unemployment rose to 10.6 percent, the highest unemployment rate in the post–World War II period. More than one person out of every ten who wanted to work could not find a job. Such unemployment levels had not been experienced since the great depression of the 1930s.

Inflation, Growth, and Unemployment: The Record

Macroeconomic performance is judged by the three broad measures we have introduced: the *inflation* rate, the *growth* rate of output, and the rate of *unemployment.* News of these three variables makes the headlines, because they affect our daily lives.

When the inflation rate is high, the prices of goods people buy are rising. Partly for this reason, inflation is unpopular, even if people's incomes rise along with the prices. Inflation is also unpopular because it is often associated with other disturbances to the economy — such as the oil price increases of the 1970s — that would make people worse off even if there were no inflation. Inflation is frequently a major political issue, as it was, for instance, in the 1980 presidential election between Presidents Carter and Reagan, when the high rate of inflation contributed to President Reagan's victory.

When the growth rate is high, the production of goods and services is rising, making possible an increased standard of living. Along with the high growth rate typically goes lower unemployment, and more jobs. High growth is a target and hope of most societies.

For the long run, the growth rate of real GNP per person is the most important of all the macroeconomic performance indicators. Per capita GNP doubles every 35 years if it grows at 2 percent a year. In that case, each generation could look forward to a material standard of living double that of its parents. If per capita GNP grows at 1 percent per annum, it takes 70 years to

---

[2] These efficiency improvements are often called productivity increases.

double. Over long periods, small differences in growth rates mount up to big differences in the material standard of living.

High unemployment rates are a major social problem. Jobs are difficult to find. The unemployed suffer a loss in their standard of living, personal distress, and sometimes a lifetime deterioration in their career opportunities. When unemployment reaches 11 percent—and even well short of that—it becomes the number one social and political issue.

Macroeconomic Performance, 1952–1985

Table 1-1 shows that economic performance in the United States deteriorated sharply from the decade of the sixties to the seventies. Inflation and unemployment increased and growth fell.

The table also shows the radical change in inflation performance since 1982. As the economy recovered from high unemployment in 1981–1982, the unemployment rate began to fall, growth increased, and inflation stayed low. Many hoped that the economy was in for another high-growth, low-inflation decade like the sixties. Collapsing oil prices in 1985–1986 reinforced that hope.

As we develop macroeconomics in this book, we are looking for answers to the questions that recent macroeconomic performance raises. Why did the inflation rate rise from the fifties to the seventies and then fall rapidly? Will the growth rate return to levels of the 1960s? Can the unemployment rate be reduced? And, of course, what economic policies, if any, can produce low inflation, low unemployment, and high growth?

TABLE 1-1 MACROECONOMIC PERFORMANCE, 1952–1985

Period	Inflation, % p.a.	Growth, % p.a.	Unemployment rate, % of the labor force
1952–1962	1.3	2.9	5.1
1962–1972	3.3	4.0	4.7
1972–1982	8.7	2.2	7.0
1981–1982	6.1	−1.9	9.7
1983–1985	3.7	4.1	8.0

Source: *Economic Report of the President, 1986. Note:* Unemployment rate is average of rates for years shown; inflation rate is for CPI, year over year; "p.a." means per annum.

The Business Cycle and the Output Gap

Inflation, growth, and unemployment are related through the *business cycle.* The business cycle is the more or less regular pattern of expansion (recovery) and contraction (recession) in economic activity around the path of trend growth. At a cyclical *peak,* economic activity is high relative to trend, and at a cyclical *trough,* the low point in economic activity is reached. **Inflation, growth, and unemployment all have clear cyclical patterns as we will show below. For the moment we concentrate on measuring the behavior of output or real GNP relative to trend over the business cycle.**

Figure 1-2 shows by the black line, the trend path of real GNP. The trend path of GNP is the path GNP would take if factors of production were fully employed. Over time real GNP will change for two reasons, as we already noted. First, more resources become available: the size of the population increases; firms acquire machinery or build plants; land is improved for cultivation; the stock of knowledge increases as new goods and new methods of production are invented and introduced. This increased availability of resources allows the economy to produce more goods and services, resulting in a rising trend level of output.

FIGURE 1-2   THE BUSINESS CYCLE. Output or GNP does not grow smoothly at its trend rate. Rather, it fluctuates irregularly around trend, showing business cycle patterns from trough, through recovery, to peak, and then from peak, through recession, back to the trough. Business cycle output movements are not regular in timing or in size.

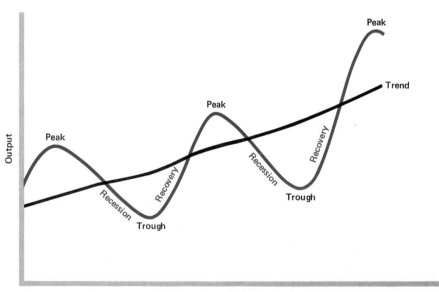

But, second, factors are not fully employed all the time.[3] Output is not always at its trend level. Rather it fluctuates around trend in the business cycle. During an *expansion* (or *recovery*) the *employment* of factors of production increases, and that is a source of increased production. Output can rise above trend because people work overtime, and machinery is used for several shifts. Conversely, during a *recession* unemployment develops and less output is produced than can in fact be produced with the existing resources and technology. The wavy line in Figure 1-2 shows these cyclical departures of output from trend. Deviations of output from trend are referred to as the *output gap*. The output gap measures the gap between actual output and the output the economy could produce at full employment given the existing resources. Full-employment output is also called *potential output.*

$$\text{Output gap} \equiv \text{potential output} - \text{actual output} \qquad (1)$$

The output gap allows us to measure how large the cyclical deviations of output from potential output or trend output (we use these terms interchangeably) are. Figure 1-3 shows actual and potential output for the United States. The shaded lines represent recessions, with the letters *P* and *T* denoting cyclical peaks and troughs.[4]

The figure shows that the output gap grows during a recession, such as in 1982. More resources become unemployed, and actual output falls below potential. Conversely, during an expansion, most strikingly in the long expansion of the 1960s, the gap declines and ultimately even becomes negative. A negative gap means that there is overemployment, overtime of workers, and more than the usual rate of utilization of machinery. It is worth noting that the gap is sometimes very sizable. For example, in 1982 it amounted to as much as 10 percent.

Establishing the level of potential output is a difficult problem. In the 1960s it was believed that full employment corresponds to a measured rate of unemployment of 4 to 4.5 percent of the labor force. Changes in the composition of the labor force toward younger workers and female workers who change jobs more frequently raised the estimate of the full employment rate of unemployment to a range around 6 percent in the early 1980s.

---

[3] Full employment of factors of production is an economic, not a physical, concept. Physically, labor is fully employed if everyone is working 16 hours a day all year. Economically, there is full employment of labor when everyone who wants a job can find one within a reasonable amount of time. Because the economic definition is not precise, we typically define full employment of labor by some convention, for example that labor is fully employed when the unemployment rate is 6 percent. Capital similarly is never fully employed in a physical sense; for example, office buildings or lecture rooms, which are part of the capital stock, are used only part of the day.

[4] Dating of the business cycle is done by the National Bureau of Economic Research (NBER). The NBER is a private, nonprofit research organization based in Cambridge, Massachusetts.

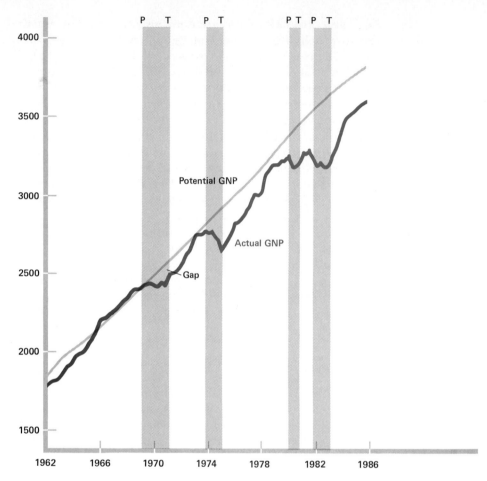

FIGURE 1-3   ACTUAL AND POTENTIAL OUTPUT, 1962–1985.
Potential output is the full employment level of output. It grows like trend
output in Figure 1-2. Actual GNP fluctuates around potential, falling
below during recession, and rising back toward the potential level during
recoveries. Shaded areas represent recessions.

The potential output data shown in Figure 1-3 are calculated by the
Bureau of Economic Analysis (BEA) of the U.S. Department of Commerce.
They correspond to the level of output that would exist if the unemployment
rate were 6 percent. The BEA does not refer to the series as potential output,
but rather as the output level corresponding to 6 percent unemployment. The
series is a benchmark for calculating what potential output or full employment
output is, but it is only a benchmark, not a rigid, undebatable rule. Even so, the

GNP gap provides an important indicator of how the economy is performing and in which direction policies should try to move the level of activity.[5]

Much of recent history can be read from the GNP gap. In the Kennedy-Johnson years (1961–1968) the output gap declined under the impact of expansionary government policies. The policies were successful in reducing the gap, but did so at the cost of building up inflationary pressures. The Nixon administration (1969–1973) inherited this inflation problem and decided to fight it by tight policies that led to a recession and thus a growing gap. In 1972–1973, highly expansionary monetary policies of the Federal Reserve System led to recovery and even overemployment shown by a negative gap, actual output exceeding potential. In 1973–1974, tight policies together with the huge increases in oil prices threw the economy into a deep recession. Recovery from that recession in the 1976–1979 period was too fast and led to sharp increases in inflation. With the aid of another rapid rise in oil prices in 1979, inflation by 1980 had come to exceed 10 percent, and again tight policies drove the economy into a recession in 1980–1981 and also in 1981–1982. The recessions, as can be seen from the gap, were very severe and in that way made a deep cut in the inflation rate. From 1982, the economy recovered fast and began to close the output gap.

1-2 RELATIONSHIPS AMONG MACROECONOMIC VARIABLES

The preliminary look at the data presented above, and our discussion of the business cycle, suggests — correctly — that we should expect to find simple relationships among the major macroeconomic variables, growth, unemployment, and inflation. There are indeed such relationships, as we now document.

Growth and Unemployment

We have already noted that changes in the employment of factors of production provide one of the sources of growth in real GNP. We would then expect high GNP growth to be accompanied by declining unemployment. That is indeed the case, as we observe from Figure 1-4. On the vertical axis, Figure 1-4 shows the growth rate of output in a particular year and on the horizontal axis the change in the unemployment rate in that year. For example, in 1984, the growth rate of output was 6.5 percent and the reduction in the unemployment rate was 2.1 percentage points. Thus we plot the point labeled 1984 in the upper left-hand region. That region corresponds to a period of expansion and falling unemployment rates.

---

[5] The BEA does not use the term *potential output* so that it is not seen as suggesting that the economy *should* have a 6 percent unemployment rate when in fact unemployment has been above 6 percent for 5 years, as it has been since 1980. That way it would seem to be criticizing the government of which it is a part.

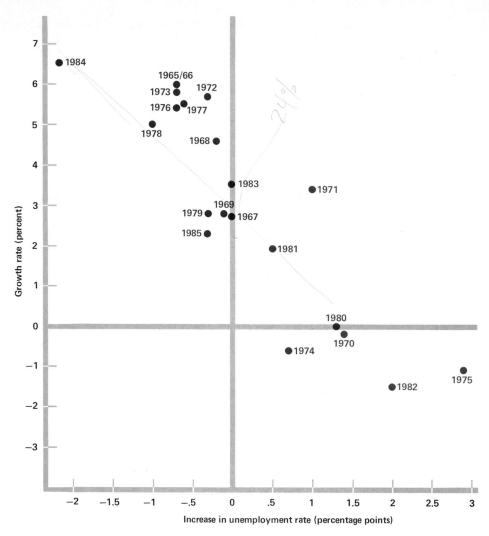

FIGURE 1-4 GROWTH AND THE CHANGE IN THE UNEMPLOY-
MENT RATE, 1965–1985. High rates of growth cause the unemployment rate to fall, and low or negative rates of growth are accompanied
by increases in the unemployment rate. The relationship shown by the
scatter of the points in this figure is summarized by *Okun's law*, linking
the growth rate to the change in the unemployment rate.

By contrast, in the lower right-hand region, points such as those labeled
1980 and 1982, are periods of recession — low growth and rising unemployment rates. Note that even when there is some growth, such as in 1981,
unemployment rates may be rising. It takes growth rates above about 3 percent to cause unemployment rates to come down. The year 1984 stands out as

having the most rapid growth and largest reduction in unemployment in 20 years.

Okun's Law

A relationship between real growth and changes in the unemployment rate is known as *Okun's law*, named after its discoverer, the late Arthur Okun of the Brookings Institution, former chairperson of the Council of Economic Advisers (CEA). Okun's law says that for every 2.2 percentage points of growth in real GNP above the trend rate that is sustained for a year, the unemployment rate declines by 1 percentage point. This 2.2 to 1 relationship, the status of which is somewhat exaggerated by calling it a law rather than an empirical regularity, provides a rule of thumb for assessing the implications of real growth for unemployment.[6] While the rule is only approximate and will not work very precisely from year to year, it still gives a sensible translation from growth to unemployment.

The relation is a useful guide to policy because it allows us to ask how a particular growth target will affect the unemployment rate over time. Suppose we were in a deep recession with 9 percent unemployment. How many years would it take us to return to, say, 6 percent unemployment? The answer depends, of course, on how fast the economy grows in the recovery. Assume the growth rate of potential output is 3 percent per year. One possible path to return to 6 percent unemployment is for output to grow at 5.2 percent per year for 3 years. On this path, each year we are growing 2.2 percent above trend, and thus each year we take 1 percentage point off the unemployment rate. An alternative recovery strategy is front-loaded: growth is high at the beginning and then slows down. Such a path might be one of growth rates in successive years equal to 6.2, 5.2, and 4.2 percent, also allowing a return to 6 percent unemployment in 3 years.

Inflation and the Cycle

Expansionary aggregate demand policies tend to produce inflation, unless they occur when the economy is at high levels of unemployment. Protracted periods of low aggregate demand tend to reduce the inflation rate. Figure 1-5 shows one measure of inflation for the U.S. economy for the period since 1960. The inflation measure in the figure is the rate of change of the *consumer price index,* the cost of a given basket of goods, representing the purchases of a typical urban consumer.[7]

---

[6] For more details on Okun's law, see Chap. 15.

[7] By contrast, the measure of inflation obtained in Fig. 1-1 by comparing nominal and real GNP is the rate of change of the GNP *deflator.* The consumer price index (CPI) rate of inflation is the most frequently used, and the GNP deflator is next most popular. Chapter 2 presents more details on the different price indexes.

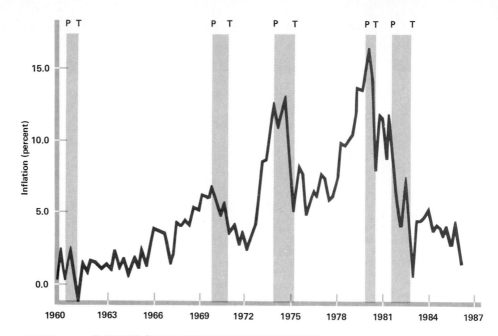

FIGURE 1-5   THE RATE OF INFLATION OF CONSUMER PRICES,
1960–1986. The inflation rate falls during and after recessions, and
then—over the period shown—tends to rise later in the recovery.
(*Source:* Citibank Database.)

The rate of inflation shown in Figure 1-5 fluctuates considerably. Just as
we could tell much about the recent history of the economy from looking at
Figure 1-3's picture of the course of actual and potential GNP, we can likewise
see much of recent economic history in Figure 1-5. In particular, there is the
period of steady inflation from 1960 through 1964 when the inflation rate
hovered around the 2 percent level. Then there is a slow climb in the inflation
rate from 1965 to 1970, followed by a slowing down till mid-1972. And finally
there are the inflationary bursts from 1972 through 1974 and 1978 to 1981 as
the inflation rate rose to 12 percent and above. In 1982–1983 inflation was
again down, under the impact of a deep recession. But this time, into 1986, the
inflation rate stayed low even as the economy grew fast out of the recession.

Figure 1-5 shows the *rate of increase* of prices. We can also look at the
level of prices. All the inflation of the 1960s and 1970s adds up to a large
increase in the price level. In the period from 1960 to 1985 the price level
more than tripled. A product that cost $1 in 1960 cost $3.65 by 1986. Much of
that increase in prices took place since the early 1970s.

Inflation, like unemployment, is a major macroeconomic problem. However, the costs of inflation are much less obvious than those of unemployment.
In the case of unemployment, potential output is going to waste, and it is
therefore clear why the reduction of unemployment is desirable. In the case of

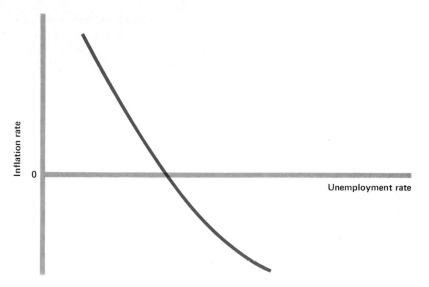

FIGURE 1-6   A PHILLIPS CURVE. The Phillips curve suggests a tradeoff between inflation and unemployment: less unemployment can always be obtained by incurring more inflation—or inflation can be reduced by allowing more unemployment. The combination of high inflation *and* high unemployment in years such as 1975 and 1981 led to skepticism about the Phillips curve. It nonetheless remains useful, as we shall show later.

inflation, there is no obvious loss of output. As we noted above, consumers in part dislike inflation because it is often associated with disturbances, such as the oil price shocks, that reduce their real incomes. It is also argued that inflation upsets familiar price relationships and reduces the efficiency of the price system. Whatever the reasons, policy makers have been willing to increase unemployment in an effort to reduce inflation—that is, to trade off some unemployment for less inflation.

Inflation-Unemployment Tradeoffs

The *Phillips curve* describes a relationship between inflation and unemployment: the higher the rate of unemployment, the lower the rate of inflation. The Phillips curve is an empirical relationship that relates the behavior of wage and price inflation to the rate of unemployment. It was made famous in the 1950s in Great Britain and has since become a cornerstone of macroeconomic discussion. Figure 1-6 presents a typical downward-sloping Phillips curve showing that high rates of unemployment are accompanied by low rates of inflation and vice versa. The curve suggests that less unemployment can always be attained by incurring more inflation and that the inflation rate can always be reduced by incurring the costs of more unemployment. In other words, the curve suggests there is a tradeoff between inflation and unemployment.

Economic events since 1970, particularly the combination of high inflation and high unemployment in 1974 or 1981, have led to considerable skepticism about the unemployment-inflation relation shown in Figure 1-6. Figure 1-7 presents the inflation and unemployment rate combinations for the years 1963 to 1985. Clearly, there is no simple relationship of the form shown in Figure 1-6.

Nonetheless, there remains a tradeoff between inflation and unemployment which is more sophisticated than a glance at Figure 1-6 would suggest, and which will enable us to make sense of Figure 1-7. In the short run, of, say, 2 years, there is a relation between inflation and unemployment of the type shown in Figure 1-6. The *short-run Phillips curve*, however, does not remain stable. It shifts as expectations of inflation change. In the long run, there is no tradeoff worth speaking about between inflation and unemployment. In the long run, the unemployment rate is basically independent of the long-run inflation rate.

The short- and long-run tradeoffs between inflation and unemployment are obviously a major concern of policy making and are the basic determinants of the potential success of stabilization policies.

1-3 MACROECONOMIC POLICY

Policy makers have at their command two broad classes of policies with which to affect the economy. *Monetary policy* is controlled by the Federal Reserve System (the Fed). The instruments of monetary policy are changes in the stock of money, changes in the interest rate — the discount rate — at which the Fed lends money to banks, and some controls over the banking system. *Fiscal policy* is under the control of the Congress and usually is initiated by the executive branch of the government. The instruments of fiscal policy are tax rates and government spending.

One of the central facts of policy is that the effects of monetary and fiscal policy on the economy are not fully predictable, neither in their *timing* nor in the *extent* to which they affect demand or supply. These two uncertainties are at the heart of the problem of stabilization policy. *Stabilization policies* are monetary and fiscal policies designed to moderate the fluctuations of the economy — in particular, fluctuations in the rates of growth, inflation, and unemployment.

Figure 1-7, which shows large fluctuations of the rates of inflation and unemployment, suggests strongly that stabilization policy has not been fully successful in keeping them within narrow bounds. The failures of stabilization policy are due both to uncertainty about the way it works and to limits on the effects of policy on the economy.

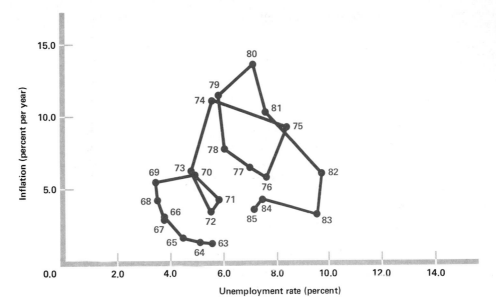

FIGURE 1-7   INFLATION AND UNEMPLOYMENT, 1963–1985. The actual history of inflation and unemployment in the United States since 1963 shows no simple Phillips curve relationship. There are periods, for instance, 1963–1969, 1976–1979, and 1980–1982, which fit the general shape of the Phillips curve, but in-between there are periods where inflation and unemployment both increase or sometimes (e.g., 1984–1985) decrease.

However, questions of political economy are also involved in the way stabilization policy has been operated. The speed at which to proceed in trying to eliminate unemployment, at the risk of increasing inflation, is a matter of judgment about both the economy and the costs of mistakes. Those who regard the costs of unemployment as high, relative to the costs of inflation, will run greater risks of inflation to reduce unemployment than will those who regard the costs of inflation as primary and unemployment as a relatively minor misfortune.

Political economy affects stabilization policy in more ways than through the costs which policy makers of different political persuasions attach to inflation and unemployment, and the risks they are willing to undertake in trying to improve the economic situation. There is also the so-called *political business cycle,* which is based on the observation that election results are affected by economic conditions. When the economic situation is improving and the unemployment rate is falling, incumbent presidents tend to be reelected. There is thus the incentive to policy makers running for reelection, or who wish to affect the election results, to use stabilization policy to produce booming economic conditions before elections.

Stabilization policy is also known as *countercyclical policy*, that is, policy to moderate the trade cycle or business cycle. Figure 1-3 shows that cycles in the past 20 years have been far from regular. The behavior, and even the existence, of the trade cycle is substantially affected by the conduct of stabilization policy. Successful stabilization policy smooths out the cycle, while unsuccessful stabilization policy may worsen the fluctuations of the economy. Indeed, one of the tenets of monetarism is that the major fluctuations of the economy are a result of government actions rather than the inherent instability of the economy's private sector.

Monetarists and Activists

We noted above that there is some controversy over the existence of a tradeoff between inflation and unemployment. That controversy arose around 1967–1968 in the context of the debate in macroeconomics between monetarists and nonmonetarists, or fiscalists. We have already identified some of the major participants in the debate as Milton Friedman on the monetarist side and Franco Modigliani and James Tobin on the nonmonetarist side. But macroeconomists cannot be neatly classified into one camp or the other. Instead, there is a spectrum of views. There are monetarists who make Friedman look like a Keynesian, and Keynesians who make Modigliani look like a monetarist. Not only that; there is no compelling unity in the views that are identified with monetarism, and the balanced economist is likely to accept some monetarist arguments and reject others. Nor is the debate one in which there is no progress. For example, both theory and empirical evidence have been brought to bear on the issue of the inflation-unemployment tradeoff, and it is no longer central to the monetarist/fiscalist debate.

Another major point of contention is the relation between *money* and *inflation. Monetarists* tend to argue that the quantity of money is the prime determinant of the level of prices and economic activity, and that excessive monetary growth is responsible for inflation and unstable monetary growth for economic fluctuations. Since they contend that variability in the growth rate of money accounts for variability of real growth, they are naturally led to argue for a monetary policy of low and constant growth in the money supply—a constant money growth rule. *Activists*, by contrast, point out that there is no close relationship between monetary growth and inflation in the short run and that monetary growth is only one of the factors affecting aggregate demand. Activists maintain that policy makers are—or at least can be—sufficiently careful and skillful to be able to use monetary and fiscal policy to control the economy effectively.

The skill and care of the policy makers are important because monetarists raise the issue of whether aggregate demand policies might not worsen the performance of the economy. Monetarists point to episodes, such as the inflationary policies followed by the Fed in the 1970s, to argue that policy makers cannot and do not exercise sufficient caution to justify using activist policy. Here the activists are optimists, suggesting that we can learn from our past mistakes.

A further issue that divides the two camps concerns the proper role of government in the economy. This is not really an issue that can be analyzed using macroeconomic theory, but it is difficult to follow some of the debate without being aware that the issue exists.

Monetarists tend to be conservatives who favor small government and abhor budget deficits and a large public debt. They favor tax cuts during recessions and cuts in public spending during booms, with the net effect of winding up with a smaller share of government in the economy. Activists, by contrast, tend to favor an active role for government and are therefore quite willing to use increased government spending and transfers as tools of stabilization policy. Differences between monetarists and activists must, therefore, be seen in a much broader perspective than their particular disagreements about the exact role of money in the short run.

Expectations, the New Classical Macroeconomics, and Activism

The monetarist challenge to Keynesian activism warmed up in the sixties and still continues today. But its importance has been superceded by the more fundamental and theoretically innovative *rational expectations equilibrium approach* to macroeconomics, or the *new classical macroeconomics.* The approach and challenge, associated with Robert Lucas and Thomas Sargent, has been developed by many other well-known economists, including Neil Wallace of the University of Minnesota and Robert Barro of the University of Rochester.

The essence of the rational expectations equilibrium approach is the assumption that markets are continuously in equilibrium. In particular, new classical macroeconomists regard as incomplete or unsatisfactory any theory that leaves open the possibility that private individuals could make themselves better off by trading among themselves.

This may not sound radical, but consider for instance unemployment. There is unemployment when people who want jobs cannot find them. It is quite easy to explain unemployment if wages do not adjust and are too high for firms who want to employ everyone who wants to work at that wage. New classical macroeconomists insist that such an assumption is too easy and unsatisfactory. After all, they say, if the unemployed are willing to work for less than existing workers, firms would increase their profits by hiring them and firing any of their existing workers who are not willing to work at the lower wage. Thus if wages are indeed slow to adjust, economists have to explain why it is not in someone's interest to adjust them more rapidly. The new classical macroeconomics has developed a sophisticated alternative explanation of unemployment that we discuss later.

The new classical macroeconomists also assume that expectations are *rational,* that is, that they are based on all economically relevant information. This is consistent with the assumption that individuals do not act arbitrarily or without thought in their economic life, in forming expectations as in other economic decisions.

New classical macroeconomists, like monetarists, tend to be conservatives, who see only a relatively small role for active government policy in the economy. This follows from the view that markets are mostly in equilibrium; people look after their own interests, leaving little for the government to do to improve the situation. They argue also that activist policy is difficult to carry out successfully because reactions of thinking firms and consumers to government actions depend on what the private sector thinks the government is trying to achieve, and may be difficult to predict.

Although they share many policy views, new classical macroeconomists are not necessarily monetarists. We discuss the equilibrium approach, rational expectations, and the new classical macroeconomics throughout the book, and in detail in Chapter 18.

1-4 AGGREGATE DEMAND AND SUPPLY

We have sketched the major issues and variables we shall be discussing and using in the book.

The key overall concepts in analyzing output, inflation and growth, and the role of policy are *aggregate demand* and *aggregate supply.* In this section we provide a brief preview of those concepts and of their interaction, with the aims of showing where we are heading and of keeping the material of Chapters 3 through 7 in perspective.

The level of output and the price level are determined by the interaction of aggregate demand and aggregate supply. Under some conditions, employment depends only on total spending, or aggregate demand. At other times, supply limitations are an important part of the policy problem and have to receive major attention. From the 1930s to the later 1960s, macroeconomics was very much demand-oriented.

But in recent years the emphasis has shifted, and aggregate supply and *supply-side economics* have gained in importance. This shift of emphasis and interest was no doubt fostered by the slow growth and high inflation experienced by the industrialized countries in the 1970s.

What are the relationships among aggregate demand and aggregate supply, output or employment, and prices? Aggregate demand is the relationship between spending on goods and services and the level of prices. If output limitations are not present, increased spending or an increase in aggregate demand will raise output and employment with little effect on prices. In such conditions, for example, during the great depression of the thirties, it would certainly be appropriate to use expansionary aggregate demand policies to increase output.

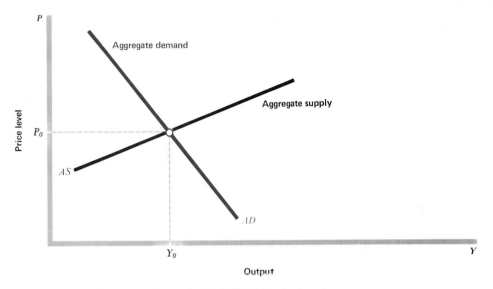

FIGURE 1-8   AGGREGATE DEMAND AND SUPPLY. The basic tools for analyzing output, inflation, and growth are the aggregate supply and demand curves. Shifts in either aggregate supply or demand will cause the level of output to change—thus affecting growth—and will also change the price level—thus affecting inflation. Through Okun's law, changes in output are linked to changes in the unemployment rate. For the first six chapters, we concentrate on aggregate demand. Then in the later chapters we introduce the aggregate supply curve, thereby completing the analysis.

But if the economy is close to full employment, increased aggregate demand will be reflected primarily in higher prices or inflation. The aggregate supply side of the economy has then to be introduced. The aggregate supply curve specifies the relationship between the amount of output firms produce and the price level. The supply side not only enters the picture in telling us how successful demand expansions will be in raising output and employment, but also has a role of its own. Supply disturbances, or *supply shocks,* can reduce output and raise prices, as was the case in the seventies when the price of oil increased sharply. Conversely, policies that increase productivity, and thus the level of aggregate supply at a given price level, can help reduce inflationary pressures.

Graphical Analysis

Figure 1-8 shows aggregate demand and supply curves. The vertical axis P is the price level, and the horizontal axis Y is the level of real output or income. Although the curves look like the ordinary supply and demand curves of microeconomics, an understanding of them will not be reached until Chapter 7.

Aggregate demand is the total demand for goods and services in the economy. It depends on the aggregate price level, as shown in Figure 1-8. It can be shifted through monetary and fiscal policy. The aggregate supply curve shows the price level associated with each level of output. It can, to some extent, be shifted by fiscal policy.

Aggregate supply and demand interact to determine the price level and output level. In Figure 1-8, P_0 is the equilibrium price level and Y_0 the equilibrium level of output. If the AD curve in the figure shifts upward to the right, then the extent to which output and prices, respectively, are changed depends on the steepness of the aggregate supply curve.[8] If the AS curve is very steep, then a given increase in aggregate demand mainly causes prices to rise and has very little effect on the level of output. If the AS curve is flat, a given change in aggregate demand will be translated mainly into an increase in output and very little into an increase in the price level.

One of the crucial points about macroeconomic adjustment is that the aggregate supply curve is not a straight line. Figure 1-9 shows that at low levels of output, below potential output Y^*, the aggregate supply curve is quite flat. When output is below potential, there is very little tendency for prices of goods and factors (wages) to fall. Conversely, for output above potential, the aggregate supply curve is steep and prices tend to rise continuously. The effects of changes in aggregate demand on output and prices therefore depend on the level of output relative to potential.

All these observations are by way of a very important warning. In Chapters 3 through 6 we focus on aggregate demand as the determinant of the level of output. We shall assume that prices are given and constant, and that output is determined by the level of demand — that there are no supply limitations. We are thus talking about the very flat part of the aggregate supply curve, at levels of output below potential.

The suggestion that output rises to meet the level of demand without a rise in prices leads to a very activist conception of policy. Under these circumstances, without any obvious tradeoffs, policy makers would favor very expansionary policies to raise demand and thereby cause the economy to move to a high level of employment and output. There are circumstances where such a policy view is altogether correct. The early 1960s are a case in point. Figure 1-3 shows that in those years output was substantially below potential. There were unused resources, and the problem was a deficiency of demand. By contrast, in the late 1960s and the early 1970s the economy was operating at full employment. There was no significant GNP gap. An attempt to expand output or real GNP further would run into supply limitations and force up prices rather than the production of goods. In these circumstances, a model that assumes that output is demand-determined and that increased demand raises output and *not* prices is simply inappropriate.

---

[8] Experiment with graphs like Fig. 1-8 to be sure you understand this fact.

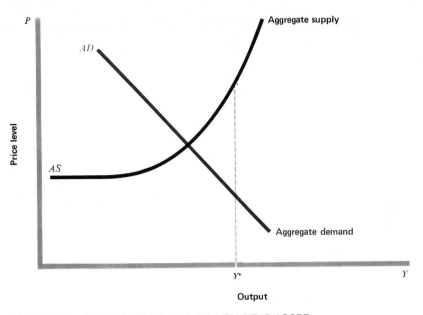

FIGURE 1-9   AGGREGATE DEMAND AND NONLINEAR AGGRE-
GATE SUPPLY. A key fact about the aggregate supply curve is that it is
not linear. At low levels of output, prices do not change much on the
aggregate supply schedule, implying that more output will be supplied
without much increase in prices. But as the economy gets close to full
employment or potential output, further increases in output will be
accompanied by increased prices.

Should we think that the model with fixed prices and demand-determined
output is very restricted and perhaps artificial? The answer is no. There are
two reasons for this. First, the circumstances under which the model is
appropriate—those of high unemployment—are neither unknown nor unimportant. Unemployment and downward price rigidity are continuing features of the United States economy. Second, even when we come to study the
interactions of aggregate supply and demand in Chapter 7 and later, we need
to know how given policy actions *shift* the aggregate demand curve at a given
level of prices. Thus all the material of Chapters 3 through 6 on aggregate
demand plays a vital part in the understanding of the effects of monetary and
fiscal policy on the price level as well as output in circumstances where the
aggregate supply curve is upward-sloping.

What, then, is the warning of this section? It is simply that the very activist
spirit of macroeconomic policy under conditions of unemployment must not
cause us to overlook the existence of supply limitations and price adjustment
when the economy is near full employment.

1-5 OUTLINE AND PREVIEW OF THE TEXT

We have sketched the major issues we shall discuss in the book. We now outline our approach to macroeconomics and the order in which the material will be presented. The key overall concepts, as already noted, are aggregate demand and aggregate supply. Aggregate demand is influenced by monetary policy, primarily via interest rates and expectations, and by fiscal policy. Aggregate supply is affected by fiscal policy and also by disturbances such as changes in the supply of oil.

Figure 1-10 presents a schematic view of the approach of the book to macroeconomics. Being schematic, the diagram is not comprehensive, but it does show the most important relationships we shall examine.

The coverage by chapters starts in Chapter 2 with national income accounting, emphasizing data and relationships that are used repeatedly later in the book. Chapters 3 to 6 are concerned with aggregate demand. Chapter 7

FIGURE 1-10   BASIC APPROACH TO MACROECONOMICS.
Aggregate demand and aggregate supply are the key elements in determining prices and output. Aggregate supply is affected by fiscal policy and by wage behavior and expectations. Aggregate demand is affected by fiscal policy and by monetary policy. There are also feedbacks through the money market—a high level of income increases the demand for money, which raises interest rates and reduces aggregate demand. This figure is a road map for the rest of the book. It will be helpful to return to it later, to see where the material being covered in later chapters fits in to the overall approach to the economy outlined here.

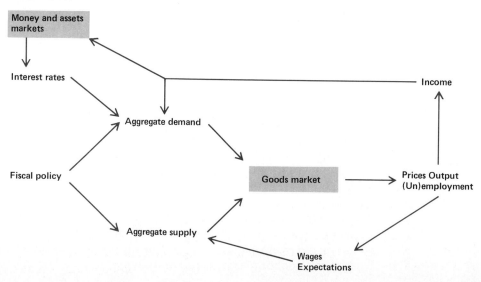

introduces aggregate supply and shows how aggregate supply and demand interact to determine both real GNP and the price level. Chapters 8 through 12 present material which clarifies and deepens understanding of aggregate demand and of the ways in which monetary and fiscal policies affect the economy. Chapters 13 through 19 perform a similar service for aggregate supply and the interactions of aggregate supply and demand. Chapter 20 extends Chapter 6's discussion of the role of international trade in macro-economics.

1-6 PREREQUISITES AND RECIPES

A few words on how to use this book are helpful in concluding this introductory chapter. First, we note that there is no mathematical prerequisite beyond high school algebra. We do use equations whenever they appear helpful, but they are not an indispensable part of the exposition. Nevertheless, they can and should be mastered by any serious student of macroeconomics.

The technically harder chapters or sections can be skipped or dipped into. Either we present them as supplementary material, or we provide sufficient nontechnical coverage to help the reader get on without them later in the book. The reason we do present more advanced material or treatment is to afford a complete and up-to-date coverage of the main ideas and techniques in macroeconomics. Even though you may not be able to grasp every point of such sections on first reading—and should not even try to—these sections should certainly be read to get the main message and an intuitive appreciation of the issues that are raised.

The main problem you will encounter comes from the interaction of several markets and many variables. As Figure 1-10 already suggests, the direct and feedback effects in the economy constitute a quite formidable system. How can you be certain to progress efficiently and with some ease? The most important thing is to ask questions. Ask yourself, as you follow the argument: Why is it that this or that variable should affect, say, aggregate demand? What would happen if it did not? What is the critical link?

There is no substitute whatsoever for an active form of learning. Reading sticks at best for 7 weeks. Are there simple rules for active study? The best way to study is to use pencil and paper and work the argument by drawing diagrams, experimenting with flowcharts, writing out the logic of an argument, working out the problems at the end of each chapter, and underlining key ideas. The Study Guide, by Richard Startz of the University of Washington, contains both much useful material and problems that will help in your studies. Another valuable exercise is to take issue with an argument or position, or to spell out the defense for a particular view on policy questions. Beyond that, if you get stuck, read on for half a page. If you are still stuck, go back five pages.

You should also learn to use the Index. Several concepts are discussed at different levels in different chapters. If you come across an unfamiliar term or concept, check the Index to see whether and where it was defined and discussed earlier in the book.

As a final word, this chapter is designed for reference purposes. You should return to it whenever you want to check where a particular problem fits or where a particular subject matter is relevant. The best way to see the forest is from Chapter 1.

KEY TERMS

Monetarists
Keynesians
New classical macroeconomists
GNP, nominal and real
Inflation
Growth
Unemployment
Business cycle
Trend or potential output
Peak
Trough

Recovery or expansion
Recession
Output gap
Okun's law
Phillips curve
Monetary policy
Fiscal policy
Stabilization policies
Activists
Rational expectations
Aggregate demand and supply

NATIONAL INCOME ACCOUNTING

Macroeconomics is ultimately concerned with the determination of the economy's total output, the price level, the level of employment, interest rates, and other variables discussed in Chapter 1. A necessary step in understanding how these variables are determined is *national income accounting*.

The national income accounts give us regular estimates of GNP, the basic measure of the economy's performance in producing goods and services. The first part of this chapter discusses the measurement and meaning of GNP, nominal and real. But the national income accounts are useful also because they provide us with a conceptual framework for describing the relationships among three key macroeconomic variables: output, income, and spending. Those relationships are described in the second part of this chapter. They are summarized in the circular flow diagram, Figure 2-1.

Figure 2-1 illustrates the interactions of firms and households in the economy. Output is produced by firms. The value of the output produced is the gross national product. GNP includes the value of goods produced, such as automobiles and eggs, along with the value of services, such as haircuts and medical services.

Firms produce the output by employing factors of production—land, labor, and capital—and paying for their use. The payments made by the firms are the *incomes* earned in the economy. The flow of income is shown in the lower bottom loop of the circular flow diagram. Thus the value of output is equal to the value of incomes received in the economy.

The goods produced by the firms are sold to households (and to other firms). Total *spending* on goods is thus also equal to the value of output. The flow of spending is also shown in Figure 2-1.

Looking at the relationships summarized in Figure 2-1, we see that *GNP is equal to total income earned in the economy, and is also equal to total spending.* That is the main lesson of this chapter, and the single most important point to remember about national income accounting. But there is considerable complexity in the actual national income accounts in relating GNP to incomes and to spending. Those complexities arise in large part from the role of the government and from the presence of foreign trade, and we shall have to explain some of them.

We start in Section 2-1 by examining GNP and its measurement. Section 2-2 returns to the distinction between real and nominal GNP, a distinction which is necessary because of inflation. Section 2-3 compares alternative

FIGURE 2-1   THE CIRCULAR FLOW OF INCOME AND SPENDING. Production of goods and services is carried out by firms, whose total output is equal to GNP. The output is produced using the services of factors of production, mostly labor, owned by households and paid for by the firms. The payments for the use of factors of production generate households' incomes. Household spending out of those incomes, in turn, generates the demand for the goods produced by the firms. Spending on goods is, in the simple case shown here where there is no government and no foreign trade, equal to GNP, and also equal to the income of households. The diagram shows the key relation: output is equal to income is equal to spending.

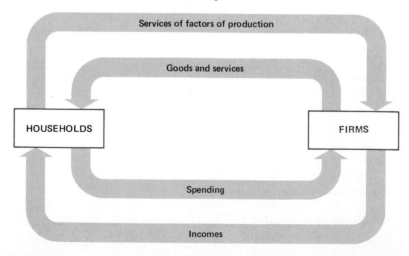

measures of inflation. Then we move in Sections 2-4 to 2-6 to the relationships among output, income, and spending summarized in the circular flow diagram.

Section 2-7 paves the way for the economic analysis of the determination of the level of output that begins in Chapter 3, by systematically setting out the national income relationships studied in this chapter.

2-1 GROSS NATIONAL PRODUCT AND NET NATIONAL PRODUCT

Calculating Gross National Product

GNP is the value of all final goods and services produced by domestically owned factors of production within a given period. It includes the value of such goods produced as houses and bourbon, and the value of services, such as brokers' services and economists' lectures. The output of each of these is valued at its market price, and the values are added together to give GNP.

Table 2-1 shows the calculation of GNP in a simple economy that produces only bananas and oranges. Twenty bananas and sixty oranges are produced. The bananas are valued at $0.30 each and the oranges at $0.25 each. GNP is equal to $21, the total value of output.

GNP in the United States in 1985 was $3,989 billion. Dividing by population, equal to 238.8 million in 1985, we obtain GNP per person or per capita, which was $16,700. We can also calculate output per person employed. In 1985 there were on average 108.9 million people employed. Thus GNP per person employed or output per person employed was $36,630.

GNP has increased rapidly in the last 20 years, as Figure 1-1 shows. GNP has grown on average at a rate of 9.0 percent per year since 1965. In that year GNP was only $705 billion, less than one-fifth of its value in 1985. Recall that much of the increase is a result of inflation.

A number of subtleties in the calculation of GNP should be kept in mind.

TABLE 2-1	CALCULATING GNP IN A SIMPLE ECONOMY, 1987			
	Output	Price per unit, $	Value of output, $	GNP, $
Bananas	20	0.30	6.00	
Oranges	60	0.25	15.00	
				21.00

FINAL GOODS AND VALUE ADDED

GNP is the value of *final* goods and services produced. The insistence on final goods and services is simply to make sure that we do not double-count. For example, we would not want to include the full price of an automobile in GNP and then also include the value of the tires that were sold to the automobile producer as part of the GNP. The components of the car, sold to the manufacturers, are called *intermediate* goods, and their value is not included in GNP. Similarly, the wheat that goes into bread is an intermediate good, and we do not count the value of the wheat sold the miller and the value of the flour sold the baker, as well as the value of the bread, as part of GNP.

In practice, double counting is avoided by working with *value added.* At each stage of the manufacture of a good, only the value added to the good at that stage of manufacture is counted as part of GNP. The value of the wheat produced by the farmer is counted as part of GNP. Then the value of the flour sold by the miller minus the cost of the wheat is the miller's value added. If we follow this process along, we will see that the sum of value added at each stage of processing will be equal to the final value of the bread sold.[1]

CURRENT OUTPUT

GNP consists of the value of output *currently produced.* It thus excludes transactions in existing commodities such as old masters or existing houses. We count the construction of new houses as part of GNP, but we do not add trade in existing houses. We do, however, count the value of realtor's fees in the sale of existing houses as part of GNP. The realtor provides a current service in bringing buyer and seller together, and that is appropriately part of current output.

MARKET PRICES

GNP values goods at *market prices.* The market price of many goods includes indirect taxes such as the sales tax and excise taxes, and thus the market price of goods is not the same as the price the seller of the good receives. The price net of indirect taxes is the *factor cost*, which is the amount received by the factors of production that manufactured the good. GNP is valued at market prices and not at factor cost. This point becomes important when we relate GNP to the incomes received by the factors of production.

Valuation at market prices is a principle that is not uniformly applied, because there are some components of GNP that are difficult to value. There is no very good way of valuing the services of housepersons, or a self-administered haircut, or, for that matter, the services of the police force or the government bureaucracy. Some of these activities are simply omitted from currently

---

[1] How about the flour that is directly purchased by households for baking in the home? It is counted as a contribution toward GNP since it represents a final sale.

measured GNP, as, for instance, housepersons' services. Government services are valued at cost, so that the wages of government employees are taken to represent their contribution to GNP. There is no unifying principle in the treatment of these awkward cases, but rather a host of conventions is used.

GNP and Gross Domestic Product

There is a distinction between GNP and *gross domestic product,* or *GDP.* GDP is the value of final goods produced within the country. What is the difference between GNP and GDP? Part of GNP is earned abroad. For instance, the income of an American citizen working in Japan is part of U.S. GNP. But it is not part of U.S. GDP because it is not earned in the United States. On the other side, the profits earned by Honda from its U.S. manufacturing operations are part of Japanese GNP and not U.S. GNP. But they are part of U.S. GDP because they are earned in the United States.

When the GNP exceeds GDP, residents of a given country are earning more abroad than foreigners are earning in that country. In the United States in recent years, GNP has slightly exceeded GDP, meaning that U.S. corporations and residents who own factories or work abroad earn more in foreign countries than foreign firms and individuals earn in the United States.

Net National Product

Net national product (NNP), as distinct from GNP, deducts from GNP the *depreciation* of the existing capital stock over the course of the period. The production of GNP causes wear and tear on the existing capital stock; for example, machines wear out as they are used. If resources were not used to maintain or replace the existing capital, GNP could not be kept at the current level. Accordingly, we use NNP as a better measure of the rate of economic activity that could be maintained over long periods, given the existing capital stock and labor force.

Depreciation is a measure of the part of GNP that has to be set aside to maintain the productive capacity of the economy, and we deduct that from GNP to obtain NNP. In 1985 depreciation was $438 billion, or about 11 percent of GNP. The figure is typically in the 10 to 12 percent range. Depreciation is called the *capital consumption allowance* in the national income accounts.

We usually work with the GNP rather than the NNP data because depreciation estimates may be quite inaccurate, and also are not quickly available, whereas the GNP estimate for each calendar quarter is available in preliminary form less than a month after the end of the quarter.[2] Indeed, from 1983 to 1985, a preliminary "flash" estimate of GNP for a given quarter was made public before the end of the quarter.

---

[2] National income account data are regularly reported in the *Survey of Current Business.* Historical data are available in *Business Statistics,* a biennial edition, and the *Economic Report of the President.*

2-2 REAL AND NOMINAL GNP

Nominal GNP measures the value of output in a given period in the prices of that period, or, as it is sometimes put, in *current dollars.* Thus 1987 nominal GNP measures the value of the goods produced in 1987 at the market prices that prevailed in 1987, and 1976 GNP measures the value of goods produced in 1976, at the market prices that prevailed in 1976. Nominal GNP changes from year to year for two reasons. The first is that the physical output of goods changes. The second is that market prices change. As an extreme and unrealistic example, one could imagine the economy producing exactly the same output in 2 years, between which all prices have doubled. Nominal GNP in the second year would be double nominal GNP in the first year, even though the physical output of the economy has not changed at all.

Real GNP measures changes in *physical* output in the economy between different time periods by valuing all goods produced in the two periods *at the same prices,* or in *constant dollars.* Real GNP is now measured in the national income accounts in the prices of 1982. That means that, in calculating real GNP, today's physical output is multiplied by the prices that prevailed in 1982 to obtain a measure of what today's output would have been worth had it been sold at the prices of 1982.[3]

We return to the simple example of Table 2-1 to illustrate the calculation of real GNP. The hypothetical outputs and prices of bananas and oranges in 1982 and 1987 are shown in the first two columns of Table 2-2. Nominal GNP in 1982 was $14, and nominal GNP in 1987 was $21, or an increase in nominal GNP of 50 percent. However, much of the increase in nominal GNP is purely a result of the increase in prices between the 2 years and does not reflect an increase in physical output. When we calculate real GNP in 1987 by valuing 1987 output at the prices of 1982, we find real GNP equal to $17.20, which is an increase of 23 percent rather than 50 percent. The 23 percent increase is a better measure of the increase in physical output of the economy than the 50 percent increase.

We see from the table that the output of bananas rose by 33 percent, while the output of oranges increased by 20 percent from 1982 to 1987. We should thus expect our measure of the increase in real output to be somewhere between 20 and 33 percent, as it is.[4]

---

[3] The shift from the prices of 1972 to those of 1982 for calculating real GNP was made at the end of 1985.

[4] The increase in real GNP that is calculated depends on the prices that are used in the calculation. If you have a calculator, you might want to compare the increase in real GNP between 1982 and 1987 if the prices of 1987 are used to make the comparison. (Using 1987 prices, real GNP rises 23.5 percent from 1982 to 1987, compared with 22.9 percent using 1982 prices.) The ambiguities that arise in comparisons using different prices to calculate real GNP are an inevitable result of the attempt to use a single number to capture the increase in output of both bananas and oranges when those two components did not increase in the same proportion. However, the ambiguity is not a major concern when there is inflation at any substantial rate, and that is precisely when we most want to use real (rather than nominal) GNP to study the performance of the economy.

TABLE 2-2	REAL AND NOMINAL GNP, AN ILLUSTRATION				
1982 nominal GNP, $		1987 nominal GNP, $		1987 real GNP*, $	
15 bananas at 0.20	3.00	20 bananas at 0.30	6.00	20 bananas at 0.20	4.00
50 oranges at 0.22	11.00	60 oranges at 0.25	15.00	60 oranges at 0.22	13.20
	14.00		21.00		17.20

* Measured in 1982 prices

Figure 2-2 shows the behavior of real and nominal GNP over the period since 1972. Note particularly that in some periods real GNP fell while nominal GNP kept on rising. That happened in the recessions of 1973–1975, 1980, and 1981–1982. The recession periods, shaded in the figure, stand out as years of low or negative real GNP growth.

It would clearly be a mistake to regard the increases in *nominal* GNP as

FIGURE 2-2   REAL AND NOMINAL GNP, 1972–1986.

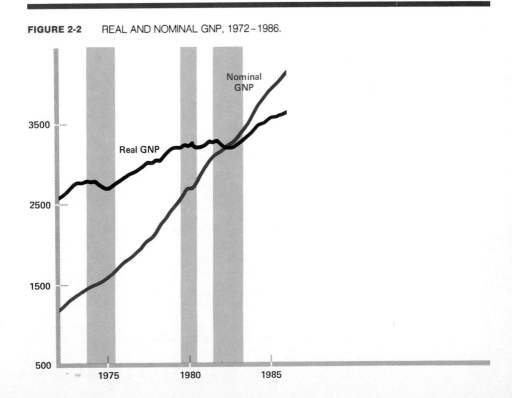

BOX

2-1

GNP MEASUREMENT

Two particular (unrelated) problems of GNP measurement are the possibility that large parts of economic activity escape being counted in GNP, and that the data are frequently and quite substantially revised. We take up the two problems in turn.

THE UNDERGROUND ECONOMY

By some estimates, as much as 30 percent of U.S. GNP may not be measured in the GNP accounts. Here are examples of transactions that generate goods and services that might not make it into measured GNP: working at a second job for cash, illegal gambling, working as an illegal immigrant, working while collecting unemployment benefits, illegal drug dealing, working for tips that are not fully reported, selling home-grown tomatoes for cash.*

There are two main types of transactions that people attempt to conceal: transactions that are not inherently illegal, but for which people are not complying with tax or immigration laws or other government regulations; and transactions that are themselves illegal, such as drug dealing. The U.S. national income accounts as a matter of principle do not include the value of illegal activities in GNP, so that part of the underground economy would not count even if it could be measured. But many other countries and economists have no objection to including illegal activities if they can be measured. The remaining activities in the underground economy occur mainly because people are trying to keep from losing some government benefit or avoid paying taxes, and these activities should be included in GNP.

How large is the underground economy, and how can it be measured? Of course, by their nature these are difficult data to estimate. Estimates range widely. For the U.S. conservative numbers are 3 to 4 percent of GNP, with a radical number of 33 percent of GNP. Estimates for foreign countries are similar, for instance for Canada from 4 to 22 percent of GNP, for Italy from 8 to 33 percent.

The largest estimates for the United States are based on the holdings of currency, on the argument that black market transactions are undertaken mainly using currency. The ratio of currency holdings to bank deposits has risen from 25 percent in 1959 to 40 percent in 1984, and it is argued that the reason is the increasing share of underground economic activity. Alternative estimates are based on inconsistencies in the GNP accounts, for instance, differences between total spending and total income (recall from Figure 2-1 that income should be equal to spending.) The Bureau of Economic Analysis that creates the GNP accounts believes the underground economy is 3 percent of GNP or less, while the Internal Revenue Service has come up with an estimate as high as 8 percent of GNP. The evidence in favor of really large corrections, say more than 10 percent, is weak.

What problems does the underground economy pose for GNP measurement? The main problem is that the relative importance of underground activities may have been changing. If, say, the underground economy was always equal to 10 percent of reported GNP, then measured GNP would show accurately the *rate* at which output *changes* over time. But if the

---

* A more complete list is provided in the excellent survey article by Carol S. Carson, "The Underground Economy: An Introduction," *Survey of Current Business*, May 1984; see also part II of the same article, in the July 1984 *Survey of Current Business*. There has been an explosion of research on the underground economy in recent years; for a review of three books on the topic see Peter M. Gutman, *Journal of Economic Literature*, March 1983, pp. 117–120.

underground economy grows relative to the measured economy, then the measured growth rate of output is below the true growth rate. It is precisely the claim that the underground economy has been growing rapidly, and that therefore slow economic growth in the seventies was in large part a statistical illusion, that has spurred research on the topic.

GNP REVISIONS AND THE ACCURACY OF GNP ESTIMATES

There are several estimates of GNP for a given period. The first estimate for a given quarter appears about 3 weeks after the end of the quarter. For example, the data for the fourth quarter of 1986 will be announced about January 18, 1987. These data are then revised a month later and once more a month after that. Then in July each year there is a major revision of all GNP data, possibly going back many years.

It is thus clear that GNP data are not, when they first appear, firm estimates. The reason is that many of the data are not measured directly, but rather are based on surveys and guesses. Considering that GNP is supposed to measure the value of *all* production of goods and services in the economy, it is not surprising that not all the data are available within a few weeks after the period of production. The data are revised as new figures come in, and as the Bureau of Economic Analysis improves its data collection and estimation methods.

Data revisions may be quite large. The estimate of how fast GNP grew from one quarter to the next can sometimes change by 2 to 3 percent (at an annual rate) between the first and third estimates of GNP.

Big changes may also be registered when a complete revision of the GNP data is undertaken, at irregular intervals. Table 1 shows the size of revisions to estimates of 1974 and 1984 GNP when new data were presented in 1985. The reasons for the revisions are described in the December 1985 *Survey of Current Business*.

With such substantial revisions possible, the preliminary data have always to be greeted with caution.

TABLE 1   GNP DATA REVISIONS, 1985

	NOMINAL GNP, $ BILLIONS			GROWTH RATE OF REAL GNP (% p.a.)		
	Prerevision	Postrevision	Percentage change	Prerevision	Postrevision	Change
1974	1,434.2	1,472.8	2.7	−0.6	−0.5	0.1
1984	3,661.3	3,774.7	3.1	6.8	6.6	−0.2

Sources: Prerevision data are from *Economic Report of the President, 1985.* Tables B-1 and B-2. Postrevision data are from "Revised Estimates of the National Income and Product Accounts of the United States, 1929–85: An Introduction," *Survey of Current Business*, December 1985, p. 2.

indicating that the performance of the economy in producing goods and services was improving from, say, 1981 to 1982. So we look at real and not nominal GNP as the basic measure for comparing output in different years.

Problems of GNP Measurement

GNP data are, in practice, used not only as a measure of how much is being produced, but also as a measure of the welfare of the residents of a country. Economists and politicians talk as if an increase in real GNP means that people are better off. But GNP data are far from perfect measures of either economic output or welfare.

Some of the problems of GNP measurement are described in Box 2-1, which discusses the underground economy and revisions in GNP data. Here we cover first inadequacies in the measurement of some outputs and then the use of GNP as a measure of economic welfare.

BADLY MEASURED OUTPUTS

Most of the difficulties of measuring GNP arise because some outputs do not go through the market. We already noted that government production is valued at cost. That is because much of government output is not sold in the market, nor is anything comparable available that would make it possible to estimate the value of government output. How would we measure the value of the output of safety from attack that defense expenditures are supposed to produce?

But there is also a conceptual problem with much of government output. We include in GNP the value of wages paid for the police and the defense forces. Suppose there was an improvement in public safety and police were taken out of the police force and put to work making candy — at their previous wage. GNP would not change. But the economy's output of useful goods and services certainly would seem to rise.

The problem in this case is that we generally do not deduct negative outputs, or *bads*, from GNP. We do not attempt to value the decline in public safety that requires increased police forces. Nor do we deduct from GNP the value of pollution produced by factories and cars. These are bads, but they do not show up in the GNP accounts. If we were somehow able to value the amount of public safety provided by society, then a shift of labor out of the police force resulting from an increase in public safety would indeed show up as an increase in GNP. Similarly, the improvement in the quality of the environment in the 1970s would show up as having raised output over that decade.

Other nonmarket activities, including do-it-yourself work and volunteer activities, are also excluded from GNP. The most important category here is the value of work done in the home by housepersons. Measured GNP would increase if someone stopped cleaning the house by himself or herself and instead hired a cleaning service to do the same thing. But the output of the economy has not really risen.

TOTAL INCOMES SYSTEM OF ACCOUNTS

Professor Robert Eisner of Northwestern University has undertaken the massive task of recalculating GNP to correct some of the main problems discussed above.[5] In particular, he excludes defense and police services from output, arguing those are just intermediate goods, and he includes the value of much work that is not now measured in the GNP accounts.

In his total incomes system of accounts (TISA), GNP for 1981 was $4,560 billion, compared with $2,954 billion for the official estimate. The biggest difference arises from his calculation that the value of meal preparation, laundry, child care, and other nonmarket work done in the home was $944 billion. He also puts a value of $284 billion on the output produced because students are learning while at school or college.

The Eisner calculations do not make a big difference to the estimated *growth rate* of real GNP over the entire 1946–1981 period for which he calculates his accounts. Real GNP grew at an annual average rate of 3.2 percent in the Eisner accounts, 3.3 percent in the regular accounts.

THE PROBLEM OF QUALITY CHANGES

There is not much difficulty in valuing real GNP when it is only a matter of counting or weighing oranges and bananas. But changes in the quality of goods over time create substantial difficulties for real GNP measurement.

A simple example is automobiles. Suppose we try to compare GNP in 1960 and 1987, using 1960 prices to value automobile production in 1987. The problem is that a 1987 car is not the same as a 1960 car, so it would certainly be a mistake to calculate the real value of 1987 automobile production (in 1960 prices) by multiplying the number of cars produced in 1987 by the average price of a car in 1960. Instead of doing that, the GNP accounts try to adjust for changes in the quality of a car by valuing its characteristics separately — horsepower, automatic transmission, air conditioning, etc. Even so there are difficulties: in 1960 there were no cars in which you were told politely by a voice in the car to buckle up, so the value of that option is hard to calculate in 1960 prices.[6]

The problem of quality change is a severe one that makes long-term

---

[5] Eisner presents his data in "The Total Incomes System of Accounts," *Survey of Current Business,* January 1985.

[6] The issue of quality change and the implications for measuring real income are even more obvious for the case of computers.

comparisons of real GNP very uncertain. For instance, although real GNP in 1985 was 430 percent higher than calculated 1929 real GNP, we should not have any great confidence that the real volume of goods produced in 1985 was exactly 5.3 times as great as that in 1929.

Real GNP as a Measure of Well-Being

The second use of GNP is as a *measure of economic welfare* (MEW) or well-being of the residents of a country. When GNP rises, it is assumed that people are materially better off. Of course, it is necessary first to divide real GNP by the number of people to use GNP in this sense: it is per capita (per person) GNP that is used as a welfare measure.

The difficulties of measuring nonmarket outputs already suggest that real GNP per capita is an imperfect measure of economic well-being. In addition, real GNP has to be adjusted to include the value of leisure. If the value of output falls because people have decided thay would like to work less, that is not necessarily a sign that they are worse off. Much economic progress over the last century is reflected in a falling workweek. One hundred years ago the average workweek was well above 60 hours — and in manufacturing it was higher still. Now it is under 40 hours. Real GNP should be adjusted to include the value of the increased leisure people have as a result of the declining workweek, if GNP is to be used as a measure of economic welfare.

Measure of Economic Welfare

Yale's William Nordhaus and James Tobin in 1972 put together estimates of real GNP, adjusting as best they could for nonmarket outputs and nonmarket bads and for the increased amount of leisure people now have.[7] The value of MEW is larger than that of GNP. But on balance, MEW has grown more slowly than real GNP. Production of bads (pollution) increased over the fifties and sixties, and the increase in leisure time has grown more slowly than the output of goods and services.

MEW and Eisner's total accounts are not published regularly, and thus we continue to use real GNP as the chief measure of the economy's output and — although we know its shortcomings — as a measure of how the economy is performing in providing material well-being. The justification for doing so, in addition to the lack of choice, is that, in the short run, changes in real GNP are probably in the same direction as changes in the other measures of output.

---

[7] William Nordhaus and James Tobin, "Is Growth Obsolete?" in National Bureau of Economic Research. *Fiftieth Anniversary Colloquium* (New York: Columbia University Press, 1972).

2-3 PRICE INDEXES

The GNP Deflator

The calculation of real GNP gives us a useful measure of inflation known as the *GNP deflator.* Returning to the hypothetical example of Table 2-2, we can get a measure of inflation between 1982 and 1987 by comparing the value of 1987 GNP in 1987 prices and 1982 prices. The ratio of nominal to real GNP in 1987 is 1.22 ($=21 \div 17.2$). In other words, output is 22 percent higher in 1987 when it is valued using the higher prices of 1987 than valued in the lower prices of 1982. We ascribe the 22 percent increase to price changes, or inflation, over the 1982–1987 period.

The GNP deflator is the ratio of nominal GNP in a given year to real GNP, and it is a measure of inflation from the period from which the base prices for calculating the real GNP are taken, to the current period. Since the GNP deflator is based on a calculation involving all the goods produced in the economy, it is a widely based price index that is frequently used to measure inflation.

The Consumer Price Index

The *consumer price index (CPI)* measures the cost of buying a fixed bundle of goods, representative of the purchases of urban consumers. The GNP deflator differs in three main ways from the CPI. First, the deflator measures the prices of a much wider group of goods than the CPI. CPI prices are measured by field-workers who go into shops and make phone calls to discuss the prices of the goods. Second, the CPI measures the cost of a given basket of goods, which is the same from year to year. The basket of goods included in the GNP deflator, however, differs from year to year, depending on what is produced in the economy in each year. When corn crops are high, corn receives a relatively large weight in the computation of the GNP deflator. By contrast, the CPI measures the cost of a fixed bundle of goods that does not vary over time.[8] Third, the CPI directly includes prices of imports, whereas the deflator includes only prices of goods *produced* in the United States.[9] The two main indexes used to compute inflation, the GNP deflator and the CPI, accordingly differ in behavior from time to time. For example, at times when the price of imported oil rises rapidly, the CPI is likely to rise faster than the deflator.

---

[8] Price indexes are, however, occasionally revised to change weights to reflect current expenditure patterns.

[9] Until 1983 there was a fourth difference: through the seventies and until 1982 the CPI undoubtedly badly miscalculated housing costs and gave too much weight to interest rate changes. The index was revised in 1983 to improve its measurement of housing costs.

The Producer Price Index

The *producer price index (PPI)* is the third price index that is widely used. Like the CPI, this is a measure of the cost of a given basket of goods. It differs from the CPI partly in its coverage, which includes, for example, raw materials and semifinished goods. It differs, too, in that it is designed to measure prices at an early stage of the distribution system. Whereas the CPI measures prices where urban households actually do their spending — that is, at the retail level — the PPI is constructed from prices at the level of the first significant commercial transaction.

This difference makes the PPI a relatively flexible price index and one that signals changes in the general price level, or the CPI, some time before they actually materialize. For this reason the PPI, and more particularly, some of its subindexes, such as the index of "sensitive materials," serves as one of the business cycle indicators that are closely watched by policy makers.

Table 2-3 shows the CPI, the PPI, and the GNP deflator for the past 35 years. Both the CPI and PPI use 1967 as their base. This means that the weights in the standard basket that is priced are those of 1967.[10] The GNP deflator expresses prices in the current year relative to 1982 prices, using quantities of the current year as weights. Note from the table that all three indexes have been increasing throughout the period. This is a reflection of the fact that the average price of goods has been rising, whatever basket we look at. Note, too, that the cumulative increase (price 1985/price 1950) differs across indexes. This difference occurs because the indexes represent the prices of different commodity baskets.

Although the indexes do not change at the same rate over the entire period, all of them show substantial — and reasonably close — annual rates of inflation. There is no sense in which one of the indexes is "correct" while the others are not. The indexes measure changing prices of different baskets of goods. We tend to focus on the deflator or the CPI, the deflator because it measures the prices of a very broad range of goods, and the CPI because the concept it tries to measure — the cost of buying a given basket of goods for the consumer — is a useful one.

We now return to the relationships summarized in the circular flow diagram Figure 2-1, among GNP or output, income, and spending.

2-4 GNP AND NATIONAL INCOME

In this section we show that *income is equal to the value of output* because the receipts from the sale of output must accrue to someone as income. The

---

[10] The mechanics of price indexes are briefly described in the appendix to this chapter. Detailed discussion of the various price indexes can be found in the Bureau of Labor Statistics, *Handbook of Methods*, and in the Commerce Department biennial edition of *Business Statistics*.

TABLE 2-3   IMPORTANT PRICE INDEXES

	CPI, 1967 = 100	PPI, 1967 = 100	GNP deflator, 1982 = 100
1950	72.1	81.8	24.0
1960	88.7	94.9	30.9
1967	100.0	100.0	42.1
1972	125.3	119.1	50.3
1980	246.8	268.8	86.1
1985	322.2	308.8	112.4
Increase:			
Price 1985/price 1950	4.47	3.78	4.68
Average annual inflation rate	4.4%	3.9%	4.5%

Source: Data Resources, Inc.

purchaser of bread is indirectly paying the farmer, the miller, the baker, and the supermarket operator for the labor and capital used in production and is also contributing to their profits.

Our statement above equating the value of output and income is correct with two qualifications:

1. The first correction arises from depreciation. As already noted, part of GNP has to be set aside to maintain the productive capacity of the economy. Depreciation should not be counted as part of income, since it is a cost of production. As a rule, depreciation, or the capital consumption allowance, amounts to about 11 percent of GNP. After subtracting depreciation from GNP, we have NNP.
2. The second adjustment arises from indirect taxes, in particular, sales taxes, that introduce a discrepancy between market price and prices received by producers. GNP is valued at market price, but the income accruing to producers does not include the sales taxes that are part of market price, and thus falls short of GNP. Indirect taxes, along with some other items of the same nature, account for about 10 percent of GNP.

With these two deductions we can derive national income from GNP, as shown in Table 2-4, which gives the dollar figures for 1985.[11] *National income*

[11] The term "Other (net)" in Table 2-4 includes a statistical discrepancy. In addition, it subtracts from NNP business transfer payments but adds subsidies to, less current surpluses of, government enterprises. The adjustment for government enterprises is required because, in the case of subsidies, market price understates the factor cost. In the case of deficits, similarly, the value of output measured at market prices falls short of the factor cost.

TABLE 2-4   GNP AND NATIONAL INCOME, 1985

	$ billions	$ billions
Gross national product		3,988.5
Less		
Capital consumption allowance	438.4	
Equals		
Net national product		3,550.1
Less		
Indirect taxes	328.4	
Other (net)	10.4	
Equals		
National income		3,211.3

Note: Numbers may not sum to totals because of rounding.
Source: Survey of Current Business, April, 1986.

gives the value of output at *factor cost* rather than market prices, which is GNP. National income measures the total income received by factors of production, before direct taxes and transfers.

Factor Shares in National Income

We next ask how national income is split (*factor shares*) among different types of incomes, as shown in Table 2-5.

The most striking fact of Table 2-5 is the very large share of wages and

TABLE 2-5   NATIONAL INCOME AND ITS DISTRIBUTION, 1985

	$ billions	Percent
National income	3,211.3	100
Compensation of employees	2,372.5	73.9
Proprietors' income	242.2	7.5
Rental income of persons	13.8	0.4
Corporate profits	295.5	9.2
Net interest	287.4	8.9

Note: Numbers may not sum to totals because of rounding.
Source: Survey of Current Business, April 1986.

salaries—compensation of employees—in national income. This accounts for 74 percent of national income. Proprietors' income is income from unincorporated businesses. Rental income of persons includes the *imputed* income of owner-occupied housing[12] and income from ownership of patents, royalties, and so on. The net interest category consists of interest payments by domestic businesses and the rest of the world to individuals and firms who have lent to them.

The division of national income into various classes is not too important for our macroeconomic purposes. If reflects, in part, such questions as whether corporations are financed by debt or equity, whether a business is or is not incorporated, and whether the housing stock is owned by persons or corporations—which, in turn, are owned by persons.[13]

National Income and Personal Income

A considerably more important question from the macroeconomic viewpoint is how much the personal sector—households and unincorporated business—actually receives as income, inclusive of transfers. This quantity is measured by *personal income. Transfers* are those payments that do *not* arise out of current productive activity. Thus, pensions, welfare payments, and unemployment benefits are examples of transfer payments. The level of personal income is important because it is a prime determinant of household consumption and saving behavior.

To go from national income to personal income, we have to remove those parts of national income that are earned by the corporate sector and add net transfer payments to the personal sector. Table 2-6 shows the steps needed to make the transition from national income to personal income.

Two items are deducted from national income:

1. Corporate profits (pretax), which clearly are not directly part of personal income.[14]
2. Contributions for social insurance. These are contributions, by both corporations and the personal sector, which are essentially taxes paid to the government sector and thus not part of personal income.

---

[12] GNP includes an estimate of the services homeowners receive by living in their homes. This is estimated by calculating the rent on an equivalent house. Thus the homeowner is treated as if she pays herself rent for living in her home.

[13] You might want to work out how Table 2-5 would be modified for each of the possibilities described in this sentence. Problem 9 asks for the answers.

[14] Corporate profits in the national income accounts are adjusted by correcting firms' estimates of *(a)* depreciation (the capital consumption adjustment) and *(b)* the costs of inventories used up in production (the inventory valuation adjustment). The second adjustment occurs because computed profits are affected by the value firms place on the goods they use up in production. In inflationary times, typical ways of valuing inventories *understate* the cost of goods sold and thus *overstate* profits. The inventory valuation adjustment is an attempt to correct that error. The corporate profits deducted from national income in Table 2-6 include the two adjustments mentioned in this footnote.

TABLE 2-6 NATIONAL INCOME AND
PERSONAL INCOME IN 1985

	$ billions	$ billions
National income		3,211.3
Less		
Corporate profits	295.5	
Social insurance contributions	354.9	
Plus		
Government and business transfers to persons	484.5	
Interest adjustment	168.9	
Dividends	78.9	
Equals		
Personal income		3,293.5

Source: *Survey of Current Business*, April 1986.

We then add back three items:

1. *Transfer payments:* These are made to persons, consisting mostly of government transfers such as Social Security benefits, state unemployment insurance benefits, and veterans' benefits, along with business transfers such as business contributions to charity.
2. *Interest adjustment:* National income measures only payments for productive services. Other payments, not classified as factor payments, still represent income receipts for households or businesses even though they do not appear in national income. Some of the interest income received by households counts as transfer payments in the national income accounts, but has now to be taken into account in calculating the income of households. We therefore add in Table 2-6 an item "interest adjustment."[15]
3. *Dividends:* (distributed after-tax corporate profits).

After making these adjustments, we have a measure of the income received by persons and unincorporated businesses. Personal income is a useful measure particularly because it is available monthly, as opposed to most national income measures which are published only quarterly. The monthly

[15] This interest adjustment is equivalent to subtracting "net interest" and adding "personal interest income." These two items can be found in the national accounts tables. Net interest is that part of interest that is included as nontransfer interest income in national income; personal interest income is the amount of interest income available to households for spending, and thus part of the household members' personal income.

TABLE 2-7   PERSONAL INCOME, DISPOSABLE PERSONAL INCOME, AND ITS DISPOSITION IN 1985

	$ billions	$ billions	Percent of disposable personal income
Personal income	3,293.5		
Less			
Personal tax and nontax payments	492.7		
Equals			
Disposable personal income		2,800.8	100
Personal outlays		2,671.8	95.4
Personal consumption expenditures	2,582.3		92.2
Interest paid by consumers	87.4		3.1
Transfers to foreigners	2.1		0.1
Personal savings		129.0	4.6

Note: Third and fourth columns show the breakdown of disposable personal income as a percentage of disposable personal income. Numbers may not sum to totals because of rounding.
Source: Survey of Current Business, April 1986.

personal income data are used as a guide to the behavior of GNP by those who follow economic events closely.

Although we have derived personal income in Table 2-6 by starting with national income and making adjustments, it is also possible to build up to an estimate of personal income by looking at its components in a way similar to that shown in Table 2-5. In particular, personal income consists of labor income, plus proprietors' income, plus persons' rental, dividend, and interest income, plus transfer payments, minus personal contributions for social insurance.

Disposable Personal Income and Its Allocation

Not all personal income is available for spending by households. The amount available for spending, *disposable personal income*, deducts from personal income the personal tax and certain nontax payments made by the household sector. The nontax payments include such items as license fees and traffic tickets.

Disposable personal income is the amount households have available to spend or save. Table 2-7 shows how households allocate their disposable income. By far the largest outlay is for personal consumption. Most of the remainder is saved. Small amounts of personal disposable income are used to make interest payments and to make transfers to foreigners.

The U.S. personal saving rate is among the world's lowest. We shall see later why this worries some economists.

Summary

This section has shown the relation between GNP and the income that accrues to the household sector. The main steps we have followed arise from taxes, transfers between sectors, depreciation, and profits.

These intermediate steps remind us that there is an important difference between GNP as the value of output at market prices and the spendable receipts of the household sector. We could have a positive disposable personal income even if GNP were zero, provided there was someone to make the necessary transfer payments. Likewise, GNP could be large, and disposable income small, if the government sector took in a lot of taxes. The larger taxes are relative to government transfers, the smaller is disposable income relative to GNP.

We summarize here in a few identities (and in the accompanying Figure 2-3) the relationships reviewed in each table:

$$\text{GNP} - \text{capital consumption allowance} \equiv \text{NNP} \qquad \text{(Table 2-4)} \qquad (1)$$

$$\text{NNP} - \text{indirect taxes} \equiv \text{national income} \qquad \text{(Table 2-4)} \qquad (2)$$

$$\begin{aligned} \text{National income} &\equiv \text{wages and salaries} + \text{proprietors' income} + \text{rental} \\ \text{income of persons} &+ \text{corporate profits} + \text{net interest} \qquad \text{(Table 2-5)} \end{aligned} \qquad (3)$$

$$\begin{aligned} \text{National income} &- \text{corporate profits} - \text{social insurance contributions} \\ &+ \text{transfer receipts} + \text{interest adjustment} + \text{dividends} \\ &\equiv \text{personal income} \qquad \text{(Table 2-6)} \end{aligned} \qquad (4)$$

$$\begin{aligned} \text{Personal income} &- \text{personal tax and nontax payments} \\ &\equiv \text{disposable personal income} \qquad \text{(Table 2-7)} \end{aligned} \qquad (5)$$

$$\begin{aligned} \text{Disposable personal income} &\equiv \text{personal outlays} \\ &+ \text{personal savings} \qquad \text{(Table 2-7)} \end{aligned} \qquad (6)$$

2-5 OUTLAYS AND COMPONENTS OF DEMAND

In the previous section, we started with GNP and asked how much of the value of goods and services produced actually gets into the hands of households. In this section we present a different perspective on GNP by asking who buys the output, rather than who receives the income. More technically, we look at the demand for output and speak of the *components* of the aggregate demand for goods and services.

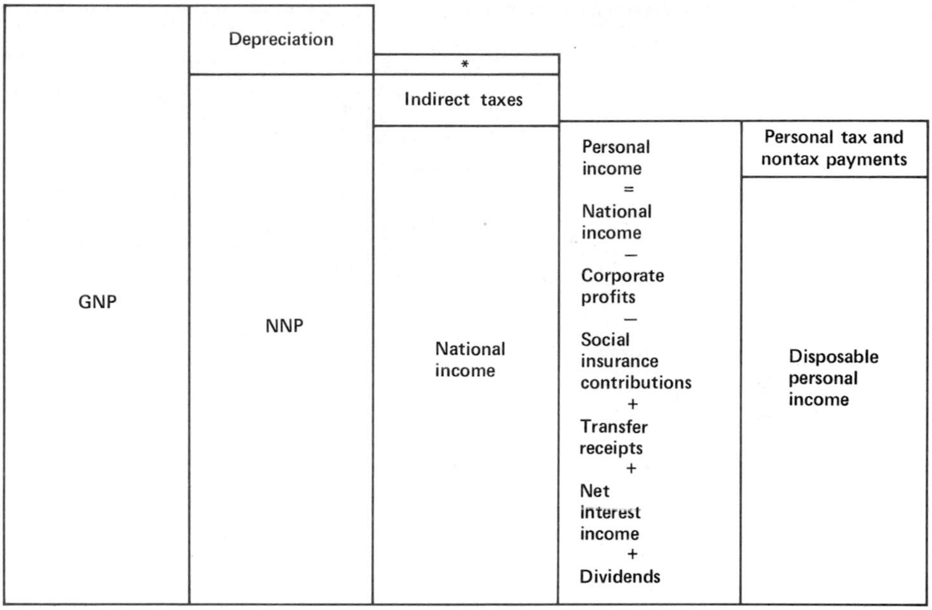

*Statistical discrepancy plus subsidies less current surplus of government enterprises.

FIGURE 2-3   THE RELATION BETWEEN GNP AND DISPOSABLE PERSONAL INCOME.

Total demand for domestic output is made up of four components: (1) consumption spending by households; (2) investment spending by businesses or households; (3) government (federal, state, and local) purchases of goods and services; and (4) foreign demand. We shall now look more closely at each of these components.

Consumption

Table 2-8 presents a breakdown of the demand for goods and services in 1985 by components of demand. The table shows that the chief component of demand is *consumption* spending by the personal sector. This includes anything from food to golf lessons, but involves also, as we shall see in discussing investment, consumer spending on durable goods such as automobiles—spending which might be regarded as investment rather than consumption.

Government

Next in importance we have *government purchases* of goods and services. Here we have such items as national defense expenditures, road paving by state and local governments, and salaries of government employees.

TABLE 2-8	GNP AND COMPONENTS OF DEMAND, 1985	
	$ billions	Percent
Personal consumption expenditures	2,582.3	64.7
Gross private domestic investment	669.3	16.8
Government purchases of goods and services	815.4	20.4
Net exports of goods and services	−78.5	−2.0
Gross national product	3,988.5	100.0

Note: Numbers do not sum to totals because of rounding.
Source: Survey of Current Business, April 1986.

We draw attention to the use of certain words in connection with government spending. We refer to government spending on goods and services as *purchases* of goods and services, and we speak of *transfers plus purchases* as *government expenditure.* The federal government budget, of the order of $1,000 billion, refers to federal government expenditure. Less than half that sum is for federal government purchases of goods and services.

Investment

Gross private domestic investment requires some definitions. First, throughout this book, *investment* means additions to the physical stock of capital. As we use the term, investment does *not* include buying a bond or purchasing stock in General Motors. Practically, investment includes housing construction, building of machinery, business construction, and additions to a firm's inventories of goods.

If we think of investment more generally as any current activity that increases the economy's ability to produce output in future, we would include not only physical investment but also what is known as investment in human capital. Human capital is the knowledge and ability to produce that is embodied in the labor force. Education can be regarded as investment in human capital. In the total incomes system of accounts (TISA), the definition of investment is broadened to include investment in human capital, which means that total investment in that system is more than one-third of GNP. But in this book we mean by investment only additions to the physical capital stock.

The classification of spending as consumption or investment remains to a significant extent a matter of convention. From the economic point of view, there is little difference between a household building up an inventory of peanut butter and a grocery store doing the same. Nevertheless, in the national income accounts, the individual's purchase is treated as a personal consumption expenditure, whereas the store's purchase is treated as investment in the form of inventory investment. Although these borderline cases clearly exist, we can apply a simple rule of thumb: that investment is associated with the business sector's adding to the physical stock of capital, including inventories.[16]

Similar issues arise in the treatment of household sector expenditures. For instance, how should we treat purchases of automobiles by households? Since automobiles usually last for several years, it would seem sensible to classify household purchases of automobiles as investments. We would then treat the *use* of automobiles as providing consumption services. (We could think of imputing a rental income to owner-occupied automobiles.) However, the convention is to treat all household expenditures as consumption spending. This is not quite so bad as it might seem, since the accounts do separate households' purchases of *durable goods* like cars and refrigerators from their other purchases. When consumer spending decisions are studied in detail, expenditures on consumer durables are usually treated separately.[17]

In passing, we note that in Table 2-8, investment is defined as "gross" and "domestic." It is gross in the sense that depreciation is not deducted. Net investment is gross investment minus depreciation. Thus NNP is equal to net investment plus the other categories of spending in Table 2-8.

The term *domestic* means that this is investment spending by domestic residents but is not necessarily spending on goods produced within this country. It may well be an expenditure that falls on foreign goods. Similarly, consumption and government spending may also be partly for imported goods. On the other hand, some of domestic output is sold to foreigners.

Net Exports

The item "Net exports" appears in Table 2-8 to show the effects of domestic spending on foreign goods and foreign spending on domestic goods on the aggregate demand for domestic output. The total demand for the goods we produce includes exports, the demand from foreigners for our goods. It excludes imports, the part of our domestic spending that is not for our own goods. Accordingly, the difference between exports and imports, called *net exports*, is a component of the total demand for our goods. Net exports were negative in 1985, reflecting a high level of imports and a low level of exports.

The point can be illustrated with an example. Assume that instead of having spent $2,582 billion, the personal sector had spent $20 billion more.

---

[16] The GNP accounts record as investment *business sector* additions to the stock of capital. Some government spending, for instance for roads or schools, also adds to the capital stock. Estimates of the capital stock owned by government are available in the *Survey of Current Business*, October 1982, pp. 33–36; this source also provides references to estimates of government investment.

[17] The convention that is adopted with respect to the household sector's purchases of houses also deserves comment. The accounts treat the building of a house as investment by the business sector. When the house is sold to a private individual, the transaction is treated as the transfer of an asset, and not then an act of investment. Even if a house is custom-built by the owner, the accounts treat the builder who is employed by the owner as undertaking the act of investment in building the house. The investment is thus attributed to the business sector.

What would GNP have been? If we assume that government and investment spending had been the same as in Table 2-8, we might be tempted to say that GNP would have been $20 billion higher. That is correct if all the additional spending had fallen on our goods. The other extreme, however, is the case where all the additional spending falls on imports. In that event, consumption would be up $20 billion *and* net exports would be down $20 billion, with *no* net effect on GNP.

Final Sales

Sometimes it is important to distinguish total spending by domestic residents from the level of output produced. The two can differ because spending can exceed output when net imports are positive or it can fall short of output when net exports are positive. In the national income accounts total spending by domestic residents is called *gross domestic purchases* and is defined as follows:

$$\text{Gross domestic purchases} \equiv \text{GNP} + \text{imports} - \text{exports}$$

Although gross domestic purchases refers to *total* spending by domestic residents, it is also useful to have a concept of spending that nets out changes in inventories. This is *final sales to domestic purchasers* and is defined as

$$\text{Final sales to domestic purchasers} \equiv \text{GNP} + \text{imports}$$
$$- \text{exports} - \text{inventory change}$$

The emphasis here is on *final* spending. The definition of final sales is useful because it helps clarify the allocation of output to alternative uses and points out that there are three separate possible sources of disturbances to output: changes in final sales, changes in net exports, and changes in inventories. This point can be seen by simply rearranging the definition to put output on the left-hand side:

$$\text{GNP} \equiv \text{final sales to domestic residents} + \text{net exports} + \text{inventory change}$$

Figure 2-4 shows final sales as a percent of GNP. There are in fact sizable swings. In 1981 and 1982 final sales were much below output, whereas in 1985 they exceeded output by more than 2 percent.

2-6 SOME IMPORTANT IDENTITIES

In this section we summarize the discussion of the preceding sections by writing down a set of relationships which we use extensively in Chapter 3. We introduce here some notation and conventions that we follow throughout the book.

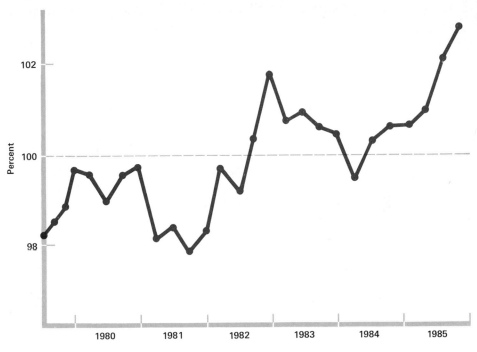

FIGURE 2-4   FINAL SALES TO DOMESTIC PURCHASERS
AS A PERCENT OF GNP. (*Source:* Data Resources, Inc.)

For analytical work in the following chapters, we simplify our analysis by omitting the distinction between GNP and national income. For the most part we disregard depreciation and thus the difference between GNP and NNP, as well as the difference between gross and net investment. We refer simply to investment spending. We also disregard indirect taxes and business transfer payments. With these conventions in mind *we refer to national income and GNP interchangeably as income or output.* These simplifications have no serious consequence and are made only for expositional convenience. Finally, and only for a brief while, we omit both the government and foreign sector. Thus the assumptions we are making conform to those of the circular flow diagram, Figure 2-1.

A Simple Economy

We denote the value of output in our simple economy, which has neither a government nor foreign trade, by Y. Consumption is denoted by C and investment spending by I. The first key identity is that between output produced and output sold. Output produced is Y, which can be written in terms of the components of demand as the sum of consumption and investment spending. (Remember, we have assumed away the government and foreign sectors.) Accordingly, we can write the identity of output sold and output produced[18]:

$$Y \equiv C + I \tag{7}$$

Now, is equation (7) really an identity? Is it inevitably true that all output produced is either consumed or invested? After all, do not firms sometimes make goods that they are unable to sell? The answer to each of the questions is yes. Firms do sometimes make output that they cannot sell, and that accumulates on their shelves. *However, we count the accumulation of inventories as part of investment* (as if the firms sold the goods to themselves to add to their inventories), and therefore, all output is either consumed or invested. Note that we are talking here about *actual* investment, which includes investment in inventories that firms might be very unhappy to make. Because of the way investment is defined, output produced is identically equal to output sold.

Identity (7) formalizes the basis of Table 2-8 (we are still assuming away the government and external sectors). The next step is to draw up a corresponding identity for Table 2-7 and identity (6), which examined the disposition of personal income. For that purpose, it is convenient to ignore the existence of corporations and consolidate or add together the entire private sector. Using this convention, we know that private sector income is Y, since the private sector receives as income the value of goods and services produced. Why? Because who else would get it? There is no government or external sector yet. Now the private sector receives, as disposable personal income, the whole of income Y. How will that income be allocated? Part will be spent on consumption, and part will be saved. Thus we can write

$$Y \equiv S + C \tag{8}$$

where S denotes private sector saving. Identity (8) tells us that the whole of income is allocated to either consumption or saving.

Next, identities (7) and (8) can be combined to read

$$C + I \equiv Y \equiv C + S \tag{9}$$

The left-hand side of equation (9) shows the components of demand, and the right-hand side shows the allocation of income. The identity emphasizes that output produced is equal to output sold. The value of output produced is equal to income received, and income received, in turn, is spent on goods or saved.

---

[18] Throughout the book we distinguish identities from equations. Identities are statements that are *always* true because they are directly implied by definitions of variables or accounting relationships. They do not reflect any economic behavior but are extremely useful in organizing our thinking. Identities, or definitions, are shown with the sign ≡, and equations with the usual equality sign =.

The identity in equation (9) can be slightly reformulated to look at the relation between saving and investment. Subtracting consumption from each part of equation (9), we have

$$I \equiv Y - C \equiv S \qquad (10)$$

Identity (10) is an important result. It shows first that in this simple economy, saving is identically equal to income less consumption. This result is not new, since we have already seen it in equation (8). The new part concerns the identity of the left and right sides: *investment is identically equal to saving.*

One can think of what lies behind this relationship in a variety of ways. In a very simple economy, the only way the individual can save is by undertaking an act of physical investment—by storing grain or building an irrigation channel. In a slightly more sophisticated economy, one could think of investors financing their investing by borrowing from individuals who save.

However, it is important to recognize that equation (10) expresses the identity between investment and saving and that some of the investment might well be undesired inventory investment, occurring as a result of mistakes by producers who expected to sell more than they actually did. The identity is really only a reflection of our definitions—output less consumption is investment, output is income, and income less consumption is saving. Even so, we shall find that identity (10) plays a key role in Chapter 3.

Reintroducing the Government and Foreign Trade

We can now reintroduce the government sector and the external sector. First, for the government we denote purchases of goods and services by G and all taxes by TA. Transfers to the private sector (including interest) are denoted by TR. Net exports (exports minus imports) are denoted by NX.

We return to the identity between output produced and sold, taking account now of the additional components of demand G and NX. Accordingly, we restate the content of Table 2-8 by writing

$$Y \equiv C + I + G + NX \qquad (11)$$

Once more we emphasize that in equation (11) we use actual investment in the identity and thus do not rule out the possibility that firms might not at all be content with the investment. Still, as an accounting identity, equation (11) will hold.

Next we turn to the derivation of the very important relation between output and disposable income. Now we have to recognize that part of income is spent on taxes and that the private sector receives net transfers TR in addition to national income. Disposable income (YD) is thus equal to income plus transfers less taxes:

$$YD \equiv Y + TR - TA \tag{12}$$

Disposable income, in turn, is allocated to consumption and saving:

$$YD \equiv C + S \tag{13}$$

Combining identities (12) and (13) allows us to write consumption as the difference between income, plus transfers minus taxes, and saving:

$$C + S \equiv YD \equiv Y + TR - TA \tag{14}$$

or
$$C \equiv YD - S \equiv Y + TR - TA - S \tag{14a}$$

Identity (14a) states that consumption is disposable income less saving or, alternatively, that consumption is equal to income plus transfers less taxes and saving. Now we use the right-hand side of equation (14a) to substitute for C in identity (11). With some rearrangement we obtain

$$S - I \equiv (G + TR - TA) + NX \tag{15}$$

Saving, Investment, the Government Budget, and Trade

Identity (15) cannot be overemphasized. Its importance arises from the fact that the first set of terms on the right-hand side $(G + TR - TA)$ is the *government budget deficit*. $(G + TR)$ is equal to government[19] purchases of goods and services (G) plus government transfer payments (TR), which is total government spending. TA is the amount of taxes received by the government. The difference $(G + TR - TA)$ is the excess of government spending over its receipts, or its budget deficit. The second term on the right-hand side is the excess of exports over imports, or the *trade surplus*.

Thus identity (15) states that the excess of savings over investment $(S - I)$ of the private sector is equal to the government budget deficit plus the trade surplus. The identity suggests — correctly — that there are important relations among the accounts of the private sector, $S - I$, and government budget $G + TR - TA$, and the external sector. For instance, if, for the private sector, saving is equal to investment, then the government's budget deficit (surplus) is reflected in an equal external deficit (surplus).

Table 2-9 shows the significance of equation (15). To fix ideas, suppose that private sector saving S is equal to $300 (billion). In the first two rows we

---

[19] *Government* throughout this chapter means the federal government plus state and local governments. A breakdown between these entities can be found in the *Economic Report of the President.* There one would see, for example, that state and local governments run surpluses in their budgets and are net recipients of interest payments.

		BD	NX
TABLE 2-9		THE BUDGET DEFICIT, TRADE, SAVING, AND INVESTMENT	
S	I	(budget deficit)	(trade surplus)
300	300	0	0
300	200	100	0
300	250	0	50
300	300	100	−100

assume that exports are equal to imports, so that the trade surplus is zero. In row 1, we assume the government budget is balanced. Investment accordingly has to equal $300 billion. In the next row we assume the government budget deficit is $100 billion. *Given the level of saving* of $300 billion and a zero trade balance, it has to be true that investment is now lower by $100 billion. Row 3 shows how this relationship is affected when there is a trade surplus.

To interpret these relationships, realize that any sector that spends more than it receives in income has to borrow to pay for the excess spending. The private sector has three ways of disposing of its saving. It can make loans to the government, which thereby pays for the excess of its spending over the income it receives from taxes. Or it can lend to foreigners, who are buying more from us than we are buying from them. They therefore are earning less from us than they need to pay for the goods they buy from us, and we have to lend to cover the difference. Or it can lend to business firms which use the funds for investment.

The last row of Table 2-9 is relevant to the change in the U.S. budget and trade deficits between 1981 and 1985. Between those years the government budget deficit increased. Private saving did not increase much, and private investment did not fall. Accordingly, as a matter of arithmetic, the United States had to be running a trade deficit. Of course, that is exactly what happened. Between 1981 and 1985 the government deficit increased by $125 billion while net exports fell by $100 billion.

2-7 SUMMARY

1. As the circular flow diagram shows, output is equal to income and spending.
2. Nominal GNP is the value of the output of final goods and services produced by domestically owned factors of production, measured at market prices.

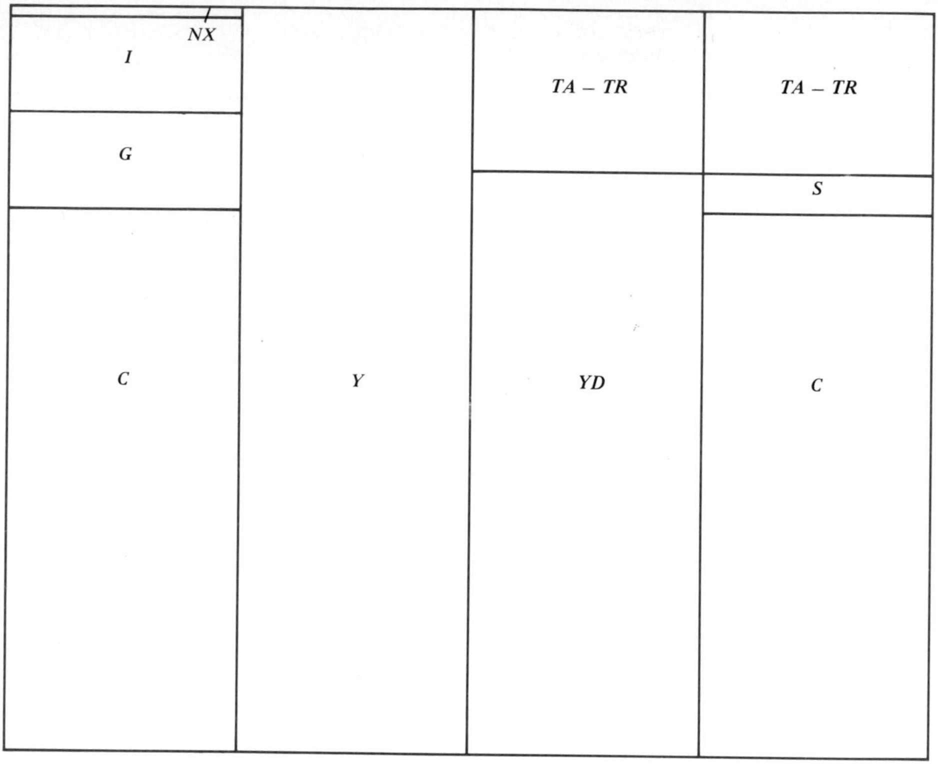

FIGURE 2-5   THE BASIC MACROECONOMIC IDENTITY.

$$C + G + I + NX \equiv Y \equiv YD + (TA - TR) \equiv C + S + (TA - TR) \quad (16)$$

The left-hand side is the demand for output by components; it is
identically equal to output supplied. Output supplied is equal to income.
Disposable income is equal to income plus transfers less taxes.
Disposable income is allocated to saving and consumption.

3. Gross domestic product is the value of output produced within the country. It differs from GNP because some of our GNP is produced abroad and because some of our domestic production is produced by foreign-owned factors of production.

4. Real GNP is the value of the economy's output measured in the prices of some base year. Real GNP comparisons, based on the same set of prices for valuing output, provide a better measure of the change in the economy's physical output than nominal GNP comparisons, which also reflect inflation.

5. The GNP deflator is the ratio of nominal to real GNP. It reflects the general rise in prices from the base date by which real GNP is valued. Other

frequently used price indexes are the consumer and producer price indexes.

6. National income is equal to the incomes received in the economy, valued at factor cost. It is equal to GNP minus depreciation and indirect taxes.
7. Spending on GNP is divided into consumption, investment, government purchases of goods and services, and net exports. The division between consumption and investment in the national income accounts is somewhat arbitrary at the edges.
8. The excess of the private sector's saving over investment is equal to the sum of the budget deficit and the foreign trade surplus.
9. For the remainder of the book we use a simplified model for expositional convenience. We assume away depreciation, indirect taxes, business transfer payments, and the difference between households and corporations. For this simplified model, Figure 2-5 and equation (16) review the *basic macroeconomic identity:*

$$C + G + I + NX \equiv Y \equiv YD + (TA - TR) \equiv C + S + (TA - TR) \qquad (16)$$

The left-hand side is the demand for output by components which is identically equal to output supplied. Output supplied is equal to income. Disposable income is equal to income plus transfers less taxes. Disposable income is allocated to saving and consumption.

KEY TERMS

Final goods
Value added
Market prices
Factor cost
Gross domestic product (GDP)
Net national product (NNP)
Depreciation
Measure of economic welfare (MEW)
The illegal economy
GNP deflator
Consumer price index (CPI)
Producer price index (PPI)
National income

Factor shares
Personal income
Transfers
Disposable personal income
Consumption
Government purchases
Government expenditure
Investment
Net exports
Final sales to domestic purchasers
Consumer durables
Government budget deficit

PROBLEMS

1. Show from national income accounting that:
    (a) An increase in taxes (while transfers remain constant) must imply a change in the trade balance, government purchases, or the saving-investment balance.

(b) An increase in disposable personal income must imply an increase in consumption or an increase in saving.

(c) An increase in both consumption and saving must imply an increase in disposable income.

[For both (b) and (c) assume there are no interest payments by households or transfer payments to foreigners.]

2. The following is information from the national income accounts for a hypothetical country.

GNP	$4,800
Gross investment	800
Net investment	300
Consumption	3,000
Government purchases of goods and services	960
National income	3,850
Wages and salaries	2,920
Proprietors' income + rental income of persons	320
Dividends	100
Net interest	260
Government budget surplus	30
Social insurance contributions	380
Personal interest income	380
Government and business transfers to persons	520
Personal tax and nontax payments	600
Interest paid by consumers and transfers to foreigners	90

What is:

(a) NNP?

(b) net exports?

(c) indirect taxes?
   [Assume "Other (net)" is zero.]

(d) corporate profits?

(e) government taxes — transfers?

(f) personal income?

(g) disposable personal income?

(h) personal saving?

3. What would happen to GNP if the government hired unemployed workers, who had been receiving amount TR in unemployment benefits, as government employees to do nothing, and now paid them TR? Explain.

4. What is the difference in the national income accounts between:

(a) A firm's buying an auto for an executive and the firm's paying the executive additional income to buy a car?

(b) Your hiring your spouse (who takes care of the house) rather than just having him or her do the work without pay?

(c) Your deciding to buy an American car rather than a German car?

5. Explain the following terms: (a) value added, (b) factor cost, (c) inventory investment, (d) GNP deflator.

6. (a) In 1985 U.S. GNP was $3,989 billion. GDP was $3,948. Why is there a difference?

(b) In 1985 U.S. GNP was $3,389 billion. NNP was $3,550. What accounts for the difference? How typical is the difference for 1984 as a fraction of GNP?

7. This question deals with price index numbers. Consider a simple economy where only three items are in the CPI: food, housing, and entertainment (fun). Assume in the base period, say, 1967, the household consumed the following quantities at the then prevailing prices:

	Quantities	Prices per unit, $	Expenditure, $
Food	5	14	70
Housing	3	10	30
Fun	4	5	20
Total			120

(a) Define the consumer price index.

(b) Assume that the basket of goods that defines the CPI is as given in the table. Calculate the CPI for 1986 if the prices prevailing in 1986 are: food, $30 per unit; housing, $20 per unit; and fun, $6 per unit.

*(c) Show that the change in the CPI relative to the base year is a weighted average of the individual price changes, where the weights are given by the base year expenditure shares of the various goods.

8. Here are some 1984 GNP data, in billions:

GNP = $3,663   Indirect taxes = $304
NNP = $3,260   Other (net) = −$4

(a) What are *(i)* depreciation and *(ii)* national income?

(b) Why are indirect taxes deducted from NNP to get national income?

9. After Table 2-5 we asked you to answer certain questions. Here they are:

(a) How would a shift by corporations from equity to debt finance affect the distribution of national income in Table 2-5?

(b) How would the incorporation of a business affect the table?

(c) What difference would it make if some existing houses were owned by corporations instead of individuals?

10. Assume that GNP is $5,000, personal disposable income is $4,100, and the government budget deficit is $200. Consumption is $3,800, and the trade deficit is $100.

(a) How large is saving S?

(b) What is the size of investment I?

(c) How large is government spending?

APPENDIX: PRICE INDEX FORMULAS

Both the PPI and CPI are price indexes which compare the current and base year cost of a basket of goods of *fixed* composition. If we denote the base year quantities of the various goods by q_0^i and their base year prices by p_0^i, the cost of the basket in the base year is $\Sigma p_0^i q_0^i$, where the summation (Σ) is over all the goods in the basket. The cost of a basket of the *same* quantities but at today's prices is $\Sigma p_t^i q_0^i$, where p_t^i is today's price. The CPI or PPI is the ratio of today's cost to the base year cost, or

$$\text{Consumer or producer price index} = \frac{\Sigma p_t^i q_0^i}{\Sigma p_0^i q_0^i} \times 100$$

---

* An asterisk denotes a more difficult problem.

This is a so-called *Laspeyres*, or *base-weighted*, price index.

The GNP deflator by contrast uses the weights of the *current* period to calculate the price index. Let q_t^i be the quantities of the different goods produced in the current year.

$$\text{GNP deflator} = \frac{\text{GNP measured in current prices}}{\text{GNP measured in base year prices}}$$

$$= \frac{\Sigma p_t^i q_t^i}{\Sigma p_0^i q_t^i} \times 100$$

This is known as a *Paasche*, or *current-weighted*, price index.

Comparing the two formulas we see that they differ only in that q_0^i, or the base year quantities, appears in both numerator and denominator of the CPI and PPI formula, whereas q_t^i appears in the formula for the deflator. In practice, the CPI, PPI, and GNP deflector indexes differ also because they involve different collections of goods.

Problem: Calculate both Laspeyres and Paasche price indexes for the information in Table 2-2.

3

AGGREGATE DEMAND AND EQUILIBRIUM INCOME AND OUTPUT

In Chapter 2 we studied the measurement of national income and output (GNP). With these fundamental concepts, we can now begin our study of the factors that determine the level of national income and product. Ultimately, we want to know why real GNP sometimes falls (and the rate of unemployment rises), as it did in the 1981–1982 recession, and why at other times income rises very rapidly (and unemployment falls), as it did in the 1983–1984 recovery.

We also want to know what determines the rate of inflation. Why was it so high in 1980? How did it come down so fast, from 13 percent in 1980 to 3 percent in 1983? We want to know whether public policies, such as changes in government spending and tax rates, or changes in the growth rate of the money supply, or changes in interest rates, can affect the level of income and the rates of inflation and unemployment. And if they can, we want to know how.

The study of those questions occupies the rest of the book. But to make progress we proceed slowly. We begin in this chapter with a simplified model of the economy that isolates the crucial concept of *aggregate demand,* while still omitting both some factors that affect aggregate demand and considerations of aggregate supply. In later chapters we gradually introduce those other factors. By the time we have completed Chapter 7, we shall be able to understand the behavior of the key macroeconomic variables—the rates of unemployment and inflation and the level of GNP.

We start from the macroeconomic identities in equation (16) of Chapter 2 and in Figure 2-4. First, GNP is equal to total spending on goods and services, consisting of consumption C, investment I, government purchases of goods and services G, and net exports NX. Second, GNP is also equal to income received in the economy.[1] Income, in turn, increased by transfers TR and reduced by taxes TA, is allocated to consumption C and saving S. Thus

$$C + I + G + NX \equiv Y \equiv C + (TA - TR) + S$$

In this chapter we go beyond that *accounting identity* to begin our study of the factors that determine the level of national product or output. In particular, we focus on the interactions between the level of output and aggregate demand. The main point of the chapter is to show that *there is a single level of equilibrium output at which the aggregate (total) demand for goods and services is equal to the level of output.*

To begin with, we simplify our task by discussing a hypothetical world without a government. $(G \equiv TA \equiv TR \equiv 0)$ and without foreign trade $(NX \equiv 0)$. In such a world, the accounting identity simplifies to

$$C + I \equiv Y \equiv C + S \tag{1}$$

where Y denotes the *real* value of output and income. Throughout this chapter a change in a macroeconomic aggregate is a change in its *real* value. For instance, when we speak of a change in consumption spending, we mean a change in real consumption spending.

The key concept of *equilibrium output* is introduced immediately, in Section 3-1. To keep the analysis as simple as possible, we assume to begin with that the demand for goods is *autonomous*—that is, independent of the level of income.[2] In fact, though, increases in income increase the demand for consumption goods. Accordingly, in Section 3-2 we extend the basic analysis by introducing the *consumption function,* which relates the demand for consumption goods to the level of income. In Sections 3-2 and 3-3 we derive explicit formulas for the equilibrium level of income.

The government sector is reintroduced in Section 3-4, which includes the first discussion of fiscal policy. The government budget is examined in Section 3-5. We do not include foreign trade in this chapter, even though exports account for about 12 percent of GNP. Instead, issues of the open economy are introduced in Chapter 6. For the impatient reader, problem 14 at the end of the chapter provides an introduction to the role of trade.

---

[1] Because output is equal to income received in the economy, economists tend to use the terms *income* and *output* interchangeably when discussing the level of economic activity.

[2] The terms *autonomous* and *induced* are traditionally used to indicate spending that is independent of the level of income and dependent on the level of income, respectively. More generally, autonomous spending is spending that is independent of the other variables explained in a given theory.

3-1 EQUILIBRIUM OUTPUT

In this chapter and the next we assume a world where all prices are given and constant.[3] In terms of Figure 1-8, the aggregate supply curve is horizontal.

What would determine the level of output actually produced if firms could supply any amount of output at the prevailing level of prices? *Demand* must enter the picture. Firms would produce at a level just sufficient to meet demand.

To develop this point, we define the concepts of *aggregate demand* and *equilibrium output*.

Aggregate Demand

Aggregate demand is the total amount of goods demanded in the economy. In general, the quantity of goods demanded, or aggregate demand, depends on the level of income in the economy and—as we shall see later—on interest rates. But for now we shall assume that the amount of goods demanded is constant, independent of the level of income.

Aggregate demand is shown in Figure 3-1 by the horizontal line *AD*. In the diagram, aggregate demand is equal to 300 (billion dollars). This means that the total amount of goods demanded in the economy is $300 billion, independent of the level of income.

But if the quantity of goods demanded is constant, independent of the level of income, what determines the actual level of income? We have to turn to the concept of equilibrium output.

Equilibrium Output

Output is at its *equilibrium* level when the quantity of output produced is equal to the quantity demanded. An equilibrium situation is one which no forces are causing to change. We now explain why output is at its equilibrium level when it is equal to aggregate demand.

In Figure 3-1 we show the level of output on the horizontal axis. The 45° line serves as a reference line that translates any horizontal distance into an equal vertical distance. For any given level of output Y on the horizontal axis, the 45° line gives the level of aggregate demand that is equal to that level of output. For instance, at point E, both output and aggregate demand are equal to 300.

Point E is the point of equilibrium output, at which the quantity of output produced is equal to the quantity demanded. To understand why this should be the equilibrium level of output, suppose that firms were producing some

---

[3] The assumption that prices are constant is made to simplify the exposition of Chaps. 3 and 4. In later chapters, starting with Chap. 7, we use the theory of aggregate demand developed here to study the factors that determine the price level and cause it to change over time.

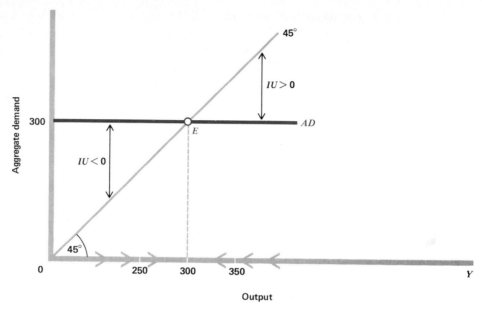

FIGURE 3-1   EQUILIBRIUM WITH CONSTANT AGGREGATE
DEMAND. Aggregate demand is shown by the *AD* line, and is equal to
300. Output is at its equilibrium level when it is equal to aggregate
demand, equal to 300. Thus the equilibrium is shown at point *E*. At any
other output level, inventories are changing in a way that causes firms
to change their production in a direction that moves output toward the
equilibrium level.

other amount, say, 350 units. Then output would exceed demand. Firms
would be unable to sell all they produce and would find their warehouses
filling with inventories of unsold goods. They would then cut their output.
This is shown by the horizontal arrow pointing left at the output level of 350 on
the horizontal axis.

Similarly, if output were less than 300, say, at 250, firms would either run
out of goods or be running down their inventories. They would therefore
increase output, as shown by the horizontal arrow pointing to the right from
the output level of 250.

Thus at point *E*, the equilibrium level of output, firms are selling as much
as they produce, people are buying the amount they want to purchase, and
there is no tendency for the level of output to change. At any other level of
output, the pressure from increasing or declining inventories causes firms to
change the level of output.

Equilibrium Output and the National Income Identity

We have defined equilibrium output as that level of output at which aggregate
demand for goods is equal to output. To clarify that definition, we have to

dispose of an unsettling issue that arises from the accounting identity in equation (1), derived from our study of national income accounting. The identity in equation (1) states that demand, $C + I$, is *identically* equal to supply Y, *whatever* the level of output. That seems to mean that demand equals supply at *any* level of output, so that any level of output could be the equilibrium level.

The issue is resolved by recalling that aggregate demand is the amount of goods people *want to buy*, whereas in the national income accounts investment and consumption are the amounts of the goods *actually* bought for investment or consumption, whether or not people wanted to or planned to buy them. In particular, the investment measured in equation (1) includes *involuntary*, or *unintended* (or *undesired*), inventory changes, which occur when firms find themselves selling more or less goods than they had planned to sell. Similarly, if households cannot buy all the goods they want, the consumption measured in equation (1) will be different from planned consumption.

We have to make a distinction between the actual aggregate demand that is measured in an accounting context and the relevant economic concept of planned (desired, intended) aggregate demand.

Actual aggregate demand $(C + I)$ is, by the accounting identity in equation (1), equal to the level of output (Y). The output level is determined by firms. In deciding how much to produce, firms calculate how much investment, including inventory investment, they want to undertake. They also produce to meet the demand for consumption they forecast will be forthcoming from households. *Planned aggregate demand* consists of the amount of consumption that households plan to carry out plus the amount of investment planned by firms.[4]

If firms miscalculate households' consumption demands, planned aggregate demand does not equal actual aggregate demand. Suppose first that firms overestimate consumption demand. In terms of Table 3-1, suppose that firms decide to produce 350 units of output, expecting to be able to sell that amount. However, aggregate demand is only 300. The firms thus sell 300 units of output. But they are left with 50, which they have to add to their inventories. It is as if they buy those extra 50 units of output themselves. In the national income accounts, additions to inventories count as investment. Of course, this is not *planned* or *desired* investment, but it does count as part of investment. Looking at the national income accounts for such an economy, we would see output equal to 350 and consumption plus investment equal to 350. But the equality of output and $(C + I)$ does not mean that 350 is the equilibrium level of output, because 50 units of investment were undesired additions to inventories.

When aggregate demand, the amount people *want* to buy, is not equal to output, there is unplanned inventory investment. We summarize this as

---

[4] From now on we shall assume that actual consumption is equal to planned consumption, so that all differences between actual and planned aggregate demand are reflected in unintended inventory changes. In practical terms, this means we are not considering situations where firms put "Sold Out" signs in their windows and customers cannot buy what they want.

TABLE 3-1	EQUILIBRIUM OUTPUT AND INVOLUNTARY INVENTORY CHANGE	
Output	Aggregate demand	Involuntary inventory changes
200	300	−100
250	300	−50
300	300	0
350	300	+50
400	300	+100

$$IU = Y - AD \qquad (2)$$

where IU is unplanned additions to inventory.

In terms of Figure 3-1, unplanned inventory investment is shown by the vertical arrows. When output exceeds 300, there is unplanned inventory investment. When output is less than 300, there are unplanned reductions in inventories. In Table 3-1, unplanned inventory investment is shown in the last column.

An alternative way of seeing the link between the national income accounting relations and the economic concepts is in equation (2a). Here we state that actual output is equal to planned spending or aggregate demand, plus involuntary inventory adjustment.

$$\text{Output} = \text{planned spending} + \text{involuntary inventory adjustment} \qquad (2a)$$

The *equilibrium* level of income is the level of income (or output) at which planned spending is equal to actual output, so that there is no involuntary inventory acumulation or decumulation.

Equilibrium Output and Demand

We can now define equilibrium output more formally, using equation (2). Output is at its equilibrium level when it is equal to aggregate demand, or when unplanned inventory accumulation is zero. That is, output is at its equilibrium level when

$$Y = AD \qquad (3)$$

There are three essential notions from this section:

1. Aggregate demand determines the equilibrium level of output.

2. At equilibrium, unintended changes in inventories are zero, and households consume the amount they want to consume.
3. An adjustment process for output based on unintended inventory changes will actually move output to its equilibrium level.[5]

Note, too, that the definition of equilibrium implies that actual spending on consumption and investment equals planned spending. In equilibrium, aggregate demand, which is planned spending, equals output. Since output identically equals income, we see also that *in equilibrium, planned spending equals income*.

3-2 THE CONSUMPTION FUNCTION AND AGGREGATE DEMAND

The preceding section studied the equilibrium level of output (and income) on the assumption that aggregate demand was simply a constant. Now we move to a more realistic specification of aggregate demand and begin to examine the economic variables that determine it.

In the simplified model we are working with, which excludes both the government and foreign trade, aggregate demand consists of the demands for consumption and investment. The demand for consumption goods is not in practice autonomous as we have so far assumed, but rather increases with income — families with higher income consume more than families with lower income, and countries where income is higher typically have higher levels of total consumption. The relationship between consumption and income is described by the *consumption function*.

The Consumption Function

We assume that consumption demand increases along with the level of income[6]:

$$C = \overline{C} + cY$$

where
$$\overline{C} > 0 \quad \text{and} \quad 0 < c < 1 \tag{4}$$

---

[5] You may have noticed that the adjustment process we describe raises the possibility that output will temporarily exceed its new equilibrium level during the adjustment to an increase in aggregate demand. This is the *inventory cycle*. Suppose firms desire to keep on hand inventories which are proportional to the level of demand. When demand unexpectedly rises, inventories are depleted. In subsequent periods, the firms have to produce not only to meet the new higher level of aggregate demand, but also to restore their depleted inventories and to raise them to a higher level. While they are rebuilding their inventories and also producing to meet the higher level of demand, their total production will exceed the new higher level of aggregate demand.

[6] Equation (4) is special because consumption is assumed to be a *linear* function of income. That means that in terms of Fig. 3-2, we can show the consumption function as a straight line. You might want to experiment with nonlinear consumption functions. Note also that because income is equal to output, we use the same symbol, Y, for both income and output.

This consumption function is shown in Figure 3-2a. The consumption function in equation (4) implies that at low levels of income consumption exceeds income, whereas at high levels of income consumption is less than income. The *intercept* of the consumption function is $\overline{C}$ and the *slope* is c. Along the consumption function the level of consumption rises with income. Box 3-1 shows that this relationship holds in practice.

The coefficient c is sufficiently important to have a special name, the *marginal propensity to consume*. The marginal propensity to consume is the increase in consumption per unit increase in income. In our case, the marginal propensity to consume is less than 1, which implies that out of a dollar increase in income, only a fraction c is spent on consumption. For example, if c is 0.8, then when income rises by $1, consumption increases by $0.80.

Consumption and Saving

What happens to the rest, the fraction $(1 - c)$ that is not spent on consumption? If it is not spent, it must be saved. Income is either spent or saved; there are no other uses to which income can be put.

More formally, look at equation (1) which says that income that is not spent on consumption is saved, or

$$S \equiv Y - C \tag{5}$$

Equation (5) tells us that by definition, *saving is equal to income minus consumption.* This means that we cannot postulate, in addition to the consumption function, an independent saving function and still expect consumption and saving to add up to income.

The consumption function in equation (4), together with equation (5), which we call the *budget constraint,* implies a saving function. The saving function is the function that relates the level of saving to the level of income. Substituting the consumption function in equation (5) into the budget constraint in equation (6) yields the saving function

$$S \equiv Y - C$$
$$= Y - (\overline{C} + cY) \tag{6}$$
$$= -\overline{C} + (1 - c)Y$$

From equation (6), saving is an increasing function of the level of income because the *marginal propensity to save,* $s = 1 - c$, is positive. For instance, suppose the marginal propensity to consume, c, is 0.8, meaning that 80 cents out of each extra dollar of income is consumed. Then the marginal propensity to save, s, is 0.2, meaning that the remaining 20 cents of each extra dollar of income is saved.

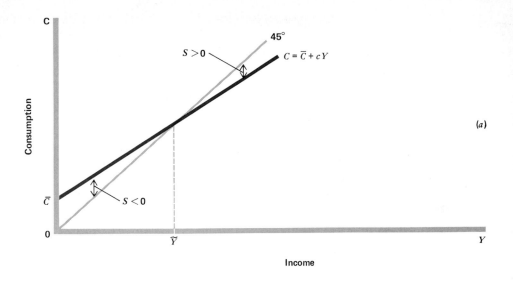

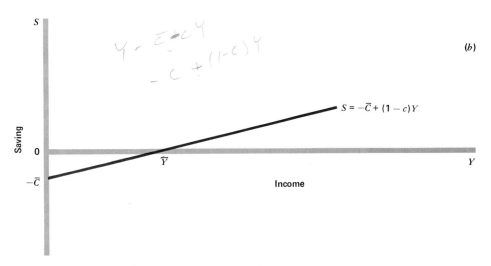

FIGURE 3-2   THE CONSUMPTION AND SAVING FUNCTIONS. *(a)*
The consumption function shows consumption increasing with income.
Its intercept is $\overline{C}$, and its slope, the marginal propensity to consume, is
c. At low levels of income, consumption is above the level of income,
implying that people spend more than they earn. At higher levels of
income, consumption is below the level of income, implying that people
save part of their income. *(b)* The saving function in Figure 3-2*b* is
consistent with the consumption function above it, at low income levels,
saving is negative, and it is positive at higher income levels. At income
level $\widetilde{Y}$, saving is exactly zero.

THE CONSUMPTION-INCOME RELATIONSHIP

The consumption function of equation (4),

$$C = \overline{C} + cY$$

provides a good first description of the consumption-income relationship. Annual consumption and disposable income data for the United States for the years since 1947 are plotted in Figure 1. Recall from Chapter 2 that disposable income is the amount of income households have available for either spending or saving after paying taxes and receiving transfers.

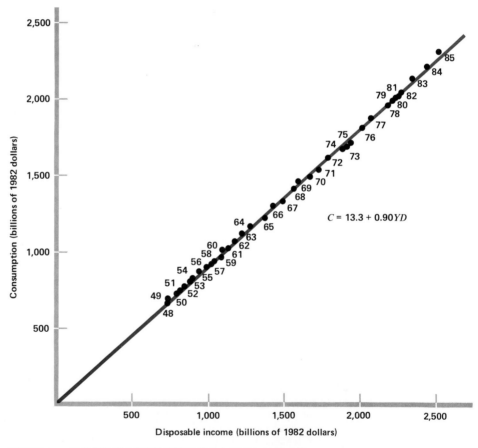

FIGURE 1   THE CONSUMPTION-INCOME RELATION, 1948–1985.
There is a close relationship in practice between consumption spending and disposable income. Consumption spending rises on average by 90 cents for every extra dollar of disposable income. The color line is the fitted regression line that summarizes the relationship shown by the points for the individual years.

The figure reveals a very close relationship between consumption and disposable income. The actual relationship is

$$C = 13.3 + 0.9YD$$

where C and YD are each measured in billions of real (1982) dollars. Although the relationship between consumption and disposable income is close, not all the points in Figure 1 lie exactly on the line. That means that something other than disposable income is affecting consumption in any given year. We turn our attention to those other factors determining consumption in Chapter 8. Meanwhile, it is reassuring that equation (4) is a quite accurate description of the real world's consumption-income relationship.

The interrelationship between the consumption and savings functions examined in equation (6) can also be seen in Figure 3-2, where the vertical distance between the consumption function and the 45° line at each level of income measures saving. At low levels of income, saving is negative, reflecting the fact that consumption exceeds income. An individual can have negative saving by using up his or her assets—bank account or stocks—to pay for purchases in excess of income. Conversely, at sufficiently high levels of income, saving becomes positive, reflecting the fact that not all income is spent on consumption.

The saving function is the mirror image of the consumption function. Figure 3-2b shows the saving function that is derived from the consumption function in Figure 3-2a by plotting the vertical distance between income and consumption spending at each level of income. Of course, Figure 3-2b is merely a representation of equation (6). Note that the slope of the saving function in Figure 3-2b is the marginal propensity to save, $s = 1 - c$, as defined above.

Planned Investment and Aggregate Demand

We have now specified one component of aggregate demand, consumption demand. We must also consider the determinants of investment spending, or an *investment function*. We cut short the discussion for the present by simply assuming that planned investment spending is at a constant level $\bar{I}$.[7]

---

[7] In Chaps. 4, 5, and 10, investment spending will become a function of the rate of interest and will gain an important place in the transmission of monetary policy.

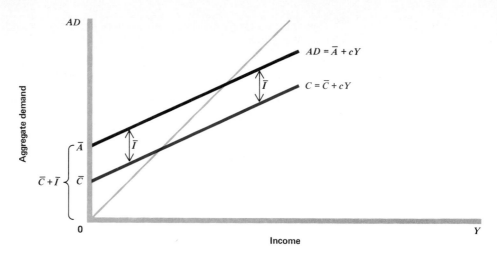

FIGURE 3-3   AGGREGATE DEMAND. Aggregate demand is the sum of the demands for consumption and investment goods. The consumption function is upward-sloping. Investment demand $\bar{I}$ is assumed constant and is added to consumption demand to obtain the level of aggregate demand at each level of income. The line AD shows how aggregate demand increases with income. Its slope is c, the marginal propensity to consume.

Aggregate demand is the sum of consumption and investment demands:

$$AD = C + \bar{I}$$
$$= \bar{C} + cY + \bar{I} \qquad (7)$$
$$= \bar{A} + cY$$

The aggregate demand function (7) is shown in Figure 3-3. Part of aggregate demand, $\bar{A}\ (=(\bar{C}+\bar{I}))$, is independent of the level of income, or autonomous. But aggregate demand also depends on the level of income. It increases with the level of income, because consumption demand increases with income.

Equilibrium Income and Output

The next step is to use the aggregate demand function AD in Figure 3-3 and equation (7) to determine the equilibrium level of output and input. We plot the AD schedule again in Figure 3-4.

Recall the basic point of this chapter: the equilibrium level of income is such that aggregate demand equals output (which in turn equals income). The 45° line in Figure 3-4 shows points at which output and aggregate demand are equal. The aggregate demand schedule in Figure 3-4 cuts the 45° line at E, and

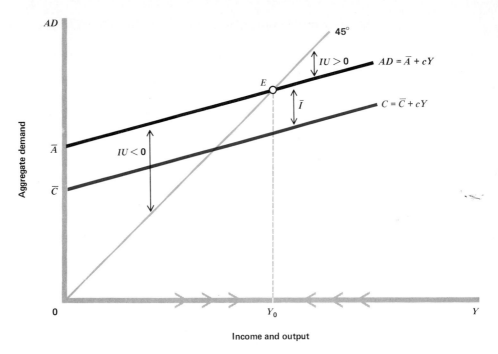

FIGURE 3-4   DETERMINATION OF EQUILIBRIUM INCOME AND
OUTPUT. Output is at its equilibrium level when aggregate demand is
equal to output. This occurs at point E, corresponding to the output
(and income) level Y_0. At any higher level of output, aggregate demand
is below the level of output, firms are unable to sell all they produce and
there is undesired accumulation of inventories. Firms therefore reduce
output, as shown by the arrows. Similarly, at any level of output below
Y_0, aggregate demand exceeds output, firms run short of goods to sell,
and they therefore increase output. Only at the equilibrium output level
Y_0 are firms producing the amount that is demanded, and there is no
tendency for the level of output to change.

it is accordingly at E that aggregate demand is equal to output (equals income).
Only at E, and at the corresponding equilibrium level of income and output,
Y_0, does aggregate demand exactly equal output.[8] At that level of output and
income, planned spending precisely matches production.

The arrows in Figure 3-4 indicate once again how we reach equilibrium. If
firms expand production whenever they face unintended decreases in their
inventory holdings, then they increase output at any level below Y_0, because
below Y_0, aggregate demand exceeds output and inventories are declining.
Conversely, for output levels above Y_0, firms find inventories piling up and
therefore cut production. This process leads to the output level Y_0, where

---

[8] We frequently use the subscript $_0$ to denote the equilibrium level of a variable.

current production exactly matches planned aggregate spending, and unintended inventory changes are therefore equal to zero. Again, the arrows in Figure 3-4 represent the dynamic process by which the economy moves to the equilibrium level of output Y_0.[9]

THE FORMULA FOR EQUILIBRIUM OUTPUT

The determination of equilibrium output in Figure 3-4 can also be described using equation (7) and the equilibrium condition in the goods market that output is equal to aggregate demand:

$$Y = AD \tag{8}$$

The level of aggregate demand AD is specified in equation (7). Substituting for AD in equation (8), we have the equilibrium condition as

$$Y = \overline{A} + cY \tag{9}$$

Since we have Y on both sides of the equilibrium condition in equation (9), we can collect the terms and solve for the equilibrium level of income and output, denoted by Y_0:

$$Y - cY = \overline{A}$$

or
$$Y(1 - c) = \overline{A}$$

Thus the equilibrium level of income, at which aggregate demand equals output, is

$$Y_0 = \frac{1}{1 - c} \overline{A} \tag{10}$$

Figure 3-4 sheds light on equation (10). The position of the aggregate demand schedule is characterized by its slope c and intercept $\overline{A}$. The intercept $\overline{A}$ is the level of autonomous spending, that is, spending that is independent of the level of income. The other determinant of the equilibrium level of income is the marginal propensity to consume, c, which is the slope of the aggregate demand schedule.

Given the intercept, a steeper aggregate demand function — as would be implied by a higher marginal propensity to consume — implies a higher level of equilibrium income. Similarly, for a given marginal propensity to consume, a higher level of autonomous spending — in terms of Figure 3-4 a larger intercept — implies a higher equilibrium level of income. These results, sug-

---

[9] Do you see that there is once more the possibility of an inventory cycle? Refer to footnote 5.

gested by Figure 3-4, are easily verified from equation (10), which gives the formula for the equilibrium level of income.

Thus, the equilibrium level of output is higher, the larger the marginal propensity to consume, c, and the larger the level of autonomous spending $\bar{A}$.

Saving and Investment

There is an alternative, useful formulation of the equilibrium condition that aggregate demand is equal to output. *In equilibrium, planned investment equals saving.* This condition applies only to an economy in which there is no government and no foreign trade.

To understand this relationship, return to Figure 3-4. The vertical distance between the aggregate demand and consumption schedules in that figure is equal to planned investment spending $\bar{I}$. Recall in addition (from Figure 3-2) that the vertical distance between the consumption schedule and the 45° line measures saving at each level of income.

We thus have two vertical distances: between the AD and C schedules in Figure 3-4 and between the 45° line and the C schedule in Figure 3-2a. The equilibrium level of income is one where AD crosses the 45° line, at E. Accordingly, at the equilibrium level of income — and only at that level — the two vertical distances are equal. Thus at the equilibrium level of income, saving equals (planned) investment. By contrast, above the equilibrium level of income Y_0, saving (the distance between the 45° line and the consumption schedule) exceeds investment, while below Y_0, investment exceeds saving.

Now, is the equality between saving and investment at equilibrium an essential characteristic of the equilibrium level of income, or is it a mere curiosity? It is an essential characteristic of equilibrium. We can see that by starting with the basic equilibrium condition, equation (8), which states that in equilibrium, $Y = AD$. If we subtract consumption from both Y and AD, we realize that $Y - C$ is saving and $AD - C$ is planned investment. In symbols,

$$Y = AD$$
$$Y - C = AD - C \tag{11}$$
$$S = \bar{I}$$

Thus, the condition $S = \bar{I}$ is merely another way of stating the basic equilibrium condition.[10]

There is also a diagrammatic derivation of the equilibrium level of income in terms of equation (11)'s balance between saving and investment. In Figure 3-5, we show the saving function that was derived in Figure 3-2. We have

---

[10] In problem 3 at the end of this chapter, we ask you to derive equation (10) for Y_0 by starting from $S = \bar{I}$ and substituting for S from equation (6).

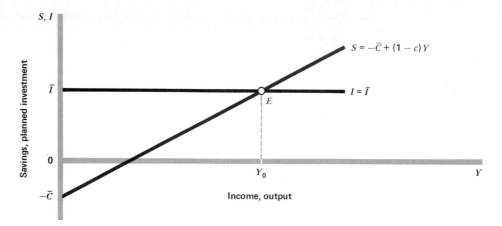

FIGURE 3-5 SAVING AND INVESTMENT. An alternative definition of the equilibrium level of output is that it occurs where saving is equal to (planned) investment. This is shown at point E, with corresponding output level Y_0. At higher levels of output, consumers want to save more than $\bar{I}$. They do not buy all of output, inventories accumulate, and actual investment is made equal to saving because firms undertake undesired inventory investment. They therefore cut output, and the economy moves to output level Y_0.

drawn, too, planned investment spending, indicated by the horizontal line with intercept $\bar{I}$. Equilibrium income is shown at the level Y_0.

3-3 THE MULTIPLIER

In this section we develop an answer to the following question: By how much does a $1 increase in autonomous spending raise the equilibrium level of income?[11] There appears to be a simple answer. Since, in equilibrium, income equals aggregate demand, it would seem that a $1 increase in (autonomous) demand or spending should raise equilibrium income by $1. That answer is wrong. Let us now see why.

Suppose first that output increased by $1 to match the increased level of autonomous spending. This increase in output and income would in turn give rise to further *induced* spending as consumption rises because the level of income has risen. How much of the initial $1 increase in income would be spent on consumption? Out of an additional dollar of income, a fraction c is

---

[11] Recall that autonomous spending $\bar{A}$ is spending that is independent of the level of income. Note also that the answer to this question is contained in equation (10). Can you deduce the answer directly from equation (10)? This section provides an explanation of that answer.

TABLE 3-2   THE MULTIPLIER

Round	Increase in demand this round	Increase in production this round	Total increase in income
1	$\Delta \overline{A}$	$\Delta \overline{A}$	$\Delta \overline{A}$
2	$c \, \Delta \overline{A}$	$c \, \Delta \overline{A}$	$(1 + c) \, \Delta \overline{A}$
3	$c^2 \, \Delta \overline{A}$	$c^2 \, \Delta \overline{A}$	$(1 + c + c^2) \, \Delta \overline{A}$
4	$c^3 \, \Delta \overline{A}$	$c^3 \, \Delta \overline{A}$	$(1 + c + c^2 + c^3) \, \Delta \overline{A}$
.	.	.	.
.	.	.	.
.	.	.	$\dfrac{1}{1 - c} \Delta \overline{A}$
1	1.0	1.0	1.0
2	0.6	0.6	1.6
3	0.36	0.36	1.96
4	0.216	0.216	2.176
5	0.1296	0.1296	2.3056
.	.	.	.
.	.	.	.
.	.	.	2.5

consumed. Assume then that production increases further to meet this induced expenditure, that is, that output and so income increase by $1 + c$. That will still leave us with an excess demand, because the very fact of an expansion in production and income by $1 + c$ will give rise to further induced spending. This story could clearly take a long time to tell. We seem to have arrived at an impasse where an expansion in output to meet excess demand leads to a further expansion in demand without an obvious end to the process.

It helps to lay out the various steps in this chain more carefully. We do this in Table 3-2. We start off in the first round with an increase in autonomous spending $\Delta \overline{A}$. Next we allow an expansion in production to meet exactly that increase in demand. Production accordingly expands by $\Delta \overline{A}$. This increase in production gives rise to an equal increase in income and, therefore, via the consumption function, $C = \overline{C} + cY$, gives rise in the second round to induced expenditures of size $c \, (\Delta \overline{A})$. Assume again that production expands to meet the increase in spending. The production adjustment this time is $c \, (\Delta \overline{A})$, and so is the increase in income. This gives rise to a third round of induced spending equal to the marginal propensity to consume times the increase in income $c(c \, \Delta \overline{A}) = c^2 \, \Delta \overline{A}$. Careful inspection of the last term shows that induced expenditures in the third round are smaller than those in the second round. Since the marginal propensity to consume, c, is less than 1, the term c^2 is less than c. This can be seen also in the lower part of the table, where we assume $c = 0.6$ and show the steps corresponding to those in the upper part of the table.

If we write out the successive rounds of increased spending, starting with the initial increase in autonomous demand, we obtain

$$\Delta AD = \Delta \overline{A} + c \, \Delta \overline{A} + c^2 \, \Delta \overline{A} + c^3 \, \Delta \overline{A} + \cdots$$
$$= \Delta \overline{A} \, (1 + c + c^2 + c^3 + \cdots) \tag{12}$$

For a value of $c < 1$, the successive terms in the series become progressively smaller. In fact, we are dealing with a geometric series, the sum of which is calculated as

$$\Delta AD = \frac{1}{1 - c} \, \Delta \overline{A} = \Delta Y_0 \tag{13}$$

From equation (13) therefore, the cumulative change in aggregate spending is equal to a multiple of the increase in autonomous spending. This could also have been deduced from equation (10).[12] The multiple $1/(1 - c)$ is called the *multiplier*. The multiplier is the amount by which equilibrium output changes when autonomous aggregate demand increases by one unit. Because the multiplier exceeds unity, we know that a \$1 change in autonomous spending increases equilibrium income and output by more than \$1.[13] The concept of the multiplier is sufficiently important to create a new notation. Defining the multiplier as α, we have

$$\alpha \equiv \frac{1}{1 - c} \tag{14}$$

Inspection of the multiplier in equation (14) shows that the larger the marginal propensity to consume, the larger the multiplier. With a marginal propensity to consume of 0.6 as in Table 3-2, the multiplier is 2.5; for a marginal propensity to consume of 0.8, the multiplier is 5. The reason is simply

---

[12] If you are familiar with the calculus, you will realize that the multiplier is nothing other than the derivative of the equilibrium level of income, Y_0, in equation (10) with respect to autonomous spending. Use the calculus on equation (10) and later on equation (22) to check the statements of the text.

[13] *Two warnings:* (1) The multiplier is necessarily greater than 1 in this very simplified model of the determination of income, but as we shall see in the discussion of "crowding out" in Chap. 4, there may be circumstances in which it is less than 1. (2) The term *multiplier* is used more generally in economics to mean the effect on some endogenous variable (a variable whose level is explained by the theory being studied) of a unit change in an exogenous variable (a variable whose level is not determined within the theory being examined). For instance, one can talk of the multiplier of a change in the income tax rate on the level of unemployment. However, the classic use of the term is as we are using it here—the effects of a change in autonomous spending on equilibrium output.

that a high marginal propensity to consume implies that a large fraction of an additional dollar income will be consumed. Accordingly, expenditures induced by an increase in autonomous spending are high and, therefore, so is the expansion in output and income that is needed to restore balance between income and demand (or spending).

Note that the relationship between the marginal propensity to consume, c, and the marginal propensity to save, s, allows us to write equation (14) in a somewhat different form. Remembering from the budget constraint that saving plus consumption adds up to income, we realize that the fraction of an additional dollar of income consumed plus the fraction saved must add up to a dollar, or $1 \equiv s + c$. Substituting $s \equiv 1 - c$ in equation (14), we obtain an equivalent formula for the multiplier in terms of the marginal propensity to save: $\alpha \equiv 1/s$.

The Multiplier in Pictures

Figure 3-6 provides a graphic interpretation of the effects of an increase in autonomous spending on the equilibrium level of income. The initial equilibrium is at point E with an income level Y_0. Now autonomous spending increases from $\overline{A}$ to $\overline{A}'$. This is represented by a parallel upward shift of the aggregate demand schedule to AD'. The upward shift means that now, at each level of income, aggregate demand is higher by an amount $\Delta\overline{A} \equiv \overline{A}' - \overline{A}$.

At the initial level of income, Y_0, aggregate demand now exceeds income or output. Consequently, unintended inventory decumulation is taking place at a rate equal to the increase in autonomous spending, equal to the vertical distance $\Delta\overline{A}$. Firms will respond to that excess demand by expanding production, say, to income level Y'. This expansion in production gives rise to induced expenditure, increasing aggregate demand to the level A'. At the same time, it reduces the gap between aggregate demand and output to the vertical distance FG. The gap between demand and output is reduced because the marginal propensity to consume is less than 1.

Thus, a marginal propensity to consume that is positive but less than unity implies that a sufficient expansion in output will restore the balance between aggregate demand and output. In Figure 3-6 the new equilibrium is indicated by point E', and the corresponding level of income is Y_0'. The change in income required is therefore $\Delta Y_0 = Y_0' - Y_0$.

The magnitude of the income change required to restore equilibrium depends on two factors. The larger the increase in autonomous spending, represented in Figure 3-6 by the parallel shift in the aggregate demand schedule, the larger the income change. Furthermore, the larger the marginal propensity to consume — that is, the steeper the aggregate demand schedule — the larger the income change.

As a further check on our results, we verify from Figure 3-6 that the change in equilibrium income exceeds the change in autonomous spending. For that purpose, we use the 45° line to compare the change in income ΔY_0

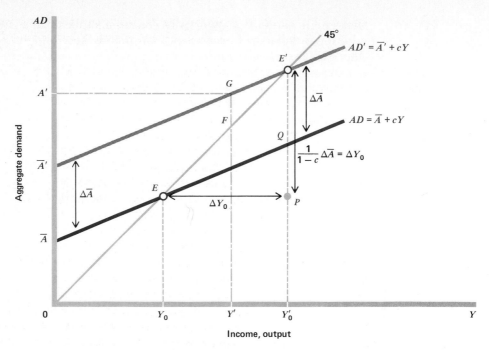

FIGURE 3-6 GRAPHICAL DERIVATION OF THE MULTIPLIER. When there is an increase in autonomous aggregate demand, the aggregate demand schedule shifts up to AD'. The equilibrium moves from E to E'. The increase in equilibrium output ($Y_0' - Y$), equal to distance PE, equal to PE', exceeds the increase in autonomous demand $E'Q$. From the diagram we see that is a result of the AD curve having a positive slope rather than being horizontal. In other words, the multiplier exceeds 1 because consumption demand increases with output—any increase in output produces further increases in demand.

($=EP=PE'$) with the change in autonomous spending that is equal to the vertical distance between the new and old aggregate demand schedule (QE'). It is clear from Figure 3-6 that the change in income PE' exceeds the change in autonomous spending QE'.

Another Derivation

Finally, there is yet another way of deriving the multiplier. Remember that in equilibrium, aggregate demand equals income or output. From one equilibrium to another, it must therefore be true that the change in income ΔY_0 is equal to the change in aggregate demand ΔAD:

$$\Delta Y_0 = \Delta AD \tag{15}$$

Next we split up the change in aggregate demand into the change in autonomous spending $\Delta \overline{A}$ and the change in expenditure induced by the consequent change in income — that is, $c \Delta Y_0$.

$$\Delta AD = \Delta \overline{A} + c \Delta Y_0 \tag{16}$$

Combining equations (15) and (16), the change in income is

$$\Delta Y_0 = \Delta \overline{A} + c \Delta Y_0 \tag{17}$$

or, collecting terms,

$$\Delta Y_0 = \frac{1}{1 - c} \Delta \overline{A} = \alpha \Delta \overline{A} \tag{18}$$

Summary

There are three points to remember from this discussion.

1. An increase in autonomous spending raises the equilibrium level of income.
2. The increase in income is a multiple of the increase in autonomous spending.
3. The larger the marginal propensity to consume, the larger the multiplier, arising from the relation between consumption and income.

As a check on your understanding of the material of this section, you should develop the same analysis, and the same answers, in terms of Figure 3-5.

3-4 THE GOVERNMENT SECTOR

So far we have ignored the role of the government sector in the determination of equilibrium income. The government affects the level of equilibrium income in two separate ways. First, government purchases of goods and, services, G, is a component of aggregate demand. Second, taxes and transfers affect the relation between output and income, Y, and the *disposable income* — income that is available for consumption or saving — that accrues to the private sector, YD. In this section, we are concerned with the way in which government purchases, taxes, and transfers affect the equilibrium level of income.

We start again from the basic national income accounting identities. The introduction of the government restores government purchases (G) on the expenditure side of equation (1) of this chapter, and taxes (TA) less transfers

(*TR*) on the allocation of income side. We can accordingly rewrite the identity in equation (1) as

$$C + I + G \equiv S + (TA - TR) + C \tag{1a}$$

The definition of aggregate demand has to be augmented to include government purchases of goods and services—the purchases of military equipment and services of bureaucrats, for instance. Thus we have

$$AD \equiv C + \bar{I} + G \tag{7a}$$

Consumption will no longer depend on income, but rather on *disposable* income *YD*.[14] Disposable income *YD* is the net income available for spending by households after paying taxes to, and receiving transfers from, the government. It thus consists of income less taxes plus transfers, $Y + TR - TA$. The consumption function is now

$$C = \bar{C} + cYD = \bar{C} + c(Y + TR - TA) \tag{4a}$$

A final step is a specification of *fiscal policy*. Fiscal policy is the policy of the government with regard to the level of government purchases, the level of transfers, and the tax structure. We assume that the government purchases a constant amount G, that it makes a constant amount of transfers, $\overline{TR}$, and that it collects a fraction t of income in the form of taxes. For example, if t equals 0.2, there is an income tax equal to 20 percent of income.

$$G = \bar{G} \qquad TR = \overline{TR} \qquad TA = tY \tag{19}$$

With this specification of fiscal policy, we can rewrite the consumption function, after substitution from equation (19) for *TR* and *TA* in equation (4a), as

$$\begin{aligned} C &= \bar{C} + c(Y + \overline{TR} - tY) \\ &= (\bar{C} + c\overline{TR}) + c(1 - t)Y \end{aligned} \tag{20}$$

Note from equation (20) that the presence of transfers raises autonomous consumption spending by the marginal propensity to consume out of disposable income c times the amount of transfers.[15] The presence of income taxes,

---

[14] The consumption function in Box 3-1 relates consumption to disposable income.

[15] We are assuming no taxes are paid on transfers from the government. As a matter of fact, taxes are paid on some transfers, such as interest payments on the government debt, and not paid on other transfers, such as welfare and unemployment benefits.

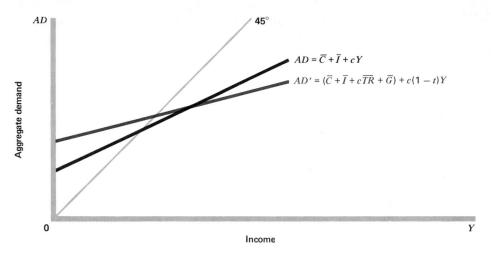

FIGURE 3-7   GOVERNMENT AND AGGREGATE DEMAND.
Government affects aggregate demand through its own purchases,
assumed here to be fixed at the autonomous level $\overline{G}$, through transfers
$\overline{TR}$, and through taxes. Taxes are assumed to be a constant proportion,
t, of income. Under these assumptions, the introduction of government
shifts the intercept of the aggregate demand curve up and flattens the
curve.

by contrast, lowers consumption spending at each level of income. That reduction arises because households' consumption is related to *disposable* income rather than income itself, and income taxes reduce disposable income
relative to the level of income.

While the marginal propensity to consume out of disposable income remains c, now the marginal propensity to consume out of income is $c(1 - t)$,
where $1 - t$ is the fraction of income left after taxes. If the marginal propensity to consume, c, is 0.8 and the tax rate is 0.25, then the marginal propensity to consume out of income, $c(1 - t)$, is 0.6 [$= 0.8 \times (1 - 0.25)$].

Combining (7a), (19), and (20), we have now

$$AD = (\overline{C} + c\overline{TR} + \overline{I} + \overline{G}) + c(1 - t)Y$$
$$= \overline{A} + c(1 - t)Y \tag{21}$$

The effects of the introduction of government on the aggregate demand
schedule are shown in Figure 3-7. The new aggregate demand schedule,
denoted AD' in the figure, starts out higher than the original schedule AD, but
has a flatter slope. The intercept is larger because it now includes both government spending $\overline{G}$ and the part of consumption resulting from transfer payments by the government, $c\overline{TR}$. The slope is flatter because households now

have to pay part of every dollar of income in taxes, and are left with only $(1 - t)$ of that dollar. Thus, as (21) shows, the marginal propensity to consume out of income is now $c(1 - t)$ instead of c.

Equilibrium Income

We are now set to study income determination when the government is included. We return to the equilibrium condition for the goods market, $Y = AD$, and using (21), write the equilibrium condition as

$$Y = \overline{A} + c(1 - t)Y$$

We can solve this equation for Y_0, the equilibrium level of income, by collecting terms in Y:

$$Y[1 - c(1 - t)] = \overline{A}$$

$$Y_0 = \frac{1}{1 - c(1 - t)} \overline{A}$$

(22)

In comparing equation (22) with equation (10), we see that the government sector makes a substantial difference. It raises autonomous spending by the amount of government purchases, $\overline{G}$, and by the amount of induced spending out of net transfers, $c\overline{TR}$.

INCOME TAXES AND THE MULTIPLIER

At the same time *income taxes lower the multiplier*. As can be seen from equation (22), if the marginal propensity to consume is 0.8 and taxes are zero, the multiplier is 5; with the same marginal propensity to consume and a tax rate of 0.25, the multiplier is cut in half to $1/[1 - 0.8(0.75)] = 2.5$. Income taxes reduce the multiplier because they reduce the induced increase of consumption out of changes in income. This can be seen in Figure 3-7, where the inclusion of taxes flattens the aggregate demand curve — recall from Figure 3-6 that the multiplier is larger, the steeper the aggregate demand schedule.

Effects of a Change in Government Purchases

We now consider the effects of changes in fiscal policy on the equilibrium level of income. We distinguish three possible changes in fiscal variables: changes in government purchases, changes in transfers, and income tax changes. The simplest illustration is that of a change in government purchases. This case is shown in Figure 3-8, where the initial level of income is Y_0.

An increase in government purchases is a change in autonomous spending and therefore shifts the aggregate demand schedule upward by an amount equal to the increase in government purchases. At the initial level of output

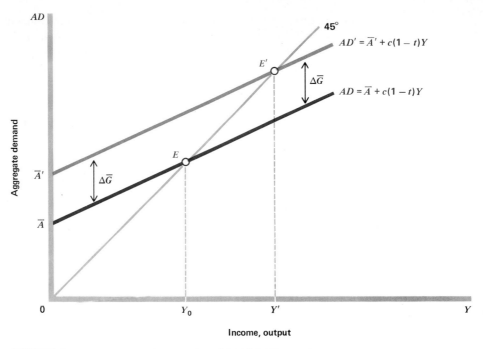

FIGURE 3-8   THE EFFECTS OF AN INCREASE IN GOVERNMENT
PURCHASES. An increase in government spending shifts the aggregate
demand schedule up from AD to AD'. Output rises from Y_0 to Y'.
The multiplier is smaller now than it was in Figure 3-6.

and income, the demand for goods exceeds output, and accordingly, firms
expand production until the new equilibrium at point E' is reached. By how
much does income expand? Recall that the change in equilibrium income will
equal the change in aggregate demand, or

$$\Delta Y_0 = \Delta \overline{G} + c(1 - t)\, \Delta Y_0$$

where the remaining terms $(\overline{C}, \overline{TR}, \text{ and } \overline{I})$ are constant by assumption. Thus,
the change in equilibrium income is

$$\Delta Y_0 = \frac{1}{1 - c(1 - t)} \Delta \overline{G} = \overline{\alpha}\, \Delta \overline{G} \tag{23}$$

where we have introduced the notation $\overline{\alpha}$ to denote the multiplier in the
presence of income taxes:

$$\overline{\alpha} \equiv \frac{1}{1 - c(1 - t)} \tag{24}$$

From equation (23) it is apparent that a $1 increase in government purchases will lead to an increase in income in excess of a dollar. Thus, as we have already seen, with a marginal propensity to consume of $c = 0.8$ and an income tax rate of $t = 0.25$, we would have a multiplier of 2.5: a $1 increase in government spending raises equilibrium income by $2.50.

INCOME TAXES AS AUTOMATIC STABILIZERS

We have just seen that a proportional income tax reduces the multiplier. This means that if any component of autonomous demand changes, output will change by less if there is a proportional income tax than in the absence of such taxes. The proportional income tax is one example of the important concept of *automatic stabilizers*. An automatic stabilizer is any mechanism in the economy that reduces the amount by which output changes in response to a change in autonomous demand.

We shall see later that one explanation of the business cycle, the more or less regular movements of real GNP around trend, is that it is caused by shifts in investment demand. Sometimes, it is argued, investors are optimistic and investment is high — and so, therefore, is output. But sometimes they are pessimistic, and both investment and output are low.

Swings in investment demand will have a smaller effect on output when automatic stabilizers are in place. This means that in the presence of automatic stabilizers we should expect output to fluctuate less than it would without them. Higher income tax rates in the post – World War II period are one reason that the business cycle has been less pronounced since 1945 than it was earlier.

The proportional income tax is not the only automatic stabilizer. Unemployment benefits enable the unemployed to continue consuming even if they do not have a job. This means that demand falls less when someone becomes unemployed than it would if there were no benefits. This too makes the multiplier smaller and output more stable. Unemployment benefits and a proportional income tax are two automatic stabilizers that keep the multiplier small, thereby protecting the economy from responding strongly to every small movement in autonomous demand and stabilizing the economy.[16]

Effects of Increased Transfer Payments

An increase in transfer payments increases autonomous demand, as can be seen from equation (21), where autonomous demand includes a term $c\overline{TR}$. A $1 increase in transfers therefore increases autonomous demand by an amount c. For instance, if the marginal propensity to consume, c, is 0.8, a $1

---

[16] Automatic stabilizers are discussed by T. Holloway, "The Economy and the Federal Budget: Guide to Automatic Stabilizers," *Survey of Current Business,* July 1984.

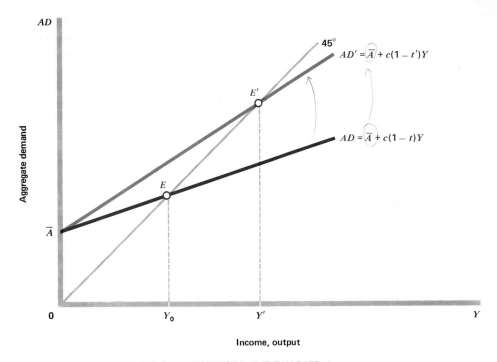

FIGURE 3-9   THE EFFECTS OF A DECREASE IN THE TAX RATE. A reduction in the income tax rate leaves the consumer with a larger proportion of every dollar of income earned. Accordingly, a larger pro-portion of every extra dollar of income is consumed. The aggregate demand curve swings upward, from AD to AD'. It becomes steeper because the income tax cut, in effect, acts like an increase in the propensity to consume. The equilibrium level of income rises from Y_0 to Y'.

increase in transfers increases autonomous demand by $0.80. The increase is less than the full $1 increase in transfers because part of the transfer — $0.20 in this case — is saved.

Given that a $1 increase in transfers increases autonomous demand by the amount c, it is clear that the multiplier for an increase in transfers is c times the multiplier for an increase in government spending. For instance, with c equal to 0.8, and a tax rate of 0.25, the government spending multiplier is 2.5. The multiplier for transfers is 0.8 times 2.5, or 2.0.

Effects of an Income Tax Change

The final fiscal policy question is the effects of a reduction in the income tax rate. This is illustrated in Figure 3-9 by an increase in the slope of the aggre-gate demand function, because that slope is equal to the marginal propensity to spend out of income, $c(1-t)$. At the initial level of income, the aggregate demand for goods now exceeds output because the tax reduction causes increased consumption. The new higher equilibrium level of income is Y'.

To calculate the change in equilibrium income, we equate the change in income to the change in aggregate demand. The change in aggregate demand has two components. The first is the change in spending at the initial level of income that arises from the tax cut. This part is equal to the marginal propensity to consume out of disposable income times the change in disposable income due to the tax cut, $cY_0 \Delta t$, where the term $Y_0 \Delta t$ is the initial level of income times the change in the tax rate. The second component of the change in aggregate demand is the induced spending due to higher income. This is now evaluated at the new tax rate t' and has the value $c(1-t')\Delta Y_0$. We can therefore write[17]

$$\Delta Y_0 = -cY_0 \, \Delta t + c(1-t') \, \Delta Y_0 \tag{25}$$

or

$$\Delta Y_0 = -\frac{1}{1-c(1-t')} \, cY_0 \, \Delta t \tag{26}$$

EXAMPLE

An example clarifies the effects of an income tax cut. Initially the level of income is $Y_0 = 100$, the marginal propensity to consume is $c = 0.8$, and the tax rate $t = 0.2$. Assume now a tax cut that reduces the income tax rate to only 10 percent, or $t' = 0.1$.

At the initial level of income, disposable income rises by $Y_0 \Delta t = 100(t - t') = \$10$. Out of the increase in disposable income of $10, a fraction $c = 0.8$ is spent on consumption, so that aggregate demand, at the initial level of income, increases by $8. This corresponds to the first term on the right-hand side of equation (25). The increase in aggregate demand causes an expansion in output and income. Per dollar increase in income, disposable income rises by a fraction $(1-t')$ of the increase in income. Furthermore, of the increase in disposable income, only a fraction, c, is spent. Accordingly, induced consumption spending is equal to $c(1-t')\Delta Y_0$, which is the second term in equation (25).

How much does the income tax cut achieve in terms of output expansion? Substituting our numbers in equation (26), we have

$$\Delta Y_0 = \frac{1}{1-0.8(1-0.1)} (0.8)(100)(0.2-0.1) = (3.57)(8)$$

$$= 28.56 \tag{26a}$$

---

[17] You should check equation (26) by using equation (22) to write out Y_0 corresponding to a tax rate of t, and Y_0' corresponding to t'. Then subtract Y_0 from Y_0' to obtain ΔY_0 as given in equation (26).

In our example, a cut in the tax rate, such that taxes fall by $10 at the initial level of income, raises equilibrium income by $28.56.

Note, however, that although taxes are initially cut by $10, the government's total taxes received fall by less than $10. Why? The reason is that the government receives 10 percent of the induced increase in income, or $2.856, as taxes. Thus the final reduction in tax receipts by the government is not the initial $10, but rather $7.144.[18]

ACTIVE FISCAL POLICY

Changes in government spending and taxes affect the level of income. This immediately raises the possibility that fiscal policy can be used to stabilize the economy. When the economy is in a recession, perhaps taxes should be cut or spending increased to get output to rise. And when the economy is booming, perhaps taxes should be increased or government spending cut to get back down to full employment.

Fiscal policy is in practice actively used to try to stabilize the economy, as we shall see in the next section when we examine the behavior of the budget. But it is also true that there is dispute over whether such fiscal policy actions really work. The disputes center on two issues: first, whether they work fast enough to help; and second, and more complicated, whether government policy actions don't merely result in private individuals taking offsetting actions. For instance, when government spending rises, private spending might fall.

We cannot at this stage evaluate the arguments against the active use of fiscal policy. But starting in Chapter 5, and continuing in Chapters 8 and 12, we resume the discussion.

Summary

1. Government purchases and transfer payments act like increases in autonomous spending in their effects on equilibrium income.
2. A proportional income tax reduces the proportion of each extra dollar of output that is received as disposable income by consumers, and thus has the same effects on equilibrium income as a reduction in the propensity to consume.[19]

---

[18] We leave it to you to calculate the multiplier relating the change in equilibrium income to the total change in taxes received by the government.

[19] It might be helpful to note that all the results we have derived can be obtained in a straightforward manner by taking the change in aggregate demand at the initial level of income times the multiplier. (Check this proposition for each of the fiscal policy changes we have considered.) You should consider, too, the effect on equilibrium income of an increase in government purchases combined with an equal reduction in transfer payments, $\Delta \overline{G} = -\Delta \overline{TR}$. (See problem 9 at the end of this chapter.)

3-5 THE BUDGET

The budget—and especially the budget deficit—became the major preoccupation of economic policy in the first half of the 1980s. By 1985 the federal government budget deficit exceeded $200 billion, or 5 percent of GNP, meaning that the federal government was spending $200 billion more per year than it was receiving in taxes. It had to borrow that $200 billion. The prospect of equally large deficits threatened for the rest of the decade unless taxes were raised or government spending cut. The fear was strong that the economy could not prosper with the threat of large deficits hanging over it. In 1985 Congress passed the Gramm-Rudman bill, requiring the budget to be balanced by 1991.

Why the concern? The fear was that the government's borrowing would make it difficult for private firms to borrow and invest, and thus slow the economy's growth. Full understanding has to wait to Chapter 9, but we start now, dealing with the government budget, its effects on output, and the effects of output on the budget. The first important concept is the *budget surplus,* denoted by *BS.* The budget surplus is the excess of the government's revenues, consisting of taxes, over its total expenditures, consisting of purchases of goods and services, and transfer payments.

$$BS \equiv TA - G - TR \tag{27}$$

A negative budget surplus, an excess of expenditure over taxes, is a *budget deficit,* denoted *BD*:

$$BD \equiv -BS = G + TR - TA$$

Of course, at the present time, government deficits are the norm, and surpluses are nowhere in prospect. But it was not always so. For most of its history the federal government has run surpluses in peacetime and deficits during wars. It is only in the last 20 years that peacetime deficits have become standard.[20]

In Box 3-2 we describe the concepts of government budget surplus and deficit that appear in the national income accounts. For that purpose, the federal government and state and local governments are added together. Thus the government sector in the national income accounts, and in the theory we are developing here, is not just the federal government. It is all government.

---

[20] We deal with the budget in more detail in Chap. 17. But we already note here the distinction between the federal government and state and local governments. In the 1950–1980 period the federal government ran a deficit averaging 0.7 percent of GNP, whereas state and local governments actually showed a surplus of 0.2 percent of GNP. From 1980 to 1985 the federal deficit sharply increased, by nearly 4 percent of GNP, and state and local governments showed some increase in the surplus. The policy discussion of the 1980s centers on correcting the federal deficit.

BOX
3-2

GOVERNMENT IN
THE NATIONAL INCOME ACCOUNTS

Three aspects of fiscal policy are distinguished in the text. G is government purchases of goods and services. TR is government transfers, and TA is taxes or government receipts. We now give the data for these variables in 1985, when GNP was $3,989 billion. We also show the breakdown of the variables between federal and state and local governments.

GOVERNMENT PURCHASES OF GOODS AND SERVICES

		$ billions	Percent of GNP
Federal government		353.9	8.9
Defense	262.0		
Nondefense	91.9		
State and local		517.1	13.0
Compensation of employees	279.2		
Building	54.2		
Other	126.9		
Total		871.0	21.9

Source: Economic Report of the President, 1986, and *Survey of Current Business*, February 1986, p. 36.

The surprise here is that state and local government purchases of goods and services are substantially larger than those of the federal government.

TRANSFER PAYMENTS

	$ billions	Percent of GNP
Federal government		
Transfers	379.7	9.5
Net interest payments	129.0	3.2
State and Local		
Transfers	98.8	2.5
Net interest	−31.0	−0.8
Total	576.5	14.5

Source: Economic Report of the President, 1986.

Federal government transfer payments are substantially larger than federal government purchases of goods and services. These transfer payments include Social Security and welfare payments.

The federal government also had to make large interest payments on the national debt. State and local governments make only small transfer payments and actually on balance *receive* interest. We see why below.

GOVERNMENT RECEIPTS

		$ billions	Percent of GNP
Federal government		785.7	19.7
Income taxes	351.1		
Contributions for social insurance	309.9		
Other	124.7		
State and local		575.4	14.4
Sales taxes	128.9		
Property taxes	104.1		
Income taxes	73.6		
Other	268.8		

Source: *Economic Report of the President*, 1986, and *Survey of Current Business*, February 1986, p. 35.

SURPLUS OR DEFICIT (−) IN GNP ACCOUNTS

	$ billions	Percent of GNP
Federal government	−197.3	−4.9
State and local	58.3	1.5
Net, government sector*	−139	−3.5

* Total not equal to sum of components because of rounding.
Source: *Economic Report of the President*, 1986.

In 1985, the government sector had a deficit in the national income accounts of $139 billion. While the federal government had a deficit, state and local governments on balance were in surplus.

State and local governments have for many years run surpluses. With their surpluses they buy assets, including federal government bonds. That is why they have positive interest earnings.

To summarize, G in 1985 was about 22 percent of GNP, TR was about 15 percent of GNP, and TA was 32.9 percent of GNP (calculated from $TA = G + TR + BS$).

However, the budget deficit on which the media and politicians focus is the federal budget deficit. Later in this section we look at the behavior of the federal budget. For now we study the behavior of the budget surplus in relation to income, in the simple theory of this chapter.

Substituting in equation (27) the assumption of a proportional income tax that yields a tax revenue $TA = tY$ gives us

$$BS = tY - G - TR \qquad (27a)$$

In Figure 3-10 we plot the budget surplus as a function of the level of income for given $G = \overline{G}$, $TR = \overline{TR}$, and income tax rate t. At low levels of income, the budget is in deficit (the surplus is negative) because payments $\overline{G} + \overline{TR}$ exceed income tax collection. For high levels of income, by contrast, the budget shows a surplus, since income tax collection outweighs expenditures in the form of government purchases and transfers.

Figure 3-10 demonstrates a significant point about budget surpluses and deficits. The point is that the budget deficit depends not only on the government's policy choices, reflected in the tax rate t, in purchases $\overline{G}$, and in transfers $\overline{TR}$, but also on anything else that shifts the level of income. For instance, suppose there is an increase in investment demand that increases the level of output. Then the budget deficit will fall, or the surplus will increase because tax revenues have risen. But the government has done nothing that changed the deficit.

We should accordingly not be surprised to see budget deficits in recessions. Those are periods when the government's tax receipts are low. And in practice, transfer payments, through unemployment benefits, also increase in recessions, even though in our model we are taking $\overline{TR}$ as autonomous.

The Effects of Government Purchases and Tax Changes on the Budget Surplus

Next we show how changes in fiscal policy affect the budget. In particular, we want to find out whether an increase in government purchases must reduce the budget surplus. At first sight, this appears obvious, because increased government purchases, from equation (27), are reflected in a reduced surplus,

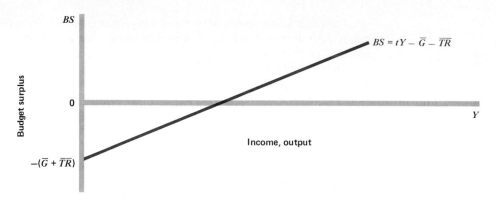

FIGURE 3-10   THE BUDGET SURPLUS. The budget surplus, or deficit, depends in part on the level of income. Given the tax rate, t, and $\overline{G}$ and $\overline{TR}$, the budget surplus will be high if income is high — because then the government takes in a lot of taxes. But if the level of income is low, there will be a budget deficit because government tax receipts are small.

or increased deficit. At further thought, however, the increased government purchases will cause an increase (multiplied) in income and, therefore, increased income tax collection. This raises the interesting possibility that tax collection might increase by more than government purchases.

A brief calculation shows that the first guess is right — increased government purchases reduce the budget surplus. From equation (23) the change in income due to increased government purchases is equal to $\Delta Y_0 \equiv \overline{\alpha}\,\Delta \overline{G}$. A fraction of that increase in income is collected in the form of taxes, so that tax revenue increases by $t\overline{\alpha}\,\Delta \overline{G}$. The change in the budget surplus, using equation (24) to substitute for $\overline{\alpha}$, is therefore

$$
\begin{aligned}
\Delta BS &= \Delta TA - \Delta \overline{G} \\
&= t\overline{\alpha}\,\Delta \overline{G} - \Delta \overline{G} \\
&= \left[\frac{t}{1 - c(1 - t)} - 1 \right]\Delta \overline{G} \\
&= -\frac{(1 - c)(1 - t)}{1 - c(1 - t)}\Delta \overline{G}
\end{aligned}
\tag{28}
$$

which is unambiguously negative.

We have, therefore, shown that an increase in government purchases will reduce the budget surplus, although by considerably less than the increase in purchases. For instance, for $c = 0.8$ and $t = 0.25$, a \$1 increase in government purchases will create a \$0.375 reduction in the surplus.[21]

In the same way, we can consider the effects of an increase in the tax rate on the budget surplus. We know that the increase in the tax rate will reduce the level of income. It might thus appear that an increase in the tax rate, keeping the level of government spending constant, could reduce the budget surplus. In fact, an increase in the tax rate increases the budget surplus, despite the reduction in income that it causes, as you are asked to show in problem 8 at the end of this chapter.[22]

A SIMULTANEOUS CHANGE IN TAXES AND PURCHASES

Finally, we can investigate the budgetary effects of simultaneous changes in taxes and government purchases. We do this by working out an example, in Table 3-3. We assume a fiscal policy change that reduces the tax rate and government purchases. The reduction is such that at the initial equilibrium level of income, of 100, the cut in taxes is exactly equal to the cut in government purchases.

What effect would we expect such a fiscal policy to have? A first reaction would be that since taxes are being cut the same amount as spending, there will be no effect. But the table shows that is not right. The combined effect of the two actions is actually to lower income.

Why? The reason is that part of the cut in taxes is saved, so that not all the tax cut goes to increase aggregate demand. But the entire cut in government spending reduces aggregate demand. Therefore this fiscal policy actually reduces aggregate demand, and therefore income.

Notice also from the table that the budget deficit in the end increases slightly — as a result of the fall in income — even though at the initial level of income the cuts in taxes and spending are equal.

BALANCED BUDGET MULTIPLIER

In the previous example, the combined tax cut and reduction of government purchases raised the budget deficit. What would happen to the level of income if government purchases and taxes changed by exactly the same amount, so that the budget surplus remained unchanged between the initial and final level of income? The answer to this question is contained in the famous *bal-*

---

[21] In this case, $\overline{\alpha} = 1/[1 - 0.8(0.75)] = 2.5$. So $\Delta BS = -2.5(0.2)(0.75) = -0.375$.

[22] The theory that tax rate cuts would increase government revenue (or tax rate increases reduce government revenue) is associated with Arthur Laffer of Pepperdine University. Laffer's argument, however, did not depend on the aggregate demand effects of tax cuts, but rather on the possibility that a tax cut would lead people to work more. This was a strand in supply-side economics, which we examine in Chap. 18.

TABLE 3-3   EFFECTS OF COMBINED TAX CUT AND GOVERNMENT SPENDING DECREASE

Parameters: Initial tax rate, $t = 0.2$

New tax rate, $t' = 0.1$

Initial level of income, $Y_0 = \$100$

Marginal propensity to consume, $c = 0.8$

Change in government spending, $\Delta \overline{G} = -10$

Multiplier: $\overline{\alpha} = \dfrac{1}{1 - c(1 - t')} = \dfrac{1}{1 - 0.72} = 3.57$

Effects of tax cut: [See equation (26)]

Change in income: $-\overline{\alpha}\, cY_0 \Delta t = -(3.57)(0.8)(100)(-0.1) = 28.56$

Effects of cut in government spending: [See equation (23)]

Change in income: $\overline{\alpha}\, \Delta \overline{G} = -35.70$

Total effect on income: $\Delta Y_0 = -35.70 + 28.56$

$= -7.14$

Therefore: $Y_0' = 100 - 7.14 = 92.86$

Effect on tax receipts: Initial taxes $= 20$

Taxes in new situation $= 0.1 \times 92.86 = 9.29$

Therefore: Change in taxes, $\Delta \text{TA} = -10.71$

Effects on budget surplus: $\Delta BS = \Delta TA - \Delta \overline{G}$

$= -10.71 + 10.00$

$= -0.71$

anced budget multiplier result. The result is that the balanced budget multiplier is exactly 1. That is, an increase in government purchases, accompanied by an equal increase in taxes, increases the level of income by exactly the amount of the increase in purchases.[23] This interesting result is derived in the appendix at the end of this chapter.

The major points of the preceding discussion are that a balanced budget cut in government purchases lowers equilibrium income and that a dollar increase in government purchases has a stronger impact on equilibrium income than a dollar cut in taxes. A dollar cut in taxes leads only to a fraction of a dollar's increase in consumption spending, the rest being saved, while government purchases are reflected dollar for dollar in a change in aggregate demand.[24]

---

[23] Note that the balanced budget multiplier may well be less than 1 in the more sophisticated models of Chap. 4, in which investment spending depends on the interest rate.

[24] Rather than go through the analysis of changes in transfer payments, we leave it to you to work through an example of the effects on the budget of a change in transfer payments in problem 10 at the end of the chapter.

3-6 THE FULL-EMPLOYMENT BUDGET SURPLUS

A final topic to be treated here is the concept of the full-employment budget surplus.[25] Recall that increases in taxes add to the surplus and that increases in government expenditures reduce the surplus. Increases in taxes have been shown to reduce the level of income, and increases in government purchases and transfers to increase the level of income. It thus seems that the budget surplus is a convenient, simple measure of the overall effects of fiscal policy on the economy. For instance, when the budget is in deficit, we would say that fiscal policy is expansionary, tending to increase GNP.

However, the budget surplus by itself suffers from a serious defect as a measure of the direction of fiscal policy. The defect is that the surplus can change passively because of changes in autonomous private spending, as we have seen. Thus, if the economy moves into a recession, tax revenue automatically declines and the budget moves into a deficit (or reduced surplus). Conversely, an increase in economic activity causes the budget to move into a surplus (or reduced deficit). These changes in the budget take place automatically for a given tax structure. This implies that we cannot simply look at the budget deficit as a measure of whether government fiscal policy is expansionary or deflationary. A given fiscal policy may imply a deficit if private spending is low and a surplus if private spending is high. Accordingly, an increase in the budget deficit does not necessarily mean that the government has changed its policy in an attempt to increase the level of income.

Since we frequently want to measure the way in which fiscal policy is being actively, rather than passively, used to affect the level of income, we require some measure of policy that is independent of the particular position of the business cycle — boom or recession — in which we may find ourselves. Such a measure is provided by the *full-employment budget surplus*, which we denote by BS^*. The full-employment (high-employment) budget surplus measures the budget, not at the actual level of income, but rather at the full-employment level of income or at potential output. Thus, a given fiscal policy summarized by $\overline{G}$, $\overline{TR}$, and t is assessed by the level of the surplus, or deficit, that is generated at full employment. Using Y^* to denote the full-employment level of income, we can write

$$BS^* = tY^* - \overline{G} - \overline{TR} \qquad (29)$$

Alternative names for the full-employment surplus have been proliferating. Included are the *cyclically adjusted surplus* (or deficit), the *high-employment surplus*, the *standardized employment surplus*, and the *structural surplus* or deficit. All these names refer to the same concept. The new names are intended to divert attention from the notion that there is a unique level of full employment output that the economy has not yet reached. They suggest

---

[25] The concept of the full-employment surplus was first used by E. Cary Brown, "Fiscal Policy in the Thirties: A Reappraisal," *American Economic Review,* December 1956.

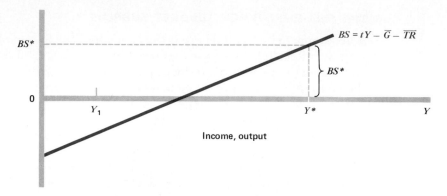

FIGURE 3-11 THE ACTUAL AND FULL-EMPLOYMENT BUDGET SURPLUSES. Y^* is the full-employment level of output. The full-employment budget surplus BS^* is the budget surplus that would exist if the economy were at full employment. If output is below the full-employment level, at a level such as Y_1, the budget surplus would be smaller than BS^*. Indeed, at income level Y_1 the actual budget is in deficit even though there is a full-employment surplus.

instead that the concept is merely a convenient measuring rod that fixes a given level of employment as the reference point. Given the difficulty of knowing exactly what is the full-employment level of output, the new names have some justification.[26]

In Figure 3-11 we show the budget surplus schedule from Figure 3-10 but add the full-employment level of income Y^*. The full-employment budget surplus is indicated by the corresponding point on the budget surplus schedule. To see the difference between the actual and the full-employment budgets, we subtract the actual budget in equation $(27a)$ from equation (29) to obtain

$$BS^* - BS = t(Y^* - Y) \qquad (30)$$

The only difference arises from income tax collection.[27] Specifically, if output is below full employment, the full-employment surplus exceeds the actual

---

[26] For a useful exposition, see Congressional Budget Office, *The Economic Outlook*, February 1984, Appendix B.

[27] In practice, transfer payments, such as welfare and unemployment benefits, are also affected by the state of the economy, so that *TR* also depends on the level of income. But the major cause of differences between the actual surplus and the full-employment surplus is taxes. Automatic movements in taxes caused by a change in income are about five times the size of automatic movements in spending. (See T. M. Holloway and J. C. Wakefield, "Sources of Change in the Federal Government Deficit, 1970–86," *Survey of Current Business*, May 1985.)

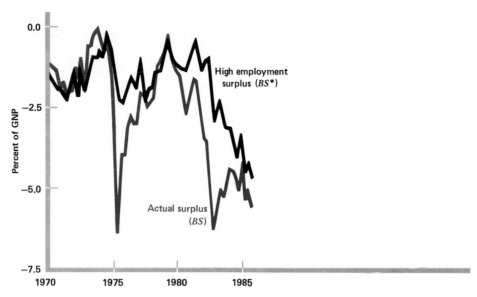

FIGURE 3-12   THE ACTUAL AND FULL-EMPLOYMENT BUDGET
SURPLUS AS A FRACTION OF GNP. (*Source: Survey of Current
Business,* April and August 1982 and March 1983.)

surplus. Conversely, if actual output exceeds full-employment (or potential)
output, the full-employment surplus is less than the actual surplus.

Budget Trends

Figure 3-12 shows the actual and full-employment budget surpluses (as a
percent of GNP) since 1970. Three facts stand out.

1. The actual budget fluctuates more than the full-employment budget. That
    is because the actual budget changes as the level of output fluctuates
    during the business cycle—and the effects of those fluctuations are ex-
    cluded from the full-employment budget. The 1974–1975 and 1980–
    1982 recessions stand out particularly as periods when the actual deficit
    was far greater than the full-employment deficit. Equivalently, in those
    years the actual budget surplus was far below the full-employment surplus.
2. Over most of this period, the actual surplus was below the full-employment
    surplus. This is because over most of the period output was below its
    full-employment level.
3. Over the period, both budgets have been moving increasingly into deficit.
    Indeed, by the mid-1980s the full-employment deficit is larger than at any
    time in the last 30 years.

BOX
3-3

CYCLICAL AND POLICY INFLUENCES ON THE BUDGET: THE FIRST HALF OF THE EIGHTIES

Big deficit changes in the first half of the 1980s show the separate influences of cyclical and full-employment budget changes. Figure 1 shows a substantial rise in the actual deficit from 1981 to 1982, at the same time as the unemployment rate increased from 7.5 to 9.5 percent. Most of the increase in the actual deficit (shown by the black lines) over that period was due to the higher unemployment and the automatic effects of a recession in reducing government revenue. But the colored lines show the full-employment deficit also increased a bit over that period.

Between 1983 and 1984, the *actual* budget deficit *de*creased as a share of GNP — from 5.4 to 4.8 percent. But the *full-employment deficit in*creased from 3.9 to 4.8 percent of GNP.

FIGURE 1   FULL-EMPLOYMENT AND ACTUAL BUDGET DEFICITS, AND THE UNEMPLOYMENT RATE, 1980–1985. The red lines show the full employment deficit as a percentage of GNP, the black lines are the actual deficit. Movements in the unemployment rate account for differences between changes in the actual and full-employment deficits. Tax and spending decisions account for changes in the full-employment deficit. (*Source:* Federal Reserve Bank of St. Louis, *Monetary Trends,* for actual and full employment budgets. Other data from *Economic Indicators.*).

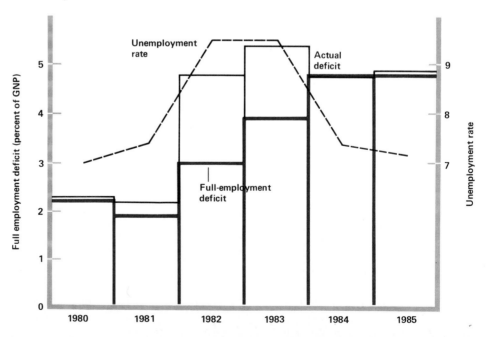

The actual deficit could fall while the full-employment deficit was increasing because the economy was in a recovery, unemployment was falling, and government revenue was increasing rapidly. Between 1984 and 1985 with almost no change in unemployment and the full-employment deficit, there is also virtually no change in the actual deficit.

Three points are important:

1. Note the steady increase in the full-employment deficit from 1981 to 1984, from 1.9 percent of GNP to 4.8 percent. The change is made up of a 2.0 percent cut in revenue, caused by tax cuts, and a 0.8 percent increase in government spending. [The discrepancy between the increase in the full-employment deficit of 2.9 percent of GNP and the sum of the effects of tax cuts and spending increases (2.8 percent) is due to rounding.]
2. A rough rule of thumb is that an increase in the unemployment rate of 1 percent increases the actual deficit by 0.75 percent of GNP.
3. In Figure 1 the 1984 and 1985 actual and full-employment deficits are shown almost equal; this means that the St. Louis Federal Reserve, which creates the full-employment data we use in Figure 1, regards an unemployment rate of 7 to 7.3 percent as full-employment. The Department of Commerce data used in Figure 3-12, however, calculate the high employment budget at a 6 percent unemployment rate. The contrast is a reminder that these data are estimates that depend crucially on the assumed rate of unemployment.

Public concern about the deficit mounted in the 1980s. For many economists, the behavior of the deficit during the high unemployment years 1982 and 1983 was not especially worrisome. The actual budget is usually in deficit during recessions. But the shift toward deficit of the full-employment budget was regarded as an entirely different matter. Discussion of that problem must wait until Chapter 17.

Two final words of warning. First, there is no certainty as to the true full-employment level of output. Various assumptions are possible about the level of unemployment that corresponds to full employment. The usual assumptions now are that full employment means an unemployment rate of 5.5 to even as high as 7 percent. But estimates of the full-employment deficit or surplus will differ depending on the assumptions made about the economy at full employment.

Second, the high-employment surplus is a better measure of the direction of active fiscal policy than the actual budget surplus. But it is not a perfect measure of the thrust of fiscal policy. The reason is that balanced budget increases in government purchases, for example, are themselves expansionary, so that an increase in government purchases matched by a tax increase that keeps the surplus constant leads to an increase in the level of income.

Because fiscal policy involves the setting of a number of variables — the tax rate, transfers, and government purchases — it is difficult to describe the thrust of fiscal policy perfectly in a single number. But the high-employment surplus is nevertheless a useful guide to the direction of fiscal policy.

3-7 SUMMARY

1. Output is at its equilibrium level when the aggregate demand for goods is equal to the level of output.
2. Aggregate demand consists of planned spending by households on consumption, firms on investment goods, and government on its purchases of goods and services.
3. When output is at its equilibrium level, there are no unintended changes in inventories and all economic units are making precisely the purchases they had planned to. An adjustment process for the level of output based on the accumulation or decumulation of inventories leads the economy to the equilibrium output level.
4. The level of aggregate demand is itself affected by the level of output (equal to the level of income), because consumption demand depends on the level of income.
5. The consumption function relates consumption spending to income. Consumption rises with income. Income that is not consumed is saved, so that the saving function can be derived from the consumption function.
6. The multiplier is the amount by which a $1 change in autonomous spending changes the equilibrium level of output. The greater the propensity to consume, the higher the multiplier.
7. Government purchases and government transfer payments act like increases in autonomous spending in their effects on the equilibrium level of income. A proportional income tax has the same effects on the equilibrium level of income as a reduction in the propensity to consume. A proportional income tax thus reduces the multiplier.
8. The budget surplus is the excess of government receipts over its expenditure. When the government is spending more than it receives, the budget is in deficit. The size of the budget surplus (deficit) is affected by the government's fiscal policy variables — government purchases, transfer payments, and tax rates.
9. The actual budget surplus is also affected by changes in tax collection and transfers resulting from movements in the level of income that occur as a result of changes in private autonomous spending. The full-employment (high-employment) budget surplus is used as a measure of the *active* use of fiscal policy. The full-employment surplus measures the budget surplus that would exist if output were at its potential (full-employment) level.

KEY TERMS

Aggregate demand
Equilibrium output
Unintended (undesired) inventory
  accumulation
Planned aggregate demand
Consumption function
Marginal propensity to consume

Marginal propensity to save
Multiplier
Automatic stabilizer
Budget surplus
Budget deficit
Balanced budget multiplier
Full-employment (high-employment) surplus

PROBLEMS

1. Here we investigate a particular example of the model studied in Sections 3-2 and 3-3 with no government. Suppose the consumption function is given by $C = 100 + 0.8Y$, while investment is given by $\bar{I} = 50$.
    (a) What is the equilibrium level of income in this case?
    (b) What is the level of saving in equilibrium?
    (c) If, for some reason, output was at the level of 800, what would the level of involuntary inventory accumulation be?
    (d) If $\bar{I}$ were to rise to 100 (we discuss what determines $\bar{I}$ in later chapters), what would the effect be on equilibrium income?
    (e) What is the multiplier α here?
    (f) Draw a diagram indicating the equilibria in both $1a$ and $1d$.
2. Suppose consumption behavior were to change in problem 1 so that $C = 100 + 0.9Y$, while $\bar{I}$ remained at 50.
    (a) Would you expect the equilibrium level of income to be higher or lower than in $1a$? Calculate the new Y' to verify this.
    (b) Now suppose investment increases to $\bar{I} = 100$ just as in $1d$. What is the new equilibrium income?
    (c) Does this change in investment spending have more or less of an effect on Y than in problem 1? Why?
    (d) Draw a diagram indicating the change in equilibrium income in this case.
3. We showed in the text that the equilibrium condition $Y = AD$ is equivalent to the $S = \bar{I}$, or saving = investment, condition. Starting from $S = \bar{I}$ and the saving function, derive the equilibrium level of income, as in equation (10).
4. This problem relates to the so-called *paradox of thrift*. Suppose that $I = \bar{I}$ and that $C = \bar{C} + cY$.
    (a) What is the saving function, that is, the function that shows how saving is related to income?
    (b) Suppose individuals want to save more at every level of income. Show, using a figure like Figure 3-5, how the saving function is shifted.
    (c) What effect does the increased desire to save have on the new equilibrium level of saving? Explain the paradox.
5. Now let us look at a model which is an example of the one presented in Sections 3-4 and 3-5; that is, it includes government purchases, taxes, and transfers. It has the same features as

the one in problems 1 and 2, except that it also has a government. Thus, suppose consumption is given by $C = 100 + 0.8YD$ and $\bar{I} = 50$, while fiscal policy is summarized by $\overline{G} = 200$, $\overline{TR} = 62.5$, and $t = 0.25$.

(a) What is the equilibrium level of income in this more complete model?

(b) What is the new multiplier $\overline{\alpha}$? Why is this less than the multiplier in problem 1e?

6. Using the same model as in problem 5, determine the following:

(a) What is the value of the budget surplus BS when $\bar{I} = 50$?

(b) What is BS when $\bar{I}$ increases to 100?

(c) What accounts for the change in BS from 6a to 6b?

(d) Assuming that the full-employment level of income $\overline{Y}$ is 1,200, what is the full-employment budget surplus BS^* when $\bar{I} = 50$? 100? (Be careful.)

(e) What is BS^* if $\bar{I} = 50$ and $\overline{G} = 250$, with $\overline{Y}$ still equal to 1,200?

(f) Explain why we use BS^* rather than simply BS to measure the direction of fiscal policy.

7. Suppose we expand our model to take account of the fact that transfer payments TR do depend on the level of income Y. When income is high, transfer payments such as unemployment benefits will fall. Conversely, when income is low, unemployment is high and so are unemployment benefits. We can incorporate this into our model by writing transfers as $TR = \overline{TR} - bY$, $b > 0$. Remember that equilibrium income is derived as the solution to $Y_0 = C + \bar{I} + \overline{G} = \overline{C} + cYD + \bar{I} + \overline{G}$, where $YD = Y + TR - TA$ is disposable income.

(a) Derive the expression for Y_0 in this case, just as equation (22) was derived in the text.

(b) What is the new multiplier now?

(c) Why is the new multiplier less than the standard one, $\overline{\alpha}$?

(d) How does the change in the multiplier relate to the concept of automatic stabilizers?

8. Now we look at the role taxes play in determining equilibrium income. Suppose we have an economy of the type in Sections 3-4 and 3-5, described by the following functions:

$$C = 50 + 0.8YD$$

$$\bar{I} = 70$$

$$\overline{G} = 200$$

$$\overline{TR} = 100$$

$$t = 0.20$$

(a) Calculate the equilibrium level of income and the multiplier in this model.

(b) Calculate also the budget surplus BS.

(c) Suppose that t increases to 0.25. What is the new equilibrium income? The new multiplier?

(d) Calculate the change in the budget surplus. Would you expect the change in the surplus to be more or less if $c = 0.9$ rather than 0.8?

(e) Can you explain why the multiplier is 1 when $t = 1$?

9. Suppose the economy is operating at equilibrium with $Y_0 = 1,000$. If the government undertakes a fiscal change so that the tax rate t increases by 0.05 and government spending increases by 50, will the budget surplus go up or down? Why?

10. Suppose Congress decides to reduce transfer payments (such as welfare), but to increase government purchases of goods and services by an equal amount. That is, it undertakes a change in fiscal policy such that $\Delta G = -\overline{TR}$.

(a) Would you expect equilibrium income to rise or fall as a result of this change? Why?

Check out your answer with the following example: Suppose initially, $c = 0.8$, $t = 0.25$, and $Y_0 = 600$. Now let $\Delta\overline{G} = 10$ and $\Delta\overline{TR} = -10$.

(b) Find the change in equilibrium income ΔY_0.

(c) What is the change in the budget surplus ΔBS? Why has BS changed?

*11. We have seen in problem 10 that an increase in G accompanied by an equal decrease in TR does not leave the budget unchanged. What would the effect on equilibrium income be if TR and G change to leave the budget surplus BS fixed? [*Hint:* Notice that $BS = TA - TR - G$. We want $\Delta BS = \Delta TA - \Delta TR - \Delta G = 0(*)$ so that $\Delta TR = \Delta TA - \Delta G$. Since t is constant, $\Delta TA = t\Delta Y_0(**)$. We also know that $Y_0 = \overline{\alpha}(\overline{C} + \overline{I} + \overline{G} + c\overline{R})$ and $\Delta Y_0 = \overline{\alpha}(\Delta\overline{G} + c\,\Delta\overline{TR})$.

[Substituting (*) and (**) into this last equation, derive an expression for ΔY in terms of ΔG. Simplify that expression, using the fact that $\overline{\alpha} = \{1/[1 - c(1 - t)]\}$, to obtain the balanced budget result in the case of changes in transfers and government spending. If you have trouble with this problem, check the appendix to this chapter.]

*12. In the preceding problem and in the appendix we derived the balanced budget multiplier result. It states that if $\Delta G = \Delta TA$ from the initial to final equilibrium, then $\Delta Y = \Delta G$. Let us look at an example of this balanced budget multiplier in action.

Consider the economy described by the following functions:

$$C = 85 + 0.75YD$$

$$\overline{I} = 50$$

$$\overline{G} = 150$$

$$\overline{TR} = 100$$

$$t = 0.20$$

(a) Derive the multiplier $\overline{\alpha}$ and the level of autonomous spending $\overline{A}$.

(b) From 12a calculate the equilibrium level of income and the budget surplus.

(c) Now suppose G rises to 250 while t increases to 0.28. Repeat step 12a for the new fiscal policy.

(d) What are ΔTA, ΔG, ΔY, and ΔBS?

(e) In view of this result and that of problem 10, what do you think the effect on income would be if we had a balanced budget change where $\Delta TR = \Delta TA$?

*13. Suppose the aggregate demand function is as in the figure on the following page. Notice that at Y_0 the slope of the aggregate demand curve is *greater* than 1. (This would happen if $c > 1$.) Complete this picture as is done in Figure 3-1 to include the arrows indicating adjustment when $Y \neq Y_0$ and show what IU is for $Y < Y_0$ and $Y > Y_0$. What is happening in this example, and how does it differ fundamentally from Figure 3-1?

*14. This problem anticipates our discussion of the open economy in Chapter 6. It is hard, and only the ambitious student should try it. You are asked to derive some of the results that will be shown there. We start with the assumption that foreign demand for our goods is given and equal to $\overline{X}$. Our demand for foreign goods or imports, denoted Q, is a linear function of income.

$$\text{Exports} = \overline{X} \qquad \text{Imports} = Q = \overline{Q} + mY$$

where m is the *marginal propensity to import*.

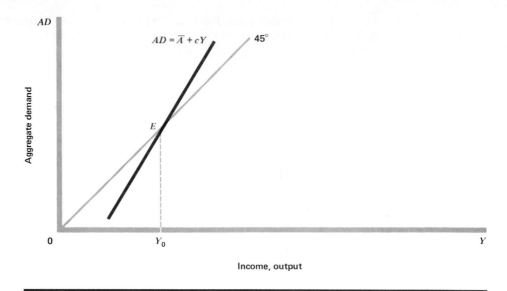

(a) The trade balance, or net exports, NX, is defined as the excess of exports over imports. Write an algebraic expression for the trade balance and show in a diagram net exports as a function of the level of income. (Put Y on the horizontal axis.)

(b) Show the effect of a change in income on the trade balance, using your diagram. Show also the effect of a change in exports on the trade balance, given income.

(c) The equilibrium condition in the goods market is that aggregate demand for *our* goods is equal to supply. Aggregate demand for our goods includes exports but excludes imports. Thus we have

$$Y = C + \bar{I} + NX$$

where we have added net exports (exports less imports) to investment and consumption. Using the expression for net exports developed in 14a and the consumption function $C = \bar{C} + cY$, derive the equilibrium level of income, Y_0.

(d) Using your expression for the equilibrium level of income in 14c, what is the effect of a change in exports, $\bar{X}$, on equilibrium income? Interpret your result and discuss the multiplier in an open economy.

(e) Using your results in 14a and d, show the effect of an increase in exports on the trade balance.

APPENDIX: THE BALANCED BUDGET MULTIPLIER

This appendix considers the balanced budget multiplier result mentioned earlier. The balanced budget multiplier refers to the effects of an increase in government purchases accompanied by an increase in taxes such that, in the new equilibrium, the budget surplus is exactly the same as in the original equilibrium. The result is that the multiplier of such a policy change, the balanced budget multiplier, is 1.

A multiplier of unity implies that output expands by precisely the amount of the increased government purchases with no induced consumption spending. It is apparent that what must be at work is the effect of higher taxes that exactly offset the effect of the income expansion, thus maintaining disposable income, and hence consumption, constant. With no induced consumption spending, output expands simply to match the increased government purchases.

We can derive this result formally by noting that the change in aggregate demand ΔAD is equal to the change in government purchases plus the change in consumption spending. The latter is equal to the marginal propensity to consume out of disposable income, c, times the change in disposable income, ΔYD; that is, $\Delta YD = \Delta Y_0 - \Delta TA$, where ΔY_0 is the change in output. Thus,

$$\Delta AD = \Delta \overline{G} + c(\Delta Y_0 - \Delta TA) \tag{A1}$$

Since from one equilibrium to another the change in aggregate demand has to equal the change in output, we have

$$\Delta Y_0 = \Delta \overline{G} + c(\Delta Y_0 - \Delta TA)$$

or

$$\Delta Y_0 = \frac{1}{1-c}(\Delta \overline{G} - c\,\Delta TA) \tag{A2}$$

Next we note that by assumption the change in government purchases between the new equilibrium and the old one is exactly matched by a change in tax collection so that $\Delta \overline{G} = \Delta TA$. It follows from this last equality, after substitution in equation (A2), that with this particular restriction on fiscal policy we have

$$\Delta Y_0 = \frac{1}{1-c}(\Delta \overline{G} - c\,\Delta \overline{G}) = \Delta \overline{G} = \Delta TA \tag{A3}$$

so that the multiplier is precisely unity.

Another way of deriving the balanced budget multiplier result is by considering the successive rounds of spending changes caused by the government policy changes. Suppose each of government purchases and taxes increased by \$1. Let $c(1-t)$, the induced increase in aggregate demand caused by a \$1 increase in income in the presence of taxes, be denoted by $\overline{c}$.

Table A3-1 shows the spending induced by the two policy changes. The first column shows the changes in spending resulting from the change in government purchases and its later repercussions. The second column similarly gives the spending effects in successive rounds of the tax increase. The third column sums the two effects for each spending round, while the final column adds all the changes in spending induced so far. Since $\overline{c}$ is less than 1, $(\overline{c})^n$ becomes very small as the number of spending rounds, n, increases, and the final change in aggregate spending caused by the balanced budget increase in governmental spending is just equal to \$1.

Finally, the balanced budget multiplier can also be thought of from a somewhat different perspective. Consider the goods market equilibrium condition in terms of saving, taxes, investment, transfers, and government purchases:

$$S + TA - TR = \overline{I} + G \tag{A4}$$

Now, using the definition of the budget surplus, $BS \equiv TA - TR - G$,

$$BS = \overline{I} - S \tag{A5}$$

TABLE A3-1   THE BALANCED BUDGET MULTIPLIER

Spending round	CHANGE IN SPENDING RESULTING FROM			
	$\Delta \overline{G} = 1$	$\Delta TA = 1$	Net this round	Total
1	1	$-\overline{c}$	$1 - \overline{c}$	$1 - \overline{c}$
2	$\overline{c}$	$-\overline{c}^2$	$\overline{c} - \overline{c}^2$	$1 - \overline{c}^2$
3	$\overline{c}^2$	$-\overline{c}^3$	$\overline{c}^2 - \overline{c}^3$	$1 - \overline{c}^3$
4	$\overline{c}^3$	$-\overline{c}^4$	$\overline{c}^3 - \overline{c}^4$	$1 - \overline{c}^4$
$\vdots$				
n	$\overline{c}^{n-1}$	$-\overline{c}^n$	$\overline{c}^{n-1} - \overline{c}_n$	$1 - \overline{c}^n$

If there is no change in the budget deficit, nor a change in investment, the equilibrium change in saving is zero. For saving not to change, disposable income must remain unchanged. This says that $\Delta YD = \Delta Y - \Delta T = 0$, and hence shows once more that the change in income equals the change in taxes. This in turn equals the change in government purchases.

Hence, the balanced budget multiplier, or more precisely, the multiplier associated with an unchanging budget surplus or deficit, is equal to unity. This perspective on the income determination process is very useful because it emphasizes the fact that a change in the surplus or deficit of one sector is matched by a corresponding change in the deficit or surplus of the remaining sectors. If the government surplus is constrained by fiscal policy to be unchanged, so too must be the private sector's surplus, $S - \overline{I}$.

MONEY, INTEREST,
AND INCOME

The stock of money, interest rates, and the Federal Reserve seemingly had no place in the model of income determination developed in Chapter 3. But money plays an important role in the determination of income and employment. Interest rates are a significant determinant of aggregate spending, and the Federal Reserve and monetary policy receive at least as much public attention as fiscal policy. For instance, the blame for the deep 1981–1982 recession and its extraordinarily high interest rates is often placed on the Federal Reserve's tight money policy. This chapter introduces money and monetary policy, and builds an explicit framework of analysis in which to study the interaction of goods and assets markets.

This new framework leads to an understanding of the determination of interest rates and of their role in the business cycle. Figure 4-1 shows the interest rate on Treasury bills. The interest rate on Treasury bills represents the payment, per dollar per year, that someone receives who lends to the U.S. government. Thus an interest rate of 10 percent means that someone who lends $100 to the government for 1 year will receive 10 percent, or $10, in interest. Figure 4-1 immediately suggests some questions: What factors cause the interest rate to increase, as occurred for example in 1980–1981, and what factors cause rates to decline as they did in 1982 and 1985? Furthermore, when interest rates increase, what are the effects on output and employment?

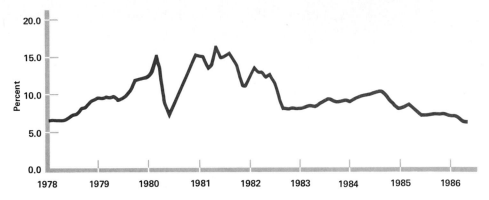

FIGURE 4-1   THE INTEREST RATE ON TREASURY BILLS (percent per year). (*Source:* Data Resources, Inc.)

The model we introduce in this chapter, the *IS-LM model,* is the core of modern macroeconomics. It maintains the spirit and, indeed, many details of the previous chapter. The model is broadened, though, by introducing the interest rate as an additional determinant of aggregate demand. In Chapter 3, autonomous spending and fiscal policy were the chief determinants of aggregate spending. Now we add the interest rate and argue that a reduction in the rate of interest raises aggregate demand. This seems a minor extension, which can readily be handled in the context of Chapter 3. This is not entirely correct, because we have to ask what determines the rate of interest. That question extends our model to include the markets for financial assets and forces us to study the interaction of goods and assets markets. Interest rates and income are jointly determined by equilibrium in goods and assets markets.

What is the payoff for that complication? The introduction of assets markets and interest rates serves three important purposes:

1. The extension shows how monetary policy works.
2. The analysis qualifies the conclusions of Chapter 3. Consider Figure 4-2, which lays out the logical structure of the model. So far we looked at the submodel of autonomous spending and fiscal policy as determinants of aggregate demand and equilibrium income. Now the inclusion of assets markets—money demand and supply, as we shall see—introduces an additional channel. An expansionary fiscal policy, for example, would in the first place raise spending and income. That increase in income, though, would affect the assets markets by raising money demand and thereby raising interest rates. The higher interest rates in turn reduce aggregate

spending and thus, as we shall show, dampen the expansionary impact of fiscal policy. Indeed, under certain conditions, the increase in interest rates may be sufficiently important to offset *fully* the expansionary effects of fiscal policy. Clearly, such an extreme possibility is an important qualification to our study of fiscal policy in Chapter 3.

3. Even if the interest rate changes just mentioned only dampen (rather than offset fully) the expansionary effects of fiscal policy, they nevertheless have an important side effect. The *composition* of aggregate demand between investment and consumption spending will depend on the rate of interest. Higher interest rates dampen aggregate demand mainly by reducing investment. Thus, an expansionary fiscal policy would tend to raise consumption through the multiplier, but it would tend to reduce investment through the induced increase in interest rates. The side effects of fiscal expansion on interest rates and investment continue to be a sensitive and important issue in policy making. Because fiscal expansion tends to reduce investment, an influential view is that fiscal policy should not be used as a tool for demand management.

These three reasons justify the more complicated model we study in this chapter. There is the further advantage that the extended model helps us to understand the functioning of financial markets.

FIGURE 4-2   THE STRUCTURE OF THE *IS-LM* MODEL. The *IS-LM* model emphasizes the interaction between goods and assets markets. The model of Chapter 3 looks at income determination by arguing that income affects spending, which in turn determines output and income. Now we add the effects of interest rates on spending and thus income, and the dependence of assets markets on income. Higher income raises money demand and thus interest rates. Higher interest rates lower spending and thus income. Spending, interest rates, and income are determined jointly by equilibrium in goods *and* assets markets.

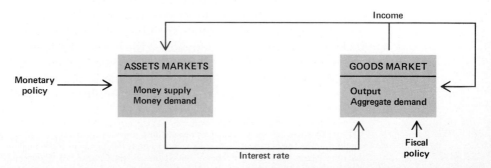

OUTLINE OF THE CHAPTER

We use Figure 4-2 once more to lay out the structure of this chapter. We start in Section 4-1 with a discussion of the link between interest rates and aggregate demand. Here we use the model of Chapter 3 directly, augmented to include an interest rate as a determinant of aggregate demand. We derive a key relationship — the *IS* curve — that shows combinations of interest rates and levels of income for which the goods markets clear. In Section 4-2, we turn to the assets markets and in particular to the money market. We show that the demand for money depends on interest rates and income and that there are combinations of interest rates and income levels — the *LM* curve — for which the money market clears.[1] In Section 4-3, we combine the two schedules to study the joint determination of interest rates and income. Section 4-4 lays out the adjustment process toward equilibrium. Monetary policy is discussed in Sections 4-5 and 4-6. Fiscal policy and the important issue of the monetary-fiscal policy mix are reserved for Chapter 5. That material is in a separate chapter only to avoid making this chapter too long.

4-1 THE GOODS MARKET AND THE *IS* CURVE

In this section we derive a *goods market equilibrium schedule.* The goods market equilibrium schedule, or *IS* schedule, shows combinations of interest rates and levels of output such that planned spending equals income. The goods market equilibrium schedule is an extension of income determination with a 45° line diagram. What is new here is that investment is no longer fully exogenous but is also determined by the interest rate. To appreciate the extension of Chapter 3 we briefly review what we found there.

In Chapter 3 we derived an expression for equilibrium income:

$$Y_0 = \frac{\overline{A}}{1 - \overline{c}} \qquad \overline{c} = c(1 - t) \tag{1}$$

Equilibrium income in this simple Keynesian model has two determinants: autonomous spending, $\overline{A}$, and the propensity to consume out of income, $\overline{c}$. Autonomous spending includes government spending, investment spending, and autonomous consumption spending. The propensity to consume out of income, as seen from (1), depends on the propensity to consume out of disposable income, c, and on the fraction of a dollar of income retained after taxes, $(1 - t)$. The higher the level of autonomous spending and the higher the propensity to consume, the higher the equilibrium level of income.

---

[1] The terms *IS* and *LM* are shorthand representations, respectively, of investment equals saving (goods market equilibrium) and money demand (*L*) equals money supply (*M*), or money market equilibrium. The classic article that introduced this model is J. R. Hicks, "Mr. Keynes and the Classics: A Suggested Interpretation," *Econometrica*, 1937, pp. 147–159.

Investment and the Interest Rate

So far, investment spending $\bar{I}$ has been treated as *entirely* exogenous — some number like $700 billion determined altogether outside the model of income determination. Now, as we make our macromodel more complete by introducing interest rates as part of the model, investment spending, too, becomes endogenous. The desired or planned rate of investment is lower the higher the interest rate.

A simple argument shows why. Investment is spending on additions to the capital stock (machinery, structures, inventories). Such investment is undertaken with the aim of making profits in the future by operating machines and factories. Suppose firms borrow to buy the capital (machines and factories) that they use. Then the higher the interest rate, the more firms have to pay out in interest each year from the earnings they receive from their investment. Thus, the higher the interest rate, the less the profits to the firm after paying interest, and the less it will want to invest. Conversely, a low rate of interest makes investment spending profitable and is, therefore, reflected in a high level of planned investment.

The Investment Demand Schedule

We specify an investment spending function of the form[2]

$$I = \bar{I} - bi \qquad b > 0 \tag{2}$$

where i is the rate of interest and b measures the interest response of investment. $\bar{I}$ now denotes autonomous investment spending, that is, investment spending that is independent of both income and the rate of interest.[3] Equation (2) states that the lower the interest rate, the higher is planned investment, with the coefficient b measuring the responsiveness of investment spending to the interest rate.

Figure 4-3 shows the investment schedule of equation (2). The schedule shows for each level of the rate of interest the rate at which firms plan to spend on investment. The schedule is negatively sloped to reflect the assumption that a reduction in the rate of interest increases the profitability of additions to the capital stock and therefore leads to a larger rate of planned investment spending.

---

[2] Here and in other places in the book, we specify linear (straight-line) versions of behavioral functions. We use the linear specifications to simplify both the algebra and the diagrams. The linearity assumption does not lead to any great difficulties so long as we confine ourselves to talking about small changes in the economy. You should often draw nonlinear versions of our diagrams to be sure you can work with them.

[3] In Chap. 3, investment spending was defined as autonomous with respect to income. Now that the interest rate appears in the model, we have to extend the definition of autonomous to mean independent of *both* the interest rate and income. To conserve notation, we continue to use $\bar{I}$ to denote autonomous investment, but recognize that the definition is broadened.

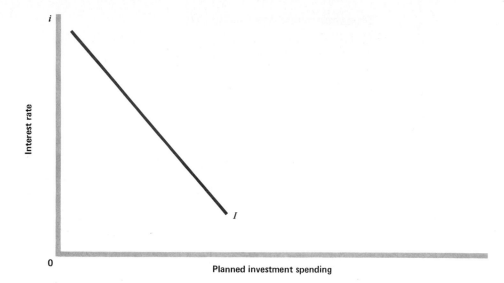

FIGURE 4-3 THE INVESTMENT SCHEDULE. The investment schedule shows the planned level of investment spending at each rate of interest. Because higher interest rates reduce the profitability of additions to the capital stock, higher interest rates imply lower planned rates of investment spending. Changes in autonomous investment shift the investment schedule.

The position of the investment schedule is determined by the slope — the term b in equation (2) — and by the level of autonomous investment spending $\bar{I}$. If investment is highly responsive to the interest rate, a small decline in interest rates will lead to a large increase in investment, so that the schedule is almost flat. Conversely, if investment responds little to interest rates, the schedule is more nearly vertical. Changes in autonomous investment spending $\bar{I}$ shift the investment schedule. An increase in $\bar{I}$ means that at each level of the interest rate firms plan to invest at a higher rate. This would be shown by a rightward shift of the investment schedule.

The Interest Rate and Aggregate Demand: The *IS* Curve

We now modify the aggregate demand function of Chapter 3 to reflect the new planned investment spending schedule. Aggregate demand still consists of the demand for consumption, investment, and government spending on goods and services. Only now investment spending depends on the interest rate. We have

$$AD \equiv C + I + G$$
$$= \overline{C} + c\overline{TR} + c(1 - t)Y + \overline{I} - bi + \overline{G} \qquad (3)$$
$$= \overline{A} + \overline{c}Y - bi$$

where
$$\overline{A} \equiv \overline{C} + c\overline{TR} + \overline{I} + \overline{G} \qquad (4)$$

From equation (3) we observe that an increase in the interest rate reduces aggregate demand at a given level of income because an interest rate increase reduces investment spending. Note that the term $\overline{A}$, which is the part of aggregate demand unaffected by either the level of income or the interest rate, does include part of investment spending, namely, $\overline{I}$. As noted earlier, $\overline{I}$ is the *autonomous* component of investment spending, which is independent of the interest rate (and income).

At any given level of the interest rate, we can still proceed as in Chapter 3 to determine the equilibrium level of income and output. As the interest rate changes, however, the equilibrium level of income changes. Figure 4-4 is used to derive the *IS* curve.

For a given level of the interest rate, say, i_1, the last term of equation (3) is a constant (bi_1), and we can in Figure 4-4a draw the aggregate demand function of Chapter 3, this time with an intercept $\overline{A} - bi_1$. The equilibrium level of income obtained in the usual manner is Y_1 at point E_1. Since that equilibrium level of income was derived for a given level of the interest rate i_1, we plot that pair (i_1, Y_1) in the bottom panel as point E_1. We now have one point, E_1, on the *IS* curve.

Consider next a lower interest rate, i_2. At a lower interest rate, aggregate demand would be higher at each level of income because investment spending is higher. In terms of Figure 4-4a, that implies an upward shift of the aggregate demand schedule. The curve shifts upward because the intercept $\overline{A} - bi$ has been increased. Given the increase in aggregate demand, the equilibrium level of income rises to point E_2, with an associated income level Y_2. At point E_2, in the bottom panel, we record the fact that an interest rate i_2 implies an equilibrium level of income, Y_2 — equilibrium in the sense that the goods market is in equilibrium (or that the goods market *clears*). Point E_2 is another point on the *IS* curve.

We can apply the same procedure to all conceivable levels of the interest rate and thereby generate all the points which make up the *IS* curve. They have in common the property that they are combinations of interest rates and income (output) such that the goods market clears. That is why the *IS* curve is called the *goods market equilibrium schedule.*

Figure 4-4 shows that the *IS* curve is negatively sloped, reflecting the increase in aggregate demand associated with a reduction in the interest rate.

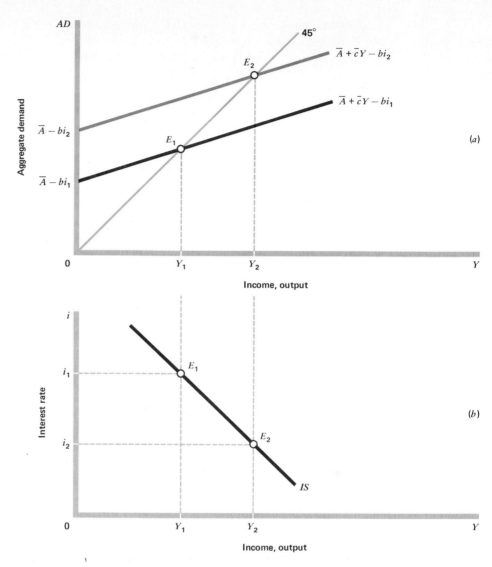

FIGURE 4-4 DERIVATION OF THE *IS* CURVE. At an interest rate i_1, equilibrium in the goods market obtains at point E_1 in the upper panel with an income level Y_1. In the lower panel this is recorded as point E_1. A fall in the interest rate to i_2 raises aggregate demand, increasing the level of spending at each income level. The new equilibrium income level is Y_2. In the lower panel, point E_2 records the new equilibrium in the goods market corresponding to an interest rate i_2.

We can also derive the *IS* curve by using the goods market equilibrium condition, income equals planned spending, or

$$Y = AD$$
$$= \bar{A} + cY - bi \tag{5}$$

which can be simplified to

$$Y = \bar{\alpha}(\bar{A} - bi) \qquad \bar{\alpha} = \frac{1}{1 - \bar{c}} \tag{6}$$

where $\bar{\alpha}$ is the multiplier of Chapter 3. Equation (6) should now be compared with (1) at the beginning of this chapter. Note from equation (6) that a higher interest rate implies a lower level of equilibrium income for a given $\bar{A}$, as Figure 4-4 shows.

The construction of the *IS* curve is quite straightforward and may even be deceptively simple. We can gain further understanding of the economics of the *IS* curve by asking and answering the following questions:

- What determines the slope of the *IS* curve?
- What determines the position of the *IS* curve, given its slope, and what causes the curve to shift?
- What happens when the interest rate and income are at levels such that we are not on the *IS* curve?

The Slope of the *IS* Curve

We have already noted that the *IS* curve is negatively sloped because a higher level of the interest rate reduces investment spending, therefore reducing aggregate demand and thus the equilibrium level of income. The steepness of the curve depends on how sensitive investment spending is to changes in the interest rate, and also on the multiplier $\bar{\alpha}$ in equation (6).

Suppose that investment spending is very sensitive to the interest rate, so that b in equation (6) is large. Then, in terms of Figure 4-4, a given change in the interest rate produces a large change in aggregate demand, and thus shifts the aggregate demand curve in Figure 4-4a up by a large distance. A large shift in the aggregate demand schedule produces a correspondingly large change in the equilibrium level of income. If a given change in the interest rate produces a large change in income, the *IS* curve is very flat. This is the case if investment is very sensitive to the interest rate, that is, if b is large. Correspondingly, with b small and investment spending not very sensitive to the interest rate, the *IS* curve is relatively steep.

THE ROLE OF THE MULTIPLIER

Consider next the effects of the multiplier $\overline{\alpha}$ on the steepness of the *IS* curve. Figure 4-5 shows aggregate demand curves corresponding to different multipliers. The coefficient $\overline{c}$ on the darker aggregate demand curves is smaller than the corresponding coefficient $\overline{c}'$ on the lighter aggregate demand curves. The multiplier is accordingly larger on the lighter aggregate demand curves. The initial levels of income, Y_1 and Y_1', correspond to the interest rate i_1 on the lower of each of the darker and lighter aggregate demand curves, respectively.

A given reduction in the interest rate, to i_2, raises the intercept of the aggregate demand curves by the same vertical distance, as shown in the top panel. However, the implied change in income is very different. For the lighter curve, income rises to Y_2', while it rises only to Y_2 on the darker line. The change in equilibrium income corresponding to a given change in the interest rate is accordingly larger as the aggregate demand curve is steeper; that is, the larger the multiplier, the greater the rise in income. As we see from the lower figure, the larger the multiplier, the flatter the *IS* curve. Equivalently, the larger the multiplier, the larger the change in income produced by a given change in the interest rate.

We have thus seen that the smaller the sensitivity of investment spending to the interest rate and the smaller the multiplier, the steeper the *IS* curve. This conclusion is confirmed using equation (6). We can turn equation (6) around to express the interest rate as a function of the level of income:

$$i = \frac{\overline{A}}{b} - \frac{Y}{\overline{\alpha}b} \tag{6a}$$

Thus, for a given change in Y, the associated change in i will be larger in size as b is smaller and $\overline{\alpha}$ is smaller.

Given that the slope of the *IS* curve depends on the multiplier, fiscal policy can affect that slope. The multiplier $\overline{\alpha}$ is affected by the tax rate: an increase in the tax rate reduces the multiplier. Accordingly, the higher the tax rate, the steeper the *IS* curve.[4]

The Position of the *IS* Curve

Figure 4-6 shows two different *IS* curves, the lighter one of which lies to the right and above the darker *IS* curve. What might cause the *IS* curve to be at *IS'* rather than at *IS*? The answer is an increase in the level of autonomous spending.

In Figure 4-6a we show an initial aggregate demand curve drawn for a level of autonomous spending $\overline{A}$ and for an interest rate i_1. Corresponding to

---

[4] In problem 3 we ask you to relate this fact to the discussion of automatic stabilizers in Chap. 3.

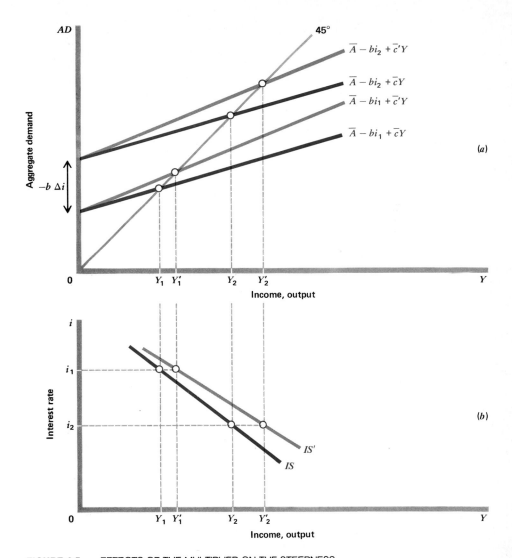

FIGURE 4-5   EFFECTS OF THE MULTIPLIER ON THE STEEPNESS
OF THE *IS* CURVE. The diagram shows that corresponding to a higher
marginal propensity to spend, and hence a steeper aggregate demand
schedule, there is a flatter *IS* schedule.

the initial aggregate demand curve is the point E_1 on the *IS* curve in Figure
4-6b. Now, at the same interest rate, let the level of autonomous spending
increase to $\overline{A}'$. The increase in autonomous spending increases the equilibrium level of income at the interest rate i_1. The point E_2 in Figure 4-6b is thus a

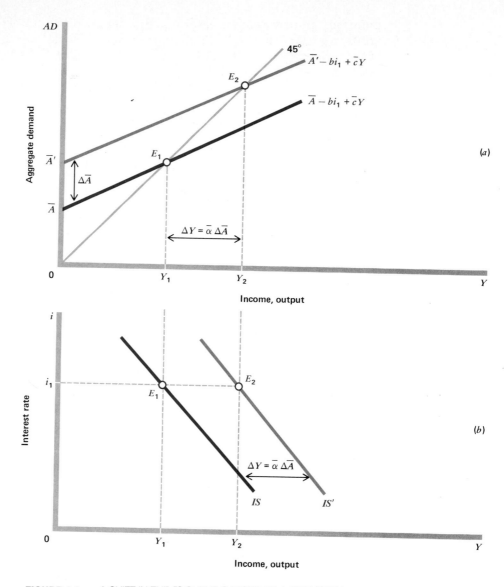

FIGURE 4-6 A SHIFT IN THE *IS* CURVE CAUSED BY A CHANGE IN AUTONOMOUS SPENDING. An increase in aggregate demand due to higher autonomous spending shifts the aggregate demand curve in (*a*) up, raising the equilibrium level of output at interest rate i_1. The *IS* schedule shifts. At each level of the interest rate, equilibrium income is now higher. The horizontal shift of the *IS* schedule is equal to the multiplier times the increase in autonomous spending.

point on the new goods market equilibrium schedule IS'. Since E_1 was an arbitrary point on the initial IS curve, we can perform the exercise for all levels of the interest rate and thereby generate the new curve IS'. Thus, an increase in autonomous spending shifts the curve out to the right.

By how much does the curve shift? The change in income, as a result of the change in autonomous spending, can be seen from the top panel to be just the multiplier times the change in autonomous spending. That means that the IS curve is shifted horizontally by a distance equal to the multiplier times the change in autonomous spending as in the lower panel.

The level of autonomous spending is, from equation (4):

$$\overline{A} \equiv \overline{C} + c\overline{TR} + \overline{I} + \overline{G}$$

Accordingly, an increase in government purchases or transfer payments will shift the IS curve out to the right, the extent of the shift depending on the size of the multiplier. A reduction in transfer payments or in government purchases shifts the IS curve to the left.

Positions off the IS Curve

We gain understanding of the meaning of the IS curve by considering points off the curve. Figure 4-7 reproduces Figure 4-4, along with two additional points — the *dis*equilibrium points E_3 and E_4. Consider first the question of what is true for points off the schedule, points such as E_3 and E_4. In Figure 4-7*b* at point E_3 we have the same interest rate i_2 as at point E_2, but the level of income is lower than at E_2. Since the interest rate i_2 at E_3 is the same as at E_2, we must have the same aggregate demand function corresponding to the two points. Accordingly, looking now at Figure 4-7*a*, we find both points are on the same aggregate demand schedule. At E_3 on that schedule, aggregate demand exceeds the level of output. Point E_3 is therefore a point of *excess demand for goods:* the interest rate is too low or output is too low for the goods market to be in equilibrium. Demand for goods exceeds output.

Next, consider point E_4 in Figure 4-7*b*. Here we have the same rate of interest i_1 as at $\mathbf{E}_1$, but the level of income is higher. Given the interest rate i_1, the corresponding point in Figure 4-7*a* is at E_4, where we have an *excess supply of goods* since output is larger than aggregate demand — that is, aggregate demand, given the interest rate i_1 and the income level Y_2.

The preceding discussion shows that points above and to the right of the IS curve — points like E_4 — are points of excess supply of goods. This is indicated by ESG (excess supply of goods) in Figure 4-7*b*. Points below and to the left of the IS curve are points of excess demand for goods (EDG). At a point like E_3, the interest rate is too low and aggregate demand is therefore too high, relative to output. EDG shows the region of excess demand in Figure 4-7.

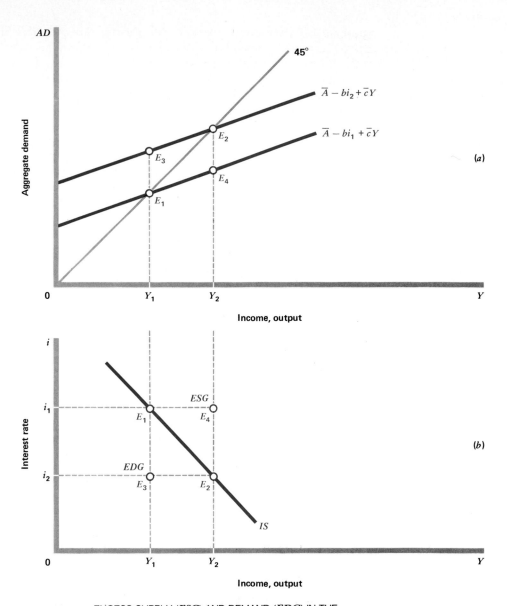

FIGURE 4-7 EXCESS SUPPLY (*ESG*) AND DEMAND (*EDG*) IN THE GOODS MARKET. Points above and to the right of the *IS* schedule correspond to an excess supply of goods, and points below and to the left to an excess demand for goods. At a point such as E_4, interest rates are higher than at E_2 on the *IS* curve. At the higher interest rates, investment spending is too low, and thus output exceeds planned spending and there is an excess supply of goods.

Summary

The major points about the *IS* curve are:

1. The *IS* curve is the schedule of combinations of the interest rate and level of income such that the goods market is in equilibrium.
2. The *IS* curve is negatively sloped because an increase in the interest rate reduces planned investment spending and therefore reduces aggregate demand, thus reducing the equilibrium level of income.
3. The smaller the multiplier and the less sensitive investment spending is to changes in the interest rate, the steeper the curve.
4. The *IS* curve is shifted by changes in autonomous spending. An increase in autonomous spending, including an increase in government purchases, shifts the *IS* curve out to the right.
5. At points to the right of the curve, there is excess supply in the goods market, and at points to the left of the curve, there is excess demand for goods.

We turn now to examine behavior in the assets markets.

4-2 THE ASSETS MARKETS AND THE *LM* CURVE

In the preceding section, we discussed aggregate demand and the goods market. In the present section, we turn to the assets markets. The assets markets are the markets in which money, bonds, stocks, houses, and other forms of wealth are traded. Up to this point in the book, we have ignored the role of those markets in affecting the level of income, and it is now time to remedy the omission.

There is a large variety of assets, and a tremendous volume of trading occurs every day in the assets markets. But we shall simplify matters by grouping all available financial assets into two groups, *money* and *interest-bearing assets*.[5] By analogy with our treatment of the goods market, we proceed in the assets markets as if there are only two assets, money and all others. It will be useful to think of the other assets as marketable claims to future income such as *bonds*.

A bond is a promise to pay to its holder certain agreed-upon amounts of money at specified dates in the future. For example, a borrower sells a bond in

---

[5] We assume in this section that certain assets, such as the capital that firms use in production, are not traded. That too is a simplification. A more complete treatment of the assets markets would allow for the trading of capital and would introduce a relative price for the capital operated by firms. This treatment is usually reserved for advanced graduate courses. For such a treatment of the assets markets, see James Tobin, "A General Equilibrium Approach to Monetary Theory," *Journal of Money, Credit and Banking,* February 1969, pp. 15–29, and by the same author, "Money, Capital, and Other Stores of Value," *American Economic Review,* May 1961, pp. 26–37.

BOX
4-1

ASSETS AND ASSET RETURNS

There are four main kinds of assets in the economy: money, bonds, equities or stocks, and real assets.

MONEY

The money stock consists of assets that can be immediately used for making payments. Money includes currency (notes and coins) and also deposits on which checks can be written. In mid-1986, the currency stock was $177 billion, or $735 per person. The stock of deposits on which checks can be written was $484 billion, or about $2,016 per person. Thus the money stock (more detail follows in Chapter 8) was $661 billion, which implies that the amount of money held in the economy was $2,750 per person.

Until the mid-1970s (and from the 1930s) no interest was paid on checkable deposits. During that period people held checkable deposits purely for the convenience. Now interest is paid on checkable deposits, which people hold both because they pay interest and because they are a convenient way of making payments.

BONDS

A bond is a promise by a borrower to pay the lender a certain amount (the principal) at a specified date (the maturity date of the bond) and in the meantime to pay a given amount of interest per year. Thus we might have a bond, issued by the U.S. Treasury, that pays $10,000 on June 1, 1989, and until that time pays 8 percent interest per year, or $800 each year. Bonds are issued by many types of borrower—the government, municipalities, corporations. The interest rates on bonds issued by different borrowers reflect the differing risk of default. Default occurs when a borrower is unable to meet the commitment to pay interest or principal. Corporations sometimes default, and during the great depression of the 1930s, so did some cities. In the late 1970s there was fear that New York City would default, and in the 1980s there was the same fear that many foreign governments would do so.

By the end of 1985, individuals in the United States held a total of about $4 trillion in the form of bonds. Well over half that amount was in the form of debt of banks—time and saving deposits. Nearly $500 billion consisted of government bonds held by individuals. Individuals held relatively small amounts of corporate bonds—under $100 billion.

EQUITIES OR STOCKS

Equities or stocks are claims to a share of the profits in an interprise. For example, a share in IBM entitles the owner to a share of the profits of that corporation. The shareholder or stockholder receives the return on equity in two forms. Most firms pay regular *dividends*, which means that stockholders receive a certain amount of dollars for each share they own. Firms may also decide not to distribute profits to the stockholders, but rather retain them and reinvest these profits by adding to their stock of machines and structures. When this occurs, the shares become more valuable since they now represent claims on the profits from a larger capital stock. Therefore, the price of the stock in the market will rise, and stockholders make *capital gains*. A capital gain is an increase, per period of time, in the price of an asset. Of course, when the outlook for a corporation turns sour, stock prices can fall and stockholders make capital losses.

Thus the return on stocks or the yield to a holder of a stock is equal to the dividend (as a percent of price) plus the capital gain.

Suppose we look at 1987 and 1988 and consider the yield on a stock in an imaginary company, BioMiracles, Inc. In 1987 the stock trades for $15. In 1988 the stock pays a dividend of $0.75 and the stock prices increases to $16.50. What is the yield on the stock? The yield per year is equal to 15.0 percent, which is the dividend as a percent of initial price [5 percent = (0.75/15) × 100] plus 10.0 percent, which is the $1.50 capital gain as a percent of initial price.

At the end of 1985 the value of equity held by individuals in the United States was $1.8 trillion.

REAL ASSETS

Real assets, or tangible assets, are the machines, land, and structures owned by corporations, and the consumer durables (cars, washing machines, stereos, etc.) and houses owned by households. These assets carry a return that differs from one asset to another. Owner-occupied houses provide a return to owners who enjoy living in them and not paying monthly rent; the machines a firm owns contribute to producing output and thus making profits. The assets are called *real* to distinguish them from *financial* assets (money, stocks, bonds). The total value of tangible assets at the end of 1985 was $12.5 trillion, or over $52,000 per person.

The value of equities and bonds held by individuals cannot be added to tangible wealth to get the total wealth of individuals. The reason is that the equities and bonds they hold are claims on part of the tangible wealth, that part held by corporations. The equity share gives an individual a part ownership in the factory and machinery.

In macroeconomics, to make things manageable, we lump assets into two categories. On one side we have money, with the specific characteristic that it is the only asset that serves as a means of payment. On the other side we have all other assets. Because money offers the convenience of being a means of payment, it carries a lower return than other assets, but that differential depends on the relative supplies of assets. As we see in this chapter, when the Fed reduces the money stock and increases the supply of other assets (we say "bonds"), the yield on other assets increases.

The appendix to Chapter 9 develops the relationship between interest rates and asset prices or present values. The appendix can be read independently of Chapter 9, and the interested student can study that material now.

exchange for a given amount of money today, say, $100, and promises to pay a fixed amount, say, $6, each year to the person who owns the bond, and to repay the full $100 (the principal) after some fixed period of time, such as 3 years, or perhaps longer. In this example, the interest rate is 6 percent, for that is the percentage of the amount borrowed that the borrower pays each year.

The Wealth Constraint

An any given time, an individual has to decide how to allocate his or her financial wealth between alternative assets. The more bonds held, the more interest received on total financial wealth. The more money held, the less likely the individual is not to have money available when he or she wants to make a purchase. The person who has $1,000 in financial wealth has to decide whether to hold, say, $900 in bonds and $100 in money, or rather, $500 in each type of asset, or even $1,000 in money and none in bonds. Decisions on the form in which to hold assets are *portfolio decisions.*

The example makes it clear that the portfolio decision on how much money to hold and the decision on how many bonds to hold are really the same decision. Given the level of financial wealth, the individual who has decided how many bonds to hold has implicitly also decided how much money to hold. There is thus a *wealth budget constraint* which states that the sum of the individual's demand for money and demand for bonds has to add up to that person's total financial wealth.

Real and Nominal Money Demand

At this stage we have to reinforce the crucial distinction between *real* and *nominal* variables. The nominal demand for money is the individual's demand for a given number of dollars, and similarly, the nominal demand for bonds is the demand for a given number of dollars' worth of bonds. The real demand for money is the demand for money expressed in terms of the number of units of goods that money will buy: it is equal to the nominal demand for money divided by the price level. If the nominal demand for money is $100 and the price level is $2 per good — meaning that the representative basket of goods costs $2 — then the real demand for money is 50 goods. If the price level later doubles to $4 per good and the demand for nominal money likewise doubles to $200, the real demand for money is unchanged at 50 goods.

Real money balances — real balances for short — are the quantity of nominal money divided by the price level, and the real demand for money is called the *demand for real balances.* Similarly, real bond holdings are the nominal quantity of bonds divided by the price level.

The wealth budget constraint in the assets markets states that the demand for real balances, which we denote L, plus the demand for real bond holdings, which we denote DB, must add up to the real financial wealth of the individual. Real financial wealth is, of course, simply nominal wealth WN divided by the price level P:

$$L + DB \equiv \frac{WN}{P} \tag{7}$$

Note, again, that the wealth budget constraint implies, given an individual's real wealth, that a decision to hold more real balances is also a decision to hold less real wealth in the form of bonds. This implication turns out to be both important and convenient. It will allow us to discuss assets markets entirely in terms of the money market. Why? Because, given real wealth, when the money market is in equilibrium, the bond market will turn out also to be in equilibrium. We now show why that should be.

The total amount of real financial wealth in the economy consists of real money balances and real bonds in existence. Thus, total real financial wealth is equal to

$$\frac{WN}{P} \equiv \frac{M}{P} + SB \tag{8}$$

where M is the stock of nominal money balances and SB is the real value of the supply of bonds. Total real financial wealth consists of real balances and real bonds. The distinction between equations (7) and (8) is that equation (7) is a constraint on the amount of assets individuals wish to hold, whereas equation (8) is merely an accounting relationship which tells us how much financial wealth there is in the economy. There is no implication in the accounting relationship in equation (8) that individuals are necessarily happy to hold the amounts of money and bonds that actually exist in the economy.

Now substitute equation (7) into equation (8) and rearrange terms to obtain

$$\left(L - \frac{M}{P}\right) + (DB - SB) \equiv 0 \tag{9}$$

Let us see what equation (9) implies. Suppose that the demand for real balances L is equal to the existing stock of real balances M/P. Then the first term in parentheses in equation (9) is equal to zero, and therefore the second term in parentheses must also be zero. Thus, if the demand for real money balances is equal to the real money supply, the demand for real bonds DB must be equal to the supply of real bonds SB.

Stating the same proposition in terms of "markets," we can say the following: The *wealth budget constraint* implies that when the money market is in equilibrium ($L = M/P$), the bond market, too, is in equilibrium ($DB = SB$). Similarly, when there is excess demand in the money market, so that $L > M/P$, there is an excess supply of bonds; $DB < SB$. We can therefore fully discuss the assets markets by concentrating our attention on the money market.

The Demand for Money

We now turn to the money market and initially concentrate on the demand for real balances.[6] The demand for money is a demand for *real* balances because the public holds money for what it will buy. The higher the price level, the more nominal balances a person has to hold to be able to purchase a given quantity of goods. If the price level doubles, then an individual has to hold twice as many nominal balances in order to be able to buy the same amount of goods.

---

[6] The demand for money is studied in depth in Chap. 10; here we only briefly present the arguments underlying the demand for money.

The demand for real balances depends on the level of real income and the interest rate. It depends on the level of real income because individuals hold money to finance their expenditures, which, in turn, depend on income. The demand for money depends also on the cost of holding money. The cost of holding money is the interest that is foregone by holding money rather than other assets. The higher the interest rate, the more costly it is to hold money, rather than other assets and, accordingly, the less cash will be held at each level of income.[7] Individuals can economize on their holdings of cash, when the interest rate rises, by being more careful in managing their money, by making transfers from money to bonds whenever their money holdings reach any appreciable magnitude. If the interest rate is 1 percent, then there is very little benefit from holding bonds rather than money. However, when the interest rate is 10 percent, one would probably go to some effort not to hold more money than needed to finance day-to-day transactions.

On these simple grounds, then, the demand for real balances increases with the level of real income and decreases with the interest rate. The demand for real balances is accordingly written[8]

$$L = kY - hi \qquad k > 0 \qquad h > 0 \tag{10}$$

The parameters k and h reflect the sensitivity of the demand for real balances to the level of income and the interest rate, respectively. A $5 increase in real income raises money demand by $5k$ real dollars. An increase in the interest rate by 1 percentage point reduces real money demand by h real dollars.

The demand function for real balances, equation (10), implies that for a given level of income, the quantity demanded is a decreasing function of the rate of interest. Such a demand curve is shown in Figure 4-8 for a level of income Y_1. The higher the level of income, the larger the demand for real balances, and therefore the further to the right the demand curve. The demand curve for a higher level of real income Y_2 is also shown in Figure 4-8.

The Supply of Money, Money Market Equilibrium, and the *LM* Curve

Now we study equilibrium in the money market. For that purpose we have to say how the supply of money is determined. The nominal quantity of money M is controlled by the Federal Reserve System, and we take it as given at the level

---

[7] As we discuss in Chap. 11, changes in financial regulations in the early 1980s led to the payment of interest on some forms of money holdings. In Chap. 10 we discuss the effects of such changes on the demand for money and on the *LM* curve. But there do remain sizable parts of money holding — including currency — on which no interest is paid, so that overall, money earns less interest than other assets and the analysis of this chapter is still applicable.

[8] Once again, we use a linear equation to describe a relationship. You should experiment with an alternative form, for example, $L = kY + h'/i$, where k and h' are positive. How would the equivalent of Fig. 4-8 look for this demand function?

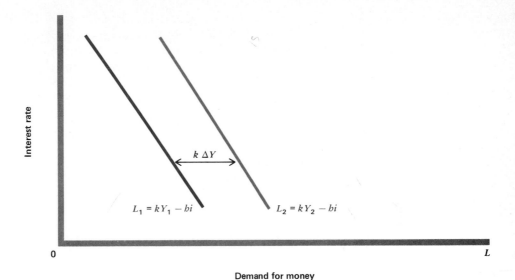

Demand for money

FIGURE 4-8   THE DEMAND FOR REAL BALANCES AS A FUNCTION
OF THE INTEREST RATE AND REAL INCOME. The demand for real
balances is drawn as a function of the rate of interest. The higher the
rate of interest, the lower the quantity of real balances demanded, given
the level of income. An increase in income raises the demand for
money. This is shown by a rightward shift of the money demand schedule.

$\overline{M}$. We assume the price level is constant at the level $\overline{P}$, so that the real money
supply is at the level $\overline{M}/\overline{P}$.[9]

In Figure 4-9, we show combinations of interest rate and income levels
such that the demand for real balances exactly matches the available supply.
Starting with the level of income Y_1, the corresponding demand curve for real
balances L_1, is shown in Figure 4-9b. It is drawn, as in Figure 4-8, as a decreasing function of the interest rate. The existing supply of real balances $\overline{M}/\overline{P}$ is
shown by the vertical line, since it is given and therefore is independent of the
interest rate. The interest rate i_1 has the property that it clears the money
market. At that interest rate, the demand for real balances equals the supply.
Therefore, point E_1 is an equilibrium point in the money market. That point is
recorded in Figure 4-9a as a point on the *money market equilibrium schedule,*
or the *LM curve.*

---

[9] Since for the present we are holding constant the money supply and price level, we refer to them as exogenous
and denote that fact by a bar.

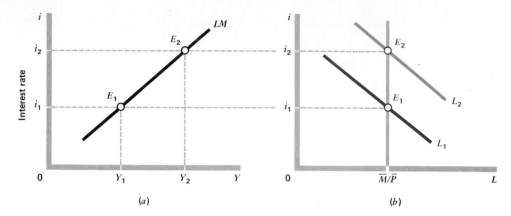

FIGURE 4-9 DERIVATION OF THE *LM* CURVE. The right-hand panel shows the money market. The supply of real balances is the vertical line $\overline{M}/\overline{P}$. The nominal money supply $\overline{M}$ is fixed by the Fed, and the price level $\overline{P}$ is assumed given. Demand for money curves L_1 and L_2 corresponds to different levels of income. When the income level is Y_1, L_1 applies, and the equilibrium interest rate is i_1. This gives point E_1 on the *LM* schedule in (*a*). At income level Y_2, greater than Y_1, the equilibrium interest rate is i_2, yielding point E_2 on the *LM* curve.

Consider next the effect of an increase in income to Y_2. In Figure 4-9*b* the higher level of income causes the demand for real balances to be higher at each level of the interest rate, and so the demand curve for real balances shifts up and to the right, to L_2. The interest rate increases to i_2 to maintain equilibrium in the money market at that higher level of income. Accordingly, the new equilibrium point is E_2. In Figure 4-9*a* we record point E_2 as a point of equilibrium in the money market. Performing the same exercise for all income levels, we generate a series of points that can be linked to give us the *LM* schedule.

The *LM* schedule, or money market equilibrium schedule, shows all combinations of interest rates and levels of income such that the demand for real balances is equal to the supply. Along the *LM* schedule, the money market is in equilibrium.

The *LM* curve is positively sloped. An increase in the interest rate reduces the demand for real balances. To maintain the demand for real balances equal to the fixed supply, the level of income has, therefore, to rise. Accordingly, money market equilibrium implies that an increase in the interest rate is accompanied by an increase in the level of income.

The *LM* curve can be obtained directly by combining the demand curve for real balances, equation (10), and the fixed supply of real balances. For the money market to be in equilibrium, demand has to equal supply, or

$$\frac{\overline{M}}{P} = kY - hi \qquad (11)$$

Solving for the interest rate:

$$i = \frac{1}{h}\left(kY - \frac{\overline{M}}{P}\right) \qquad (11a)$$

The relationship $(11a)$ is the *LM* curve.

Next we ask the same questions about the properties of the *LM* schedule that we asked about the *IS* curve.

The Slope of the *LM* Curve

The larger the responsiveness of the demand for money to income, as measured by k, and the lower the responsiveness of the demand for money to the interest rate h, the steeper the *LM* curve will be. This point can be established by experimenting with Figure 4-9. It can also be confirmed by examining equation $(11a)$, where a given change in income ΔY has a larger effect on the interest rate i, the larger is k and the smaller is h. If the demand for money is relatively insensitive to the interest rate, so that h is close to zero, the *LM* curve is nearly vertical. If the demand for money is very sensitive to the interest rate, so that h is large, then the *LM* curve is close to horizontal. In that case, a small change in the interest rate is accompanied by a large change in the level of income to maintain money market equilibrium.

The Position of the *LM* Curve

The real money supply is held constant along the *LM* curve. It follows that a change in the real money supply will shift the *LM* curve. In Figure 4-10, we show the effect of an increase in the real money supply. In Figure 4-10b, we draw the demand for real money balances for a level of income Y_1. With the initial real money supply $\overline{M}/\overline{P}$, the equilibrium is at point E_1, with an interest rate i_1. The corresponding point on the *LM* schedule is E_1.

Consider the effect of an increase in the real money supply to $\overline{M}'/\overline{P}$, which is represented by a rightward shift of the money supply schedule. At the initial level of income and, hence, on the demand schedule L_1, there is now an excess supply of real balances. To restore money market equilibrium at the income level Y_1, the interest rate has to decline to i_2. The new equilibrium is, therefore, at point E_2. This implies that in Figure 4-10a, the *LM* schedule shifts to the right and down to *LM'*. At each level of income the equilibrium interest rate has to be lower to induce people to hold the larger real quantity of money.

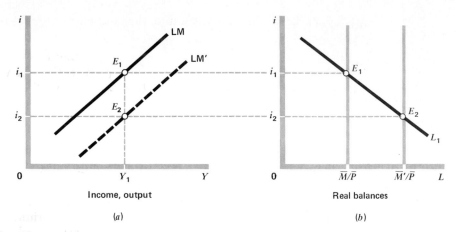

FIGURE 4-10   AN INCREASE IN THE SUPPLY OF MONEY FROM $\overline{M}$ TO $\overline{M}'$ SHIFTS THE *LM* CURVE TO THE RIGHT. An increase in the stock of real balances shifts the supply schedule in the right panel from $\overline{M}/\overline{P}$ to $\overline{M}'/\overline{P}$. At the initial income level Y_1, the equilibrium interest rate in the money market falls to i_2. In the left panel we show point E_2 as one point on the new *LM* schedule, corresponding to the higher money stock. Thus an increase in the real money stock shifts the *LM* schedule down and to the right.

Alternatively, at each level of the interest rate the level of income has to be higher so as to raise the transactions demand for money and thereby absorb the higher real money supply. These points can be noted, too, from inspection of the money market equilibrium condition in equation (11).

Positions off the *LM* Curve

Next we consider points off the *LM* schedule, to characterize them as points of excess demand or supply of money. For that purpose, look at Figure 4-11, which reproduces Figure 4-9 but adds the disequilibrium points E_3 and E_4. Look first at point E_1, where the money market is in equilibrium. Next assume an increase in the level of income to Y_2. This will raise the demand for real balances and shift the demand curve to L_2. At the initial interest rate, the demand for real balances would be indicated by point E_4 in Figure 4-11b, and we would have an excess demand for money—an excess of demand over supply—equal to the distance $E_1 E_4$. Accordingly, point E_4 in Figure 4-11a is a point of excess demand for money: the interest rate is too low and/or the level of income too high for the money market to clear. Consider, next, point E_3 in Figure 4-11b. Here we have the initial level of income Y_1, but an interest rate that is too high to yield money market equilibrium. Accordingly, we have an excess supply of money equal to the distance $E_3 E_2$. Point E_3 in Figure 4-11a therefore corresponds to an excess supply of money.

More generally, any point to the right and below the LM schedule is a point of excess demand for money, and any point to the left and above the LM curve is a point of excess supply. This is shown by the EDM and ESM notations in Figure 4-11a.

Summary

The following are the major points about the LM curve.

1. The LM curve is the schedule of combinations of the interest rate and level of income such that the money market is in equilibrium.
2. When the money market is in equilibrium, so is the bond market in equilibrium. The LM curve is, therefore, also the schedule of combinations of the level of income and the interest rate such that the bond market is in equilibrium.

FIGURE 4-11   EXCESS DEMAND (EDM) AND SUPPLY (EDM) OF MONEY. Points above and to the left of the LM schedule correspond to an excess supply of real balances; points below and to the right to an excess demand for real balances. Starting at point E_1 in the left panel, an increase in income takes us to E_4. AT E_4 in the right panel, there is an excess demand for money—and thus at E_4 in the left panel there is an excess demand for money. By a similar argument, we can start at E_2 and move to E_3, at which the level of income is lower. This creates an excess supply of money.

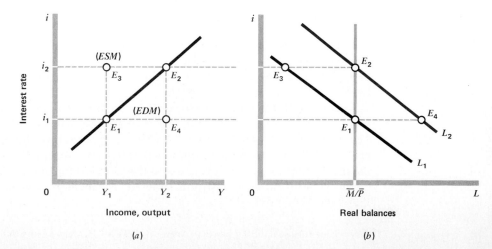

3. The *LM* curve is positively sloped. Given the fixed money supply, an increase in the level of income, which increases the quantity of money demanded, has to be accompanied by an increase in the interest rate. This reduces the quantity of money demanded and thereby maintains money market equilibrium.
4. The *LM* curve is shifted by changes in the money supply. An increase in the money supply shifts the *LM* curve to the right.
5. At points to the right of the *LM* curve, there is an excess demand for money, and at points to its left, there is an excess supply of money.

We are now ready to discuss the joint equilibrium of the goods and assets markets.

4-3 EQUILIBRIUM IN THE GOODS AND ASSETS MARKETS

The conditions that have to be satisfied for the goods and money markets, respectively, to be in equilibrium are summarized by the *IS* and *LM* schedules. The task now is to determine how these markets are brought into *simultaneous* equilibrium. For simultaneous equilibrium, interest rates and income have to be such that *both* the goods market *and* the money market are in equilibrium. That condition is satisfied at point *E* in Figure 4-12. The equilibrium interest rate is therefore i_0, and the equilibrium level of income is Y_0, given the exogenous variables, in particular, the real money supply and fiscal policy.[10] At point *E*, both the goods market and the assets markets are in equilibrium.

Figure 4-12 summarizes our analysis: the interest rate and the level of output are determined by the interaction of the assets (*LM*) and goods (*IS*) markets.

It is worth stepping back now to review our assumptions and the meaning of the equilibrium at *E*. The major assumption is that the price level is constant and that firms are willing to supply whatever amount of output is demanded at that price level. Thus, we assume the level of output Y_0 in Figure 4-12 will be willingly supplied by firms at the price level $\bar{P}$. We repeat that this assumption is one that is temporarily needed for the development of the analysis; it will be dropped in Chapter 7 when we begin to study the determinants of the price level.

At the point *E*, in Figure 4-12, the economy is in equilibrium, given the price level, because both the goods and money markets are in equilibrium. The demand for goods is equal to the level of output on the *IS* curve. And on the *LM* curve, the demand for money is equal to the supply of money. That also means the supply of bonds is equal to the demand for bonds, as the discussion of the wealth budget constraint showed. Accordingly, at point *E*, firms are

---

[10] Recall that exogenous variables are those whose values are not determined within the system being studied.

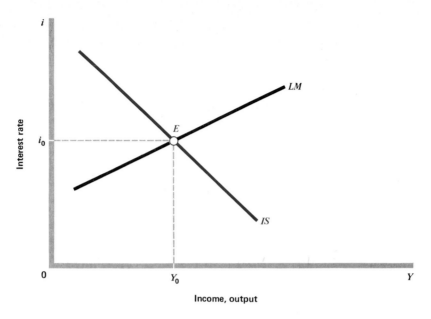

FIGURE 4-12   GOODS AND ASSETS MARKET EQUILIBRIUM.
Goods and assets markets clear at point E. Interest rates and income
are such that the public holds the existing stock of money and planned
spending equals output.

producing the amount of output they plan to (there is no unintended inventory
accumulation or decumulation), and individuals have the portfolio composi-
tions they desire.

Changes in the Equilibrium Levels of Income and the Interest Rate

The equilibrium levels of income and the interest rate change when either the
IS or the LM curve shifts. Figure 4-13, for example, shows the effects of an
increase in the rate of autonomous consumption $\overline{C}$ on the equilibrium levels of
income and the interest rate. Such an increase raises autonomous spending $\overline{A}$
and therefore shifts the IS curve to the right. That results in a rise in the level of
income and an increase in the interest rate at point E'.

Recall that an increase in autonomous spending $\Delta\overline{C}$ shifts the IS curve to
the right by the amount $\overline{\alpha}\,\Delta\overline{C}$, as we show in Figure 4-13. In Chapter 3, where
we dealt only with the goods market, we would have argued that $\overline{\alpha}\,\Delta\overline{C}$ would
be the change in the level of income resulting from the change of $\Delta\overline{C}$ in
autonomous spending. But it can be seen in Figure 4-13 that the change in

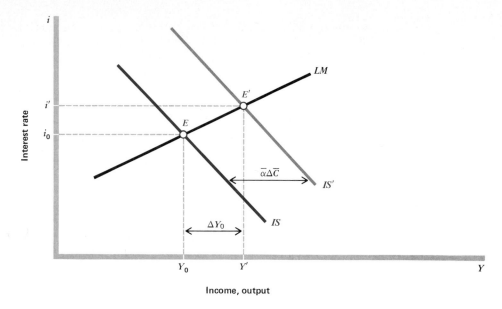

FIGURE 4-13 EFFECTS OF AN INCREASE IN AUTONOMOUS
SPENDING ON INCOME AND THE INTEREST RATE. An increase in
autonomous spending shifts the *IS* schedule out and to the right.
Income increases, and the equilibrium income level rises. The increase
in income is less than is given by the simple multiplier $\bar{\alpha}$. This is
because interest rates increase and dampen investment spending.

income here is only ΔY_0, which is clearly less than the shift in the *IS* curve
$\bar{\alpha} \, \Delta \bar{C}$.

What explains the fact that the increase in income is smaller than the
increase in autonomous spending $\Delta \bar{C}$ times the simple multiplier $\bar{\alpha}$? Diagrammatically, it is clear that it is the slope of the *LM* curve. If the *LM* curve were
horizontal, there would be no difference between the extent of the horizontal
shift of the *IS* curve and the change in income. If the *LM* curve were horizontal,
then the interest rate would not change when the *IS* curve shifts.

What is the economics of what is happening? The increase in autonomous
spending does tend to increase the level of income. But an increase in income
increases the demand for money. With the supply of money fixed, the interest
rate has to rise to ensure that the demand for money stays equal to the fixed
supply. When the interest rate rises, investment spending is reduced because
investment is negatively related to the interest rate. Accordingly, the equilib-
rium change in income is less than the horizontal shift of the *IS* curve, $\bar{\alpha} \, \Delta \bar{C}$.

We have now provided an example of the use of the *IS-LM* apparatus. That
apparatus is most useful for studying the effects of monetary and fiscal policy

on income and the interest rate, and we so use it in Sections 4-5 and 4-6 and Chapter 5. Before we do, however, we discuss how the economy moves from one equilibrium, such as E, to another, such as E'.

4-4 ADJUSTMENT TOWARD EQUILIBRIUM

Suppose the economy were initially at a point like E in Figure 4-13, and that one of the curves then shifted, so that the new equilibrium was at a point like E'. How would that new equilibrium actually be reached? The adjustment will involve changes in both the interest rate and the level of income. To study how they move over time, we make two assumptions:

1. Output increases whenever there is an excess demand for goods and contracts whenever there is an excess supply of goods. This assumption reflects the adjustment of firms to undesired decumulation and accumulation of inventories.
2. The interest rate rises whenever there is an excess demand for money and falls whenever there is an excess supply of money. This adjustment occurs because an excess demand for money implies an excess supply of other assets (bonds). In attempting to acquire more money, people sell off bonds and thereby cause their prices to fall or their yields (interest rate) to rise.

A detailed discussion of the relationship between the price of a bond and its yield is presented in the appendix to Chapter 9. Here we give only a brief explanation. For simplicity, consider a bond which promises to pay the holder of the bond $5 per year forever. The $5 is known as the bond *coupon,* and a bond which promises to pay a given amount to the holder of the bond forever is known as a *perpetuity.* If the yield available on other assets is 5 percent, the perpetuity will sell for $100 because at that price it too yields 5 percent (= $5/$100). Now suppose that the yield on other assets rises to 10 percent. Then the price of the perpetuity will drop to $50, because only at that price does the perpetuity yield 10 percent; that is, the $5 per year interest on a bond costing $50 gives its owners a 10 percent yield on their $50. This example makes it clear that the price of a bond and its yield are inversely related, given the coupon.

In point 2 above we assumed that an excess demand for money causes asset holders to attempt to sell off their bonds, thereby causing their prices to fall and their yields to rise. Conversely, when there is an excess supply of money, people attempt to use their money to buy up other assets, raising their prices and lowering their yields.

In Figure 4-14 we apply the analysis to study the adjustment of the economy. Four regions are represented, and they are characterized in Table 4-1. We know from Figure 4-11 that there is an excess supply of money above the LM curve, and hence we show ESM in regions I and II in Table 4-1.

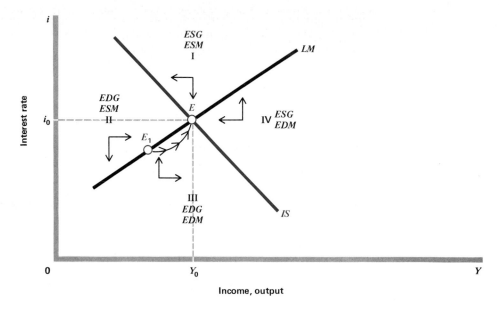

FIGURE 4-14 DISEQUILIBRIUM AND DYNAMICS IN THE GOODS AND MONEY MARKETS. Income and interest rates adjust to the disequilibrium in goods markets and assets markets. Specifically, interest rates fall when there is an excess supply of money and rise when there is an excess demand. Income rises when aggregate demand for goods exceeds output and falls when aggregate demand is less than output. The system converges over time to the equilibrium at E.

Similarly, we know from Figure 4-7 that there is an excess demand for goods below the *IS* curve. Hence, we show *EDG* for regions II and III in Table 4-1. You should be able to explain the remaining entries of Table 4-1.

The adjustment directions specified in assumptions 1 and 2 above are represented by arrows. Thus, for example, in region IV we have an excess demand for money that causes interest rates to rise as other assets are sold off for money and their prices decline. The rising interest rates are represented by the upward-pointing arrow. There is, too, an excess supply of goods in region IV, and, accordingly, involuntary inventory accumulation to which firms respond by reducing output. Declining output is indicated by the leftward-pointing arrow. The adjustments shown by the arrows will lead ultimately, perhaps in a cyclical manner, to the equilibrium point E. For example, starting at E_1 we show the economy moving to E, with income and the interest rate increasing along the *adjustment path* indicated.

TABLE 4-1   DISEQUILIBRIUM AND ADJUSTMENT

	GOODS MARKET		MONEY MARKET	
Region	Disequilibrium	Adjustment: output	Disequilibrium	Adjustment: interest rate
I	ESG	Falls	ESM	Falls
II	EDG	Rises	ESM	Falls
III	EDG	Rises	EDM	Rises
IV	ESG	Falls	EDM	Rises

Rapid Asset Market Adjustment

For many purposes it is useful to restrict the dynamics by the reasonable assumption that the money market adjusts very quickly and the goods market adjusts relatively slowly. Since the money market can adjust merely through the buying and selling of bonds, the interest rate adjusts rapidly and the money market effectively is always in equilibrium. Such an assumption implies that we are always on the *LM* curve: any departure from the equilibrium in the money market is almost instantaneously eliminated by an appropriate change in the interest rate. In disequilibrium, we therefore move along the *LM* curve, as is shown in Figure 4-15.

The goods market adjusts relatively slowly because firms have to change their production schedules, which takes time. For points below the *IS* curve, we move up along the *LM* schedule with rising income and interest rates, and for points above the *IS* schedule, we move down along the *LM* schedule with falling output and interest rates until point *E* is reached. The adjustment process is *stable* in that the economy does move to the equilibrium position at *E*.

The adjustment process shown in Figure 4-15 is very similar to that of Chapter 3. To the right of the *IS* curve, there is an excess supply of goods, and firms are therefore accumulating inventories. They cut production in response to their inventory buildup, and the economy moves down the *LM* curve. The difference between the adjustment process here and in Chapter 3 is the following: here, as the economy moves toward the equilibrium level of income, with a falling interest rate, desired investment spending is actually rising.[11]

---

[11] In a more detailed analysis, one would want to allow for the possibility that desired investment would be cut back in response to excess inventories. This again raises the possibility of the inventory cycle, referred to in Chap. 3.

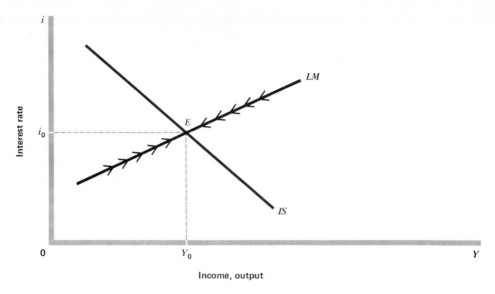

FIGURE 4-15   ADJUSTMENT TO EQUILIBRIUM WHEN THE MONEY
MARKET ADJUSTS QUICKLY. If the money market adjusts very rapidly,
then the economy is always in monetary equilibrium. In the diagram this
corresponds to always being on the *LM* schedule. When there is
excess demand for goods, output and interest rates are rising, and
when there is excess supply of goods, output and interest rates are falling.

Now that we have established that the economy does adjust toward its
equilibrium position, we turn to examine the effects of monetary and fiscal
policy on the equilibrium interest rate and level of income.

4-5 MONETARY POLICY

In this section we are concerned with the effect of an increase in the real
quantity of money on the interest rate and level of income. We break up that
inquiry into two separate questions. First, what is the ultimate effect of the
increase in the money supply when the new equilibrium is reached? Second,
how is that new equilibrium reached, or what is the transmission mechanism?

Through monetary policy the Federal Reserve affects the quantity of
money and thereby the interest rate and income. The chief instrument, studied in more detail in Chapter 12, is *open market operations*. In an open market
operation the Federal Reserve purchases bonds in exchange for money, thus
increasing the stock of money, or it sells bonds in exchange for money paid by
the purchasers of the bonds, thus reducing the money stock.

We take here the case of an open market purchase of bonds. The purchase is made by the Federal Reserve System, which pays for its purchases with money that it can create. One can usefully think of the Fed printing money with which to buy bonds, even though that is not strictly accurate, as we shall see in Chapter 11. The purpose of an open market operation is to change the available *relative* supplies of money and bonds and thereby change the interest rate or yield at which the public is willing to hold this modified composition of assets. When the Fed buys bonds, it reduces the supply of bonds available in the market and thereby tends to increase their price, or lower their yield. Only at a lower interest rate will the public be prepared to hold a larger fraction of its given wealth in the form of money, and a lower fraction in the form of bonds.

In Figure 4-16 we show graphically how the open market purchase works. The initial equilibrium at point E is on the initial LM schedule that corresponds to a real money supply, $\overline{M}/\overline{P}$. Consider next an open market operation that increases the nominal quantity of money, and given the price level, the real quantity of money. We showed before that, as a consequence, the LM schedule will shift to LM'. Therefore, the new equilibrium will be at point E' with a lower interest rate and a higher level of income. The equilibrium level of income rises because the open market purchase reduces the interest rate and thereby increases investment spending.

By experimenting with Figure 4-16, you will be able to show that the steeper the LM schedule, the larger the change in income. If money demand is very sensitive to the interest rate, then a given change in the money stock can be absorbed in the assets markets with only a small change in the interest rate. The effects of an open market purchase on investment spending would then be small. By contrast, if the demand for money is not very sensitive to the interest rate, a given change in the money supply will cause a large change in the interest rate and have a big effect on investment demand.[12] Similarly, if the demand for money is very sensitive to income, a given increase in the money stock can be absorbed with a relatively small change in income.

Consider next the adjustment process to the monetary expansion. At the initial equilibrium point E, the increase in the money supply creates an excess supply of money to which the public adjusts by attempting to reduce its money holdings by buying other assets. In the process, asset prices increase and yields decline. By our assumption that the assets markets adjust rapidly, we move immediately to point E_1, where the money market clears, and where the public is willing to hold the larger real quantity of money because the interest rate has declined sufficiently. At point E_1, however, there is an excess demand for goods. The decline in the interest rate, given the initial income level Y_0, has raised aggregate demand and is causing inventories to run down. In response,

---

[12] In problem 3, we ask you to provide a similar explanation of the role of the slope of the IS curve—which is determined by the multiplier and the interest sensitivity of investment demand—in determining the effect of monetary policy on income.

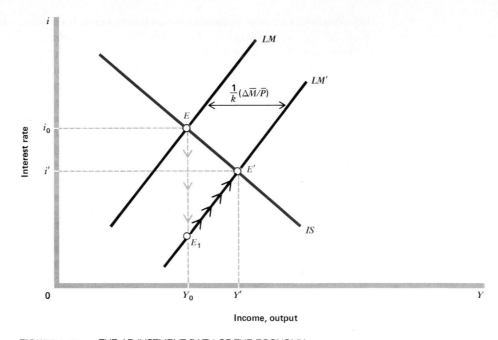

FIGURE 4-16   THE ADJUSTMENT PATH OF THE ECONOMY
FOLLOWING AN INCREASE IN THE MONEY STOCK. An increase in
the real money stock shifts the *LM* schedule down and to the right.
Interest rates immediately decline from E to E_1 and then, through their
effect on investment, cause spending and income to rise until a new
equilibrium is reached at E'. Once all adjustments have taken place, a
rise in the real money stock raises equilibrium income and lowers
equilibrium interest rates.

output expands and we start moving up the *LM'* schedule. Why does the
interest rate rise in the adjustment process? Because the increase in output
raises the demand for money and that increase has to be checked by higher
interest rates.

Thus the increase in the money stock first causes interest rates to fall as
the public adjusts its portfolio and then—through lower interest rates—increases aggregate demand.

The Transmission Mechanism

Two steps in the *transmission mechanism*—the process by which changes in
monetary policy affect aggregate demand—are essential. The first is that an
increase in real balances generates a *portfolio disequilibrium*—at the prevailing interest rate and level of income, people are holding more money than

TABLE 4-2	THE TRANSMISSION MECHANISM		
(1)	**(2)**	**(3)**	**(4)**
Change in real money supply	Portfolio adjustments lead to a change in asset prices and interest rates	Spending adjusts to the change in interest rates	Output adjusts to the change in aggregate demand

they want. This causes portfolio holders to attempt to reduce their money holdings by buying other assets, thereby changing asset prices and yields. In other words, the change in the money supply changes interest rates. The second stage of the transmission process occurs when the change in interest rates affects aggregate demand.

These two stages of the transmission process are essential in that they appear in almost every analysis of the effects of changes in the money supply on the economy. The details of the analysis will often differ — some analyses will have more than two assets and more than one interest rate; some will include an influence of interest rates on other categories of demand, in particular consumption and spending by local government.[13]

Table 4-2 provides a summary of the stages in the transmission mechanism. There are two critical links between the change in real balances and the ultimate effect on income. First, the change in real balances, by bringing about portfolio disequilibrium, must lead to a change in interest rates. Second, that change in interest rates must change aggregate demand. Through those two linkages, changes in the real money stock affect the level of output in the economy. But that immediately implies the following: if portfolio imbalances do not lead to significant changes in interest rates — for whatever reason — or if spending does not respond to changes in interest rates, the link between money and output does not exist.[14] We now study these linkages in more detail.

---

[13] Some analyses also include a mechanism by which changes in real balances have a direct effect on aggregate demand through the real balance effect. The argument is that wealth affects consumption demand (as we shall see in Chap. 8) and that an increase in real balances increases wealth and therefore consumption demand. This effect would not apply in the case of an open market purchase, which merely exchanges one asset for another (bonds for money) without changing wealth. The real balance effect is not very important empirically because the relevant real balances are only a small part of wealth.

[14] We refer to the responsiveness of aggregate demand — rather than investment demand — to the interest rate because consumption demand may also respond to the interest rate. Higher interest rates may lead to more saving and less consumption at a given level of income. Empirically, it has been difficult to isolate such an interest rate effect on consumption.

The Liquidity Trap

In discussing the effects of monetary policy on the economy, two extreme cases have received much attention. The first is the *liquidity trap*, a situation in which the public is prepared, at a given interest rate, to hold whatever amount of money is supplied. This implies that the *LM* curve is horizontal and that changes in the quantity of money do not shift it. In that case, monetary policy carried out through open market operations[15] has no effect on either the interest rate or level of income. In the liquidity trap, monetary policy is powerless to affect the interest rate.

There is a liquidity trap at a zero interest rate. At a zero interest rate, the public would not want to hold any bonds, since money, which also pays zero interest, has the advantage over bonds of being usable in transactions. Accordingly, if the interest rate ever, for some reason, was zero, increases in the quantity of money could not induce anyone to shift into bonds and thereby reduce the interest rate on bonds even below zero. An increase in the money supply in that case would have no effect on the interest rate and income, and the economy would be in a liquidity trap.

The belief that there was a liquidity trap at low positive (rather than zero) interest rates was quite prevalent during the forties and fifties. It was a notion associated with the Keynesian followers and developers of the theories of the great English economist John Maynard Keynes — although Keynes himself did state that he was not aware of there ever having been such a situation.[16] The importance of the liquidity trap stems from its presenting a circumstance under which monetary policy has no effect on the interest rate and thus on the level of real income. Belief in the trap, or at least the strong sensitivity of the demand for money to the interest rate, was the basis of the Keynesian belief that monetary policy has no effects on the economy. There is no strong evidence that there ever was a liquidity trap, and there certainly is not one now.

The Classical Case

The polar opposite of the horizontal *LM* curve — which implies that monetary policy cannot affect the level of income — is the vertical *LM* curve. The *LM* curve is vertical when the demand for money is entirely unresponsive to the interest rate. Under those circumstances, any shift in the *LM* curve has a maximal effect on the level of income. Check this by moving a vertical *LM* curve to the right and comparing the resultant change in income with the change produced by a similar horizontal shift of a nonvertical *LM* curve.

---

[15] We say "through open market operations" because an increase in the quantity of money carried out simply by giving the money away increases individuals' wealth and, through the real balance effect, has some effect on aggregate demand. An open market purchase, however, increases the quantity of money and reduces the quantity of bonds by the same amount, leaving wealth unchanged.

[16] J. M. Keynes, *The General Theory of Employment, Interest and Money* (New York: Macmillan, 1936), p. 207.

The vertical *LM* curve is called the *classical case.* It implies that the demand for money depends only on the level of income and not at all on the interest rate. The classical case is associated with the classical *quantity theory of money,* which argues that the level of nominal income is determined solely by the quantity of money. We return to this view in Chapter 5. As we shall see, a vertical *LM* curve implies not only that monetary policy has a maximal effect on the level of income, but also that fiscal policy has no effect on income. The vertical *LM* curve, implying the comparative effectiveness of monetary policy over fiscal policy, is sometimes associated with the view that "only money matters" for the determination of output. Since the *LM* curve is vertical only when the demand for money does not depend on the interest rate, the interest sensitivity of the demand for money turns out to be an important issue in determining the effectiveness of alternative policies.

These two extreme cases, the liquidity trap and the classical case, suggest that the slope of the *LM* curve is a key determinant of the effectiveness of monetary policy in affecting output. The slope of the *LM* curve in turn depends on the interest sensitivity of money demand. The more sensitive to the interest rate is the quantity of money demanded, the flatter the *LM* curve.

4-6 AN APPLICATION OF MONETARY POLICY: THE 1979 POLICY SWITCH

From 1975 to 1979 the U.S. economy expanded rapidly under the impact of monetary and some fiscal stimulus. The unemployment rate had been as high as 9 percent in 1975; by the middle of 1979 it was down to 5.6 percent. At the same time the inflation rate had risen from an annual rate of 4.8 percent in 1976 to 13.3 percent in 1979.

With unemployment low, the Fed saw the rapid inflation as the prime problem facing the economy and decided to try to reduce inflation by reducing aggregate demand.[17] In October 1979 the Fed announced a major change in monetary policy, the ultimate aim of which was to bring much lower inflation to the U.S. economy. In terms of the *IS-LM* diagram in Figure 4-17, the *LM* schedule was shifted to the left.

Table 4-3 shows data on the growth rates of money and GNP, the Treasury bill rate, and the share of investment spending in GNP in the period from the second quarter of 1979 to the fourth quarter of 1980. The quantity of money was growing at more than 10 percent per year in the second and third quarters of 1979, with the Treasury bill rate below 10 percent. About 16 percent of GNP was being invested.

In the next three quarters the growth rate of money was cut back sharply. The interest rate rose to more than 13 percent by the first quarter of 1980. In response there was a fall in investment, to 13.8 percent of GNP in the second

---

[17] Although we have not yet studied inflation, it suffices for now to know that policies that reduce aggregate demand tend to reduce the inflation rate.

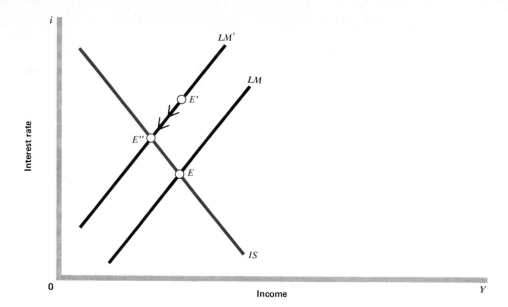

FIGURE 4-17 THE EFFECTS OF TIGHT MONEY. At the end of 1979 the Fed tightened monetary policy. The *LM* curve shifted to *LM'*. Interest rates rose, and then as the economy moved from *E'* to *E"*, real GNP fell.

quarter of 1980. Correspondingly, GNP fell dramatically in the second quarter of 1980, creating a very sharp recession. As investment and GNP fell, the demand for money was reduced and the Treasury bill rate fell back to the 9 to 10 percent range in the second quarter of 1980, even though money growth was still slow.

Afraid of creating a massive recession, the Fed reversed direction drastically in the third quarter of 1980. The money stock was increased rapidly, and investment and GNP soon began to climb again. But so did inflation, with the result that just a year later monetary policy put the economy into another recession. The 1981–1982 recession lasted for over a year but this time did reduce the inflation rate substantially.

In terms of Figure 4-17, the Fed's policy switch shifted the *LM* curve from *LM* to *LM'*. The economy moved from a point like *E* to *E'* in the fourth quarter of 1979 and first quarter of 1980. Under the pressure of the high interest rate, investment and GNP fell, as did the interest rate when the economy went into a sharp slide in the second quarter of 1980. Then the Fed shifted policy, moving the *LM* curve to the right again, setting the stage for a recovery and rising interest rates.

Two important points emerge from this episode:

1. There is a *lag* between the time the Fed changes policy and the time the policy takes effect. The interest rate rose sharply in the fourth quarter of 1979, but it was not until the third quarter of 1980 that the full effect on investment is visible. Lags imply that monetary policy cannot work very quickly — say in the same quarter — on aggregate demand. Tight money, if sustained for some time will reduce investment, but it can take well over half a year for those effects to become visible. The reason is that much of the investment spending that takes place in a given quarter is based on plans and even financing that were prepared some time ago. For instance, someone starting to build a house this quarter certainly drew up the plans earlier and probably arranged a loan some months back too. Thus high interest rates today primarily affect plans for investment drawn up now but that will take place over months to come.
2. It follows that the Fed can easily miscalculate and make economic performance worse rather than better when it tries to stabilize the economy. In particular, many believe that the Fed overreacted in the second quarter of 1980 when it sharply reduced the growth rate of money and undertook other restrictive policies, precisely at the time when the economy was already going into a deep slide. And it may then have overreacted in the opposite direction in the third quarter of 1980 when it changed policy so rapidly. The analogy is to a driver who swings the wheel sharply to the left to avoid an obstacle, heads to the ditch, then swings sharply to the right to avoid the ditch on the left, and ends up looking like a drunk driver and quite likely in the ditch as well.

TABLE 4-3	THE CHANGE IN MONETARY POLICY, 1979			
	Money growth	Treasury bill rate	Investment/ GNP, %	GNP growth
1979:2	10.2	9.4	16.4	−0.9
1979:3	10.9	9.7	16.0	4.8
1979:4	4.3	11.8	15.1	0.7
1980:1	6.1	13.4	15.0	1.9
1980:2	−3.5	9.6	13.8	−9.0
1980:3	16.9	9.2	13.5	0.8
1980:4	11.5	13.6	14.2	3.8

Notes: 1. All growth rates are quarter over quarter at annual rate.
2. Money stock is $M1$.
3. GNP growth is for real (1972 prices) GNP.
Source: Data Resources, Inc.

4-7 SUMMARY

1. The *IS-LM* model presented in this chapter is the basic model of aggregate demand that incorporates the assets markets as well as the goods market. It lays particular stress on the channels through which monetary and fiscal policy affect the economy.

2. The *IS* curve shows combinations of the interest rate and level of income such that the goods market is in equilibrium. Increases in the interest rate reduce aggregate demand by reducing the demand for investment goods. Thus at higher interest rates, the level of income at which the goods market is in equilibrium is lower: the *IS* curve slopes downward.

3. The demand for money is a demand for *real* balances. The demand for real balances increases with income and decreases with the interest rate, the cost of holding money rather than other assets. With an exogenously fixed supply of real balances, the *LM* curve, representing money market equilibrium, is upward-sloping. Because of the wealth constraint, equilibrium of the money market implies equilibrium of the remaining assets markets — summarized here under the catchall "bond market."

4. The interest rate and level of output are jointly determined by simultaneous equilibrium of the goods and money markets. This occurs at the intersection point of the *IS* and *LM* curves.

5. Assuming that output is increased when there is an excess demand for goods and that the interest rate rises when there is an excess demand for money, the economy does move toward the new equilibrium when one of the curves shifts. Typically we think of the assets markets as clearing rapidly so that, in response to a disturbance, the economy tends to move along the *LM* curve to the new equilibrium.

6. Monetary policy affects the economy in the first instance by affecting the interest rate, and then by affecting aggregate demand. An increase in the money supply reduces the interest rate, increases investment demand and aggregate demand, and thus increases equilibrium output.

7. There are two extreme cases in the operation of monetary policy. In the classical case the demand for real balances is independent of the rate of interest. In this case monetary policy is highly effective. The other extreme is the liquidity trap, where the public is willing to hold *any* amount of real balances at the going interest rate. In that case changes in the supply of real balances have no impact on interest rates and therefore do not affect aggregate demand and output.

8. *A final warning:* We are assuming here that any level of output that is demanded can be produced by firms at the constant price level. Price level behavior, including inflation, is discussed in substantially more detail first in Chapter 6 and then in Chapters 13 and 14. Those chapters build on the analysis of the *IS-LM* model.

KEY TERMS

IS curve

LM curve

Bond

Money

Portfolio decisions

Real balances (real money balances)

Wealth budget constraint

Open market operation

Transmission mechanism

Liquidity trap

Classical case

PROBLEMS

1. The following equations describe an economy. (Think of C, I, G, etc., as being measured in billions and i as percent; a 5 percent interest rate implies $i = 5$.)

$$C = 0.8(1 - t)Y \qquad 1$$
$$t = 0.25 \qquad 2$$
$$I = 900 - 50i \qquad 3$$
$$\overline{G} = 800 \qquad 4$$
$$L = 0.25Y - 62.5i \qquad 5$$
$$\frac{\overline{M}}{P} = 500 \qquad 6$$

   (a) What is the equation that describes the *IS* curve?

   (b) What is the general definition of the *IS* curve?

   (c) What is the equation that describes the *LM* curve?

   (d) What is the general definition of the *LM* curve?

   (e) What are the equilibrium levels of income and the interest rate?

   (f) Describe in words the conditions that are satisfied at the intersection of the *IS* and *LM* curves, and why this is an equilibrium.

2. Continue with the same equations.

   (a) What is the value of $\overline{\alpha}$, which corresponds to the simple multiplier (with taxes) of Chapter 3?

   (b) By how much does an increase in government spending of $\Delta\overline{G}$ increase the level of income in this model, which includes the assets markets?

   (c) By how much does a change in government spending of $\Delta\overline{G}$ affect the equilibrium interest rate?

   (d) Explain the difference between your answers to 2a and b.

3. (a) Explain in words how and why the multiplier $\overline{\alpha}$ and the interest sensitivity of aggregate demand affect the slope of the *IS* curve.

   (b) Explain why the slope of the *IS* curve is a factor in determining the working of monetary policy.

4. Explain in words how and why the income and interest sensitivities of the demand for real balances affect the slope of the *LM* curve.

5. (a) Why does a horizontal *LM* curve imply that fiscal policy has the same effects on the economy as we derived in Chapter 3?

   (b) What is happening in this case in terms of Figure 4-2?

   (c) Under what circumstances might the *LM* curve be horizontal?

6. We mentioned in the text the possibility that the interest rate might affect consumption spending. An increase in the interest rate could, in principle, lead to increases in saving and therefore a reduction in consumption, given the level of income. Suppose that consumption were in fact reduced by an increase in the interest rate. How would the IS curve be affected?

7. Suppose that the money supply, instead of being constant, increased (slightly) with the interest rate.

    (a) How would this change affect the construction of the LM curve?

    (b) Could you see any reason why the Fed might follow a policy of increasing the money supply along with the interest rate?

8. (a) How does an increase in the tax rate affect the IS curve?

    (b) How does it affect the equilibrium level of income?

    (c) How does it affect the equilibrium interest rate?

9. Draw a graph of how i and Y respond over time (that is, use time as the horizontal axis) to an increase in the money supply. You may assume that the money market adjusts much more rapidly than the goods market.

10. (a) Show that a given change in the money stock has a larger effect on output the less interest sensitive the demand for money.

    (b) How does the response of the interest rate to a change in the money stock depend on the interest sensitivity of money demand?

FISCAL POLICY, CROWDING OUT, AND THE POLICY MIX

Whenever governments run a budget deficit, borrowing to pay for the excess of their spending over the tax revenue they receive, the talk turns to *crowding out.* Crowding out occurs when expansionary fiscal policy causes interest rates to rise, thereby reducing private spending, particularly investment.

When we introduced fiscal policy in Chapter 3, we had not yet included the assets markets in the analysis. Thus we could not discuss the effects of changes in fiscal policy on interest rates. In this chapter we focus on how fiscal policy works when the interdependence of goods and assets markets is taken into account in the *IS-LM* model introduced in Chapter 4.

Our aim is to see how explicit consideration of interest rates affects the conclusions we reached in Chapter 3 about fiscal policy. Is it still the case that an increase in government spending raises output and employment? Do tax cuts still increase output? Or is it possible that the effects of fiscal policy on interest rates are so important that our previous conclusions about the effects of fiscal policy on the economy are reversed?

Figure 5-1 shows how fiscal policy fits into the *IS-LM* model. Fiscal policy affects aggregate demand directly. For instance, an increase in government spending increases aggregate demand, tending to raise output. But the higher output level raises the interest rate in the assets markets and thereby dampens the effects of the fiscal policy on output. The higher interest rates reduce the

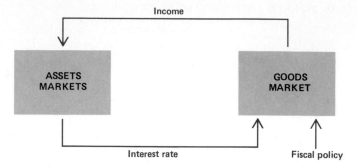

FIGURE 5-1   FISCAL POLICY IN THE *IS-LM* MODEL. Fiscal policy affects aggregate demand and thus has an impact on output and income. But changes in income affect the demand for money and thereby equilibrium interest rates in assets markets. These interest rate changes feed back to the goods market and dampen the impact of fiscal policy.

level of investment spending, or crowd out investment. Thus a fiscal policy that increases output may actually reduce the rate of investment.

Once we have discussed crowding out, we turn to the issue of the *monetary-fiscal policy mix.* The policy mix is the combination of monetary and fiscal policies. For instance, monetary policy may be easy, with rapid monetary growth, and fiscal policy tight or restrictive, with taxes being increased. We ask what alternative mixes imply for the economy. The question of the appropriate mix is frequently at the center of political controversy.

Table 5-1 shows possible combinations and indicates for each case when, in recent U.S. history, the combination prevailed.

TABLE 5-1   MONETARY-FISCAL POLICY MIXES

	MONETARY POLICY	
Fiscal policy	Tightening	Easing
Tightening	1974, 1981	1976–1977
Easing	1982	1982–1984

5-1 FISCAL POLICY AND CROWDING OUT

This section shows how changes in fiscal policy shift the *IS* curve, the curve that describes goods market equilibrium. Recall from Chapter 4 that the *IS* curve slopes downward because a decrease in the interest rate increases the demand for investment, thereby increasing aggregate demand and the level of output at which the goods market is in equilibrium. Recall also that changes in fiscal policy shift the *IS* curve.

The equation of the *IS* curve, derived in Chapter 4, is repeated here for convenience:

$$Y = \overline{\alpha}(\overline{A} - bi) \qquad \overline{\alpha} \equiv \frac{1}{1 - c(1 - t)} \tag{1}$$

Note that $\overline{G}$, the level of government spending, is a component of autonomous spending $\overline{A}$ in (1). The income tax rate t is part of the multiplier. Thus both government spending and the multiplier affect the *IS* schedule. We now show in Figure 5-2 how fiscal expansion raises equilibrium income and the interest rate.

An Increase in Government Spending

At unchanged interest rates, higher levels of government spending will increase the level of aggregate demand. To meet the increased demand for goods, output must rise. In Figure 5-2, we show the effect of a shift of the *IS* schedule. At each level of the interest rate, equilibrium income must rise by $\overline{\alpha}$ times the government spending. For example, if government spending rises by 100 and the multiplier is 2, then equilibrium income must increase at each level of the interest rate by 200. Thus the *IS* schedule shifts to the right by 200.

If the economy is initially in equilibrium at point E and now government spending rises by 100, we would move to point E'' *if the interest rate stayed constant.* At E'' the goods market is in equilibrium in that planned spending equals output. But the assets market is no longer in equilibrium. Income has increased, and therefore the quantity of money demanded is higher. At interest rate i_0, the demand for real balances now exceeds the given real money supply. Because there is an excess demand for real balances, the interest rate rises. But as interest rates rise, private spending is cut back. Firms' planned investment spending declines at higher interest rates, and thus aggregate demand falls off.

What is the complete adjustment, taking into account the expansionary effect of higher government spending and the dampening effects of higher interest rates on private spending? Figure 5-2 shows that only at point E' do *both* the goods and assets markets clear. Only at point E' is planned spending equal to income and, at the same time, the quantity of real balances demanded

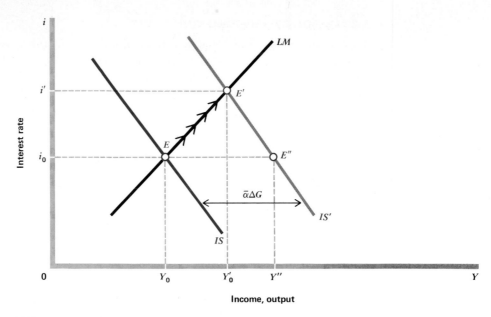

FIGURE 5-2 EFFECTS OF AN INCREASE IN GOVERNMENT
SPENDING. An increase in government spending raises aggregate
demand at each level of the interest rate and thus shifts the *IS* schedule
out and to the right to *IS'*. At point *E* there is now an excess demand
for goods. Output rises, and with it the interest rate, because the
income expansion raises money demand. The new equilibrium is at
point *E'*. The increase in income $(Y'_0 - Y_0)$ is less than the amount
indicated by the simple multiplier $(Y'' - Y_0)$ because higher interest
rates crowd out some investment spending.

equal to the given real money stock. Point E' is therefore the new equilibrium
point.

The Dynamics of Adjustment

We continue to assume that the money market clears fast and continuously,
while output adjusts only slowly. This implies that as government spending
increases, we stay initially at point E, since there is no disturbance in the
money market. The excess demand for goods, however, leads firms to increase
output, and that increase in output and income raises the demand for money.
The resulting excess demand for money, in turn, causes interest rates to be bid
up, and we proceed up along the *LM* curve with rising output and rising
interest rates, until the new equilibrium is reached at point E'.

The Extent of Crowding Out

Comparing E' to the initial equilibrium at E, we have seen that increased government spending raises both income and the interest rate. But another important comparison is between points E' and E'', the equilibrium in the goods market at unchanged interest rates. Point E'' corresponds to the equilibrium we studied in Chapter 3 where we neglected the impact of interest rates on the economy. In comparing E'' and E' it becomes clear that the adjustment of interest rates and their impact on aggregate demand dampen the expansionary effect of increased government spending. Income, instead of increasing to the level Y'', rises only to Y_0'. This leads us to the following question: What factors determine the extent to which interest rate adjustments dampen the output expansion induced by increased government spending?

The extent to which a fiscal expansion raises income and the interest rate depends on the slopes of the IS and LM schedules and on the size of the multiplier. By drawing for yourself different IS and LM schedules you will be able to show the following:

1. Income increases more, and interest rates increase less, the flatter the LM schedule.
2. Income increases less, and interest rates increase less, the flatter the IS schedule.
3. Income and interest rates increase more the larger the multiplier $\bar{\alpha}$ and thus the larger the horizontal shift of the IS schedule.

To illustrate these conclusions, we turn to the two extreme cases we discussed in connection with monetary policy, the liquidity trap and the classical case.

The Liquidity Trap

If the economy is in the liquidity trap so that the LM curve is horizontal, then an increase in government spending has its full multiplier effect on the equilibrium level of income. There is no change in the interest rate associated with the change in government spending, and thus no investment spending is cut off. There is therefore no dampening of the effects of increased government spending on income.

You should draw your own IS-LM diagrams to confirm that if the LM curve is horizontal, monetary policy has no impact on the equilibrium of the economy and fiscal policy has a maximal effect on the economy. Less dramatically, if the demand for money is very sensitive to the interest rate, so that the LM curve is almost horizontal, fiscal policy changes have a relatively large effect on output, while monetary policy changes have little effect on the equilibrium level of output.

So far, we have taken the money supply to be constant at the level $\overline{M}$. It is possible that the Fed might instead manipulate the money supply so as to keep the interest rate constant. In that case the money supply is responsive to the interest rate: the Fed increases the money supply whenever there are signs of an increase in the interest rate, and reduces the money supply whenever the interest rate seems about to fall. The more responsive the money supply with respect to the interest rate, the flatter will be the *LM* curve, and fiscal policy will again have large impacts on the level of output.

The Classical Case and Crowding Out

If the *LM* curve is vertical, then an increase in government spending has *no* effect on the equilibrium level of income. It only increases the interest rate. This case is shown in Figure 5-3a, where an increase in government spending shifts the *IS* curve to *IS'* but has no effect on income. If the demand for money is not related to the interest rate, as a vertical *LM* curve implies, then there is a unique level of income at which the money market is in equilibrium.

Thus with a vertical *LM* curve, an increase in government spending cannot change the equilibrium level of income, but only raises the equilibrium

FIGURE 5-3 FULL CROWDING OUT. With a vertical *LM* schedule, a fiscal expansion, shifting out the *IS* schedule, raises interest rates, not income. Government spending displaces, or crowds out, private spending, one-for-one.

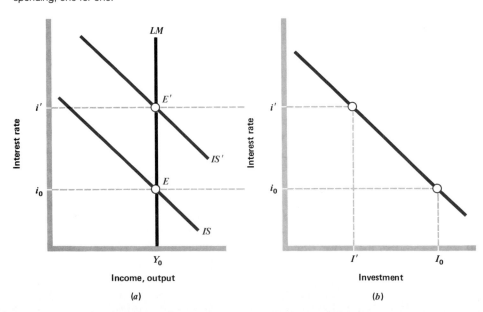

interest rate. But if government spending is higher and output is unchanged, there must be an offsetting reduction in private spending. The increase in interest rates *crowds out* private investment spending. Crowding out, as defined earlier, is the reduction in private spending (and particularly investment) associated with the increase in interest rates caused by fiscal expansion. There will be full crowding out if the *LM* curve is vertical.[1]

In Figure 5-3 we show the crowding out in panel (*b*), where the investment schedule of Figure 4-3 is drawn. The fiscal expansion raises the equilibrium interest rate from i_0 to i' in panel (*a*). In panel (*b*), as a consequence, investment spending declines from the level I_0 to I'. Now it is easy to verify that if the *LM* schedule were positively sloped rather than vertical, interest rates would rise less with a fiscal expansion and as a result investment spending would decline less. The extent of crowding out thus depends on the slope of the *LM* curve and therefore on the interest responsiveness of money demand. The less interest-responsive is money demand, the more a fiscal expansion crowds out investment rather than raising output.

The view that increased government spending crowds out private spending, largely or even completely, is held by most monetarists.[2] They believe money determines income or, as we saw above, that money demand does not depend on the interest rate, implying a vertical *LM* schedule. However, there is also another case where crowding out can be complete, as we shall see in Chapter 7. If the economy is at full employment so that output cannot expand, then, of course, increased purchases of goods and by the government must mean that some other sector uses less goods and services. Interest rates increase to crowd out private spending by an amount exactly equal to the higher level of government spending.

Is Crowding Out Likely?

How seriously must we take the possibility of crowding out? Here three points must be made. First, in an economy with unemployed resources there will *not* be full crowding out because the *LM* schedule is not, in fact, vertical. A fiscal expansion will raise interest rates, but income will also rise. Crowding out thus, rather than being full, is a matter of degree. The increase in aggregate demand raises income, and with the rise in income, it raises the level of saving. This expansion in saving, in turn, makes it possible to finance a larger budget deficit without *completely* displacing private borrowing or investment.

---

[1]Note that in principle consumption spending could be reduced by increases in the interest rate, and then both investment and consumption would be crowded out. Further, as we will see in Chap. 6, fiscal expansion can crowd out net exports, increasing the trade deficit.

[2] We discuss monetarism in Chap. 11.

We can look at this proposition with the help of equation (2), which states the equilibrium condition in the goods market already studied in Chapter 3:[3]

$$S \equiv I + (G + TR - TA) \tag{2}$$

Here the term $G + TR - TA$ is the budget deficit. Now from (2) an increase in the deficit, given saving, must lower investment. In simple terms, when the deficit rises, the government has to borrow to pay for its excess spending. That borrowing "uses up" part of saving, leaving less available for firms to borrow to finance their investment plans. But it is equally apparent that if saving rises with a government spending increase, because income rises, then there need not be a one-for-one decline in investment. In an economy with unemployment, crowding out is incomplete because increased demand for goods raises real income and output; saving rises and interest rates do not rise enough (because of interest-responsive money demand) to choke off investment.

The second point is that, with unemployment and thus a possibility for output to expand, interest rates need not rise at all when government spending rises, and there need not be any crowding out. This is because the monetary authorities can *accommodate* the fiscal expansion by an increase in the money supply. Monetary policy is *accommodating* when, in the course of a fiscal expansion, the money supply is increased so as to prevent interest rates from increasing. Monetary accommodation is also referred to as *monetizing budget deficits*, meaning that the Federal Reserve prints money to buy the bonds with which the government pays for its deficit.[4] When the Fed accommodates a fiscal expansion, both the *IS* and the *LM* schedule shift to the right as in Figure 5-4. Output will clearly increase, but interest rates need not rise. Accordingly, there need not be any adverse effects on investment. On some occasions, as in the 1960s, the Fed has been willing to accommodate, as we see in Section 5-3 below.

The third comment on crowding out is an important warning. So far we are assuming an economy with given prices. When we talk about fully employed economies in Chapter 14, crowding out becomes a much more realistic possibility, and accommodating monetary policy may turn into an engine of inflation.

---

[3] In (2) we look at a closed economy. We saw in Chap. 2 and shall see in Chap. 6, in the open economy the identity reads $S = I + (G + TR - TA) + NX$, where NX stands for net exports or net foreign lending. Thus borrowing abroad can supplement saving to finance a budget deficit without the need for crowding out. This was particularly important in the United States in 1983 to 1986.

[4] The term *accommodation* is also used more generally. For instance, when oil prices increased in the 1970s, there was much discussion of whether the Fed should accommodate the higher prices by raising the money stock. The issue, and the meaning of *accommodation* in that context, is discussed in Chap. 14.

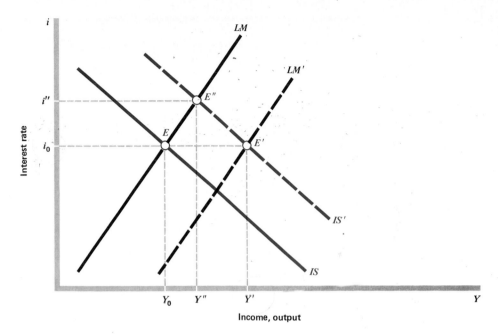

FIGURE 5-4   MONETARY ACCOMMODATION OF FISCAL
EXPANSION. A fiscal expansion shifts the *IS* curve to *IS'*, and moves
the equilibrium of the economy from *E* to *E"*. Because the higher level
of income has increased the quantity of money demanded, the interest
rate rises from i_0 to $i"$, thereby crowding out investment spending. But
the Fed can accommodate the fiscal expansion, creating more money
and shifting the *LM* curve to *LM'*, and the equilibrium of the economy to
E'. The interest rate remains at level i_0, and the level of output rises to *Y'*.

5-2 THE COMPOSITION OF OUTPUT

We have now seen that both monetary and fiscal policy can be used to expand
aggregate demand and thus raise the equilibrium level of output. Since the
liquidity trap and the classical case represent, at best, extremes useful for
expositional purposes, it is apparent that policy makers can use either monetary or fiscal policy to affect the level of income.

Table 5-2 summarizes the effects of expansionary monetary and fiscal
policy on output and the interest rate. These are the effects shown in Figures
5-2 and 5-3.

We now examine the policy choices of an economy that is in equilibrium
with an output level Y_0, below the full-employment level $\overline{Y}$. What can be done
to raise output? From the preceding analysis and Table 5-3, it is obvious that

TABLE 5-2	SUMMARY: POLICY EFFECTS ON INCOME AND INTEREST RATES	
Policy	Equilibrium income	Equilibrium interest rate
Monetary expansion	+	−
Fiscal expansion	+	+

we could use an expansionary monetary policy. By increasing the money supply, we could shift the *LM* curve down and to the right, lower interest rates, and raise aggregate demand. Alternatively, we can use an expansionary fiscal policy to shift the *IS* curve up and to the right. Finally, we can use a combination of monetary and fiscal policy. What package should we choose?

The choice of monetary and fiscal policy as tools of stabilization policy is an important and controversial topic. In Chapter 12 we address some technical issues that deal with the flexibility and speed with which these policies can be implemented and can take effect. Here we do not discuss speed and flexibility, but rather look at what these policies do to the composition of aggregate demand.

In that respect, there is a sharp difference between monetary and fiscal policy. Monetary policy operates by stimulating interest-responsive components of aggregate demand, primarily investment spending and, in particular, residential construction. There is strong evidence that the earliest and strongest effect of monetary policy is on residential construction.

Fiscal policy, by contrast, operates in a manner that depends on precisely what goods the government buys or what taxes and transfers it changes. Here we might be talking of government purchases of goods and services such as defense spending, or a reduction in the corporate profits tax, sales taxes, or Social Security contributions. Each policy affects the level of aggregate demand and causes an expansion in output, except that the type of output and the beneficiaries of the fiscal measures differ. An investment subsidy, discussed below, increases investment spending. An income tax cut has a direct effect on consumption spending. Given the quantity of money, all expansionary fiscal policies have in common that they will raise the interest rate.

An Investment Subsidy

Table 5-3 shows examples of the impact of different fiscal policies on key variables. One interesting case is an *investment subsidy,* shown in Figure 5-5. When the government subsidizes investment, it essentially pays part of the cost of each firm's investment. A subsidy to investment shifts the investment

TABLE 5-3	ALTERNATIVE FISCAL POLICIES			
	Interest rate	Consumption	Investment	GNP
Income tax cut	+	+	−	+
Government spending	+	+	−	+
Investment subsidy	+	+	+	+

schedule in panel (a). At each interest rate, firms now plan to invest more. With investment spending higher, aggregate demand increases.

In panel (b), the IS schedule shifts by the multiplier times the increase in autonomous investment brought about by the subsidy. The new equilibrium is at point E', where goods and money markets are again in balance. But note

FIGURE 5-5   AN INVESTMENT SUBSIDY. An investment subsidy shifts the investment schedule in panel (a) at each interest rate out and to the right. The increase in planned investment shows in panel (b) as a shift of the IS curve. Equilibrium income rises to Y_0', and the interest rate increases to i_0'. At the higher interest rate, investment is still higher, I_0', than it was initially. Thus an investment subsidy raises interest rates, income, and investment.

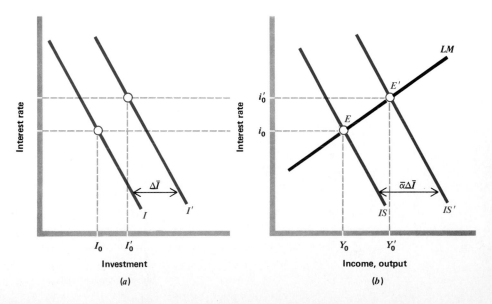

(a)   (b)

now that although interest rates have risen, we see in panel (*a*) that investment is higher. Investment is at the level I_0' up from I_0. The interest rate increase thus has only dampened but not reversed the impact of the investment subsidy. Here is an example where both consumption, induced by higher income, and investment rise as a consequence of fiscal policy.

The Policy Mix

In Figure 5-6 we show the policy problem of reaching full-employment output Y° for an economy that is initially at point E with unemployment. Should we choose a fiscal expansion, moving to point E_1 with higher income and higher interest rates? Or should we choose a monetary expansion, leading to full employment with lower interest rates at point E_2? Or should we pick a policy

FIGURE 5-6   EXPANSIONARY POLICIES AND THE COMPOSITION OF OUTPUT. In an economy with output Y_0 below the full-employment level Y*, there is a choice of using monetary or fiscal expansion to move to full employment. Monetary expansion would move the *LM* curve to the right, putting the equilibrium at E_2. Fiscal expansion shifts the *IS* curve, putting the new equilibrium at E_1. The expansionary monetary policy reduces the interest rate, while the expansionary fiscal policy raises it. The lower interest rate in the case of monetary policy means that investment is higher at E_2 than it is at E_1.

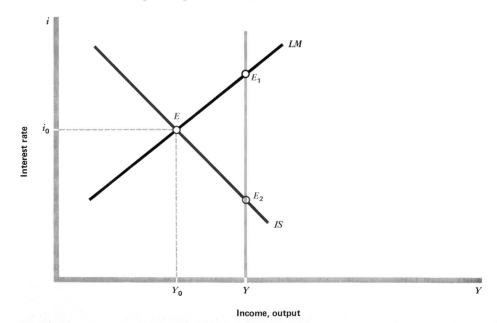

Income, output

mix of fiscal expansion and accommodating monetary policy, leading to an intermediate position?

Once we recognize that all the policies raise output but differ significantly in their impact on different sectors of the economy, we open up a problem of political economy. Given the decision to expand aggregate demand, who should get the primary benefit? Should the expansion take place through a decline in interest rates and increased investment spending, or should it take place through a cut in taxes and increased personal spending, or should it take the form of an increase in the size of government?

Questions of speed and predictability of policies apart, the issues have been settled by political preferences. Conservatives will argue for a tax cut anytime. They will favor stabilization policies that in a recession cut taxes and in a boom cut government spending. Over time, given enough cycles, the government sector becomes very small, just as a conservative would want it to be. The counterpart view belongs to those who believe that there is much scope for government spending on education, environment, job training and rehabilitation, and the like, and who, accordingly, favor expansionary policies in the form of increased government spending. Growth-minded people and the construction lobby finally argue for expansionary policies that operate through low interest rates.

The recognition that monetary and fiscal policy changes have different effects on the composition of output is important. It suggests that policy makers can choose a *policy mix* that will both get the economy to full employment and also make a contribution to solving some other policy problem. We anticipate here several subsequent discussions in which we point out two other targets of policy which have been taken into account in setting monetary and fiscal policy — growth and balance of payments equilibrium.

5-3 THE POLICY MIX IN ACTION

In this section we review several episodes of monetary and fiscal policy in recent U.S. economic history. We first look at the great economic expansion in the 1960s, originating in the 1964 tax cut. We conclude with the monetary-fiscal policy mix in the 1980s.

The 1964 Tax Cut

In the early 1960s the U.S. economy was in a recession with a GNP gap of 3.2 percent in 1963. To help the economy recover, the Kennedy-Johnson administration proposed a package of fiscal expansion. The program had two parts, a cut in the personal income tax rates and a cut in corporate profit taxes. The program, enacted in February 1964, complemented an investment subsidy that had already gone into effect in late 1962. The Revenue Act of 1964 provided for a permanent cut in income tax rates for all individual and corporate taxpayers. Personal taxes were cut by more than 20 percent and corporate

TABLE 5-4	THE 1964 TAX CUT		
	1963	1964	1965
GNP gap, %	3.2	1.8	−0.2
GNP growth, %	4.0	5.3	6.0
Full-employment surplus, % of GNP	1.2	0.2	0.1
Interest rate, %	4.26	4.40	4.49

taxes by about 8 percent. Before the cut, the marginal personal tax rates ranged from 20 to 91 percent; afterward, the range was 14 to 70 percent. For most corporations, the rate fell from 52 to 48 percent.

In terms of the *IS-LM* diagram the fiscal expansion moves the *IS* schedule out and to the right. Monetary policy determines the extent to which interest rates rise. Table 5-4 summarizes some of the relevant data.

Note from Table 5-4 the large fiscal expansion, visible in the decline of the full-employment surplus of 1 percent of GNP. The effects of the fiscal expansion show up in high real growth and a declining GNP gap. To judge monetary policy we look at the behavior of interest rates. Interest rates in Table 5-4 are measured by the yield on high quality corporate bonds (AAA-rated bonds). The interest rate moves up only very slightly. Thus monetary policy on balance was accommodating, keeping interest rates relatively constant. The fiscal expansion was therefore allowed to push up aggregate demand, without adverse side effects on interest rates that would lead to a decline in investment. This is precisely the policy combination shown in Figure 5-4.

Arthur Okun in commenting on the monetary-fiscal policy mix in the period summarized the experience as follows.[5]

> In short, the strong economic expansion of 1964–65 would not have taken place in the face of a highly restrictive monetary strategy. Moreover, the job could in principle have been accomplished by a very expansionary monetary strategy without a stimulative fiscal policy. But the monetary policy that was actually pursued would not in itself have quickened the pace of the economy. It supplied a good set of tires for the economy to move on, but fiscal policy was the engine of growth.

The 1969–1970 Contraction

The expansion of economic activity in response to stimulative fiscal policy led to a significant reduction of unemployment over the 1960s. By 1968 the

---

[5] *The Political Economy of Prosperity* (New York: Norton, 1970), p. 59.

unemployment rate had fallen to only 3.4 percent. At that unemployment rate, output was above its full-employment level. The boom in activity not only reduced unemployment, but also increased the inflation rate. With unemployment no longer a problem and inflation uncomfortably high — 4½ to 5 percent in 1968 and 1969, up from only 1 percent at the beginning of the 1960s — monetary and fiscal policy turned to restraint.

Figure 5-7 shows the policy changes. Fiscal policy moved to correct the budget deficits caused by stimulative fiscal policy and the defense spending associated with the Vietnam War. Monetary policy tightened, pushing up interest rates.

The fiscal contraction, starting at the end of 1968, was a long delayed measure to help reduce the war-inflated budget deficits by increasing tax revenues. The Revenue and Expenditure Control Act of 1968, becoming effective in June 1968, had been recommended by the administration as early as January 1967. The chief measure was a 10 percent surtax on personal income taxes and on corporate incomes. The surtax, for example, implied that any individual who had, at a given income, previously paid $1,000 in taxes would now have to pay an extra 10 percent of those taxes, or $1,100 in taxes in total. Fiscal revenues thus increased strongly, and the budget deficit declined. These surtaxes were supplemented on the government spending side. When the Nixon administration came into power in 1969, expenditure increases were sharply curtailed, thus further increasing the full-employment surplus.

In Figure 5-7 we show the effects of the monetary-fiscal policy mix. Tight money shows up in rising interest rates throughout 1969. The tightening of fiscal policy is indicated by the large shift in the full-employment budget. From the last quarter of 1968 to the first quarter of 1969, fiscal policy swings by a full percentage point of GNP, from a deficit of 0.6 percent to a surplus of that magnitude. If we compare annual averages (not shown in the figure), the shift is even larger: from a deficit that averaged 1.3 percent of GNP in 1968 to a surplus of 0.5 percent of GNP in 1969, which is a shift of nearly 2 percent. Clearly, fiscal policy took a decidedly restrictive course, thus complementing tight money.

Figure 5-7 also shows the unemployment rate for the period. It is interesting to observe here the lags between the restrictive policies and their effects on unemployment. Throughout 1969, the tightening of policies not withstanding, unemployment hardly changed. But by late 1969 the restraint of demand through increased taxes and high interest rates has clearly built up, and unemployment increased rapidly throughout 1970.

The business cycle timing in this recession was as follows. The longest peacetime expansion, which started in December 1961, came to an end in December 1969, the peak of the 1960s expansion. The recession, reflected in the mounting unemployment, had its trough in November 1970. From that trough a new expansion lasting exactly 3 years took place. Thus, using the business cycle dates for reference purposes, there is a very significant lag between the tightening of policies and their impact on aggregate demand.

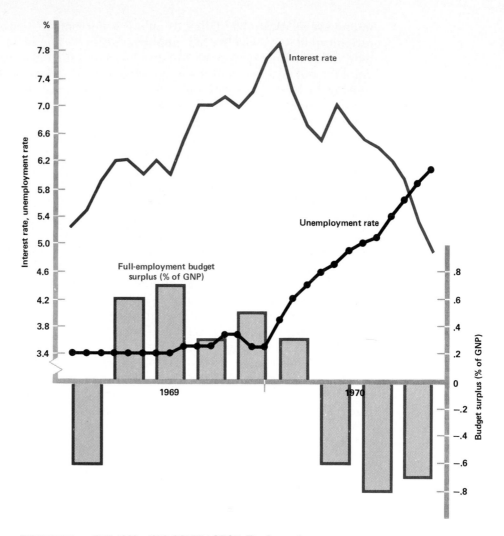

FIGURE 5-7   THE 1969–1970 CONTRACTION. The figure shows
monthly data for the Treasury bill rate and the unemployment rate.
Quarterly data are shown for the full-employment budget surplus,
expressed as a fraction of GNP. (*Source: Business Statistics*, 1977,
pp. 246 and 256; *Survey of Current Business*, April 1982, p. 27.)

The 1980–1984 Policy Mix

Economic policy in the early 1980s departed radically from the policies of the
previous two decades. First, tight money was implemented at the end of 1979
to fight an inflation that had reached record peacetime levels; then in 1981 an

expansionary fiscal policy was put in place as President Reagan's program of tax cuts and increased defense spending began.

With inflation as a central concern of policy in the early 1980s, this section serves both to discuss the highly unusual policy mix and to introduce the problem of inflation. Systematic study of inflation begins in Chapter 6 when we introduce aggregate supply and drop the assumption that the price level is fixed.

For this section, we need to know that policies that reduce aggregate demand, such as reducing the growth rate of money, or reducing government spending, tend to reduce the inflation rate along with the level of output. Expansionary policy increases inflation together with the level of output. Recall also that inflation is unpopular, and that governments for that reason will generally try to reduce the inflation rate after it has risen.

In 1973 the United States and the rest of the world were hit by the first oil shock, in which the oil exporting countries raised the price of oil fourfold. The oil price increase raised other prices, and in the United States it helped create inflation and also a recession in which unemployment increased to the then post–World War II record rate of 8.9 percent. The recession ended in 1975. Economic policy under the Carter administration (1977–1981) was generally expansionary; by 1979 unemployment was below 6 percent and thus perhaps below the full-employment level. Inflation increased with the expansionary policy over the period, and in 1979 it increased sharply as the second oil shock hit and the price of oil doubled.

The rising inflation was extremely unpopular, and in October 1979 the Fed acted, turning monetary policy in a highly restrictive direction. The monetary squeeze was tightened in the first half of 1980, at which stage the economy went into a minirecession. Fiscal policy in this episode remained unchanged.

Table 5-5 shows the key data. Note the extremely high inflation rates at the beginning of 1980, the sharp reduction in the growth rate of money in

TABLE 5-5	THE 1980 MINIRECESSION				
	1979:4	1980:1	1980:2	1980:3	1980:4
Unemployment	5.9	6.2	7.2	7.6	7.3
Inflation*	12.2	18.4	13.7	6.8	11.1
Money growth[†]	7.6	7.9	4.3	5.7	7.5
Full-employment deficit (% of GNP)	1.9	2.2	2.2	2.3	2.2

* CPI, last month of quarter relative to last month of previous quarter, at annual percent rate.
[†] M1 growth, over same quarter a year before.
Source: Data Resources, Inc.

mid-1980, and the immediate rise in unemployment and fall in inflation. The unemployment rate peaked in the third quarter of 1980 and then declined for the next four quarters, back to 7.3 percent. The inflation rate fell sharply from the second to the third quarter of 1980, but then increased again.

The recession is called a *minirecession* because it lasted only two quarters, from the peak in January 1980 to the trough in July 1980. But the recovery did not make much of an inroad into unemployment. On the contrary another recession starting in July 1981 raised unemployment to a new postwar high of 10.7 percent by the end of 1982.

The reason for the renewed decline in activity was tight money. Because inflation was still above 10 percent and the money stock was growing at only 5.1 percent in 1981, the real money supply was falling. Interest rates continued to climb. Table 5-6 shows the mortgage interest rate rising in 1981 and 1982 to 15 percent. Not surprisingly investment, and especially construction, collapsed. The economy was dragged into a deep recession with a trough in December 1982.

Table 5-6 shows the second component of the early 1980s policy mix: the full-employment deficit increased rapidly from 1981 to 1984. The 1981 tax bill set in motion cuts in tax rates for individuals; the cuts came into effect over the next three years and increased investment subsidies for corporations. The full-employment deficits in those years are the largest in peacetime U.S. history.

With the policy mix of easy fiscal and tight monetary policy, the analysis around Figure 5-6 tells us to expect a rise in the interest rate. With investment subsidies increased, Figure 5-5 tells us to look for the possibility that investment increases along with the interest rate.

NOMINAL AND REAL INTEREST RATES

The first element — a rise in the interest rate — indeed occurred. That may be a surprise if you look only at the mortgage interest rate in Table 5-6, which came down from 15.1 percent in 1982 to 12.4 percent in 1984. But when there is inflation, the correct interest rate to consider is not the *nominal* rate but the *real* rate. The real interest rate is the nominal (stated) rate of interest minus the rate of inflation.

To understand the distinction between real and nominal interest rates, realize that when prices are rising, when there is inflation, borrowers pay back in dollars that have lost value compared with the dollars they borrowed. If prices are rising 10 percent and we can borrow at 6 percent, then we can take the dollars we borrow, buy goods or invest, sell the goods a year later for 10 percent more dollars than we paid (because prices have risen 10 percent in the meantime), and pay back only the 6 percent interest. We would be ahead by 4 percent. In this case the real cost of borrowing is negative even though we are paying 6 percent nominal interest. To calculate the *real* cost of borrowing, deduct the inflation rate from the interest rate.

TABLE 5-6	MONEY GROWTH AND THE FULL EMPLOYMENT BUDGET, 1981–1984			
	1981	1982	1983	1984
Money growth*	5.1	8.8	10.4	5.2
Full-employment deficit	1.9	3.0	3.9	4.8
Mortgage rate	14.7	15.1	12.6	12.4
Inflation†	10.4	6.1	3.2	4.3
Unemployment rate	7.5	9.5	9.5	7.4

* Fourth quarter to fourth quarter growth rate of M1.

† CPI, year relative to previous year.

Over the period 1981 to 1984 the *real* interest rate increased sharply even as the *nominal* rate declined. The real cost of borrowing went up though the nominal cost went down.

INVESTMENT

Figure 5-8 shows fixed investment as a ratio to GNP as well as the nominal and real interest rate on long-term corporate bonds.[6] Two dents in investment, one for each recession, are clearly visible. Both nominal and real interest rates fell in each recession. Nominal and real interest rates increased after the 1980 minirecession, and investment fell. But even as tight money sent the economy into recession in 1981, fiscal policy started shifting into the opposite direction. Between 1981 and 1983 the cyclically adjusted budget moved by a full 2 percent of GNP in the direction of expansion. Tax cuts for households and subsidies for business investment soon overcame the restrictive impact of tight money, raising aggregate demand, output, and employment.

The unemployment rate peaked in the last quarter of 1982 and from then on steadily declined under the impact of the huge fiscal expansion. The policy mix produced rising real interest rates, even though the nominal rate remained at roughly the same level to which it had fallen in 1982.[7] Even so,

---

[6] The real interest rate in Fig. 5-8 is measured as the nominal interest rate minus the average of the inflation rate over the previous 2 years. The real interest rate relevant to borrowing should be the nominal interest rate minus the inflation borrowers *expect* during the period they are borrowing—that is, the real interest they expect to pay. Of course, we do not know how much inflation they expect, so the calculated real interest rates in the figure are only a reasonable guess as to the real rates borrowers actually expected.

[7] The policy mix had another important consequence: it strengthened the dollar, making imports cheap and reducing U.S. net exports. Understanding the mechanism through which the policy mix affected the exchange rate will have to wait till we open the economy to international trade, in Chapter 6.

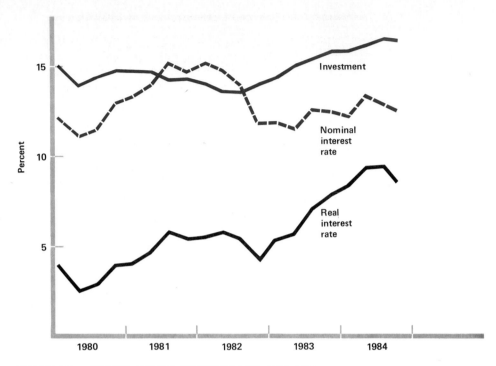

FIGURE 5-8   INVESTMENT AND INTEREST RATES, 1980–1984.
(*Source:* Data Resources, Inc.)

investment boomed, rising sharply as a percentage of GNP. The prospect of a fast recovery encouraged firms to invest. So did the investment subsidies put in place in 1981 that reduced the cost of investing for firms even though the real interest rate had risen.

Summary

The policy mix in the early 1980s featured extremely expansionary fiscal policy and tight money. The tight money succeeded in reducing the inflation of the late seventies, 1980, and 1981 at the expense of a serious recession. Expansionary fiscal policy then drove a recovery, during which real interest rates increased sharply. Despite the increasing real interest rates, investment increased in part because investment subsidies reduced the cost of investing.

*5-4 A FORMAL TREATMENT OF THE *IS-LM* MODEL

Our exposition so far has been a verbal and graphic one, and has been supplemented by looking at several policy applications in recent U.S. history. We now round off the analysis with a more formal treatment that uses the equations of the *IS* and *LM* schedules to derive and discuss fiscal and monetary policy multipliers.

Equilibrium Income and the Interest Rate

The intersection of the *IS* and *LM* schedules determines equilibrium income and the equilibrium interest rate. We can derive expressions for these equilibrium values by using the equations of the *IS* and *LM* schedules. From Chapter 4 we remember the equation of the *IS* schedule or goods market equilibrium schedule as

IS schedule: $$Y = \overline{\alpha}(\overline{A} - bi) \tag{3}$$

and the equation describing money market equilibrium as[8]

LM schedule: $$i = \frac{1}{h}\left(kY - \frac{\overline{M}}{P}\right) \tag{4}$$

The intersection of the *IS* and *LM* schedules in the diagrams corresponds to a situation where both the *IS* and *LM* equations hold — the *same* interest rate and income levels assure equilibrium in *both* the goods and money market. In terms of the equations, that means we can substitute the interest rate from the *LM* equation (4) into the *IS* equation (3):

$$Y = \overline{\alpha}\left[\overline{A} - \frac{b}{h}\left(kY - \frac{\overline{M}}{P}\right)\right] \tag{5}$$

Collecting terms and solving for the equilibrium level of income, we obtain

$$Y_0 = \frac{h\overline{\alpha}}{h + kb\overline{\alpha}}\overline{A} + \frac{b\overline{\alpha}}{h + kb\overline{\alpha}}\frac{\overline{M}}{P} \tag{5a}$$

Equation (5a) shows the equilibrium level of income depending on two exogenous variables: autonomous spending $\overline{A}$, including fiscal policy parame-

---

[8] To deal with the case where liquidity preference is not only high but at some rate, say i', *perfectly* elastic, we could rewrite the *LM* equation as $\overline{M}/P = kY - h(i - i')$, so that real money demand depends on the excess of the interest rate above some floor level i'. With this formulation, (4) becomes $i = i' + (1/h)[kY - \overline{M}/P]$. If h is extremely high, the interest rate is $i = i'$ or the *LM* schedule is horizontal at the level i'.

ters $(\overline{C}, \overline{I}, \overline{G}, t, \overline{TR})$ and the real money stock $\overline{M}/\overline{P}$. Equilibrium income is higher the higher the level of autonomous spending $\overline{A}$ and the higher the stock of real balances.

The equilibrium rate of interest, i_0, is obtained by substituting the equilibrium income level Y_0 from (5a) into the equation of the LM schedule, (4):

$$i_0 = \frac{k\overline{\alpha}}{h + kb\overline{\alpha}} \overline{A} - \frac{1}{h + kb\overline{\alpha}} \frac{\overline{M}}{\overline{P}} \tag{6}$$

Equation (6) shows that the equilibrium interest rate depends on the parameters of fiscal policy captured in the multiplier and the term $\overline{A}$, and on the real money stock. A higher real money stock implies a lower equilibrium interest rate.

For policy questions we are interested in the precise relation between changes in fiscal policy or changes in the real money stock and the resulting changes in equilibrium income. The *monetary* and *fiscal policy multipliers* provide the relevant information.

The Fiscal Policy Multiplier

The fiscal policy multiplier shows how much an increase in government spending changes the equilibrium level of income, holding the real money supply constant. Examine equation (5a) and consider the effect of an increase in government spending on income. The increase in government spending $\Delta\overline{G}$ is a change in autonomous spending, so that $\Delta\overline{A} = \Delta\overline{G}$. The effect of the change in $\overline{G}$ is given by

$$\frac{\Delta Y_0}{\Delta \overline{G}} = \frac{h\overline{\alpha}}{h + bk\overline{\alpha}} \tag{7}$$

We note that the expression in equation (7) is zero if h is very small and will be equal to $\overline{\alpha}$ if h approaches infinity. This corresponds, respectively, to vertical and horizontal LM schedules. Similarly, a large value of either b or k serves to reduce the effect on income of government spending. Why? A high value of k implies a large increase in money demand as income rises and hence a large increase in interest rates in order to maintain money market equilibrium. In combination with a high b, this implies a large reduction in private aggregate demand. Equation (7) thus presents the algebraic analysis that corresponds to the graphical analysis of Figures 5-2 and 5-3.

The Monetary Policy Multiplier

The monetary policy multiplier shows how much an increase in the real money supply increases the equilibrium level of income, keeping fiscal policy unchanged. Using equation (5a) to examine the effects of an increase in the real money supply on income, we have

$$\frac{\Delta Y_0}{\Delta(\overline{M}/\overline{P})} = \frac{b\overline{\alpha}}{h + bk\overline{\alpha}} \tag{8}$$

The smaller h and k and the larger b and $\overline{\alpha}$, the more expansionary the effect of an increase in real balances on the equilibrium level of income. Large b and $\overline{\alpha}$ correspond to a very flat *IS* schedule. Equation (8) thus corresponds to the graphic analysis presented in Figure 4-16.

The Classical Case and the Liquidity Trap

We now turn to two special cases that demonstrate the role of the demand function for real balances in the effectiveness of monetary and fiscal policies. Consider first the possibility that money demand does not depend at all on interest rates and is simply proportional to real income. This happens if the parameter h is zero, so that real money demand is simply

$$L = kY \tag{9}$$

In this case monetary equilibrium, equating the demand and supply of money, leads to[9]

$$Y = \frac{1}{k}\frac{\overline{M}}{\overline{P}} \tag{10}$$

This case is called the *classical case* because classical (that is, nineteenth-century) economists" did not give much emphasis to the interest response of money demand. The case is important because it has the following implication: If money demand does not depend on the interest rate and only on the level of income, as in (9), the money supply alone determines income.

In this classical case the level of nominal income, $\overline{P}Y$, is proportional to the nominal money stock. Changes in the nominal money stock lead to changes in income in the same proportion. Furthermore, while income does respond to money, it is *totally* unresponsive to fiscal policy. We also can see the point from (5a) by setting $h = 0$.

Interest Rates and Fiscal Policy

How is it possible that fiscal policy should have no effect at all on income? After all, if the government were to spend more, how is it possible that the

---

[9] The demand for real balances is $L = kY$ and the supply $\overline{M}/\overline{P}$. Thus with demand equal to supply, $\overline{M}/\overline{P} = kY$ or $Y = (1/k)\overline{M}/\overline{P}$.

increased spending should *not* raise income? The reasoning is as follows. An increase in government spending does lead to an incipient rise in aggregate demand and income, but that immediately raises the demand for money. With the money supply unchanged, interest rates will shoot up to clear the money market. As interest rates rise because of the excess demand for money, investment spending declines. The fall in investment spending compensates exactly for the higher government spending, and the level of income is unchanged.

We can see this by looking at the investment equation (11), obtained by substituting in the equilibrium interest rate from (6):

$$I = \bar{I} - bi_0 = \bar{I} - \frac{bk\bar{\alpha}}{h + bk\bar{\alpha}} \bar{A} + \frac{b}{h + bk\bar{\alpha}} \frac{\bar{M}}{\bar{P}} \tag{11}$$

In the case where $h = 0$, the coefficient multiplying $\bar{A}$ in (11) is 1. This means that a \$1 increase in $\bar{A}$, given the real money stock, leads to an equal reduction of investment. That is what we call *full* crowding out. In general, with h not equal to zero, the coefficient of $\bar{A}$ is a fraction, as shown in (11). The larger h, the smaller the fraction of an extra dollar of government spending that is offset by reduced investment spending.

Liquidity Trap

The other extreme for monetary and fiscal policy is represented by a world where h is infinite. Then money and other assets are effectively perfect substitutes. In such a world, equation (5a) reduces to

$$Y = \bar{\alpha}\bar{A} \tag{12}$$

This is the "multiplier world" of Chapter 3, where autonomous spending entirely determines the level of real income. It occurs if the economy is in a liquidity trap.

In the liquidity trap, money does not matter for income determination because money demand is *so* responsive to interest rates. The smallest change in interest rates is sufficient to eliminate imbalances in the money market that might arise from changes in money supply or in income. And because these corrective changes in interest rates are so small, they do not even affect aggregate demand. The interest rate effect can be verified from (11). With h extremely high, investment spending is not influenced by either monetary or fiscal policy.

5-5 SUMMARY

1. Taking into account the effects of fiscal policy on the interest rate modifies the multiplier results of Chapter 3. Fiscal expansion, except in ex-

treme circumstances, still leads to an income expansion. However, the rise in interest rates that comes about through the increase in money demand caused by higher income dampens the expansion.

2. Fiscal policy is more effective the smaller are the induced changes in interest rates and the smaller is the response of investment to these interest rate changes.

3. In the liquidity trap, the interest rate is constant because money demand is completely elastic with respect to the interest rate. Monetary policy has no effect on the economy, whereas fiscal policy has its full multiplier effect on output — and no effect on interest rates.

4. In the classical case, the demand for money is independent of the interest rate. In that case, changes in the money stock change income. But fiscal policy has no effect on income — it affects only the interest rate. In this case there is complete crowding out of private spending by government spending.

5. Neither the liquidity trap nor the classical case applies in practice. But they are useful extremes to study to show what determines the magnitude of monetary and fiscal policy multipliers.

6. A fiscal expansion, because it leads to higher interest rates, displaces or crowds out some private investment. The extent of crowding out is a sensitive issue in assessing the usefulness and desirability of fiscal policy as a tool of stabilization policy.

7. In an economy that is less than fully employed, crowding out need not occur. The monetary authorities can provide an accommodating monetary policy that avoids the rise in interest rates associated with the output expansion.

8. The question of the monetary-fiscal policy mix arises because expansionary monetary policy reduces the interest rate while expansionary fiscal policy increases the interest rate. Accordingly, expansionary fiscal policy increases output while reducing the level of investment; expansionary monetary policy increases output and the level of investment.

9. Governments have to choose the mix in accordance with their objectives for economic growth, or increasing consumption, or from the viewpoint of their beliefs about the desirable size of the government.

10. The real interest rate is the nominal rate minus the inflation rate.

KEY TERMS

Crowding out
Monetary-fiscal policy mix
Monetary accommodation
Monetizing budget deficits
Composition of output

Investment subsidy
Monetary policy multiplier
Fiscal policy multiplier
Real interest rate

PROBLEMS

1. The economy is at full employment. Now the government wants to change the composition of demand toward investment and away from consumption without, however, allowing aggregate demand to go beyond full employment. What is the required policy mix? Use the *IS-LM* diagram to show your policy proposal.

2. Discuss the role of the parameters $\bar{\alpha}$, h, b, and k in the transmission mechanism linking an increase in government spending to the resulting change in equilibrium income. In developing the analysis use the following table:

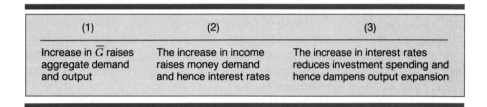

(1)	(2)	(3)
Increase in $\bar{G}$ raises aggregate demand and output	The increase in income raises money demand and hence interest rates	The increase in interest rates reduces investment spending and hence dampens output expansion

3. Suppose the government cuts income taxes. Show in the *IS-LM* model the impact of the tax cut under two assumptions: One, the government keeps interest rates constant through an accommodating monetary policy; two, the money stock remains unchanged. Explain the difference in results.

4. Discuss the circumstances in which the monetary and fiscal policy multipliers are, respectively, equal to zero. Explain in words why this can happen and how likely you think this is.

5. Consider an economy where the government considers two alternative programs for contraction. One is the removal of an investment subsidy; the other is a rise in income tax rates. Use the *IS-LM* schedule and the investment schedule, as shown in Figure 5-5, to discuss the impact of these alternative policies on income, interest rates, and investment.

*6. Suppose the parameters k and $\bar{\alpha}$ are 0.5 and 2, respectively. Assume there is an increase of $1 billion in government spending. By how much must the real money stock be increased to hold interest rates constant?

7. Discuss the circumstances where fiscal expansion leads to *full* crowding out.

8. In Figure 5-6 the economy can move to full employment by an expansion in either money or the full-employment deficit. Which policy leads to E_1 and which to E_2? How would you expect the choice to be made? Who would most strongly favor moving to E_1? E_2? What policy would correspond to "balanced growth"?

9. "We can have the GNP path we want equally well with a tight fiscal policy and an easier monetary policy, or the reverse, within fairly broad limits. The real basis for choice lies in many subsidiary targets, besides real GNP and inflation, that are differentially affected by fiscal and monetary policies." What are some of the subsidiary targets referred to in the quote? How would they be affected by alternative policy combinations?

10. Explain why:
    (a) A rise in interest rates reduces the quantity of real balances demanded.
    (b) A fall in interest rates raises investment spending.

6

INTERNATIONAL LINKAGES

International macroeconomic linkages play a powerful role in the U.S. economy. And even more, U.S. policies have substantial effects on foreign economies. Whether the U.S. economy grows or moves into recession makes all the difference to Japan or to Mexico, and whether other industrial countries shift to fiscal stimulus, or on the contrary to budget surpluses, makes a lot of difference to the U.S. economy. In this chapter we present the key linkages of an open economy and introduce some first pieces of analysis. There is more detail on international aspects of macroeconomics in Chapter 20.

Any economy is linked to the rest of the world through two broad channels: *trade* and *finance*. The *trade* linkage arises from the fact that some of a country's production is exported to foreign countries, while some goods that are consumed or invested at home are produced abroad and imported. In 1984–1985 U.S. exports amounted to 9.5 percent of GNP, while imports were equal to 11.5 percent of GNP. By comparison with other countries the United States engages in relatively little international trade — or is a relatively closed economy. For the Netherlands, at the other extreme — a very open economy — imports and exports each come to about 60 percent of GNP.

The trade linkages are nonetheless important for the United States. Spending on imports escapes from the circular flow of income, while exports appear as an increase in the demand for domestically produced goods. Thus income determination and the multiplier analysis must be amended to include international effects.

The trade channel also opens up an international influence on prices in the U.S. economy. We have not yet analyzed the determinants of the price level, but it is worthwhile noting here how trade linkages affect domestic prices and the demand for our goods. Foreign prices matter in two main respects. First, the prices of commodities or raw materials (oil, tin, copper, agricultural products), which are inputs in production and an element of producers' costs, are heavily affected by worldwide supply and demand conditions. Changes in commodity prices affect costs and prices in the United States. The most striking examples are the oil price increases of the 1970s. When oil prices were increased manyfold by the oil producers' cartel in 1973–1974 and 1979–1980, U.S. inflation rose sharply.

Foreign prices matter in a second way. The prices of foreign manufactured goods, such as cars, VCRs, and machine tools, affect the demand for domestically produced goods. A decline in the dollar prices of our competitors, relative to the prices at which U.S. firms sell, shifts demand away from U.S. goods toward goods produced abroad. Our imports rise and exports fall. This is precisely what happened in the United States between 1980 and 1985 as the value of the dollar increased relative to foreign currencies. Conversely, if foreign prices in dollars rise relative to our prices, demand here and abroad shifts toward our goods, exports rise, and imports decline.

There are also strong international links in the area of *finance*. U.S. residents, whether households, banks, or corporations, can hold U.S. assets such as Treasury Bills or corporate bonds, or they can hold assets in foreign countries, say in Canada or in Germany. Most U.S. households, in fact, hold almost exclusively U.S. assets, but that is certainly not true for banks or large corporations. Portfolio managers will shop around the world for the most attractive yields, and they may well decide at a particular time that holding German government bonds, Yen bonds issued by the Japanese government, or Swiss bonds offers a better yield—all things considered—than U.S. bonds.

International investors provide a link between asset markets here and abroad and their actions have fundamental effects on the determination of income, exchange rates, and the ability of monetary policy to affect interest rates. We show in this chapter how the *IS-LM* analysis has to be modified to take international trade and finance linkages into account. A first step is to discuss exchange rates and the balance of payments.

6-1 THE BALANCE OF PAYMENTS AND EXCHANGE RATES

The *balance of payments* is the record of the transactions of the residents of a country with the rest of the world. There are two main accounts in the balance of payments: the current account and the capital account.

The *current account* records trade in goods and services, as well as transfer payments. Services include freight, royalty payments, and interest payments. Transfer payments consist of remittances, gifts, and grants. We talk of a current account surplus if exports exceed imports plus net transfers to foreigners, that is, if receipts from trade in goods and services and transfers exceed payments on this account. The *trade balance* simply records trade in goods. Adding trade in services and net transfers, we arrive at the current account balance.

The *capital account* records purchases and sales of assets, such as stocks, bonds, and land. There is a capital account surplus, or a net capital inflow, when our receipts from the sale of stocks, bonds, land, bank deposits, and other assets exceed our payments for our own purchases of foreign assets.

Surpluses and Deficits

The simple rule for balance of payments accounting is that any transaction that gives rise to a payment by U.S. residents is a deficit item. Thus, imports of cars, use of foreign shipping, gifts to foreigners, purchase of land in Spain, or making a deposit in a bank in Switzerland are all deficit items. Surplus items, by contrast, would be U.S. sales of airplanes abroad, payments by foreigners for U.S. licenses to use American technology, pensions from abroad received by U.S. residents, and foreign purchases of GM stock.

The overall *balance of payments* is the sum of the current and capital accounts. If both the current account and the capital account are in deficit, then the overall balance of payments is in deficit. When one account is in surplus and the other is in deficit to precisely the same extent, the overall balance of payments is zero—neither in surplus nor in deficit. We record these relationships as[1]

Balance of payments surplus

$$= \text{current account surplus} + \text{capital account surplus} \qquad (1)$$

Table 6-1 presents the U.S. balance of payments accounts. We show the accounts since the 1960s. In the sixties the current account was in surplus, in the seventies it was in a slight deficit, and in the eighties it has been in a large deficit. The U.S. capital account was in deficit through the end of the seventies. There was a net capital *outflow*, meaning that U.S. residents purchased more assets abroad than foreigners bought in the United States. But that capital account deficit turned around in the eighties. There has been a massive capital *inflow* as foreigners have on balance bought more U.S. assets than Americans have acquired foreign assets.

Making International Payments

Any transaction which gives rise to a payment by U.S. residents to foreigners is a deficit item. An overall deficit in the balance of payments—the sum of the current and capital accounts—means, therefore, that U.S. residents make

---

[1] In using equation (1), recall that a deficit is a negative surplus.

TABLE 6-1 THE UNITED STATES BALANCE OF PAYMENTS
(Billions of Dollars, Annual Averages)

	1960–1969	1970–1979	1980–1984	1985
Current account	3.3	−0.2	−28.4	−117.7
Trade balance	3.6	−1.1	−52.1	−124.3
Capital account*	−4.6	−14.0	26.2	125.9
Balance of payments	−1.3	−14.2	−2.2	8.3

* Including errors and omissions.
Source: Economic Report of the President, various issues, and *Economic Indicators,* April 1986.

more payments to foreigners than they receive from foreigners. Since foreigners want to be paid in their own currencies, the question arises of how these payments are to be made.

When the overall balance of payments is in deficit[2] — when the sum of the current and capital accounts is negative — Americans have to pay more foreign currency to foreigners than is received. The Fed and foreign central banks provide the foreign currency to make payments to foreigners, and the net amount supplied is "official reserve transactions."[3] When the U.S. balance of payments is in surplus, foreigners have to get the dollars with which to pay for their excess of payments to the United States over their receipts from sales to the United States. The dollars are provided by the central banks.

Fixed Exchange Rates

We now examine in more detail the way in which central banks, through their official transactions, *finance,* or provide the means of paying for, balance of payments surpluses and deficits. At this point we distinguish between fixed and floating exchange rate systems.

In a fixed exchange rate system, foreign central banks stand ready to buy and sell their currencies at a fixed price in terms of dollars. The major countries had fixed exchange rates against one another from the end of World War II until 1973.

---

[2] We include in Table 6-1 the statistical discrepancies that arise from incomplete recording of actual trade in goods and services and assets. The data are reconciled by an entry called "errors and omissions" which are believed to arise largely from unreported capital flows.
[3] The official presentation of balance of payments statistics as in Table 6-1 was stopped in mid-1976 after a review committee suggested that official reserve transactions are not a full measure of foreign exchange transactions by central banks. Nonetheless everyone but the government presents the data as in the table.

In Germany, for example, the central bank, the Bundesbank, would buy or sell any amount of dollars in the 1960s at 4 deutsche marks (DM) per U.S. dollar. The French central bank, the Banque de France, stood ready to buy or sell any amount of dollars at 4.90 French francs (FF) per U.S. dollar. The fact that the central banks were prepared to buy or sell *any* amount of dollars at these fixed prices or exchange rates meant that market prices would indeed be equal to the fixed rates. Why? Because nobody who wanted to buy U.S. dollars would pay more than 4.90 FF per dollar when francs could be gotten at that price from the Banque de France. Conversely, nobody would part with dollars in exchange for francs for less than 4.90 francs per dollar if the Banque de France, through the commercial banking system, was prepared to buy dollars at that price.

In a fixed rate system, the central banks have to finance any balance of payments surplus or deficit that arises at the official exchange rate. They do that simply by buying or selling all the foreign currency that is not supplied in private transactions. If the United States were running a deficit in the balance of payments vis-à-vis Germany, so that the demand for marks in exchange for dollars exceeded the supply of dollars in exchange for marks from Germans, the Bundesbank would buy the excess dollars, paying for them with marks.

Fixed exchange rates thus operate like any other price support scheme, such as in agricultural markets. Given market demand and supply, the price fixer has to make up the excess demand or take up the excess supply. In order to be able to ensure that the price (exchange rate) stays fixed, it is obviously necessary to hold an inventory of foreign exchange that can be provided in exchange for domestic currency.[4]

RESERVES

Foreign central banks held *reserves* — inventories of dollars, and gold that could be sold for dollars — that they would sell in the market when there was an excess demand for dollars. Conversely, when there was an excess supply of dollars, they would buy up the dollars, as in our example of the U.S. balance of payments deficit vis-à-vis Germany.

INTERVENTION

Intervention is the buying or selling of foreign exchange by the central bank. What determines the amount of intervention that a central bank has to do in a

---

[4] We have so far avoided being specific on exactly which central banks did the intervening in the foreign exchange market in the fixed rate system. It is clear that if there were an excess supply of dollars and an excess demand for marks, either the Bundesbank could buy the dollars in exchange for marks, or the Fed could sell marks in exchange for dollars. In practice, during the fixed rate period, each foreign central bank undertook to *peg* (fix) its exchange rate vis-à-vis the dollar, and most foreign exchange intervention was undertaken by the foreign central banks. The Fed was nonetheless involved in the management of the exchange rate system, since it frequently made dollar loans to foreign central banks that were in danger of running out of dollars.

fixed exchange rate system? We already have the answer to that question. The balance of payments measures the amount of foreign exchange intervention needed from the central banks. So long as the foreign central bank has the necessary reserves, it can continue to intervene in the foreign exchange markets to keep the exchange rate constant. However, if a country persistently runs deficits in the balance of payments, the central bank eventually will run out of reserves of foreign exchange and will be unable to continue its inter vention.

Before that point is reached, the central bank is likely to decide that it can no longer maintain the exchange rate, and will devalue the currency. In 1967, for instance, the British devalued the pound from $2.80 per pound to $2.40 per pound. That meant it became cheaper for Americans and other foreigners to buy British pounds, and the devaluation thus affected the balance of payments.

Flexible Exchange Rates

We have seen that the central banks have to provide whatever amounts of foreign currency are needed to finance payments imbalances under fixed exchange rates. In flexible rate systems, by contrast, the central banks allow the exchange rate to adjust to equate the supply and demand for foreign currency. If today's exchange rate against the mark were 50 cents per mark, and German exports to the United States increased, thus increasing the demand for marks by Americans, the Bundesbank could simply stand aside and let the exchange rate adjust. In this particular case, the exchange rate could move from 50 cents per mark to a level such as 52 cents per mark, making German goods more expensive in terms of dollars and thus reducing the demand for them by Americans. We shall later in this chapter examine the way in which exchange rate changes under floating rates affect the balance of payments. The terms *flexible rates* and *floating rates* are used interchangeably.

Floating, Clean and Dirty

In a system of *clean floating*, central banks stand aside completely and allow exchange rates to be freely determined in the foreign exchange markets. The central banks do not intervene in the foreign exchange markets in a system of clean floating, and official reserve transactions would, accordingly, be zero in such a situation. That means the balance of payments would be zero in a system of clean floating: The exchange rate would adjust to make the current and capital accounts sum to zero.

In practice, the flexible rate system, since 1973, has not been one of clean floating. Instead, the system has been one of *managed*, or *dirty*, *floating*. Under managed floating, central banks intervene to buy and sell foreign currencies, in attempts to influence exchange rates. Official reserve transactions are, accordingly, not equal to zero. The reasons for this central bank intervention under floating rates are discussed in Chapter 20.

Terminology

The use of language with respect to exchange rates can be very confusing. In particular, the terms *depreciation* and *appreciation* and *devaluation* and *revaluation* recur in any discussion of trade.

Figure 6-1 shows the dollar-sterling exchange rate since 1960. We use the figure to clarify some points of terminology. The vertical axis shows the exchange rate measured as $U.S. per pound sterling. First note that we show two subperiods, the fixed rate period lasting through the 1960s until 1973 and then the flexible rate regime. During the fixed rate period the dollar price of

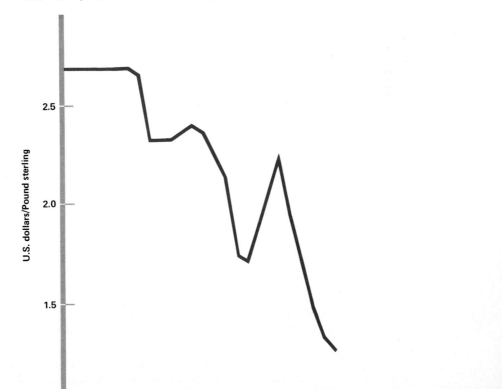

FIGURE 6-1   THE DOLLAR-STERLING EXCHANGE RATE, 1960–1985. (*Source:* Data Resources, Inc.)

sterling remained constant. It was constant, or pegged, at a given level by the Bank of England except for two adjustments. Until 1967 the exchange rate was $2.80 per pound sterling, but in that year sterling was devalued and the rate became $2.40 per pound. In 1971 sterling was revalued to $2.60 per pound. A *devaluation* takes place when the price of foreign currencies under a fixed rate regime is increased by official action. A devaluation thus means that foreigners pay less for the devalued currency or that residents of the devaluing country pay more for foreign currencies. The opposite of a devaluation is a *revaluation*.

Changes in the price of foreign exchange under flexible exchange rates are referred to as *currency depreciation* or *appreciation*. A currency *depreciates* when, under floating rates, it becomes less expensive in terms of foreign currencies. For instance, if the exchange rate of the pound sterling changes from $1.50 per pound to $1.47 per pound, the pound is depreciating. By contrast, the currency *appreciates* when it becomes more expensive in terms of foreign money.

For example, in Figure 6-1 we see that in 1975–1976 and again in 1982–1985 sterling was depreciating, meaning that it took fewer and fewer dollars to buy a pound sterling. By contrast, in 1977–1980 sterling was appreciating. Although the terms devaluation/revaluation and depreciation/appreciation are used in fixed and flexible rate regimes, respectively, there is no economic difference. These terms describe the direction in which an exchange rate moves.

Summary

1. The balance of payments accounts are a record of the transactions of the economy with other economies. The capital account describes transactions in assets, while the current account covers transactions in goods and services and transfers.
2. Any payment to foreigners is a deficit item in the balance of payments. Any payment from foreigners is a surplus item. The balance of payments deficit (or surplus) is the sum of the deficits (or surpluses) on current and capital accounts.
3. Under fixed exchange rates, central banks stand ready to meet all demands for foreign currencies arising from balance of payments deficits or surpluses at a fixed price in terms of the domestic currency. They have to *finance* the excess demands for, or supplies of, foreign currency (that is, the balance of payments deficits or surpluses, respectively) at the pegged (fixed) exchange rate by running down, or adding to, their reserves of foreign currency.
4. Under flexible exchange rates, the demands for and supplies of foreign currency are equated through movements in exchange rates. Under clean floating, there is no central bank intervention and the balance of payments is zero. But central banks sometimes intervene in a floating rate system, engaging in so-called dirty floating.

6-2 EXCHANGE RATE MEASURES AND THE U.S. DOLLAR

Since 1973 the U.S. dollar has floated more or less freely. Although there has been some intervention for much of the time, except in the early years of the Reagan administration, the dollar exchange rate has fluctuated substantially. Table 6-2 shows movements of the dollar relative to the yen and the deutsch mark (DM) over the period 1976 to 1986. The dollar depreciated sharply from 1976 to 1980, and then appreciated even more (against the DM) through 1985. In the first quarter of 1986 another sharp reversal set in, with the dollar depreciating rapidly against other currencies.

Table 6-2 shows several measures of exchange rates. The first two columns are the conventional measure, the price of the foreign currency in terms of the dollar. For example, one DM cost 34 cents in 1985. These are also called *bilateral, nominal* exchange rates. They are bilateral in the sense that they are exchange rates for one currency against another, and they are nominal because they specify the exchange rate in nominal terms, as so many dollars per DM or cents per yen.

Often we want to characterize the movement of the dollar relative to all other currencies in a single number rather than by looking at the separate exchange rates for the DM, the yen, the French franc, etc. That is, we want an index for the exchange rate against other currencies, just as we use a price index to show how the prices of goods in general have changed.

The third and fourth columns in Table 6-2 present indexes of the *multilateral or effective exchange rate.* The effective or multilateral rate represents the price of a representative basket of foreign currencies, each weighted by its importance to the United States in international trade. Thus the yen receives a large weight, as does the Canadian dollar, because large shares of our trade are with Japan and Canada. By contrast Germany or France or Italy receive much smaller weights.

TABLE 6-2	NOMINAL AND REAL EXCHANGE RATES FOR THE U.S. DOLLAR			
			EFFECTIVE RATE INDEX (1980 = 100)	
	$/Yen	$/DM	Nominal	Real
1976	0.00337	0.35	89	87
1980	0.00441	0.55	100	100
1985	0.00419	0.34	67	74

Source: International Financial Statistics, various issues.

Figure 6-2 shows the effective dollar index with a base 1980 = 100. The effective exchange rate index shows the very large appreciation of the dollar relative to the currencies of our trading partners in the 1980s—more than 40 percent between 1980 and 1985—followed by a decline in the 1985–1986 period.

The effective exchange rate index measures the average nominal exchange rate. But to know whether our goods are becoming relatively cheaper or more expensive than foreign goods, we have to take into account, too, what happened to prices here and abroad. To do so we look at the *real effective exchange rate* or simply the *real exchange rate.*

The real exchange rate measures a country's competitiveness in international trade. It is given by the ratio of prices of goods abroad, measured in dollars, relative to prices of goods at home:

$$\text{Real exchange rate} \equiv R = \frac{eP_f}{P} \tag{2}$$

where P and P_f are the prices here and abroad and e is the dollar price of foreign exchange. A rise in the real exchange rate, or a real depreciation, means that foreign prices in dollars have increased relative to the prices of goods pro-

FIGURE 6-2   THE U.S. REAL EXCHANGE RATE. (Index, 1980 = 100.)
(*Source: International Financial Statistics.*)

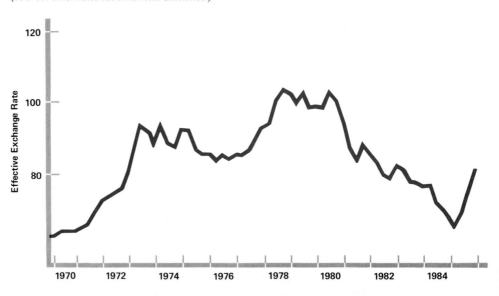

duced here, and implies, other things equal, a gain in our external competitiveness. That is, our goods become cheaper relative to foreign goods, both for us and for foreigners. For instance, if the exchange rate stays constant and prices abroad rise more than prices in the United States, the real exchange rate depreciates or rises, indicating that our goods have become cheaper relative to foreign goods. Conversely a decline in R or a real appreciation means that our goods have become relatively more expensive or that we have lost competitiveness.

Figure 6-2 shows in addition to the effective exchange rate, the U.S. real exchange rate for the 1970s and 1980s. The measure reported here shows the dollar prices of our trading partners for manufactures relative to our own prices of manufactures, eP_f/P. Changes in U.S. competitiveness were extreme in the 1980–1985 period. Note also how closely the nominal and real effective exchange rates move together. The reason is that movements in nominal rates, not changes in prices here and abroad, have been the main cause of changes in competitiveness. Inflation rates were not substantially different in various countries, but exchange rates moved a lot.

6-3 TRADE IN GOODS, MARKET EQUILIBRIUM, AND THE BALANCE OF TRADE

We now study the effects of trade in goods on the level of income and the effects of various disturbances on both income and the trade balance — which, from now on, we use as shorthand for the current account. We also examine policy problems which arise when the balance of trade and the level of income require different corrective actions. We do not at this stage include the capital account, so that for the present the current account and the balance of payments are the same.

In this section we fit foreign trade into *IS-LM* framework. As in Chapters 3 to 5, we assume that the price level is given and that output that is demanded will be supplied. It is both conceptually and technically easy to relax the fixed price assumption, and we shall do so in Chapter 20. But it is important to be clear on how the introduction of trade modifies the analysis of aggregate demand, and for that reason we start from a familiar and basic level.

Domestic Spending and Spending on Domestic Goods

In this subsection we want to establish how foreign trade fits into the *IS* schedule. In an open economy, part of domestic output is sold to foreigners (exports), and part of spending by domestic residents falls on foreign goods (imports). We accordingly have to modify our analysis of aggregate demand.

The most important change is that it is no longer true that domestic spending determines domestic output. What is true now is that *spending on domestic goods* determines domestic output. Spending by domestic residents falls in part on domestic goods but also in part on imports. Part of the typical American's spending is for imported beer, for instance. Demand for domestic goods that determines output, by contrast, includes exports or foreign demand along with part of spending by domestic residents.

The way in which external transactions affect the demand for domestic output was examined in Chapter 2. Recall the definitions:

$$\text{Spending by domestic residents} \equiv A \equiv C + I + G \tag{3}$$

$$\text{Spending on domestic goods} \equiv A + NX \equiv (C + I + G) + X - Q$$
$$= (C + I + G) + NX \tag{4}$$

where X is the level of exports, Q is imports, and NX is the trade balance (goods and services) surplus. The definition of spending by domestic residents $(C + I + G)$ remains that of the earlier chapters. Spending on domestic goods is total spending by domestic residents *less* their spending on imports *plus* foreign demand or exports. Since exports minus imports is the trade surplus, or net exports NX, spending on domestic goods is spending by domestic residents plus the trade surplus.

With this clarification we can return to our model of income determination. We will assume, as in Chapter 4, that domestic spending depends on the interest rate and income, so that we can write

$$A = A(Y, i) \tag{5}$$

Further, we assume now that net exports depend on our income, which affects import spending, on foreign income Y_f which affects foreign demand for our exports, and on the real exchange rate R defined above. A rise in R or a real depreciation improves our trade balance as demand shifts from foreign goods to those produced at home:[5]

$$NX = X(Y_f, R) - RQ(Y, R) = NX(Y, Y_f, R) \tag{6}$$

We can immediately state three important results:

1. A rise in foreign income, other things being equal, improves the home country's trade balance and therefore raises aggregate demand.
2. A real depreciation by the home country improves the trade balance and therefore increases aggregate demand.

---

[5] Note two points about net exports in equation (6). First, we measure net exports in terms of domestic output. To do so we must multiply the volume of imports Q by the relative price of imports $eP_f/P = R$. Second, we *assume* that a real appreciation worsens the trade balance, and a real depreciation (a rise in R) improves the trade balance. This is a matter of assumption since there are opposing effects of changes in volume and in price. We return to this point in Chap. 20.

As we see below, a rise in foreign income or a real depreciation each causes a rightward shift in the *IS* curve since aggregate demand is now higher at each income level. Finally the third result is:

3. A rise in home income raises import spending and hence worsens the trade balance.

Figure 6-3 shows the net export schedule. The schedule is drawn for a given level of foreign income and a given real exchange rate. It is downward sloping since a higher level of home income raises imports and thus reduces net exports. At low levels of home income net exports are positive since import spending is very low, but as income rises so does import spending, and hence net exports fall off and ultimately become negative. The schedule is steeper the greater the increase in import spending per dollar increase in income or the larger the *marginal propensity to import.*

An increase in foreign income shows up as an exogeneous increase in exports and hence as an upward and rightward shift of the net export schedule. The same applies to a real depreciation. A real depreciation raises net exports at each level of income and hence shifts the net export schedule upward. A real appreciation by contrast, because it reduces exports and raises imports implies

FIGURE 6-3   THE NET EXPORT SCHEDULE. Net exports are a declining function of the level of income. A rise in income raises imports and hence reduces net exports. The schedule is steeper the larger the marginal propensity to import. The schedule is drawn for a given level of foreign income, Y_f, and for a given real exchange rate, R.

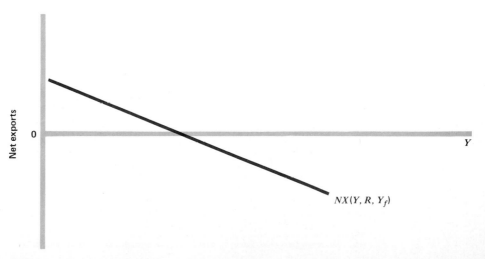

$NX(Y, R, Y_f)$

a worsening of net exports at each income level and hence a downward shift of the schedule.

Goods Market Equilibrium

The open economy *IS* curve now includes net exports as a component of aggregate demand. Thus we write

$$\text{IS curve:} \qquad\qquad Y = A(Y, i) + NX(Y, Y_f, R) \qquad\qquad (7)$$

It is immediately clear from (7) that the equilibrium level of income will now depend on both foreign income and the real exchange rate. We will therefore have to ask how disturbances in foreign income, or real exchange rate changes, affect the equilibrium level of income.

Figure 6-4 shows the effects of an increase in foreign income. Income abroad rises, say because of a tax cut or increased government spending. As a result, foreign demand for our goods and net exports rises at each level of our income. This results in a rightward shift of the *IS* curve in Figure 6-4. The new equilibrium level of income is Y'. Thus a rise in foreign income unambiguously raises home income. The lower panel of Figure 6-4 shows the impact on net exports. The increased foreign income causes an upward shift of the *NX* schedule. At the new equilibrium level of income Y', net exports have increased.

In the same way we can show that a real depreciation by the home country shifts the *IS* schedule to the right and hence leads to a rise in equilibrium income and to an improvement in net exports.

Table 6-3 summarizes the effects of different disturbances on the equilibrium levels of income and net exports. Each of these examples can be worked out using the *IS-LM* schedule in conjunction with the net export schedule.

Repercussion Effects

So far we have looked at the effects of disturbances such as a depreciation on the home country. We have not, however, taken account of the interdepen-

TABLE 6-3	EFFECTS OF DISTURBANCES ON INCOME AND NET EXPORTS		
	Increase in home spending	Increase in foreign income	Real depreciation
Income	+	+	+
Net exports	−	+	+

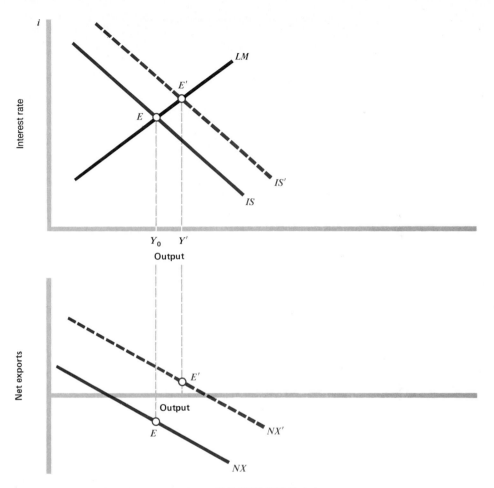

FIGURE 6-4   THE EFFECT OF A RISE IN FOREIGN INCOME. A rise
in foreign income shifts the *IS* schedule out and to the right. Equilibrium
income rises from E to E'. In the lower panel the increased foreign
income shows up as an upward shift of the *NX* schedule. At the new
equilibrium level of income the level of net exports has risen, though by
less than the rise in exports because with domestic income rising there
is also some increase in imports.

dence among economies. When we increase government spending, our income rises; part of the increase in income will be spent on imports, which
means that income will rise abroad too. The increase in foreign income will
then raise their demand for our goods, which in turn adds to the domestic
income expansion brought about by higher government spending and so on.

TABLE 6-4   INTERNATIONAL MULTIPLIERS (Percentage Increase in GNP Due to Increased Government Spending Equal to 1 Percent of GNP)

Effect on	INITIATING COUNTRY		
	U.S.	Japan	Germany
U.S.	2.0	0.1	0.1
Japan	0.6	1.8	0.1
Germany	0.5	0.2	1.5
Canada	0.8	0.1	0.1

Source: OECD Economic Studies No. 1, Autumn 1983, pp. 72–73.

These *repercussion effects* are very important in practice. When the United States expands it will, as a locomotive, pull the rest of the world into an expansion. Likewise, if the rest of the world expands, we share in the expansion. To get an idea of the size of these interdependence effects, we look at estimates of international multipliers. Table 6-4 shows multipliers for a one percentage point of GNP increase in government spending in various countries.

First note that each country responds most to its own expansion. For instance for the United States an increase in its own level of government spending raises income much more than a foreign rise in spending. But foreign spending increases *do* spill over. A rise in government spending in Japan or in Germany will raise output in the United States and a U.S. rise in spending will have a very sizable effect on Canada, a country from which we import a significant share of our total imports.

There is an asymmetry in the table: Why does an extra 1 percent of GNP increase in government spending in the United States raise Japanese or German income more than a 1 percent increase in their spending raises income in the United States? The reason is that we are much larger, so that a spending increase of 1 percent of our income represents a much larger increase in world demand than 1 percent of their GNP extra spending in Germany or Japan.

In Table 6-5 we show the impact of changes in real exchange rates on real GNP. Note that the impact on output in the depreciating country is always positive, just as we assumed above. Thus for the United States, for example, a 10 percent real depreciation will raise output by almost half a percentage point. But the effect abroad is the opposite. U.S. real depreciation draws demand away from the rest of the world and hence reduces income there. The table shows that a U.S. real depreciation will reduce output sizably in Europe

TABLE 6-5   IMPACT OF REAL DEPRECIATION (Percentage Increase in GNP Due to a 10 Percent Depreciation)

Impact on	DEPRECIATING COUNTRY		
	U.S.	Japan	Germany
U.S.	0.4	−0.2	−0.1
Japan	−0.9	1.7	−0.3
OECD Europe	−0.5	−0.4	1.3*

* Impact on Germany.
Source: OECD Economic Studies, No. 1, Autumn 1983, p. 82.

and Japan. Clearly then real exchange rate changes are an important element in the determination of income and of international linkages.

6-4 CAPITAL MOBILITY AND THE POLICY MIX

So far, we have been assuming that trade is confined to goods and services and does not include assets. Now we allow for trade in assets and see the effects of such trade on the equilibrium of the economy and its desired policy mix.

One of the striking facts about the international economy is the high degree of integration or linkage among financial or capital markets — the markets in which bonds and stocks are traded. The capital markets are very fully integrated among the main industrial countries. Yields on assets in New York and yields on comparable assets in Canada, for example, move closely together. If rates in New York rose relative to those in Canada, investors would turn to lending in New York, while borrowers would turn to Toronto. With lending up in New York and borrowing up in Toronto, yields would quickly fall into line.

Figure 6-5 shows the yields on U.S. short-term securities and their Canadian counterparts.[6] The yield differential is consistently small. There is impressive evidence in Figure 6-5 of the linkage of international capital markets that ensures consistency among interest rates in different countries. That consistency arises because the flow of capital — lending to and by foreigners — to countries with higher interest rates soon equalizes such rates.

---

[6] The yield on Canadian securities in Fig. 6-5 is "covered," which means that it is without exchange risk. Any yield differential in Fig. 6-5 is *not* a reflection of exchange risk.

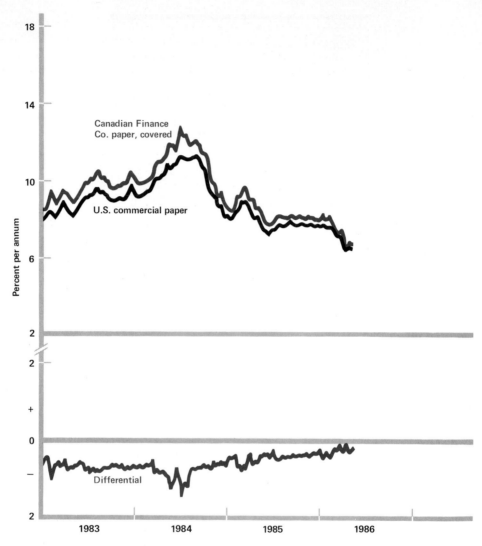

FIGURE 6-5   INTERNATIONAL INTEREST RATE LINKAGES.
(*Source:* Board of Governors of the Federal Reserve, *Selected Interest Rates and Exchange Rates.*)

The high degree of capital market integration that is reflected in Figure 6-5 suggests that any one country's interest rates cannot get too far out of line from those in the rest of the world without bringing about capital flows that tend to restore yields to the world level. As we have noted, if Canadian yields fell relative to U.S. yields, there would be a capital outflow from Canada because lenders would take their funds out of Canada and borrowers would try to raise funds in Canada. From the point of view of the balance of payments, this implies that a relative decline in interest rates — a decline in our rates relative to those abroad — will worsen the balance of payments because of the capital outflow — lending abroad by U.S. residents.

The recognition that interest rates affect capital flows and the balance of payments has important implications for stabilization policy. First, because monetary and fiscal policies affect interest rates, they have an effect on the capital account and therefore on the balance of payments. The effects of monetary and fiscal policies on the balance of payments are *not* limited to the trade balance effects discussed above but extend to the capital account. The second implication is that the way in which monetary and fiscal policies work in affecting the domestic economy and the balance of payments changes when there are international capital flows. We will examine the monetary-fiscal policy mix that can be used to achieve internal and external balance, and we will see that capital flows can be used to *finance* the trade balance and thus help in achieving overall balance of payments.

The Balance of Payments and Capital Flows

We introduce the role of capital flows in a framework in which we assume that the home country faces a given price of imports and a given export demand. In addition, we assume that the world rate of interest is given and that capital flows into the home country at a rate that is higher, the higher the home country's rate of interest. That is, foreign investors purchase more of our assets the higher the interest rate our assets pay relative to the world interest rate. The rate of capital inflow, CF, or the capital account surplus, is an increasing function of our rate of interest. At a level equal to the world rate, $i = i_f$, there are no capital flows. If the domestic interest rate is higher, there will be an inflow, and conversely, if the domestic interest rate is lower, there will be a capital outflow.

Next we look at the balance of payments. The balance of payments surplus BP is equal to the trade surplus NX plus the capital account surplus CF:

$$BP = NX(Y, \ . \ . \ .) + CF(i, i_f) \tag{8}$$

In equation (8) we have shown the trade balance as a function of income and the capital account as a function of the domestic interest rate. An increase in income worsens the trade balance, and an increase in the interest rate raises capital inflows and thus improves the capital account. It follows that when income increases, an increase in interest rates could maintain overall balance of payments equilibrium. The trade deficit would be financed by a capital inflow.

That idea is extremely important. Countries frequently face the following dilemma: domestic output is low, and they want to expand, *but* the balance of payments is in difficulty and they do not believe they can run a larger balance of payments deficit. If the level of income increases, net exports will fall as domestic demand rises, thereby tending to worsen the balance of payments — which the country wants to avoid. The presence of interest-sensitive capital flows suggests that a country can undertake an expansionary domestic policy without necessarily running into balance of payments problems.

A country can afford an increase in domestic income and import spending, provided it is accompanied by an increase in interest rates so as to attract a capital inflow. But how can an expansion in domestic income be achieved at the same time that interest rates are increased? The answer is to use fiscal policy to increase aggregate demand to the full-employment level and monetary policy to get the right amount of capital flows.[7]

Internal and External Balance

Countries typically want their balance of payments to be close to balance. Otherwise the central bank is either losing reserves — which it cannot keep on doing — or gaining reserves, which it does not want to do forever. The goal of balance of payments equilibrium is called *external balance.* In addition, countries want to maintain *internal balance,* or full employment. In this section and the next we discuss policy mixtures that will produce both internal and external balance.

In Figure 6-6 we show the positively sloped schedule $BP = 0$, derived from equation (8), along which we have balance of payments equilibrium. To derive the slope of the $BP = 0$ line, start with an income expansion, which raises imports and worsens the balance of payments. To restore balance of payments equilibrium, interest rates have to be higher to attract the capital flows that finance the trade deficit. Thus to maintain payments balance, an income increase has to be matched by a higher interest rate, and the $BP = 0$ line is therefore upward-sloping.

The schedule is drawn for given exports and a given foreign interest rate. The higher the degree of capital mobility, the flatter the schedule. If capital is very highly responsive to interest rates, then a small increase in the interest rate will bring about very large capital flows and thus allow the financing of large trade deficits. The larger the marginal propensity to import, the steeper the schedule. An increase in income worsens the trade balance by the increase in income times the marginal propensity to import. Thus, a high propensity to import means that a given increase in income produces a large deficit and thus

---

[7] The idea of the policy mix for internal and external balance was suggested by Robert Mundell in his important paper, "The Appropriate Use of Monetary and Fiscal Policy under Fixed Exchange Rates," *I.M.F. Staff Papers,* March 1962. Mundell's work on international macroeconomics has been extraordinarily important, and the adventurous student should certainly consult his two books: *International Economics* (New York: Macmillan, 1967) and *Monetary Theory* (Pacific Palisades, Calif.: Goodyear, 1971).

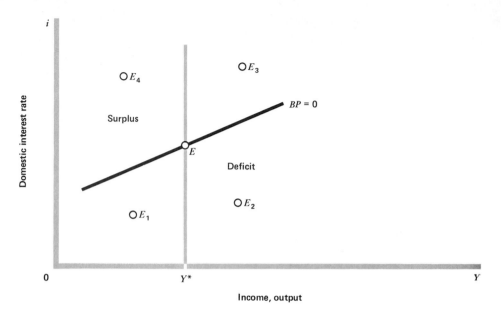

FIGURE 6-6 INTERNAL AND EXTERNAL BALANCE Full employment obtains at an output level Y^*. The internal balance schedule is
therefore the vertical line at Y^*. Along $BP = 0$ the balance of payments
is in equilibrium. A rise in income worsens the trade balance, and
therefore higher interest rates are required to attract capital inflows that
finance the trade deficit. Points above and to the left of the BP schedule
correspond to surpluses and points below and to the right to deficits in
the balance of payments. The higher the degree of capital mobility, the
flatter the BP schedule, since then a small increase in our interest rates
creates large capital flows.

requires a large increase in interest rates to bring about the right amount of
capital flows to offset the trade deficit. Points above and to the left of the
$BP = 0$ schedule correspond to a surplus, and points below and to the right to a
deficit. We have also drawn, in Figure 6-6, full-employment output Y^*. The
full equilibrium with both internal and external balance is at point E.

We can talk about policy problems in terms of points in the four quadrants
of Figure 6-6. Each such point would be an intersection of an IS and an LM
curve, and the question is how to use monetary and fiscal policy — shifting the
IS and LM curves — to get full equilibrium. Thus, point E_1, for example,
corresponds to a case of unemployment and a balance of payments deficit.
Point E_2, by contrast, is a case of deficit and overemployment. What are points
E_3 and E_4?

The Policy Mix

Suppose that the economy is at point E_1. The appropriate policy to produce internal and external balance requires a higher level of employment for internal balance and higher interest rates and/or a lower level of income for external balance.

There is a policy dilemma at E_1 because employment considerations suggest income should be raised and balance of payments considerations suggest it should be reduced. However, there is a way out of the dilemma. Suppose we reduce the money supply and thus raise interest rates. To offset the effects of the higher interest rates on income, we could use expansionary fiscal policy. Clearly, we would keep income constant and reach balance of payments equilibrium by getting interest rates high enough. However, we can do better. We can use fiscal policy to get us all the way to full employment and use tight money, in the form of higher interest rates, to achieve balance of payments equilibrium. Thus we can get to point E with both internal and external balance.

The lesson we have just derived is that, under fixed exchange rates, we should expand income through fiscal policy whenever there is unemployment and use tight money whenever there is a balance of payments deficit. The combination of policies moves us to both internal and external balance. With a situation like point E_4, we want to use the same principle, but the economic conditions are different. Here we have a surplus and unemployment. Accordingly, we need expansionary fiscal policy to achieve full employment and expansionary monetary policy to reduce interest rates. Point E_4 is actually *not* a dilemma situation, since any form of expansionary policy moves us in the right direction with respect to both targets.

We leave it to you to work through the remaining cases and note here merely the principle: Under fixed exchange rates and with capital mobility, we use monetary policy to achieve external balance and fiscal policy to achieve full employment. What is the experience with such a rule? There is little doubt that tight money, for balance of payments reasons, is the oldest remedy in the policy maker's medicine chest. Since monetary policy is a flexible tool, attainment of external balance in the short run through tight money is relatively easy.

Limitations of the Policy Mix

The argument for a fiscal-monetary policy mix to handle both internal and external balance problems is persuasive but overlooks two important limitations.

First, a country will typically not be indifferent to the level of domestic interest rates. Even if fiscal policy were sufficiently flexible to implement the policy mix, it would still be true that the composition of domestic output would depend on the mix. Thus, a country that attempts an expansion in aggregate demand, together with tight money, effectively restricts the construction sector and investment spending in general. The notion of a policy mix with monetary policy devoted to the balance of payments therefore overlooks the fact that the interest rate determines the *composition* as well as the level of aggregate spending.

The second consideration concerns the composition of the balance of payments. Countries are not indifferent about the makeup of their balance of payments between the current account deficit and the capital account surplus. Even if the overall balance is in equilibrium so that one target is satisfied, there is still the problem that a capital account surplus or capital inflow means net external borrowing: our country's debts to foreigners are increasing. Those debts will eventually have to be repaid.

Under a system of fixed exchange rates, there are circumstances under which a country — much like an individual — will find it useful to borrow in order to finance, say, a transitory shortfall of export earnings. But continued large-scale borrowing from abroad is not consistent with a fixed exchange rate over long periods. Large-scale borrowing eventually places the country in a position where the interest payments to foreigners become a major burden. Faced with the prospect of continued foreign borrowing on a large scale in order to maintain its exchange rate fixed, a country would be well advised to implement adjustment policies that improve the current account balance.

6-5 PERFECT CAPITAL MOBILITY UNDER FIXED EXCHANGE RATES

So far we have assumed that an increase in the interest differential in favor of the home country will attract *some* extra capital inflow. But what happens when the response of capital flows to interest differentials becomes huge? A useful benchmark case is one where capital is *perfectly mobile.* Under perfect capital mobility the slightest interest differential provokes literally infinite capital flows. This situation arises if domestic and foreign assets are *perfect substitutes* — portfolio holders are completely indifferent which asset they hold and hence they will choose to hold the one which has the higher rate of return. Even the slightest shift in the interest differential will provoke a shift of everybody's portfolio into the highest yielding asset.

In a situation of perfect capital mobility central banks cannot conduct an independent monetary policy under fixed exchange rates. The reason is the following. Suppose a country wishes to raise interest rates. Monetary policy is tightened, and as a result interest rates rise. Immediately portfolio holders worldwide see the higher rate and shift their wealth into the country with the high interest rates. As a result of the huge capital inflow the balance of payments shows a gigantic surplus; the resulting pressure for currency appreciation forces the central bank to intervene, buying foreign money and selling domestic money in exchange. The intervention implies that the home money stock is increased. As a result the initial monetary contraction is undone. The process comes to an end when home interest rates have been pushed back down to the initial level.

The conclusion is: *Under fixed exchange rates and perfect capital mobility a country cannot pursue an independent monetary policy. Interest rates cannot move out of line with those prevailing in the world market. Any attempt at independent monetary policy leads to capital flows and a need to intervene until interest rates are back in line with those in the world market.*

Table 6-6 shows the steps in the argument. Step 4—the pressure for appreciation—occurs because the capital inflow means foreigners are trying to buy the domestic currency in exchange for their currency, thereby tending to raise the price of the domestic currency in terms of their currencies. The commitment to a fixed rate involves step 5. With the exchange rate tending to appreciate because foreigners are trying to buy the domestic currency, the central bank has to provide the domestic currency. Just as in an open market operation the central bank buys and sells bonds for money so does intervention in the foreign exchange market mean buying and selling foreign money (yen or DM or Canadian dollars) for domestic money. Thus the money supply is linked to the balance of payments. Surpluses imply *automatic* monetary expansion; deficits imply monetary contraction.

It is worthwhile to look at this point in terms of the open economy *IS-LM* model. In Figure 6-7 we show the *IS* and *LM* schedules as well as the *BP* = 0 schedule which now, because of perfect capital mobility, is a horizontal line. Only at a level of interest rates equal to those abroad, $i = i_f$, can we have payments balance. Any slight increase in interest rates brings in infinite capital inflows, pressure for appreciation, intervention, and hence monetary expansion. Conversely, any tendency for interest rates to fall below the world level leads to capital outflows, pressure on the exchange rate toward depreciation, intervention, and monetary contraction. Thus the *LM* schedule, rather than staying put, moves in response to the changing money supply. Any time the interest rate is above i_f, the central bank will be buying foreign exchange and selling home money, leading to a rightward shift of the *LM* schedule. Conversely, when interest rates fall below i_f, the central bank is selling foreign exchange and buying home money, and hence the *LM* schedule is shifting to the left.

TABLE 6-6	PAYMENTS IMBALANCES, INTERVENTION, AND THE MONEY SUPPLY
1. Tightening of money	5. Intervention selling home money, buying foreign money
2. Increased interest rates	6. Monetary expansion due to intervention lowers interest rate
3. Capital inflow, payments surplus	7. Back to initial interest rates and payments balance
4. Pressure for appreciation	

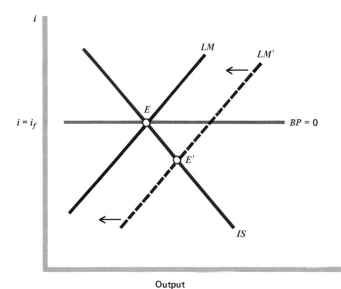

FIGURE 6-7   MONETARY EXPANSION UNDER FIXED RATES AND
PERFECT CAPITAL MOBILITY. Under perfect capital mobility the
balance of payments can only be in equilibrium at the interest rate
$i = i_f$. At even slightly higher rates there are massive capital inflows; at
lower rates there are capital outflows. A monetary expansion that cuts
interest rates to point E' causes downward pressure on the exchange
rate. The monetary authorities must intervene, selling foreign exchange
and buying domestic money until the LM schedule has shifted back to
its initial position.

Monetary Expansion

Consider now a monetary expansion that starts from point E. The LM schedule
shifts down and to the right, and the economy moves to point E'. But at E' there
is a large payments deficit and hence pressure for the exchange rate to depreciate. The central bank must intervene, selling foreign exchange and buying
home money. As a result, the LM schedule shifts back up and to the left. The
process continues until the initial equilibrium at E is reestablished.

Indeed, with perfect capital mobility the economy never even gets to
point E'. The response of capital flows is so large and rapid that the central
bank is forced to reverse the initial contraction of the money stock as soon as it
attempts it. Conversely, any attempt to expand the money stock would immediately lead to vast reserve losses, forcing a contraction of the money stock and
a return to the initial equilibrium.

Fiscal Expansion

Fiscal expansion under fixed exchange rates with perfect capital mobility is by contrast extremely effective. We describe the effects in terms of the *IS-LM* model, but we do not draw the diagram, leaving that for the problem set.

With the money supply initially unchanged, a fiscal expansion moves the *IS* curve up to the right, tending to increase both the interest rate and the level of output. The higher interest rate sets off a capital inflow that would appreciate the exchange rate. To maintain the exchange rate, the central bank has to expand the money supply, thus increasing income further. Equilibrium is restored when the money supply has increased enough to drive the interest rate back to its original level, $i = i_f$.

The Endogenous Money Stock

Although the assumption of perfect capital mobility is extreme, it us a useful benchmark case that in the end is not too far from reality. The commitment to maintain a fixed exchange rate makes the money stock endogenous, because the central bank has to provide the foreign exchange or domestic money that is demanded at the fixed exchange rate. Thus even when capital mobility is less than perfect, the central bank has only limited ability to change the money supply without having to worry about maintaining the exchange rate.

6-6 PERFECT CAPITAL MOBILITY AND FLEXIBLE EXCHANGE RATES: THE MUNDELL-FLEMING MODEL

In this section we explore how monetary and fiscal policy work for an economy that has fully flexible exchange rates and perfect capital mobility. The analysis is once again an extension to the open economy of the standard *IS-LM* model. It has a special name, the *Mundell-Fleming model.* Robert Mundell, now a professor at Columbia University, and the late Marcus Fleming, who was a researcher at the International Monetary Fund, developed this analysis in the 1960s, well before flexible exchange rates came into operation.[8] Although later research has refined their analysis, the initial Mundell-Fleming formulation shown here remains essentially intact as a way of understanding how policies work under high capital mobility and flexible rates.

Under fully flexible exchange rates the central bank does not intervene in the market for foreign exchange. The exchange rate must adjust to clear the

---

[8] See Robert A. Mundell "Capital Mobility and Stabilization Policy under Fixed and Flexible Exchange Rates," *Canadian Journal of Economics,* November 1963, and Marcus Fleming "Domestic Financial Policies under Fixed and under Floating Exchange Rates," International Monetary Fund *Staff Papers,* vol. 9, 1962, pp. 369–379. An up-to-date discussion can be found in Jacob Frenkel and Michael Mussa, "Asset Markets, Exchange Rates and the Balance of Payments," in R. W. Jones and P. Kenen (eds.), *Handbook of International Economics,* vol. 2 (Amsterdam, North-Holland, 1985).

market so that the demand and supply for foreign exchange balance. Without central bank intervention, therefore, the balance of payments must be equal to zero.

Under fully flexible exchange rates the absence of intervention implies a zero balance of payments. Any current account deficit must be financed by private capital inflows, a surplus by capital outflows. Adjustments in the exchange rate assure the balancing of the current and capital account.

The second implication of fully flexible exchange rates is that the central bank can set the money supply at will. Since there is no obligation to intervene, there is no longer any link between the balance of payments and the money supply.

Perfect capital mobility implies that there is only one interest rate at which the balance of payments will balance:

$$i = i_f \tag{9}$$

Only when the home interest rate is equal to that abroad will there not be infinite capital inflows or capital outflows. Thus balance of payments equilibrium requires $i = i_f$. We show this in Figure 6-8 by the line $BP = 0$, which is a horizontal schedule at the level of the world interest rate i_f. From equation (7) we remember that the real exchange rate is a determinant of aggregate demand and hence appears as a shift variable in the *IS* schedule. Given prices, P and P_f, a depreciation makes the home country more competitive, improves net exports, and hence shifts the *IS* schedule to the right. Conversely, a real appreciation means our goods become relatively more expensive, and hence the trade balance worsens and demand for domestic goods declines so that the *IS* schedule shifts to the left.

The arrows in Figure 6-8 link the movement of aggregate demand to the interest rate. If the home interest rate were higher than i_f, capital inflows would cause currency appreciation. At any point above $BP = 0$ the exchange rate is appreciating, competitiveness is declining, and aggregate demand is falling. Thus the *IS* schedule will be shifting to the left. Conversely, any point below $BP = 0$ corresponds to depreciation, improving competitiveness, and increasing aggregate demand. The *IS* schedule will therefore be shifting to the right. We now see how various disturbances affect output and the exchange rate.

Adjustment to a Real Disturbance

We have now completed our model, represented by equations (7) and (8) and Figure 6-9, and can ask how the economy will adjust to disturbances. In particular, we want to know how various changes affect our level of output, the interest rate, and the exchange rate. The first change we look at is an exogenous rise in the world demand for our goods, or an increase in exports. The change in export demand is a real disturbance to the economy, or a disturbance that originates in the goods market.

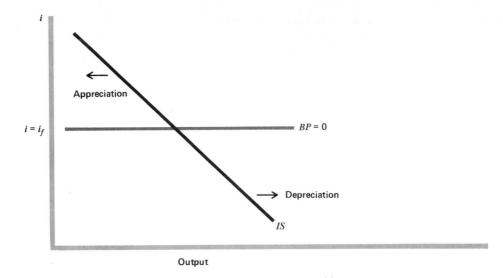

FIGURE 6-8   THE EFFECT OF EXCHANGE RATES ON AGGRE-
GATE DEMAND. With perfect capital mobility and flexible rates, capital
flows have a strong impact on demand. If home rates fall below i_f,
there are capital outflows leading to exchange depreciation, a gain in
competitiveness, and hence a rise in demand for domestic goods
shown by the rightward shift of the *IS* schedule. Conversely, if interest
rates go above i_f the capital inflows lead to appreciation, loss of
competitiveness, and a decline in demand for domestic goods shown
by the leftward shifting *IS* curve.

Starting from an initial equilibrium at point E in Figure 6-9, we see that
the increase in foreign demand implies an excess demand for our goods. At the
initial interest rate, exchange rate, and output level, demand for our goods
now exceeds the available supply. For goods market equilibrium, at the initial
interest rate and exchange rate, we require a higher level of output. Accordingly, the *IS* schedule shifts out and to the right.

Now consider for a moment point E', where the goods and money markets
clear. Here output has increased to meet the increased demand. The rise in
income has increased money demand and thus raised equilibrium interest
rates. But is point E' an equilibrium? It is not, because the balance of payments
is not in equilibrium. In fact, we would not reach point E' at all. The tendency
for the economy to move in that direction, as we show now, will bring about an
exchange rate appreciation that will take us all the way back to the initial
equilibrium at E.

THE ADJUSTMENT PROCESS

Suppose, then, that the increase in foreign demand takes place and that, in response, there is a tendency for output and income to increase. The induced increase in money demand will raise interest rates and thus will bring us out of line with interest rates internationally. The resulting capital inflows immediately put pressure on the exchange rate. The capital inflow causes our currency to appreciate.

FIGURE 6-9   EFFECTS OF AN INCREASE IN THE DEMAND FOR EXPORTS. A rise in foreign demand for our goods, at the initial exchange rate and interest rate at point E, creates an excess demand for goods. The IS schedule shifts out to IS', and the new goods and money market equilibrium is at point E'. But at E' our interest rate exceeds that abroad. Capital will tend to flow into our country in response to the increased interest rate, and the resulting balance of payments surplus leads to currency appreciation. The appreciation means that we become less competitive. The IS schedule starts shifting back as a result of the appreciation, and the process continues until the initial equilibrium at E is reached again. In the end, increased exports (or a fiscal expansion) do not change output. They simply lead to currency appreciation and thereby to an offsetting change in net exports.

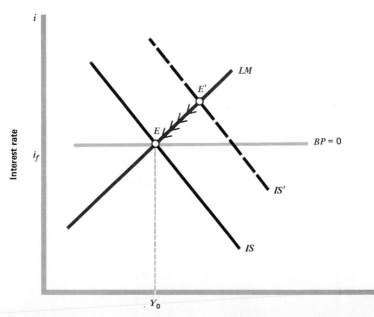

BOX

6-1

FISCAL POLICY AND THE DOLLAR 1980–1985

In the early 1980s the U.S. dollar, as we saw before, appreciated massively in world markets. A ready explanation is given by the behavior of fiscal policies in the United States and abroad. In the United States the budget shifted toward a large full-employment deficit. Abroad, by contrast, fiscal policies shifted toward restraint. The Mundell-Fleming model implies that, as a result, the U.S. dollar should have appreciated while the U.S. current account should have worsened. This is, of course, exactly what happened.

Table 1 shows the shifts in the full employment budget for the United States, for Germany, and for Japan.

TABLE 1 CUMULATIVE CHANGE IN FULL-EMPLOYMENT BUDGET DEFICITS, 1980–1985 (Percent of GNP)		
United States	Germany	Japan
4.5	−4.2	−3.2

The accompanying figure shows the impact of the fiscal policy changes on the real exchange rate and on the current account (measured as a percent of GNP). The dollar appre-

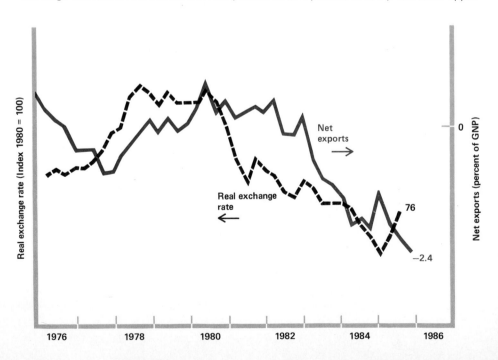

ciated strongly, and the external balance worsened steadily. It is interesting to note that the United States expanded strongly *despite* so large a deterioration in the external balance. The reason is that the deterioration in the current account only partly *crowded out* or offset the fiscal stimulus. The net effect of the fiscal expansion and the resulting deterioration in net exports was still an above average recovery from the 1982 recession.

But the recovery was not shared equally by all sectors. In particular, the loss in external competitiveness was keenly felt in manufacturing. While economy-wide employment over the 1979–1985 period increased by 10 percent, employment in manufacturing actually fell by 8 percent. The openness of the economy, and the loss in competitiveness brought about by appreciation thus left manufacturing largely out of the strong recovery. The result was powerful pressure for protection. Many manufacturing firms and, as a result, many in Congress, called for protection against import competition. The pressure for protection was one of the reasons Congress and the administration became more actively concerned about the need to correct the budget deficit and with it dollar overvaluation and excessive external deficits.

The exchange appreciation means, of course, that import prices fall and that domestic goods become relatively more expensive. Demand shifts away from domestic goods, and net exports decline. In terms of Figure 6-9, the appreciation implies that the *IS* schedule shifts back from *IS′* to the left. Next, we have to ask how far the exchange appreciation will go and to what extent it will therefore dampen the expansionary effect of increased net exports.

The exchange rate will keep appreciating as long as our interest rate exceeds the world level. This implies that the exchange appreciation must continue until the *IS* schedule has shifted back all the way to its initial position. Thus adjustment is shown by the arrows along the *LM* schedule. Only when we return to point *E* will output and income have reached a level consistent with monetary equilibrium at the world rate of interest.

We have now shown that under conditions of perfect capital mobility, an expansion in exports has no lasting effect on equilibrium output. With perfect capital mobility the tendency for interest rates to rise, as a result of the increase in export demand, leads to currency appreciation and thus to a complete offset of the increase in exports. Once we return to point *E*, net exports are back to their initial level. The exchange rate has, of course, appreciated. Imports will increase as a consequence of the appreciation, and the initial expansion in exports is in part offset by the appreciation of our exchange rates.

FISCAL POLICY

We can extend the usefulness of this analysis by recognizing that it is valid not only for an increase in exports. The same analysis applies to a fiscal expansion. A tax cut or an increase in government spending would lead to an expansion in demand in just the same way as increased exports do. Again, the tendency for interest rates to rise leads to appreciation and therefore to a fall in exports and increased imports. There is, accordingly, complete crowding out here. The crowding out takes place not as in Chapter 5 because higher interest rates reduce investment, but because the exchange appreciation reduces net exports.

The important lesson here is that real disturbances to demand do not affect equilibrium output under flexible rates with perfect capital mobility. We can drive the lesson home by comparing a fiscal expansion under flexible rates with the results we derived for the fixed rate case. In the previous section, we showed that with fixed rates, fiscal expansion under conditions of capital mobility is highly effective in raising equilibrium output. For flexible rates, by contrast, a fiscal expansion does not change equilibrium output. Instead, it produces an offsetting exchange rate appreciation and a shift in the composition of domestic demand toward foreign goods and away from domestic goods.

We turn next to the analysis of a monetary disturbance.

Adjustment to a Monetary Disturbance

We now show that under flexible exchange rates, an increase in the money stock leads to an increase in income and a depreciation of the exchange rate. The analysis uses Figure 6-10. We start from an initial position at point E and consider an increase in the nominal quantity of money, M. Since prices are given, we have an increase in the real money stock, M/P. At E there will be an excess supply of real balances. To restore equilibrium, interest rates would have to be lower or income would have to be larger. Accordingly, the LM schedule shifts down and to the right to LM'.

We ask once again whether point E' is the new equilibrium. At E', goods and money markets are in equilibrium (at the initial exchange rate), but it is clear that interest rates have fallen below the world level. Capital outflows will therefore put pressure on the exchange rate. The exchange depreciation caused by the low level of interest rates implies that import prices increase, domestic goods become more competitive, and, as a result, demand for our output expands. The exchange depreciation therefore shifts the IS curve out and to the right. As the arrows indicate, exchange depreciation continues until the relative price of domestic goods has fallen enough to raise demand and output to the level indicated by point E''. Only at E'' do we have goods and money market equilibrium compatible with the world rate of interest. Consequently, there is no further tendency for exchange rates and relative prices, and hence demand, to change.[9]

We have now shown that a monetary expansion leads to an increase in output and a depreciation of the exchange rate under flexible rates. One way

---

[9] In the problem set at the end of this chapter we ask you to show that the current account improves between E and E'', even though the increased level of income increases imports.

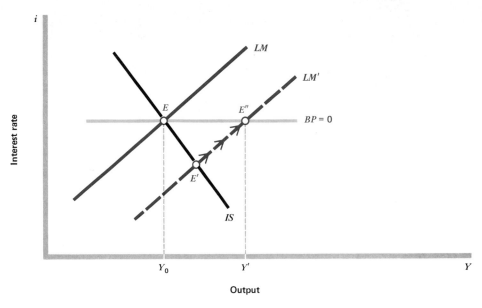

FIGURE 6-10   EFFECTS OF AN INCREASE IN THE MONEY STOCK.
A monetary expansion shifts the *LM* schedule to *LM'*. At point *E'* the
goods and money markets clear, but out interest rate is below the world
level. Therefore capital will tend to flow out, the balance of payments
goes into deficit, and the exchange rate depreciates. The depreciation
means that we become more competitive. Net exports rise, and
therefore the *IS* curve shifts out and to the right. The process continues
until we reach point *E''*. Interest rates are again at the world level, and
the depreciation has led to a higher level of income. Monetary policy
thus works by increasing net exports.

of thinking about this result is that with P fixed, an increase in M increases M/P.
The demand for real balances is, from equation (4), equal to $L(i, Y)$. Since i
cannot differ from the world rate of interest, Y has to rise to equate the demand for money to the supply. The exchange depreciation raises net exports,
and that increase in net exports, in turn, sustains the higher level of output and
employment. One interesting implication of our analysis, then, is the proposition that monetary expansion improves the current account through the induced depreciation.

How do our results compare with those of a fixed exchange rate world?
Under fixed rates, the monetary authorities cannot control the nominal money
stock, and an attempt to expand money will merely lead to a reserve loss as the
central bank attempts to prevent the tendency for the exchange rate to depreciate in response to declining interest rates. Under flexible rates, by contrast,

the central bank does not intervene, and so the money stock increase is *not* reversed in the foreign exchange market. The depreciation and expansion in output actually do take place, given the assumed sticky prices. The fact that the central bank *can* control the money stock under flexible rates is one of the most important aspects of that exchange rate system.

Beggar-Thy-Neighbor Policy and Competitive Depreciation

We extend the analysis of the fixed price variable employment model with a brief discussion of the international implications of exchange depreciation and changes in net exports. We showed that a monetary expansion in the home country leads to exchange depreciation, an increase in net exports, and therefore an increase in output and employment. But our increased net exports correspond to a deterioration in the trade balance abroad. The domestic depreciation shifts demand from foreign goods toward domestic goods. Abroad, output and employment therefore decline. It is for this reason that the depreciation-induced change in the trade balance has been called a *beggar-thy-neighbor policy* — it is a way of exporting unemployment or of creating domestic employment at the expense of the rest of the world.

The recognition that exchange depreciation is mainly a way of shifting demand from one country to another, rather than changing the level of world demand, is important. It implies that exchange rate adjustment can be a useful policy when countries find themselves in different stages of a business cycle — for example, one in a boom (with overemployment) and the other in a recession. In that event, a depreciation by the country experiencing a recession would shift world demand in that direction and thus work to reduce divergences from full employment in each country.

By contrast, when countries' business cycles are highly synchronized, such as in the 1930s or in the aftermath of the oil shock in 1973, exchange rate movements will not contribute much toward world full employment. The problem is then one of the level of total world spending being deficient or excessive while exchange rate movements affect only the allocation of a *given* world demand between countries. Nevertheless, from the point of view of an individual country, exchange depreciation works to attract world demand and raise domestic output. If every country tried to depreciate to attract world demand, we would have *competitive depreciation* and a shifting around of world demand rather than an increase in the world level of spending. Coordinated monetary and/or fiscal policies are needed to increase demand and output in each country.

6-7 SUMMARY

1. The balance of payments accounts are a record of the international transactions of the economy. The current account records trade in goods and

services as well as transfer payments. The capital account records purchases and sales of assets. Any transaction that gives rise to a payment by U.S. residents is a deficit item for the United States.

2. The overall balance of payments is the sum of the current and capital accounts. If the overall balance is in deficit, we have to make more payments to foreigners than they make to us. The foreign currency for making these payments is supplied by central banks.

3. Under fixed exchange rates, the central bank maintains constant the price of foreign currencies in terms of the domestic currency. It does this by buying and selling foreign exchange at that fixed exchange rate. For that purpose, it has to keep reserves of foreign currency.

4. Under floating or flexible exchange rates, the exchange rate may change from moment to moment. In a system of clean floating, the exchange rate is determined by supply and demand without central bank intervention to affect the rate. Under dirty floating, the central bank intervenes by buying and selling foreign exchange in an attempt to influence the exchange rate.

5. The introduction of trade in goods means that some of the demand for our output comes from abroad and that some spending by our residents is on foreign goods. The demand for our goods depends on the real exchange rate as well as the levels of income at home and abroad. A real depreciation or increase in foreign income increases net exports and shifts the *IS* curve out to the right. There is equilibrium in the goods market when the demand for domestically produced goods is equal to the output of those goods.

6. The introduction of capital flows points to the effects of monetary and fiscal policy on the balance of payments through interest rate effects on capital flows. An increase in the domestic interest rate relative to the world interest rate leads to a capital inflow that can finance a balance of trade deficit.

7. A country facing the policy dilemma that it wants to expand output but cannot allow the balance of payments to deteriorate can handle that problem by combining restrictive monetary policy to raise the interest rate and attract foreign capital, with fiscal expansion to increase domestic employment.

8. When capital mobility is perfect, interest rates in the home country cannot diverge from those abroad. This has major implications for the effects of monetary and fiscal policy under fixed and floating exchange rates. These effects are summarized in Table 6-7.

9. Under fixed exchange rates and perfect capital mobility, monetary policy is powerless to affect output. Any attempt to, say, reduce the domestic interest rate by increasing the money stock would lead to a huge outflow of capital, tending to cause a depreciation which the central bank would then have to offset by buying the domestic money in exchange for foreign money. This reduces the domestic money stock, until it returns to its

TABLE 6-7	THE EFFECTS OF MONETARY AND FISCAL POLICY UNDER PERFECT CAPITAL MOBILITY	
	Fixed rates	Flexible rates
Monetary expansion	No output change; reserve losses equal to money increase	Output expansion; trade balance improves; exchange depreciation
Fiscal expansion	Output expansion; trade balance worsens	No output change; reduced net exports; exchange appreciation

original level. Under fixed exchange rates with capital mobility, the central bank cannot run an independent monetary policy.

10. Fiscal policy is highly effective under fixed exchange rates with complete capital mobility. A fiscal expansion tends to raise the interest rate, thereby leading the central bank to increase the money stock to maintain the exchange rate constant, reinforcing the expansionary fiscal effect.

11. Under floating rates, monetary policy is highly effective and fiscal policy ineffective in changing output. A monetary expansion leads to depreciation, increased exports, and increased output. Fiscal expansion however causes an appreciation and completely crowds out net exports.

12. If an economy with floating rates finds itself with unemployment, the central bank can intervene to depreciate the exchange rate and increase net exports and thus aggregate demand. Such policies are known as beggar-thy-neighbor policies, because the increase in demand for domestic output comes at the expense of demand for foreign output.

KEY TERMS

Exchange rate
Current account
Capital account
Balance of payments
Fixed exchange rate
Floating exchange rate
Intervention
Dirty floating

Nominal and real exchange rate
Depreciation
Appreciation
Repercussion effects
Capital mobility
Internal and external balance
Mundell-Fleming model
Beggar-thy-neighbor policy

PROBLEMS

1. This problem formalizes some of the questions about income and trade balance determination in the open economy. (Before doing it, read the appendix to this chapter.) We assume, as a simplification, that the interest rate is given and equal to $i = i_0$.

We assume aggregate spending by domestic residents is

$$A = \bar{A} + cY - bi$$

and net exports, NX are given by

$$NX \equiv X - Q$$

Import spending is given by

$$Q = \bar{Q} + mY$$

where $\bar{Q}$ is autonomous import spending. Exports are given and equal to

$$X = \bar{X}$$

(a) What is the total demand for domestic goods? The balance of trade?
(b) What is the equilibrium level of income?
(c) What is the balance of trade at that equilibrium level of income?
(d) What is the effect of an increase in exports on the equilibrium level of income? What is the multiplier?
(e) What is the effect of increased exports on the trade balance?

2. Suppose that, in problem 1,

$$\bar{A} = 400 \qquad c = 0.8 \qquad b = 30 \qquad i_0 = 5 (\text{percent}) \qquad \bar{Q} = 0$$
$$m = 0.2 \qquad \bar{X} = 250$$

(a) Calculate the equilibrium level of income.
(b) Calculate the balance of trade.
(c) Calculate the open economy multiplier, that is, the effect of an increase in $\bar{A}$ on equilibrium output.
(d) Assume there is a reduction in export demand of $\Delta \bar{X} = 1$ (billion). By how much does income change? By how much does the trade balance worsen?
(e) How much does a one percentage point increase in the interest rate (from 5 to 6 percent) improve the trade balance? Explain why the trade balance improves when the interest rate rises.
(f) What policies can the country pursue to offset the impact of reduced exports on domestic income and employment as well as the trade balance?

3. It is sometimes said that a central bank is a necessary condition for a balance of payments deficit. What is the explanation for this argument?

4. Consider a country that is in a position of full employment and balanced trade. Which of the following types of disturbance can be remedied with standard aggregate demand tools of stabilization? Indicate in each case the impact on external and internal balance as well as the appropriate policy response.
(a) A loss of export markets
(b) A reduction in saving and a corresponding increase in demand for domestic goods
(c) An increase in government spending
(d) A shift in demand from imports to domestic goods
(e) A reduction in imports with a corresponding increase in saving.

5. (a) Use the formula $1/(m + s)$ for the foreign trade multiplier (see the appendix) to discuss the impact on the trade balance of an increase in autonomous domestic spending.
   (b) Comment on the proposition that the more open the economy, the smaller the domestic income expansion.

6. Consider a world with some capital mobility: The home country's capital account improves as domestic interest rates rise relative to the world rate of interest. Initially, the home country is in internal and external balance. (Draw the IS, LM, and $BP = 0$ schedules.) Assume now an increase in the rate of interest abroad.
   (a) Show the effect of a foreign interest rate increase on the BP schedule.
   (b) What policy response would immediately restore internal and external balance?

7. Consider again the case of a country that faces some capital mobility. What monetary-fiscal policy mix should be prusued to offset the following disturbances?
   (a) A gain in exports
   (b) A decline in autonomous spending
   (c) An increased rate of capital outflow (at each level of domestic interest rates)

8. This question is concerned with the repercussion effects of a domestic expansion once we recognize that as a consequence output abroad will expand. Suppose that at home there is an increase in autonomous spending, $\Delta \bar{A}$, that falls entirely on domestic goods. (Assume constant interest rates throughout this problem.)
   (a) What is the resulting effect on income, disregarding repercussion effects? What is the impact on our imports, ΔQ?
   (b) Using the result for the increase in imports, we now ask what happens abroad. Our increase in imports appears to foreign countries as an increase in their exports and therefore as an increase in demand for their goods. In response, their output expands. Assuming the foreign marginal propensity to save is s^* and the foreign propensity to import is m^*, by how much will a foreign country's income expand as a result of an increase in its exports?
   (c) Now combine the pieces by writing the familiar equation for equilibrium in the domestic goods market: change in supply, ΔY, equals the total change in demand, $\Delta \bar{A} + \Delta X - m \, \Delta Y + (1 - s) \, \Delta Y$, or

$$\Delta Y = \frac{1}{s + m} (\Delta \bar{A} + \Delta X)$$

   Noting that foreign demand ΔX depends on our increased imports, we can replace ΔX with the answer to 8b to obtain a general expression for the multiplier with repercussions.
   (d) Substitute your answer for 8b in the formula for the change in foreign demand, $\Delta X = m^* \, \Delta Y^*$.
   (e) Calculate the complete change in our income, including repercussion effects. Now compare your result with the case where repercussion effects are omitted. What difference do repercussion effects make? Is our income expansion larger or smaller with repercussion effects?
   (f) Consider the trade balance effect of a domestic expansion with and without repercussion effects. Is the trade deficit larger or smaller once repercussion effects are taken into account?

9. Assume that capital is perfectly mobile, the price level is fixed, and the exchange rate is flexible. Now let the government increase purchases. Explain first why the equilibrium levels of output and the interest rate are unaffected. Then show whether the current account

improves or worsens as a result of the increased government purchases of goods and services.

10. Assume that there is perfect mobility of capital. How does the imposition of a tariff affect the exchange rate, output, and the current account? (*Hint:* Given the exchange rate, the tariff reduces our demand for imports.)

11. Explain how and why monetary policy retains its effectiveness when there is perfect mobility of capital.

12. Show graphically how fiscal policy works with capital mobility and fixed exchange rates.

13. Was U.S. policy from 1980 to 1985 consistent with a beggar-thy-neighbor approach to trade policy?

APPENDIX

In this appendix we set out the open economy *IS-LM* model. We start by assuming a simple form for the net export equation:

$$NX = \overline{X} - mY + vR \qquad R = \frac{eP^*}{P} \tag{A1}$$

where $\overline{X}$ is a constant collecting all other influences including the role of foreign income. Note that because the coefficient of the real exchange rate, v, is positive, a real depreciation or a rise in R improves the trade balance. The trade balance is more responsive to the real exchange rate the larger is v. Note, too, the influence of home income on the trade balance: A rise in income raises imports and hence worsens the trade balance. The coefficient m denotes the marginal propensity to import. It indicates the rise in imports per dollar increase in income.

With this formulation equilibrium in the goods market becomes

IS curve: $$Y = A + NX = \overline{A} + cY - bi + \overline{X} - mY + vR \tag{A2}$$

or $$Y = \frac{\overline{A} - bi + \overline{X} + vR}{1 - c + m} \tag{A2a}$$

Now note that the marginal propensity to consume, c, plus the marginal propensity to save, s, must be equal to unity: $1 = c + s$. Hence, substituting $1 - c = s$ in (A2a) we have

$$Y = \frac{\overline{A} - bi + \overline{X} + vR}{s + m} \tag{A2b}$$

We refer to the term $1/(s + m)$ as the simple open economy multiplier. It indicates the impact on home income, given interest rates, foreign income, and the real exchange rate, of an increase in domestic autonomous spending, A. Equation (A2b) also shows the impact of real depreciation on home income: A rise in the real exchange rate, R, raises home income by $v/(s + m)$. The rise is larger the more responsive the trade balance to the real exchange rate and the larger the simple open economy multiplier.

Consider next how the open economy model works under flexible exchange rates and perfect capital mobility. We simply add the *LM* schedule and the assumption $i = i_f$.

$$\frac{M}{P} = kY - hi_f \tag{A3}$$

In (A3) we have already made the substitution $i = i_f$. Thus we can determine from (A3) that the equilibrium level of income is

$$Y = \frac{1}{k}\left(\frac{M}{P} + hi_f\right) \tag{A4}$$

The home real money supply and the world interest rate thus determine the equilibrium level of income. The exchange rate adjusts to clear the goods market. Equating (A2b) and (A4) allows us to solve for the equilibrium real exchange rate:

$$R = \frac{s+m}{kv}\frac{M}{P} + \left[\frac{(s+m)h}{kv} + \frac{b}{v}\right]i_f - \frac{\overline{A} + \overline{X}}{v} \tag{A5}$$

Thus a fiscal expansion or a rise in $\overline{X}$ leads to real appreciation, while a monetary expansion leads to real depreciation.

AGGREGATE SUPPLY
AND DEMAND:
AN INTRODUCTION

So far our analysis has assumed that the price level is fixed. We studied the impacts of changes in the money supply, or of taxes, or of government spending, assuming that whatever amount of goods was demanded would be supplied, *at the existing price level.*

To put the same point in different words, we have not yet analyzed *inflation.* But, of course, inflation is one of the major concerns of citizens, policy makers, and macroeconomists. The time has therefore come to bring the price level and the inflation rate — the rate of change of the price level — into the center of our analysis of the economy. We have to study the determination of both the level of output — on which we have concentrated thus far — and the price level.

Figure 7-1 shows the model of *aggregate demand and supply* that we shall use to study the joint determination of the price level and the level of output. The aggregate demand curve *AD*, which is downward-sloping, is based entirely on the material of the earlier chapters, in particular Chapters 4 and 5. We define the aggregate demand curve in this chapter, and show why it slopes downward and what causes it to shift. The aggregate supply curve will be introduced in this chapter and developed further in Chapter 13. The intersection of the *AD* and *AS* schedules at *E* determines the equilibrium level of output, Y_0, and the equilibrium price level, P_0. Shifts in either schedule cause the price level and the level of output to change.

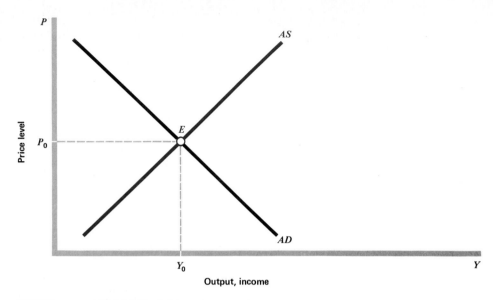

FIGURE 7-1   AGGREGATE SUPPLY AND DEMAND. The diagram shows the complete model of aggregate demand and supply that is used to explain the joint determination of the levels of output and prices. The aggregate demand curve, *AD*, is based on the *IS-LM* model studied in earlier chapters. The aggregate supply curve *AS* is developed in this chapter and Chapter 13. Their intersection at point *E* determines the level of output Y_0 and the price level P_0.

The aggregate demand-supply model is the basic macroeconomic model for studying output and price level determination — just as in microeconomics, demand and supply curves are the essential tools for studying output and price determination in a single market. But the aggregate demand and supply curves are not as simple as the microeconomic demand and supply curves. There is more going on in the background of the aggregate curves than there is in that of the microeconomic curves.[1]

7-1 INTRODUCING AGGREGATE DEMAND AND SUPPLY

Before we go deeply into the factors underlying the aggregate demand and supply curves, we show how the curves will be used. Suppose that the money

---

[1] The aggregate demand curve is sometimes referred to as the *macroeconomic demand curve*, both to emphasize that it is different from a regular demand curve in microeconomics and to distinguish it from the aggregate demand schedule in Chap. 3. We stay with the same name *AD* here after warning that the present *AD* schedule represents a considerable extension of that in Chap. 3 since it makes interest rates endogenous along the curve.

supply is increased. What effects will that have on the price level and output? In particular, does an increase in the money supply cause the price level to rise, thus producing inflation? Or does the level of output rise, as it did in the analysis of earlier chapters? Or do both output and the price level rise?

Figure 7-2 shows that an increase in the money supply shifts the aggregate demand curve AD to the right, to AD'. We see later in this chapter why that should be so. The shift of the aggregate demand curve moves the equilibrium of the economy from E to E'. The price level rises from P_0 to P', and the level of output from Y_0 to Y'. Thus an increase in the money stock causes both the level of output and the price level to rise.

The Slope of the Aggregate Supply Curve

What determines how much the price level rises and how much output increases? Looking at Figure 7-3a we see that if the aggregate supply curve is relatively flat, a shift in the AD curve raises output a lot and prices very little. By contrast, in Figure 7-3b we see that when the aggregate supply curve is nearly vertical, an increase in the money supply mainly causes prices to rise and hardly increases output at all.

FIGURE 7-2   THE EFFECTS OF AN INCREASE IN THE NOMINAL MONEY STOCK. An increase in the money stock shifts the aggregate demand curve from AD to AD'. The equilibrium moves from E to E', resulting in higher levels of both prices and output. Thus an increase in the money stock in part results in higher prices and not entirely in higher output.

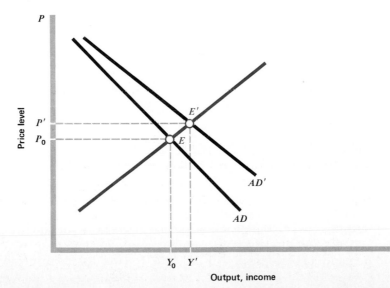

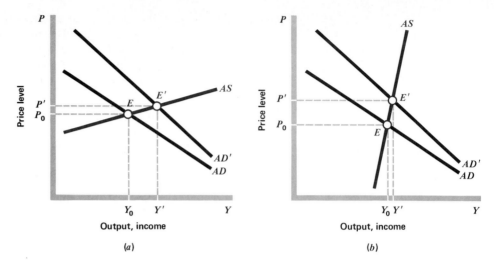

FIGURE 7-3   THE INTERACTION OF AGGREGATE SUPPLY AND
DEMAND. The effects of a shift in the aggregate demand curve from
AD to AD' depend on the slope of the aggregate supply curve. If the AS
curve is relatively flat, as in panel (a), the shift in the aggregate demand
curve results mainly in an increase in output. By contrast, in panel (b),
the shift in the aggregate demand curve results almost entirely in an
increase in the price level and very little in an increase in output.

If the aggregate supply curve is vertical, or nearly so as in Figure 7-3b,
then the analysis of the earlier chapters that showed an increase in the money
stock raising output could be very misleading. For example, if the aggregate
supply curve is vertical, an increase in the money stock will lead only to higher
prices, not to more output. Thus one of the key questions on which we shall
concentrate is what determines the shape of the aggregate supply curve.
When is it vertical, or nearly so as in Figure 7-3b? When is the aggregate
supply curve more nearly horizontal as in Figure 7-3a?

We start the analysis here by defining aggregate demand and supply.

Aggregate Demand and Supply Defined

The *aggregate demand curve* shows the combinations of the price level and
level of output at which the goods and assets markets are simultaneously in
equilibrium. At any point on the aggregate demand curve, for instance point B
in Figure 7-4, we see that for the given price level, P_B in this case, the level of
output at which the goods and assets markets are in equilibrium is Y_B.

We can already give a preliminary explanation of why the aggregate
demand curve slopes downward, based on the discussion of monetary policy in

Chapter 4. Suppose that the goods and assets markets are in equilibrium at a level of output like Y_B, with given price level P_B. Now suppose the price level falls. With a given nominal stock of money, a fall in the price level creates an increase in the quantity of *real balances*. Recall from Chapter 4 that an increase in the quantity of real balances reduces interest rates, increases investment demand, and therefore increases aggregate spending. Accordingly, when the price level falls, the equilibrium level of spending rises; therefore the *AD* curve slopes down. We go into the details in Section 7-3.

   We can also see, from the definition of the aggregate demand curve, why the analysis of the previous chapters is not at all wasted. The aggregate demand curve describes the joint equilibrium of the goods and assets markets. That is precisely what the *IS-LM* analysis describes. Thus the material we studied in earlier chapters is an essential part of the aggregate demand and supply model we shall use to analyze the simultaneous determination of the levels of output and prices.

FIGURE 7-4   AGGREGATE DEMAND AND SUPPLY CURVES DEFINED. At any point on the aggregate demand curve, such as point B, both the goods and assets markets are in equilibrium. This is the equilibrium described by the intersection of *IS* and *LM* curves in Chapter 4. For instance, with price level P_B, the level of output at which both goods and assets markets are in equilibrium is Y_B. The aggregate supply curve *AS* describes the relation between the price level and the amount of output firms wish to supply. For instance, at price level P_C, firms want to supply output Y_C.

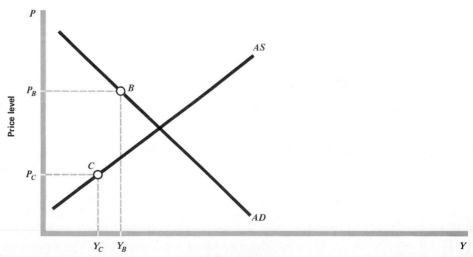

The *aggregate supply curve* describes the combinations of output and the price level such that firms are willing, at the given price level, to supply the given quantity of output. For instance, at point C in Figure 7-4, with price level P_C, firms are willing to supply output equal to Y_C. The amount of output firms are willing to supply depends on the prices they receive for their goods and the amounts they have to pay for labor and other factors of production. *Accordingly, the aggregate supply curve reflects conditions in the factor markets — especially the labor market — as well as the goods markets.*

7-2 AGGREGATE SUPPLY: TWO SPECIAL CASES

In this chapter we concentrate on two special cases in discussing aggregate supply. The first, the *Keynesian case*, shown in Figure 7-5a, is a horizontal aggregate supply curve. The *Keynesian aggregate supply curve* is horizontal, indicating that firms will supply at the existing price level whatever amount of goods is demanded.

The idea underlying the Keynesian aggregate supply curve is that because there is unemployment, firms can obtain as much labor as they want at the current wage. Their average costs of production therefore are assumed not to change as their output levels change. They are accordingly willing to supply as much as is demanded at the existing price level.

The Classical Supply Curve

Figure 7-5b shows the opposite extreme, of a vertical supply curve. In the *classical case*, the *aggregate supply curve* is vertical, indicating that the same amount of goods will be supplied whatever the price level.

The classical supply curve is based on the assumption that the labor market is always in equilibrium with full employment of the labor force. If the entire labor force is being employed, then output cannot be raised above its current level even if the price level rises. There is no more labor available to produce any extra output. Thus the aggregate supply curve will be vertical at a level of output corresponding to full employment of the labor force, Y^* in Figure 7-5b.

Underlying the vertical schedule is the assumption that the labor market is always in equilibrium because the wage adjusts rapidly to maintain equilibrium. For example, suppose that the economy is in equilibrium and the aggregate demand curve shifts to the right, as in Figure 7-2. At the existing price level, the quantity of goods demanded increases.

Now firms try to obtain more labor. Each firm attempts to hire more labor, offering to pay higher wages if necessary. But there is no more labor available in the economy, and so firms are unable to obtain more workers. Instead, in competing against each other for workers, they merely bid up wages. Because

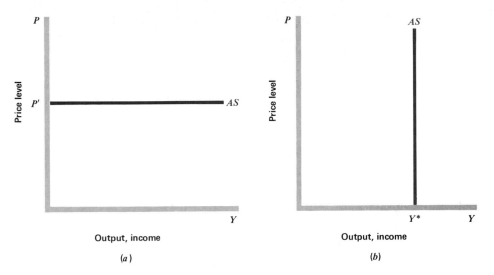

FIGURE 7-5   KEYNESIAN AND CLASSICAL SUPPLY FUNCTIONS.
The Keynesian aggregate supply curve is horizontal, implying that any
amount of output will be supplied at the existing price level. This is
shown in panel (*a*), where the *AS* curve is horizontal at price level *P'*.
The classical supply function is based on the assumption that there is
always full employment of labor, and thus that output is always at the
level of output corresponding to full employment of labor, *Y**, and
independent of the price level. This is shown by the vertical
aggregate supply curve in panel (*b*).

wages are higher, the prices the firms charge for their output will also be
higher. But output will be unchanged.

The difference between the classical and Keynesian aggregate supply
curves is that the classical supply curve is based on the belief that the labor
market works smoothly, always maintaining full employment of the labor
force. Movements in the wage are the mechanism through which full employment is maintained. The Keynesian aggregate supply curve is instead based on
the assumption that the wage does not change much or at all when there is
unemployment, and thus that unemployment can continue for some time.

These two cases — the classical, representing continuing labor market
equilibrium, and the Keynesian, assuming wages do not adjust — are the two
extremes. In Chapter 13 we develop the theory of aggregate supply and show
why the aggregate supply curve is in practice positively sloped — in between
the Keynesian and classical cases.

7-3 THE AGGREGATE DEMAND SCHEDULE

The aggregate demand curve, or schedule, shows, for each price level, the level of output at which the goods and assets markets are simultaneously in equilibrium. At any given price level, we use the *IS-LM* model to determine the level of output at which the goods and assets markets are in equilibrium.

In Figure 7-6 we show the *IS-LM* model. The position of the *IS* curve depends on fiscal policy. The *LM* schedule is drawn for a given nominal money stock M and a given price level P_0 and thus for a given real money stock M/P_0. The equilibrium interest rate is i_0, and the equilibrium level of income and spending is shown as Y_0.

A Change in the Price Level

Consider the effect of a fall in the price level from P_0 to P'. This reduction in the price level increases the real money stock from M/P_0 to M/P'. To clear the money market with an increased real money stock, either interest rates must fall, inducing the public to hold more cash balances, or output must rise, thus increasing the transactions demand for money.

Accordingly, the *LM* curve shifts downward and to the right, to *LM'*. The new equilibrium is shown at point E', where once again both the money market clears—because we are on the *LM* curve—and the goods market clears—because we are on the *IS* curve. The new equilibrium level of output is Y', corresponding to the lower price level P'. Thus a reduction in the price level, *given the nominal quantity of money*, results in an increase in equilibrium income and spending. The derivation of the *AD* schedule can be seen in Figure 7-6. The economy is initially in equilibrium at points E in both the upper and lower panels. The equilibrium interest rate is i_0, the level of output is Y_0, and the corresponding price level is P_0. Now the price level drops to P'. In the upper panel, the equilibrium moves to E', as a result of the shift of the *LM* curve to *LM'*. Corresponding to point E' in the upper panel is point E' in the lower panel, at price level P' and the level of income and output Y'.

Thus E and E' in the lower panel are both points on the *AD* schedule. We could now consider all possible price levels and the corresponding levels of real balances. For each level of real balances there is a different *LM* curve in the upper panel. Corresponding to each *LM* curve is an equilibrium level of income, which would be recorded in the lower panel at the price level that results in the *LM* curve in the upper panel. Connecting all these points gives us a downward-sloping aggregate demand curve *AD*, as shown in Figure 7-6.

The *AD* curve is downward-sloped because there is a definite relation between equilibrium spending and the price level: The higher the price level, the lower are real balances, and hence the lower the equilibrium level of spending and output.

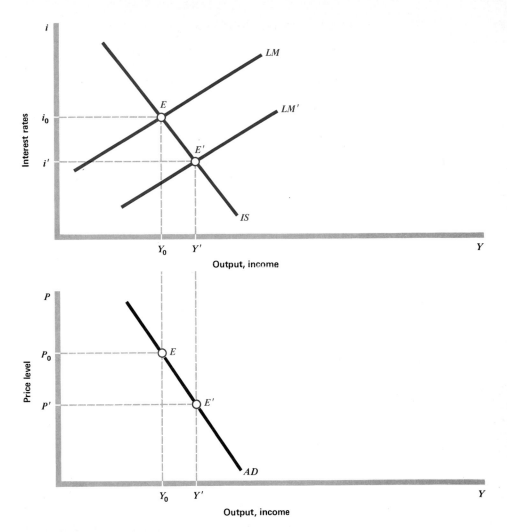

FIGURE 7-6 DERIVATION OF THE AGGREGATE DEMAND
SCHEDULE. The upper panel shows the IS schedule and the initial LM
schedule drawn for the real money stock M/P_0. Equilibrium is at point
E. In the lower panel we record that at a price level P_0 the equilibrium
level of income and spending is Y_0. This is shown by point E. At a
lower level of prices, say, P', the real money stock is M/P', and
therefore the LM schedule shifts to LM'. Equilibrium income now is Y'.
Again in the lower panel we show at point E' the combination of the
price level P' and the corresponding equilibrium level of income and
spending Y'. Considering different levels of prices and connnecting the
resulting points such as E and E', we derive the aggregate demand
schedule AD. The schedule shows the equilibrium level of spending at
each level of prices, given the nominal money stock and fiscal policy.

Properties of the *AD* Schedule

The *AD* schedule shows how the level of real spending changes with the level of prices, given fiscal policy, the quantity of money, and autonomous private spending. What are the precise properties of the *AD* schedule? We start with the slope, which tells us how much real spending changes in response to a change in the level of prices.

THE SLOPE OF THE *AD* SCHEDULE

In Figure 7-6 we derived the *AD* schedule by considering the effect of changes in the price level, and hence in real balances, on the *LM* schedule and hence on equilibrium income and spending. The slope of the *AD* curve therefore reflects the extent to which a change in real balances changes the equilibrium level of spending, taking both assets and goods markets into account.

But we have already examined the effects of a change in the stock of real balances on the level of output that equilibrates the goods and assets markets. In Chapters 4 and 5 we showed the effect of an increase in the nominal stock of money on equilibrium spending and output, with the price level given. Now we ask what is the effect of a change in real balances due to lower prices, given nominal money.

In discussing monetary policy in Chapters 4 and 5 we showed the following results using the *IS-LM* schedules:

> An increase in real balances leads to a larger increase in equilibrium income and spending, the smaller the interest response of money demand and the higher the interest response of investment demand.

> An increase in real balances leads to a larger increase in equilibrium income and spending, the larger the multiplier and the smaller the income response of money demand.

Because the slope of the AD curve is determined by the effect of a change in real balances on equilibrium spending and output, the same factors that determine the effects of a change in the stock of money on equilibrium output and spending also determine the slope of the AD curve. If a given change in real balances has a large impact on equilibrium spending, then the *AD* curve will be very flat—because a small change in the price level creates a large change in equilibrium spending. But if a given change in real balances has a small effect on equilibrium spending and output, then the *AD* curve will be steep: in that case it takes a large change in the price level to create a small change in spending and output.

Accordingly, we see that:

1. The *AD* curve is flatter (*a*) the smaller the interest responsiveness of the demand for money, and (*b*) the larger the interest responsiveness of investment demand.

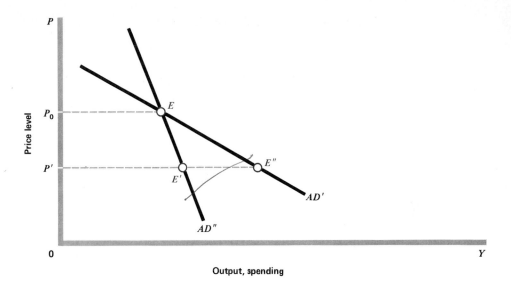

FIGURE 7-7   THE SLOPE OF THE *AD* SCHEDULE. The diagram
shows two possible *AD* schedules. Along *AD″* a change in prices from
P_0 to P' has a smaller effect on spending than along *AD′*. The former
corresponds to the case where changes in real balances have little
impact on equilibrium income and spending: the latter to the case
where real balance changes exert significant effects.

2. The *AD* curve is flatter (*a*) the larger the multiplier, and (*b*) the smaller the
   income responsiveness of the demand for money.

   To fix ideas further, it is useful to think for a moment about the *AD*
schedule in terms of the extreme classical and liquidity trap cases that we
learned about in Chapter 4. In the classical case, where money demand is
entirely unresponsive to interest rates and the *LM* curve is vertical, changes in
real balances have a big effect on income and spending. In Figure 7-7 that
corresponds to a very flat *AD* schedule, such as *AD′*, as we should expect based
on point 1*a* above. Conversely, in the liquidity trap case, where the public is
willing to hold any amount of real balances at unchanged interest rates, a fall in
prices and a rise in the real money stock have very little effect on income and
spending.[2] In Figure 7-7 that would correspond to an almost vertical *AD*

---

[2] The reason a reduction in prices increases output in this case is the *real balance effect*: with lower prices, the
value of real balances held by the public is higher, their wealth is accordingly higher, and therefore their
consumption spending and output are higher. The real balance effect is central to monetary theory as developed
in the classical treatise by Don Patinkin, *Money, Interest, and Prices* (New York: Harper & Row, 1965).

curve, as suggested again by point $1a$ above. A vertical AD curve means that the planned level of spending is unresponsive to the price level.

You should now experiment with alternative IS and LM schedules to see how the effects of a change in the price level depend on the slopes of the IS and LM curves and the factors underlying those slopes. In doing so you will confirm the points summarized above. In problem 4 at the end of the chapter, we ask you to demonstrate these links.

Next we consider the factors that determine the position of the AD curve.

THE EFFECT OF A FISCAL EXPANSION

We noted above that the same factors that determine the positions of the IS and LM schedules also determine the position of the AD curve. We now show how changes in fiscal and monetary policy shift the AD curve, starting with a fiscal expansion.

In Figure 7-8 the initial LM and IS schedules correspond to a given nominal quantity of money and the price level P_0. Equilibrium obtains at point E, and there is a corresponding point on the AD schedule in the lower panel.

Now the government increases the level of spending, say, on defense. As a consequence, the IS schedule shifts outward and to the right. At the initial price level there is a new equilibrium at point E' with higher interest rates and a higher level of income and spending. Thus at the initial level of prices, P_0, equilibrium income and spending now are higher. We show this by plotting point E' in the lower panel. Point E' is a point on the new schedule AD' reflecting the effect of higher government spending.

Of course, we could have started with any other point on the original AD curve, and we would then have shown how in the lower panel the rise in government spending leads to a higher equilibrium level of output at each price level. In that way we trace out the entire AD' schedule, which lies to the right of AD.

In fact, we can say more: At each level of prices, and hence of real balances, the AD schedule shifts to the right by an amount indicated by the fiscal policy multiplier developed in Chapter 5. As we saw there, a fiscal expansion leads to a higher level of income and spending, the larger the interest response of money demand, the smaller the interest response of aggregate demand, and the larger the marginal propensity to consume.

Thus if the fiscal policy multiplier derived in Chapter 5 was, for example, 1.5, then a \$1 (billion) dollar increase in government spending would increase equilibrium income and spending by \$1.5 billion, at the given price level. In response to any change in government spending, the AD schedule would shift to the right by 1.5 times the increase in G.[3]

---

[3] In Chap. 5 we showed that the fiscal policy multiplier is given by the expression $h\bar{\alpha}/(h + kb\bar{\alpha})$, where h is the interest responsiveness of money demand, $\bar{\alpha}$ the simple Keynesian multiplier, k the income response of money demand, and b the interest response of investment demand.

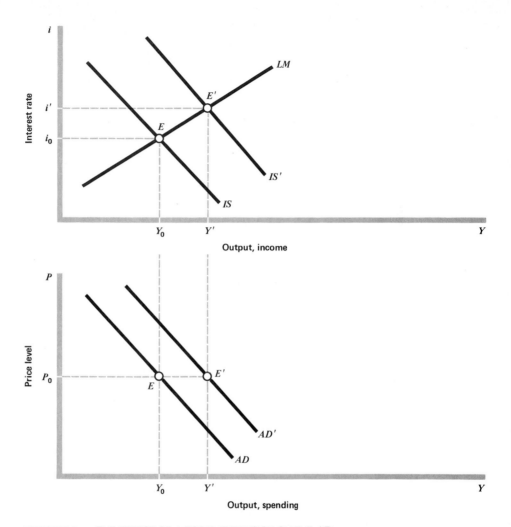

FIGURE 7-8   THE EFFECT OF A FISCAL EXPANSION ON THE AD
SCHEDULE. A fiscal expansion, such as an increase in government
spending, shifts the IS curve in the upper panel to IS'. At any given price
level, such as P_0, the equilibrium in the upper panel shifts to E', with
higher level of output Y' and higher interest rate i'. Point E' in the lower
panel is a point on the new aggregate demand schedule AD'
corresponding to price level P_0. We could similarly trace the effect of
increased government spending on the equilibrium level of output and
spending in the lower panel for every price level, and thus show that the
AD curve shifts out to AD' when fiscal policy is expansionary.

THE EFFECT OF A MONETARY EXPANSION ON THE *AD* SCHEDULE

An increase in the nominal money stock implies, at each level of prices, a higher real money stock. In the assets markets interest rates decline to induce the public to hold higher real balances. That decline in interest rates, in turn, stimulates aggregate demand and thus raises the equilibrium level of income and spending. In Figure 7-9 we show that an increase in the nominal money stock shifts the *AD* schedule up and to the right.

The extent to which an increase in nominal money shifts the *AD* schedule to the right depends on the monetary policy multiplier. If the monetary policy multiplier is large, say, because money demand is not very interest elastic and goods demand is, the *AD* schedule will shift a lot. Conversely, if the *LM* schedule is nearly flat, in which case monetary policy in ineffective, the *AD* schedule will shift very little.

We can also ask about the *upward* shift of the schedule. Here an interesting and important point emerges. Recall that what matters for equilibrium income and spending is the *real* money supply M/P. If an increase in nominal money is matched by an equiproportionate increase in prices, M/P is unchanged, and hence interest rates, aggregate demand, and equilibrium income and spending will remain unchanged. This gives us the clue to the vertical shift of the *AD* schedule.

An increase in the nominal money stock shifts the **AD** *schedule up exactly in proportion to the increase in nominal money.* Thus if, starting at point *E* in the lower panel of Figure 7-9, we have a 10 percent increase in *M*, real spending will be unchanged only if prices also rise by 10 percent, thus leaving real balances unchanged. Therefore the *AD* schedule shifts upward by 10 percent. At point *K* in Figure 7-9, *real* balances are the same as at *E*, and therefore interest rates and equilibrium income and spending are the same as at *E*.

We now have completed the derivation of the aggregate demand schedule. The important points to recall are that the *AD* schedule is shifted to the right both by increases in the money stock and by expansionary fiscal policy. In the remainder of this chapter we show how to use this tool to discuss the effects of monetary and fiscal policy *on both the level of output and the price level* under alternative assumptions about the supply side.

7-4 MONETARY AND FISCAL POLICY UNDER ALTERNATIVE SUPPLY ASSUMPTIONS

In Figure 7-2 we showed how the aggregate supply and demand curves together determine the equilibrium level of income and prices in the economy. Now that we have shown how the aggregate demand curve is derived, and how it is shifted by policy changes, we use the aggregate demand and supply model to study the effects of monetary and fiscal policy in the two extreme supply cases—Keynesian and classical.

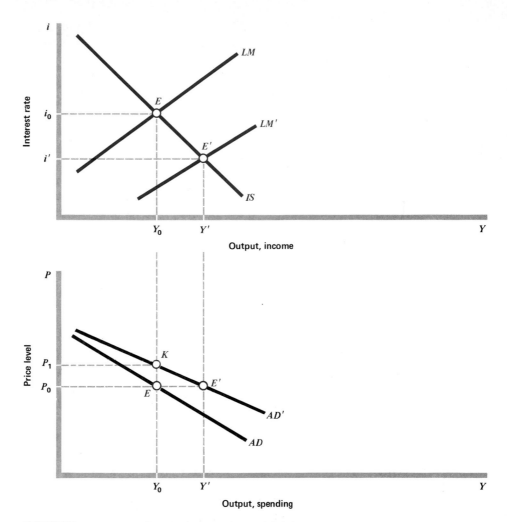

FIGURE 7-9   THE EFFECTS OF AN INCREASE IN THE MONEY
STOCK ON THE AD SCHEDULE. An increase in the money stock shifts
the LM curve to LM' in the upper panel. The equilibrium level of
income rises from Y_0 to Y' at the initial price level P_0. Correspondingly,
the AD curve moves out to the right, to AD', with point E' in the lower
panel corresponding to E' in the upper panel. The AD curve shifts up in
exactly the same proportion as the money stock increases. For
instance, at point K the price level P_1 is higher than P_0 in the same
proportion that the money supply has risen. Real balances at K on AD'
are therefore the same as at E on AD.

We should expect that the conclusions we reach in the Keynesian supply case are precisely the same as those reached in Chapters 4 and 5. In those chapters, in developing the *IS-LM* model, we assumed that whatever amount of goods was demanded would be supplied at the existing price level. And of course, as Figure 7-5*a* shows, the Keynesian supply curve implies that any amount of goods demanded will be supplied at the existing price level.

The Keynesian Case

In Figure 7-10 we combine the aggregate demand schedule with the Keynesian aggregate supply schedule. The initial equilibrium is at point *E*, where *AS* and *AD* intersect. At that point the goods and assets markets are in equilibrium.

Consider now a fiscal expansion. As we have already seen, increased government spending, or a cut in tax rates, shifts the *AD* schedule out and to the right from *AD* to *AD'*. The new equilibrium is at point *E'*, where output has increased. Because firms are willing to supply *any* amount of output at the level of prices P_0, there is no effect on prices. The only effect of higher government spending in Figure 7-10 is to increase output and employment. In addition, as we know from the *IS-LM* model that lies behind the *AD* schedule,

FIGURE 7-10   A FISCAL EXPANSION: THE KEYNESIAN CASE. In the Keynesian case, with output in perfectly elastic supply at a given price level, a fiscal expansion increases equilibrium income from *Y* to *Y'*. This is exactly the result already derived with *IS* and *LM* schedules.

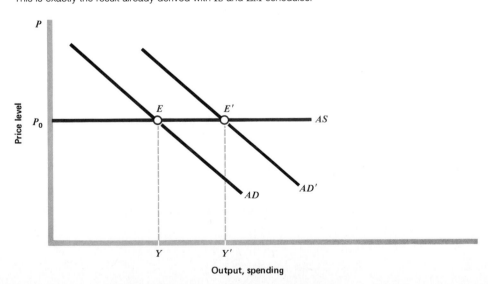

the fiscal expansion will raise equilibrium interest rates. Because interest rates do increase, the fiscal expansion raises output less than suggested by the simple multiplier of Chapter 3.

We leave it to you to show that in the Keynesian case an increase in the nominal quantity of money likewise leads to an expansion in equilibrium output. With a horizontal *AS* schedule there is again no impact on prices. The magnitude of the output expansion then depends, in this Keynesian case, only on the monetary policy multiplier that determines the extent of the horizontal shift of the *AD* schedule.

Thus, as we expected, all our conclusions about the effects of policy changes in the Keynesian supply case are those of the simple *IS-LM* model.

The Classical Case: Fiscal Policy

In the classical case the aggregate supply schedule is vertical at the full-employment level of output. Firms will supply the level of output Y^* whatever the price level. Under this supply assumption we obtain results very different from those reached using the Keynesian model. Now the price level is not given, but rather depends on the interaction of supply and demand.

In Figure 7-11 we study the effect of a fiscal expansion under classical supply assumptions. The aggregate supply schedule is *AS*, with equilibrium initially at point *E*. Note that at point *E* there is full employment because, by assumption, firms supply the full-employment level of output at any level of prices.

The fiscal expansion shifts the aggregate demand schedule from *AD* to *AD'*. At the initial level of prices, P_0, spending in the economy rises to point *E'*. At price level P_0 the demand for goods has risen. But firms cannot obtain the labor to produce more output, and output supply cannot respond to the increased demand. As firms try to hire more workers, they only bid up wages and their costs of production, and therefore they charge higher prices for their output. The increase in the demand for goods therefore leads only to higher prices, and not to higher output.

The increase in prices reduces the real money stock and leads to an increase in interest rates and a reduction in spending. The economy moves up the *AD'* schedule until prices have risen enough, and real balances have fallen enough, to raise interest rates and reduce spending to a level consistent with full-employment output. That is the case at a price level P'. At point E'' aggregate demand, at the higher level of government spending, is once again equal to aggregate supply.

Crowding Out Again

Note what has happened in Figure 7-11: output is unchanged at the full-employment level Y^*, but government spending is higher. That must imply less spending by the private sector. There is thus *full*, or complete, *crowding out*.

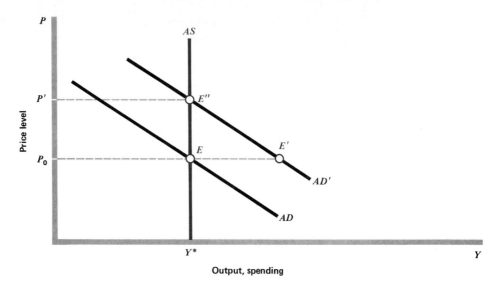

FIGURE 7-11   A FISCAL EXPANSION: THE CLASSICAL CASE. The supply of output is perfectly inelastic at the full-employment level of output, Y^*. A fiscal expansion raises equilibrium spending, at the initial price level P_0, from E to E'. But now there is an excess demand because firms are unwilling to supply that much output. Prices increase, and that reduces real balances until we reach point E''. At E'' government spending is higher, but the higher price level means lower real balances, higher interest rates, and hence reduced private spending. At E'' increased government spending has crowded out an equal amount of private spending.

Recall that crowding out occurs when an increase in government spending results in less spending by the private sector. Typically, as we showed in Chapter 5, government spending crowds out investment. In the case shown in Figure 7-11, with a classical supply curve, every dollar increase in real government spending is offset by a dollar reduction in private spending, so that crowding out is complete.

We thus reach the following important result: *In the classical case increased real government spending leads to full crowding out.* We now explain the mechanism through which crowding out occurs.

Figure 7-12 shows the *IS-LM* diagram, augmented with the line Y^* at the full-employment level of output. The initial equilibrium is at point E, where the money market clears and planned spending equals output. The fiscal expansion shifts the *IS* schedule to *IS'*. At an unchanged price level, and assuming firms were to meet the increase in demand by expanding production, we would move to point E'. But this is not possible under classical supply assumptions. Faced with an excess demand for goods, firms end up raising prices rather than output. The price increase, in turn, reduces real balances and therefore shifts the *LM* schedule up. Prices will increase until the excess demand has been eliminated. That means the *LM* schedule shifts up and to the left until we reach a new equilibrium at point *E''*.

At *E''* the goods market clears at the full-employment level of output. Interest rates have increased compared with the initial equilibrium at *E*, and that increase in interest rates has reduced private spending to make room for increased government purchases. Note that the money market is also in equilibrium. Output and income are the same as at point *E*. The higher interest rate reduces the demand for real balances, matching the decline in the real money stock.

Note that we have now seen two mechanisms that produce full crowding out. In Chapter 5, crowding out is complete if the *LM* curve is vertical. In that case, crowding out occurs because money demand is interest inelastic. In this

FIGURE 7-12   CROWDING OUT IN THE CLASSICAL CASE. A fiscal expansion in the classical case leads to full crowding out. The fiscal expansion shifts the *IS* schedule to *IS'*. At the initial price level the economy would move to point *E'*, but there is excess demand since firms supply only *Y**. Prices increase, shifting the *LM* schedule up and to the left until *LM'* is reached. The new equilibrium is at point *E''*, where interest rates have risen enough to displace an amount of private spending equal to the increase in government demand.

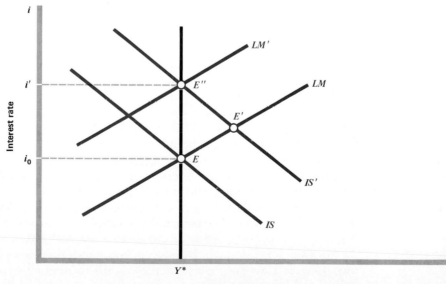

TABLE 7-1	THE EFFECTS OF A FISCAL EXPANSION		
Aggregate supply	Output	Interest rate	Prices
Keynesian	+	+	0
Classical	0	+	+

chapter, full crowding out occurs because aggregate supply limits total output. In brief, in Chapter 5 crowding out is a demand phenomenon; here it is a supply phenomenon.

We summarize in Table 7-1 the effects of a fiscal expansion in the cases of classical and Keynesian supply conditions. In each case we show what happens to output, interest rates, and the price level.

The table reinforces our understanding of the two models; in one case only prices adjust; in the other case only output. These models are clearly extremes, and we would expect that often adjustment occurs in both output and prices. That is the adjustment process we study in Chapter 13. We shall see there that the Keynesian case comes close to describing the short-run effects of a fiscal expansion, while the classical case more accurately predicts what happens in the long run after all adjustments have taken place.

Monetary Expansion under Classical Conditions

We have already seen the impact of monetary policy under Keynesian supply conditions: With prices given, a rise in the nominal money stock is a rise in the real money stock. Equilibrium interest rates decline as a consequence, and output rises. Consider now the adjustments that occur in response to a monetary expansion when the aggregate supply curve is vertical and the price level is no longer fixed.

In Figure 7-13 we study an expansion in the nominal money stock under classical supply conditions. The initial full-employment equilibrium is at point E, where the AD and AS schedules intersect. Now the nominal money stock is increased, and accordingly, the aggregate demand schedule shifts up and to the right to AD'. If prices were fixed, the economy would move to E', the Keynesian equilibrium. But now output is in fixed supply. The increase in aggregate demand leads to an excess demand for goods. Firms that attempt to expand, hiring more workers, bid up wages and costs. Prices increase in response to the excess demand, and that means real balances fall back toward their initial level. In fact prices keep rising until the excess demand for goods disappears. Thus they must increase until the economy reaches point E'', where AS intersects the new aggregate demand schedule AD'. Only when

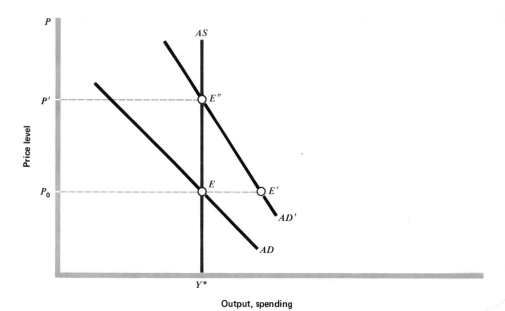

FIGURE 7-13   THE EFFECT OF A MONETARY EXPANSION UNDER
CLASSICAL SUPPLY ASSUMPTIONS. Starting from the full-employment
equilibrium at point E, an increase in the nominal money stock shifts the
aggregate demand schedule to AD'. At the initial price level there is
now an excess demand for goods. Prices increase, and thus the real
money stock declines toward its initial level. Price increases continue
until the economy reaches point E''. Here the *real* money stock has returned to its initial level, and with output unchanged, interest rates are
again at their initial level. Thus a monetary expansion affects only
prices, not output or interest rates.

aggregate demand is again equal to full-employment supply does the goods
market clear and the pressure for prices to rise disappear.

Consider now the adjustment that takes place in moving from E to E''.
There is no change in output, only a change in the price level. Note, moreover,
that prices rise in exactly the same proportion as the nominal quantity of
money.[4] This we know because we saw earlier than in response to an increase
in nominal money the AD schedule shifts upward in the same proportion as the
increase in money. Thus at point E'' the real money stock M/P is back to its
initial level. At E'' both nominal money and the price level have changed in the

---

[4] In problem 7 we ask you to use the IS and LM curves to show how the change in the money supply works. To
answer the problem you have to use Fig. 7-9 along with the fact that the LM schedule shifts as the price level
changes.

TABLE 7-2	THE EFFECTS OF AN INCREASE IN THE NOMINAL MONEY STOCK			
Aggregate supply	Output	Interest rate	Prices	Real balances
Keynesian	+	−	0	+
Classical	0	0	+	0

same proportion, leaving real money and hence interest rates and aggregate demand unchanged. We thus have an important implication of the classical model: *Under classical supply conditions an increase in nominal money raises the price level in the same proportion, but leaves interest rates and real output unchanged.*

In Table 7-2 we summarize the effects of an increase in the nominal money stock under Keynesian and classical supply conditions. Once again we look at the effects on output, prices, and interest rates. In addition we show the effect on real balances M/P. The table brings out the fact that under classical supply conditions, none of the *real* variables, such as output, interest rates, or real balances, are affected by a change in the nominal money stock. Only the price level changes.

7-5 THE QUANTITY THEORY AND THE NEUTRALITY OF MONEY

The classical model of supply, in combination with the *IS-LM* model describing the demand side of the economy, has extremely strong implications. Because, by assumption, output is maintained at the full-employment level by full wage and price flexibility, monetary and fiscal policy do not affect output. Fiscal policy affects interest rates and the *composition* of spending between the government and the private sector and between consumption and investment. Monetary policy only affects the price level.

These implications about the effects of monetary policy on output are consistent with the *quantity theory of money.* The quantity theory of money in its strongest form asserts that the price level is proportional to the stock of money. For instance, in the case of the classical supply curve, an increase in the quantity of money produces, in equilibrium, a proportional increase in the price level. In this case, money is *neutral.*

The Neutrality of Money

Money is *neutral* when changes in the money stock lead only to changes in the price level, with no real variables (output, employment, and interest rates) changing. For instance, money is neutral in the second row of Table 7-2, where in response to a change in the money stock, only the price level changes, with output, interest rates, and real balances remaining unchanged.

We saw above that the classical supply curve has the powerful and important implication that fiscal policy cannot affect output. The neutrality of money likewise has strong policy implications. For instance, if money were neutral, there would be an easy way to reduce the inflation rate if we ever wanted to do that. All we would have to do would be to reduce the rate at which the money stock is growing.

In practice, it is very difficult to change the inflation rate without producing a recession, as for instance in the 1979–1983 period in the United States. When a lower growth rate of money leads first to unemployment, and only later to lower inflation, as it did in the recession in 1982, then we know that money is not neutral. Changes in the quantity of money then have real effects — monetary policy affects the level of output. This means that the aggregate supply curve cannot be vertical in the short run. In Chapter 13 we develop the aggregate supply curve, showing why in the short run it is quite flat, whereas over longer periods it is more nearly vertical.

The Modern Quantity Theory: Monetarism

The strict quantity theory asserts that the price level is proportional to the quantity of money. Although the quantity theory is centuries, and perhaps millennia, old, few have believed in the strict quantity theory. That is, few have believed that the price level is strictly proportional to the money stock, or that money is the *only* factor affecting the price level. Rather, quantity theorists argued and argue that the money stock is, in practice, the single most important factor producing inflation.

Box 7-1 presents quotations from Irving Fisher (1867–1947), widely thought to be the greatest American economist of his time, and from Milton Friedman, the leading exponent of the quantity theory and the importance of money in the modern era. The two differ in emphasis: Fisher comes close to asserting that *only* changes in the quantity of money affect the price level; Friedman is more clear in arguing that other factors can affect the price level, but that these other factors are of secondary importance.

Friedman is the recognized intellectual leader of an influential group of economists, called *monetarists,* who emphasize the role of money and monetary policy in affecting the behavior of output and prices. Leading monetarists include Professor Karl Brunner and Robert Barro of the University of Rochester, Allan Meltzer of Carnegie Mellon University, William Poole of Brown University, and Anna Schwartz of the National Bureau of Economic Research and Hunter College. Another prominent monetarist is Beryl Sprinkel, Chairman of the Council of Economic Advisers in the second Reagan Administration (1985–1989), whose views are strongly reflected in the emphasis on monetary policy in the 1986 report of the Council of Economic Advisers.

BOX
7-1

THE QUANTITY THEORY OF MONEY

Irving Fisher (1867–1947) and Milton Friedman (born 1912) are two of the foremost monetary economists in the United States in this century. Both strongly advocated the quantity theory of money as the right model of price level determination.

Fisher stated:*

In recent popular discussions a great variety of reasons have been assigned for the "high cost of living," *e.g.,* "profiteering"; speculation; hoarding; the middleman; . . . the tariff; cold storage; longer hauls on railroads; marketing by telephone; the free delivery system; the individual package; the enforcement of sanitary laws; the tuberculin testing of cattle; the destruction of tainted meat; sanitary milk; the elimination of renovated butter and of "rots" and "spots" in eggs; food adulteration; advertising; unscientific management; extravagance; higher standards of living; the increasing cost of government; the increasing cost of old-age pensions, and of better pauper institutions, hospitals, insane asylums, reformatories, jails and other public insitutitions; . . .

I shall not discuss in detail this list of alleged explanations. While some of them are important factors in raising particular prices, none of them . . . has been important in raising the *general* scale of prices. . . .

The ups and downs of prices roughly correspond with the ups and downs of the money supply. Throughout all history this has been so. For this general broad fact the evidence is sufficient even where we lack the index numbers by which to make accurate measurements. Whenever there have been rapid outpourings from mines, following discoveries of the precious metals used for money, prices have risen with corresponding rapidity. This was observed in the sixteenth century, after great quantities of the precious metals had been brought to Europe from the New World, and again in the nineteenth century, after the Californian and Australian gold mining of the fifties; and, still again, in the same centruy after the South African, Alaskan, and Cripple Creek mining of the nineties. Likewise when other causes than mining, such as paper money issues, produce violent changes in the quantity or quality of money, violent changes in the price level usually follow.

Friedman wrote:†

Since men first began to write systematically about economic matters they have devoted special attention to the wide movements in the general level of prices that have intermittently occurred. Two alternative explanations have usually been offered. One has attributed the changes in prices to changes in the quantity of money. The other has attributed the changes in prices to war or to profiteers or to rises in wages or to some other special circumstance of the particular time and place and has regarded any accompanying change in the quantity of money as a common consequence of the same special circumstance. The first explanation has generally been referred to as the quantity theory of money, although that designation conceals the variety of forms the explanation has taken, the different levels of sophistication on which it has been developed, and the wide range of the claims that have been made for its applicability.

In its most rigid and unqualified form the quantity theory asserts strict proportionality between the quantity of what is regarded as money and the level of prices. Hardly anyone has held the theory in that form, although statements capable of being so interpreted have often been made in the heat of argument or for expository simplicity. Virtually every quantity theorist has recognized that changes in the quantity of money that correspond to changes in the volume of trade or of output have no tendency to produce changes in prices. Nearly as many have recognized also that changes in the willingness of the community to hold money can occur for a variety of reasons and can introduce disparities between changes in the quantity of money per unit of trade or of output and changes in prices. What quantity theorists have held in common is the belief that these qualifications are of secondary importance for substantial changes in either prices or the quantity of money, so that the one will not in fact occur without the other.

---

* Irving Fisher, *Stabilizing the Dollar* (New York: Macmillan, 1920), pp. 10–11 and 29.
† Milton Friedman, "Money: The Quantity Theory," in *The International Encyclopedia of the Social Sciences*, vol. X, 1968, pp. 432–447.

Modern quantity theorists differ also from the strict quantity theory in not believing that the supply curve is vertical in the short run. Monetarists such as Friedman argue that a reduction in the money stock does in practice *first* reduce the level of output, and only later have an effect on prices.

Thus Friedman and other monetarists make an important distinction between the short- and long-run effects of changes in money. They argue that in the long run money is more or less neutral. Changes in the money stock, after they have worked their way through the economy, have no real effects and only change prices: the quantity theory and the neutrality of money are, from this long-run perspective, not just theoretical possibilities, but instead a reasonable description of the way the world works. But in the short run, they argue, monetary policy and changes in the money stock can and do have important real effects.

There is more to monetarism than the argument that money is the most important determinant of macroeconomic performance, but we leave the evidence on this and the other tenets of monetarism for further discussion in Chapters 12 and 18.

7-6 AGGREGATE SUPPLY: THE QUESTIONS AHEAD

The theory of aggregate supply is among the most controversial and the least settled of any in macroeconomics. Here is the difficulty. From the viewpoint of logic and simplicity, the classical theory of supply — that the labor market clears all the time and that output is always at the full employment level — is compelling. After all, if output is below the full employment level, there are some workers who want to work but cannot find a job. Surely they could find a job by offering to work at lower real wage. Much of microeconomics suggests that markets are mostly in equilibrium (quantity demanded is equal to quantity supplied) and, if not, are at least moving that way. So economists have a professional bias in favor of equilibrium.

But the facts do not support the classical theory of supply.

- Output is not always at the full employment level. The unemployment rate varies, and is sometimes very high; there are many people wanting work who cannot find it, and therefore the quantity of labor supplied exceeds the quantity demanded.

- Further, if output is always at the full employment level, then changes in the money stock affect only prices and not output: Money is neutral. But changes in monetary policy in fact frequently appear not to be neutral. Sharp reductions in money growth, for instance when governments try to reduce inflation, almost always cause recessions. And increases in money growth often appear to cause rapid growth of real output.

Indeed, the broad facts come closer to supporting the Keynesian aggregate supply curve than the classical view. Increases in aggregate demand, caused, for instance, by expansionary fiscal or monetary policy, in the short run raise real output much more than prices.

However, the assumption that prices are completely fixed, which underlies the Keynesian supply function, is bothersome. When prices are fixed and markets do not clear, people can benefit from changing prices. The unemployed would be willing to work at a wage below that earned by the currently employed. Employers should be happy to employ labor at a lower wage. Why do not employers and the unemployed get together, agree on a lower wage, and get rid of the unemployment? In other words, why does the labor market not move quickly to equilibrium?

In a nutshell, the difficulty facing the theory of aggregate supply is that logic and simple microeconomic theory lead us to believe we should be in a classical world, but the real world appears not to be classical. The challenge for macroeconomics is to explain the real world.

There are three leading approaches to explaining the short-run stickiness of wages and prices, the short-run nonneutrality of money, and varying and often persistently high rates of unemployment that exist in the real world. We give the flavor of the arguments here, and take them up more systematically in Chapters 13, 14, and 18.

Modern Keynesian Approaches

The original Keynesian approach was to assume that the wage is fixed.[5] Modern Keynesian theories argue that the wage and price levels are very slow to change rather than fixed. The aggregate supply curve is viewed as being close to flat in the short run and close to vertical in the long run. Attention focuses mainly on wages and on the adjustment process to explain why adjustment is not immediate or at least very fast.

CONTRACTS

Wages are slow to change because they are fixed in long-term contracts. These contracts may be explicit, as with the 3-year union contracts that are found in the United States. Or they may be implicit, an unwritten agreement between firm and employee that the wage will remain fixed for a period of a year and will not be cut.

If wages (and prices) are adjusted at different times for different firms and

---

[5] In the *General Theory of Employment, Interest and Money* (London: Macmillan, 1936) Keynes assumed for most of the book that the nominal wage was fixed. But he also argued that flexible wages would not succeed in stabilizing output and employment and that the active use of monetary policy was a preferable means of maintaining full employment.

industries, then the economy-wide average wage and the aggregate price level adjust only slowly to policy changes or other changes. This is so because they are made up of many wages or many prices and only a small part them will be adjusted at any one time.

COORDINATION

The nonneutrality of money can be accounted for by the difficulty of coordinating wage and price changes when wages and prices are not all adjusted simultaneously. When the quantity of money is changed, the extent to which any individual should change his or her own price or wage depends on how much others change their prices. If everyone else changes prices in proportion to the change in the money supply, then the last remaining firm would do the same. But if no one else or only a few firms do, then the firm raising its price in proportion to an increase in the money stock will lose customers because its price is out of line with the others. Because all the firms in an economy cannot get together to coordinate, they will raise prices slowly as the effects of the change in money are felt through increased demand for their goods at the existing prices.

EFFICIENCY WAGES

Another strand of modern Keynesian supply theory, efficiency wage theory, focuses on the wage as a means of motivating labor. The amount of effort workers make on the job is related to how well the job pays relative to alternatives. Firms may want to pay employees wages above the market clearing wage to ensure that they work hard in order not to lose their "good" jobs. By the same token, firms are reluctant to cut wages because that affects worker morale and output. This theory does not explain why the average wage is slow to change, but it does help explain the existence of unemployment.

These are not the only recent models that seek to explain aggregate supply along broadly Keynesian lines in which markets may not always clear. Aggregate supply is an area of intensive research. There is not as yet a dominant, completely persuasive microeconomic explanation of the positively sloped aggregate supply curve, but there are many suggestive theories. We will examine the main explanations of upward sloping, but not vertical, supply curves in Chapter 13.

The Imperfect Information – Market Clearing Approach

An alternative explanation for the effects of changes in the money supply on real output is associated with the *rational expectations equilibrium* approach to macroeconomics. This approach, which we review further in later Chapters, assumes that markets are in equilibrium even in the short run, but that people typically have imperfect information about the economy.[6]

A frequent assumption made in this approach is that people do not know the aggregate price level but do know the absolute (dollar) price at which they can buy and sell. For instance, at a given moment of time, a worker knows that the going wage rate is $12 per hour but does not know all prices in the economy and hence the aggregate price level, and thus does not know the real wage (the nominal wage divided by the price level, equal to the amount of goods the wage will buy). Since it is the real wage, not the absolute wage, that determines whether and how many working hours are wanted, the worker has somehow to estimate the aggregate price level.

With these assumptions it is possible to explain why changes in the stock of money affect real output. Suppose the stock of money increases *unexpectedly*, and begins to affect the demand for goods and labor, raising the price level and wages. Each firm and worker knows the price at which it can sell goods or labor. However workers and firms do not know as a fact that the aggregate price level has risen. Each believes that the increase in the absolute price at which it can sell is at least in part an increase in the relative price at which it sells. Workers think their real wage has risen, and want to work more. Because the labor market is always in equilibrium, they can work more. Thus there is an increase in the amount of work and output, because workers think their real wage has risen.

Of course, the workers were wrong. Their real wage had not in fact risen. If they had known the facts, they would not have worked more, prices would have risen in proportion to the money stock, and money would have been neutral. But they had imperfect information, and as a result the increase in the money stock was not neutral.

The imperfect information–market clearing approach does not assert that people make *stupid* mistakes in deciding how much to work and produce. Rather people do their best to understand the situation in which they find themselves but lack the full information to make the correct decision.

SEARCH

The imperfect information–market clearing approach can also be used to explain unemployment. Suppose that workers who become unemployed search for a new job, staying unemployed until they find a suitable job at the right real wage. Suppose further that they do not know the aggregate price level exactly. Now suppose that the money supply increases, that the aggregate price level goes up (though less than proportionately), and that firms raise the wages they are willing to pay.

---

[6] Robert E. Lucas of the University of Chicago is the intellectual founder of this approach. See his famous article "Some International Evidence on Output-Inflation Tradeoffs," *American Economic Review*, June 1973 for an example of the approach.

Workers are unaware that the price level is up. They find higher wages when they look for a job, think that the real wage is higher, and take the job. The unemployment rate falls as a result of the increase in the money stock. What might look like a Keynesian effect of an increase in the money stock on unemployment is instead explained by imperfect information: The real wage is lower than the worker thought it was when taking the job.

Real Business Cycles and the Role of Money

A third approach, real business cycle theory, starts from the market-clearing view, assuming that markets are always in equilibrium. Its distinctive feature is the argument that changes in the money stock play no serious role in the business cycle.[7] Real business cycle theorists recognize that output fluctuates over time, but argue that the fluctuations are a result of *real* shocks to the economy.

Real shocks are taken as coming mainly from the supply side of the economy. Changes in the weather, or the price of oil, or new methods of production affect the level of output. On the demand side, changes in government spending can also affect the level of output. But real business cycle theory by definition does not give a causal role to changes in the money stock in affecting output.

Rather the argument is that the quantity of money adjusts itself to the level of output. Thus real business cycle theorists argue that changes in output cause changes in the quantity of money rather than the other way around. The explanation is that when the level of output rises, people demand more real balances, and that the banks can generally create more money.

A Look Ahead

We will not evaluate the different approaches here, but we keep returning to them in subsequent chapters, especially Chapter 18 where we discuss the interactions of events and ideas in macroeconomics.

In Chapter 13 we develop a theory of aggregate supply which produces a positively sloped aggregate supply curve that is relatively flat in the short run while vertical in the long run. We base the theory largely on the modern Keynesian approach, but combine that with the emphasis on expectations that comes from the rational expectations approach to macroeconomics.

7-7 SUMMARY

1. The aggregate supply and demand model is used to show the determination of the equilibrium levels of *both* output and prices.

---

[7] Carl Walsh "New View of the Business Cycle: Has the Past Emphasis on Money Been Misplaced?", *Business Review*, Federal Reserve Bank of Philadelphia, Jan./Feb. 1986, provides an excellent introduction to the topic.

2. The aggregate supply schedule *AS* shows at each level of prices the quantity of real output or GNP firms are willing to supply.

3. The Keynesian supply schedule is horizontal, implying that firms supply as much goods as demanded at the existing price level. The classical supply schedule is vertical. It would apply in an economy that has full price and wage flexibility. In such a frictionless economy, employment and output are always at the full-employment level.

4. The aggregate demand schedule *AD* shows at each price level the level of output at which the goods and assets markets are in equilibrium. This is the quantity of output demanded at each price level. Along the *AD* schedule fiscal policy is given, as is the nominal quantity of money. The *AD* schedule is derived using the *IS-LM* model.

5. Moving down and along the *AD* schedule, lower prices raise the real value of the money stock. Equilibrium interest rates fall, and that increases aggregate demand and equilibrium spending.

6. A fiscal expansion or an increase in the nominal quantity of money shifts the *AD* schedule outward and to the right.

7. Under Keynesian supply conditions, with prices fixed, both monetary and fiscal expansion raise equilibrium output. A monetary expansion lowers interest rates, while a fiscal expansion raises them.

8. Under classical supply conditions a fiscal expansion has no effect on output. But a fiscal expansion raises prices, lowers real balances, and increases equilibrium interest rates. That is, under classical supply conditions there is full crowding out. Private spending declines by exactly the increase in government demand.

9. A monetary expansion, under classical supply conditions, raises prices in the same proportion as the rise in nominal money. All real variables, specifically output and interest rates, remain unchanged. When changes in the money stock have no real effects, money is said to be *neutral*.

10. The strict quantity theory of money states that prices move in proportion to the nominal money stock. Modern quantity theorists or monetarists accept that there is no exact link between money and prices, but argue that changes in the money stock are, in practice, the most important single determinant of changes in the price level.

KEY TERMS

Aggregate supply curve

Aggregate demand curve

Keynesian aggregate supply curve

Classical aggregate supply curve

Efficiency wage theory

Full crowding out

Quantity theory of money

Neutrality of money

Monetarism

Rational expectations equilibrium approach

PROBLEMS

1. Define the aggregate demand and supply curves.
2. Explain why the classical supply curve is vertical and explain the mechanisms that ensure continued full employment of labor in the classical case.
3. Discuss, using the IS-LM model, what happens to interest rates as prices change along a given AD schedule.
4. Show graphically that the AD curve is steeper (a) the larger the interest responsiveness of the demand for money and (b) the smaller the multiplier.
5. Suppose full-employment output increases from Y^* to $Y^{*\prime}$. What does the quantity theory predict will happen to the price level?
6. In goods market equilibrium in a closed economy, $S + T = I + G$. Use this equation to explain why, in the classical case, a fiscal expansion must lead to full crowding out.
7. Show, using IS and LM curves, why money is neutral in the classical supply case. (Refer to footnote 4 for hints.)
8. Suppose the government reduces the personal income tax rate from t to t'.
   (a) What is the effect on the AD schedule?
   (b) What is the effect on the equilibrium interest rate?
   (c) What happens to investment?
9. Suppose there is a decline in the demand for money. At each output level and interest rate the public now wants to hold lower real balances.
   (a) In the Keynesian case, what happens to equilibrium output and to prices?
   (b) In the classical case, what is the effect on output and on prices?
10. In question 9, use the quantity theory of money to explain the effect of the money demand shift on prices.
11. Suppose the government undertakes a balanced budget increase in spending. Government spending rises from G to G', and there is an accompanying increase in tax rates so that at the initial level of output the budget remains balanced.
    (a) Show the effect on the AD schedule.
    (b) Discuss the effect of the balanced budget policy on output and interest rates in the Keynesian case.
    (c) Discuss the effect in the classical case.
12. (a) Define the strict quantity theory.
    (b) Define monetarism.
    (c) What type of statistical evidence would you need to collect to support or refute the major argument of monetarism presented in this chapter?
13. Explain the basic difficulty facing the theory of aggregate supply.

PART TWO

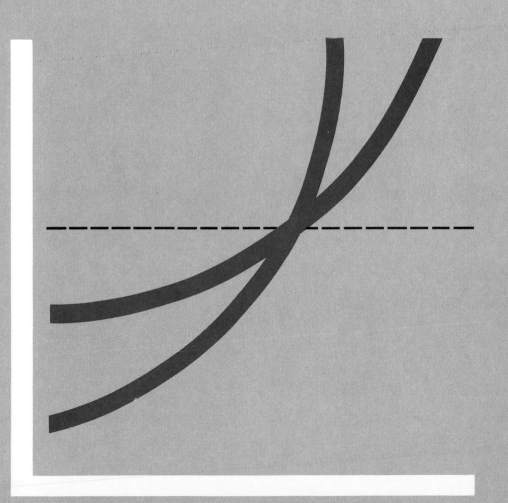

CONSUMPTION AND SAVING

The *IS-LM* model provides a comprehensive framework for understanding the interactions of the main macroeconomic variables that determine aggregate demand. Now we retrace our steps to present a more detailed and sophisticated treatment of the key relationships in the *IS-LM* model. The present chapter deals with the consumption function and with saving—since consumption purchases account for more than 60 percent of aggregate demand, this is the natural place to begin. The following three chapters flesh out the behavior of investment, money demand, and money supply, and thus move us to a more realistic and reliable understanding of the working of the economy.

Our starting point in examining consumption behavior is the consumption function we have been using in previous chapters. Thus far we have assumed that consumption is a linear function of disposable income:

$$C = \overline{C} + cYD \qquad \overline{C} > 0 \qquad 1 > c > 0 \tag{1}$$

We have already seen in the figure in Box 3-1 that the facts support the relationship described by equation (1). Figure 8-1 reproduces the Box 3-1 figure, which shows a very close link between consumption and disposable income. To find numerical estimates of the intercept ($\overline{C}$) and the marginal propensity to consume (c), we "fit" a regression line to the observations. The regression line is fitted to the data using the method of least squares, which produces the linear equation that best characterizes the relation between consumption and disposable income contained in the data.[1]

The estimated regression line is shown in Figure 8-1 as the solid line and is reported in equation (2). The estimate of the intercept is $\overline{C} = 13.3$ (13.3 billion 1982 dollars), and the estimate of the marginal propensity to consume is 0.90.

$$C = 13.3 + 0.90YD \qquad \text{(annual data, 1948–1985)} \qquad (2)$$

Two characteristics of a consumption function such as equation (1) are borne out by the empirical equation (2). There is a positive intercept ($\overline{C} = 13.3$), and the marginal propensity to consume ($c = 0.90$) is positive and less than unity.

If we divide through by YD in equation (2), we obtain an equation that gives the average propensity to consume (C/YD) as a function of disposable income:

$$\frac{C}{YD} = \frac{13.3}{YD} + 0.90 \qquad (3)$$

Equation (3) indicates that the average propensity to consume declines as disposable income rises.[2] However, although the intercept, 13.3, is positive, it is very small relative to disposable income, which is \$2,509 billion 1982 dollars, in 1985.[3] If the intercept were actually zero, then we see from equations (1) and (3) that consumption would be proportional to disposable income, with $C/YD = c$. The marginal and average propensities to consume would be equal. The relationship shown by Figure 8-1 and equation (2) is essentially one of proportionality, with the average and marginal propensities to consume out of disposable income equal to each other, at about 0.91.

Inspection of the regression line in Figure 8-1 suggests that the estimated equation fits well. There are no points far off the fitted line. As a first approxi-

---

[1] It is frequently useful to summarize a relationship, such as that of Fig. 8-1, between consumption expenditures and disposable income by writing an equation such as equation (2), which has specific numerical values in it, rather than the more general form of equation (1), which does not specify numerical values of the coefficients $\overline{C}$ and c. The line drawn in Fig. 8-1 is the line represented by equation (2). That line is calculated by minimizing the sum of the squares of the vertical distances of the points in Fig. 8-1 from the line, and it provides a good description of the general relationship between the two variables. [Those familiar with the method should note that we have corrected for serial correlation in calculating equation (2).] For further details on the fitting of such lines, called least-squares regression lines, see Robert S. Pindyck and Daniel L. Rubinfeld, *Econometric Models and Economic Forecasts,* 2d ed. (New York: McGraw-Hill, 1980).

[2] You should check a data source, such as the *Economic Report of the President,* to see how well the predicted average propensity to consume from equation (3) matches the actual propensity for 1986 and later years.

[3] Technically, the intercept is statistically not significantly different from zero. See Pindyck and Rubinfeld, op. cit., for the meaning of tests of significance.

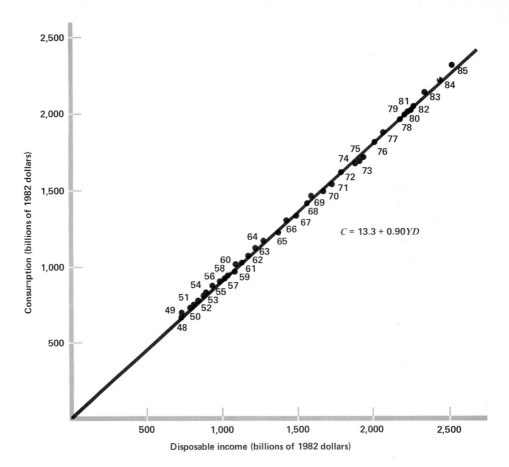

FIGURE 8-1   THE CONSUMPTION-INCOME RELATION, 1948–1985.
There is a close relationship in practice between consumption spending
and disposable income. Consumption spending rises on average by 90
cents for every extra dollar of disposable income. The solid line is the
fitted regression line that summarizes the relationship shown by the
points for the individual years.

mation then, equation (2) provides a reasonable summary of consumption
behavior. The next step is to ask whether equation (2) can be improved upon,
and if so, to determine how.

Figure 8-2 shows the average propensity to consume, as calculated from
equation (3), the smooth line, and the actual propensity to consume in each
year. The smooth line, the predicted average propensity to consume, declines
slightly over time as YD rises. The actual propensity to consume jumps around

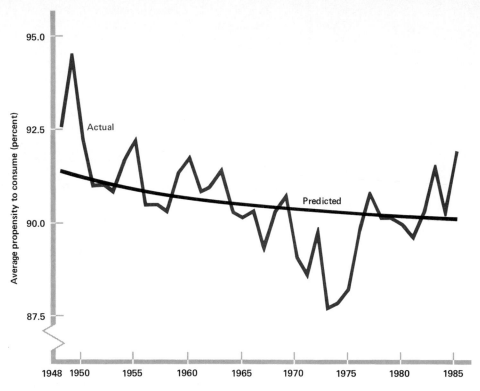

FIGURE 8-2   THE ACTUAL AND PREDICTED AVERAGE PROPEN-
SITY TO CONSUME, 1948–1985. The average propensity to consume
implied by equation (3) is shown by the black "predicted" line. The
actual average propensity to consume fluctuates more than that implied
by the equation.

a good deal, and stays above or below the predicted line for years at a time, for
example, from 1959 to 1963, or 1970 to 1976.

The deviations of the actual ratio from the predicted one in Figure 8-2
forcefully raise the question of how well the simplest consumption function
predicts consumption behavior. The answer is that it is a good first approximation, but that it can make large errors. For example, in 1973 the actual propensity to consume was only 0.882, whereas the predicted propensity was
0.906. The difference of 0.024 translates into an error in predicting consumption of over $45 billion (1982 dollars) or nearly 1.5 percent of GNP.[4] Errors of
that size strongly suggest that the simplest consumption function can be improved upon.

---

[4] Disposable income in 1973 was $1,916.3 billion, measured in 1982 dollars.

BOX
8-1

A CONSUMPTION FUNCTION PUZZLE

The puzzle consists of two types of evidence that made their appearance in the late 1940s and that were apparently in conflict. The first type of evidence came from estimates of the standard consumption function, equation (1), using annual data for the 1929–1941 period. (No earlier data were available then.) The estimated equation (in 1972 dollars) is

$$C = 47.6 + 0.73YD \qquad \text{(annual data, 1929–1941)} \qquad (B1)$$

This equation implies that the average propensity to consume falls as the level of income rises. It also has a low marginal propensity to consume. If we used this equation to predict today's average propensity to consume, the estimate would be 0.78, which of course is far off the actual ratio of about 0.9.

The second piece of evidence was the finding by Nobel Prize winner, Simon Kuznets (1901–1985), using averages of data over long periods—10 and 30 years—that there was near proportionality between consumption and income.* This is consistent with the intercept term in equation (1) being zero. The average propensity to consume that he found for three overlapping 30-year periods is shown in Table 1. The Kuznets results suggest, using long-term averages, that there is little variation in the ratio of consumption to income and, in particular, that there is no tendency for the average propensity to decline as disposable income rises.

TABLE 1   THE KUZNETS FINDING

	1869–1898	1884–1913	1904–1933
Average propensity	0.867	0.867	0.879

Source: Simon Kuznets, *National Income, A Summary of Findings* (New York: National Bureau of Economic Research, 1946), table 16.

There is clearly a conflict between the implications of the consumption function in equation (B1) and Kuznets' findings. The Kuznets results suggest that the average propensity to consume is constant over long periods, whereas equation (B1) suggests it falls as income rises. It is also clear that the consumption function estimated above on the basis of the prewar data is inconsistent with he same function estimated on the basis of postwar data, that is, equation (2).

The puzzle of the discrepancy was well known by the time the alternative theories we outline below were developed. In resolving the puzzle, both theories draw on the notion that consumption is related to a broader income measure than just current income. The broader measures go under the names of *lifetime income* and *permanent income*. These concepts have in common the recognition that consumption spending is maintained relatively constant in the face of fluctuations of current income. Consumption spending is not geared to what we earn today, but to what we earn on average. The important question obviously is what "average" means in this context. This is analyzed in the theories developed in the following sections.

* Simon Kuznets, *National Product Since 1869* and *National Income, A Summary of Findings* (New York: National Bureau of Economic Research, 1946).

We develop the two basic modern theories of consumption in the remainder of this chapter. They are the *life-cycle* theory, associated primarily with Franco Modigliani[5] of MIT, 1985 Nobel Prize winner in economic science, and the *permanent income* theory, associated primarily with Milton Friedman of the University of Chicago, the 1976 winner of the Nobel Prize in economics. These theories are quite similar. Like much of good macroeconomics, they have in common a careful attention to microeconomic foundations. The life-cycle theory in particular starts from an individual's lifetime consumption planning, and develops from there a macroeconomic theory of consumption and saving.

Box 8-1 describes an empirical puzzle about the simple consumption function that was historically important in leading to the new theories of the consumption function.[6]

8-1 THE LIFE-CYCLE THEORY OF CONSUMPTION AND SAVING

The consumption function (1) is based on the simple notion that individuals' consumption behavior in a given period is related to their income in that period. The *life-cycle hypothesis* views individuals, instead, as planning their consumption and saving behavior over long periods with the intention of allocating their consumption in the best possible way over their entire lifetimes.

The life-cycle hypothesis views savings as resulting mainly from individuals' desires to provide for consumption in old age. As we shall see, the theory points to a number of unexpected factors affecting the saving rate of the economy, for instance, the age structure of the population is, in principle, an important determinant of consumption and saving behavior.

To anticipate the main results of this section, we can already state here that we will derive a consumption function of the form

$$C = aWR + cYL \qquad (4)$$

where WR is real wealth, *a* is the marginal propensity to consume out of wealth, YL is *labor income*, and *c* is the marginal propensity to consume out of

---

[5] Modigliani developed the life cycle theory together with Richard Brumberg, who died tragically young, and Albert Ando of the University of Pennsylvania. His Nobel Prize lecture, "Life Cycle, Individual Thrift, and the Wealth of Nations," appears in the June 1986 *American Economic Review*.

[6] The theories of the consumption function developed hereafter are also useful for explaining another empirical puzzle that we shall not go into in detail. In *cross-sectional* studies of the relationship between consumption and income—studies in which the consumption of a sample of families is related to their income—the marginal propensity to consume out of disposable income also appears to be lower than the average propensity to consume, with the average propensity to consume falling as the level of income rises. If you are interested in the reconciliation of this evidence with the long-run evidence of Kuznets, you should look at the ingenious explanation advanced by Milton Friedman through the permanent-income hypothesis. Follow up the reference given in footnote 11.

labor income. Labor income is the income that is earned by labor, as opposed to the income earned by other factors of production, such as the rent earned by land or the profits earned by capital.

In developing the life-cycle hypothesis of saving and consumption, we show what determines the marginal propensities a and c in equation (4), why wealth should affect consumption, and how the life-cycle hypothesis helps explain the Kuznets puzzle described in Box 8-1.

Consider a person who expects to live for NL years, work and earn income for WL years, and be in retirement for $(NL - WL)$ years. The individual's year 1 is the first year of work. We shall, in what follows, ignore any uncertainty about either life expectancy or the length of working life. We shall assume, too, that no interest is earned on savings, so that current saving translates dollar for dollar into future consumption possibilities. With these assumptions, we can approach the saving or consumption decision with two questions. First, what are the individual's lifetime consumption possibilities? Second, how will the individual choose to distribute his or her consumption over a lifetime?

Consider now the consumption possibilities. For the moment we ignore property income (income from assets) and focus attention on labor income YL. Income, YL, and consumption, C, are measured in real terms. Given WL years of working, *lifetime income* (from labor) is $(YL \times WL)$, income per working year times the number of working years. Consumption over someone's lifetime cannot exceed this lifetime income unless that person is born with wealth, which we initially assume is not the case. Accordingly, we have determined the first part of the consumer's problem in finding the limit of lifetime consumption.

We assume the individual will want to distribute consumption over a lifetime so that he or she has a flat or even flow of consumption. Rather than consume a lot in one period and very little in another, the preferred profile is to consume exactly equal amounts in each period.[7] Clearly, this assumption implies that consumption is not geared to *current* income (which is zero during retirement), but rather to *lifetime income.*

Lifetime consumption equals lifetime income. This means that the planned level of consumption C, which is the same in every period, times the number of years in life NL equals lifetime income:

$$C \times NL = YL \times WL \qquad (5)$$

---

[7] Why? The basic reason is the notion of diminishing marginal utility of consumption. Consider two alternative consumption plans. One involves an equal amount of consumption in each of two periods; the other involves consuming all in one period and none in the other. The principle of diminishing marginal utility of consumption implies that in the latter case, we would be better off by transferring some consumption from the period of plenty toward that of starvation. The loss in utility in the period of plenty is *more* than compensated by the gain in utility in the period of scarcity. And there is a gain to be made by transferring consumption so long as there is any difference in consumption between the two periods. The principle of diminishing marginal utility of consumption conforms well with the observation that most people choose stable life styles — not, in general, saving furiously in one period to have a big bust in the next, but rather, consuming at about the same level every period.

where *WL* is working life. Lifetime income is equal to (*YL* × *WL*). Dividing through by *NL*, we have planned consumption per year, *C*, which is proportional to labor income:

$$C = \frac{WL}{NL} \times YL \tag{6}$$

The factor of proportionality in equation (6) is *WL/NL*, the fraction of lifetime spent working. Accordingly, equation (6) states that in each year of working life a fraction of labor income is consumed, where that fraction is equal to the proportion of working life in total life.

NUMERICAL EXAMPLE

Suppose a person starts working at age 20, plans to work till 65, and will die at 80. The working life *WL* is thus 45 years (= 65 − 20) and the number of years of life, *NL*, is 60 years (= 80 − 20). Annual labor income *YL* is $20,000. Then

$$
\begin{aligned}
\text{Lifetime income} &= YL \times WL \\
&= \$20,000 \times 45 \\
&= \$900,000
\end{aligned}
$$

This person will receive a total of $900,000 over a working lifetime.

The lifetime income, $900,000, has to be spread over the 60 years of life. The consumer wants to spread it evenly, and so

$$
\begin{aligned}
C &= \frac{\$900,000}{60} = \$15,000 = \frac{WL}{NL} \times YL \\
&= \frac{45}{60} \times 20,000 \\
&= 0.75 \times 20,000
\end{aligned}
$$

In this example, 0.75 of labor income is consumed each year the person works. Why is the propensity to consume out of labor income in this example equal to 0.75? Because that is the fraction of lifetime that the person works.

Saving and Dissaving

The counterpart of equation (6) is the saving function. Remembering that saving is equal to income less consumption, we have

$$S \equiv YL - C = YL \frac{NL - WL}{NL} \tag{7}$$

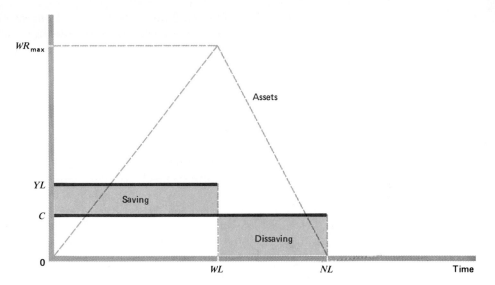

FIGURE 8-3   LIFETIME INCOME, CONSUMPTION, SAVINGS, AND WEALTH IN THE LIFE-CYCLE MODEL. During the working life, lasting WL years, the individual saves, building up assets. At the end of the working life, the individual begins to live off these assets, dissaving for the next $(NL - WL)$ years, till the end of life. Consumption is constant at level C throughout the lifetime. All assets have been used up at the end of life.

Equation (7) states that saving during the period in which the individual works is equal to a fraction of labor income, with that fraction being equal to the proportion of life spent in retirement.

Figure 8-3 shows the lifetime pattern of consumption, saving, and *dissaving*.[8] Over the whole lifetime, there is an even flow of consumption at the rate of C, amounting in total to $C \times NL$. That consumption spending is financed during working life out of current income. During retirement the consumption is financed by drawing down the savings that have been accumulated during working life. Therefore the shaded areas $(YL - C) \times WL$ and $C \times (NL - WL)$ are equal, or equivalently, saving during working years finances dissaving during retirement.

The important idea of lifetime consumption theory is apparent from Figure 8-3. It is that consumption plans are made so as to achieve a smooth or even level of consumption by saving during periods of high income and dissaving

[8] Figure 8-3 was developed by Franco Modigliani in "The Life Cycle Hypothesis of Saving, the Demand for Wealth and the Supply of Capital," *Social Research*, vol. 33, no. 2, 1966.

during periods of low income. This is, therefore, an important departure from consumption based on current income. It is an important difference because, in addition to current income, the whole future profile of income enters into the calculation of lifetime consumption. Before developing that aspect further, however, we return to Figure 8-3 to consider the role of assets.

ASSETS

During the working years, the individual saves to finance consumption during retirement. The saving builds up assets, and we accordingly show in Figure 8-3 how the individual's wealth or assets increase over working life and reach a maximum at retirement age. From that time on, assets decline because the individual sells assets to pay for current consumption.

What is the maximum level that assets reach? Remember that assets are built up to finance consumption during retirement. Total consumption during retirement is equal to $C \times (NL - WL)$. All that consumption is financed out of the assets accumulated by the date of retirement, which is when assets are at their peak.

Denote the maximum level of assets by WR_{max}. Then,

$$WR_{max} = C \times (NL - WL)$$

For instance, in the numerical example above, where C was \$15,000 and $(NL - WL)$ was equal to 15, the individual would have \$15,000 $\times$ 15 = \$225,000 saved at the date of retirement. Equivalently, the person has worked for 45 years, saving \$5,000 each year, meaning an accumulation of \$225,000 at age 65.

This simple case gives the spirit of the life-cycle hypothesis of consumption and saving. People do not want to consume over their lifetimes at precisely the same times and amounts they earn income. Thus they save and dissave so as to consume their lifetime incomes in the pattern they want. Typically, the theory argues, they will save while working, and then use the savings to finance spending in their retirement years.

SAVING

The life-cycle theory of consumption is also of course a theory of life-cycle saving. In its simplest version, as in Figure 8-3, the theory implies that individuals save for their retirement while working. But there is a more general theory of saving implied by the life-cycle theory. Namely, individuals aim to have smooth patterns of consumption over their lifetimes. Their income patterns may not be so smooth: they may go to school at one stage, or retire at another, or take a year off to find themselves at the age of forty. *The life-cycle theory of saving predicts that people save a lot when their income is high relative to lifetime average income, and dissave when their income is low relative to the lifetime average.*

Introducing Wealth

The next step is to extend this model and allow for initial assets, assuming the individual is born to wealth.[9] We can draw on the previous insight that the consumer will spread any existing resources to achieve an even lifetime consumption profile. The individual who has assets in addition to labor income will plan to use these assets to add to lifetime consumption. A person who is at some point T in life, with a stock of wealth WR and labor income accruing for another $(WL - T)$ years at the rate of YL, and with a life expectancy of $(NL - T)$ years to go, will behave as follows. The person's lifetime consumption possibilities are

$$C(NL - T) = WR + (WL - T)YL \qquad (8)$$

where we have included wealth WR along with lifetime labor income as a source of finance for lifetime consumption. From equation (8), consumption in each period is equal to

$$C = aWR + cYL \qquad a \equiv \frac{1}{NL - T} \qquad c \equiv \frac{WL - T}{NL - T} \qquad WL > T \qquad (9)$$

where the coefficients a and c are, respectively, the marginal propensities to consume out of wealth and out of labor income.

In the numerical example above we considered a person starting to work at age 20, who will retire at 65 and die at 80. Thus, $WL = 65 - 20 = 45$; and $NL = 80 - 20 = 60$. We also assumed $YL = 20,000$.

Now suppose the person is 40 years old. Accordingly $T = 20$, meaning that the person is in the twentieth year of working life. We can calculate the propensity to consume out of wealth a and the propensity to consume out of income c from equation (9). For this person, at age 40 (i.e., for $T = 20$):

$$a = \frac{1}{NL - T} = \frac{1}{60 - 20} = 0.025$$

$$c = \frac{WL - T}{NL - T} = \frac{45 - 20}{60 - 20} = 0.625$$

Suppose now that the individual's wealth is $200,000. Then from the consumption function, equation (9), we find:

$$
\begin{aligned}
C &= (0.025 \times 200,000) + (0.625 \times 20,000) \\
&= 5,000 + 12,500 \\
&= 17,500
\end{aligned}
$$

---

[9] The individual may receive wealth early in life through gifts or bequests. In the fully developed life-cycle model, the individual, in calculating lifetime consumption, has also to take account of any bequests he or she may want to leave. We discuss the role of bequests in Box 8-2.

Note that the consumption level here is higher than in the previous example. That is because this individual has more wealth at age 40 than he or she would have if all this wealth came from saving out of labor income. (That amount, at age 40, would from the previous example be \$100,000 — since the individual in the previous example saved \$5,000 per year and at $T = 20$ has been working 20 years.) We can conclude that we are dealing here with someone who inherited wealth and started out working life with some wealth.

Thus, in our model of individual lifetime consumption, we have derived a consumption function like equation (4), where both wealth and labor income affect the individual's consumption decisions. It is important to recognize from equation (9) that the marginal propensities are related to the individual's position in the life cycle. The closer a person is to the end of lifetime, the higher the marginal propensity to consume out of wealth. Thus, someone with 2 more years of life will consume half his or her remaining wealth in each of the remaining 2 years. The marginal propensity to consume out of labor income is related both to the remaining number of years during which income will be earned, $WL - T$, and to the number of years over which these earnings are spread, $NL - T$. It is quite clear from equation (9) that an increase in either wealth or labor income will raise consumption expenditures. It is apparent, too, that lengthening working life relative to retirement will raise consumption because it increases lifetime income and reduces the length of the period of dissaving. The most basic point, however, is that equation (9) shows both (lifetime) income and wealth as determinants of consumption spending.

To summarize where we have come so far, we note that in this form of the life-cycle model:

1. Consumption is constant over the consumer's lifetime.
2. Consumption spending is financed by lifetime income plus initial wealth.
3. During each year a fraction $1/(NL - T)$ of wealth will be consumed.
4. Current consumption spending depends on current wealth and lifetime income.

Extensions

The model as outlined makes very strong simplifying assumptions. It can be extended to remove most of the strong assumptions without affecting the underlying result of equation (9), that consumption is related to both labor income and wealth.

First, it is necessary to take account of the possibility that saving earns interest, so that a dollar not consumed today will provide more than a dollar's consumption tomorrow. Second, the analysis has to be extended to allow for the fact that individuals are uncertain of the length of their lifetimes, and also that they sometimes want to leave bequests to their heirs. In this latter case, they would not plan to consume all their resources over their own lifetimes. Similarly, the model has to be extended to take account of the composition of the family over time, so that some consumption is provided for children before they begin to work. But, to repeat, these extensions do not change the basic results contained in equation (9).

A final extension is very important. In practice, one never knows exactly what one's lifetime labor income will be, and lifetime consumption plans have to be made on the basis of predictions of future labor income. This, of course, raises the issue of how income is to be predicted. We do not pursue this important issue here, but leave it to the next section on permanent income, which is an estimate of lifetime income. However, *expected* lifetime labor income would be related to *current* disposable labor income, leading to a form of the consumption function like equation (4), perhaps with other variables also included.

Indeed, it is useful to think of the life-cycle and permanent-income theories as being fundamentally the same, with the life-cycle theory developing most carefully the implications of the model for the role of wealth and other variables in the consumption function,[10] and the permanent-income theory concentrating on the best way to predict lifetime income.

Aggregate Consumption and Saving

The theory as so far outlined is strictly a microeconomic theory about consumption and saving by individuals over the course of their lifetimes. How does it relate to aggregate consumption, which is, after all, the focus of macroeconomic interest in consumption? Imagine an economy in which population and the GNP were constant through time. Each individual in that economy would go through the life cycle of saving and dissaving outlined in Figure 8-3. The economy as a whole, though, would not be saving. At any one time, the saving of working people would be exactly matched by the dissaving of retired people. However, if the population were growing, there would be more young people than old, thus more saving in total than dissaving, and there would be net saving in the economy. Thus, aggregate consumption depends in part on the age composition of the population. It also depends on such characteristics of the economy as the average age of retirement and the presence or absence of Social Security. These surprising implications of the theory indicate the richness of the approach.

Implications

We want to return to equation (4) to emphasize again the role of wealth. Note from equation (4) that if there were an increase in wealth, the ratio of consumption to disposable income would rise. This has a bearing on the puzzle described in Box 8-1, where the average propensity to consume seems, on the

---

[10] The other variables indicated here will be discussed in the next paragraph.

basis of equation (3), to decline with income and, on the basis of Kuznets' findings, to remain constant on average over long periods.

If we divide through in equation (4) by YD, we obtain

$$\frac{C}{YD} = a\frac{WR}{YD} + c\frac{YL}{YD} \tag{10}$$

Now, if the ratio of wealth to disposable income and the ratio of disposable labor income to total disposable income are constant, then equation (10) shows that the ratio of consumption to disposable income will be constant. However, if the ratio of wealth to disposable income is changing, the average propensity to consume will also be changing.

This suggests, as an explanation of the Kuznets puzzle, the possibility that the ratio of wealth to disposable income is roughly constant over long periods, and that it varies considerably in the short run. This also helps explain the fluctuations in the average propensity to consume shown in Figure 8-2 as resulting from short-run changes in the wealth-income ratio.

One further interesting implication of the life-cycle hypothesis is that it provides a route for the stock market to affect consumption behavior. The value of stocks held by the public is part of wealth and is included in WR in equation (4). When the value of stocks is high—when the stock market is booming—WR is high and tends to increase consumption, and the reverse occurs when the stock market is depressed.

We continue now to the permanent-income theory of consumption, bearing in mind that we have not yet discussed the determinants of expected lifetime labor income in equation (9) in any detail, and recalling that the two theories should be thought of as complementary rather than competing.

8-2 PERMANENT-INCOME THEORY OF CONSUMPTION

In the long run, the consumption-income ratio is very stable, but in the short run, it fluctuates. The life-cycle approach explains this by pointing out that people want to maintain a smooth profile of consumption even if their lifetime income profile is uneven, and thus emphasizes the role of wealth in the consumption function. Another explanation, which differs in details but entirely shares the spirit of the life-cycle approach, is the permanent-income theory of consumption.

The theory, which is the work of Milton Friedman,[11] argues that people gear their consumption behavior to their permanent or long-term consumption opportunities, not to their current level of income. A suggestive example provided by Friedman involves someone who is paid or receives income only once a week, on Fridays. We do not expect that individual to concentrate his or her entire consumption on the one day on which income is received, with zero

---

[11] Milton Friedman, *A Theory of the Consumption Function* (Princeton, N.J.: Princeton University Press, 1957).

BOX
8-2

THE LIFE-CYCLE HYPOTHESIS, CONSUMPTION OF THE ELDERLY, AND BEQUESTS

Although the life-cycle hypothesis remains the leading microeconomic theory of consumption behavior, recent empirical evidence raises questions about the particular form of the theory developed in this chapter. In the form of the theory developed by Modigliani, the assumption is that people save mainly for retirement, and draw down their savings during retirement.

Two recent papers question the assumed motive for saving and the implication that people draw down their savings when old. Laurence Kotlikoff and Lawrence Summers* have made calculations suggesting that most saving is done to provide bequests rather than to provide for consumption when old. Of course, the savings are there for the old to use in retirement, but, they argue, the amount of wealth in the economy is far too large for people to have been saving only for their retirement. Rather, they conclude, people are saving mainly to pass wealth on to their descendants.

A detailed examination of the consumption propensities of the elderly by Sheldon Danziger, Jacques van der Gaag, Eugene Smolensky, and Michael Taussig† contains the remarkable conclusion that the elderly save a higher proportion of their incomes than the young. This fact is inconsistent with the simple form of the life-cycle hypothesis set out in the chapter.

How might this evidence be reconciled with existing theories? First, the facts are not yet definitive. Franco Modigliani in his Nobel Prize lecture (*American Economic Review*, June 1986) takes strong issue with the detailed calculations that underlie the Kotlikoff-Summers claim. In Japan, where similar results have been found,‡ the elderly typically move in and pool their wealth with their children. They thus probably are drawing down wealth during their retirement, but their wealth cannot be distinguished from that of the children who are saving.

If the basic evidence that the elderly who remain on their own accumulate wealth holds up, an explanation will have to take into account their increasing fears of being left alone without financial help from family, and with possibly large medical expenses, as they get older. The need for wealth may increase with age if complete insurance against medical expenses is not available — as it is not.

Whether people save for their own lifetimes, or also save to pass wealth on to their children, does not affect the fact that wealth belongs in the consumption function, as in equation (3). But as we shall see below, it has potentially important implications for the effects of fiscal policy on the economy.

---

* "The Role of Intergenerational Transfers in Aggregate Capital Accumulation," *Journal of Political Economy,* August 1981.

† In their research paper from the University of Wisconsin, "The Life Cycle Hypothesis and the Consumption Behavior of the Elderly," 1982.

‡ See Albert Ando and Arthur Kennickell, "How Much (or Little) Life Cycle Saving Is There in Micro Data?" in Rudiger Dornbusch, and Stanley Fischer (eds.), *Macroeconomics and Finance: Essays in Honor of Franco Modigliani* (Boston: MIT Press, 1986).

consumption on every other day. Again we are persuaded by the argument that individuals prefer a smooth consumption flow rather than plenty today and scarcity tomorrow or yesterday. On that argument, consumption on any one day of the week would be unrelated to income on that particular day but would rather be geared to average daily income — that is, income per week divided by the number of days per week. It is clear that in this extreme example, income for a period longer than a day is relevant to the consumption decision. Similarly, Friedman argues, there is nothing special about a period of the length of one quarter or one year that requires the individual to plan consumption within the period solely on the basis of income within the period; rather, consumption is planned in relation to income over a longer period.

The idea of consumption spending that is geared to long-term or average or permanent income is appealing and essentially is the same as the life-cycle theory. It leaves two further questions. The first concerns the precise relationship between current consumption and permanent income. The second question is how to make the concept of permanent income operational, that is, how to measure it.

In its simplest form the permanent-income hypothesis of consumption behavior argues that consumption is proportional to permanent income:

$$C = cYP \tag{11}$$

where YP is permanent (disposable) income. From equation (11), consumption varies in the same proportion as permanent income. A 5 percent increase in permanent income raises consumption by 5 percent. Since permanent income should be related to long-run average income, this feature of the consumption function is clearly in line with the observed long-run constancy of the consumption-income ratio.

Estimating Permanent Income

The next problem is how to think of and measure permanent income. We define permanent income as follows:[12] *Permanent income* is the steady rate of consumption a person could maintain for the rest of his or her life, given the present level of wealth and income earned now and in the future.

To think about the measurement of permanent income, imagine someone trying to figure out what his or her permanent income is. The person has a current level of income, and has formed some idea of the level of consumption he or she can maintain for the rest of life. Now income goes up. The person has to decide whether that income increase represents a permanent increase, or

---

[12] There is no standard definition of permanent income in Friedman's exposition of his theory. The definition given above is similar to average lifetime income. But it is not quite the same, because it effectively converts wealth into income in defining permanent income. Someone with no labor income, and only wealth, is defined as having permanent income equal to the amount he or she could consume each year by using up wealth at a steady rate over the remainder of his or her life.

merely a *transitory* change, one that will not persist. In any particular case, the individual may know whether the increase is permanent or transitory. A government official who is promoted one grade will know that the increase in income is likely to be maintained. Or the worker who has exceptionally high overtime in a given year will likely regard that year's increased income as transitory. But in general, a person is not so certain about what part of any change in income is likely to be maintained, and is therefore permanent, and what part is not likely to be maintained, and is therefore transitory. Transitory income is assumed not to have any substantial effect on consumption.

The question of how to infer what part of an increase in income is permanent is typically resolved in a pragmatic way by assuming that permanent income is related to the behavior of current and past incomes. To give a simple example, we might estimate permanent income as being equal to last year's income plus some fraction of the change in income from last year to this year:

$$
\begin{aligned}
YP &= Y_{-1} + \theta(Y - Y_{-1}) \qquad 0 < \theta < 1 \\
&= \theta Y + (1 - \theta) Y_{-1}
\end{aligned}
\tag{12}
$$

where θ is a fraction and Y_{-1} is last year's income. The second line in equation (12) shows permanent income as a *weighted average* of current and past income. The second formulation is, of course, equivalent to that in the first line. To understand equation (12), assume we had a value of $\theta = 0.6$ and that this year's income was $Y = \$25,000$ and last year's income was $Y_{-1} = \$24,000$. The value of permanent income would be $YP = \$24,600$ ($= 0.6 \times \$25,000 + 0.4 \times \$24,000$). Thus, permanent income is an average of the two income levels. Whether it is closer to this year's or last year's income depends on the weight θ given to current income. Clearly, in the extreme with $\theta = 1$, permanent income is equal to current income.

Some special features of equation (12) deserve comment. First, if $Y = Y_{-1}$, that is, if this year's income is equal to last year's, then permanent income is equal to the income earned this year and last year. This guarantees that an individual who had always earned the same income would expect to earn that income in the future. Second, note that if income rises this year compared with last year, then permanent income rises by *less* than current income. The reason is that the individual does not know whether the rise in income this year is permanent. Not knowing whether the increase in income will be maintained or not, the individual does not immediately increase the expected or permanent income measure by the full amount of the actual or current increase in income.

Rational Expectations and Permanent Income

An estimate of permanent income that uses only current and last year's income is likely to be an oversimplification. Friedman forms the estimate by looking at incomes in many earlier periods, as well as current income, but with weights that are larger for the more recent, as compared with the more distant, incomes.[13]

The rational expectations approach, discussed in Chapter 7 and in the following section, emphasizes that there is no simple theory that would tell us how expectations are or should be formed without looking at how income changes in practice. If, in practice, changes in income are typically permanent or long-run changes, then a consumer who sees a given change in his income will believe that it is mostly permanent. Such a consumer would have a high θ as in equation (12). If the consumer's income is usually very variable, then he or she will not pay much attention to current changes in income in forming an estimate of permanent income. Such a consumer will have a low value of θ.[14]

At the same time, any sensible theory of expectations, including rational expectations, would emphasize that a formula like (12), based on the behavior of income in the past, cannot include all the factors that influence a person's beliefs about future income. The discovery of a vast amount of oil in a country, for instance, would raise the permanent incomes of the inhabitants of the country as soon as it was announced, even though a (mechanical) formula like equation (12) based on past levels of income would not reflect such a change.

Permanent Income and the Dynamics of Consumption

Using equations (11) and (12), we can now rewrite the consumption function:

$$C = cYP = c\theta Y + c(1 - \theta)Y_{-1} \qquad (13)$$

The marginal propensity to consume out of *current* income is then just $c\theta$, which is clearly less than the long-run average propensity to consume, c. Hence, the permanent-income hypothesis implies that there is a difference between the short-run marginal propensity to consume and the long-run marginal (equal to the average) propensity to consume.

We shall see shortly that this implication is supported by the data. But first we explore it in more detail. The reason for the lower short-run marginal propensity to consume is that when current income rises, the individual is not sure that the increase in income will be maintained over the longer period on which consumption plans are based. Accordingly, the person does not fully adjust consumption spending to the higher level that would be appropriate if the increase in income were permanent. However, if the increase turns out to be permanent, that is, if next period's income is the same as this period's, then the person will (next year) fully adjust consumption spending to the higher

---

[13] Friedman also adjusted permanent income by taking into account the growth of income over time.
[14] Recall that although we restricted our measure of permanent income to a 2-year average, there is no reason why the average should not be taken over longer periods. If current income is unstable, an appropriate measure of permanent income may well be an average over 5 or more years.

level of income. Note, though, that the adjustment here is completed in 2 years only because we have assumed, in equation (12), that permanent income is an average of 2 years' income. Depending on how expectations of permanent income are formed, the adjustment could be much slower.

The argument is illustrated in Figure 8-4. Here we show the long-run consumption function as a straight line through the origin with slope c, which is the constant average and marginal propensity to consume out of permanent income. The lower flat consumption function is a short-run consumption function drawn for a given history of income which is reflected in the intercept $c(1 - \theta)Y_0$. Assume that we start out in long-run equilibrium with actual and permanent income equal to Y_0 and consumption therefore equal to cY_0, as is shown at the intersection of long-run and short-run consumption functions at point E. Assume next that income increases to the level Y'. In the short run, which means during the current period, we revise our estimate of permanent income upward by θ times the increase in income and consume a fraction c of

FIGURE 8-4   THE EFFECTS ON CONSUMPTION OF A SUSTAINED INCREASE IN INCOME. The short-run consumption functions, shown in color, have marginal propensity to consume of $c\theta$. The position of the short-run consumption function depends on the level of income in the previous period. The long-run consumption function is shown by the black line and has average and marginal propensity to consume equal to c. When the level of income rises from Y_0 to Y', consumption rises only to E' in the short run, because consumers are not sure the change in income is permanent. But with income remaining at Y', the short-run consumption function shifts up and consumption rises to point E'', as consumers realize their permanent income has changed.

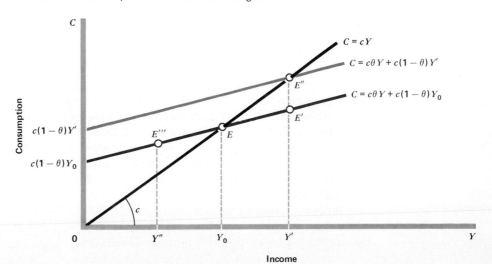

that increase in permanent income. Accordingly, consumption moves up along the short-run consumption function to point E'.

Note immediately that in the short run the ratio of consumption to income declines as we move from point E to E'. Going one period ahead and assuming that the increase in income persists so that income remains at Y', we get a shift in the consumption function. The consumption function shifts upward because, as of the given higher level of income, the estimate of permanent income is now revised upward to Y'. Accordingly, consumers want to spend a fraction of c of their new estimate of permanent income Y'. The new consumption point is E'', where the ratio of consumption to income is back to the long-run level. The example makes clear that in the short run, an increase in income causes a decline in the average propensity to consume because people do not anticipate that the increase in income will persist or be permanent. Once they do observe that the increase in income does persist, however, they fully adjust consumption to match their higher permanent income.

Like the life-cycle hypothesis, the permanent-income hypothesis has some unexpected and interesting implications. For instance, we noted above that an individual whose income is very unstable would have a low value of θ, whereas one whose income is more stable would have a higher value of θ. Looking at equation (13), this means that the short-run marginal propensity to consume of someone whose income is very variable will be relatively low — because the short-run marginal propensity to consume is $c\theta$. Friedman shows that this implication is borne out by the facts. Farmers, for instance, have very variable incomes and a low marginal propensity to consume out of current income.

The Life-Cycle and Permanent-Income Hypotheses

To conclude this section, it is worth considering again the relationship between the life-cycle and permanent-income hypotheses briefly. The two hypotheses are not mutually exclusive. The life-cycle hypothesis pays more attention to the motives for saving than the permanent-income hypothesis does, and provides convincing reasons to include wealth as well as income in the consumption function. The permanent-income hypothesis, on the other hand, pays more careful attention to the way in which individuals form their expectations about their future incomes than the original life-cycle hypothesis does. Recall that current labor income entered the life-cycle consumption function to reflect expectations of future income. The more detailed analysis of the determinants of expected future income that is provided by the permanent-income hypothesis can be, and has been, included in the life-cycle consumption function.

Indeed, modern theories of the consumption function combine the expectations formation emphasized by the permanent-income approach with the emphasis on wealth and demographic variables suggested by the life-cycle approach. A simplified version of a modern consumption function would be

$$C = aWR + b\theta YD + b(1 - \theta)YD_{-1} \qquad (14)$$

where YD in equation (14) would be disposable labor income. Equation (14) combines the main features that are emphasized by modern consumption theory.[15] It also shows the role of wealth, which is an important influence on consumption spending.

We end this section by repeating a warning that is important enough for us to risk overstating. An equation like (14) performs quite well on average in predicting consumption. But it is always important to remember the underlying theory when using it. Equation (14) embodies the estimate of permanent income implied by equation (12). If we have knowledge about some particular change in income—for example, that it is transitory—then we should use that knowledge in predicting consumption. For instance, as we shall see, a temporary 1-year tax increase that reduced current disposable income would reduce current consumption by much less than a tax increase of the same size that was known to be permanent, even though equation (14) does not show that.

8-3 RATIONAL EXPECTATIONS, EXCESS SENSITIVITY, AND LIQUIDITY CONSTRAINTS

One of the most fascinating areas of research in modern consumption theory concerns the question of whether consumption responds excessively to changes in current income. Modern research in this area, originating with work by Robert Hall of Stanford University and Marjorie Flavin of the University of Virginia, focuses on the combined implications of rational expectations and the life-cycle–permanent-income theory of consumption.[16]

In the previous section we noted that if expectations are rational, consumers' estimates of their permanent incomes should be consistent with the way income actually changes in the real world. When current income increases, it is usually impossible to be certain whether this increase represents a transitory or a permanent rise in income. But the consumer can use experience

---

[15] To fix ideas, you should draw a graph of equation (14) with consumption on the vertical axis and current disposable labor income on the horizontal axis. What is the intercept? How does the diagram differ from Fig. 8-4? Show the effects of (1) a transitory increase in income, (2) a sustained increase in income, and (3) an increase in wealth.

[16] See Robert E. Hall, "Stochastic Implications of the Life Cycle-Permanent Income Hypothesis: Theory and Evidence," *Journal of Political Economy*, vol. 86, December 1978, and Marjorie Flavin, "The Adjustment of Consumption to Changing Expectations about Future Income," *Journal of Political Economy*, vol. 89, October 1981.

to determine what is the expected relationship between changes in current and changes in permanent income. For example historically a $1 increase in current income might typically have represented a 25 cent increase in permanent income, with the remaining 75 cents being transitory. Let θ be the fraction of a dollar increase in current income that represents the permanent increase. Then the consumption function in (11) together with this extra information about the current–permanent income relation will yield a propensity to consume out of current income equal to $c\theta$. Thus if $c = 0.9$ and $\theta = 0.25$ the marginal propensity to consume out of current income should be 0.225.

The researcher determines the value of θ, the proportion of a current change in income that is permanent, by examining the past behavior of income.[17] The next step is to see whether consumption reacts to the change in income by the right amount, $c\theta$, implied by the combined rational-expectations–permanent-income theory. The striking finding, for instance in Flavin's 1981 paper referred to above, is that consumption *systematically* responds too much to current income, or is excessively sensitive. When income rises, consumption goes up by more than $c\theta$, and when income falls, consumption goes down by more than $c\theta$.

Still accepting the permanent-income hypothesis as a correct framework of consumption behavior, there are two possible explanations for this over-reaction. The first is that households do not correctly understand how changes in income are divided between permanent and transitory changes. This shortcoming is called a failure of the rational expectations hypothesis (RE) because it implies households have not done their homework and are not forecasting in the best possible way and using all available information about how income behaves. The alternative hypothesis is that, while households in fact understand how income changes are divided between permanent and transitory, they fail to adjust to these changes properly because of liquidity constraints.

Excess Sensitivity and Liquidity Constraints

A liquidity constraint exists when a consumer cannot borrow to sustain current consumption in the expectation of higher future income. Students in particular should appreciate the possibility that liquidity constraints exist. Most students can look forward to much higher income in future than they receive as students. The life-cycle theory says they should be consuming on the basis of their lifetime incomes, which means they should be spending much more than they earn. To do that, they have to borrow. They can borrow to some extent, through student loans. But it is entirely possible they cannot borrow enough to support consumption at its permanent level.

---

[17] Income changes over time in a more complicated way than is implied by equation (12), but that does not affect the principle that the test figures out how *estimated* permanent income should change with current income, and then sees whether changes in consumption are in accord with that estimate.

Such students are liquidity-constrained. When they leave college and take jobs, their incomes will rise, and their consumption will rise too. According to the life-cycle theory, consumption should not rise much when income rises, so long as the increase was expected. In fact, because of the liquidity constraint, consumption will rise a lot when income rises. Thus consumption will be more closely related to *current* income than is implied by the theory.

Or consider a household that suffers a decline in current income and that believes the decline is transitory because in the past, on average, falls in income have been mostly transitory. The household would therefore maintain consumption substantially unchanged, dissaving today. If there are no assets to run down to finance the excess of consumption over income, the household would borrow today, repaying the loan when income rises again as expected. Here imperfect capital markets come in. If the household cannot borrow because nobody wants to lend against uncertain (though likely) future income, then it faces liquidity constraints and for that reason is forced to consume according to current rather than permanent income. Consumption will then fall substantially along with current income — an overreaction in terms of the permanent income theory which occurs because of the impossibility of borrowing.

How serious are these liquidity constraints in fact? There is substantial evidence that liquidity constraints account for the excess sensitivity of consumption to income, and separate evidence that low income households are indeed liquidity-constrained.[18] When liquidity constraints are present, consumption behaves more like the simple Keynesian consumption function equation (2) than life-cycle theory implies.

The strength of liquidity constraints will depend on economic conditions. Suppose the government initiates a tax cut. If we are in a period of deep recession where many households have already run down their assets, the tax cut will translate into a large increase in spending: Liquidity-constrained household members, by definition, are spending less than they would like and hence will spend every extra penny they can lay their hands on. By contrast a tax cut that occurs in a period of prosperity will have much less of an impact because few households are in a liquidity-constrained position where they spend, at the margin, all of an extra dollar of income.

8-4 FURTHER ASPECTS OF CONSUMPTION BEHAVIOR

In this section we briefly review three topics in consumption, starting with international comparisons of saving behavior.

---

[18] For instance, Marjorie Flavin, "Excess Sensitivity of Consumption to Current Income: Liquidity Constraints or Myopia?," *Canadian Journal of Economics,* vol. 18, February 1985, and Fumio Hayashi, "The Effect of Liquidity Constraints on Consumption: A Cross-Sectional Analysis," *Quarterly Journal of Economics,* vol. 100, February 1985.

TABLE 8-1	INTERNATIONAL COMPARISONS OF SAVING RATES, 1970–1980					
	U.S.	Japan	France	U.K.	Italy	Canada
Gross household saving	12.6	25.0	16.7	10.9	25.1	13.8
Gross national saving	18.6	35.0	24.1	19.0	22.3	22.1
Adjusted national saving	26.1	38.9	33.5	25.1	28.2	31.3

Source. "Alternative Measures of Saving," *OECD Economic Outlook, Occasional Studies,* June 1983. Household saving rates are a percentage of disposable income; national saving rates are essentially percentages of GDP.

International Differences in Saving Rates

Consumers in the United States save a lower proportion of their disposable income than consumers in many other countries, as Table 8-1 shows. The most commonly quoted comparison is that in the first row. Households in the United States save a lower proportion of their disposable income than households in other major countries, except the United Kingdom.[19] North American households save only half as much of their disposable income as Japanese households.

A first question is why a low saving rate is a matter for concern. The answer is that the amount of investment in the economy, which determines how much capital — factories and machines — is available for production, depends on the saving rate. If an economy is at full employment, then an increase in the saving rate will lead to more investment and more future production, as we will see in Chapter 19. It is thus not a coincidence that the countries with lower saving rates in Table 8-1 are also the slower growing among the six major economies listed there.

A second question is why the saving rates differ. We do not go into that question in any detail. But Table 8-1 does provide some evidence, suggesting that the differences in saving rates are not quite as serious as the *household* saving rates indicate. The second row of the table examines *national* saving rates, which include saving by corporations and government. Corporations save when they retain profits and use them for investing, rather than paying them out as dividends. Corporate saving rates differ among countries, and it is therefore entirely possible for household saving rates in a country to be low even though corporations are saving a lot. Similarly, governments which run budget surpluses are saving and contributing to national saving.

---

[19] The major missing country is Germany, for which comparable data were not available. However, German saving ratios are substantially higher than those in the United States.

The comparison among national saving rates does not much affect the international comparison. Now the United States has the *lowest* national saving rate among the six countries in the table.

The third row shows a comparison that adjusts national saving rates for three factors, two of which we discuss. First, it counts spending on consumer durable goods as saving rather than consumption. When you buy a stereo or a car, you get to use that machine over several years. It thus is more an investment purchase (which produces its yield over a prolonged period) than a consumption purchase (which is used up immediately). Purchases of consumer durables make up a larger share of income in the United States than in the other countries. Second, it includes in saving some expenses on research and development. These expenditures, too, produce a yield over several years and thus can be thought of as investment rather than consumption.

Once these adjustments are made, the differences in national saving rates appear smaller than in the first row. It nonetheless remains true that the United States is a low saver and Japan an extraordinarily high saver.

These comparisons raise an interesting question, that is, whether households adjust their saving rates in accord with the saving carried out by other economic units. For instance, do households reduce their saving rates when corporations increase theirs? *Denison's Law* of saving, which shows a reasonably constant national saving rate for the United States over long periods, asserts that households do adjust their saving rates to offset the effect of changes in saving by government and business.[20] Later in this section we discuss further the relationship between household saving and government budget deficits.

Consumption, Saving, and Interest Rates

What can be done about a low saving rate? One suggestion is to make saving more worthwhile for the saver. Anyone who saves receives a return in the form of interest, or dividends and capital gains (an increase in the price) on stocks. It seems, then, that the natural way to raise saving is to raise the return available to savers. Think of someone saving and receiving an interest rate of 5 percent each year for each dollar saved. Surely an increase in the rate to, say, 10 percent would make that person save more? This thinking has influenced tax policy in the United States. For instance, there are many saving schemes which exempt the interest received on savings from the payment of taxes. This means the return received by the saver is raised compared with what it would be if taxes had to be paid on the interest received.

---

[20] Paul David and Jon Scadding, "Private Savings: Ultrarationality, Aggregation, and 'Denison's Law,' " *Journal of Political Economy*, March/April, vol. 82, 1974.

But should we really expect an increase in the interest rate to increase savings? It is true that when the interest rate rises, saving is made more attractive. But it is also made less necessary. Consider someone who has decided to save an amount that will ensure $10,000 per year is available for retirement. Suppose the interest rate is now 5 percent, and the person is saving $1,000 per year. Now let the interest rate rise to 10 percent. With such a high interest rate, the individual needs to save less now to provide the given $10,000 per year during retirement. It may be possible to provide the same retirement income by saving only about $650 a year. Thus an increase in the interest rate might reduce saving.

What do the facts show? Does saving rise when the interest rate increases, because every dollar of saving generates a higher return? Or does saving fall because there is less need to save to provide a given level of future income? The answers from the data are ambiguous. Many researchers have examined this question, but few have found strong positive effects of interest rate increases on saving. Typically, research suggests the effects are small and certainly hard to find.[21]

Tax Cuts, the Barro-Ricardo Hypothesis and Saving

The Reagan administration cut personal income tax rates by 30 percent in 1981 to 1983 on the argument that increased incentives to save and invest would enhance the productive capacity of the U.S. economy. But the question of crowding out was raised. Would so large a tax cut not mean that consumption spending and interest rates would rise and thus crowd out investment? Advocates of the tax cuts argued that on the contrary the tax cuts would be saved and that there was no risk of crowding out. Indeed, higher interest rates would lead to more saving.

We already reviewed above the view that interest rates affect saving and found out that there is no evidence to support the existence of a strong effect of interest rates on saving. We have not explicitly discussed the argument that tax cuts might be saved rather than spent. In fact, the analysis of *temporary* tax cuts suggests those are primarily saved rather than consumed. But there was no suggestion in 1981 that the tax cuts were expected to be only temporary or transitory.

The debate about tax cuts centers around an argument originally noted and rejected by David Ricardo in the nineteenth century, but revived and supported in 1974 by Robert Barro of the University of Rochester.[22] Suppose

---

[21] The best known study finding positive interest rate effects is that of Michael Boskin, "Taxation, Saving, and the Rate of Interest," *Journal of Political Economy*, pt. 2, April 1978. For more typical results, see Gerald A. Carlino, "Interest Rate Effects and Intertemporal Consumption," *Journal of Monetary Economics*, March 1982.

[22] "Are Government Bonds Net Wealth?" *Journal of Political Economy*, vol. 82, November/December 1974. Recent empirical research on this hypothesis is reported in David A. Aschauer "Fiscal Policy and Aggregate Demand," *American Economic Review*, March 1985.

the budget is balanced initially, and the government cuts taxes. There will be a budget deficit, financed by borrowing. The debt that is issued today must be retired next year or in some future year, along with the interest that it carries. To repay the debt the government will have to raise taxes in the future. Thus a tax cut today means a tax increase in the future. Hence changes in taxes should have no effect on consumption because *permanent* income is really unaffected by this intertemporal jiggling of tax rates.

But if permanent income is unaffected by the tax cut, then consumption should be unaffected. When taxes are cut today, households save the tax cut so they can pay the higher taxes tomorrow. We review this theory in more detail in Chapter 16 dealing with the government budget, but we can already run a preliminary check on the argument by studying saving behavior in the early 1980s when taxes were cut substantially.

On the Barro-Ricardo theory, the tax cuts should have been saved, and the household saving rate should have risen. Figure 8-5 shows the household saving rate lower in 1985 than it was in 1980. How can we interpret the behavior of the saving rate? Liquidity constraints already noted above are one element in the explanation. Another is that households may not in fact behave exactly in the way prescribed by the Barro-Ricardo hypothesis. They see themselves as recipients of present tax cuts, but (perhaps rationally) they do not see themselves but rather future generations (in whose well-being they are not especially interested) as paying the future taxes.[23] A third possibility is that the Barro-Ricardo view is correct and that national saving did not fall despite the decline in government and household saving, because corporations increased their saving. In fact, though, the national saving rate did fall over this period.

The evidence thus suggests that tax cuts *do* have an effect on consumption and saving, quite likely as a result of liquidity constraints.

8-5 CONSUMPTION AND THE *IS-LM* FRAMEWORK

In this section we discuss briefly how the more sophisticated theories of consumption we have developed in this chapter affect the *IS-LM* analysis of Chapters 4 and 5. We focus on two implications. The first is that consumption is a function of wealth, and not only income as we assumed previously. The second is that the response of consumption to various changes—for instance, in autonomous spending—may take time, as individuals gradually adjust their estimates of permanent income.

---

[23] We noted above that whether individuals save for their children affects fiscal policy. If parents are concerned enough about their children, they will regard future taxes to be paid by their children as equivalent to taxes on themselves.

FIGURE 8-5   THE PERSONAL SAVING RATE, 1979–1985. The diagram shows personal saving as a percentage of disposable income. Despite tax cuts starting in 1981, the personal saving rate did not increase as the Barro-Ricardo hypothesis suggests it should have.

Wealth in the Consumption Function

The life-cycle hypothesis, and estimated consumption functions of a form like equation (14), show that the rate of consumption depends on the level of wealth, as well as disposable income. This means that the position of the *IS* curve, representing equilibrium in the goods market, depends on the level of wealth.

Figure 8-6 shows how an increase in the level of wealth affects equilibrium output and the interest rate. The economy is initially in equilibrium at point *E*. There is then an increase in wealth: perhaps the stock market has gone up, because everyone is optimistic that the economy is recovering from a recession. The higher wealth raises consumption spending, and the *IS* curve thus shifts up to *IS'*. The new equilibrium is at *E'*.

At E', the interest rate and level of output are higher than at E. Thus an increase in wealth raises equilibrium output. Since the increase in wealth was assumed to result from expectations that the economy was recovering from a recession, we see that the expectations is partly self-fulfilling. A self-fulfilling prophecy is one which, purely as a result of being made, produces the prophesied result.

How large are such wealth effects? Estimates are that a 1 dollar increase in wealth is likely to increase consumption by about 3 cents. Households own about $3 trillion of equities. If the value of these equities rises by 10 percent, consumption will rise by 3 percent of $300 billion, or $9.0 billion. With consumption spending at an annual rate of about $2,500 billion, this is just under 0.4 percent of consumption spending. The effect of wealth on consumption spending is thus likely to be relatively unimportant, except for very large changes in stock prices.

The Dynamics of Adjustment

In Section 8-3 and Figure 8-4, we examined the dynamic response of consumption spending to a shift in disposable income. Now we want to embody that dynamic adjustment in a full *IS-LM* model. The slow adjustment of consumption to a given change in disposable income will mean that income itself

FIGURE 8-6   THE EFFECTS OF A SHIFT IN WEALTH. An increase in wealth shifts the consumption function, raising consumption demand at any level of income. Accordingly, the *IS* curve shifts to *IS'*, the level of output rises from Y_0 to Y', and the interest rate rises from i_0 to i'.

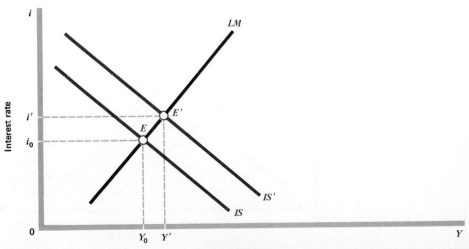

adjusts slowly to any given shift in autonomous spending that is not at first recognized as permanent, as we now show.

We assume here that people do not know whether the shift in autonomous demand is permanent or transitory. Rather, the only way they can figure that out is by seeing whether the change in demand persists or goes away. Figure 8-7 illustrates the effects of a permanent shift in autonomous demand, the nature of which (permanent or transitory) is not known to consumers.

Suppose that the economy is initially in equilibrium at point E. Now there is a shift in autonomous investment demand. In the long run, such a shift will move the IS curve to IS'. The extent of the shift is determined by the *long-run* multiplier $[1/(1 - c)]$, where c is the long-run propensity to consume. When expectations of income have fully adjusted, the economy will be at position E', with output level Y' and interest rate i'.

But in the short run the marginal propensity to consume is not c, but only $c\theta$. Thus the short-run multiplier is only $[1/(1 - c\theta)]$. In the short run, the IS

FIGURE 8-7   THE DYNAMICS OF ADJUSTMENT TO A SHIFT IN INVESTMENT DEMAND. Autonomous investment demand rises by amount ΔI, but it is not known whether the shift is permanent or transitory. It is in fact permanent, so that the IS curve will eventually be at IS', shifted to the right by an amount $[\Delta I/(1 - c)]$, where $[1/(1 - c)]$ is the long-run multiplier. But in the first period, the IS curve shifts only to IS'', by amount $[\Delta I/(1 - c\theta)]$, determined by the short-run consumption function and multiplier. Over time, the economy moves gradually from E'' to E', as individuals come to recognize that the shift in investment demand is permanent.

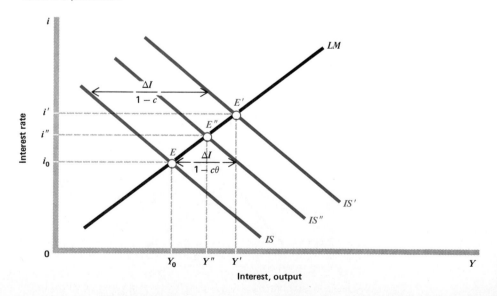

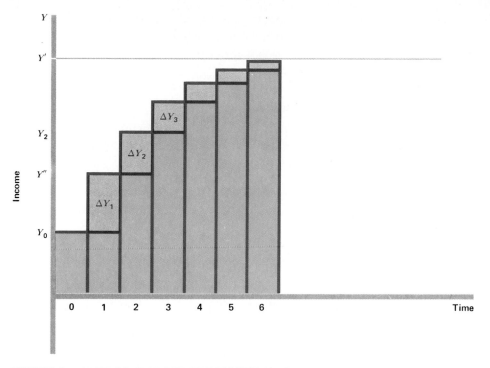

FIGURE 8-8   THE INCOME ADJUSTMENT PROCESS. The figure shows the *dynamic multiplier* of investment spending on income. This is how a given change in autonomous investment spending affects the level of output over time. Income rises in the first period from Y_0 to Y''. Then in subsequent periods it continues to rise toward its long-run equilibrium level Y'.

curve shifts only to *IS''*. Thus the immediate effect of the shift in investment demand is to raise income to Y'' and the interest rate to i''.

Next period, the *IS* curve shifts again. It does not shift all the way to *IS'* though. Consumers have adjusted their estimate of permanent income up, but they have not yet adjusted it all with way to Y', because income last period was only Y'' and not Y'. (To keep the diagram simple, we do not show the *IS* curve for the second or later periods.) Income and the interest rate will rise above Y'' and i'', but still fall short of Y' and i'.

This process continues, with the consumption function gradually shifting up over time, as people come to realize that their permanent incomes have risen. A single shock to autonomous demand therefore produces a slow, or *distributed lag*, effect on output. Figure 8-8 shows how income adjusts gradually to its new equilibrium level. The time pattern of changes in income caused by the increase in investment demand is called the *dynamic multiplier* of income with respect to autonomous investment.

Policy Implications

Suppose we have a permanent decline in investment expenditure. As we have seen, the decline in spending would lead to a fall in output and employment, occurring over a period of time.

Suppose the government wants to offset the reduction in aggregate demand by using tax cuts to keep income at the full-employment level. Since consumption adjusts only gradually to the changes in income resulting from both the initial fall in investment and tax cuts, the policy maker who wants to stabilize output *over time* will have to know about the adjustment pattern of consumption so as not to overreact. The problems may be further complicated, as we discuss in Chapter 12, by the fact that frequently the policy maker too reacts only with a lag to changed circumstances.

In the short run, consumption does not respond fully to changes in income. Therefore it takes a relatively large tax cut to obtain a given change in consumption with which to offset the decline in investment. Over time, though, consumption adjusts to the change in disposable income, and the tax cut that was initially just sufficient to offset reduced investment now turns out to be too generous. The compensating policy must therefore be one of a tax cut that is *front-loaded* and gradually phased down to the long-run level. The difference between the short-run and the long-run tax cuts is determined by the relative size of the short-run and long-run tax multipliers.

Indeed, the observant reader will recall that we assumed consumers had no special knowledge about the nature of the changes in income they experienced as a result both of the initial change in investment and of subsequent tax adjustments. Remarkably enough, if consumers know that the investment shift was permanent, and if they could be persuaded that the change in government policy was permanent, a one-time reduction in taxes, calculated using the long-run multiplier implied by the consumption function, would precisely stabilize income. For, in that case, the response to the fall in investment would recognize the permanent nature of the change, implying the long-run multiplier is relevant, and the response to the tax change would also recognize the permanent nature of the change. Consumption would adjust immediately, rather than gradually over the course of time.

The conclusion of this section is that policy making, and understanding of the behavior of the economy, cannot be successful unless careful attention is paid to expectations formation—bearing in mind that expectations depend in part on how the policy makers are perceived to be acting. This is the message of rational expectations, to which we return in Chapters 14 and 18.

8-7 SUMMARY

1. The simple Keynesian consumption function

$$C = 13.3 + 0.90YD \qquad (2)$$

accounts well for observed consumption behavior. The equation suggests that out of an additional dollar of disposable income, 90 cents is spent on consumption. The consumption function implies, too, that the ratio of consumption to income, C/YD, declines somewhat with the level of income.

2. Early empirical work on consumption showed that the average propensity to consume declined with the level of income. Postwar studies, by contrast, find a relatively constant average propensity to consume of about 0.9.

3. The evidence is reconciled by a reconsideration of consumption theory. Individuals want to maintain relatively smooth consumption profiles over their lifetime. Their consumption behavior is geared to their long-term consumption opportunities — permanent income or lifetime income plus wealth. With such a view, current income is only one of the determinants of consumption spending. Wealth and expected income play a role, too. A consumption function that represents this idea is

$$C = aWR + b\theta YD + b(1 - \theta)YD_{-1} \qquad (14)$$

which allows for the role of real wealth WR, current disposable income YD, and lagged disposable income YD_{-1}.

4. The life-cycle hypothesis suggests that the propensities of an individual to consume out of disposable income and out of wealth depend on the person's age. It implies that saving is high (low) when income is high (low) relative to lifetime average income. It also suggests that aggregate saving depends on the growth rate of the economy and on such variables as the age distribution of the population.

5. The permanent-income hypothesis emphasizes the formation of expectations of future income. It implies that the propensity to consume out of permanent income is higher than the propensity to consume out of transitory income.

6. Both theories do well, in combination, in explaining aggregate consumption behavior. But there are still some consumption puzzles, including the excess sensitivity of consumption to current income and the fact that the aged do not appear to draw down their savings as they age.

7. The excess sensitivity of consumption to current income may be caused by liquidity constraints that prevent individuals from borrowing enough to maintain smooth consumption patterns.

8. The rate of consumption, and thus of saving, could in principle be affected by the interest rate. But the evidence for the most part shows little effect of interest rates on saving.
9. The Barro-Ricardo hypothesis implies that cuts in tax rates that produce deficits will not affect consumption.
10. Lagged adjustment of consumption to income results in a gradual adjustment of the level of income in the economy to changes in autonomous spending and other economic changes. An increase in autonomous spending raises income. But the adjustment process is spread out over time because the rising level of income raises consumption only gradually. This adjustment process is described by dynamic multipliers that show by how much income changes in each period following a change in autonomous spending (or other exogenous variables).

KEY TERMS

Life-cycle hypothesis
Dissaving
Permanent income
Rational expectations

Liquidity constraints
Dynamic multiplier
Excess sensitivity
Barro-Ricardo hypothesis

PROBLEMS

1. What is the significance of the ratio of consumption to GNP in terms of the level of economic activity? Would you expect it to be higher or lower than normal during a recession (or depression)? Do you think the ratio would be higher in developed or underdeveloped countries? Why?

The Life-Cycle Hypothesis

2. The text implies that the ratio of consumption to accumulated savings declines over time until retirement.
   (a) Why? What assumption about consumption behavior leads to this result?
   (b) What happens to this ratio after retirement?
3. (a) Suppose you earn just as much as your neighbor but are in much better health and expect to live longer than she does. Would you consume more or less than she does? Why? Derive your answer from equation (6).
   (b) According to the life-cycle hypothesis, what would the effect of the Social Security system be on your average propensity to consume out of (disposable) income?
   (c) How would equation (9) be modified for an individual who expects to receive $X per year of retirement benefits? Verify your result in 3b.
4. Give an intuitive interpretation of the marginal propensity to consume out of wealth and income at time T in the individual's lifetime in equation (9).

5. In equation (6), consumption in each year of working life is given by

$$C = \frac{WL}{NL} \times YL \tag{6}$$

In equation (9), consumption is given as

$$C = aWR + cYL \qquad a \equiv \frac{1}{NL - T} \qquad c \equiv \frac{WL - T}{NL - T} \tag{9}$$

Show that equations (6) and (9) are consistent for an individual who started life with zero wealth and has been saving for T years. [*Hint:* First calculate the individual's wealth after T years of saving at rate $YL - C$. Then calculate the level of consumption implied by equation (9) when wealth is at the level you have computed.]

Permanent-Income Hypothesis

6. In terms of permanent-income hypothesis, would you consume more of your Christmas bonus if (a) you knew there was a bonus every year; (b) this was the only year such bonuses were given out?
7. Suppose that permanent income is calculated as the average of income over the past 5 years; that is,

$$YP = \tfrac{1}{5}(Y + Y_{-1} + Y_{-2} + Y_{-3} + Y_{-4})$$

Suppose, further, that consumption is given by $C = 0.9YP$.
(a) If you have earned $10,000 per year for the past 10 years, what is your permanent income?
(b) Suppose next year (period $t + 1$) you earn $15,000. What is your new YP?
(c) What is you consumption this year and next year?
(d) What is your short-run marginal propensity to consume (MPC)? Long-run MPC?
(e) Assuming you continue to earn $15,000 starting in period $t + 1$, graph the value of your permanent income in each period using the equation above.
8. Explain why good gamblers (and thieves) might be expected to live very well even in years when they don't do well at all.
9. The graph (below) shows the lifetime earnings profile of a person who lives for four periods and earns income of $30, $60, and $90 in the first three periods of the life cycle. There are no earnings during retirement. Assume that the interest rate is 0.
(a) You are asked to determine the level of consumption, compatible with the budget constraint, for someone who wants an even consumption profile throughout the life cycle. Indicate in which periods the person saves and dissaves and in what amounts.
(b) Assume now that, contrary to 9a, there is no possibility for borrowing. The credit markets are closed to the individual. Under this assumption, what is the flow of consumption the individual will pick over the life cycle? In providing an answer, continue to assume that if possible, an even flow of consumption is preferred. (*Note:* You are assuming here that there are liquidity constraints.)
(c) Assume next that the person described in 9b receives an increase in wealth or nonlabor income. The increase in wealth is equal to $13. How will that wealth be allocated over the life cycle with an without access to the credit market? How would your answer differ if the increase in wealth were $23?

(d) Relate your answer to the problem of excess sensitivity of consumption to current income.

10. Consider the consumption function in equation (14). Assume autonomous investment spending is constant, as is government spending. The economy is close to full employment and the government wishes to maintain aggregate demand precisely constant. In these circumstances, assume there is an increase in real wealth of $10 billion. What change in income taxes will maintain constant the equilibrium level of income in the present period? What change is required to maintain income constant in the long run?

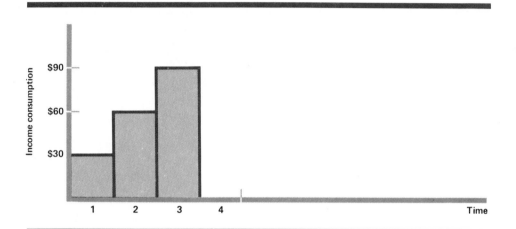

11. Equation (14) shows consumption as a function of wealth and current and lagged disposable income. To reconcile that consumption function with permanent-income expectations formation, you are asked to use equation (12) and the consumption function

$$C = 0.045WR + 0.55YD + 0.17YD_{-1}$$

to determine the magnitude of θ and $(1 - \theta)$ that is implied by equation (14).

12. (a) Explain why the interest rate might affect saving.
    (b) Why does it matter?

*Adjustment and Dynamics

13. Here is a challenge to your ability to develop diagrams. You are asked to show short-run and long-run income determination in the 45° diagram of Chapter 3. Assume that investment demand is totally autonomous and does not respond to the interest rate. Thus you do not need to use the full *IS-LM* model.
    (a) Draw the short-run and long-run consumption functions and the aggregate demand schedule with $I = \bar{I}$.
    (b) Show the initial full equilibrium.
    (c) Show the short-run and long-run effects of increased investment on equilibrium income.

INVESTMENT SPENDING

Consumption spending in the United States is on average about 62 percent of GNP and thus acounts for most of aggregate demand. Investment spending is typically less than 20 percent of GNP in the United States. But investment spending fluctuates much more than consumption and that gives it particular interest.

Table 9-1 shows how the components of aggregate demand changed in the 1981–1982 recession and in the subsequent recovery. From the third quarter of 1981 to the fourth quarter of 1982, consumption and government spending increased despite the recession. (Recall from Chapter 8 that consumption is affected by permanent or lifetime disposable income and not only by current GNP.) But GNP nevertheless fell sharply, mostly because gross investment spending declined by more than total GNP.[1]

In the subsequent recovery investment boomed, increasing by even more than consumption spending in the 3 years following the trough of the recession. The fluctuations in investment between 1981 and 1985 far exceed the fluctuations in consumption.

---

[1] There was also a sharp fall in net exports during the recession and in the subsequent recovery. This was because the exchange rate of the dollar appreciated, and American goods became more expensive relative to foreign goods. The relationship between the exchange rate and net exports was developed in Chap. 6.

TABLE 9-1	REAL GNP AND ITS COMPONENTS IN RECESSION AND RECOVERY (Billions of 1982 Dollars)	
	Change 1981 III – 1982 IV	Change 1982 IV – 1985 IV
GNP	−105.3	445.7
Consumption	47.2	250.0
Government	29.9	81.6
Investment	−151.9	253.4
Net exports	−30.4	−139.3

Source: Data Resources, Inc.

Figure 9-1 shows that the major role played by the decline in investment in the most recent recession is typical. In every recession or shortly before it, the share of investment in GNP falls sharply, and then investment begins to recover as the recovery gets under way. The cyclical relationships shown in Figure 9-1 extend much further back in history: For instance, in the great depression, gross investment fell to less than 4 percent of GNP in both 1932 and 1933. Understanding investment, then, will go a long way in helping us understand the business cycle.

In this chapter we continue our in-depth analysis of the components of aggregate demand. We both provide a foundation for the essential component of the simple investment function of Chapter 4 — that investment demand is reduced by increases in the interest rate — and go further than that investment function, by discussing the roles of output and taxes in determining investment. While much of the reason for studying investment spending is that its fluctuations help account for the business cycle, another reason is that investment spending can be significantly affected by policy. High interest rates, caused by restrictive monetary policy and expansive fiscal policy, reduce investment spending; policies that reduce interest rates and provide tax incentives for investment can increase investment spending.

One simple relationship is vital to the understanding of investment. Investment is spending devoted to increasing or maintaining the stock of capital. The stock of capital consists of the factories, machines, offices, and other durable products used in the process of production. The capital stock also includes residential housing as well as inventories. Investment is spending that adds to these components of capital stock. Recall the distinction drawn in Chapter 2 between *gross* and *net investment.* Gross investment represents total additions to the capital stock. Net investment subtracts depreciation — the reduction in the capital stock that occurs each period through wear and tear and the simple ravages of time, equal to about 11 percent of GNP—from gross investment. Net investment thus measures the increase in the capital stock in a given period of time.

In this chapter we disaggregate investment spending into three categories. The first is *business fixed investment,* consisting of business firms' spending on durable machinery, equipment, and structures, such as factories and machines. The second is *residential investment,* consisting largely of investment in housing. And the third is *inventory investment,* with which we start.

Table 9-2 shows the changes in the three categories of investment in the 1981–1982 recession and the subsequent recovery, and the share of each type of investment in GNP in 1985. Business fixed investment is the largest component of investment. Inventory investment is on average a very small part of aggregate demand (as can be seen in Figure 9-1) but fluctuates substantially. Inventory investment is frequently negative during recessions, when businesses decide the stocks of goods they have available for sale are too large and reduce them. Housing investment, too, fluctuates a good deal.

In the remainder of this chapter we develop theories and discuss evidence about the determinants of the rate of investment in each of the three major categories shown in Figure 9-1 and Table 9-2. We will develop what look like

FIGURE 9-1   COMPONENTS OF INVESTMENT SPENDING AS A PERCENTAGE OF GNP.

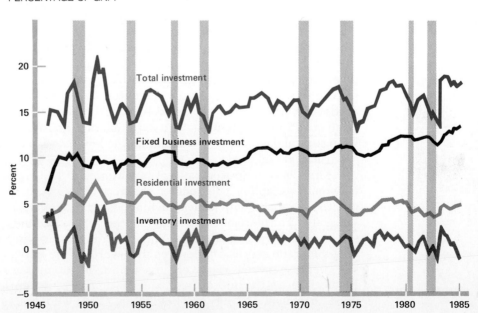

TABLE 9-2	GROSS DOMESTIC PRIVATE INVESTMENT (Billions of 1982 Dollars)		
	Change 1981 III–1982 IV	Change 1982 IV–1985 IV	Level as % of GNP, 1985
Business fixed investment	−50.4	133.1	13.2
Residential investment	−6.5	60.9	4.8
Change in inventories	−95.0	59.4	0.0

Source: Data Resources Inc.

different models to explain each of the categories of investment spending. However, the theories are essentially similar, sharing a common view of the interaction between a desired capital stock and the rate at which the economy adjusts toward that desired stock.

9-1 INVENTORY INVESTMENT

Inventories consist of raw materials, goods in the process of production, and completed goods held by firms in anticipation of their sale. The ratio of inventories to annual final sales in the United States has been in the range of 25 to 35 percent over the past 20 years. That is, on average, firms hold inventories that constitute 3 to 4 months' worth of their final sales.

The inventories of interest to us are those held to meet future demands for goods. Firms hold such inventories because goods cannot be instantly manufactured or obtained from the manufacturer to meet demand. Some inventories are held as an unavoidable part of the production process; there is an inventory of meat and sawdust inside the sausage machine during the manufacture of sausage, for example. Inventories are also held because it is less costly for a firm to order goods less frequently in large quantities than to order small quantities frequently — just as the average householder finds it useful to keep several days' supplies on hand in the house so as not to have to visit the supermarket daily.

Firms have a desired ratio of inventories to final sales that depends on economic variables. The smaller the cost of ordering new goods and the greater the speed with which such goods arrive, the smaller the inventory-sales ratio. The more uncertainty about the demand for the firm's goods, given the expected level of sales, the higher the inventory-sales ratio. The inventory-sales ratio may also depend on the level of sales, with the ratio falling with sales because there is relatively less uncertainty about sales as sales increase. Finally, there is the interest rate. Since firms carry inventories over time, they must tie up money to buy and hold them. There is an interest cost involved in such inventory holding, and the desired inventory-sales ratio should be expected to fall with increases in the interest rate.

Anticipated versus Unanticipated Inventory Investment

The most interesting aspect of inventory investment lies in the distinction betwen anticipated (desired) and unanticipated (undesired) investment. Inventory investment could be high in two circumstances. First, if sales are unexpectedly low, firms would find unsold inventories accumulating on their shelves; that constitutes unanticipated inventory investment. This is the type of inventory investment discussed in Chapter 3. Second, inventory investment could be high because firms plan to restore depleted inventories. The two circumstances obviously have very different implications for the behavior of aggregate demand. Unanticipated inventory investment is a result of unexpectedly low aggregate demand. On the other hand, planned inventory investment can be a response to recent, unexpectedly high aggregate demand. That is, rapid accumulation of inventories could be associated with either rapidly declining aggregate demand or rapidly increasing aggregate demand.

Inventories in the Business Cycle

Inventory investment fluctuates substantially in the business cycle — proportionately more than any other component of aggregate demand. In every post–World War II recession in the United States there has been a decline in inventory investment — the rate at which firms add to their inventories — between peak and trough. Table 9-3 gives the data on the change in the rate of inventory investment in column 2. At the end of every recession, firms have been reducing their inventories, meaning that inventory investment has been negative in the final quarter of every recession. (This information is not shown in Table 9-3 but may be visible in Figure 9-2.)

The last column of Table 9-3 gives an indication that the change in inventory investment typically plays a significant role in the decline in GNP during a recession. Column 3 of the table calculates how much less GNP grew in fact between peak and trough than it would have grown had GNP kept on growing at a trend rate of 3.2 percent per annum. That is a rough measure of the fall in output during the recession. Typically 20 to 40 percent or more of that decline is directly attributable to a decline in inventory investment.

The role of inventories in the business cycle is a result of a combination of unanticipated and anticipated inventory change. Figure 9-2 illustrates the combination using data from the most recent recessions. The behavior of sales and output for the 1981–1982 recession were more typical. Before the recession began, GNP increased rapidly, recovering from the previous recession. That meant firms were running down their inventories. From the beginning of 1981 firms began to accumulate inventories, as GNP exceeded their sales. Firms were probably anticipating high sales in the future and decided to build up

TABLE 9-3 INVENTORY DECUMULATION IN RECESSIONS
(Billions of 1982 dollars)

RECESSION		(1) Change in real GNP	(2) Change in rate of inventory investment	(3) Change in real GNP relative to trend	(2)/(3), %
Peak	Trough				
48.4	49.4	−22.2	−28.3	−47.2	60.0
53.2	54.2	−43.7	−18.4	−89.9	20.5
57.3	58.1	−55.4	−22.5	−82.4	28.0
60.2	61.1	+4.5	−14.4	−35.7	40.3
69.4	70.4	−9.7	−7.3	−87.3	8.4
73.4	75.1	−78.1	−120.1	−231.3	51.9
80.1	80.3	−74.3	−33.6	−126.0	26.7
81.3	82.4	−105.3	−95.0	−236.7	40.1

Notes: 1. Change in real GNP relative to trend is calculated by assuming GNP would have continued to grow at a quarterly level rate of 0.8% from the peak level of income.
2. Dates for peaks and troughs are for years and quarters (for example, 48.4 is fourth quarter of 1948.)

Source: Data Resources, Inc.

their stocks of goods for future sale. Thus there was *intended* inventory accumulation.

Final sales turned down at the beginning of 1981, but GNP stayed high until the third quarter. Then firms realized they had too much inventory and cut production to get inventories back in line. In the first quarter of 1982, firms had cut output way back and finally were successfully and *intentionally* reducing their inventories, as sales exceed output.

The behavior seen in the 1981–1982 recession explains much of the role of inventories in recessions. Before the recession there is a reduction in aggregate demand, reflected in a slowdown in sales. But output does not respond much, and inventories build up unintentionally. Then firms decide to get rid of their inventories, reducing production and planning to sell out of inventories; this is *intended* inventory decumulation. In almost all post–World War II recessions there has been a stage at which output falls quite sharply as firms intentionally cut back production to get inventories back in line. And this cutback accentuated the recession.

Note that the behavior of inventories reflects the adjustment mechanism for output that we discussed in Chapter 3. When there is a fall in aggregate demand, firms unanticipatedly accumulate inventories. They cut back production in order to get output back in line with demand. As we noted in the footnotes in Chapter 3, though, in the process of reducing production to cut back inventories, firms may cause a larger reduction in GNP for a while than would have happened had inventories not been unintentionally accumulated. This is known as the *inventory cycle*.

To understand the inventory cycle, consider the case of a hypothetical automobile dealer who sells, say, thirty cars per month, and holds an average of 1 month's sales—namely, thirty cars—in inventory. As long as sales stay steady at thirty cars per month, the dealer will be ordering thirty cars per month from the factory. Now suppose sales drop to twenty-five cars per month, and it takes the dealer 2 months to respond to the change. During those 2 months inventory will have climbed to forty cars. In the future the dealer will want an inventory of only twenty-five cars on hand. Thus when responding to the fall in demand, the dealer cuts the order from the factory from thirty to 10 in the third month, to get the inventory back to 1 month's sales. After the desired inventory-sales ratio has been restored, the order will be twenty-five cars per month from the factory. We see in this extreme case how the drop in

FIGURE 9-2   SALES AND OUTPUT IN RECESSION AND RECOVERY.
(*Source:* Data Resources, Inc.)

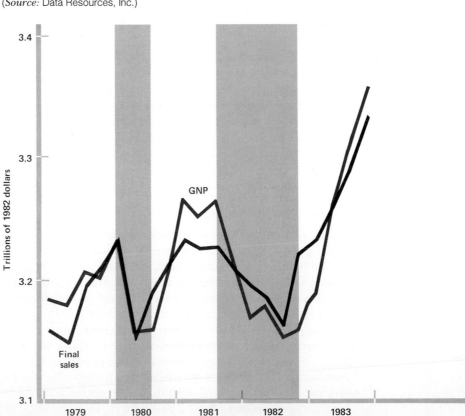

demand of five cars, instead of leading to a simple drop in car output of five cars per month, causes a drop in output of 20 cars in 1 month, followed by the longer-run drop in output of five cars per month.

The 1980 recession is one exception to the standard pattern of inventory behavior during a recession. In that recession there were only small movements in inventories. Sales and output basically moved together, and there is no pattern of an inventory cycle. This helps account for the brevity of the recession.

If inventories could be kept more closely in line with sales, or aggregate demand, fluctuations in inventory investment and in GNP would be reduced.

9-2 BUSINESS FIXED INVESTMENT: THE NEOCLASSICAL APPROACH

The machinery, equipment, and structures used in the production of goods and services constitute the *stock* of business fixed capital. Our analysis of business fixed investment in this section proceeds in two stages. First, we ask how much capital firms would like to use, given the costs and returns of using capital and the level of output they expect to produce. That is, we ask what determines the *desired capital stock.* The desired capital stock is the capital stock that firms would like to have in the long run, abstracting from the delays they face in adjusting their use of capital. However, because it takes time to order new machines, build factories, and install the machines, firms cannot instantly adjust the stock of capital used in production. Second, therefore, we discuss the rate at which firms adjust from their existing capital stock toward the desired level over the course of time. The rate of adjustment determines how much firms spend on adding to the capital stock in each period; that is, it determines the rate of investment.

The Desired Capital Stock: Overview

Firms use capital, along with labor, to produce goods and services for sale. The firms' goal is, of course, to maximize their profits. In deciding how much capital to use in production, they have to balance the contribution that more capital makes to their revenues against the cost of using more capital. The *marginal product of capital* is the increase in output produced by using one more unit of capital in production. The *rental (user) cost of capital* is the cost of using one more unit of capital in production.

To derive the rental cost of capital, we think of the firm as financing the purchase of the capital (whether the firm produces the capital itself or buys it from some other firm) by borrowing, at an interest cost i. In order to obtain the services of an extra unit of capital, in each period the firm must pay the interest cost i for each dollar of capital that it buys. Thus the basic measure of the rental cost of capital is the interest rate.[2] Later we shall go into more detail about the rental cost of capital, but for the meantime we shall think of the interest rate as determining the rental cost.

In deciding how much capital they would like to use in production, firms compare the value of the marginal product of capital with the user or rental cost of capital. The value of the marginal product of capital is the increase in the *value* of output obtained by using one more unit of capital. For a competitive firm, it is equal to the price of output times the marginal product of capital. So long as the value of the marginal product of capital is above the rental cost, it pays the firm to add to its capital stock. Thus the firm will keep investing until the value of the output produced by adding one more unit of capital is equal to the cost of using that capital — the rental cost of capital. In equilibrium, we must have

$$\text{Value of marginal product of capital} = \text{rental cost of capital} \qquad (1)$$

To give content to this relationship, we have to specify what determines the productivity of capital and what determines the user (rental) cost of capital. The marginal product of capital is examined next, and then we turn to the rental cost of the capital.

The Marginal Productivity of Capital

In understanding the marginal productivity of capital, it is important to note that firms can substitute capital for labor in the production of output. Different combinations of capital and labor can be used to produce a given level of output. If labor is relatively cheap, the firm will want to use relatively more labor, and if capital is relatively cheap, the firm will want to use relatively more capital.

The general relationship among the desired capital stock (K^*), the rental cost of capital (rc), and the level of output is given by

$$K^* = g(rc, Y) \qquad (2)$$

Equation (2) indicates that the desired capital stock depends on the rental cost of capital and the level of output. The lower the rental cost of capital, the larger the desired capital stock. And the greater the level of output, the larger the desired capital stock.[3]

---

[2] Even if the firm finances the investment out of profits it has made in the past — retained earnings — it should still think of the interest rate as the cost of using the new capital, since it could otherwise have lent out those funds and earned interest on them, or paid them out as dividends to shareholders.

[3] In writing equation (2), we assume that the real wage paid to labor is given and does not change as the rental cost of capital changes. In general, the rental cost of capital *relative to* the real wage determines the desired capital stock, given Y.

The relationship shown in equation (2) makes complete sense. It says that firms want to have more capital on hand if they have to produce more output, and that they want to have more capital the cheaper it is to use capital. We now explain in more detail the factors underlying equation (2).

As the firm combines progressively more capital with relatively less labor in the production of a *given* amount of output, the marginal product of capital declines. This relation is shown in the downward-sloping schedules in Figure 9-3. Those schedules show how the marginal product of capital falls as more capital is used in producing a given level of output. The schedule YY_1 is drawn for a level of output Y_1. The schedule YY_2 is drawn for the higher output level Y_2. The marginal product of capital, given the capital stock, say, K_0, is higher on the schedule YY_2 than on YY_1. That is because more labor is being used in combination with the given amount of capital K_0 to produce the level of output Y_2 than to produce Y_1.

Figure 9-3 shows the marginal product of capital in relation to the level of output and the amount of capital being used to produce that output. Figure 9-4 is a similar diagram which shows the desired capital stock as related to the rental cost of capital and the level of output. Given the level of output, say, Y_1,

FIGURE 9-3   THE MARGINAL PRODUCT OF CAPITAL IN RELATION TO THE LEVEL OF OUTPUT AND THE CAPITAL STOCK. The marginal product of capital decreases as relatively more capital is used in producing any given level of output. Thus the schedules YY, and YY_2 are downward sloping. The higher the level of output, for any given capital input, the higher the marginal product of capital. Thus schedule YY_2, with output level Y_2 greater than Y_1, is above schedule YY_1.

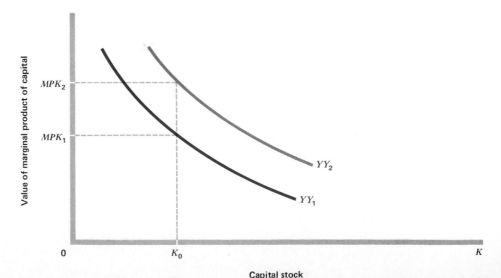

the firm will want to use more capital the lower the rental cost of capital — because at low rental costs of capital, it can afford to use capital even when its marginal productivity is quite low. If the rental cost of capital is high, the firm will be willing to use capital only if its marginal productivity is high — which means that the firm will not want to use very much capital and will instead substitute labor for capital. In producing a higher level of output, say, Y_2, the firm will use both more capital and more labor, given the rental cost of capital. Therefore, at higher levels of output, the desired capital stock is higher.

THE COBB-DOUGLAS PRODUCTION FUNCTION

While equation (2) provides the general relationship determining the desired capital stock, a particular form of the equation, based on the *Cobb-Douglas production function*,[4] is frequently used in studies of investment behavior. The particular equation that is used is[5]

$$K^\circ = \frac{\gamma Y}{rc} \tag{3}$$

where γ is a constant. In this case, the desired capital stock varies in proportion to output. Given output, the desired capital stock varies inversely with the rental cost of capital.

ESTIMATING THE RETURN TO CAPITAL

The value of the marginal product of capital is the increase in the value of output that is obtained by increasing the capital stock by one unit. If the capital stock were increased by $1 today, the marginal product of capital would be the

---

[4] The Cobb-Douglas production function is written in the form

$$Y = N^{1-\gamma}K^\gamma \qquad 1 > \gamma > 0$$

where N is the amount of labor used. This production function is particularly popular because it is easy to handle, and also because it appears to fit the facts of U.S. economic experience quite well. The coefficient γ appearing in eq (3) is the same as the γ of the production function. The reader trained in calculus will want to show that γ is the share of capital in total income.

[5] We draw attention here to a very subtle point: Equation (3) gives the marginal product of capital *(MPK)* when the *input of labor* is held fixed, while in Figs. 9-3 and 9-4 we work with the *MPK* when labor is being adjusted so that *output* is kept fixed. The desired capital stock that corresponds to Figs. 9-3 and 9-4 is

$$K^\circ = \left[\frac{\gamma\omega}{(1-\gamma)rc}\right]^{1-\gamma} Y \tag{3a}$$

where ω is the real wage.

  Equation (3a), like equation (3), implies that desired capital is proportional to Y and varies inversely with the rental cost of capital. We use equation (3) rather than equation (3a) in the text because it is the form that has been used in empirical studies. Note however that we should certainly expect equations (3a)'s implication that a higher wage rate increases K° to hold in practice.

TABLE 9-4	RETURN TO CAPITAL, %				
	1955–1959	1960–1969	1970–1979	1980–1981	1982
Average annual return	16.2	18.5	13.0	10.8	9.5

Source: Economic Report of the President, 1983.

increase in the real value of output in subsequent years. An estimate of this return to capital is shown in Table 9-4.

The numbers are typically in the 10 to 20 percent range, meaning that $1 of capital generates a return of 10 to 20 cents per year. The number varies from year to year, and according to the table has been falling, particularly since the 1960s. The return to capital is lower in recessions.[6]

The estimates of the return to capital in Table 9-4 will reappear later when we discuss the reasons for the slowdown of the real growth of the economy in the seventies and what can be done about it. One proposed remedy is to attempt, through tax policy, to increase the rate of investment. A $1 increase in the capital stock would generate a return of about 10 cents or more in the form of increased output. Thus there are many who argue that one of the keys to reviving growth in the United States is to increase investment and thus the capital stock.

Expected Output

In determining the desired stock, we have to specify the relevant time period for which the decision on the capital stock applies. In this section we are discussing the capital stock that the firm desires to hold at some future time. Accordingly, the level of output in equations (2) and (3) should be the level of

---

[6] An alternative estimate of the marginal product of capital can be obtained using the fact that the share of output received by capital is about 0.25. The share of capital in output, in turn, is equal to the marginal product of capital (MPK) times the capital stock, divided by the level of output:

$$\text{Share of capital} = MPK \times \frac{K}{Y}$$

With the capital output ratio (K/Y) in manufacturing at about 2 and the share of capital at 25 percent, we obtain

$$MPK = \frac{0.25}{2.0} = 12.5\%$$

This 12.5 percent confirms, in a ballpark figure way, the estimates in Table 9-3.

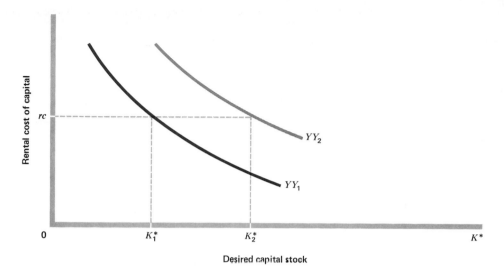

FIGURE 9-4   THE DESIRED CAPITAL STOCK IN RELATION TO THE
LEVEL OF OUTPUT AND THE RENTAL COST OF CAPITAL. Firms'
desired capital stock is chosen at the point at which the value of the
marginal product of capital is equal to the rental cost of capital. At rental
cost rc and output level Y_1, the firm's desired capital stock is K_1^*. An
increase in the level of output to Y_2 raises the desired capital stock to
K_2^*. An increase in the rental cost of capital (not shown) would reduce
the desired capital stock at each level of output.

output which firms expect to be producing at that time. For some investments
the future time at which the output will be produced is a matter of months or
only weeks. For other investments — such as power stations — the future time
at which the output will be produced is years away.

   This suggests that the notion of permanent income (in this case, permanent output) introduced in Chapter 8 is relevant to investment as well as
consumption. For longer-lived investments, the firm's capital demand is governed primarily by its views on the level of output it will be producing on
average in the future. The firm's long-run demand for business fixed capital,
depending on the normal or permanent level of output, is thus relatively
independent of the current level of output, and depends on *expectations* of
future output levels. However, it is affected by current output to the extent
that current output affects expectations of permanent output.[7]

---

[7] The role of permanent income in investment has been emphasized by Robert Eisner. Much of his work is
summarized in his book *Factors in Business Investment* (Cambridge, Mass.: Ballinger, 1978).

Summary on the Desired Capital Stock

It is worthwhile stepping back for a moment to summarize the main results so far:

1. The firm's demand for capital — the desired capital stock K° — depends on the rental cost of capital, rc, and the expected level of output.
2. Firms balance the costs and benefits of using capital. The lower the rental cost of capital, the larger the optimal level of capital relative to output. This relation reflects the lower marginal productivity of capital when it is used relatively intensively. The intensive use of capital will be profitable only if the rental cost of capital is low.
3. The higher the level of output, the larger the desired capital stock.
4. The firm plans its capital stock in relation to expected future or permanent output.
5. Current output affects capital demand to the extent that it affects expectations about future output.

The Rental Cost of Capital Again

We have already introduced the notion of the rental or user cost of capital in determining the firm's desired capital stock. As a first approximation, we identified the rental cost of capital with the interest rate, on the argument that firms would have to borrow to finance their use of capital. Now we go into more detail on the cost per period of using capital.

To use capital for a single period, say, a year, the firm can be thought of as buying the capital with borrowed funds and paying the interest on the borrowing. At the end of the year, the firm will still have some of the capital left. But the capital is likely to have depreciated over the course of the year. We shall assume that the firm intends to continue using the remaining capital in production in future years and that its depreciation simply represents the using up of the capital in the process of production — physical wear and tear. We now examine the rental cost, taking into account interest costs and depreciation. Later we will show that taxes also affect the rental cost of capital.

Leaving aside taxes, the rental cost of using capital consists of interest and depreciation costs.[8] We assume that the rate of depreciation is a constant, equal to d, implying that a fixed proportion d of the capital is used up per period. The rental cost, or user cost, of capital per dollar's worth of capital, which we denote by rc, is therefore

$$rc = \text{interest rate} + d \tag{4}$$

where d is the depreciation rate.

---

[8] Why is depreciation considered as a cost? The firm continues using the capital and therefore has to devote expenditures to maintaining the productive efficiency of capital, thus offsetting wear and tear. We are assuming that, per dollar of capital, d dollars per period are required to maintain productive efficiency.

The Real Rate of Interest

We have now to take a careful look at the interest rate term in equation (4). The distinction between the *real* and *nominal* interest rates is essential here. The real interest rate is the nominal (stated) rate of interest minus the rate of inflation.

The *notion of the real rate of interest is extremely important.* Suppose that the nominal interest rate, the rate stated in the loan agreement, is 10 percent. Then suppose also that prices are rising at 10 percent. Someone borrowing $100 at the beginning of the year pays back $110 at the end of the year. But those dollars in which repayment is made buy less goods than the dollars lent at the beginning of the year when the loan was made. If the inflation rate is 10 percent, then the $110 paid at the end of the year buys the same amount of goods that could have been bought with the original $100 at the beginning of the year. In *real* terms, in terms of the goods which the money can buy, the lender has no more at the end than at the beginning of the year. Thus the *real* interest rate actually received was zero, even though the *nominal* interest rate was 10 percent. Given the nominal interest rate, the real interest rate is lower the higher the rate of inflation becomes. In practice, nominal interest rates tend to be higher when inflation is higher.

It is the *expected real* rate of interest that should enter the calculation of the rental cost of capital. Why? The firm is borrowing in order to produce goods for sale. On average, across all firms, it is reasonable to believe that the prices of the goods the firms sell will be rising along with the general price level. Thus the value of what the firm will be producing in the future will be rising with the price level, but the nominal amount of interest it has to pay back on account of its borrowings does not rise with the price level. The real value of the debt it has incurred by borrowing will be falling over time, as a result of inflation, and it should take that reduction in the real value of its outstanding debts into account in deciding how much capital to employ.

Accordingly, we can be more precise in the way we write equation (4) for the rental cost of capital. We write the rental cost of capital, taking account of expected inflation at the rate π^e, as

$$rc \equiv r + d \equiv i - \pi^e + d \qquad (5)$$

where r is the real interest rate, i the nominal interest rate, and

$$r \equiv i - \pi^e \qquad (6)$$

Equation (6) states that the real rate of interest is the nominal interest rate minus the expected rate of inflation. Implicitly, equation (6) refers to the expected real rate of interest.[9] At the end of the period, when the rate of

---

[9] Some loans to firms carry *variable* interest rates, so that the amount of interest the firm has to pay changes over time as the general level of interest rates changes. In these cases the rate i in equation (6) would be the expected interest rate over the life of the loan.

inflation is known, we can also state what the *actual* or realized real rate of interest for the period was — namely, the nominal interest rate i minus the actual rate of inflation.

To reiterate, it is important to note that the interest rate relevant to the firm's demand for capital is the *real* rate, and not the nominal rate. This makes it clear that the nominal rate of interest is not a good guide to the rental cost of capital. If the rate of inflation is zero and is expected to be zero and the nominal interest rate is 5 percent, then the real interest rate is 5 percent. By contrast, if the nominal interest rate is 10 percent and inflation is at the rate of 10 percent, the real interest rate is zero. Other things equal, the desired capital stock in this example would tend to be higher with the nominal interest rate of 10 percent than with the nominal rate of 5 percent — because those rates correspond to real rates of zero and 5 percent, respectively. As you have no doubt deduced, and as we shall show, investment spending tends to be higher when the rental cost of capital is lower. But because of the distinction between real and nominal interest rates, that is *not* the same as saying that investment tends to be higher when the nominal rate of interest is lower.

Taxes and the Rental Cost as Capital

The rental cost of capital is affected by tax variables as well as by the interest rate and depreciation. The two main tax variables to consider are the corporate income tax and the investment tax credit. The corporate income tax is an essentially proportional tax on profits,[10] whereby the firm pays a proportion, say, t, of its profits in taxes. The investment tax credit was in place for most of the period 1962–1986 but was discontinued in 1986. It allowed firms to deduct from their taxes a certain fraction, say, τ, of their investment expenditures in each year. Thus a firm spending $1 million for investment purposes in a given year could deduct 10 percent of the $1 million, or $100,000, from the taxes it would otherwise have to pay the federal government.

We want to know what effects the corporate income tax and the investment tax credit have on the rental cost of capital. The easier case is the investment tax credit. The investment tax credit reduces the price of a capital good to the firm by the ratio τ, since the Treasury returns to the firm a proportion τ of the cost of each capital good. The investment tax credit therefore reduces the rental cost of capital.

To a first approximation, the corporate income tax, surprisingly, has no effect on the desired stock of capital. In the presence of the corporate income tax, the firm will want to equate the *after-tax* value of the marginal product of capital with the *after-tax* rental cost of capital in order to ensure that the marginal contribution of the capital to profits is equal to the marginal cost of using it.

---

[10] The 1986 Tax Reform Act cut the top corporate tax rate from 46 percent to 34 percent.

Let us focus on the interest component of the rental cost. The basic point is that interest cost is treated as a deduction from revenues in the calculation of the corporation's taxes. Suppose there were no corporate income tax, no inflation, no depreciation, and an interest rate of 10 percent. The desired capital stock would be that level of the capital stock, say, K_0^*, such that the marginal product of capital was 10 percent. Now suppose that the corporate income tax rises to 34 percent and the interest rate remains constant. At the capital stock K_0^*, the after-tax marginal product of capital is now 6.6 percent (since 34 percent of the profits are paid in taxes). But if the interest rate stays at 10 percent and the firm gets to deduct 34 percent of its interest payments from taxes, the after-tax cost of capital will be 6.6 percent too. In this case, the desired capital stock is unaffected by the rate of corporate taxation.

However, there are complexities in the tax laws, which we do not go into here, which make the total effect of the corporate income tax on the desired capital stock ambiguous. The ambiguities arise when the special tax treatment of depreciation,[11] of inflation, and of investment financing other than through borrowing is taken into account.[12]

We conclude by noting the two main points. The investment tax credit reduces the rental cost of capital and increases the desired stock of capital. The corporate income tax has ambiguous effects on the desired stock of capital.

The Stock Market and the Cost of Capital

We have so far assumed that the firm finances its investment by borrowing. But a firm can also finance investment by selling shares or equity. That way it raises the capital it needs to pay for the investment. The people buying the shares expect to earn a return from dividends and/or, if the firm is successful, from the increase in the market value of their shares, that is *capital gains*.

When the stock market is high, a company can raise a lot of money by selling relatively few shares. When stock prices are low, the firm has to sell more shares to raise a given amount of money. The owners of the firm, existing shareholders, will be more willing for the firm to sell shares to raise new money if they have to sell few shares to do so. If they have to sell many shares in the company, they will own a smaller share of the company in the future. Thus we expect corporations to be more willing to sell equity to finance investment when the stock market is high than when it is low.

In estimating the rental cost of capital, economists sometimes assume that

---

[11] Internal Revenue Service counts depreciation as a business expense, but these allowances follow complicated rules and are not generally equal to the depreciation that the capital stock actually undergoes. Depreciation allowances were substantially changed by major tax acts in 1981, 1982, and 1986.

[12] As we describe below, some investment is financed through the sale of equities. Part of the return to equity holders typically takes the form of dividend payments. However, dividends are not treated as a deduction from profits in the calculation of corporate income taxes. Thus the basic argument presented in the case of interest payments, that the corporate income tax does not affect the desired capital stock, would not apply for equity-financed investment.

the investment project will be financed by a mixture of borrowing and equity. The cost of equity capital is frequently measured by the ratio of the firm's dividends to the price of its stock.[13] Then obviously the higher the price of the stock, the lower the cost of equity capital, and the lower the overall cost of capital.[14] That is why a booming stock market is good for investment.

Summary and Effects of Fiscal and Monetary Policy on the Desired Capital Stock

We summarize, using equation (2), which gives the desired capital stock as a function of the rental cost of capital and the expected level of output, and the preceding discussion of the rental cost of capital. From equation (2) we note that the desired capital stock increases when the expected level of output rises and when the rental cost of capital falls.

The rental cost of capital falls when the real interest rate and the rate of depreciation fall. It likewise falls when the investment tax credit rises. Changes in the rate of corporate taxation have ambiguous effects on the desired capital stock.

The major significance of these results is their implication that monetary and fiscal policy affect the desired capital stock. Fiscal policy exerts an effect through both the corporate tax rate t and the investment tax credit τ. Both these instruments are used to affect capital demand and thus investment spending.

Fiscal policy affects capital demand by its overall effects on the position of the *IS* curve, as discussed in Chapter 5. A high tax – low government-spending policy keeps the real interest rate low and encourages the demand for capital. (At this point you want to refer to Figure 5-6.) A high government-spending – low-tax policy that produces large deficits raises the real interest rate and discourages the demand for capital.

Monetary policy affects capital demand by affecting the market interest rate.[15] A lowering of the nominal interest rate by the Federal Reserve System (given the expected inflation rate), as reflected in a downward shift in the *LM* curve, will induce firms to desire more capital. This expansion in capital demand, in turn, will affect investment spending, as we shall now see.

---

[13] An alternative measure is the ratio of the firm's *earnings* (some of which are not paid out to shareholders) to the price of its stock. However neither measure is really correct, for the cost of equity capital is the amount the investment is expected to yield *in the future* to the people who buy it now.

[14] An alternative approach to the firm's investment decision, Tobin's *q* theory of investment focuses on the stock market as the primary source of funds. The basic approach is outlined in James Tobin, "A General Equilibrium Approach to Monetary Theory," *Journal of Money, Credit and Banking*, February 1969. For an empirical implementation, see Lawrence H. Summers, "Taxation and Corporate Investment: A q-Theory Approach." *Brookings Papers on Economic Activity*, 1981.

[15] We should note that the Federal Reserve System is able to affect *nominal* interest rates directly by its sales and purchases of bonds. Its ability to control *real* interest rates is more limited.

From Desired Capital Stock to Investment

We have now put more content into the general form of equation (2) for the desired capital stock by discussing the rental cost of capital in detail. The actual capital stock will often differ from the capital stock firms would like to have. At what speed do firms change their capital stocks in order to move toward the desired capital stock? In particular, is there any reason why firms do not attempt to move to their desired capital stocks immediately?

Since it takes time to plan and complete an investment project, and because attempts to invest quickly are likely to be more expensive than gradual adjustment of the capital stock, it is unlikely that firms would attempt to adjust their capital stocks to the long-run desired level instantaneously. Very rapid adjustment of the capital stock would require crash programs by the firm which would distract management from its routine tasks and interfere with ongoing production. Thus, firms generally plan to adjust their capital stocks gradually over a period of time rather than immediately.

Capital Stock Adjustment

There are a number of hypotheses about the speed with which firms plan to adjust their capital stock over time; we single out the *gradual adjustment hypothesis* here.[16] The basic notion behind the gradual adjustment hypothesis is that the larger the gap between the existing capital stock and the desired capital stock, the more rapid a firm's rate of investment. The hypothesis is that firms plan to close a fraction λ of the gap between the desired and actual capital stocks each period. Denote the capital stock at the end of the last period by K_{-1}. The gap between the desired and actual capital stocks is $(K^* - K_{-1})$. The firm plans to add to last period's capital stock K_{-1}, a fraction λ of the gap $K^* - K_{-1}$ so that the capital stock at the end of current period, K, will be

$$K = K_{-1} + \lambda(K^* - K_{-1}) \tag{7}$$

Equation (7) states that the firm plans to have the capital stock at the end of the period (K) be such that a fraction λ of the gap (between the desired capital stock K^* and the capital stock K_{-1} that existed at the end of last period) is closed. To increase the capital stock from K_{-1} to the level of K indicated by equation (7), the firm has to achieve an amount of net investment, $I \equiv K - K_{-1}$, indicated by equation (7). We can therefore write net investment as

$$I = \lambda(K^* - K_{-1}) \tag{8}$$

---

[16] The gradual adjustment hypothesis is a generalized form of the older *accelerator* model of investment, in which investment is proportional to the change in the level of GNP. The accelerator model is examined in Sec. 9-3.

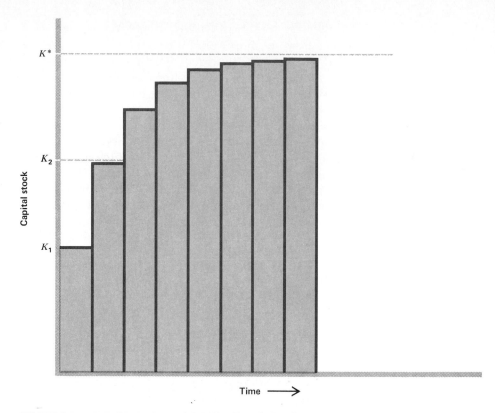

FIGURE 9-5   THE GRADUAL ADJUSTMENT OF THE CAPITAL
STOCK. The desired capital stock is K^*, and the current capital stock is
K_1. The firms plans to close half the gap between the actual and the
desired capital stock each period ($\lambda = 0.5$). Thus, in period one it
moves to K_2, with (net) investment equal to ($K_2 - K_1$), which in turn is
equal to one half of ($K^* - K_1$). In each subsequent period it closes half
the gap between the capital stock at the beginning of the period and
the desired capital stock, K^*.

which is the gradual adjustment formulation of net investment. Notice that
equation (8) implies that investment is larger, the larger the gap between
actual and desired capital stocks.[17] With a zero gap net investment is zero.

In Figure 9-5 we show the adjustment process of capital in a circumstance
where the initial capital stock is K_1 and the given desired capital stock is K^*.
The assumed speed of adjustment is $\lambda = 0.5$. Starting from K_1, one-half the

---

[17] Gross investment, as opposed to net investment described in equation (8), includes, in addition, depreciation.
Thus, gross investment is $I + dK_{-1}$, where d is again the rate of depreciation.

discrepancy between target capital and current actual capital is made up in every period. First-period net investment is therefore $0.5(K^* - K_1)$. In the second period, investment will be less because the previous period's investment reduces the gap. Investment continues until the actual capital stock reaches the level of target capital. The speed with which this process allows actual capital to reach target capital is determined by λ. The larger λ is, the faster the gap is reduced.

In equation (8), we have reached our goal of deriving an investment function that shows current investment spending determined by the desired stock of capital K^* and the actual stock of capital K_{-1}. According to the flexible accelerator hypothesis, any factor that increases the desired stock increases the rate of investment. Therefore an increase in expected output, or a reduction in the real interest rate, or an increase in the investment tax credit will each increase the rate of investment. We thus have derived a quite complete theory of business fixed investment that includes many of the factors we should expect to affect the rate of investment. And the theory of investment embodied in equation (8) also contains aspects of *dynamic behavior*—that is, of behavior that depends on values of economic variables in periods other than the current period.

There are two sources of dynamic behavior in equation (8). The first arises from expectations. The K^* term depends on the firm's estimate of future or permanent output. To the extent that the firm forms its estimates of permanent output as a weighted average of past output levels, there will be lags in the adjustment of the level of permanent output to the actual level of output. In turn, investment will therefore also adjust slowly to a change in the level of output. The second source of dynamic behavior arises from adjustment lags. Firms plan to close only a proportion of the gap between the actual and desired capital stocks each period, as shown in Figure 9-5. The adjustment lags produce a lagged response of investment to changes in the variables that affect the desired capital stock.

The Timing of Investment and the Investment Tax Credit

The flexible accelerator model provides a useful summary of the dynamics of investment. But it does not sufficiently emphasize the *timing* of investment. Because investment is undertaken for the long run and often requires several years to complete, there is flexibility in the dates on which the actual investment is undertaken. For example, suppose a firm wanted to have some machinery in place within 3 years. Suppose that it knew the investment tax credit would be raised substantially a year from now. Then the firm might be wise to delay the investment for a year and to make or acquire the machinery at a faster rate during the next 2 years, receiving the higher investment tax credit as the reward for waiting the extra year. Similarly, if a firm anticipated that the cost of borrowing next year would be much lower than this year, it might wait a year to undertake its investment project.

BOX
9-1

USING THE INVESTMENT TAX CREDIT FOR STABILIZATION

Since the investment tax credit affects the cost of capital, it affects the rate of investment. And since we have seen that investment fluctuates a great deal, it is tempting to think that a cyclically varying investment tax credit could stabilize fluctuations in GNP.

Why not, for instance, make the rate of the investment tax credit high when the economy is in a recession and low when the economy is in a boom? That way investment would be increased in recessions and reduced in booms.

There are two problems with that approach. The first is that firms would anticipate the operation of the credit and possibly increase fluctuations. Suppose for instance that GNP is growing slowly, and the economy appears headed for a recession. But it is not at all certain that a recession will occur. Partly that depends on firms' investment plans.

If there were a cyclically varying investment tax credit, firms in this example would wait to invest until times got worse. But that way the recession becomes more likely.

The other problem is that it takes time for firms to get their investment projects into action. A firm contemplating investing at the bottom of a recession has to figure out whether there will still be an investment tax credit (that means also a recession) by the time it gets its building started. If there are sizable lags in the investment project, the cyclically varying credit may not provide much incentive to invest at the cyclically appropriate times.

Because the investment tax credit is a delicate instrument, some economists suggest it should be set to the level that is appropriate for the long run and varied infrequently or not at all.

There is also an issue of whether the investment tax credit should be used at all. Is there any reason to subsidize corporate investment? Those who favor investment subsidies point to the 10 percent real rate of return earned by capital (see Table 9-4) and say that surely society wants to encourage investments with such a high rate of return. Those who are opposed argue that the government should stay out and let the markets decide how much investment there should be.*

---

* For further discussion see Alan Auerbach and Larry Summers, "Anticipated Tax Changes and the Timing of Investment," unpublished manuscript, National Bureau of Economic Research, February 1986. See too, Robert S. Chirinko, "The Ineffectiveness of Effective Tax Rates on Business Investment," National Bureau of Economic Research, Working Paper No. 1704, September 1985.

The flexibility in the timing of investment leads to an interesting contrast between the effects of the investment tax credit and the income tax on investment and consumption, respectively. We saw in Chapter 8 that a *permanent* change in the income tax has a much larger effect on consumption than a *transitory* change. However, the rate of investment *during the period* that a *temporary* investment tax credit is in effect would be higher than the rate of investment that would occur over the same period during which a *permanent* credit of the same magnitude was in effect. Why? If firms knew the investment tax credit were temporary, they would advance the timing of their planned investments in order to take advantage of the higher credit during the current period. If there were a permanent change in the investment tax credit, then the desired capital stock would rise and there would on that account be more investment, but there would not be a bunching of investment.

It is for this reason that temporary changes in the investment tax credit have been suggested as a highly effective countercyclical policy measure. However, this is not a simple policy tool, as expectations about the timing and duration of the credit might conceivably worsen the instability of investment.

Summary on the Neoclassical Theory of Business Fixed Investment

The main conclusions of the theory of business fixed investment as developed here are:

1. Over time, net investment spending is governed by the discrepancy between actual and desired capital.
2. Desired capital depends on the rental (user) cost of capital and the expected level of output. Capital demand rises with expected output and the investment tax credit, and declines with an increase in *real* interest rates.
3. Monetary and fiscal policies exert effects on investment via the desired capital stock, although the short-run impact is likely to be minor. The longer-run effects are larger. The lags with which these investment effects occur are important to bear in mind in shaping stabilization policy.
4. Investment theory, like consumption theory, emphasizes the role of expected or permanent income or output as a determinant of capital demand.

9-3 BUSINESS FIXED INVESTMENT: ALTERNATIVE APPROACHES AND EMPIRICAL RESULTS

In this section we briefly discuss the way a firm approaches its investment decisions and also describe the standard *accelerator theory of investment*. Then we go on to examine some empirical evidence on investment.

The Business Investment Decision: The View from the Trenches

Business people making investment decisions typically use *discounted cash flow analysis*. The principles of discounting are described in the appendix to this chapter. Consider a business person deciding whether to build and equip a new factory. The first step is to figure out how much it will cost to get the factory into working order, and how much revenue the factory will bring in each year after it starts operation.

For simplicity we consider a very short-lived project, one that costs $100 in the first year to set up and that then generates $50 in revenue (after paying for labor and raw materials) in the second year and a further $80 in the third year. By the end of the third year the factory has disintegrated.

The manager wants to know whether to undertake such a project. Discounted cash flow analysis says that the revenues received in later years should be *discounted* to the present in order to calculate their present value. As the

TABLE 9-5	DISCOUNTED CASH FLOW ANALYSIS AND PRESENT VALUE ($)			
	Year 1	Year 2	Year 3	Present discounted value
Cash or revenue	−100	+50	+80	
Present value of $1	1	$1/1.12$ $= 0.893$	$(1/1.12^2)$ $= 0.797$	
Present value of costs or revenue	−100	50×0.893 $= 44.60$	80×0.797 $= 63.76$	$(-100 +$ $44.60 + 63.76)$ $= 8.36$

appendix on discounting shows, if the interest rate is 10 percent, $110 a year from now is worth the same as $100 now. Why? Because if $100 were lent out today at 10 percent, a year from now the lender would end up with $110. Thus to calculate the value of the investment project, the businessperson calculates its present discounted value at the interest rate at which the business can borrow. If the present value is positive, then the project is undertaken.

Suppose that the relevant interest rate is 12 percent.[18] The calculation of the present discounted value of the investment project is shown in Table 9-5. The $50 received in year 2 is worth only $44.50 today: $1 a year from now is worth $1/1.12 = 0.893 today, and so $50 a year from now is worth $44.60. The present value of the $80 received in year 3 is calculated similarly. The table shows that the present value of the net revenue received from the project is positive ($8.36) and thus that the firm should undertake the project.

Note that if the interest rate had been much higher — say, 18 percent — the decision would have been *not* to undertake the investment decision. We thus see how the interest rate affects the investment decision of the typical firm. The higher the interest rate, the less likely the firm will be to undertake any given investment project.

Each firm has at any time an array of possible investment projects, and estimates of the costs and the revenues from those projects. Depending on the level of the interest rate, it will want to undertake some of the projects and not undertake others. Taking all firms in the economy together and adding their investment demands, we obtain the total demand for investment in the economy at each interest rate.

This approach to the investment decision, which, of course, can be applied to investment projects of any duration and complexity, seems far from

---

[18] The interest rate here is nominal, because we are calculating the present value of dollars to be received in the future.

the description of Section 9-2 in terms of a desired capital stock and rate of adjustment.

Actually, the two approaches are quite consistent. First, we should think of the desired capital stock as being the stock of capital that will be in place when the firms have their factories and new equipment on-line. Second, the adjustment speed tells us how rapidly firms on average succeed in installing that capital.

We started with the formulation in terms of the desired capital stock because the framework provides a very clear way of including the different factors that affect investment. For instance, it is easy to see how expectations of future output and taxes affect investment.

But because the two approaches are consistent, the same factors could be included using discounted cash flow analysis. The effects of expectations of future output can be analyzed using the discounted cash flow approach by asking what determines the firms' projections of their future revenues (corresponding to the $50 in year 2 and $80 in year 3 in the example above); expected demand for their goods and their output must be relevant. Similarly, taxes can be embodied by analyzing how taxes affect the amount of revenue the firm has left after taxes in each future year; the investment tax credit reduces the amount the firm has to lay out in the early years when it is actually building the project—because the Treasury provides a refund of part of the cost of the project through taxes.

Finally, the firm makes decisions about the speed of adjustment by considering the cash flows associated with building the project at different speeds. If the project can be built more rapidly, the firm will decide on the speed with which it wants the project brought on-line by considering the present discounted costs and revenues associated with speeding it up.

The Accelerator Model of Investment

The *accelerator model of investment* asserts that the rate of investment is proportional to the *change* in the economy's output. To derive the accelerator model of investment, assume that there is complete adjustment of the capital stock to its desired level within one period (that is, that $\lambda = 1$), so that $K = K^*$; that there is no depreciation, so that $d = 0$; and that the desired capital-output ratio is a constant, independent of the rental cost of capital:

$$K^* = vY \tag{9}$$

In equation (9), v is a constant equal to the desired capital-to-output ratio. Substituting equation (9) into equation (8), setting $\lambda = 1$, and noting that $K_{-1} = K^*_{-1}$, we obtain

$$I = v(Y - Y_{-1}) \tag{10}$$

which is precisely the accelerator model of investment.

The accelerator model creates the potential for investment spending to fluctuate a good deal. If investment spending is proportional to the *change* in GNP, then when the economy is in a recovery, investment spending is positive, and when the economy is in a recession, investment will be negative.[19] Thus the accelerator model predicts that investment will fluctuate considerably, as Figure 9-1 shows it does.

Empirical Results

We now examine how the investment models we have developed, particularly the neoclassical model summarized in equation (8), perform empirically.

To use equation (8), it is necessary to substitute some specific equation for K^*, the desired capital stock. Frequently the Cobb-Douglas form is chosen. Using equation (3) in equation (8) yields a (net) investment function of the form

$$ I = \lambda \left(\frac{\gamma Y}{rc} - K_{-1} \right) \tag{11} $$

The rental cost of capital, rc in equation (11), is as in equation (5), but adjusted for taxes.

Early empirical evidence, in particular that of Dale Jorgenson and his associates,[20] showed that an investment function including the variables in equation (11) provided a reasonable explanation of the behavior of business fixed investment. However, the form shown in equation (11) could be improved upon by allowing more scope for investment to respond slowly to changes in output. The empirical evidence suggests that the adjustment of investment to output takes the bell-shaped form in Figure 9-6. The major impact of a change in output on actual investment occurs with a 2-period (year) lag. The impact in the first year is less than the impact 2 years later.

There are two, not mutually exclusive, explanations for the behavior shown in Figure 9-6, corresponding to the two sources of dynamic behavior in equation (8) that we discussed above. The first possibility is that the lag pattern of Figure 9-6 reflects the way in which expectations about future output, and thus the long-run desired capital stock, are formed. In that view, only a sustained increase in output will persuade firms that the capital stock should be increased in the long run. Figure 9-6 would then imply that it takes about 2 years for changes in the variables that determine the desired capital stock to have a major impact on expectations.

---

[19] The accelerator is not in practice a complete model of investment, for gross investment spending cannot be negative.

[20] See Dale W. Jorgenson, "Econometric Studies of Investment Behavior: A Survey," *Journal of Economic Literature*, December 1971.

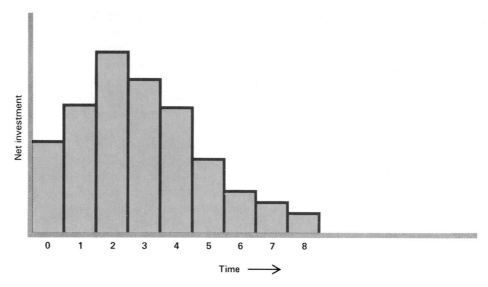

FIGURE 9-6   EFFECTS OF AN INCREASE IN OUTPUT IN PERIOD ZERO ON NET INVESTMENT IN SUBSEQUENT PERIODS (years).

The second explanation relies less on expectations and more on the physical delays in the investment process. That interpretation would be that Figure 9-6 reflects the long time it takes for a change in the desired capital stock to be translated into investment spending. In industries in which investment can be undertaken quickly, there may be some response within a year. In other industries there may be long lags between the time machinery is ordered and the time it is ready to be delivered. In the economy as a whole, the maximum impact on investment of a change in the desired capital stock happens only 2 years after the change in the desired stock.

For many purposes, it does not matter which explanation of the form of Figure 9-6 is correct, and it is difficult to tell the explanations apart empirically. It is undoubtedly true that both explanations are relevent. The important point is that lags in the determination of the level of business fixed investment are long.

THE ACCELERATOR MODEL AND COST OF CAPITAL EFFECTS

Controversy about the determinants of investment continues. (Box 9-2 discusses an attempt to explain the extraordinary investment boom from 1982 to 1985.) Note from equation (11) that the neoclassical model relates investment to the ratio of output to the rental cost of capital (Y/rc). Thus, by the way the equation is set up, both output and the rental cost of capital have similar effects on investment. The issue is whether the rental cost of capital matters in fact as much for investment as the neoclassical model implies.

Some research[21] suggests that the accelerator model of equation (10)—somewhat expanded—does about as good a job of explaining investment behavior as the neoclassical model. The accelerator model is expanded in empirical work to make the rate of investment depend not only on the change in income this period but also on the change in income in earlier periods. In empirical applications this simple accelerator model therefore differs from the neoclassical model mainly in that it omits the cost of capital.

There are also findings that the rental cost of capital does affect investment.[22] It is clear from the conflicting findings that the evidence is not strong enough to decide the precise relative roles of the cost of capital and expectations of future output. No doubt both are major determinants of investment spending. Certainly theory suggests that the rental cost of capital should play an important role in affecting investment.

We now discuss some other aspects of investment behavior.

SALES AND PROFITS AS DETERMINANTS OF INVESTMENT

Some studies find either the level of sales or total profits to be factors explaining the level of investment. The level of sales could be interpreted as affecting expectations of future output and thus affecting the desired capital stock. Note that output and sales differ by the amount of inventory accumulation.

The role of profits can be interpreted similarly. High profits may provide an indication of future demand for the firm's product, and thus of future output. Alternatively, it is often argued that firms prefer to use retained profits to finance investment, rather than borrow. The preference might result from the expense of having to raise outside funds relative to using inside funds. However, in using its retained profits to finance investment rather than borrow, the firm has also to consider the possibility of paying out its profits to the firm's owners, who can invest in other firms. Thus even when using retained earnings, firms have to take into account the level of interest rates—as a measure of the returns their owners could receive if the earnings were paid out.

Why Does Investment Fluctuate?

The facts with which we started this chapter show that investment fluctuates much more than consumption spending. The accelerator model provides one

---

[21] Peter K. Clark, "Investment in the 1970's: Theory, Performance and Predictions," *Brookings Papers on Economic Activity*, 1979:1.

[22] For example, Martin Feldstein, "Inflation, Tax Rules and Investment: Some Econometric Evidence," *Econometrica*, July 1982, and Ben Bernanke, "The Determinants of Investment: Another Look," *American Economic Review*, Papers and Proceedings, May 1983.

explanation of these fluctuations. There are two other basic explanations: the uncertain basis for expectations and the flexibility of the timing of investment.

UNCERTAIN EXPECTATIONS

Keynes, in the *General Theory*, emphasized the uncertain basis on which investment decisions are made. In his words, ". . .we have to admit that our basis of knowledge for estimating the yield ten years hence of a railway, a copper mine, a textile factory, the goodwill of a patent medicine . . . amounts to little and sometimes to nothing. . . ."[23] Thus, he argued, investment decisions are very much affected by how optimistic or pessimistic the investors feel.

The term "animal spirits" is sometimes used to describe the optimism or pessimism of investors, where "animal spirits" indicates that there may be no good basis for the expectations on which investors base their decisions. If there is no good basis for the expectations, then they could change easily — and the volume of investment along with the expectations.

THE TIMING OF INVESTMENT DECISIONS

The second possible reason for fluctuations in investment is that investment decisions can be delayed if the project will take a long time to come on-line. Suppose a firm has an investment project it would like to undertake, but the economy is currently in a recession and the firm is not sure when the recession will end. Further, at the current time it cannot even usefully fully employ all the capital it already has. Such a firm might choose to wait until the prospects for the economy look better — when the recovery gets under way — before deciding to start the investment project.

Either or both of these factors could help account for the substantial fluctuations that are seen in business investment spending. Indeed, they may also explain the success of the accelerator theory of investment, for if firms wait for a recovery to get under way before investing, their investment will be closely related to the change in GNP.

9-4 RESIDENTIAL INVESTMENT

We study residential investment separately from business fixed investment both to introduce a slightly different model of investment[24] and because residential investment shows large cyclical fluctuations, as can be seen in Figure 9-7.

---

[23] J. M. Keynes, *The General Theory of Employment, Interest and Money* (London: Macmillan, 1936), pp. 149–150.

[24] We relate the model of this section to the model of investment behavior of Sec. 9-3 in the concluding section of this chapter.

BOX
9-2

THE 1982–1985 INVESTMENT BOOM: WHAT CAUSED IT?

We saw in Table 9-1 that increased investment accounted for over half the increase in GNP during the 3 years following the trough of the recession in 1982. Investment typically grows fast during recovery, but this recovery was nonetheless exceptional. GNP grew no faster in the first 2 years of the recovery than it normally does. Business fixed investment grew twice as fast as it normally does during those 2 years.

Table 1 shows an estimate of the real rate of interest along with the ratio of business fixed investment to GNP and the real (adjusted for inflation) Standard and Poor's index of stock prices. The real interest rate rose sharply in the early eighties: indeed, interest rates were at record post–World War II levels during this period. The high real interest rates should have been expected to produce sluggish, not booming, investment. What happened?

TABLE 1 INVESTMENT AND INTEREST RATES, 1976–1985, %

	$(I/Y)_N$	Real bond rate	Stock price index	$(I/Y)_R$
1976–1979	11.1	0.2	142.9	11.3
1980	11.8	3.8	138.6	11.9
1981	12.1	6.7	136.2	12.2
1982	11.6	6.8	119.7	11.6
1983	10.5	5.6	154.5	11.0
1984	11.3	7.2	148.4	12.3
1985	11.9	6.9	167.2	13.2

Source: Economic Report of the President, 1986. First column is ratio of nominal business fixed investment spending to nominal GNP. Second column is Moody's Aaa corporate bond rate for the given year, minus the average inflation rate (of the GNP deflator) over the past 3 years, the current year, and the next 2 years. Third column is the Standard and Poor composite stock market index divided by the GNP deflator (and multiplied by 100). Column 4 is the ratio of *real* investment spending to *real* GNP.

In a careful study, Barry Bosworth of the Brookings Institution concludes that the rental cost of capital did not increase between 1982 and 1984 even though the real interest rate rose substantially.* Four factors affected the rental cost of capital:

1. One, which we have not noted above, is the purchase price of capital goods. The prices of capital goods fell sharply during the 1982–1984 period. Prices of computers in particular fell. This made investment cheaper for firms to carry out.
2. Tax treatment of investment — changes in depreciation allowances and the investment tax credit — was made substantially more favorable in the 1981 and 1982 tax bills.

---

* Taxes and the Investment Recovery," *Brookings Papers on Economic Activity,* 1985:1.

3. The stock market boomed, making equity financing cheaper.
4. Real interest rates rose sharply, making debt finance more expensive.

The contrast between the first and fourth columns of the table brings out sharply the effects of the fall in the price of investment goods. Measured in nominal terms, using current prices, the share of business fixed investment in GNP in 1985 was at practically the same level as in 1980; but measured in constant prices, there was a full 1.3 percent of GNP increase in the share of business fixed investment in GNP between 1980 and 1985. The stock market boom that started in 1983 and the rise in real interest rates are also clearly visible in the table.

The net effect, Bosworth concludes, is that the rental cost of capital did not increase over this period, and indeed fell for many types of investment. But that is not sufficient to account for an investment boom—only for the fact that there was not an investment slump. Indeed, Bosworth points out that a large share of the investment boom was in business purchases of computers and automobiles, neither of which benefited from improved tax treatment.

So what caused the investment boom? Expectations of a booming economy or animal spirits may both have played a part. So, too, may subtleties in the tax law that made debt finance less expensive than the simple increase in the real interest rate implies.

Figure 9-7 shows residential investment spending as a percentage of GNP for the 1965–1985 period, together with the mortgage interest rate. Residential investment declines in all recessions. Thus in 1969–1970, 1973–1975, 1980, and 1981–1982, there is a dip in residential investment. The same is true for the 1966–1967 minirecession.

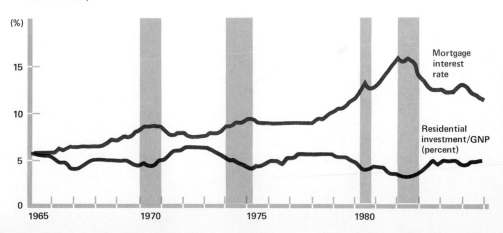

FIGURE 9-7 HOUSING INVESTMENT AND THE MORTGAGE INTEREST RATE. (*Source:* Data Resources, Inc. Mortage rate is for new houses.)

Theory

Residential investment consists of the building of single-family and multifamily dwellings, which we call housing for short. Housing is distinguished as an asset by its long life. Consequently, investment in housing in any one year tends to be a very small proportion — about 3 percent — of the existing stock of housing. The theory of residential investment starts by considering the demand for the existing stock of housing. Housing is viewed as one among the many assets that a wealth holder can own.

In Figure 9-8a we show the demand for the stock of housing in the downward-sloping DD_0 curve. The lower the price of housing (P_H), the greater the quantity demanded. The position of the demand curve itself depends on a number of economic variables: First, the greater wealth is, the greater the demand for housing. The more wealthy individuals are, the more housing they desire to own. Thus an increase in wealth would shift the demand curve from DD_0 to DD_1. Second, the demand for housing as an asset depends on the real return available on other assets. If returns on other forms of holding wealth — such as bonds — are low, then housing looks like a relatively attractive form in which to hold wealth. The lower the return on other assets, the greater the demand for housing. A reduction in the return on other assets, such as bonds or common stock, shifts the demand curve from DD_0 to DD_1.

FIGURE 9-8   THE HOUSING MARKET: DETERMINATION OF THE ASSET PRICE OF HOUSING AND THE RATE OF HOUSING INVESTMENT. The supply and demand for the stock of housing determine the asset price of housing (P_H^0) in panel (a). The rate of housing investment (Q_H^0) is determined by the flow supply of housing at price P_H^0, in panel (b).

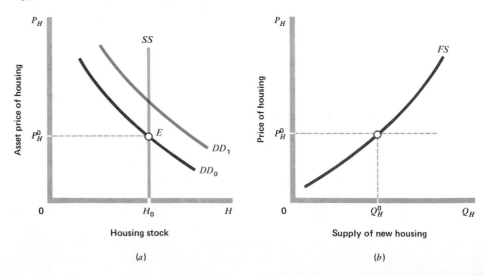

(a)   (b)

Third, the demand for the housing stock depends on the net real return obtained by owning housing. The gross return—before taking costs into account—consists of rent, if the housing is rented out, or the implicit return that the homeowner receives by living in the home, plus capital gains arising from increases in the value of the housing. In turn, the costs of owning the housing consist of interest costs, typically the mortgage interest rate, plus any real estate taxes, and depreciation. These costs are deducted from the gross return and, after tax adjustments, constitute the net return. An increase in the net return on housing, caused, for example, by a reduction in the mortgage interest rate, makes housing a more attractive form in which to hold wealth and shifts up the demand curve for housing from DD_0 to DD_1.

The price of housing is determined by the interaction of this demand with the stock supply of housing. At any time the stock supply is fixed—there is a given stock of housing that cannot be adjusted quickly in response to price changes. The supply curve of the stock of housing is the SS curve of Figure 9-8a. The equilibrium *asset price of housing,* P_H^0, is determined by the intersection of the supply and demand curves. The asset price of housing is the price of a typical house or apartment. At any one time, the market for the stock of housing determines the asset price of housing.

THE RATE OF INVESTMENT

We now consider the determinants of the rate of investment in housing, and for the purpose turn to Figure 9-8b. The curve FS represents the supply of new housing as a function of the price of housing. This curve is the same as the regular supply curve of any industry. The supply curve shows the amount of a good that suppliers want to sell at each price. In this case, the good being supplied is new housing. The position of the FS curve is affected by the costs of factors of production used in the construction industry and by technological factors affecting the cost of building.

The curve FS is sometimes called the flow supply curve, since it represents the *flow* of new housing into the market in a given time period. In contrast, the *stock* supply curve SS represents the total amount of housing in the market at a moment of time.

Given the price of housing established in the asset market, P_H^0, building contractors supply the amount of new housing, Q_H^0, for sale at that price. The higher the asset price, the greater the supply of new housing. Now the supply of new housing is nothing other than gross investment in housing—total additions to the housing stock. Figure 9-8 thus represents our basic theory of the determinants of housing investment.

Any factor affecting the demand for the existing stock of housing will affect the asset price of housing, P_H, and thus the rate of investment in housing. Similarly, any factor shifting the flow supply curve FS will affect the rate of investment. We have already investigated the major factors shifting the DD demand curve for housing, but will briefly repeat that analysis.

Suppose the interest rate — the rate potential homeowners can obtain by investing elsewhere — rises. Then the asset demand for housing falls and the price of housing falls; that, in turn, induces a decline in the rate of production of new housing, or a decline in housing investment. Or suppose that the mortgage interest rate rises: once again there is a fall in the asset price of housing and a reduction in the rate of construction.

Because the existing stock of housing is so large relative to the rate of investment in housing, we can ignore the effects of the current supply of new housing on the price of housing in the short run. However, over time, the new construction shifts the SS curve of the left-hand panel to the right as it increases the housing stock. The long-run equilibrium in the housing industry would be reached, in an economy in which there was no increase in population or wealth over time, when the housing stock was constant. Constancy of the housing stock requires gross investment to be equal to depreciation, or net investment to be equal to zero. The asset price of housing would have to be at the level such that the rate of construction was just equal to the rate of depreciation of the existing stock of housing in long-run equilibrium. If population or income and wealth were growing at a constant rate, the long-run equilibrium would be one in which the rate of construction was just sufficient to cover depreciation and the steadily growing stock demand. In an economy subjected to continual nonsteady changes, that long-run equilibrium is not necessarily ever reached.

Minor qualifications to the basic theoretical structure arise chiefly because new housing cannot be constructed immediately in response to changes in P_H; rather, it takes a short time for that response to occur. Thus, the supply of new housing responds, not to the actual price of housing today, but to the price expected to prevail when the construction is completed. However, the lags are quite short; it takes less than a year to build a typical house. Another qualification stems from that same construction delay. Since builders have to incur expenses before they sell their output, they need financing over the construction period. They are frequently financed at the mortgage interest rate by the thrift institutions, that is, savings and loan associations and mutual savings banks. Hence, the position of the flow supply curve is affected by the mortgage interest rate as well as the amount of lending undertaken by the thrift institutions.[25]

THE Q THEORY OF INVESTMENT

We sidestep for a moment to note that the model of the housing market which emphasizes the asset market and the rate of addition to the stock can similarly

---

[25] The theory of housing investment of this section is the basis of the study of the housing market undertaken by Brigham Young University's James Kearl in his 1975 MIT Ph.D. dissertation, "Inflation-Induced Distortions of the Real Economy: An Econometric and Simulation Study of Housing and Mortgage Innovation." See, too, James Poterba, "Tax Subsidies to Owner-Occupied Housing: An Asset-Market Approach," *Quality Journal of Economics*, November 1984.

be used to analyze business fixed investment. Indeed, an increasingly used view of business fixed investment is the q theory that focuses on the stock market (see footnote 14). It can be cast in terms very similar to that of the housing model. At any one moment all the shares in the economy are in inelastic supply, just like the housing stock. Stock market investors place a value on those shares, with the price of shares in the stock market corresponding to P_H in Figure 9-8.

The price of a share in a company is the price of a claim on the capital in the company. The managers of the company can then be thought of as responding to the price of the stock by producing more new capital — that is, investing — when the price of shares is high and producing less new capital or not investing at all when the price of shares is low.

What is q? It is an estimate of the value the stock market places on a firm's assets relative to the cost of producing those assets. When the ratio is high, firms will want to produce more assets, so that investment will be rapid. Similarly, P_H can be thought of as the price of an existing house relative to the cost of building a new one. When that ratio is high, there will be lots of building.

Monetary Policy and Housing Investment

Monetary policy has powerful effects on housing investment. Part of the reason is that most houses are purchased with the aid of mortgage financing. Since the 1930s, a mortgage has typically been a debt instrument of very long maturity, 20 to 30 years, with a fixed rate and with monthly nominal repayments which remain fixed for the 20 to 30 years to maturity.[26]

Monetary policy has powerful effects on housing investment because the demand for housing is sensitive to the interest rate. There is sensitivity to both the *real* and *nominal* interest rates. The reason for this sensitivity can be seen in Table 9-6, which shows the monthly payment that has to be made by someone borrowing $50,000 through a conventional mortgage at different interest rates. All these interest rates have existed at some time the last 25 years: 5 percent at the beginning of the sixties, 10 percent at the end of the seventies and in 1986, and 15 percent in 1981 and 1982.

The monthly repayment by the borrower approximately doubles when the interest rate doubles. Thus an essential component of the cost of owning a home rises almost proportionately with the interest rate. It is therefore not surprising that the demand for housing is very sensitive to the interest rate.

The above statements have to be qualified. In the first place, there are substantial tax advantages to the homeowner who finances through a mortgage, because the interest payments can be deducted from income before

---

[26] So-called ARMs (adjustable rate mortgages) became increasingly popular in the 1980s. As the name suggests, the interest rate on such mortgages is adjusted, in accordance with some reference rate such as a 1-year Treasury bill rate. Nonetheless the standard mortgage is still as described in the text.

TABLE 9-6	MONTHLY PAYMENTS ON MORTGAGES		
Interest rate, %	5	10	15
Monthly payment, $	292	454	640

Note: The assumed mortgage is a loan for $50,000, paid back over 25 years, with equal monthly payments for those 25 years.

calculating taxes. Second, of course, we should be concerned with the *real* and not the nominal interest cost of owning a house — and certainly much of the rise of the mortgage interest rate is a result of increases in the expected rate of inflation.

But the *nominal* interest rate also affects the homeowner. The reason has to do with the form of the mortgage. The conventional mortgage makes the borrower pay a fixed amount each month over the lifetime of the mortgage. Even if the interest rate rises only because the expected rate of inflation has risen — and thus the real rate is constant — the payments that have to be made *today* by a borrower go up. But the inflation has not yet happened. Thus the real payments made today by a borrower rise when the *nominal* interest rate rises, even if the real rate does not rise.[27] Given the higher real monthly payments when the *nominal* interest rate rises, we should expect the nominal interest rate also to affect housing demand. And the data shown in Figure 9-6 are quite consistent with the nominal interest rate affecting housing demand.

Disintermediation, Mortgage Availability, and Regulation Q

Before 1978 monetary policy affected housing demand through a channel known as *disintermediation.* Mortgage financing is provided mostly by savings and loans institutions. These institutions have assets (mortgages) that have very long lives. Up to 1978 they obtained the funds they loaned out mainly from depositors, who made savings deposits in the institutions. The depositors had the right to remove their funds immediately, sometimes on payment of a penalty, or within a short time at no charge.

At that time the Fed controlled the interest rates that savings and loans (and banks and other financial institutions) could pay to their depositors.[28] The

---

[27] How can the real payments rise if the real interest rate stays the same? The explanation is that today's real payments rise, but the real present value of future payments falls: the repayment stream tilts toward the present. For more on this feature, see Franco Modigliani and Donald Lessard (eds.), *New Mortgage Designs for Stable Housing in an Inflationary Environment,* Federal Reserve Bank of Boston, Conference Series #14, 1975.

[28] These controls were phased out between 1980 and 1986 under the terms of the 1980 Depository Institutions Decontrol and Monetary Control Act.

control was exercised through Regulation Q. Reg Q, as it was called, in effect set the interest rate maximum to be paid on deposits by savings and loans at 5.5 percent. The financial institutions were generally in favor of Reg Q, since it limited the amount they had to pay to borrow.

The savings and loans in particular were concerned that the rate of interest they paid depositors should not rise. This was because they had made long-term loans (mortgages) at low interest rates. Thus they knew that they would for a long time be earning only 5 or 6 percent on the loans they had made. They could not afford to pay out more than 5 percent to their depositors.

But when market interest rates started rising, depositors limited to 5.5 percent at the financial institutions went elsewhere with their money. This is the process of disintermediation. As the depositors withdrew their deposits, for instance, buying Treasury bills instead, the savings and loans had nothing left to loan. There were no mortgages available, even though the interest rate that the savings and loans were quoting (this was the rate they would charge if they could find the money to lend) was not especially high.

With housing loans unavailable, there was a *credit crunch.* The first serious crunch took place in 1966–1967. (Note the dip in residential investment in Figure 9-6 even though there is no evident increase in the mortgage rate.) Disintermediation happened again in 1969–1970 and in the 1973–1975 recession. But then the savings and loans invented new ways of borrowing, and since then, monetary policy has affected housing investment directly through interest rates, rather than through the round-about route of disintermediation.

What about the problem that the savings and loans, borrowing by paying high interest rates to depositors, would be paying out more than they were earning on the loans they had made? This was a very real problem in the late seventies and early eighties. Several saving and loans institutions failed (went bankrupt) and were bought out by other financial institutions. Savings and loans had to close in Ohio and Maryland in 1985, though this was mainly a result of some bad loans rather than their having made fixed interest loans at times when the interest rate was low.

By the mid-eighties many of the thrift institutions were in better health than they had been five years before. In part this was because of the development of new types of mortgages.[29] It was also because markets had developed for the resale of mortgages. Savings and loans who have made mortgage loans to individuals can now bundle those mortgages together, and sell a package of them to someone else who wants to hold a long-term asset. That way the thrift institution can obtain more funding when it needs it.

Now monetary policy affects housing investment through interest rates, but not through disintermediation. Indeed, this is one reason the interest rate in the late seventies and early eighties went so high: The Fed wanted to reduce

---

[29] See footnote 26.

aggregate demand and had to do so through the direct rate route and not through the indirect disintermediation route.

9-5 CONCLUDING REMARKS

We have presented several different models to explain the different categories of investment behavior in this chapter. Nonetheless, there is a basic common element in the models, the interaction of the demand for the stock of capital with investment. In each case we started by examining the determinants of the desired stock—capital or housing. The discussion of inventory investment started by examining the determinants of the desired inventory-sales ratio. Then, in each case, we went on to analyze or describe the determinants of the rate per year of that type of investment.

We come now to the question of why there is a difference between the theoretical models used to explain the level of business fixed investment and residential investment. The fundamental difference arises from the degree of standardization of the capital and the associated question of the existence of a good market for the used capital goods. Much of business fixed investment is in capital that is specifically designed for a given firm and is not of much use to other firms. It is, accordingly, difficult to establish a market price for the stock of that type of capital, and the theory used in discussing residential investment would be difficult to apply in that case. Although housing, too, varies a good deal, it is, nonetheless, possible to talk of a price of housing. Further, used housing is a very good substitute for new housing, whereas that is less often true for many capital goods.

To look ahead, note that the emphasis in this chapter has been on investment as a component of aggregate demand. But the definition of investment as adding to the capital stock suggests that it is also a key in understanding aggregate supply. We turn to the supply-side aspect of investment in Chapter 19.

9-6 SUMMARY

1. Investment constitutes less than 20 percent of aggregate demand, but fluctuations in investment account for a large share of business cycle movements in GNP. We analyze investment in three categories: business fixed investment, residential investment, and inventory investment.
2. Investment is spending that adds to the capital stock.
3. Inventory investment fluctuates proportionately more than any other class of investment. Firms have a desired inventory-to-sales ratio. That may get out of line if sales are unexpectedly high or low, and then firms change their production levels to adjust inventories. For instance, when aggregate demand falls at the beginning of a recession, inventories build

up. Then when firms cut back production, output falls even more than did aggregate demand. This is the inventory cycle.

4. The neoclassical theory of business fixed investment sees the rate of investment being determined by the speed with which firms adjust their capital stocks toward their desired levels. The desired capital stock is larger the more output the firm expects to produce, and the smaller is the rental or user cost of capital. Since investment is undertaken for *future* production, it is expected future (permanent) output that determines the desired capital stock.

5. The real interest rate is the nominal (stated) intererest rate minus the inflation rate.

6. The rental cost of capital is higher, the higher the real interest rate, the lower the price of the firm's stock, and the higher the rate of depreciation of capital. Taxes also affect the rental cost of capital, in particular through the investment tax credit. The investment tax credit is, in effect, a government subsidy for investment.

7. In practice, firms decide how much to invest using discounted cash flow analysis. This analysis gives answers that are consistent with those of the neoclassical approach.

8. The accelerator model of investment is a special case of the gradual adjustment model of investment. It predicts that investment demand is proportional to the *change* in GNP.

9. Empirical results show that business fixed investment responds with long lags to changes in output. The accelerator model, which does not take into account changes in the rental cost of capital, does almost as good a job of explaining investment as the more sophisticated neoclassical model.

10. The theory of housing investment starts from the demand for the *stock* of housing, affected by wealth, the interest rates available on alternative investments, and the mortgage rate. Increases in wealth increase the stock demand for housing; increases in either the interest rate on alternative assets or the mortgage rate reduce the stock demand. The price of housing is determined by the interaction of the stock demand and the given stock supply of housing available at any given time.

11. The rate of housing investment is determined by the rate at which builders supply housing at the going price.

12. Housing investment is affected by monetary policy under current conditions because housing demand is sensitive to the interest rate (real and nominal), and in the past also because of disintermediation.

13. We now summarize the common elements of the different models. First, aggregate investment is the sum of the different types of investment spending. Thus any variable that affects any of the categories of investment analyzed also affects aggregate investment. Second, monetary and fiscal policy both affect investment, particularly business fixed investment and housing investment. The effects take place through changes in the real (and nominal in the case of housing) interest rates and through tax

incentives for investment. Third, there are substantial lags in the adjustment of investment spending to changes in output and other determinants of investment. This is true particularly for business fixed investment and inventory investment. Such lags are likely to increase fluctuations in GNP.

KEY TERMS

Business fixed investment	Real interest rate
Residential investment	Gradual adjustment hypothesis
Inventory investment	Discounted cash flow analysis
Desired capital stock	Accelerator model of investment
Marginal product of capital	Inventory cycle
Rental (user) cost of capital	Present discounted value
Cobb-Douglas production function	q theory

PROBLEMS

1. (a) Explain how final sales and output can differ.
   (b) Point out from Figure 9-2 periods of planned and unplanned inventory investment and decumulation.
   (c) During a period of slow but steady growth, how would you expect final sales and output to be related? Explain. Draw a hypothetical figure like Figure 9-2 for such a period.
2. At the end of 1985 the inventory-to-sales ratio was very low. Business cycle forecasters argued this was a sign that 1986 would not see a recession. Why? Were they correct?
3. We have seen in Chapters 8 and 9 that *permanent* income and output, rather than current income and output, determine consumption and investment.
   (a) How does this affect the *IS-LM* model built in Chapter 4? (Refer to Figure 8-4.)
   (b) What are the policy implications of the use of "permanent" measures?
4. In Chapter 4 it was assumed that investment rises during periods of low interest rates. That, however, was not the case during the 1930s, when investment and interest rates were both very low. Explain how this can occur. What would have been appropriate fiscal policy in such a case?
5. According to the description of business fixed investment in this chapter, how would you expect a firm's investment decisions to be affected by a sudden increase in demand for its product? What factors would determine the speed of its reaction?
6. It is often suggested that investment spending is dominated by "animal spirits" — the optimism or pessimism of investors. Is this argument at all consistent with the analysis of Sections 9-2 and 9-3?
7. Here are the cash flows for an investment project:

Year 1	Year 2	Year 3
−200	100	120

Should this firm undertake the project:
(a) If the interest rate is 5 percent?
(b) If the interest rate is 10 percent?

8. Is there any relation between the neoclassical theory of investment and the way firms make their investment decisions in practice?

9. Explain how the two panels of Figure 9-8 react together over time. What would happen if the demand for housing stock (DD) shifts upward and to the right over time?

10. Trace carefully the step-by-step effects on the housing market (using Figure 9-8) of an increase in interest rates. Explain each shift and its long-run and short-run effects.

11. (a) Explain why the housing market usually prospers when (real) mortgage rates are low.
    (b) In some states, usury laws prohibit (nominal) mortgage rates in excess of a legal maximum. Explain how this could lead to an exception to the conclusion in part a.
    (c) Could this happen in the absence of inflation? Explain.

12. Suppose that an explicitly temporary tax credit is enacted. The tax credit is at the rate of 10 percent and lasts only 1 year.
    (a) What is the effect of this tax measure on investment in the long run (say, after 4 or 5 years)?
    (b) What is the effect in the current year and the following year?
    (c) How will your answers under a and b differ if the tax credit is permanent?

*13. For this question use the Cobb-Douglas production function and the corresponding desired capital stock given by equation (3). Assume that $\gamma = 0.3$, $Y = 2.5$ trillion, and $rc = 0.15$.
    (a) Calculate the desired capital stock K^*.
    (b) Now suppose that Y is expected to rise to 3 trillion. What is the corresponding desired capital stock?
    (c) Suppose that the capital stock was at its desired level before the change in income was expected. Suppose further that $\lambda = 0.4$ in the gradual adjustment model of investment. What will the rate of investment be in the first year after expected income changes? In the second year?
    (d) Does your answer in c refer to gross or net investment?

*APPENDIX: INTEREST RATES, PRESENT VALUES, AND DISCOUNTING

In this appendix we deal with the relationships among bond coupons, interest rates and yields, and the prices of bonds. In doing so, we shall introduce the very useful concept of present discounted value (PDV).

Section 1

We start with the case of a perpetual bond, or perpetuity. Such bonds have been issued in a number of countries, including the United Kingdom, where they are called Consols. The Consol is a promise by the British government to pay a fixed amount to the holder of the bond every year and forever. Let us denote the promised payment per Consol by Q_c, the *coupon*.[30]

---

[30] The *coupon rate* is the coupon divided by the face value of the bond, which is literally the value printed on the face of the bond. Bonds do not necessarily sell for their face value, though customarily the face value is close to the value at which the bonds are sold when they first come on the market.

The *yield* on a bond is the return per dollar that the holder of the bond receives. The yield on a savings account paying 5 percent interest per year is obviously just 5 percent. Someone paying $25 for a Consol that has a coupon of $2.5 obtains a yield of 10 percent [($2.5/25) × 100%].

The yield on a Consol and its price are related in a simple way. Let us denote the price of the Consol by P_c and the coupon by Q_c. Then, as the above example suggests, the yield i is just

$$i = \frac{Q_c}{P_c} \tag{A1}$$

which says that the yield on a perpetuity is the coupon divided by the price. Alternatively, we can switch equation (A1) around to

$$P_c = \frac{Q_c}{i} \tag{A2}$$

which says that price is the coupon divided by the yield. So, given the coupon and the yield, we can derive the price, or given the coupon and the price, we can derive the yield.

None of this is a theory of the determination of the yield or the price of a perpetuity. It merely points out the relationship between price and yield. Our theory of the determination of the yield on bonds is presented in Chapter 4. The interest rate in Chapter 4 corresponds to the yield on bonds, and we tend to talk interchangeably of interest rates and yields.

We shall return to the Consol at the end of this appendix.

Section 2

Now we move to a short-term bond. Let us consider a bond which was sold by a borrower for $100, on which the borrower promises to pay back $108 after 1 year. This is a 1-year bond. The yield on the bond to the person who bought it for $100 is 8 percent. For every $1 lent, the lender obtains both the $1 principal and 8 cents extra at the end of the year.

Next we ask a slightly different question. How much would a promise to pay $1 at the end of the year be worth? If $108 at the end of the year is worth $100 today, then $1 at the end of the year must be worth $100/108, or 92.6 cents. That is the value today of $1 in 1 year's time. In other words, it is the present discounted value of $1 in 1 year's time. It is the present value because it is what would be paid today for the promise of money in 1 year's time, and it is discounted because the value today is less than the promised payment in a year's time.

Denoting the 1-year yield or interest rate by i, we can write that the present discounted value of a promised payment Q_1, 1 year from now, is

$$PDV = \frac{Q_1}{1+i} \tag{A3}$$

Let us return to our 1-year bond and suppose that the day after the original borrower obtained the money, the yield on 1-year bonds rises. How much would anyone *now* be willing to pay for the promise to receive $108 after 1 year? The answer must be given by the general formula (A3). That means that the price of the 1-year bond will fall when the interest rate or yield on such bonds rises. Once again, we see that the price of the bond and the yield are inversely related, given the promised payments to be made on the bond.

As before, we can reverse the formula for the price in order to find the yield on the bond, given its price and the promised payment Q_1. Note that the price P is equal to the present discounted value, so that we can write

$$1 + i = \frac{Q_1}{P} \tag{A4}$$

Section 3

Next we consider a 2-year bond. Such a bond would typically promise to make a payment of interest, which we shall denote Q_1, at the end of the first year, and then a payment of interest and principal (usually the amount borrowed), Q_2, at the end of the second year. Given the yield i on the bond, how do we compute its PDV, which will be equal to its price?

We start by asking first what the bond will be worth 1 year from now. At that stage, it will be a 1-year bond, promising to pay the amount Q_2 in 1 year's time, and yielding i. Its value 1 year from now will accordingly be given by equation (A3), except that Q_1 in equation (A3) is replaced by Q_2. Let us denote the value of the bond 1 year from now by PDV_1, and note that

$$PDV_1 = \frac{Q_2}{1 + i} \tag{A5}$$

To complete computing the PDV of the 2-year bond, we can now treat it as a 1-year bond, which promises to pay Q_1 in interest 1 year from now, and also to pay PDV_1 1 year from now, since it can be sold at that stage for that amount. Hence, the PDV of the bond, equal to its price, is

$$PDV = \frac{Q_1}{1 + i} + \frac{PDV_1}{1 + i} \tag{A6}$$

or

$$PDV = \frac{Q_1}{1 + i} + \frac{Q_2}{(1 + i)^2} \tag{A6a}$$

As previously, given the promised payments Q_1 and Q_2, the price of the bond will fall if the yield rises, and vice versa.

It is now less simple to reverse the equation for the price of the bond to find the yield than it was before; that is because from equation (A6), we obtain a quadratic equation for the yield, which has two solutions.

Section 4

We have now provided the outline of the argument whereby the present discounted value of *any* promised stream of payments for any number of years can be computed. Suppose that a bond, or any other asset, promises to pay amounts Q_1, Q_2, Q_3 . . . , Q_n in future years, 1, 2, 3, . . . , n years away. By pursuing the type of argument given in Section 3, it is possible to show that the PDV of such a payments stream will be

$$PDV = \frac{Q_1}{1 + i} + \frac{Q_2}{(1 + i)^2} + \frac{Q_3}{(1 + i)^3} + \cdots + \frac{Q_n}{(1 + i)^n} \tag{A7}$$

As usual, the price of a bond with a specified payments stream will be inversely related to its yield.

Section 5

The formula (A7) is the general formula for calculating the present discounted value of any stream of payments. Indeed, the payments may also be negative. Thus in calculating the PDV of an investment project, we expect the first few payments, for example, Q_1 and Q_2, to be negative. Those are the periods in which the firm is spending to build the factory or buy machinery. Then in later years the Q_i become positive as the factory starts generating revenues.

Firms undertaking discounted cash flow analysis are calculating present values using a formula such as (A7).

Section 6

Finally, we return to the Consol. The Consol promises to pay the amount Q_c forever. Applying the formula, we can compute the present value of the Consol by

$$PDV = Q_c \left[\frac{1}{(1+i)} + \frac{1}{(1+i)^2} + \frac{1}{(1+i)^3} + \cdots + \frac{1}{(1+i)^n} + \cdots \right] \qquad \text{(A8)}$$

The contents of the parentheses on the right-hand side are infinite series, the sum of which can be calculated as $1/i$. Thus,

$$PDV = \frac{Q_c}{i} \qquad \text{(A9)}$$

This section casts a slightly different light on the commonsense discussion of Section 1 of this appendix. Equations (A8) and (A9) show that the Consol's price is equal to the PDV of the future coupon payments.

THE DEMAND FOR MONEY

Money is a means of payment or medium of exchange. In the United States, the basic measure of the money stock is currency plus checkable deposits, or $M1$. This is the amount that people keep in order to make payments for their purchases. $M1$ in the United States was about $650 billion in the middle of 1986. With a population of 240 million, this means that average money holdings per person were above $2,700.

We start discussing the topic of money demand with a review of the concept of the demand for *real balances*. One of the essentials of money demand is that individuals are interested in the purchasing power of their money holdings — the value of their cash balances in terms of the goods the cash will buy. They are not concerned with their *nominal* money holdings, that is, the number of dollar bills they hold. What this means in practice is that (1) *real* money demand is unchanged when the price level increases, but *all* real variables, such as the interest rate, real income, and real wealth, remain unchanged; and (2) *nominal* money demand increases in proportion to the increase in the price level, given the constancy of the real variables just specified.[1]

---

[1] Be sure you understand that (1) and (2) say the same thing in slightly different ways.

We have a special name for behavior that is not affected by changes in the price level, all real variables remaining unchanged. An individual is free from *money illusion* if a change in the level of prices, holding all real variables constant, leaves real behavior, including real money demand, unchanged. By contrast, an individual whose real behavior is affected by a change in the price level, all real variables remaining unchanged, is said to suffer from money illusion.

We shall see that empirical evidence supports the theoretical argument that the demand for money is a demand for real balances — or that the demand for nominal balances, holding real variables constant, is proportional to the price level.

In Chapter 4, we also assumed that the demand for money increases with the level of real income and decreases with the nominal interest rate. Recall that the response of the demand for money to interest rates is important in determining the effectiveness of fiscal policy. Changes in fiscal variables, such as tax rates or government spending, affect aggregate demand if the demand for money changes when the interest rate changes — if the demand for money is interest-elastic. If the demand for money does not react at all to changes in the interest rate, increases in government spending totally *crowd out* private spending and leave the level of income unaffected.

The demand for money has been studied very intensively at both the theoretical and empirical levels. There is by now almost total agreement that the demand should, as a theoretical matter, increase as the level of real income rises and decrease as the nominal interest rate rises. Empirical work bears out these two properties of the demand-for-money function.

However, the money demand function has been a problem for over a decade. Until 1973, empirical work showed a very *stable* simple demand for money function, with real balances demanded increasing with the level of income and decreasing with interest rates. But then from about 1974 on, the demand for money function seemed to shift several times. Through the early 1980s the shifts generally showed less real balances being demanded at given levels of income and interest rates than before. But twice in the first half of the 1980s there have also been shifts in the opposite direction, in which the quantity of real balances demanded appears to have increased at given levels of income and interest rates. Explaining these shifts in money demand is a major area for research. Much of the blame is undoubtedly due to a series of changes in the financial system that we discuss below.

10-1 COMPONENTS OF THE MONEY STOCK

The money supply concept we use in most of this chapter is $M1$, which consists of currency plus checkable deposits (including traveler's checks). Table 10-1 shows that $M1$ in March 1986 was equal to $638 billion, of which $174 billion was currency and the remaining $465 billion checkable deposits.

TABLE 10-1   COMPONENTS OF THE MONEY STOCK, MARCH 1986 (In Billions of Dollars, Seasonally Adjusted)

(1) Currency	(2) Checkable deposits (incl. traveler's checks)	(3) M1 = (1) + (2)	(4) Money market mutual funds and deposit accounts	(5) Savings and small time deposits	(6) Overnight RP's and Eurodollars	(7) M2 = (3) + (4) + (5) + (6)*
173.9	464.5	638.4	776.9	1,201.6	66.4	2,621.6

* Total is seasonally adjusted, and is not equal to sum of components because (4) and (6) are not seasonally adjusted.
Sources: Economic Indicators and Data Resources, Inc.

Currency consists of notes and coin in circulation, most of it in the form of notes. "Checkable" deposits are, as the name suggests, deposits against which checks can be written. They are held in commercial banks and thrift institutions.[2] The financial institutions referred to as thrifts are savings and loan associations, mutual savings banks, and credit unions. Before 1980, only demand deposits at commercial banks were included in what was *then* called *M*1. However, because there is no obvious difference in economic function served by checkable deposits at commercial banks and other thrift institutions, the definition of *M*1 was expanded in 1980. Now *M*1 includes other checkable deposits, such as NOW accounts.[3]

We concentrate on *M*1 because it is the definition of the money supply that corresponds most closely to the role of money as a *medium of exchange,* or as the means of making payments. Payments can be made directly with coin and notes and also, for most transactions, with a check. To make a payment using a passbook savings account, it is generally necessary first to transfer money out of the savings account into a checking account and then to write the check. That is why savings and similar accounts are not included in the basic definition of the money supply.

Information on the distribution of the ownership of demand deposits is available,[4] but there are no systematic records of the ownership of currency. About a third of demand deposits are held by consumers, with businesses holding most of the rest.

---

[2] Not all demand deposits held in U.S. banks are part of *M*1. Demand deposits held by foreign official institutions, foreign commercial banks, the U.S. government, and other commercial banks are excluded.
[3] A NOW account is an interest-bearing checking account. Box 10-1 gives details of the different types of assets.
[4] The data, available each quarter, are published in the *Federal Reserve Bulletin.*

A 1984 survey of cash holdings of U.S. households, undertaken for the Federal Reserve System, showed that the average amount of currency held per person surveyed was about $100.[5] At that time, total currency outstanding divided by population was $675. Thus the vast majority of the currency outstanding is not held by U.S. households — or at least they are not admitting to holding it. Some currency is held by legitimate businesses, but large amounts must be held to finance illegal activities, or held outside the United States. In many foreign countries $100 bills are regularly used to conduct large, perhaps illegal, transactions.

Although the money supply concepts have often been revised, the present definition of $M1$ still does not correspond exactly to the role of money as a means of making payments. For instance, there is a question of whether credit cards should not be regarded as a means of making payment. If so — and the argument is certainly compelling — we should probably count the amount that people are allowed to charge by using their credit cards as part of the money stock.

Historically, there have often been changes in the type of assets which can be used as means of payment, and simultaneous disagreements about what constitutes money in those circumstances. When checks first began to be widely used in England early in the nineteenth century, there was a disagreement over whether demand deposits should be regarded as part of the money stock. Now that point is not disputed. We can expect there to be continuing changes in the financial structure over the years, with consequent changes in the definitions of the various money supply concepts.

$M2$ and Other Monetary Aggregates

Anyone visiting a bank to make a deposit knows that there is a wide variety of ways of holding assets. Thus there are many substitutes that individuals might hold instead of the assets that make up $M1$. The major forms of monetary assets as of the beginning of 1986 are described in Box 10-1.

All the assets described in Box 10-1 are to some extent substitutes for one another. The Fed therefore publishes data for wider definitions of the money supply than $M1$. The wider definitions, from $M2$, to $M3$, to L, are for aggregates that are seen as increasingly less *liquid* substitutes for $M1$. An asset is liquid if it can immediately, conveniently, and cheaply be used for making payments.

$M2$ adds to $M1$ assets that are close to being usable as a medium of exchange. The largest part of $M2$ consists of savings and small (less than $100,000) time deposits at banks and thrift institutions. These can be used almost without difficulty for making payments. In the case of a savings deposit, the bank has to be notified to transfer funds from the savings deposit to a checking account; for time deposits, it is necessary to wait until the time deposit matures, or else to pay an interest penalty.

---

[5] "The Use of Cash and Transaction Accounts by American Families," *Federal Reserve Bulletin*, February 1986.

The second largest category of assets in $M2$ consists of money market mutual funds and deposit accounts. A money market mutual fund (MMMF) is a fund that invests its assets in short-term interest-bearing securities, such as certificates of deposit (CDs)[6] and Treasury bills. MMMFs pay interest and permit the owner of the account to write checks (typically the checks have to be for more than $500) against the account. Money market deposit accounts (MMDAs) are MMMFs held in commercial banks. A limited number of checks can be written against MMDAs each month. Obviously MMDAs and MMMFs are close to being checkable deposits — only the limits on the size and number of checks that can be written against these accounts keep them out of $M1$.

$M2$ is an alternative definition of the money supply, whose behavior is watched almost as closely as that of $M1$. And as we shall see in Chapter 11, it is also an aggregate for which the Fed sets target levels in advance, just as it does for $M1$. Thus $M2$ receives considerable attention from the Fed and from market watchers who are trying to figure out what the Fed is doing in its monetary policy. The fact that there are $M1$ and $M2$ definitions of the money supply (and also $M3$) reflects the difficulty of defining *uniquely* a set of assets used as the medium of exchange when other assets are very close substitutes.

Financial Innovation

It is worth discussing briefly the reasons for changes in money supply definitions. The definitional changes followed financial innovations that changed the nature of the assets that banks and thrifts issued. For instance, thrifts, which pay interest on deposits and had been forbidden to have checkable accounts, invented NOW accounts as a way of getting around the prohibition. A NOW, a negotiable order of withdrawal, looks and smells like a check, but is not, legally speaking, a check. Banks were trying to compete with one another and thrifts by finding ways of paying interest on demand deposits, again something they were forbidden from doing. As ways around the prohibitions were found, deposits formerly called savings deposits, such as NOW accounts, became, in fact, demand deposits, and eventually the definitions changed. Similarly, money market mutual funds were invented only in 1973. Until 1982, banks were not allowed to issue money market deposit accounts, but as soon as they were permitted to do so, there was a rapid inflow of such deposits to banks: MMDA deposits rose from zero in November 1982 to $320 billion in March 1983.

In summary, there is no unique set of assets which will always constitute the money supply. At present, there are arguments for using a broader definition of the money stock than $M1$. For instance, a limited number of checks can be written against MMDAs each month; maybe they belong in $M1$. And there are even arguments for using a less broad definition — should $1,000 bills be

---

[6] CDs are liabilities of the banks that can be bought and sold in the open market like other securities. Typically they come in large denominations of $100,000 or more.

BOX
10-1

COMPONENTS OF
THE MONETARY AGGREGATES

A wide and growing variety of liquid assets, which can be held by individuals and businesses, are included in the monetary aggregates. We list them here, giving brief discriptions and amounts outstanding in March 1986.

1. *Currency:* Consists of coins and notes in circulation. ($173.9 billion.)
2. *Demand deposits:* Noninterest-bearing checking accounts at commercial banks, excluding deposits of other banks, the government, and foreign governments. ($273.5 billion.)
3. *Traveler's checks:* The total is only of such checks issued by nonbanks (such as American Express). Traveler's checks issued by banks are included in demand deposits. ($6.1 billion.)
4. *Other checkable deposits:* Interest-earning checking accounts, including NOW and ATS accounts. ($185.2 billion.) ATS means automatic transfers from savings accounts. With ATS a deposit holder keeps assets in a savings account, and the bank transfers them automatically to the checking account when a payment has to be made.

$$M1 = (1) + (2) + (3) + (4)$$

5. *Overnight repurchase agreements* (RPs): Borrowing by a bank from a nonbank customer. The bank sells a security (for example, a Treasury bill) to the customer today and promises to buy it back at a fixed price tomorrow. That way the bank gets to use the amount borrowed for a day.
6. *Overnight Eurodollars:* Deposits that pay interest and mature the next day, held in Caribbean branches of U.S. banks. (Overnight RPs and Eurodollars together = $66.4 billion.)
7. *Money market mutual fund shares:* Interest-earning checkable deposits in mutual funds that invest in short-term assets. Some MMMF shares are held by institutions; these are excluded from $M2$ but included in $M3$. (MMMF shares in $M2$ = $256.8 billion.)
8. *Money market deposit accounts:* MMMFs run by banks, with the advantage that they are insured up to $100,000. Introduced at the end of 1982 to allow the banks to compete with MMMFs. ($520.5 billion.)
9. *Savings deposits:* Deposits at banks and other thrift institutions that are not transferrable by check, often recorded in a separate passbook kept by the depositor. ($306.9 billion.)
10. *Small time deposits:* Interest-bearing deposits with a specific maturity date. Before that date they can be used only if a penalty is paid. "Small" means less than $100,000. ($894.7 billion.)

$$M2 = M1 + (5) + (6) + (7) + (8) + (9) + (10)$$

11. *Large-denomination time deposits:* Interest-earning deposits of more than $100,000 denomination. The total excludes amounts held by MMMFs or MMDAs (and some other institutions) to make sure the same asset is not counted twice in the monetary aggregates. ($450.4 billion.)
12. *Term repurchase agreements:* These are RPs sold by thrift institutions, typically for longer than overnight. ($70.6 billion.)

$$M3 = M2 + (11) + (12) + \text{MMMFs held by institutions}$$

13. *Other Eurodollar deposits:* Longer-term (than overnight) Eurodollars. ($81.6 billion.)

14. *Savings bonds:* U.S. government bonds, typically sold to the small saver. ($81.1 billion.)
15. *Banker's acceptances:* These are orders to pay a specific amount at a specific time that are obligations of banks. They arise largely in international trade. ($41.6 billion.)
16. *Commercial paper:* Short-term liabilities of corporations. ($209.5 billion.)
17. *Short-term Treasury securities:* Securities issued by the U.S. Treasury that have less than 12 months to maturity. ($299.9 billion.)

$$L = M3 + (13) + (14) + (15) + (16) + (17)$$

Sources: Economic Indicators; Daniel J. Larkins, "The Monetary Aggregates: An Introduction to Definitional Issues," *Survey of Current Business,* January 1983; *Handbook of Securities of the United States Government and Federal Agencies,* First Boston Corporation; Data Resources, Inc.

included, for example? And over the course of time, the particular assets that serve as a medium of exchange, or means of payment, will certainly change further.

10-2 THE FUNCTIONS OF MONEY

Money is so widely used that we rarely step back to think how remarkable a device it is. It is impossible to imagine a modern economy operating without the use of money or something very much like it. In a mythical barter economy in which there is no money, every transaction has to involve an exchange of goods (and/or services) on both sides of the transaction. The examples of the difficulties of barter are endless. The economist wanting a haircut would have to find a barber wanting to listen to a lecture on economics; the actor wanting a suit would have to find a tailor wanting to watch movies; and so on. Without a medium of exchange, modern economies could not operate.

Money, as a medium of exchange, makes it unnecessary for there to be a "double coincidence of wants" in exchanges. By the double coincidence, we have in mind the above examples. The wants of two individuals would have to be identically matched for the exchange to take place. For instance, the man selling movie tickets would have to find a buyer whose goods he wanted to buy (the suit) while, at the same time, the woman selling suits would have to find a buyer whose goods she wanted to buy (the movie tickets).

There are four traditional functions of money, of which the medium of exchange is the first.[7] The other three are store of value, unit of account, and standard of deferred payment. These stand on a different footing from the medium of exchange function.

---

[7] See W. S. Jevons, *Money and the Mechanism of Exchange* (London: Routledge, Kegan, Paul, 1910).

A *store of value* is an asset that maintains value over time. Thus, an individual holding a store of value can use that asset to make purchases at a future date. If an asset were not a store of value, then it would not be used as a medium of exchange. Imagine trying to use ice cream as money in the absence of refrigerators. There would hardly ever be a good reason for anyone to give up goods for money (ice cream) if the money were sure to melt within the next few minutes. And if the seller were unwilling to accept the ice cream in exchange for his or her goods, then the ice cream would not be a medium of exchange. But there are many stores of value other than money—such as bonds, stocks, and houses.

The *unit of account* is the unit in which prices are quoted and books kept. Prices are quoted in dollars and cents, and dollars and cents are the units in which the money stock is measured. Usually, the money unit is also the unit of account, but that is not essential. In the German hyperinflation of 1922–1923, dollars were the unit of account for some firms, whereas the mark was the medium of exchange.

Finally, as a *standard of deferred payment,* money units are used in long-term transactions, such as loans. The amount that has to be paid back in 5 or 10 years is specified in dollars and cents. Dollars and cents are acting as the standard of deferred payment. Once again, though, it is not essential that the standard of deferred payment be the money unit. For example, the final payment of a loan may be related to the behavior of the price level, rather than being fixed in dollars and cents. This is known as an indexed loan.

The last two of the four functions of money are, accordingly, functions which money *usually* performs, but not functions that it *necessarily* performs. And the store of value function is one that many assets perform.

There are fascinating descriptions of different types of money that have existed in the past that we do not have room to review here.[8] But there is one final point we want to emphasize. *Money is whatever is generally accepted in exchange.* However magnificently a piece of paper may be engraved, it will not be money if it is not accepted in payment. And however unusual the material of which it is made, anything that is generally accepted in payment is money. The only reason money is accepted in payment is that the recipient believes that it can be spent at a later time. There is thus an inherent circularity in the acceptance of money. Money is accepted in payment because it is believed that it will also be accepted in payment by others.

10-3 THE DEMAND FOR MONEY: THEORY

In this section we review the three major motives underlying the demand for money. In doing so, we will concentrate on the effects of changes in income and changes in the interest rate on money demand.

---

[8] See Paul Einzig, *Primitive Money* (New York: Pergamon, 1966).

The three theories we are about to review correspond to Keynes's famous three motives for holding money[9]: (1) the transactions motive, which is the demand for money arising from the use of money in making regular payments; (2) the precautionary motive, which is the demand for money to meet unforeseen contingencies; and (3) the speculative motive, which arises from the uncertainties about the money value of other assets that an individual can hold. In discussing the transactions and precautionary motives, we are mainly discussing $M1$, whereas the speculative motive refers more to $M2$, as we shall see.

Although we examine the demand for money by looking at the three motives for holding it, we cannot separate a particular person's money holdings, say, $500, into three neat piles of, say, $200, $200, and $100, that are being held from each motive. Money being held to satisfy one motive is always available for another use. The person holding unusually large balances for speculative reasons also has those balances available to meet an unexpected emergency, so that they serve too as precautionary balances. All three motives influence an individual's holdings of money, and as we shall see, each leads to the prediction that the demand for money should fall as the interest rate on other assets increases.

This final point is worth emphasizing. Money ($M1$) generally earns no interest (currency and some checkable deposits) or less interest than other assets. Anyone holding money is giving up interest that could be earned by holding some other asset, such as a savings deposit or a bond. The higher the interest loss from holding a dollar of money, the less money we expect the individual to hold. The demand for money will thus be higher, the greater the interest rate on money itself if interest is paid on demand deposits, and will be lower, the higher the interest rate on alternative assets. In practice, we can measure the cost of holding money as the difference between the interest rate paid on money (perhaps zero) and the interest rate paid on the most nearly comparable other asset, such as a savings deposit or, for corporations, a certificate of deposit or commercial paper.

For most of the remainder of the chapter, we shall write as if money earns no interest. This is true of much of the $M1$ stock. Further, it is easy to modify the analysis to take account of the payment of interest on other parts of $M1$. All that is necessary is to substitute the difference between the interest rate on the alternative asset and the interest rate on money in places we mention only the interest rate on the alternative asset.

The Transactions Demand

The transactions demand for money arises from the use of money in making regular payment for goods and services. In the course of each month, an individual makes a variety of payments for such items as rent or mortgage,

---

[9] J. M. Keynes, *The General Theory of Employment, Interest and Money* (New York: Macmillan, 1936), chap. 13.

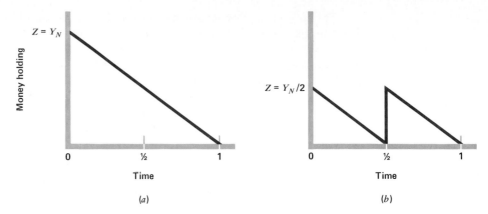

FIGURE 10-1   THE AMOUNT OF CASH HELD DURING THE MONTH
RELATED TO THE NUMBER OF WITHDRAWALS. Panel (*a*) shows the
pattern of money holding during the month when the individual makes
just one transaction from the savings account to cash during the month.
At the beginning of the month the individual transfers the entire amount
to be spent, Y_N, into cash, and then spends it evenly over the month.
Panel (*b*) shows the pattern of money holding when there are two
transactions, one at the beginning of the month and one in the middle
of the month. In panel (*a*), average cash holdings for the month are
$Y_N/2$; in panel (*b*) they are $Y_N/4$.

groceries, the newspaper, and other purchases. In this section we examine
how much money an individual would hold for such purchases.

In analyzing the transactions demand, we are concerned with a tradeoff
between the amount of interest an individual forgoes by holding money and
the costs and inconveniences of holding a small amount of money. To make the
problem concrete, consider a man who is paid, say, $1,800 each month. As-
sume that he spends the $1,800 evenly over the course of the month, at the
rate of $60 per day. Now at one extreme, the individual could simply leave his
$1,800 in cash (whether currency or demand deposits) and spend it at the rate
of $60 per day. Alternatively, on the first day of the month the individual could
take his $60 to spend that day and put the remaining $1,740 in a daily-interest
savings account. Then every morning he could go to the bank to withdraw that
day's $60 from the savings account. By the end of the month he would have
earned interest on the money he had each day in the savings account. This
would be the *benefit* of keeping his money holdings down as low as $60 at the
beginning of each day. The *cost* of keeping money holdings down is simply the
cost and inconvenience of the trips to the bank to withdraw the daily $60. To
decide on how much money to hold for transactions purposes, the individual
has to weigh the costs of holding small balances against the interest advantage
of doing so.

We now study the tradeoff in more detail and derive a formula for the demand for money. Suppose the nominal monthly income[10] of the individual is Y_N. We make the simplifying asumption that Y_N is paid in to his savings account, rather than his checking account, each month. The money is spent at a steady rate over the course of the month. To spend it, the individual has to get it out of the savings account and into cash, which may be currency or a checking account. If left in the savings account, the deposit earns interest at a rate of i per month. It earns zero interest as cash. The cost to the individual of making a transfer between cash and the savings account (which we henceforth call bonds for convenience) is $tc. That cost may be the individual's time, or it may be a cost that he explicitly pays someone else to make the transfer. For convenience we refer to it as a broker's fee.

THE INVENTORY APPROACH

The approach we are describing is known as the *inventory-theoretic approach*.[11] You should think of this inventory-theoretic approach applying equally well, with small changes in terminology and assumptions, to firms and households.

The individual has to decide how many transactions to make between bonds and cash each month. If he makes just one transaction, transferring Y_N into cash at the beginning of the month, his cash balance over the course of the month will be as shown in Figure 10-1a. It starts at Y_N, is spent evenly over the month, and is down to zero by the end of the month, at which time a new payment is received by the individual and transferred into his checking account. If he makes two withdrawals from the savings account, he first transfers $Y_N/2$ into cash at the beginning of the month, resulting in a cash balance that is run down to zero in the middle of the month, at which time another $Y_N/2$ is transferred into cash and spent evenly over the rest of the month.[12] Figure 10-1b shows the individual's cash holdings in that case.

We shall denote the size of a cash withdrawal from the bond portfolio (savings account) by Z and the number of withdrawals from the bond portfolio by n. Thus, n is the number of times the individual adds to his cash balance

---

[10] As a reminder, nominal income Y_N is defined as real income Y times the price level P: $Y_N \equiv PY$.

[11] The approach was originally developed to determine the inventories of goods a firm should have on hand. In that context, the amount Y_N would be the monthly sales of the good, tc the cost of ordering the good, and i the interest rate for carrying the inventory. The analogy between money as an inventory of purchasing power, standing ready to buy goods, and an inventory of goods, standing ready to be bought by customers, is quite close. The inventory-theoretical approach to the demand for money is associated with the names of William Baumol and James Tobin. (William Baumol, "The Transactions Demand for Cash: An Inventory Theoretic Approach," *Quarterly Journal of Economics*, November 1952; and James Tobin, "The Interest Elasticity of Transactions Demand for Cash," *Review of Economics and Statistics*, August 1956.) The most famous result of Baumol's and Tobin's work is the *square-root law* of the demand for money, which is presented later in equation (4).

[12] With simple interest being paid on the savings account, the individual's transactions between bonds and cash should be evenly spaced over the month. We leave the proof of that for the case where there are two transactions to the problem set.

during the month. If he makes n equal-sized withdrawals during the month, transferring funds from his savings account to his checking account, then the size of each transfer is Y_N/n, since a total of Y_N has to be transferred from the savings account into cash. For example, if Y_N is $1,800$, and n, the number of transactions, is 3, then Z, the amount transferred to cash each time, is $600. Accordingly, we can write

$$nZ = Y_N \qquad (1)$$

Suppose that the amount Z is transferred from bonds to cash at each withdrawal. What then is the *average* cash balance over the course of the month? We want to find the size of the average cash balance in order to measure the interest that is lost as a result of holding cash; if that amount were not held as cash, it could be held as interest-earning bonds. In Figure 10-1a, the average cash balance held during the month is $Y_N/2 = Z/2$, since the cash balance starts at Y_N and runs down in a straight line to zero.[13] In the case of Figure 10-1b, the average cash balance for the first half of the month is $Y_N/4 = Z/2$, and the average cash balance for the second half of the month is also $Z/2$. Thus, the average cash balance for the entire month is $Y_N/4 = Z/2$. Similarly, if three withdrawals were made, the average cash balance would be $Y_N/6 = Z/2$. In general, the average cash balance is $Z/2$, as you might want to confirm by drawing diagrams similar to Figure 10-1 for $n = 3$ or other values of n.

The interest cost of holding money is the interest rate times the average cash balance, or $iZ/2$. From equation (1), that means the total interest cost is $iY_N/2n$. The other component of the cost of managing the portfolio is the brokerage cost, or the cost in terms of the individual's time and inconvenience in managing his money. That cost is just the number of withdrawals made, n, times the cost of each withdrawal, tc, and is thus equal to $n \times tc$. The total cost of managing the portfolio is the interest cost plus the total brokerage cost:

$$\text{Total cost} = n \times tc + \frac{iY_N}{2n} \qquad (2)$$

Equation (2) shows formally that the brokerage cost $n \times tc$ increases as the number of withdrawals (transactions between bonds and money) rises, and that the interest cost decreases as the number of withdrawals increases. It thus emphasizes the tradeoff faced in managing money, and suggests that there is an optimal number of withdrawals the individual should make to minimize the total cost of holding money to meet transactions requirements for buying goods.

---

[13] The average cash balance is the average of the amount of cash the individual holds at each moment during the month. For instance, if he held $400 for 3 days and zero for the rest of the month, the average cash balance would be $40, or one-tenth (3 days divided by 30 days) of the month times $400.

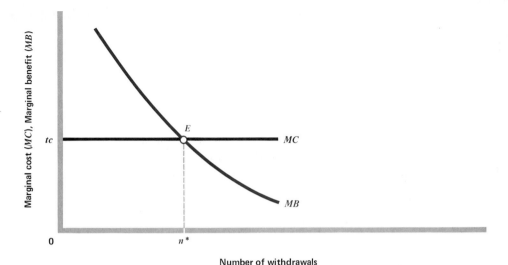

FIGURE 10-2   OPTIMAL CASH MANAGEMENT DETERMINING THE
OPTIMAL NUMBER OF WITHDRAWALS. The marginal cost of making
another transaction is the constant amount, tc, as shown by the MC
curve. The marginal benefit of making another transaction is the amount
of interest saved by holding smaller money balances. The marginal
benefit decreases as the number of withdrawals from the savings
account increases. Point E is the point at which the cost of managing
money holdings is minimized. Corresponding to point E is n^*, the
optimal number of transactions to make between the savings account
and money.

To derive that optimal point, we want to find the point at which the
benefit of carrying out another withdrawal is less than, or just equal to, the cost
of making another transaction between bonds and money. If the benefit of
making another transaction were greater than the cost, then another withdrawal should be made, and the original point could not have been optimal.
The cost of making another transaction is always equal to tc. In Figure 10-2, we
show the costs of making a further transaction by the marginal cost curve MC,
which is horizontal at the level tc. The financial benefit from making another
transaction is represented by the MB (marginal benefit) curve in Figure 10-2,
which represents the interest *saved* by making another withdrawal and thus
having a smaller cash balance on average during the month.

The more transactions between money and bonds an individual makes,
the lower is the total interest cost. But the reduction of the interest cost that is
obtained by making more transactions falls off rapidly as the number of withdrawals increases. There is a substantial saving in interest costs by making two

withdrawals rather than one, but very little saving in interest costs by making thirty-one transactions rather than thirty.

This suggests that the marginal benefit of making more withdrawals decreases as the number of withdrawals becomes large. The *MB* curve in Figure 10-2 is, accordingly, downward-sloping.[14]

In Figure 10-2, the optimal number of transactions is given by n^*, the number at which the marginal benefit in terms of interest saved is equal to the marginal cost of making a transaction. Given the number of transactions and the individual's income, we also know the average cash balance M, using the relationship between average money holdings and the size of each transfer which we derived earlier:

$$M = \frac{Z}{2} = \frac{Y_N}{2n} \tag{3}$$

PROPERTIES OF MONEY DEMAND

From Figure 10-2 we can see two important results. First, suppose the brokerage cost rises. That shifts the *MC* curve up, decreases the number of withdrawals n, and therefore [from equation (3), where M is inversely related to n] *increases* the average holding of money. Second, an increase in the interest rate shifts up the *MB* curve, therefore increases n, and thus [again, from equation (3)] reduces the holding of money: when the interest rate is higher, the individual is willing to make more trips to the bank to earn the higher interest now available. Figure 10-2 thus shows one of the key results we wanted to establish — that the demand for money is inversely related to the interest rate.

In the case of an increase in income, Figure 10-2 is unfortunately less useful. An increase in income shifts up the *MB* curve and increases the number of transactions. But from equation (3), we see that an increase in the number of transactions accompanying an increase in income does not necessarily imply that the demand for money rises, since it seems that n could increase proportionately more than Y_N. However, more complete algebraic analysis of the individual's optimal behavior will show that the demand for money in this model rises when income rises.

The famous *square-root formula* for money demand, developed by William Baumol and James Tobin,[15] both makes the results of the graphical analysis of Figure 10-2 more precise and resolves the ambiguity about the effects of

---

[14] Two points about Fig. 10-2: First, note that we have, for convenience, drawn the curves as continuous, even though you will recognize that it is possible to make only an integral number of transactions, and not, for example, 1.6 or 7.24 transactions. Second, if you can use the calculus, try to derive the equation of the marginal benefit curve from the component of costs in equation (2) that is due to interest lost.

[15] See the references in footnote 11.

income on the demand for money. The formula gives the demand for money that is obtained as a result of minimizing the total costs in equation (2) with respect to the number of withdrawals and then using equation (3) to derive the cash balance.[16] The formula is

$$M^* = \sqrt{\frac{tc \times Y_N}{2i}} \qquad (4)$$

Equation (4) shows that the transactions demand for money increases with the brokerage fee, or the cost of transacting, and with the level of income. The demand for money decreases with the interest rate.

MONEY DEMAND ELASTICITIES

Equation (4) also shows that an increase in income raises the demand for money proportionately less than the increase in income itself. To put the same point somewhat differently, the ratio of income to money, Y_N/M, rises with the level of income. A person with a higher level of income than another holds proportionately less money than the other person. This point is sometimes put in different words by saying that there are *economies of scale* in cash management.

Yet another way of saying the same thing is that the income elasticity of the demand for money is less than 1 [it is equal to ½ in equation (4)]. The income elasticity measures the percentage change in the demand for money due to a 1 percent change in income.[17]

Similarly, equation (4) implies that the elasticity of the demand for money with respect to the brokerage fee is ½, and the elasticity with respect to the interest rate is −½.

What accounts for the fact that people can somehow manage with less cash per dollar of spending as income increases? The reason is that cash management is more effective at high levels of income because the average cost per dollar of transaction is lower with large-size transactions. In turn, the lower average cost of transactions results from the fixed brokerage fee per transaction; it costs as much to transfer $10 as $10 million, so that the average cost per dollar transferred is lower for large transfers.

However, in the case of households, we should recognize that the "brokerage cost" *tc*, the cost of making withdrawals from a savings account, is in part the cost of time and the nuisance of having to go to the bank. Since the cost of time to individuals is likely to be higher the higher their income, *tc* may rise

---

[16] If you can handle calculus, try to derive equation (4) by minimizing total cost in equation (2).

[17] The income elasticity of demand is $\dfrac{\Delta(M/P)}{M/P} \Big/ \dfrac{\Delta Y}{Y}$. Similarly, the interest elasticity is $\dfrac{\Delta(M/P)}{M/P} \Big/ \dfrac{\Delta i}{i}$.

with Y_N. In that case, an increase in income would result in an increase in the demand for money by more than the income elasticity of ½ indicates because *tc* goes up together with Y_N.

THE DEMAND FOR REAL BALANCES

We started this chapter by emphasizing that the demand for money is a demand for real balances. It is worth confirming that the inventory theory of the demand for money implies that the demand for real balances does not change when all prices double (or increase in any other proportion). When all prices double, both Y_N and *tc* in equation (4) double — that is, both nominal income and the nominal brokerage fee double. Accordingly, the demand for nominal balances doubles, so that the demand for real balances is unchanged. The square-root formula does not imply any money illusion in the demand for money. Thus we should be careful when saying the income elasticity of demand for money implied by equation (4) is ½. The elasticity of the demand for *real* balances with respect to *real* income is ½. But if income rises only because all prices (including *tc*) rise, then the demand for *nominal* balances rises proportionately.

INTEGER CONSTRAINTS

So far we have ignored the important constraint that it is possible to make only an integral number of transactions, such as 1, 2, 3, etc., and that it is not possible to make 1.25 or 3.57 transactions. However, when we take account of this constraint, we shall see that it implies that many people do not make more than the essential one transaction between money and bonds within the period in which they are paid.[18] Consider our previous example of the person who received $1,800 per month. Suppose, realistically, that the interest rate per month on savings deposits is ½ percent. The individual cannot avoid making one initial transaction, since income initially arrives in the savings account. The next question is whether it pays to make a second transaction. That is, does it pay to keep half the monthly income for half a month in the savings account and make a second withdrawal after half a month? With an interest rate of ½ percent per month, interest for half a month would be ¼ percent. Half the income would amount to $900, and the interest earnings would, therefore, be $900 × ¼ percent = $2.25.

Now if the brokerage fee exceeds $2.25, the individual will not bother to make more than one transaction. And $2.25 is not an outrageous cost in terms of the time and nuisance of making a transfer from the savings to the checking account. Thus, for many individuals whose monthly net pay is below $1,800,

---

[18] If we had assumed that individuals were paid in cash, it would turn out that many people would not make any transactions between money and bonds in managing their transactions balances.

we do not expect formula (4) to hold exactly. Their cash balance would instead simply be half their income. They would make one transfer into cash at the beginning of the month; Figure 10-1*a* would describe their money holdings. For such individuals, the income elasticity of the demand for money is 1, since their demand for money goes up precisely in proportion with their income. The interest elasticity is zero, so long as they make only one transaction.

The very strong restrictions on the income and interest elasticities of the demand for money of equation (4) are not valid when the integer constraints are taken into account. Instead, the income elasticity is an average of the elasticities of different people, some of whom make only one transaction from bonds to money, and the elasticity is therefore between ½ and 1. Similarly, the interest elasticity is also an average of the elasticities across different individuals, being between − ½ and zero.[19] Because firms deal with larger amounts of money, they are likely to make a large number of transactions between money and bonds, and their income and interest elasticities of the demand for money are therefore likely to be close to the ½ and − ½ predicted by equation (4).

THE PAYMENT PERIOD

Once the integer constraints are taken into account, it can also be seen that the transactions demand for money depends on the frequency with which individuals are paid (the payment period). If one examines the square-root formula (4), the demand for money does not seem to depend on how often a person is paid, since an increase in the payments period increases both Y_N and i in the same proportion. Thus the demand for money appears unaffected by the length of the period. However, consider a person who makes only one transaction from bonds to money at the beginning of each month. Her money demand is $Y_N/2$. If such a person were paid weekly, her demand for money would be only one-quarter of the demand with monthly payments. Thus we should expect the demand for money to increase with the length of the payment period.

SUMMARY

The inventory-theoretic approach to the demand for money gives a precise formula for the transactions demand for money: The income elasticity of the demand for money is ½, and the interest elasticity is − ½. When integer constraints are taken into account, the limits on the income elasticity of demand are between ½ and 1, and the limits on the interest elasticity are between − ½ and zero. We have outlined the approach in terms of an individual's demand for money, but a similar approach is relevant for firms.

---

[19] See Robert J. Barro, "Integer Constraints and Aggregation in an Inventory Model of Money Demand," *Journal of Finance*, 1976.

Some of the assumptions made in deriving the square-root formula are very restrictive. People do not spend their money evenly over the course of the month, and they do not know exactly what their payments will be. Their checks are not paid into savings accounts, and so on. It turns out, though, that the major results we have derived are not greatly affected by the use of more realistic assumptions. There is thus good reason to expect the demand for money to increase with the level of income and to decrease as the interest rate on other assets (or, generally, the cost of holding money) increases.

The Precautionary Motive

In discussing the transactions demand for money, we focused on transactions costs and ignored uncertainty. In this section, we concentrate on the demand for money that arises because people are uncertain about the payments they might want to, or have to, make.[20] Suppose, realistically, that an individual did not know precisely what payments he would be receiving in the next few weeks and what payments he would have to make. He might decide to have a hot fudge sundae, or need to take a cab in the rain, or have to pay for a prescription. If he did not have money with which to pay, he would incur a loss. The loss could be missing a fine meal, or missing an appointment, or having to come back the next day to pay for the prescription. For concreteness, we shall denote the loss incurred as a result of being short of cash by q. The loss clearly varies from situation to situation, but as usual we simplify.

The more money an individual holds, the less likely he or she is to incur the costs of illiquidity (that is, not having money immediately available). But the more money he or she holds, the more interest he or she is giving up. We are back to a tradeoff situation similar to that examined in relation to the transactions demand. Somewhere between holding so little money for precautionary purposes that it will almost certainly be necessary to forgo some purchase (or to borrow in a hurry) and holding so much money that there is little chance of not being able to make any payment that might be necessary, there must be an optimal amount of precautionary balances to hold. That optimal amount will involve the balancing of interest costs against the advantages of not being caught illiquid.

Once more, we write down the total costs of holding an amount of money M.[21] This time we are dealing with expected costs, since it is not certain what the need for money will be. We denote the probability that the individual is illiquid during the month by $p(M, \sigma)$. The function $p(M, \sigma)$ indicates that the probability of the person's being illiquid at some time during the month depends on the level of money balances M being held and the degree of uncer-

---

[20] See Edward H. Whalen, "A Rationalization of the Precautionary Demand for Cash," *Quarterly Journal of Economics*, May 1966.
[21] This paragraph contains technical material that is optional and can easily be skipped.

tainty σ about the net payments that will be made during the month. The probability of illiquidity is lower, the higher is M, and higher, the higher is the degree of uncertainty σ. The *expected cost* of illiquidity is $p(M, \sigma)q$—the probability of illiquidity times the cost of being illiquid. The interest cost associated with holding a cash balance of M is just iM. Thus, we have

$$\text{Expected costs} = iM + p(M, \sigma)q \qquad (5)$$

To determine the optimal amount of money to hold, we compare the marginal costs of increasing money holding by $1 with the expected marginal benefit of doing so. The marginal cost is again the interest forgone, or i. That is shown by the MC curve in Figure 10-3. The marginal benefit of increasing money holding arises from the lower expected costs of illiquidity. Increasing precautionary balances from zero has a large marginal benefit, since that takes care of small, unexpected disbursements that are quite likely. As we increase

FIGURE 10-3   THE PRECAUTIONARY DEMAND FOR MONEY. The MC schedule shows the marginal cost of holding an extra dollar of money: holding an extra dollar means losing interest, and so the MC curve is horizontal at a level equal to the interest rate (or, more generally, the difference between the interest rate on money and alternative assets). The marginal benefit (MB) of holding an extra dollar is that the consumer is less likely to be short of money when it is needed. The marginal benefit declines with the amount of money held. The optimal amount of money to hold is shown by M^*, where marginal cost is equal to marginal benefit.

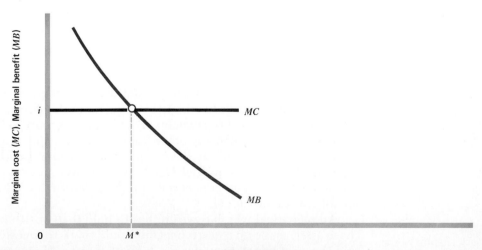

cash balances further, we continue to reduce the probability of illiquidity, but at a decreasing rate. We start to hold cash to insure against quite unlikely events. Thus, the marginal benefit of additional cash is a decreasing function of the level of cash holdings — more cash on hand is better than less, but at a diminishing rate. The marginal benefit of increasing cash holdings is shown by the *MB* curve in Figure 10-3.

The optimal level of the precautionary demand for money is reached where the two curves intersect. That level of money is shown as M^* in Figure 10-3. Now we can use Figure 10-3 to examine the determinants of the optimal level of the precautionary demand. It is, first, apparent that precautionary balances will be larger when the interest rate is lower. A reduction in the interest rate shifts the *MC* curve down and increases M^*. The lower cost of holding money makes it profitable to insure more heavily against the costs of illiquidity. An increase in uncertainty leads to increased money holdings because it shifts up the *MB* curve. With more uncertainty about the flow of spending, there is more scope for unforeseen payments and thus a greater danger of illiquidity. It therefore pays to insure more heavily by holding larger cash balances. Finally, the lower the costs of illiquidity, *q*, the lower the money demand. A reduction in *q* moves the *MB* curve down. Indeed, if there were no cost to illiquidity, no one would bother to hold money. There would be no penalty for not having it, while at the same time, holding it would mean a loss of interest.

The model of precautionary demand can be applied to goods other than money. It is a broad theory that applies to any commodity inventory that is held as insurance against contingencies. For instance, cars carry spare tires. You can work out circumstances under which one would want to have more than one spare tire in a car, and even circumstances in which zero would be the optimal number. The idea of the precautionary demand for money or for goods is quite general. So, too, are the determinants of the precautionary demand: the alternative cost in terms of interest forgone, the cost of illiquidity, and the degree of uncertainty that determines the probability of illiquidity.

The Speculative Demand for Money

The transactions demand and the precautionary demand for money emphasize the medium of exchange function of money, for each refers to the need to have money on hand to make payments. Each theory is more relevant to the *M*1 definition of money than any other, though the precautionary demand could certainly explain part of the holding of savings accounts and other relatively liquid assets which are part of *M*2. Now we move over to the store of value function of money and concentrate on the role of money in the investment portfolio of an individual.

An individual who has wealth has to hold that wealth in specific assets. Those assets make up a *portfolio.* One would think an investor would want to hold the asset which provides the highest returns. However, given that the return on most assets is uncertain, it is unwise to hold the entire portfolio in a single *risky asset*. You may have the hottest tip that a certain stock will surely double within the next 2 years, but you would be wise to recognize that hot tips are far from infallible, and that you could lose a lot of money in that stock as well as make money. A prudent, risk-averse investor does not put all his or her eggs in one basket. Uncertainty about the returns on risky assets leads to a diversified portfolio strategy.

As part of that diversified portfolio, the typical investor will want to hold some amount of a safe asset as insurance against capital losses on assets whose prices change in an uncertain manner. The safe asset would be held precisely because it is safe, even though it pays a lower expected return than risky assets. Money is a safe asset in that its nominal value is known with certainty.[22] In a famous article, James Tobin argued that money would be held as the safe asset in the portfolios of investors.[23] The title of the article, "Liquidity Preference as Behavior towards Risk," explains the essential notion. In this framework, the demand for money — the safest asset — depends on the expected yields, as well as on the riskiness of the yields, on other assets. The riskiness of the return on other assets is measured by the variability of the return. Using reasonable assumptions, Tobin shows that an increase in the expected return on other assets — an increase in the opportunity cost of holding money (that is, the return lost by holding money) — lowers money demand. By contrast, an increase in the riskiness of the returns on other assets increases money demand.

An investor's aversion to risk certainly generates a demand for a safe asset. The question we want to consider is whether that safe asset is money. That is, we want to ask whether considerations of portfolio behavior do generate a demand for money. The relevant considerations in the portfolio are the returns and the risks on assets. From the viewpoint of the yield and risks of holding money, it is clear that time or savings deposits or MMDAs have the same risks as currency or checkable deposits. However, they generally pay a higher yield. The risks in both cases are the risks arising from uncertainty about inflation. Given that the risks are the same, and with the yields on time and savings deposits higher than on currency and demand deposits, portfolio diversification explains the demand for assets such as time and savings deposits better than the demand for $M1$. We therefore regard the speculative demand as applying primarily to $M2$.

The implications of the speculative, or risk-diversifying, demand for money are similar to those of the transactions and precautionary demands. An increase in the interest rate on nonmoney assets, such as long-term bond yields or equity yields, will reduce the demand for $M2$. An increase in the rate paid on

---

[22] Of course, when the rate of inflation is uncertain, the real value of money is also uncertain, and money is no longer a safe asset. Even so, the uncertainties about the values of equity are so much larger than the uncertainties about the rate of inflation that money can be treated as a relatively safe asset.

[23] James Tobin, "Liquidity Preference as Behavior towards Risk," *Review of Economic Studies*, February 1958.

time deposits will increase the demand for time deposits, perhaps even at the cost of the demand for $M1$, as people take advantage of the higher yields they can earn on their investment portfolios to increase the size of those portfolios. One important difference between the speculative and the other two categories of demand is that here the level of wealth is clearly relevant to the demand for $M2$. The level of wealth determines the size of the total portfolio, and we expect that increases in wealth lead to increases in the demand for the safe asset, and thus in $M2$ demand.

One final point on the speculative demand. Many individuals with relatively small amounts of wealth will indeed hold part of that wealth in savings accounts in order to diversify their portfolios. But bigger investors are sometimes able to purchase other securities which pay higher interest and also have fixed (that is, risk-free) nominal values. Large CDs (in excess of $100,000) are sometimes an example of such assets, as are Treasury bills on occasion. For such individuals or groups, the demand for a safe asset is not a demand for money.

10-4 EMPIRICAL EVIDENCE

This section examines the empirical evidence — the studies made using actual data — on the demand for money. We know that the *interest elasticity* of the demand for money plays an important role in determining the effectiveness of monetary and fiscal policies. We showed in Section 10-3 that there are good theoretical reasons for believing the demand for real balances should depend on the interest rate. The empirical evidence supports that view very strongly. Empirical studies have established that the demand for money is responsive to the interest rate. An increase in the interest rate reduces the demand for money.

The theory of money demand also predicts that the demand for money should depend on the level of income. The response of the demand for money to the level of income, as measured by the *income elasticity* of money demand, is also important from a policy viewpoint. As we shall see below, the income elasticity of money demand provides a guide to the Fed as to how fast to increase the money supply to support a given rate of growth of GNP without changing the interest rate.

Lagged Adjustment

The empirical work on the demand for money has introduced one complication that we did not study in the theoretical section — that the demand for money adjusts to changes in income and interest rates *with a lag*. When the level of income or the interest rate changes, there is first only a small change in the demand for money. Then, over the course of time, the change in the demand for money increases, slowly building up to its full long-run change.

TABLE 10-2	ELASTICITIES OF REAL MONEY DEMAND		
	Y	i_{TD}	i_{CP}
Short run	0.19	−0.045	−0.019
Long Run	0.68	−0.16	−0.067

Source: S. Goldfeld, "The Demand for Money Revisited," *Brookings Papers on Economic Activity*, 1973:3 (Washington, D.C.: The Brookings Institution, 1973), p. 602, Regression A.

Reasons for this lag are not yet certain. The two usual possibilities exist in this case too. The lags may arise because there are costs of adjusting money holdings, or they may arise because money holders' expectations are slow to adjust. If people believe that a given change in the interest rate is temporary, they may be unwilling to make a major change in their money holdings. As time passes and it becomes clearer that the change is not transitory, they are more willing to make a larger adjustment.

Empirical Results

The standard demand-for-money function until the mid-1970s was that estimated by Stephen Goldfield of Princeton University in a comprehensive 1973 study.[24] Goldfeld studied the demand for $M1$ using quarterly postwar data and, of course, the 1973 definition of $M1$. Table 10-2 summarizes the major conclusions from that early empirical work. The table shows the elasticities of the demand for real balances with respect to real income Y (real GNP) and interest rates. The rate on time deposits, i_{TD}, and the rate on commercial paper, i_{CP}, are the interest rates used by Goldfeld. Commercial paper represents short-term borrowing by corporations. That interest rate is relevant to the demand for money because commercial paper is an asset which is very liquid for corporations that hold it instead of money for short periods of time.

In the short run (one quarter), the elasticity of demand with respect to real income is 0.19. This means that a 1 percent increase in real income raises money demand by 0.19 percent, which is considerably less than proportionately. The table shows that the elasticity of money demand with respect to interest rates is negative: an increase in interest rates reduces money demand.

---

[24] Stephen M. Goldfeld, "The Demand for Money Revisited," *Brookings Papers on Economic Activity*, 1973:3 (Washington, D.C.: The Brookings Institution, 1973). A review of other work on the demand for money is contained in the very readable book by David Laidler, *The Demand for Money: Theories and Evidence*, 2d ed. (New York: Dun-Donnelley, 1977). For recent work on the demand for money, see V. Vance Roley, "Money Demand Predictability," *Journal of Money, Credit and Banking*, part 2, November 1985.

TABLE 10-3	DYNAMIC PATTERNS OF ELASTICITIES OF MONEY DEMAND WITH RESPECT TO REAL INCOME AND INTEREST RATES		
Quarters elapsed	Y	i_{TD}	i_{CP}
1	0.19	−0.045	−0.019
2	0.33	−0.077	−0.033
3	0.43	−0.100	−0.042
4	0.50	−0.117	−0.049
8	0.63	−0.148	−0.062
Long run	0.68	−0.160	−0.067

Source: S. Goldfeld, "The Demand for Money Revisited," *Brookings Papers on Economic Activity,* 1973:3 (Washington, D.C.: The Brookings Institution, 1973).

The short-run interest elasticities are quite small. An increase in the rate on time deposits from 4 percent to 5 percent, that is, a 25 percent increase ($5/4 = 1.25$), reduces the demand for money by only 1.12 percent ($= 0.045 \times 25$ percent). An increase in the rate on commercial paper from 4 to 5 percent would reduce money demand by only 0.47 percent.

The long-run elasticities exceed the short-run elasticities by a factor of more than 3, as Table 10-2 shows. The long-run real income elasticity is 0.68, meaning that in the long run the increase in real money demand occurring as a result of a given increase in real income is only 68 percent as large as the proportional increase in income. Real money demand thus rises less than proportionately to the rise in real income. The long-run interest elasticities sum to a little over 0.2, meaning that an increase in *both* i_{TD} and i_{CP} from 4 percent to 5 percent would reduce the demand for money by a little over 5 percent.

How long is the long run? That is, how long does it take the demand for money to adjust from the short-run elasticities of Table 10-2 to the long-run elasticities shown in the table? Actually, it takes forever for the full long-run position to be reached. Table 10-3, however, shows the elasticities of the demand for real balances in response to changes in the level of income and interest rates after one, two, three, four, and eight quarters. Three-fourths of the adjustment is complete within the first year, and over 90 percent of the adjustment is complete within the first 2 years.

In summary, we have so far described three essential properties of money demand, as estimated by Goldfeld:

1. The demand for real money balances responds negatively to the rate of interest. An increase in interest rates reduces the demand for money.

2. The demand for money increases with the level of real income. However, the income elasticity of money demand is less than 1 so that money demand increases less than proportionately with income.
3. The short-run responsiveness of money demand to changes in interest rates and income is considerably less than the long-run response. The long-run elasticities are estimated to be over three times the size of the short-run elasticities.

There is one more important question Goldfeld considered. This is the question of how money responds to an increase in the level of prices. Here, Goldfeld, like other researchers before and since, finds strong evidence that an increase in prices raises nominal money demand in the same proportion. We can add, therefore, a fourth conclusion:

4. The demand for nominal money balances is proportional to the price level. There is no money illusion; in other words, the demand for money is a demand for *real* balances.

Money Demand Instability

Until 1973 the demand for real money balances was considered one of the best understood and highly stable equations in the U.S. macroeconomy. Since then new evidence has shaken that belief and opened up a debate over reasons for shifts in money demand in the 1970s and 1980s.

The point of the discussion can be seen from Table 10-4. Here we show the values of the determinants of real money demand in 1970 and in 1980. We also show the percentage changes in real balances that are implied by the percentage changes in these determinants applying the long-run elasticities of

TABLE 10-4	ACTUAL AND PREDICTED CHANGE IN REAL BALANCES, 1970–1980	
	Percentage change in variable	Percentage change in real money demand
Real income	35.9	24.4
Commercial paper rate	59.4	−4.0
Time deposit rate	18.8	−3.0
Predicted change in real balances		17.4
Actual change		−30.3

Source: Table 10-2, *Economic Report of the President,* 1986, and MPS Data Bank.

Table 10-2. To understand the table, consider for example the first row. Real income per capita increased 35.9 percent between 1970 and 1980. With the income elasticity from Table 10-2 equal to 0.68, real money demand should have risen 24.4 percent (=0.68 × 35.9 percent) over that 10-year period. The entries in the other rows are calculated similarly. Altogether, these three factors should have caused real balances to rise 17.4 percent. In fact per capita real balances *fell* by 30.3 percent over the 10-year period. The discrepancy is striking.

Goldfeld's estimates of the money demand equation in 1973 imply that the increase in real income over the 1970 – 1980 period would have increased real money demand by substantially more than the reduction in money demand stemming from increased interest rates. The net effect should have been a *rise* in money demand, not the observed 30 percent decline. The very large discrepancy between actual and predicted means that money demand shifted: at each interest rate and income level households chose to hold less real balances. Most research on money demand in the last decade has tried to explain the puzzle of the missing money. In the meantime, in 1982 – 1983 and 1985 there were episodes in which the shift seemed to go the other way, with the demand for real balances increasing *more* than expected.[25]

There are several explanations for the shift. The first is that the financial innovations mentioned earlier led to changes in money demand. For example, in 1975 it became possible to make transfers between accounts by telephone instruction rather than by actually going to the bank. This reduces the brokerage cost, *tc*, and reduces the demand for $M1$. Similarly, during this period corporations were for the first time allowed to own savings deposits, leading them to reduce holdings of $M1$. In addition, the invention of money market mutual funds (see Section 8-1) reduced the demand for money. Such explanations do appear to account for part of the shift in money demand.

An associated explanation argues that there have been permanent shifts in money demand associated with the very high interest rates of 1973 – 1974 and 1978 – 1982. The argument here is that when interest rates became very high, firms undertook studies of how to economize on money, developing new methods of *cash management.* These are sophisticated methods for firms to reduce the amount of money held in the normal course of business. Among these methods are "sweep accounts," where the bank undertakes to monitor the account and automatically invests any excess balances in short-term financial assets.

Adoption of the new methods leads to a permanent reduction in the demand for money even after interest rates have fallen from their record

---

[25] Two recent papers review the discussion and various explanations. See Robert J. Gordon, "The Short-run Demand for Money: A Reconsideration," *Journal of Money, Credit and Banking,* November 1984, part 1, and V. Vance Roley, "Money Demand Predictability," *Journal of Money, Credit and Banking,* November 1985, part 2. Both these papers discuss in addition possible statistical problems in estimating money demand.

levels. This is because once the firm has figured out the new methods of managing its cash, it continues to use them. It is clear that firms have increasingly used sophisticated methods of cash management. The explanation that centers on cash management obtains further support from two facts: First, the shift in money demand in 1974–1976 can be traced mostly to a shift in the demand for demand deposits rather than currency; and second, a substantial role in the shift can be traced to reduced demand for money by corporations.

The second main possibility is that the Goldfeld demand function omits some relevant variables. Here the leading candidate has been the long-term interest rate. It has been argued that since all assets are potentially substitutes for money in the portfolios of money holders, there is no reason why only short-term interest rates should enter the demand function for money. Inclusion of the long-term interest rate and an estimate of the return on equity does improve the fit of the money-demand function.[26]

An alternative explanation focuses on what is the right transactions variable, income or spending. Income and spending can diverge because of additions to inventories or because of imbalances in the current account. Thus rather than including GNP in the money demand equation, the right variable might be gross domestic purchases (=GNP + reductions in inventories + current account deficit). In periods where inventories are run down and the current account is in large deficit, there may be significant discrepancies between income and spending. This goes in the direction of explaining why money demand rose in 1982–1983 and 1985 when the current account deficit was growing—but the effects are just too small to provide a full explanation of the instability of the money-demand function.

Finally, amid all the excitement we should remember that, despite the recent shifts in money demand, empirical work still finds that the demand for money is positively related to income and negatively related to interest rates.

10-5 THE INCOME VELOCITY OF MONEY AND THE QUANTITY THEORY

The *income velocity of money* is the number of times the stock of money is turned over per year in financing the annual flow of income. Thus in 1985 GNP was about $4,000 billion, the money stock (*M*1) averaged $625 billion, and velocity was therefore 6.4. The average dollar of money balances financed $6.40 of spending on final goods and services, or the public held on average just under $0.16 of *M*1 per dollar of income. While we usually calculate velocity for the economy as a whole, we can also calculate it for an individual. For instance, for someone earning $20,000 per year, who has average money

[26] This is shown by Michael Hamburger, "Behavior of the Money Stock: Is There a Puzzle?" *Journal of Monetary Economics,* July 1977.

balances during the year of $2,000, the income velocity of money holdings is 10.[27]

Income velocity (from now on we shall refer to velocity rather than income velocity) is defined as

$$V \equiv \frac{Y_N}{M} \tag{6}$$

the ratio of nominal income to nominal money stock. An alternative way of writing equation (6) recognizes that Y_N, nominal GNP, is equal to the price level P times real income Y. Thus

$$M \times V = P \times Y \tag{7}$$

The Quantity Theory

Equation (7) is the famous *quantity equation,* linking the product of the price level and the level of output to the money stock. The quantity equation became the (classical) *quantity theory of money* when it was argued that both V, the income velocity of money, and Y, the level of output, were fixed. Real output was taken to be fixed because the economy was at full employment, and velocity was assumed not to change much. Neither of these assumptions holds in fact, but it is, nonetheless, interesting to see where they lead. *If both V and Y are fixed, then it follows that the price level is proportional to the money stock.* Thus the classical quantity theory was a theory of inflation. The classical quantity theory argued that the price level was proportional to the money stock:

$$P = V \frac{M}{Y} \tag{7a}$$

The classical quantity theory applies in the *classical case* supply function examined in Chapter 7.[28] Recall that in that case, with a vertical aggregate supply function, changes in the quantity of money result in changes in the price level, with the level of output remaining at its full employment level. When the aggregate supply function is not vertical, increases in the quantity of money increase both the price level and output, and the price level is there-

---

[27] Why do we say income velocity and not plain velocity? There is another concept, transactions velocity, that is, the ratio of total transactions to money balances. Total transactions far exceed GNP for two reasons. First, there are many transactions involving the sale and purchase of assets that do not contribute to GNP. Second, a particular item in final output typically generates total spending on it that exceeds the contribution of that item to GNP. For instance, 1 dollar's worth of wheat generates transactions as it leaves the farm, as it is sold by the miller, as it leaves the baker for the supermarket, and then as it is sold to the household. One dollar's worth of wheat may involve several dollars of transactions before it is sold for the last time. Transactions velocity is thus higher than income velocity.

[28] For more on the quantity theory, see Chap. 7.

fore not proportional to the quantity of money. Of course, if velocity is constant, *nominal GNP* (the price level times output) is proportional to the money stock.

Velocity and Policy

Velocity is a useful concept in economic policy making. We see how to use it by rewriting (6) as

$$Y_N \equiv VM \tag{6a}$$

Given the nominal money stock (M) and given velocity, we know the level of nominal GNP. Thus if we can predict the level of velocity, we can predict the level of nominal income, given the money stock.

Further, *if* velocity were constant, changing the money supply would result in proportionate changes in nominal income. Any policies, including fiscal policies, that did not affect the money stock would not affect the level of income. You will probably now recognize that we have previously discussed a case of constant velocity. In Chapter 5, we discussed the effectiveness of fiscal policy when the demand for money is not a function of the interest rate and the *LM* curve is therefore vertical. That vertical *LM* curve is the same as the assumption of constant velocity.

Velocity and the Demand for Money

The discussion of constant velocity is closely related to the behavior of the demand for money. Indeed, the notion of velocity is important because it is a convenient way of talking about money demand.

We now examine the relationship between velocity and the demand for money. Let the demand for real balances be written $L(i, Y)$, consistent with Chapter 4. Recall that Y is real income. When the supply of money is equal to the demand for money, we have

$$\frac{M}{P} = L(i, Y) \tag{8}$$

or $M = PL(i, Y)$. Now we can substitute for the nominal money supply into equation (6) to obtain

$$V = \frac{Y_N}{PL(i, Y)} = \frac{Y}{L(i, Y)} \tag{6b}$$

where we have recognized that Y_N/P is the level of real income. Income velocity is the ratio of the level of real income to the demand for real balances.

From equation (6*b*) we note that velocity is a function of real income and the interest rate. Consider first the effects of a change in the interest rate on velocity. An increase in the interest rate reduces the demand for real balances and therefore increases velocity: when the cost of holding money increases, money holders make their money do more work and thus turn it over more often.

The way in which changes in real income affect velocity depends on the income elasticity of the demand for money. If the income elasticity of the demand for real balances were 1, then the demand for real balances would change in the same proportion as income. In that case, changes in real income would not affect velocity. Suppose that real income Y increased by 10 percent. The numerator Y in equation (6*b*) would increase by 10 percent, as would the denominator, and velocity would be unchanged. However, we have seen that the income elasticity of the demand for money is less than 1. That means that velocity *increases* with increases in real income. For example, suppose that real income rose 10 percent, and the demand for real balances increased only by 6.8 percent ($=0.68 \times 10$ percent), as Goldfeld's results suggest. Then the numerator of equation (6*b*) would increase by more than the denominator, and velocity would rise.

The empirical work reviewed in Section 10-4 makes it clear that the

FIGURE 10-4   THE INCOME VELOCITY OF MONEY, 1973–1985
(*M*1). (*Source:* Data Resources Inc.)

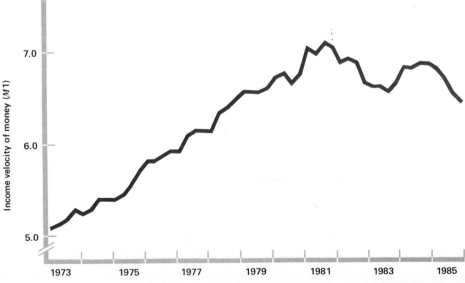

demand for money and, therefore, also velocity do react systematically to changes in interest rates and the level of real income. The empirical evidence therefore decisively refutes the view that velocity is unaffected by changes in interest rates and that fiscal policy is, accordingly, incapable of affecting the level of nominal income. In terms of equation (6*b*), and using the analysis of Chapter 4, expansionary fiscal policy can be thought of as working by increasing interest rates, thereby increasing velocity, and thus making it possible for a given stock of money to support a higher level of nominal GNP.

Velocity in Practice

The empirical evidence we reviewed in Section 10-4 is useful in interpreting the behavior of velocity. Figure 10-4 shows a general rise in velocity over the period since 1973. Indeed, that increase is even more marked over longer periods: in the mid-fifties velocity was about 3, whereas it is now above 6. The average dollar of $M1$ finances twice the income flow now than it did in the mid-fifties.

This increase in velocity can, of course, be explained by the same factors that explain the demand for money. Velocity has risen because income has risen (since the income elasticity of demand is less than 1) and because interest rates have risen. In addition, the financial innovations that reduced money demand in the seventies increased velocity. A look at equation (6*b*) shows that anything which reduces the demand for money, in the denominator, for a given level of Y in the numerator, increases velocity.

Figure 10-4 shows velocity increasing steadily during the 1970s: the rate of increase averaged about 3.5 percent per year in that decade. But in the 1980s velocity no longer shows this trend growth. Velocity was lower in 1985 than in 1980, as we see from Figure 10-4 and Table 10-5. Not only did the trend of velocity appear to change, but in the meantime it has shown very large fluctuations.

We saw above the money-demand puzzle, the question of why money demand has shifted from the well-established behavior of the pre-1973 period. There is a similar *velocity puzzle* in the 1980s. Why did velocity in the 1980s stay basically flat rather than rising at the 3.5 percent rate it had been

TABLE 10-5	THE INCOME VELOCITY OF MONEY: 1980–1985				
1980	1981	1982	1983	1984	1985
6.58	6.91	6.58	6.44	6.75	6.39

Source: Economic Report of the President, 1986.

BOX
10-2

MONEY DEMAND AND HIGH INFLATION

The demand for real balances depends on the alternative cost of holding money. That cost is normally measured by the yield on alternative assets, say Treasury bills, commercial paper, or money market funds. But there is another margin of substitution. Rather than holding their wealth in financial assets, households or firms can also hold real assets: stocks of food, or houses, or machinery. This margin of substitution is particularly important in countries where inflation is very high and capital markets do not function well. In that case it is quite possible that the return on holding goods can even be higher than that on financial assets.

Consider a household deciding whether to hold $100 in currency or a demand deposit or else to hold it in the form of groceries on the shelf. The advantage of holding groceries is that, unlike money, they maintain their real value. Rather than having the purchasing power of money balances eroded by inflation, the household gets rid of money, buying goods and thus avoiding a loss.

This "flight out of money" occurs systematically when inflation rates become high. In a famous study of hyperinflations (defined in the study as inflation rates of more than 50 percent *per month*) Phillip Cagan of Columbia University found large changes in velocity taking place as inflation increased. In the most famous hyperinflation, that in Germany in 1922–1923,* the quantity of real balances at the height of the hyperinflation had fallen to one-twentieth of its preinflation level. The increased cost of holding money leads to a reduction in real money demand and with it to changes in the public's payments habits as everybody tries to pass on money like a hot potato. We shall see more on this in Chapter 16 where we study money and inflation.

In well developed capital markets interest rates will reflect expectations of inflation and hence it will not make much difference whether we measure the alternative cost of holding money by interest rates or inflation rates. But when capital markets are not free because interest rates are regulated or have ceilings, it is often appropriate to use inflation, not interest rates as the measure of the alternative cost. Franco Modigliani has offered the following rule of thumb: The right measure of the opportunity cost of holding money is the higher of the two, interest rates or inflation.

---

* Phillip Cagan, "The Monetary Dynamics of Hyperinflation," in Milton Friedman (ed.), *Studies in the Quantity Theory of Money* (Chicago: The University of Chicago Press, 1956).

---

increasing in the 1980s? To put the same point in terms of the demand for money: Why did real money demand grow nearly as strongly as real income over the 1980–1985 period?[29] Figure 10-4 shows velocity decreasing particularly from 1981 to 1983, and from 1984 to 1985.

One ready explanation is the decline in interest rates. The Treasury bill rate, for example, declined from a 1980 average of 11.5 percent to only 7.5 percent in 1985. Another reason, mentioned earlier, is the discrepancy be-

---

[29] In addition to the references in footnote 25 see Lawrence Radecki and John Wenninger, "Recent Instability in M1's Velocity," Federal Reserve Bank of New York *Quarterly Review*, Autumn 1985, and Robert L. Hetzel, "The Behavior of the M1 Demand Function in the Early 1980s," Federal Reserve Bank of Richmond *Economic Review*, November/December 1984.

tween income and spending. If real money demand depends on spending, then a rise in spending relative to income would reduce velocity, as for example occurred in 1985.

But Figure 10-4 and Table 10-5 also draw attention to the short-run fluctuations in velocity. These are much larger in the 1980s than they used to be in the past. The fall in velocity in 1985 compared with 1984, for example, amounts to 5.3 percent. That means that, given the growth rate of money, nominal GNP increased 5.3 percent less in 1985 than it would have had velocity remained at its 1984 level.

If the Fed had based its 1985 money growth on the behavior of velocity in 1984, it would have found GNP growing more slowly than expected in 1985. It could — and did — in response increase the growth rate of money to offset the decline in velocity. But unexpected changes in velocity create serious difficulties for monetary policy. Unexpected shifts in money demand, or equivalently, in velocity force the central bank to depart from its planned path of money growth, as we shall see in the next chapter.

10-6 SUMMARY

1. The demand for money is a demand for real balances. It is the purchasing power, not the number, of their dollar bills that matters to holders of money.
2. The money supply $M1$ is made up of currency and checkable deposits. A broader measure, $M2$, includes savings and time deposits at depository institutions as well as some other interest-bearing assets.
3. The chief characteristic of money is that it serves as a means of payment.
4. There are two broad reasons why people hold money and thus forgo interest that they could earn by holding alternative assets. These reasons are transactions costs and uncertainty.
5. Transactions costs are an essential aspect of money demand. If it were costless to move (instantaneously) in and out of interest-bearing assets, nobody would hold money. Optimal cash management would involve transfers from other assets (bonds or saving deposits) just before outlays, and it would involve immediate conversion into interest-bearing form of any cash receipts. The existence of transactions costs — brokerage costs, fees, and time costs — makes it optimal to hold some money.
6. The inventory-theoretic approach shows that an individual will hold a stock of real balances that varies inversely with the interest rate but increases with the level of real income and the cost of transactions. The income elasticity of money demand is less than unity, implying that there are economies of scale.
7. Transactions costs, in combination with uncertainty about payments and receipts, give rise to a precautionary demand for money. Money holdings

provide insurance against illiquidity. Optimal money holdings are higher, the higher the variability of net disbursements and the higher the cost of illiquidity. Since holding money implies forgoing interest, optimal money holdings will vary inversely with the rate of interest.

8. Portfolio diversification involves the tradeoff between risk and return. Saving deposits form part of an optimal portfolio because they are not risky — their nominal value is constant. Saving deposits dominate currency or demand deposits, which are also safe nominal assets, because they bear interest. Thus the speculative portfolio demand for money is a demand for saving or time deposits.

9. The empirical evidence provides strong support for a negative interest elasticity of money demand and a positive income elasticity. Because of lags, short-run elasticities are much smaller than long-run elasticities. The long-run income elasticity is about 0.7, and the long-run interest elasticity is about -0.2.

10. Over the decade 1970–1980 the demand for money shifted; less money ($M1$) was demanded than should have been demanded according to the standard demand-for-money equation. The reduction in money demand was a result of both the introduction of new assets and improvements in cash management methods. During the 1980s there have been episodes of unexpected increases in the demand for money.

11. The income velocity of money is defined as the ratio of income to money or the rate of turnover of money. Since the fifties, velocity has doubled to a level in excess of 6.

12. The empirical evidence implies that an increase in real income raises velocity, as does an increase in the rate of interest. At higher levels of income or at higher interest rates, there is a lower demand for money in relation to income. Higher interest rates lead people to economize on cash balances.

13. Inflation implies that money loses purchasing power, and inflation thus creates a cost of holding money. The higher the rate of inflation, the lower the amount of real balances that will be held. Hyperinflations provide striking support for this prediction. Under conditions of very high expected inflation, money demand falls dramatically relative to income. Velocity rises as people use less money in relation to income.

KEY TERMS

Real balances
Money illusion
$M1$
$M2$
Liquidity
Medium of exchange

Store of value
Unit of account
Standard of deferred payments
Transactions demand
Inventory-theoretic approach
Square-root formula

Precautionary demand
Speculative demand
Income velocity of money

Quantity equation
Quantity theory of money
Hyperinflation

PROBLEMS

1. To what extent would it be possible to design a society in which there was no money? What would the problems be? Could currency at least be eliminated? How? (Lest all this seems too unworldly, you should know that some people are beginning to talk of a "cashless economy" in the next century.)

2. Evaluate the effects of the following changes on the demand for $M1$ and $M2$. Which of the functions of money do they relate to?
   (a) "Instant cash" machines which allow 24-hour withdrawals from savings accounts at banks
   (b) The employment of more tellers at your bank
   (c) An increase in inflationary expectations
   (d) Widespread acceptance of credit cards
   (e) Fear of an imminent collapse of the government
   (f) A rise in the interest rate on time deposits

3. (a) Do you think credit card credit limits should be counted in the money stock?
   (b) Should MMDAs be part of $M1$?

4. (a) Determine the optimal strategy for cash management for the person who earns $1,600 per month, can earn 0.5 percent interest per month in a savings account, and has a transaction cost of $1.
   (b) What is the individual's average cash balance?
   (c) Suppose income rises to $1,800. By what percentage does the individual's demand for money change? (Pay attention to the integer constraints.)

5. Discuss the various factors that go into an individual's decision regarding how many traveler's checks to take on a vacation.

6. In the text, we said that the transactions demand-for-money model can also be applied to firms. Suppose a firm sells steadily during the month and has to pay its workers at the end of the month. Explain then how it would determine its money holdings.

7. In the text we argued that the demand for money fell when corporations received permission to hold savings accounts.
   (a) For which money-demand concept is this true? For which is it false?
   (b) Explain why this change would have been more important for small firms than for large ones.

8. Explain why the demand-for-money function shifted during the seventies and early eighties.

9. (a) Is V high or low relative to trend during recessions? Why?
   (b) How can the Fed influence velocity?

10. This chapter emphasizes that the demand for money is a demand for real balances. Thus the demand for nominal balances rises with the price level. At the same time, inflation causes the real demand to fall. Explain how these two assertions can both be correct.

11. "Muggers favor deflation." Comment.

*12. The assumption was made in the text that, in the transactions demand for cash model, it is optimal to space transactions evenly throughout the month. Prove this as follows in the case where $n = 2$. Since one transaction must be made immediately, the only question is when to make the second one. For simplicity, call the beginning of the month $t = 0$ and the end of the month $t = 1$. Then consider a transaction strategy which performs the second transaction at the time t_0. If income is Y_N, then this will require moving $t_0 Y_N$ into cash now and $(1 - t_0)Y_N$ at time t_0. Calculate the total cost incurred under this strategy, and try various values of t_0 to see which is optimal. (If you are familiar with calculus, prove that $t_0 = \frac{1}{2}$ minimizes total cost.)

*13. For those students familiar with calculus, derive equation (4) from equation (2) by minimizing total costs with respect to n.

THE MONEY SUPPLY, THE FED, AND MONETARY POLICY

We have so far taken the money supply to be given and determined by the Federal Reserve System. By and large, the Fed is able to determine the money supply quite accurately, but it does not set it directly. In this chapter we study the way in which the actions of the Fed, financial institutions, and the public interact to determine the stock of money.

In conducting monetary policy, the Fed pays attention to the behavior of both interest rates and the money stock. Some monetarist critics of the Fed argue that this practice makes monetary policy wrong. They claim the Fed is continually distracted from its main task of keeping the money stock growing steadily by its habit of worrying about changes in interest rates. Other critics argue that the Fed *should* worry more about the behavior of interest rates, and not slavishly follow announced target paths for the money stock.

We start this chapter with the mechanics of money supply determination. Then we go on to discuss monetary policy: both how the Fed conducts monetary policy and controversies about how it should conduct monetary policy.

11-1 DEFINITIONS

The money stock $M1$ is the sum of checkable deposits CD plus currency held by the public, CU.

$$M1 = CD + CU \qquad (1)$$

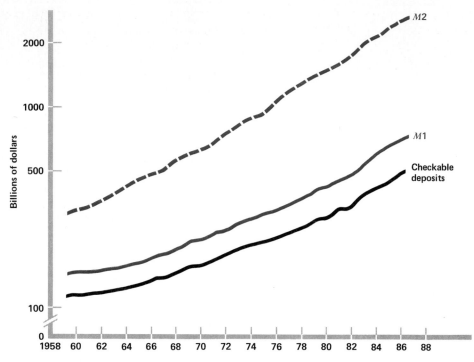

FIGURE 11-1   MONETARY AGGREGATES. *Note:* Scale is logarithmic. (*Source:* Data Resources, Inc.)

A broader measure of the money supply is $M2$, which adds **MMMF** shares, **MMDAs**, and time and savings and other deposits to $M1$ (see footnote 1):

$$M2 = M1 + LD \tag{2}$$

Figure 11-1 shows the history of these aggregates and their components. (Currency is not shown but is the difference between $M1$ and checkable deposits.) Because time and savings deposits, and especially **MMDAs** and **MMMFs**, have been growing more rapidly than the other components of the money supply, $M2$ has grown more rapidly than $M1$. Over the 1972–1985 period, $M1$ grew at 7.2 percent per annum and $M2$ at 9.3 percent. The 7.2 percent growth rate of $M1$ from 1972 to 1985 is well above the average rate of growth of $M1$ of 4.9 percent from 1960 to 1972.

---

[1] We are using CD to stand for "checkable deposits" and LD for "liquid deposits"; there is no generally accepted term as yet for the sum of the assets we are calling LD.

Table 11-1 reproduces part of Table 10-1 and shows the March 1986 components of the money stock. $M1$ is about \$640 billion, more than a quarter of that consisting of currency. The difference between $M2$ and $M1$ of \$1,953 billion is composed chiefly of time and savings deposits.

For simplicity, we ignore the distinction between checkable deposits and the assets grouped in column (4) in Table 11-1 and consider the money supply process as if there were only a uniform class of deposits D. Using that simplification, we define money as deposits plus currency:

$$M \equiv CU + D \tag{3}$$

Starting from equation (3), we begin to develop the details of the process of money stock determination. It is apparent from equation (3) that both the public and the depository institutions (which we shall refer to simply as banks in the rest of this chapter) have an influence on the determination of the money supply. The public has a role because its demand for currency affects the currency component CU. The banks have a role because the other component of money stock, deposits D, is a liability of the banks, that is, a debt the banks owe their customers. We know too that the Fed has a part (the most important) in determining the money supply. The interactions among the actions of the public, the banks, and the Fed determine the money supply. We shall summarize the behavior of the public, the banks, and the Fed in the money supply process by three separate variables.

The Public

From the viewpoint of money supply determination, the variable on which we concentrate as representing the behavior of the public is the *currency-deposit ratio*, that is, the ratio of the public's holdings of currency to their holdings of deposits. In March 1986, that ratio was 0.37 (\$174 billion currency ÷ \$465

TABLE 11-1   COMPONENTS OF THE MONEY STOCK, MARCH 1986
(In Billions of Dollars, Seasonally Adjusted)

(1) Currency	(2) Checkable deposits	(3) $M1 = (1) + (2)$	(4) Time and savings deposits, MMMFs, MMDAs, etc.	(5) $M2 = M1 + (4)$
173.9	464.5	638.4	1,952.9	2,591.3

Source: Economic Indicators.

billion of checkable deposits), using the $M1$ definition of the money stock. We denote the currency-deposit ratio CU/D by cu.

The Banks

The behavior of the banks is summarized by the *reserve-deposit ratio. Reserves* are assets held by the banks to meet (1) the demands of their customers for cash and (2) payments their customers make by checks which are deposited in other banks. Reserves consist of notes and coin held by the banks — *vault cash* — and also of deposits held at the Fed.

Banks that have accounts at the Fed can use them to make payments among themselves. Thus, when my bank has to make a payment to your bank because I paid you with a check drawn on my bank account, it makes the payment by transferring money from its account at the Fed to your bank's account at the Fed.

We examine the determinants of the bank's demand for reserves, RE, in more detail in Section 11-5, but in the meantime we summarize that behavior by the reserve-deposit ratio $RE/D \equiv re$.[2] The reserve ratio is less than 1, since banks hold assets other than reserves, such as loans they make to the public and securities, in their portfolios. Banks in March 1986 held $46.3 billion of reserves. With checkable deposits of $465 billion, the reserve-deposit ratio was $re = 10.0$ percent.

The Fed

The Fed's behavior is summarized by the stock of *high-powered money*, or the *monetary base, H*. High-powered money consists of currency (notes and coin) and banks' deposits at the Fed. Part of the currency is held by the public — that is, the $174 billion previously referred to. The remaining currency, $22.5 billion, is held by banks as vault cash. The notes that constitute most of the outstanding stock of currency are issued by the Fed[3] and the reserves held by member banks as Fed deposits are a liability of the Fed — that is, a debt of the Fed to the member banks. Banks' reserves at the Fed were $23.8 billion in March 1986.

---

[2] Until the Depository Institutions Decontrol Act and Monetary Control Act of 1981, the Fed had more power to control the behavior of member banks of the Federal Reserve System than it had over nonmembers. In particular, the Fed could set reserve requirements for members but not for nonmembers. In return, members had access to services, such as borrowing from the Fed and using the Fed's check-clearing system, that nonmembers did not have. The new law allowed the Fed to impose reserve requirements on *all* deposit-issuing financial institutions. The Fed now is supposed to supply its services on equal terms to all banks, members or not. There is thus little to choose for a bank between belonging or not belonging to the Fed, since both reserve requirements and the ability to use the Fed's services are independent of whether a bank belongs to the Federal Reserve System.

[3] Coins are minted by the Treasury and sold to the Fed by the Treasury. This detail complicates the bookkeeping but is of no real importance to the process of money supply determination.

11-2 THE MONEY MULTIPLIER

In this section we develop a simple approach to money stock determination. The approach is organized around the supply of and the demand for *high-powered money*. The Fed can control the *supply* of high-powered money. The total *demand* for high-powered money comes from the public, who want to use it as currency, and the banks, who need it as reserves. Because the public has a preferred ratio of currency to deposits and because the banks have a desired ratio of reserves to deposits, we can calculate the total money stock that can be supported by any given stock of high-powered money.

Before going into details, we want to think briefly about the relationship betwen the money stock and the stock of high-powered money (Figure 11-2). At the top of the figure we show the stock of high-powered money. At the bottom we show the stock of money. They are related by the *money multiplier*. The money multiplier is the ratio of the stock of money to the stock of high-powered money.

The money multiplier is larger than 1. It is clear from the diagram that the multiplier is larger the larger are deposits as a fraction of the money stock. That is because currency uses up 1 dollar of high-powered money per dollar of money. Deposits, by contrast, use up only amount *re* of high-powered money (in reserves) per dollar of money stock. For instance, if the reserve ratio *re* is 10 percent, every dollar of the money stock in the form of deposits uses up only 10 cents of high-powered money.

It is thus clear that (1) *the money multiplier is larger, the smaller is the reserve ratio* re. In addition, (2) *the money multiplier is larger, the smaller is the currency deposit ratio* cu. That is because the smaller is *cu*, the smaller the

FIGURE 11-2   THE MONEY MULTIPLIER. The money multiplier is the ratio of the money stock (the base of the diagram) to high-powered money. The multiplier is larger than 1. It is larger, the smaller the ratio of currency to deposits and the smaller the ratio of reserves to deposits.

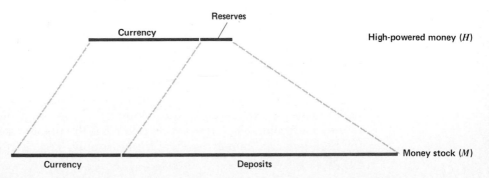

proportion of the high-powered money stock that is being used as currency (which translates high-powered money only one for one into money) and the larger the proportion that is available to be reserves (which translate much more than one for one into money).

The precise relationship between the money stock M, the stock of high-powered money H, the reserve-deposit ratio re, and the currency-deposit ratio cu is derived in the appendix to this chapter. Here we present the resulting expression for the money supply expressed in terms of its principal determinants, re, cu, and H:

$$M = \frac{1 + cu}{re + cu} H \equiv mm \cdot H \tag{4}$$

where mm is the money multiplier given by

$$mm \equiv \frac{1 + cu}{re + cu} \tag{5}$$

Careful examination of the formula for the money multiplier (5) shows that the multiplier is higher the smaller the reserve ratio and the smaller the currency-deposit ratio — as our earlier discussion suggested.

EXAMPLE

We can calculate the money multiplier as given by equation (5) using the actual values of the currency-deposit ratio, $cu = 0.37$, and the reserve ratio, $re = 0.10$, that existed at the beginning of 1986. That gives

$$mm = \frac{1 + 0.37}{0.10 + 0.37} = 2.91$$

You should confirm that you get the same result using the definition that the money multiplier is the ratio of money stock to high-powered money. (In March 1986, the money stock was \$638.4 billion, reserves were \$46.3 billion, and currency was \$173.9 billion.)

Graphical Analysis

Figure 11-3 shows how the money multiplier works. The supply of high-powered money, $\overline{H}$, is shown by the horizontal black line. The demand for high-powered money, HD, is an upward-sloping line with slope equal to 1 over the money multiplier. The intersection point E is the point at which the demand for high-powered money is equal to the supply. The corresponding money supply is shown by M_0.

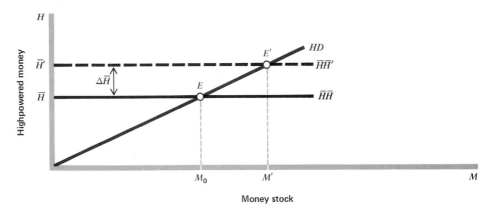

FIGURE 11-3   THE MONEY MULTIPLIER AND AN INCREASE IN THE MONETARY BASE. The HD schedule shows the demand for high-powered money, as related to the money stock M. The slope of the HD schedule is 1 over the money multiplier [see equation (4)]. The supply of high-powered money is shown by the $\overline{HH}$ schedule. At point E the demand for high-powered money is equal to supply. The corresponding money supply is M_0. An increase in the stock of high-powered money by $\Delta \overline{H}$ shifts the $\overline{HH}$ schedule up to $\overline{HH}'$, resulting in a new equilibrium money stock M'. The ratio of the distance $(M' - M_0)$ (the increase in the money stock) to $\Delta \overline{H}$ (the increase in the base) is equal to the money multiplier.

Now suppose the stock of high-powered money increases to H'. The $\overline{HH}$ schedule moves up by the amount $\Delta \overline{H}$ to $\overline{HH}'$. The money supply increases until we reach point E', with new money stock M'. Because the slope of the HD schedule is less than 1, the distance between M_0 and M' is greater than $\Delta \overline{H}$. Indeed, the ratio of the distance $(M' - M_0)$, which is the increase in the money stock, to $\Delta \overline{H}$ is equal to the money multiplier.[4]

The Multiplier in Practice

Since the Fed controls $\overline{H}$, it would be able to control the money stock M exactly if the multiplier were constant or fully predictable. Actual data for the money multiplier are shown in Figure 11-4. It is clear that the money multiplier is far from constant. Further, it is not possible for the Fed to predict the money

---

[4] In problem 1, we ask you to use Fig. 11-3 to show the effects of increases in the currency-deposit ratio (cu) and the reserve-deposit ratio (re) on the money multiplier and the money stock. Changes in these ratios change the slope of the HD line in Fig. 11-3.

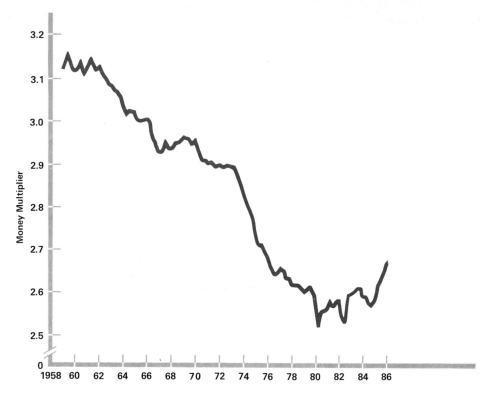

FIGURE 11-4   THE M1 MONEY MULTIPLIER, 1959–1986, (*Source:* Data Resources, Inc.)

multiplier exactly.[5] This means that the Fed cannot exactly determine the money stock in any period by setting the base at a specific level. For instance, suppose it wants the money stock to be $700 billion, and therefore sets the base at $240.5 billion (= $700 billion/2.91, which is the value of the multiplier we calculated above). The multiplier might turn out to be 2.86. Then the money stock would be $687.8 billion (2.86 × 240.5), which means that the money stock would differ by more than 1 percent from the value the Fed intended.

In much of the remainder of this chapter we take a closer look at the reasons the money multiplier varies. To do that we examine more closely the

---

[5] A sophisticated method of predicting the money multiplier is presented in James M. Johannes and Robert H. Rasche, "Predicting the Money Multiplier," *Journal of Monetary Economics*, July 1979.

TABLE 11-2 SIMPLIFIED FORM OF THE FED BALANCE SHEET, SHOWING SOURCES AND USES OF HIGH-POWERED MONEY, MARCH 1986 (In Billions of Dollars)*

Assets (sources)			Liabilities (uses)		
Gold and foreign exchange		$ 15.7	Currency		$192.4
Federal reserve credit		200.0	Held by the public	$169.7	
Loans and discounts	$ 0.8		Vault cash	22.7	
Government securities	183.0		Bank deposits at the Fed		27.5
Net other credit	16.2				
Plus					
Net other assets		4.2			
Monetary base (sources)		$219.9	Monetary base (uses)		$219.9

* These data are not seasonally adjusted and do not adjust reserves for changes in reserve requirements. Thus they differ substantially from data in Section 11-2, which show the currency held by the public as $173.9 billion and the monetary base as $220.2 billion.
Source: Federal Reserve Bulletin, June 1986.

process by which the Fed determines $\overline{H}$ and the portfolio behavior of households and banks.

11-3 THE STOCK OF HIGH-POWERED MONEY

Table 11-2 shows a highly simplified form of the Fed's balance sheet, designed to illustrate the sources of the monetary base—the way the Fed creates high-powered money—and the uses of, or demand for, the base. The Fed's main assets appear on the left-hand side and its liabilities appear on the right.[6]

The fundamental reason for examining the Fed's balance sheet is this: High-powered money is created when the Fed acquires assets and pays for these assets by creating liabilities. The two main classes of liabilities, or *uses* of the base, are currency and member bank deposits.

An Open Market Purchase

The method by which the Fed most often changes the stock of high-powered money is an open market operation. We examine the mechanics of an open market *purchase*, an operation in which the Fed buys, say $1 million of govern-

---

[6] We have simplified the balance sheet by lumping together a number of assets in the entry "Net other assets." More detail on the Fed's balance sheet and the monetary base can be obtained by examining the tables in the *Federal Reserve Bulletin*.

ment bonds from a private individual. An open market purchase *increases* the monetary base.

The accounting for the Fed's purchase is shown in Table 11-3. The Fed's ownership of government securities rises by $1 million, which is reflected in the "Government securities" entry on the assets side of the balance sheet. How does the Fed pay for the bond? It writes a check on itself. In return for the bond, the seller receives a check instructing the Fed to pay (the seller) $1 million. This individual takes the check to his bank, which credits the depositor with the $1 million, and then deposits the check at the Fed. That bank has an account at the Fed, which is credited for $1 million, and the bank deposits entry of the "Liabilities" side of the balance sheet rises by $1 million. The commercial bank has just increased its reserves by $1 million, held in the first instance as a deposit at the Fed.[7]

The only strange part of the story of the open market purchase is that the Fed can write checks on itself. The check instructs the Fed to pay $1 million to the order of the seller of the bond. The payment is made by giving the eventual owner of the check a deposit at the Fed. That deposit can be used to make payments to other banks, or it can be exchanged for currency. Just as the ordinary deposit holder at a commercial bank can obtain currency in exchange for deposits, the bank deposit holder at the Fed can acquire currency in exchange for its deposits. When the Fed pays for the bond with a deposit at the Fed, it creates high-powered money with a stroke of the pen. Further, since it is the issuer of currency, it also creates high-powered money with the printing press. In either event, the Fed can create high-powered money at will merely by buying assets, such as government bonds, and paying for them with its liabilities.

The Fed Balance Sheet

We return now to the balance sheet, starting by examining the assets. The purchase of assets generates high-powered money. The gold and foreign exchange that the Fed owns were acquired in the past, when the Fed paid for them by writing checks on itself. There is, accordingly, almost no difference between the way in which an open market purchase of gold affects the balance sheet and the way in which an open market purchase of bonds affects the balance sheet. The Fed's 1986 holdings of gold were about $11 billion, valued at $42 an ounce. The market value of the gold is much higher, since the market price of gold is far above $42 per ounce.[8]

---

[7] In problem 2 we ask you to trace through the effects of an open market sale that reduces $\bar{H}$.

[8] In the problem set, you are asked to show how the balance sheet would be affected if the Fed decided to value its gold at the free market price. For that purpose you will have to adjust the item "Net other assets" appropriately.

TABLE 11-3	EFFECTS OF AN OPEN MARKET PURCHASE ON THE FED BALANCE SHEET		
Assets (millions of dollars)		**Liabilities** (millions of dollars)	
Government securities	+1	Currency	0
All other assets	0	Bank deposits at Fed	+1
Monetary base (sources)	+1	Monetary base (uses)	+1

Foreign Exchange and the Base

Table 11-2 points to the effects of Fed purchases of foreign exchange on the monetary base. The Fed sometimes buys and sells foreign currencies in an attempt to affect exchange rates. These purchases and sales of foreign exchange—*foreign exchange market intervention*—affect the base. Note from the balance sheet that if the central bank buys gold or foreign exchange, there is a corresponding increase in high-powered money, as the Fed pays with its own liabilities for the gold or foreign exchange that is purchased. The first point to note, then, is the direct impact of foreign exchange market operations on the base.[9]

The second point concerns *sterilization.* By that term we denote attempts by the Fed to neutralize the effects of its intervention in the foreign exchange market, outlined above, on the base. What the Fed does here is to conduct an open market operation that offsets the effects of its intervention *on the base.* For instance, if the Fed sells foreign exchange (thereby reducing the monetary base when purchasers of foreign exchange pay the Fed), it, at the same time, makes an open market purchase of bonds (thereby restoring the base to its original level). The net effect, therefore, is to leave the base unchanged but to change the portfolio composition of the Fed's balance sheet. There will be an increase in the gold and foreign exchange entry and an offsetting reduction in Federal Reserve credit. Thus, by sterilization, the Fed breaks the link between foreign exchange operations and the money supply.

The Discount Rate

The Fed's role as a lender is reflected by the "Loans and discounts" item in Table 11-2. The Fed provides high-powered money to banks that need it by

---

[9] Details of this impact may be complicated by the fact, which we shall not pursue, that the Fed and the Treasury usually cooperate in foreign exchange intervention.

lending to them (crediting their account at the Fed) against the collateral of government securities. The rate at which the Fed typically lends is called the *discount rate,* and it is a rate set by the Fed. If a bank is short of reserves, it can try to borrow from the Fed. The Fed does not automatically lend to banks that want to borrow, even if they are willing and able to pay the discount rate for the borrowing, in part because it does not want banks to use the Fed habitually as a source of reserves. The willingness of banks to borrow from the Fed is partially affected by the rate the Fed charges, and the discount rate accordingly influences the volume of borrowing. Since borrowed reserves are also part of high-powered money, the Fed's discount rate has some effect on the monetary base.[10]

The Treasury and the Fed

The balance sheet of Table 11-2 conceals one important item in the "Net other assets" entry. Among those net assets are deposits that the Treasury holds at the Fed. (Actually, Treasury deposits are Fed *liabilities*, which are negative net assets.) The Treasury makes almost all its payments for the purchases of goods and services and repays maturing government debt out of its accounts at the Fed. That has the interesting implication that Treasury purchases affect the stock of high-powered money. For instance, suppose the Treasury, to buy weapons, makes a payment of $1 billion out of its Fed account by writing a check on that account. Such a check would look much like any other check, except that it would instruct the Fed, rather than a commercial bank, to pay $1 billion to the bearer of the check. The seller of the weapons deposits the check in a commercial bank, which, in turn, presents it to the Fed. The Fed then credits the commercial bank account at the Fed for $1 billion. Member bank deposits have risen. We show these changes in the balance sheet in Table 11-4.

Because payments by the Treasury from its Fed accounts affect the stock of high-powered money, the Treasury attempts to prevent those accounts from fluctuating excessively. For that purpose, it also keeps accounts at commercial banks, the so-called *tax and loan accounts.* When the Treasury receives tax payments, it typically deposits them in commercial banks, rather than the Fed, so that it does not affect the stock of high-powered money; then, before it has to make a payment, it moves the money from the commercial bank to the Fed. If the payment is made fairly soon after the money is moved into the Fed, the stock of high-powered money is only temporarily affected by the Treasury purchase. The Treasury's degree of concern over the effects of its operations on the stock of high-powered money has varied over the years.

---

[10] At one time, the discount rate had considerable importance as a signal of the Fed's intentions with regard to the behavior of interest rates. More recently, the Fed has tended to use discount policy passively, letting the discount rate adjust occasionally as the general level of interest rates changes.

TABLE 11-4	FED BALANCE SHEET: EFFECT OF TREASURY PAYMENT (In Billions of Dollars)		
Assets		**Liabilities**	
Net other assets*	+1	Currency	0
Other asets	0	Bank account at Fed	+1
Monetary base (sources)	+1	Monetary base (uses)	+1

* The Treasury's payment *reduces* Fed liabilities by $1 billion, therefore *increasing* assets by $1 billion.

Financing Federal Deficits

The relationship between the Fed and the Treasury is important also in understanding the financing of government budget deficits. Such deficits can be financed by the Treasury's borrowing from the public. In that case, the Treasury sells bonds to the public. The public pays for the bonds with checks, which are deposited in a tax and loan account. This, accordingly, does not affect the stock of high-powered money. When the Treasury makes payments, it moves the money in and out of its Fed account, leaving the monetary base the same after it has made its payments as it was before the money was transferred into the Fed from the tax and loan account. Thus, Treasury deficit financing through borrowing from the public has only a temporary effect on the monetary base, and no effect on the base after the Treasury has used the borrowed funds to make the payments for which the funds were raised.

Alternatively, the Treasury can finance its deficit by borrowing from the Fed. It is simplest to think of the Treasury's selling a bond to the Fed instead of to the public. When the bond is sold, the Fed's holdings of government securities increase, and simultaneously the asset "Net other assets" falls because Treasury deposits, a liability of the Fed, have risen. But then when the Treasury uses the borrowed money to make a payment, the stock of high-powered money rises, just as in Table 11-4. Accordingly, when a budget deficit is financed by Treasury borrowing from the Fed, the stock of high-powered money is increased. We sometimes talk of central bank financing of government deficits as financing through the printing of money. It is not necessarily true that the deficit is literally financed by the central bank through the printing of money, but it is true that central bank financing increases the stock of high-powered money, which comes to much the same thing.

The Fed is not legally obliged to finance government deficits by buying bonds. Thus it still retains its ability to control the stock of high-powered money even when the Treasury is running a budget deficit.

Summary

1. The main point of this section is that the Fed controls the stock of high-powered money primarily through open market operations.
2. The Fed has some influence over the stock of high-powered money through the indirect route of changing the discount rate and thereby affecting the volume of member bank borrowing.
3. Treasury financing of its deficits through borrowing from the public leaves the stock of high-powered money unaffected, whereas Treasury financing by borrowing from the Fed increases the monetary base.

11-4 THE CURRENCY-DEPOSIT RATIO

The next element in the money multiplier formula (5) is the currency-deposit ratio, which reflects the behavior of the public. The currency-deposit ratio is determined primarily by payment habits and has a strong seasonal pattern; it is highest around Christmas. The ratio increases when the ratio of consumption to GNP increases, since currency demand is more closely linked to consumption than GNP, while deposit demand is more closely linked to GNP.

The currency-deposit ratio has been increasing, as can be deduced from the behavior of currency and demand deposits since 1970, as shown in Figure 11-1. The increase in the currency-deposit ratio accounts for some of the decline in the money multiplier shown in Figure 11-4. For the remainder of the chapter we shall treat the currency-deposit ratio as independent of interest rates and constant. It is possible, though, that with interest paid on demand deposits, the currency-deposit ratio is negatively related to the interest rate.

11-5 THE RESERVE-DEPOSIT RATIO

The banking system affects the supply of money through the reserve-deposit ratio *re*. The reserve-deposit ratio is determined by two sets of considerations. First, the banking system is subject to Fed regulation in the form of *minimum reserve requirements*. The reserve requirements vary by type of deposit and also by bank size and location. The reserve requirements against time deposits are lower than those against demand deposits; reserve requirements are lower for smaller banks than for larger banks, and so on. The variety of the reserve requirements creates some difficulties for control of the money stock because shifts of deposits between different categories of deposits change the level of required reserves even if the level of deposits is unaffected. There is no compelling logic to the way in which the reserve requirements have evolved, and we shall not discuss them further.[11]

---

[11] Reserve requirements and their recent history are published in the *Federal Reserve Bulletin*. In March 1980, the Congress passed the important Depository Institutions Deregulation and Monetary Control Act, which among other things requires all depository institutions to hold the same reserve ratios. Before March 1980, reserve requirements varied, depending on whether a bank belonged to the system or was instead state-chartered.

TABLE 11-5   COMMERCIAL BANK BALANCE SHEET

Assets	Liabilities
Reserves	Deposits
Commercial bank credit	
Loans	
Investments	
Less	
Borrowing from Fed	
Borrowing in the Fed funds market (net)	

Second, banks may want to hold *excess reserves* beyond the level of required reserves. In deciding how much excess reserves to hold, a bank's economic problem is very similar to the problem of the individual in deciding on a precautionary demand for money. Banks hold reserves to meet demands on them for cash or payments to other banks.[12] If they cannot meet those demands, they have to borrow either from the Fed or from other banks that happen to have spare reserves.

The explicit cost of borrowing from the Fed is the discount rate, while the implicit cost is Fed disapproval of the bank's imprudent behavior (if it is short of reserves frequently) and possible future refusal of the borrowing privilege. The cost of borrowing from other banks is the *federal funds rate*. Federal funds are simply reserves that some banks have in excess and others need. The federal funds rate varies with the overall availability of reserves to the banking system, and can be affected by the Fed through open market operations. When the Fed buys assets in the open market, it increases the availability of reserves and reduces the federal funds rate. In brief, there is a cost to a bank of being short of reserves, and that cost is affected by the Fed's actions.

There is also a cost to a bank of holding reserves. Reserves do not earn interest. By holding smaller reserves, a bank is able to invest in interest-earning assets and increase its profits. A simplified commercial bank balance sheet is shown in Table 11-5. By reducing its reserves, the bank is able to increase its loans or investments on which it earns interest. There is thus a tradeoff of the sort examined in Chapter 10 in discussing the precautionary demand for money. The more reserves a bank holds, the less likely it is to have to incur the costs of borrowing. But the more reserves it holds, the more interest it forgoes.

---

[12] Many banks, particularly small ones, hold deposits at other banks to facilitate transactions of this sort. These *interbank deposits* serve the same function as reserves but are not included in our measure of reserves. They are excluded from the definitions of the money stock.

The bank's choice of reserve ratio therefore depends on three factors in addition to the required reserve ratio, which we denote r_R. The first is the uncertainty of its net deposit flow. The more variable the inflows and outflows of cash a bank experiences, the more reserves it will want to hold. The second is the cost of borrowing when the bank runs short of reserves. We shall take the discount rate i_D to be the cost of borrowing. The third factor is the interest forgone by holding reserves, which we shall take as the market interest rate i. We can therefore write the bank's reserve-deposit ratio re as a function of the market interest rate, the discount rate, the required reserve ratio r_R, and σ:

$$re = r(i, i_D, r_R, \sigma) \tag{6}$$

where σ indicates the uncertainty characteristics of the bank's deposit inflows and outflows.

How does each of the factors in equation (6) affect the reserve ratio? An increase in the market interest rate on earnings assets decreases the reserve ratio, since it makes reserves more costly to hold. An increase in the discount rate increases the ratio, since it raises the cost of running short of reserves.[13] And an increase in the required reserve ratio increases the actual reserve ratio. We thus see that the reserve ratio is a function of market interest rates, which suggests that the supply of money itself may also be a function of market interest rates.

Excess Reserves

Excess reserves in the last 10 years have averaged less than 1 percent of total reserves. Indeed, in the entire postwar period, they have been small compared with levels reached in the 1930s. The thirties were a period of great economic uncertainty, during which there were many bank failures: that is, banks were unable to meet the demands of their depositors for cash. If you have a deposit in a failed bank, you cannot "get your money (currency) out."

In the thirties, it became necessary for banks to hold large reserves. The reason is that a bank that holds relatively few reserves, with most of its assets in loans or securities, cannot quickly meet its depositors' demands for currency. Banks that hold low reserves are exposed to the risk that a run by depositors —an attempt to convert their deposits into currency—will drive the bank

---

[13] The precise behavior of excess reserves depends on how the Fed is conducting monetary policy. One possible method is for the Fed to allow banks to borrow as much as they want to meet the required reserve ratio, r_R. If banks hold exactly to that ratio, there are never any excess reserves, so excess reserves are unaffected by the discount rate. In this case, an increase in the discount rate would reduce *total* reserves, because banks want to borrow less, but would not affect *excess* reserves, which would remain at zero, nor the reserve ratio, which would remain equal to r_R. More generally, we should expect the relationship stated in the text, in which the reserve ratio declines with increases in the discount rate.

into default. But it is precisely when depositors are afraid that a bank is in danger of defaulting that they are likely to attempt to withdraw their money from that bank before it is too late. That is to say that a run may occur on a bank precisely because its depositors believe that a run on the bank is likely to occur.

In a general atmosphere of instability — such as prevailed in the thirties — it therefore becomes important for banks to demonstrate their ability to meet cash withdrawals by holding large reserves, that is, by holding excess reserves. Only by being in a position to meet large cash demands can the banks avoid their depositors actually making those demands. The massive bank failures of the thirties, as a consequence of runs on banks, gave rise to an important institutional reform, the creation of the *Federal Deposit Insurance Corporation* (FDIC). That institution insures bank deposits, so that depositors get paid even if a bank fails.

In form, the FDIC operates like an insurance company. Banks pay premiums to insure their deposits. In principle, insurance applies only for up to $100,000 on an account. In fact, the FDIC is more than a private insurance company. When banks fail, the FDIC steps in to arange the sale of the bank and to ensure that all depositors do not lose, not only those with small accounts. Further, the FDIC itself is too small to pay out all depositors if there should be a massive run on many banks. It remains effective though because there is little doubt the U.S. government would intervene to support the FDIC if its own funds began to run short.

There are three main reasons why excess reserves are now so small. First, bank deposits are insured, mainly through FDIC. Individual depositors now know that their deposit will ultimately be paid back. The threat of runs on banks is accordingly much reduced, and banks do not have to hold large reserves to guard against runs.[14] Second, the development of financial markets and communications has reduced the cost to banks of managing their balance sheets in such a way as to keep excess reserves small. Third, the relatively high level of interest rates makes it costly for banks to hold idle reserves rather than to earn assets.

11-6 THE MULTIPLIER AND THE ADJUSTMENT PROCESS

To this point the money multiplier looks like a mystery: The Fed puts in a dollar of high-powered money and out comes more than a dollar increase in the money supply. We now put more economics into the money multiplier by showing how the interactions of the banks and the public produce a multiple expansion of the money stock. We sketch the argument here and develop it in full analytical detail in the appendix to this chapter.

---

[14] See Milton Friedman and Anna Schwartz, *A Monetary History of the United States* (Princeton, N.J.: Princeton University Press, 1963).

The monetary expansion following an open market operation involves adjustments by banks and the public. When the Fed buys securities from the public, the monetary base is increased. To start with, the increase in the base shows up as an increase in bank reserves. This is because the Fed pays for the securities by writing a check on itself, which the seller of the securities deposits in his or her bank account. The bank in turn will present the check for collection to the Fed and will be credited with an increase in its reserve position at the Fed.

At this stage the public has an increase in deposits without an increase in currency. That means the currency deposit ratio is out of line — it is too low. The public will therefore convert deposits into currency, thus reducing bank reserves and deposits.

More important in the story is the fact that the bank in which the original check was deposited now has a reserve ratio that is too high. Its reserves and deposits have gone up by the same amount. Therefore its ratio of reserves to deposits has risen. To reduce the ratio of reserves to deposits, it chooses to expand its loans.

When the bank makes a loan, the person receiving the loan gets a bank deposit. It is at that stage that the money supply has risen by more than the amount of the open market operation. The person who sold the security to the Fed has increased his or her holdings of money — some in currency and some in deposits — by the value of the bonds sold. The person receiving the loan has a new bank deposit — and thus the process has already generated a multiple expansion of the money stock.

In the subsequent adjustment part of the increase in high-powered money finds its way into the public's holdings of currency, and part serves as the basis for an expansion of credit by the banking system.[15] When banks make loans, they do so by crediting the deposits of their loan customers with the loan. Since deposits are part of the money supply, banks therefore create money whenever they make loans. The expansion of loans, and hence money, continues until the banking system has increased loans to the point where the reserve-deposit ratio has fallen to the desired level and the public again has achieved its desired currency-deposit ratio. The money multiplier summarizes the total expansion of money created by a dollar increase in the monetary base.

11-7 THE MONEY SUPPLY FUNCTION AND THE INSTRUMENTS OF MONETARY CONTROL

We have, in Sections 11-3 to 11-5, gone behind formula (4) for the determinants of the money supply and studied the behavior of the three variables in

---

[15] Bank loans and purchases of securities are described as *bank credit.* It is the existence of bank credit that makes the money stock larger than the stock of high-powered money. If banks did not extend credit (that is, did not make loans or buy securities), the entire multiple expansion process would never get off the ground, and we would have $M = H$.

that formula. We now return to equation (4) to summarize the discussion by writing a *money supply function* that takes account of the behavior of the banking system and the public:

$$M = \frac{1 + cu}{cu + re} \overline{H} \qquad (7)$$

$$= mm(i, i_D, r_R, cu, \sigma) \overline{H}$$

In equation (7) we have written the money multiplier *mm* as a function of interest rates, the discount rate, required reserves, the currency-deposit ratio, and the variability of deposit flows.

Given the stock of high-powered money, the supply of money increases with the money multiplier *mm*. The multiplier, in turn, increases with the level of market interest rates and decreases with the discount rate, the required reserve ratio, and the currency-deposit ratio. We refer to equation (7) as a supply *function* because it describes the behavior that determines the money supply, given $\overline{H}$. Note that the Fed affects the money supply through three routes: $\overline{H}$, controlled primarily through open market operations; the discount rate i_D; and the required reserve ratio r_R.

Of these three *instruments of monetary control*, open market operations are the most frequently used. Until 1986 there was a fourth instrument of monetary control. Through its Regulation Q, the Fed controlled the interest rates paid on deposits. By changing the permissible interest rates, the Fed could affect the currency deposit ratio, *cu*, and thus affect the multiplier. Regulation Q was phased out between 1980 and 1986, leaving the Fed with three major instruments of monetary control: open market operations, required reserve ratios, and the discount rate.

Why can the Fed not control the money stock exactly? The reasons emerge by looking at the money multiplier formula in equation (7). We have assumed *cu* is constant — but in fact *cu* varies from month to month, and the Fed does not know in advance exactly what its value will be. The public does not keep an exactly constant ratio of currency to deposits. Similarly, the reserve ratio *re* varies, both because deposits move among banks with different reserve ratios and because banks change the amount of excess reserves they want to hold.

In brief, the Fed cannot control the money stock exactly because the money multiplier is not constant, nor is it fully predictable.

11-8 EQUILIBRIUM IN THE MONEY MARKET

We can now combine the money supply function in equation (7) with the money demand function developed in Chapter 10 to study money market equilibrium. For that purpose we will assume that the price level is given at the level $\overline{P}$. Furthermore, for the purposes of this section, we will take the level of real income as given, $Y = Y_0$. With both the price level and level of income fixed, money demand depends only on the interest rate, while the money market equilibrium will determine the equilibrium interest rate and quantity of money for given $\bar{P}$ and Y_0.

The equilibrium condition in the money market is that the real money supply M/P equals the demand for real balances, or

$$\frac{M}{P} = L(i, Y) \qquad (8)$$

Substituting expression (7) for M in the money market equilibrium condition (8), and noting $P = \bar{P}$ and $Y = Y_0$ by assumption, we obtain

$$mm(i, i_D, r_R, cu, \sigma) \frac{\bar{H}}{\bar{P}} = L(i, Y_0) \qquad (9)$$

We now have the money market equilibrium condition in terms of interest rates and the other variables affecting the supply of, and demand for, money.

In Figure 11-5 we show the real money demand function (LL) as a downward-sloping schedule, drawn for a given level of real income. The real money supply function (MS), given $\bar{P}$, σ, cu, i_D, and r_R, is upward-sloping and is drawn for a given stock of high-powered money $\bar{H}$. The positive slope of MS reflects the fact that, at higher interest rates, banks prefer to hold fewer reserves, so that the money multiplier is higher.[16] The equilibrium money supply and interest rate are jointly determined at point E.

Figure 11-5 studies the effects of monetary policy on interest rates, given the price level and the level of income. An increase in the monetary base of $\Delta \bar{H}$ shifts the MS curve to the right to MS', increasing the money stock and reducing the interest rate. Because the interest rate falls, the money multiplier declines as a result of the increase in $\bar{H}$. But there is no question, despite the decline in the interest rate, that the money stock increases.

In Figure 11-5, we, in effect, look at the effects of a change in the stock of high-powered money on the LM curve. Figure 11-6 shows the IS-LM curves. The LM curve represents the combinations of income levels and the interest rate at which the money market is in equilibrium. What happens to the LM curve when the stock of high-powered money is increased? In Figure 11-5 we saw that for any given level of income (Y_0), an increase in $\bar{H}$ reduces the equilibrium interest rate. That means that the LM curve in Figure 11-6 shifts down to LM' when $\bar{H}$ increases. The equilibrium shifts from E to E', with output rising and the interest rate falling. Thus our analysis confirms that the

---

[16] At sufficiently high interest rates, the money supply schedule becomes vertical. This is because excess reserves become zero at very high interest rates and the banks cannot squeeze out any more loans on the basis of the reserves they have.

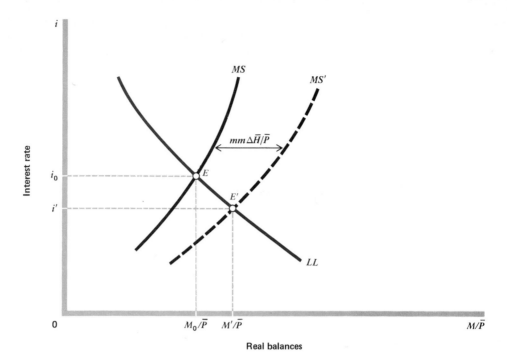

FIGURE 11-5   EQUILIBRIUM IN THE MONEY MARKET. The downward-sloping curve is the demand for money. The quantity of money demanded is greater the lower the interest rate. The upward-sloping curve is the money supply function. This slopes up because, given the quantity of high-powered money, banks reduce their demand for excess reserves when the interest rate rises. Thus the reserve ratio is lower and the money multiplier bigger at higher interest rates. The equilibrium interest rate and stock of money are determined at the intersection point E. An increase in the stock of high-powered money shifts the money supply curve out to the right, with a new equilibrium at E'. The money stock increases, and the interest rate decreases.

Fed, by increasing the stock of high-powered money, can reduce the interest rate and increase the level of income.

This is basically what we concluded in Chapter 4, except there we assumed the Fed controlled the money supply directly. Now we know the Fed does not have such direct control; nonetheless it can shift the LM curve and affect output and the interest rate.

Changes in the Discount Rate

We can also analyze the effects of an increase in the discount rate on the position of the LM curve and thus on the interest rate and output. We know

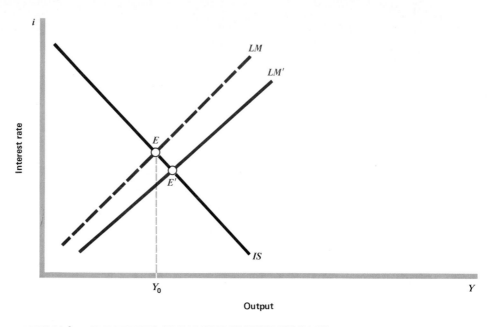

FIGURE 11-6   THE EFFECTS OF AN INCREASE IN THE STOCK OF
HIGH-POWERED MONEY. As Figure 11-5 shows, an increase in the
stock of high-powered money reduces the interest rate at which the
money market is in equilibrium, for any given level of output. That
means the *LM* curve shifts down when $\overline{H}$ is increased. The equilibrium
interest rate falls and the level of output rises as the economy moves
from *E* to *E'*.

from our analysis of the demand for reserves that banks will hold higher
reserves when the discount rate rises, because it is more expensive to run short
of reserves when the cost of borrowing to cover the shortage is higher.

An increase in the discount rate therefore reduces the money multiplier.
Figure 11-7 shows in terms of the money market, at a given level of income,
that the money supply curve shifts up to *MS'*. The interest rate rises at the
given level of income. In terms of the *IS-LM* analysis, the *LM* curve would
therefore move to the left (we do not show this here, but ask you to do so in
problem 13), the interest rate would rise, and output would fall. Thus an
increase in the discount rate is a contractionary monetary policy.

11-9 CONTROL OF THE MONEY STOCK AND CONTROL OF THE INTEREST RATE

We make a simple but important point in this section: The Fed cannot simultaneously set both the interest rate and the stock of money at any given target

levels that it may choose. If the Fed wants to achieve a given interest rate target, such as 5 percent, it has to supply the amount of money that is demanded at that interest rate. If it wants to set the money supply at a given level, say, $800 billion in the month of June 1988, it has to allow the interest rate to adjust to equate the demand for money to that supply of money.

Figure 11-8 illustrates the point. Suppose that the Fed, for some reason, decides that it wants to set the interest rate at a level i^* and the money stock at a level M^*, but that the demand-for-money function is as shown in LL. The Fed is able to move the money supply function around, as in Figure 11-6, but it is not able to move the money demand function around. It therefore has to accept that it can set only the combinations of the interest rate and the money supply that lie along the money demand function. At the interest rate i^*, it can have the money supply $M_0/\bar{P}$. At the target money supply $M^*/\bar{P}$, it can have the interest rate i_0. But it cannot have both $M^*/\bar{P}$ and i^*.

FIGURE 11-7   THE EFFECTS OF AN INCREASE IN THE DISCOUNT RATE. An increase in the discount rate increases the amount of reserves that banks want to hold at each level of market interest rates i. Thus the money multiplier is reduced, and the money supply function shifts from MS to MS'. Accordingly, the market interest rate rises, and the quantity of real balances falls. An increase in the discount rate is a contractionary monetary policy.

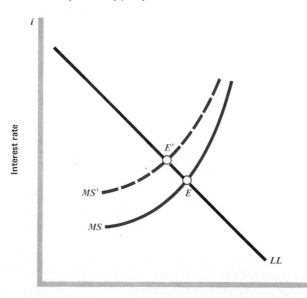

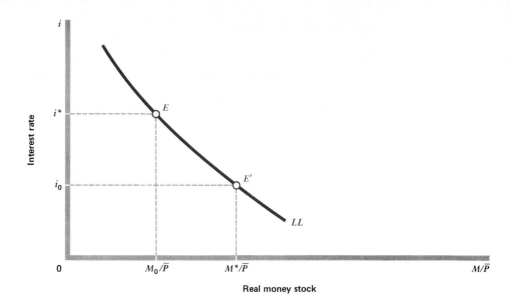

FIGURE 11-8   CONTROLLING THE MONEY STOCK AND INTEREST
RATES. The Fed cannot simultaneously set both the interest rate and
the money stock levels it wants. Suppose it wanted the interest rate to
be i^* and the money stock to be M^*. These two levels are inconsistent
with the demand for money, LL. If the Fed insists on the interest rate
level i^*, it will have to accept a money stock equal to M_0. If instead the
Fed wants to set the money stock at M^*, it will end up with an interest
rate equal to i_0.

The point is sometimes put more dramatically as follows. When the Fed
decides to set the interest rate at some given level and keep it fixed — a policy
known as *pegging* the interest rate — it loses control over the money supply. It
has to supply whatever amount of money is demanded at that interest rate. If
the money demand curve were to shift, because of income growth, say, the
Fed would have to increase the stock of high-powered money to increase the
money supply.

As an operational matter, the Fed, in its day-to-day operations, can more
easily control interest rates exactly than it can control the money stock exactly.
The Fed buys and sells government securities — primarily Treasury bills —
from its *open market desk* in the New York Fed every day. If the Fed wanted to
raise the price of government securities (lower the interest rate), it would have
to buy the securities at the price it wanted. If it wanted to reduce prices of
government securities (raise the interest rate), it would sell a sufficient amount

of securities from its large portfolio. Thus, on a day-to-day basis, the Fed can determine interest rates quite accurately.[17]

However, the Fed cannot determine the money supply precisely on a day-to-day basis. For one thing, there is a lag in obtaining data on the money stock. Some time must pass before reasonably good money supply data for a given date become available. That would not affect the Fed's ability to control the money stock if the money multiplier were constant, for then it would be able to deduce, from the behavior of the monetary base, what the money stock was. But as we have seen earlier, the multiplier is not constant. It varies as a result of changes in the currency-deposit and reserve-deposit ratios.

These are *technical* reasons the Fed cannot control the money supply exactly in the sense that the Fed cannot hit the target stock of money exactly even if it wants to. But over a slightly longer period, the Fed can determine the money supply fairly accurately. As data on the behavior of the money stock and the money multiplier become available, the Fed can make midcourse corrections to its setting of the base. For example, if the Fed were aiming for monetary growth of 5 percent over a given period, it might start the base growing at 5 percent. If it found halfway into the period that the multiplier had been falling, and the money stock therefore growing less than 5 percent, it would step up the growth rate of the base to compensate.

The main reasons the Fed does not hit its money growth targets are not technical, but rather have to do with its having both interest rate *and* money stock targets, and as we have seen in this section, it cannot hit them both at the same time.

11-10 MONEY STOCK AND INTEREST RATE TARGETS

Over the period since the 1950s, the Fed has moved from an emphasis on the interest rate as a target of monetary policy to a much greater emphasis on the money stock as the variable it tries to control. Indeed, it was not until 1959 that the Fed even began to publish money stock data. In this section we discuss the issues involved in the choice between interest rate and money stock targets.

Making Monetary Policy

Monetary policy is made by the Fed's Open Market Committee, which meets about every 6 weeks and also holds frequent consultations between meetings. At these meetings the Fed issues a *monetary policy directive* to the open market desk in New York describing the type of monetary policy it wants.

---

[17] For a description of techniques of monetary control, see Paul Meek, *U.S. Monetary Policy and Financial Markets*, Federal Reserve Bank of N.Y., 1982.

BOX
11-1

WEEKLY MONEY STOCK ANNOUNCEMENTS AND INTEREST RATES

On Thursdays at 4 P.M. the Fed announces the money supply. The announcements are eagerly awaited by financial markets and have immediate effects — within minutes or even seconds — on interest rates, the stock market, commodity prices, and exchange rates. When the money stock is unexpectedly high, short-term interest rates rise; when the money stock is unexpectedly low, interest rates fall.

Why should markets be so curious about money supply announcements and why do asset prices and interest rates react to these announcements? More puzzling, what the Fed announces is not that day's money stock, or the following week's money stock, but merely what the money stock was 2 weeks prior to the announcement! How is it possible that announcements about money 2 weeks ago moves markets today? This is called the money supply puzzle. It has kept quite a few researchers busy formulating and testing alternative explanations.*

The point of departure is a distinction between expected and unexpected announcements. Let M be the actual announcement and M' the market's expectations or guess beforehand of what the announcement would turn out to be. The difference between these two is called the *unanticipated increase in the money supply*, or simply *news*; thus $M - M' =$ news. Researchers can actually measure news because there are weekly survey data on the market's expectations, M', which, in combination with the actual announcement, M, yield a series for news.

There are systematic relationships between news and asset price changes. Whenever the money supply announcement comes out large relative to the expected money supply, interest rates increase, the dollar strengthens, and stock prices fall. Why does an unexpectedly large money supply lead to these immediate adjustments in asset prices? The reason must be that the announcement presents *new and relevant information* for market participants even though the announcement concerns money 2 weeks ago.

Note first the apparent reversal of the normal relationship between the money stock and interest rates. Increases in the money stock *reduce* interest rates, accordng to the *IS-LM* model. Yet the announcement that the money stock is high *increases* the interest rate.

Three theories have been advanced. Each relies on the fact that markets look forward and are trying to predict the state of the money market — in particular, interest rates — over the coming weeks and months. They are trying to predict what money demand and money supply will be.

The first hypothesis focuses on the Fed. If the Fed follows a target path for money and it turns out that money was unexpectedly high relative to that path, the market will assume that in the period ahead the Fed will try to pull money growth back down to the target path. The announcement of high $M - M'$ therefore conveys the news that the Fed will tighten monetary policy, reducing the supply of money. This implies future interest rates will be higher. Anyone who had expected to borrow will immediately rush to do so before rates rise. And, of course, the rush will raise rates instantly. This explanation would be expected to have particular force when the Fed sticks very tightly to targets for monetary aggregates, as for example in the period 1979–1982.

The second hypothesis focuses on money demand. Market participants do not know exactly the demand for money and hence, even knowing the broad setting of monetary policy, they cannot predict future interest rates with certainty. If money demand turns out high, interest rates will be high and vice versa. In this case an announcement of unanticipatedly high money

---

* A good summary is presented in R. Sheehan, ''Weekly Money Supply Announcements: New Information and Its Effects,'' *Federal Reserve Bank of St. Louis Review*, August/September 1985. See, too, the comment by B. Falk and P. Orazem and the reply by B. Cornell in the June 1985 issue of the *American Economic Review*.

tells the market that money demand is high and hence that future interest rates must be expected to be high. Thus rates are immediately pushed up to reflect that new information. Of course, the argument works only if money demand disturbances are relatively persistent. Otherwise learning that money demand was high 2 weeks ago tells the market nothing about money demand a week from now.

The third argument draws on a tight and rapid link between changes in the money supply and inflation: Unanticipatedly high money leads the market to revise upward its estimate of inflation. At going interest rates it becomes more profitable to borrow and hold goods or stocks that are expected to appreciate. The increased borrowing in turn pushes up interest rates immediately.

Empirical research has focused on three issues. First, is it *only* the news that explains changes in interst rates or asset prices, or does the anticipated part of the announcement also have an effect? The evidence suggests that both the news and the expected change in money affects interest rates. Second, is there any significant differences in the response, depending on the Fed's policy regime? Specifically does the 1979–1982 period when aggregates were targeted stand out as one where news has stronger effects? There is no strong evidence that responses were stronger in that period. Third, research attempts to identify which of the three hypotheses is most likely to explain the facts. Here there is no consensus yet, though the third argument has less empirical support than the first two.

In recent years, the directive has instructed the open market desk to conduct open market operations to produce money stock growth within given target ranges. The target ranges since 1976, for $M1$ and $M2$, are given in Table 11-6.[18] In addition, the Committee specifies a range within which it expects interest rates to be during the period until the next meeting. If interest rates threaten to move outside the range, the Committee members will typically consult (on the telephone) and decide whether to change the instructions to the open market desk.

Comparison of actual money growth rates with target ranges makes it hard to believe the Fed has taken the targets very seriously — or else it has remarkably bad aim. In only 3 of the 10 years has the Fed come within the target ranges for $M1$; in all the remaining years money growth was more rapid than targeted. It is this record that leads monetarist critics of the Fed to argue that it pays only lip service to money targeting.

The next question is whether it should pay more than lip service.

Interest Rate or Money Targets?

There are two levels on which the discussion of interest rate versus money targets proceeds. The first is at the technical level of the open market desk.

---

[18] The Fed specifies, in addition, target ranges for $M3$ and, since 1982, for total nonfinancial debt in the economy. This latter total is the amount of lending to spending units in the economy.

TABLE 11-6   TARGET AND ACTUAL GROWTH RATES OF MONEY*

Period	M1 target range	M1 actual	M2 target range	M2 actual
1976	4.5–7.5	5.8	7.5–10.5	10.9
1977	4.5–6.5	7.9	7–10	9.8
1978	4–6.5	7.2	6.5–9	8.7
1979	1.5–4.5	5.5	5–8	8.3
1980	4–6.5	7.2	6–9	9.0
1981	3.5–6	5.1	6–9	9.4
1982	2.5–5.5	8.5	6–9	9.2
1983	4–8	9.8	7–10	12.0
1984	4–8	5.8	6–9	8.4
1985	4–7	11.8	6–9	8.1
1986	3–8		6–9	

* Money definitions are those in effect at the time targets were set. Rates are for a 1-year period ending in the fourth quarter of the specified year.

Source: Various *Federal Reserve Bulletins,* and Federal Reserve Bank of Boston.

The question here is whether a given target level of the money stock can be attained more accurately by holding the interest rate fixed or by fixing H. The second level is that of the economy as a whole. The question here is whether the Fed makes the economy more stable by aiming for a particular money stock or for a particular interest rate.

The analyses for evaluating these questions are similar. We start with and discuss in more detail the second issue.

THE BROAD VIEW

We assume that the Fed aims for the economy to reach a particular level of output. The question is whether it can do that more accurately by targeting the money stock or by fixing interest rates. We should think of the analysis as applying to a reasonably short period such as 3 to 9 months.[19]

Figure 11-9a starts with the *IS* and *LM* curves. Recall that the *LM* curve shows combinations of the interest rate and output at which the money market is in equilibrium. The *LM* curve labeled *LM(M)* is the *LM* curve that exists when the Fed fixes the money stock. The *LM* curve labeled *LM(i)* describes

---

[19] The analysis we are presenting here is based on William Poole, "Optimal Choice of Monetary Policy Instruments in a Simple Stochastic Macro Model," *Quarterly Journal of Economics,* May 1970.

money market equilibrium when the Fed fixes the interest rate. It is horizontal at the chosen level of the interest rate i°.

The problem for policy is that the IS and LM curves shift in ways that cannot be predicted. When they shift, output ends up at a level different from the target level. In Figure 11-9a we show two alternative positions for the IS curve, IS_1, and IS_2. We assume that the Fed does not know in advance which IS curve will obtain: the position depends, for instance, on investment demand, which is difficult to predict. The Fed's aim is to have income come out as close as possible to the level Y°.

In Figure 11-9a we see that the level of output stays closer to Y° if the LM curve is $LM(M)$. In that case the level of output will be Y_1 if the IS curve is IS_1

FIGURE 11-9 MONEY AND INTEREST RATE TARGETS. In panel (*a*), the IS curve shifts. If the Fed targets the money stock, the LM curve is shown by $LM(M)$. $LM(i)$ is the LM curve when the interest rate is held constant. The aim of policy is to hit output level Y^*. If the LM curve is $LM(M)$, the output levels will be either Y_1 or Y_2, depending on where the IS curve turns out to be. In the case of an interest rate target, the corresponding levels of output are Y'_1 and Y'_2, both further from the desired level of output Y^*. Thus monetary targeting leads to more stable output behavior. In panel (*b*) it is the LM curve that is shifting, because of shifts in the demand for money. With LM shifting and the IS curve stable, output will be at the target level Y^* if the interest rate is held constant at i^*, but will be at either Y_1 or Y_2 if the money stock is held constant. Therefore the Fed should target the interest rate if the demand-for-money function is unstable.

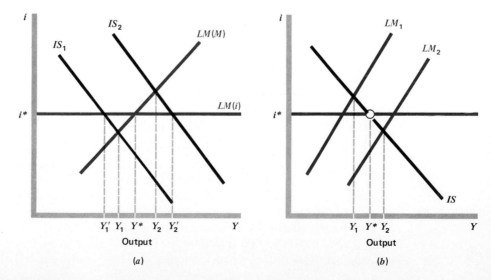

and Y_2 if the IS curve is IS_2. If policy had kept the interest rate constant, we would in each case have a level of income that is further from Y^*: Y_1' instead of Y_1, and Y_2' instead of Y_2.

Thus we have our first conclusion: If output deviates from its equilibrium level mainly because the IS curve shifts about, then output is stabilized by keeping the money stock constant. The Fed should, in this case, have monetary targets.

We can see from Figure 11-9a why it is more stabilizing to keep M than i constant. When the IS curve shifts to the right and the $LM(M)$ curve applies, the interest rate rises, thereby reducing investment demand and moderating the effect of the shift. But if the $LM(i)$ curve applies, there is no resistance from monetary policy to the effects of the IS shift. Monetary policy is thus automatically stabilizing in Figure 11-9a when the IS curve shifts, and the money stock is held constant.

In Figure 11-9b we assume that the IS curve is stable. Now the uncertainty about the effects of monetary policy results from shifts in the LM curve. Assuming that the Fed can fix the money stock, the LM curve shifts because the money demand function shifts. The Fed does not know when it sets the money stock what the interest rate will be. The LM curve could end up being either LM_1 or LM_2. Alternatively the Fed could simply fix the interest rate at level i^*. That would ensure that the level of output is Y^*.

If the Fed were to fix the money stock, output could be either Y_1 or Y_2. If it fixes the interest rate, output will be Y^*. Thus we have our second conclusion: If output deviates from its equilibrium level mainly because the demand-for-money function shifts about, then the Fed should operate monetary policy by fixing the interest rate. That way it automatically neutralizes the effects of the shifts in money demand. In this case the Fed should have interest rate targets.

It is important to note that the argument discusses Fed targeting over short periods. The Fed should readjust its targets in light of the changing behavior of the economy. It is *not* to be thought of as announcing or desiring that the interest rate will be, say, 5 percent forever. Rather, the target interest rate might be 5 percent at the bottom of a recession and 15 percent when the economy is overheating. Similarly, the money growth targets could also be adjusted in response to the state of the economy.

THE SHORT RUN AND THE LONG RUN

This analysis describes well the reasons why the Fed might choose either the money stock or the interest rate as a target at which to aim over a period of less than a year. In particular, at a time when money demand is shifting a lot — as it did in the seventies and eighties — the Fed should pay attention to the behavior of interest rates. The reason is that when money demand is shifting, it is hard to evaluate the meaning of money stock data.

Suppose the Fed is aiming for nominal GNP to increase only 2 percent, and we find ourselves in a recession. How could we tell things are going wrong? By looking at interest rates. If there has been a shift in money demand, increasing the quantity demanded at any interest rate, the interest rate will rise. If the Fed were paying attention to the behavior of the interest rate, it would automatically adjust the money stock to account for that shift in money demand. That is why interest rate targets are useful.

But monetarist proponents of money stock targeting have another argument in favor of targeting the money stock. They might concede that in the short run the Fed may do better targeting interest rates. But they say, a policy of targeting interest rates can over long periods lead to big trouble, by steadily raising the growth rate of money. They point, rightly, to the fact that changes in monetary policy take a long time to affect the economy. They argue that increases in the money stock lead eventually to inflation, and that the only way to avoid inflation in the long run is by keeping money growth moderate. The problem with focusing on interest rates, they suggest, is that while the Fed keeps its eye on interest rates, the growth rate of money and the inflation rate increase.[20] This argument appears to fit the facts of the 1960s and 1970s well.

It is for that reason that the Fed moved to a two-track targeting system. It has *long-run* targets for money growth. Thus it has continually to worry whether it is following monetary paths consistent with desired low rates of inflation.[21] At the same time it pays attention to interest rates in case its monetary targets lead in the short run to recession or inflation if there are shifts in money demand.

By "pays attention" we mean that the Fed has target ranges for both money and interest rates. When either moves close to the limits of the range, the Fed has a meeting to discuss why this is happening. And then it gives fresh instructions to the open market desk. Typically these instructions are to compromise on both targets. For instance, if the interest rate is very high, the Fed would allow the growth rate of money to increase slightly. Or if the growth rate of money is high, the Fed would increase the target range for the interest rate.

MONETARY CONTROL

We noted at the beginning of this section that there were two levels at which the issue of interest rates versus money targets arose. We have already dis-

---

[20] Another argument for money targeting arises from the distinction between real and nominal interest rates. The nominal interest rate can rise because inflation is expected. If the Fed fights this increase in the nominal rate by increasing the money stock, it is only feeding the inflation. We examine this argument in more detail in Chap. 14.

[21] A comprehensive discussion of monetary policy and the Fed's operating procedures, generally critical of monetary targeting, is presented in Ralph C. Bryant, *Controlling Money. The Federal Reserve and Its Critics,* The Brookings Institution, 1983. See also Bennett T. McCallum, "On Consequences and Criticisms of Monetary Targeting," *Journal of Money, Credit and Banking,* November 1985, part 2, and the subsequent comments and discussion.

cussed the economywide issue. There is also a much narrower question: If the Fed has already decided that it wants to target the money stock, will it come closer to target by setting the interest rate at a given level, or will it do better by fixing H? Here the horizon is a very short one, of a few weeks—about the period between meetings of the Open Market Committee.

We do not go into the full analysis, but sketch the arguments, which rely on a diagram like Figure 11-5, and an analysis very similar to that used in Figure 11-9. The result of such an analysis involves the relative stability of money demand and the money multiplier and shows the following:

1. If the demand-for-money function is stable, then fixing interest rates ensures that the Fed will come closest to hitting the target money stock.
2. If the demand-for-money function is relatively unstable (compared with the money multiplier), then the Fed should target H if it wants to hit its target level of the money stock most closely.

Note again that we are talking about a very short period. In this context, the Fed may want to target an interest rate in the short run *in order to hit the target money stock most closely.* More generally, this analysis suggests again why the Fed should pay attention to the behavior of both interest rates and the money stock. Shifts in money demand may reveal themselves first in movements in interest rates—and if the Fed wants to stabilize the economy, it should respond to shifts in money demand.

The Monetary Policy Shift of 1979

In October 1979 the Fed announced a major change in monetary policy: it would henceforth stay close to its target path for the money stock and allow interest rates to fluctuate more than in the past. The change was made at a time of high inflation (the CPI inflation rate over 1979 was more than 13 percent).

The Fed made the change as part of its program to fight inflation. It wanted to get the inflation rate down, and it wanted everyone to understand that it was committed to doing so, even if that meant interest rates had to reach very high levels.

The change in monetary policy was most evident in the increase in the ranges the Fed presented for target levels of the interest rate. Up to the end of 1979, the Fed had specified a narrow range of about ½ percent within which the interest rate (the federal funds rate) would be allowed to move. And the rate was kept reasonably close to the target range. After the reform the range increased to 5 percent, and large swings in interest rates indeed occurred. Thus the announced change in monetary policy operating procedures was certainly followed by much larger interest rate fluctuations than before.

But the change did not lead to more stable monetary growth. Figure 11-10 shows graphically what can also be seen in Table 11-6: the Fed came no closer to hitting its money targets after 1979 than it did before. Note also that the Fed typically went above its target range for the money stock.

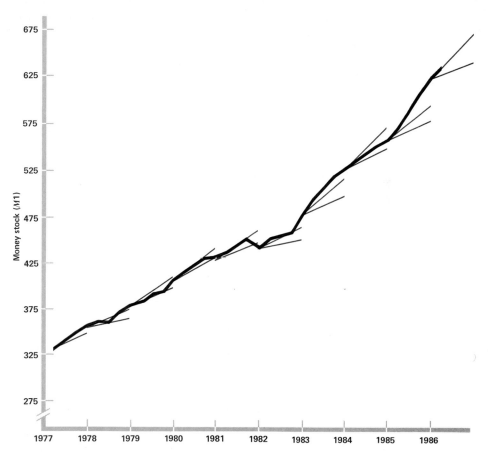

FIGURE 11-10   TARGET AND ACTUAL MONEY STOCK (M1),
1977 – 1986. (*Source:* Various issues of the *Federal Reserve Bulletin.*)
Notes: (1) Money stocks and targets are as of definitions of M1 when
target was set. (2) Target ranges for money stock are shown in color, and
the actual path of money stock is shown in black. Target ranges are set
at the end of one year to apply 1 year later. New targets are set each year.

In the fall of 1982 the Fed announced that it was increasing its money
targets for the year above the level that had been announced at the end of
1981. Similarly, in the middle of 1985 the money target for 1985 was increased. On both occasions the reason was an apparent shift in the demand
function for money, a reduction in velocity. In the fall of 1982 the economy
was in a deep recession, which the Fed feared would get worse unless the
growth rate of money were sharply increased to offset the apparent decline in
velocity. In 1985 the Fed feared that the recovery would be aborted because

of the unexpected velocity decline, and it pumped up money growth accordingly.

In both cases the Fed seems to have done the right thing. Further monetary restraint in the fall of 1982 would have worsened the recession. Instead the rapid money growth aided a vigorous recovery. In the middle of 1985 the economy was growing slowly, a recession was possible, and the Fed acted. GNP growth for the remainder of the year was moderate and there was no resurgence of inflation as critics of the Fed had predicted.

The Fed's willingness to give up its money targets when circumstances warrant suggests that the 1979 change in monetary policy is over, and was over by 1982. During that period the Fed succeeded in creating the recession that brought the inflation rate down from around 12 percent per year to the present 3 to 4 percent. With inflation lower, the Fed felt able to reduce the emphasis on money growth. By now the Fed's target ranges for the money stock do little other than describe what the Fed will be doing until it seems reasonable to change policy.

The Monetarist Critique

Monetarist critics of the Fed describe its use of monetary targets as "rhetorical camouflage," [22] a perfectly reasonable comment. Their criticisms of the Fed's monetary policy take place at several levels. First, as noted above, monetarists argue that the Fed's propensity to try to stabilize interest rates tends to make it follow inflationary policies. Whether that is a justified criticism in the eighties is unclear: certainly the inflation rate from 1982 to 1985 stayed remarkably low even as the economy recovered rapidly from the recession.

In reply to the previous analysis that shows the interest rate as a good guide for monetary policy when money demand is unstable, critics of the Fed argue that velocity changes are infrequent. [23] Further, they contend, money demand would be more stable if the Fed followed steady policies.

At a second level, monetarist critics argue that the Fed's operating procedures are technically defective. [24] Changes would enable it to hit its targets more accurately — if it wanted to.

---

[22] Milton Friedman, "The Fed Hasn't Changed Its Ways," *Wall Street Journal,* August 20, 1985.

[23] The Fed has dealt with expected shifts in velocity by changing its money targets. For instance, the target range of 1.5 to 4.5 percent for *M*1 for 1979 in Table 11-6 was so low because the Fed estimated that there would be a reduction in M1 demand of 3 percent as new types of accounts (alternative to *M*1) were introduced. Alfred Broaddus and Marvin Goodfriend, "Base Drift and Longer Run Growth of M1: Experience from a Decade of Monetary Targeting," Federal Reserve Bank of Richmond, *Economic Review,* November/December 1984, detail several such adjustments.

[24]For descriptions of alternative techniques of control, see R. Alton Gilbert, "Operating Procedures for Conducting Monetary Policy," Federal Reserve Bank of St. Louis *Review,* February 1985, and Robert H. Rasche, "Interest Rate Volatility and Alternative Monetary Control Procedures," Federal Reserve Bank of San Francisco, *Economic Review,* Summer 1985.

There is a more basic monetarist criticism. It argues that the Fed should simply attempt to keep the growth rate of money constant, quarter by quarter and year by year, rather than change its targets frequently. The argument is that policy that reacts to the way the economy is behaving ends up causing more instability rather than less. This intriguing argument is taken up in the next chapter where we discuss the difficulties of policy making in general.

Within this overall criticism, a particular complaint about the Fed's targeting procedure has received considerable attention.

Base Drift and the Fan

The criticism is that the Fed's money targeting procedures provide no long-run assurance of what the money supply will be. The argument can be seen in Figure 11-11. The key point is that the Fed sets its target range for a given year on the basis of where the money stock is at the end of the previous year.

Suppose the starting point for 1987 is *A*, with a target range of 4 to 7

FIGURE 11-11   THE FAN VERSUS THE BAND IN MONEY TARGET-ING, OR BASE DRIFT. The Fed's target range for 1987, starting from *A*, is shown by the fan *ABC*. At the end of the year the money stock is *B*. The Fed then announces a new target range, which implies the fan *BDE*. The alternative is to fix a band around a target path for the money stock, as shown by the dashed lines. That way the money stock cannot wander far from its original target path.

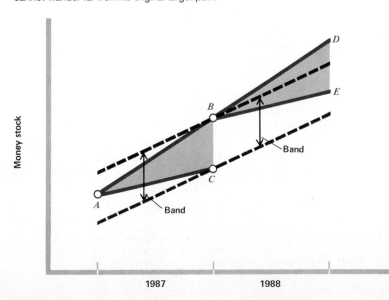

percent money growth over the next year. The figure shows values of the money stock consistent with the target range by the shaded fan-shaped area *ABC*. One year later the Fed is at *B*, the top of its range. At that point the Fed will announce its targets for 1988, *starting from point B.* Now there is a new fan-shaped target area, *BDE,* also shaded. Keeping going, we see that the procedure of starting from wherever the money stock is at the end of the year allows the money stock to wander very far from a path growing at the rate of 5.5 percent per year, which presumably is the target that the Fed intends when it announces a range of 4 to 7 percent. In effect, the fan keeps fanning.

The alternative preferred by critics of the Fed's procedure is that the Fed should announce a target *band* around a growth path of, say, 5.5 percent. That band is shown in Figure 11-11 by the dashed lines. The money stock will always be within say, 1.5 percent of the target path of 5.5 percent growth under the band procedure. The difference between the fan and the band procedures is that under the band, the Fed commits itself each year to try to come back to the original target path by correcting the deviation of the previous year. Under the fan approach, past misses are ignored, and the target is reset each year.

The process followed by the Fed allows *base drift.* The base is not the monetary base, but rather the baseline to which the money stock target is reset. Under the band, the base stays fixed. Under the fan, the base shifts, or drifts.[25]

Which is the better procedure? That depends on the reason the Fed missed the target in the first place. If it was responding to shifts in velocity, the choice depends on the nature of shocks to velocity. If velocity shocks are transitory, then fanning allows nominal GNP to wander over time from its target path. If shocks to velocity are permanent, then fanning is better because it keeps nominal GNP closer to its target level over time. In practice some velocity shocks will be permanent — for instance those associated with changes in regulations — and some transitory. So there is no hard and fast rule for whether a particular velocity change should be incorporated in the target money stock.[26]

Our own views in this area are that rigid commitment to monetary targets is unwise in light of shifts in the money demand function, and that the Fed should target interest rates as well as the stock of money. We note also that on a year-to-year basis the Fed has maintained quite stable monetary growth — not much different from that of other leading countries, such as Japan and Germany. The Fed thus does not let money growth get out of hand: if the growth rate is very high for a short time — as in Figure 11-10 — the growth rate will

---

[25] For more on base drift, see the article by Broaddus and Goodfriend referred to in footnote 23.

[26] The Fed may also miss the monetary target because of poor monetary control. What it should do then depends in part on how quickly the effects of the errors can be reversed.

BOX
11-2

CREDIT RATIONING

In the *IS-LM* model interest rates are the only channel of transmission between financial markets and aggregate demand. An important additional channel in the real world is *credit rationing*. Credit rationing takes place when banks limit the amount individuals can borrow, even though the individuals are willing to pay the going interest rate on their loans.

When banks relax the limits on borrowing by their customers, investment spending by firms and spending on consumer durables by households increases and hence demand and output increase. Conversely, when banks tighten credit constraints, spending falls off because households and firms cannot finance their spending.*

Credit rationing can appear in one of two forms. Banks routinely practice credit rationing, for a very good reason. A bank often cannot tell whether a particular customer (or the project the customer is financing) is good or bad. A bad customer will default on the loan and not repay it. Given the risk of default, the obvious answer seems to be to raise the interest rate.

However, raising interest rates to provide the bank with a risk premium works the wrong way: honest customers are deterred from borrowing because they realize their investments are not profitable at high interest rates. But customers who are reckless or dishonest will borrow because they do not expect to pay the interest in the first place. Even if banks screen their customers carefully, they cannot altogether escape this *moral hazard* problem of finding themselves lending to many borrowers who have no intention of repaying. The answer is to limit the amount lent to any one customer. Most customers get broadly the same interest rate (with some adjustments), but the amount of credit they are allowed is rationed both according to the kind of security the customer can offer and to the prospects of the economy that the bank perceives.

When times are good, banks lend cheerfully because they believe that the average customer will not default. When the economy turns down, credit rationing intensifies because banks feel that their loans become less safe.

These shifts in credit rationing are reinforced when banks see a change in monetary policy. If they perceive that the Fed is shifting to restraint and higher interest rates so as to cool down the economy, they help it along by tightening credit. Conversely, if they believe policy is expansionary, they ease credit, both via lower interest rates and via expanded credit rations. Lower interest rates increase the profitability of investment and hence raise demand. More liberal credit rations also help finance spending. Credit rationing thus is another channel for monetary policy.

A second type of credit rationing can occur by the central bank imposing credit constraints on commercial banks. Central banks often impose credit ceilings. Banks are then not allowed to expand their loans over a given period by more than, say, 5 percent, or even less. Such a credit limit can put an abrupt end to a boom. A striking example occurred in the United States in early 1980. Concerned with the risk of double-digit inflation the Fed clamped on credit controls. In no time the economy fell into a recession with output falling at an annual rate of 9 percent.

Credit controls thus are an emergency brake for the central bank. They work, but they do so in a very blunt way. For that reason their use is very infrequent and remains reserved for occasions when dramatic, fast effects are desired.

---

* An early and important reference to credit rationing is D. Jaffe and R. Russell, "Imperfect Information, Uncertainty and Credit Rationing," *Quarterly Journal of Economics,* November 1966. More recently the importance of credit rationing has been emphasized by A. Blinder and J. Stiglitz, "Money, Credit Constraints, and Economic Activity," *American Economic Review,* May 1983.

typically later be reduced to compensate for the high growth and bring the money stock closer to target.

11-11 WHICH TARGETS FOR THE FED?

The Fed sets target ranges for $M1$, $M2$, $M3$, and debt growth, as well as ranges for interest rates. It typically fails to hit most of the targets. Why would it need so many targets, should it have fewer or only one, and if so which?

There are three points to note before we get down to the details:

1. A key distinction is between *ultimate targets* of policy and *intermediate targets* illustrated in Figure 11-12. Ultimate targets are variables such as the inflation rate and the unemployment rate (or real output) whose behavior matters. The interest rate or the rate of growth of money are *intermediate targets* of policy — targets the Fed aims at only so it can hit the ultimate targets more accurately. The discount rate, open market operations, and reserve requirements are the instruments the Fed has with which to hit the targets.
2. It is also essential to know how often the targets are reset. If the target is reset frequently, such as every month, it does not much matter what intermediate target is being used, provided the ultimate targets — for example, inflation and unemployment — are given. That is because the intermediate target can be reset as needed to be consistent with the ultimate targets. But if the intermediate targets are held constant for a long period, then the choice of target matters. For instance, if the Fed were to commit itself to a 5.5 percent money growth forever, changes in velocity would affect the growth rate of nominal GNP consistent with the target money growth.
3. In an ideal world, there would be no need for targeting. If the Fed had the right ultimate goals in mind and knew how the economy worked, it would do whatever was needed to keep the economy as close to its ultimate targets as possible.

So what is the point of targeting? Intermediate targets give the Fed something concrete and specific to aim for in the next year. That has the advantage

FIGURE 11-12   FEDERAL RESERVE INSTRUMENTS AND TARGETS

of enabling the Fed itself to know where it wants to go. They also help the private sector know what to expect for the future. If the Fed announces and will stick to its targets, firms and consumers have a better idea of what future levels of prices and output will be and can make their investment and savings plans accordingly.

Further, critics of the Fed say it has to be given a clearly defined task so that it can be held *accountable* for its actions. It has a job to do. By announcing targets it makes it possible for outsiders to discuss whether it is aiming in the right direction. In addition, the targets make it possible to judge whether it succeeds in its aims.

The ideal intermediate target is a variable that the Fed can control exactly and which at the same time has an exact relationship with the ultimate targets of policy. For instance, if the ultimate target could be expressed as some particular level of nominal GNP, and if the money multiplier and velocity were both constant, the Fed could hit its ultimate target by having the money base as its intermediate target.

In practice life is not so simple. Rather, in choosing intermediate targets, the Fed has to trade off between those targets it can control exactly and those targets that are most closely related to its ultimate targets.

Sometimes proposed, and at one extreme, is *monetary base targeting*. The Fed can essentially control the monetary base exactly. If that were the intermediate target, the Fed would have no trouble hitting the bull's eye. Further, it could certainly be held accountable for not hitting the target, since it could not plausibly blame factors beyond its control for any failures.

The problem with monetary base targeting is that the Fed might be hitting the bull's eye on the money base target while completely missing the ultimate targets of policy. Unpredictable changes in the money multiplier and in velocity break the tight link between the money base and nominal GNP.

Nominal GNP targeting is at the other end of the tradeoff. In this scheme the Fed would announce a target path for nominal GNP—for instance, that it wants nominal GNP to grow 10 percent—and then set the money stock to try to achieve that goal. By targeting nominal GNP growth, the Fed would be aiming at both inflation and real output goals. Relative to money stock targeting, nominal GNP targeting implies that the Fed automatically adjusts money targets for velocity shifts.

In addition, nominal GNP targeting builds in an automatic policy tradeoff between inflation and output. If inflation turns out high, the nominal income growth target implies that the Fed will be aiming for a lower level of output growth than it otherwise would have.[27]

Nominal GNP targeting is close to the ultimate targets but far from what the Fed controls directly. It would not be plausible to blame the Fed if nominal

---

[27]John B. Taylor provides a technical discussion of nominal income targeting in "What Would Nominal GNP Targeting Do to the Business Cycle," in Carnegie-Rochester Conference Series on Public Policy, Karl Brunner and Allan H. Meltzer (eds.), *Understanding Monetary Regimes*, vol. 22 (Amsterdam: North-Holland, 1985).

GNP does not hit the target — fiscal policy or supply shocks just as much as monetary policy could be responsible. Thus those who believe the main problem in monetary policy is controlling the Fed typically argue for monetary base or money stock rules. Those who believe the Fed can be trusted to do the right thing tend to prefer nominal GNP targeting.

Beyond the issue of trusting the Fed, lie questions of whether the economy would be more stable if over periods of a year or so nominal GNP growth were held constant or if money or base growth interest rates were held constant. There are no simple answers at this stage: the answer depends both on what shocks hit the economy and on the dynamic pattern of adjustment of the economy to shocks.

To start with, we asked why the Fed has so many targets and which it should have. One view is that the many targets exist to give the Fed flexibility to vary monetary policy. With so many targets, it is likely to hit one of them — and can then claim success. Equally plausibly, it may have many targets because the relationship between each intermediate money target and the ultimate targets is uncertain. By having many targets, it in effect reduces the risk of making a big mistake.

Which target should the Fed have? The goals of targeting can be achieved if the Fed announces several money stock targets, and also interest rate targets, for the next year and explains why those targets are consistent with the ultimate targets of policy.

11-12 SUMMARY

1. The stock of money is determined by the Fed through its control of the monetary base (high-powered money); the public, through its preferred currency-deposit ratio; and the banks, through their preferred reserve holding behavior.
2. The money stock is larger than the stock of high-powered money because part of the money stock consists of bank deposits, against which the banks hold less than 1 dollar of reserves per dollar of deposits.
3. The money multiplier is the ratio of the money stock to high-powered money. It is larger the smaller the reserve-deposit ratio and the smaller the currency-deposit ratio.
4. The Fed creates high-powered money when it buys assets (for example, Treasury bills, gold, foreign exchange) by creating liabilities on its balance sheet. Purchases of these assets by the Fed increase banks' reserves held at the Fed and lead through the multiplier process to a larger increase in the money stock.
5. The money multiplier builds up through an adjustment process in which banks make loans (or buy securities) because deposits have increased their reserves to more than desired levels.

6. The Fed has three basic policy instruments: open market operations, the discount rate, and its ability to fix reserve requirements for the banks.

7. Because the desired reserve-deposit ratio of banks decreases as the interest rate rises, the supply-of-money function is interest-elastic.

8. The Fed cannot control both the interest rate and the money stock exactly. It can only choose combinations of the interest rate and money stock that are consistent with the demand-for-money function.

9. The Fed operates monetary policy by specifying target ranges for both the money stock and the interest rate. In order to hit its target level of output, the Fed should concentrate on its money targets if the *IS* curve is unstable or shifts about a good deal. It should concentrate on interest rate targets if the money demand function is the major source of instability in the economy.

10. In 1979 the Fed announced a major change in monetary policy whereby it would stick closely to money targets and allow interest rates to fluctuate more. Over the next 3 years interest rates indeed fluctuated more than before, but money growth did not hit targets more accurately. Since the fall of 1982 the Fed has again been paying less attention to money targets, adjusting them as it believes appropriate in the light of shifts in money demand and conditions in the economy.

11. In choosing the targets for monetary policy, the Fed faces a tradeoff between targets that it can hit exactly but may be far from the ultimate targets of policy, and targets that are closer to ultimate targets, but are more difficult to hit. Critics of the Fed argue that in addition targets should be chosen so that the Fed can be held accountable for its actions — this suggests intermediate targets that the Fed can hit quite accurately.

KEY TERMS

Currency-deposit ratio

Reserve-deposit ratio

High-powered money (monetary base)

Money multiplier

Discount rate

Excess reserves

FDIC

Multiple expansion of bank deposits

Money supply function

Money stock and interest rate targets

Intermediate targets

Ultimate targets

Base drift

Fan versus band

PROBLEMS

1. Use Figure 11-3 to show how (a) an increase in the currency-deposit ratio and (b) an increase in the reserve-deposit ratio affect the money stock, given the monetary base.

2. Show how an open market sale affects the Fed's balance sheet and also the balance sheet of the commercial bank of the purchaser of the bond sold by the Fed.

3. When the Fed buys or sells gold or foreign exchange, it automatically offsets or sterilizes the impact of these operations on the monetary base by compensating open market operations. Show the effects on the Fed balance sheet of a purchase of gold and a corresponding sterilization through an open market operation.

4. How much do bank loans and security purchases increase when the Fed increases the monetary base by $1? Give the answer in terms of cu and re.

5. Explain how the Fed's balance sheet would be affected if it valued gold at the market price.

6. A proposal for "100 percent banking" involves a reserve-deposit ratio of unity. Such a scheme has been proposed for the United States in order to enhance the Fed's control over the money supply.

   (a) Indicate why such a scheme would help monetary control.

   (b) Indicate what bank balance sheets look like under this scheme.

   (c) Under 100 percent money, how would banking remain profitable?

7. Discuss the impact of credit cards on the money multiplier.

8. By using Figures 11-5 and 11-6 show the effect of an increase in required reserves on (a) the equilibrium money supply, (b) interest rates, and (c) the equilibrium level of income.

9. The Federal Deposit Insurance Corporation insures commercial bank deposits against bank default. Discuss the implications of that deposit scheme for the money multiplier.

10. Assume required reserves were zero. Would banks hold any reserves?

11. Under what circumstances should the Fed conduct monetary policy by targeting mainly (a) interest rates or (b) the money stock?

12. (a) Why does the Fed not stick more closely to its target paths for money?

    (b) Should the Fed use a fan or a band approach to monetary targeting?

13. Show the effect of a discount rate increase (a) on the money supply and (b) on income and interest rates.

14. The Fed's target for monetary policy should be to produce constant growth of real GNP at a rate of 3.5 percent per year. Discuss.

APPENDIX

We derive the equilibrium money stock and the multiplier by looking at the demand and supply of money and of high-powered money. Consider, first, equilibrium between the supply of money and the demand for money, which, in turn, equals currency plus deposits:

$$M = CU + D \equiv (cu + 1)D \qquad (A1)$$

where we have substituted for $CU = cuD$, denoting the public's desired ratio of currency to deposits cu.

Equilibrium between the supply of high-powered money and the demand for high-powered money which equals currency plus reserves implies

$$\overline{H} = CU + RE \equiv (cu + re)D \qquad (A2)$$

Again we have expressed the demand side in terms of the desired ratio of currency to deposits and of the banks' desired reserve-deposit ratio re. When (A1) and (A2) both hold, we are in monetary equilibrium because people hold the composition of their money balances in the preferred ratio and banks hold just the right ratio of reserves to deposits.

Dividing (A2) by (A1) yields an expression for the money multiplier:

$$\frac{M}{\overline{H}} \equiv mm = \frac{1 + cu}{cu + re} \qquad\qquad (A3)$$

The money multiplier thus depends on the cu ratio and the re ratio. We can also use (A3), multiplying both sides by $\overline{H}$, to obtain the money supply in terms of the principal determinants mm and $\overline{H}$:

$$M = mm\, \overline{H} \qquad\qquad (A4)$$

In writing (A4) we remember that mm is dependent on the currency-deposit preferences of the public and the reserve-deposit preferences of banks. It thus takes into account preferences about the composition of balance sheets.

The Multiplier Process

Suppose the stock of high-powered money has been increased by 1 dollar through an open market purchase. We now trace the process by which that increase in H affects the money stock.

We start by considering the individual who sold the bond to the Fed. That person is paid with a check, which he or she takes to her bank. But, like all portfolio holders, this person has a currency-deposit ratio of cu. Therefore, of the 1 dollar received from the Fed, he or she wants to keep the fraction $[cu/(1 + cu)]$ as currency. For instance, with cu equal to 0.37, the person keeps 27.0 cents ($=0.37/1.37$ dollars) as currency and deposits 73.0 cents.

At this stage the money stock has increased by only 1 dollar as a result of the increase in the stock of high-powered money. The effect of the deposit on the bank's balance sheet is shown in Table A11-1. The bank has increased its reserves by 73.0 cents. This is a result of its depositing at the Fed the check it received from its customer, which increased reserves by 1 dollar, and then paying out 27.0 cents in currency—leaving it with an extra 73.0 cents of reserves.

Now comes the crucial stage. The bank does not want to hold the *entire* extra 73 cents as reserves. The bank's reserve ratio is only re, which means that it wants to hold only re of every extra dollar of assets it receives in the form of reserves. It wants to hold the rest $(1 - re)$ in some other form. For instance, if re is equal to 0.10, it wants to hold 10 cents of every dollar of its

---

TABLE A11-1   A BANK LOAN*

(a)		(b)	
Assets	Liabilities	Assets	Liabilities
Reserves 73.0¢	Deposits 73.0¢	Reserves 7.3¢	Deposits 73.0¢
		Loans 65.7¢	

---

* In (a), reserves and deposits both increase by $\$(1/1 + cu)$.
In (b), the bank lends out fraction $(1 - re)$ of the reserves.
$cu = 0.37;\ re = 0.10$

portfolio as reserves and 90 cents in some other form. As we see from Table 11-5, the bank's other assets are loans and securities. We assume the bank wants to lend 90 cents of every extra dollar of assets it receives. When it has received 73 cents, it will want to lend 65.7 cents ($=0.9 \times 73.0$) cents.

This loan is shown in Table A11-1. For simplicity we think of the borrower receiving the loan in the form of currency. The loan is equal to 65.7 cents. *It is at this stage that the bank's lending activities have increased the money stock by more than the increase in high-powered money.* Why? The person who sold the bond to the Fed has 1 more dollar in money — 27.0 cents in currency and the rest in deposits. But the person who took a loan from the commercial bank also has more money holdings — the 65.7 cents lent by the bank. The money stock is up by $1.657, which is, of course, more than 1 dollar.

The person taking the loan probably wanted to spend it. Thus assume the 65.7 cents is spent. The person receiving the 65.7 cents now wants to hold a fraction ($cu/1 + cu$) as bank deposits. But of that amount deposited in that person's bank, the bank will want to lend out a fraction ($1 - re$). Clearly the process can keep going for a long time.

Table A11-2 shows the successive steps by which the money multiplier builds up as a result of the decisions of individuals to deposit part of their increased money holdings in the banks, and the decision of the banks to make loans (or buy securities). Round 1 is the process described in Table A11-2, ending with the bank making a loan. Round 2 starts when the borrower spends the loan, and the person receiving the proceeds holds some of that amount as currency and deposits the rest in a bank. Round 2 ends once again with a bank loan, and so forth.

TABLE A11-2   MULTIPLE EXPANSION OF BANK DEPOSITS, BANK LOANS, AND THE MONEY MULTIPLIER

Increase in H	Increase in currency	Increase in deposits	Increase in reserves	Increase in bank loans	Stage
1	$\dfrac{cu}{1 + cu}$	$\dfrac{1}{1 + cu}$	$\dfrac{re}{1 + cu}$	$\dfrac{1 - re}{1 + cu}$	Round 1
	$\dfrac{cu}{1 + cu}\left(\dfrac{1 - re}{1 + cu}\right)$	$\dfrac{1}{1 + cu}\left(\dfrac{1 - re}{1 + cu}\right)$	$\dfrac{re}{1 + cu}\left(\dfrac{1 - re}{1 + cu}\right)$	$\dfrac{1 - re}{1 + cu}\left(\dfrac{1 - re}{1 + cu}\right)$	Round 2
	$\dfrac{cu}{1 + cu}\left(\dfrac{1 - re}{1 + cu}\right)^2$	$\dfrac{1}{1 + cu}\left(\dfrac{1 - re}{1 + cu}\right)^2$	$\dfrac{re}{1 + cu}\left(\dfrac{1 - re}{1 + cu}\right)^2$	$\dfrac{1 - re}{1 + cu}\left(\dfrac{1 - re}{1 + cu}\right)^2$	Round 3
	$\dfrac{cu}{1 + cu}\left(\dfrac{1 - re}{1 + cu}\right)^n$	$\dfrac{1}{1 + cu}\left(\dfrac{1 - re}{1 + cu}\right)^n$	$\dfrac{re}{1 + cu}\left(\dfrac{1 - re}{1 + cu}\right)^n$	$\dfrac{1 - re}{1 + cu}\left(\dfrac{1 - re}{1 + cu}\right)^n$	Round $n + 1$
	$\dfrac{cu}{1 + cu}SUM$	$\dfrac{1}{1 + cu}SUM$	$\dfrac{re}{1 + cu}SUM$	$\dfrac{1 - re}{1 + cu}SUM$	Total*
	$\dfrac{cu}{cu + re}$	$\dfrac{1}{cu + re}$	$\dfrac{re}{cu + re}$	$\dfrac{1 - re}{cu + re}$	After substituting for *SUM* from equation (A5)

* *SUM* is defined by equation (A5).

We can now add up the increases in currency, deposits, reserves, and bank credit occurring over all the rounds together, that is, during the entire process. As in the Appendix to Chapter 9, we are now dealing with the sum of an infinite series, denoted here as SUM. That sum is given by[28]

$$SUM = 1 + \left(\frac{1-re}{1+cu}\right) + \left(\frac{1-re}{1+cu}\right)^2 + \left(\frac{1-re}{1+cu}\right)^3 + \cdots$$

$$= \frac{1+cu}{cu+re}$$

(A5)

We use equation (A5) in arriving at the bottom row of Table A11-2, which shows that currency increases by the fraction $[cu/(cu+re)]$ of $1 following the increase in H of $1, that deposits increase by $[1/(cu+re)]$, that reserves increase by $[re/(cu+re)]$, and finally, that credit increases by $[(1-re)/(cu+re)]$.

Adding the increases in currency and deposits, we discover that the two together have risen by the amount $[(1+cu)/(cu+re)]$, which is nothing other than the money multiplier. Table A11-2 thus provides another way of thinking about the money multiplier. The table also shows how, and by how much, the banking system creates loans (or buys securities) when the Fed increases high-powered money, thereby causing the money supply to increase by a multiple of the increase in H.

Example

With cu equal to 0.37 and re equal to 0.10, we have currency increasing by $0.79 $[cu/(cu+re)]$, deposits by $2.13 $[1/(cu+re)]$, reserves by $0.21 $[re/(cu+re)]$, and bank loans by $1.91 $[(1-re)/(cu+re)]$. The money stock increases by $2.92, or 2.92 times the increase in the stock of high-powered money. This is (approximately) the value of the money multiplier calculated earlier.

Multiple Expansion of Bank Deposits

Table A11-2 illustrates the process known as the *multiple expansion of bank deposits*. It shows how an increase in deposits leads to further deposits, and therefore how the money multiplier works. There is one further interesting aspect of the results shown in Table A11-2. It is

---

[28] *Technical note:* The formula for the sum of a geometric series, which can in general be written

$$SUM = 1 + a + a^2 + \cdots$$

where a is a number between minus and plus 1, is

$$SUM = \frac{1}{1-a}$$

If you have not met geometric series before, you may want to take an example, say, $a = \frac{1}{4}$, and start adding the terms in the first formula in the footnote. You will soon find your answer coming close to $\frac{4}{3}$, which is the answer given by the second formula in the footnote.

possible to say that the banking system creates money in the sense that if there were not a banking system, a $1 increase in H would increase the money stock only by $1. With the banking system, the $1 increase in H leads to more than a $1 increase in M.

The interesting point is that at each stage of the process, no one bank believes it is, or can be said to be, creating money. At each stage, each bank in the process is only lending out money that has been deposited with it. Each bank manager would rightly, and no doubt vehemently, deny that the bank is creating money. The system as a whole, though, is creating money through the successive rounds of loans and subsequent further bank deposits.

STABILIZATION POLICY: PROSPECTS AND PROBLEMS

Figure 12-1, which shows the unemployment rate over the period 1926–1985, gives the clear impression that stabilization policy has left something to be desired. Standing out is the disaster of the great depression decade of the thirties, when the unemployment rate peaked at almost 25 percent of the labor force. But unemployment has sometimes been high even in the post–World War II period, as in the 1973–1975 and 1981–1982 recessions.

The historical record forcefully raises the question of why the economy has not done better. The preceding chapters have laid out a clear body of theory that seems to show exactly the measures that can be used to maintain full employment. High unemployment, or a large GNP gap, can be reduced by expansionary monetary or fiscal policy. Similarly a boom and inflation can be contained by restrictive monetary or fiscal policies.

The policies needed to prevent the fluctuations in unemployment seen in Figure 12-1 accordingly appear to be simple. The policy maker knows the full-employment level of output. If there is unemployment a policy maker can use a model, such as the *IS-LM* model, to calculate the level of government spending or taxes needed to get income to the full-employment level. But if it is all so simple, how did the fluctuations in Figure 12-1 occur?

The answer must be that policy making is far from simple. Part of the difficulty arises from the possible *conflict between the maintenance of full*

FIGURE 12-1 THE CIVILIAN UNEMPLOYMENT RATE IN THE
UNITED STATES, 1926–1985 (*Sources:* Data Resources, Inc., and
Historical Statistics of the United States, Bureau of the Census, 1976.)

employment and the target of low inflation. Because expansionary fiscal or
monetary policy raises both output and prices, policy to reduce unemployment may increase inflation. We pursue that problem, which can be seen in the
aggregate supply-demand analysis of Chapter 7, in more detail in Chapters 14
and 15.

In this chapter we discuss both the optimistic prospects for stabilization
policy and problems in the execution of policy. The mainline approach to
stabilization policy developed out of the great depression. We set the scene by
describing the events of the great depression, and the New Economics that it
spawned, with its emphasis on the potential for active policy to help stabilize
the economy.

Then we turn to technical problems in policy making, which imply that
policy cannot be expected to keep the economy always close to full employment with low inflation. We begin by discussing the types of disturbance that
cause the economy to move away from the full-employment level of output in

the first place. Then we briefly describe *econometric models*, models of the economy with specific numerical values for parameters and multipliers, that can be used to assist policy making. The bulk of the chapter is taken up by a discussion of three factors that in large measure account for the failure of policy continually to achieve its targets. The three *handicaps of policy making are:*

1. Lags in the effects of policy
2. The role of expectations in determining private sector responses to policy
3. Uncertainty about the effects of policy

In a nutshell, we will argue that a policy maker who (1) observes a disturbance, (2) does not know whether it is permanent or not, and (3) takes time to develop a policy which (4) takes still more time to affect behavior and (5) has uncertain effects on aggregate demand, is very poorly equipped to do a perfect job of stabilizing the economy.

12-1 THE GREAT DEPRESSION

The great depression of the 1930s is the event that shaped both many institutions in the economy, including the Fed, and modern American macroeconomics. The essential facts about the depression are shown in Figure 12-2 and in Table 12-1. Between 1929 and 1933, GNP fell by nearly 30 percent. Over the same period, the unemployment rate rose from 3 to 25 percent. For the 10 years 1931 to 1940, the unemployment rate averaged 18.8 percent, ranging between a low of 14.3 percent in 1937 and a high of 24.9 percent in 1933. By contrast, the post–World War II high, reached in 1982, was under 11 percent. Investment collapsed in the great depression, indeed, net investment was negative from 1931 to 1935. The consumer price index fell nearly 25 percent from 1929 to 1933; the stock market fell 80 percent between September 1929 and March 1933. From 1933 to 1937, real GNP grew fast, at an annual rate of nearly 9 percent, but even that did not get the unemployment rate down to normal levels. Then, in 1937–1938 there was a major recession within the depression, pushing the unemployment rate back up to nearly 20 percent. In the second half of the decade, short-term interest rates, such as the commercial paper rate, were near zero.

Facts such as those in Table 12-1 raise a host of questions. The two most important are, Why did this happen? and, Could it have been prevented? Underlying these questions is one that many economists are asked whenever the economy is in recession, and that they ask themselves in their bad moments: Could it happen again?

The depression and the stock market crash of October 1929 are popularly thought of as almost the same thing. In fact, the economy started turning down before the stock market crash. The peak of the business cycle is estimated to

TABLE 12-1   ECONOMIC STATISTICS OF THE GREAT DEPRESSION

Year	GNP (billion 1972 $)	I/GNP (%)	G (billion 1972 $)	Unemployment rate (%)	CPI (1929 = 100)	Commercial paper rate (%)	AAA rate (%)	Stock market index	M1 (1929 = 100)	Full-employment surplus/Y* (%)
1929	314.7	17.8	40.9	3.2	100	5.9	4.7	83.1	100	−0.8
1930	285.2	13.5	44.6	8.7	97.4	3.6	4.6	67.2	96.2	−1.4
1931	263.3	9.0	46.2	15.9	88.7	2.6	4.6	43.6	89.4	−3.1
1932	226.8	3.5	44.0	23.6	79.7	2.7	5.0	22.1	78.0	−0.9
1933	222.1	3.8	42.8	24.9	75.4	1.7	4.5	28.6	73.5	1.6
1934	239.4	5.5	48.7	21.7	78.0	1.0	4.0	31.4	81.4	0.2
1935	260.8	9.2	49.8	20.1	80.1	0.8	3.6	33.9	96.6	−0.1
1936	296.1	10.9	58.5	16.9	80.9	0.8	3.2	49.4	110.6	−1.1
1937	309.8	12.8	56.3	14.3	83.3	0.9	3.3	49.2	114.8	1.8
1938	297.1	8.1	61.3	19.0	82.3	0.8	3.2	36.7	115.9	0.6
1939	319.7	10.5	63.8	17.2	81.0	0.6	3.0	38.5	127.3	−0.1

Note: Stock market index is the Standard & Poor's composite index, which includes 500 stocks, September 1929 set equal to 100. Y^* denotes full-employment output.

Sources:

Cols. 1, 2, 3: The National Income and Product Accounts of the United States. 1929–1974, U.S. Department of Commerce.

Col. 4: Revised Bureau of Labor Statistics data taken from Michael Darby, "Three-and-a-Half Million Employees Have Been Mislaid: Or, an Explanation of Unemployment, 1934–1941," *Journal of Political Economy,* February 1976.

Cols. 5, 6, and 7: Economic Report of the President. 1957.

Col. 8: Security Price Index Record, 1978, Standard & Poor's Statistical Service.

Col. 9: Milton Friedman and Anna J. Schwartz, *A Monetary History of the United States, 1867 – 1960* (Princeton, N.J.: Princeton University Press, 1963), table A1, col. 7.

Col. 10: E. Cary Brown, "Fiscal Policy in the Thirties: A Reappraisal," *American Economic Review,* December 1956, table 1, cols. 3, 5, and 19.

FIGURE 12-2   OUTPUT AND PRICES IN THE GREAT DEPRESSION.
(*Sources:* U. S. Department of Commerce, *The National Income and Product Accounts of the United States,* 1929–1974, and *Economic Report of the President,* 1957.)

have been in August 1929, and the stock market itself peaked in September 1929. Standard & Poor's composite stock price index, calculated using September 1929 as the base period, fell from 100 in September to 66 in November. It rose again through March 1930, but then the collapse continued until the index fell to 15 in June 1932.

By early 1931, the economy was suffering from a very severe depression, but not one that was out of the range of the experience of the previous century.[1] It was in the period from early 1931 until Franklin Roosevelt became President in March 1933 that the depression became "great."

[1] The classic work by Milton Friedman and Anna J. Schwartz, *A Monetary History of the United States, 1867–1960* (Princeton, N.J.: Princeton University Press, 1963), gives a very detailed account of the great depression, comparing it with other recessions and emphasizing the role of the Fed. For a more general economic history of the period, see Robert A. Gordon, *Economic Instability: The American Record* (New York: Harper & Row, 1974), chap. 3.

Economic Policy

What was economic policy during this period? The money stock fell from 1929 to 1930, and then fell rapidly in 1931 and 1932 and continued falling through April 1933. At the same time, the composition of the money stock changed. In March 1931 the currency-demand deposit ratio was 18.5 percent; 2 years later, it was 40.7 percent.

The fall in the money stock was the result of large-scale bank failures. Banks failed because they did not have the reserves with which to meet customers' cash withdrawals, and in failing they destroyed deposits and hence reduced the money stock. But the failures went further in reducing the money stock, because they led to a loss of confidence on the part of depositors and hence to an even higher desired currency-deposit ratio. Furthermore, banks that had not yet failed adjusted to the possibility of a run by holding increased reserves relative to deposits. The rise in the currency-deposit ratio and the reserve-deposit ratio reduced the money multiplier and hence sharply contracted the money stock.

The Fed took very few steps to offset the fall in the money supply; for a few months in 1932 it did undertake a program of open market purchases, but otherwise it seemed to acquiesce in bank closings and certainly failed to understand that the central bank should act vigorously in a crisis to prevent the collapse of the financial system.[2]

Fiscal policy too was not vigorous. The natural impulse of politicians then was to balance the budget in times of trouble, and much rhetoric was devoted to that proposition. The presidential candidates in 1932 campaigned on balanced budget platforms. In fact, as Table 12-2 shows, the federal government ran enormous deficits, particularly for that time, averaging 2.6 percent of GNP from 1931 to 1933 and even more later. (These actual deficits are lower as a percentage of GNP than those projected for the mid-eighties.) The belief in budget balancing was more than rhetoric, however, for state and local governments raised taxes to match their expenditures,[3] as did the federal government, particularly in 1932 and 1933. President Roosevelt tried seriously to balance the budget—he was no Keynesian. The full-employment surplus shows fiscal policy (combined state, local, and federal) as most expansionary in 1931, and moving to a more contractionary level from 1932 to 1934. In fact, the full-employment surplus was positive in 1933 and 1934, despite the actual deficits.[4] Of course, the full-employment surplus concept had not been invented in the 1930s.

---

[2] Friedman and Schwartz speculate on the reasons for the Fed's inaction; the whodunit or "who didn't do it" on pp. 407 to 419 of their book (cited in footnote 1) is fascinating.

[3] You can calculate the surplus of state and local governments as a percentage of GNP by subtracting column 4 in Table 12-2 from column 2.

[4] Note that in this chapter, unlike Chapter 3 and elsewhere in the book, the full-employment deficit includes federal, state, and local governments.

TABLE 12-2 GOVERNMENT SPENDING AND REVENUE, 1929-1939 (In percent)

	TOTAL GOVERNMENT		FEDERAL GOVERNMENT		TOTAL GOVERNMENT
Year	Expenditure/ GNP	Actual surplus/ GNP	Expenditure/ GNP	Actual surplus/ GNP	Full employment surplus/Y*†
1929	10.0	1.0	2.5	1.2	−0.8
1930	12.3	−0.3	3.1	0.3	−1.4
1931	16.4	−3.8	5.5	−2.8	−3.1
1932	18.3	−3.1	5.5	−2.6	−0.9
1933	19.2	−2.5	7.2	−2.3	1.6
1934	19.8	−3.7	9.8	−4.4	0.2
1935	18.6	−2.8	9.0	−3.6	−0.1
1936	19.5	−3.8	10.5	−4.4	−1.1
1937	16.6	0.3	8.2	0.4	1.8
1938	19.8	−2.1	10.2	−2.5	0.6
1939	19.4	−2.4	9.8	−2.4	−0.1

† Y^* = potential output.

Sources:

Cols. 1, 2, 3, 4: *Economic Report of the President*, 1972, tables B1 and B70.

Col 5: E. Cary Brown, "Fiscal Policy in the Thirties: A Reappraisal," *American Economic Review*, December 1956, table 1, cols. 3, 5, and 19.

Economic activity recovered in the period from 1933 to 1937, with fiscal policy becoming more expansionary and the money stock growing rapidly. The growth of the money stock was based on an inflow of gold from Europe. This provided high-powered money for the monetary system. It was in the thirties that the Fed acquired most of its current holdings of gold.[5]

Institutional Change

The period from 1933 to 1937 also saw substantial legislative and administrative action — the *New Deal* — from the Roosevelt administration. The Fed was reorganized, and the Federal Deposit Insurance Corporation (FDIC) was established.

A number of regulatory agencies were also created, most notably the Securities and Exchange Commission, which regulates the securities industry. Its purpose was to prevent speculative excesses that were thought largely responsible for the stock market crash. The Social Security Administration was

---

[5] For details of the way in which the Fed acquired the gold, see Friedman and Schwartz, op. cit., p. 506.

set up so that the elderly would not in the future have to rely on their own savings to ensure themselves a minimally adequate of standard of living in retirement. The Roosevelt administration also believed that the route to recovery lay in increasing wages and prices, so it encouraged trade unionization, and price-raising, and price-fixing schemes by business, through the National Recovery Administration.

International Aspects

Another important aspect of the depression deserves mention: it was virtually worldwide. To some extent, this was the result of the collapse of the international financial system.[6] It resulted, too, from the mutual adoption of high tariff policies by many countries (including the United States), keeping out foreign goods to protect domestic producers. And, of course, if each country keeps out foreign goods, the volume of world trade declines, providing a contractionary influence on the world economy.

The experience of the thirties varied internationally. Sweden began an expansionary policy in the early thirties and reduced its unemployment relatively fast in the second half of the decade. Britain's economy suffered high unemployment in both the twenties and the thirties. Germany grew rapidly after Hitler came to power and expanded government spending. China escaped the recession until after 1931, essentially because it had a floating exchange rate. As always, there is much to be learned from the exceptions.

In 1939, real GNP in the United States rose above its 1929 level for the first time in the decade. But it was not until 1942, after the United States formally entered World War II, that the unemployment rate finally fell below 5 percent.

12-2 THE GREAT DEPRESSION: THE ISSUES AND IDEAS

In Section 12-1 we asked what caused the great depression, whether it could have been avoided, and whether it could happen again. The question of what caused the depression seems purely academic, but it is much more than that. The depression was the greatest economic crisis the Western world had experienced.

The classical economics of the time had no well-developed theory that would explain persistent unemployment, nor any policy prescriptions to solve the problem. Many economists of the time did, in fact, recommend government spending as a way of reducing unemployment, but they had no macroeconomic theory by which to justify their recommendations.

---

[6] This aspect of the depression is emphasized by Charles Kindleberger, *The World in Depression, 1929–1939* (Berkeley: University of California Press, 1986), and Gottfried Haberler, *The World Economy, Money and the Great Depression* (Washington, D.C.: American Enterprise Institute, 1976).

Keynes wrote his great work, *The General Theory of Employment, Interest and Money* in the 1930s, after Britain had suffered during the 1920s from a decade of double-digit unemployment and while the United States was in the depths of its depression. He was fully aware of the seriousness of the issues. As Don Patinkin of the Hebrew University puts it[7]:

> . . . the period was one of fear and darkness as the Western world struggled with the greatest depression that it had known. . . . [T]here was a definite feeling that by attempting to achieve a scientific understanding of the phenomenon of mass unemployment, one was not only making an intellectual contribution, but was also dealing with a critical problem that endangered the very existence of Western civilization.

Keynesian theory explained what had happened, what could have been done to prevent the depression, and what could be done to prevent future depressions. The explanation soon became accepted by most macroeconomists, in the process described as the Keynesian revolution. The Keynesian revolution did not have much impact on economic policy making in the United States until the 1960s, but it affected macroeconomics much earlier than that, setting the foundation for modern macroeconomics.

The Keynesian Explanation

The essence of the Keynesian explanation of the great depression is based on the simple aggregate demand model developed in Chapter 3. Growth in the twenties, in this view, was based on the mass production of the automobile and radio and was fueled by a housing boom. The collapse of growth in the thirties resulted from the drying up of investment opportunities and a downward shift in investment demand. The collapse of investment, shown in Table 12-1, fits in with this picture. Some researchers also believe there was a downward shift in the consumption function in 1930.[8] Poor fiscal policy, as reflected in the perverse behavior of the full-employment surplus from 1931 to 1933, shares the blame, particularly for making the depression worse.

What does this view have to say about the monetary collapse? The Fed argued in the thirties that there was little it could have done to prevent the depression, because interest rates were already as low as they could possibly go. A variety of sayings of the type, "You can lead a horse to water but you can't make it drink," were used to explain that further reductions in interest rates would have had no effect if there was no demand for investment. Invest-

---

[7] In "The Process of Writing *The General Theory*: A Critical Survey," in Don Patinkin and J. Clark Leith (eds.), *Keynes, Cambridge and the General Theory* (Toronto: University of Toronto Press, 1978), p. 3. For a short biography of Keynes, see D. E. Moggridge, *John Maynard Keynes* (New York: Penguin Books, 1976).

[8] Peter Temin, *Did Monetary Forces Cause the Great Depression?* (New York: Norton, 1976).

ment demand was thought to be very unresponsive to the rate of interest—implying a very steep *IS* curve. At the same time, the *LM* curve was believed to be quite flat, though not necessarily reaching the extreme of a liquidity trap. In this situation, as we saw in Chapter 4, monetary expansion would be relatively ineffective in stimulating demand and output.

It was also widely believed that the experience of the depression showed that the private economy was inherently unstable in that it could self-depress with no difficulty if left alone. The experience of the thirties was, implicitly or explicitly, the basis for the belief that an active stabilization policy was needed to maintain good economic performance.

The Keynesian model not only offered an explanation of what had happened, but also suggested policy measures that could have been taken to prevent the depression, and that could be used to prevent future depressions. Vigorous use of countercyclical fiscal policy was the preferred method for reducing cyclical fluctuations. If a recession ever showed signs of deteriorating into a depression, the cure would be to cut taxes and increase government spending. And those policies would, too, have prevented the depression from being as deep as it was.

There is nothing in the *IS-LM* model developed in Chapter 4 that suggests fiscal policy is more useful than monetary policy for stabilization of the economy. Nonetheless, it is true that until the 1950s, Keynesians tended to give more emphasis to fiscal than to monetary policy.

The Monetarist Challenge

The Keynesian emphasis on fiscal policy, and its downplaying the role of money, was increasingly challenged by Milton Friedman and his coworkers[9] during the 1950s. During this period Friedman was developing much of the analysis and evidence that provided the basis for monetarism, which we describe in detail in Chapter 18. The main thrust was a heavy emphasis on the role of monetary policy in determining the behavior of both output and prices.

If monetary policy was to be given an important role, though, it was necessary to dispose of the view that monetary policy had been tried in the great depression and had failed. In other words, the view that "You can lead a horse to the water, etc.," had to be challenged.

The view that monetary policy in the thirties had been impotent was attacked in 1963 by Friedman and Schwartz in their *Monetary History*. They argued that the depression, far from showing that money does not matter, "is in fact a tragic testimonial to the importance of monetary factors."[10] They

---

[9] See, in particular, Milton Friedman (ed.), *Studies in the Quantity Theory of Money* (Chicago: University of Chicago Press, 1956).

[10] Friedman and Schwartz, op. cit., p. 300.

argued, with skill and style, that the failure of the Fed to prevent bank failures and the decline of the money stock from the end of 1930 to 1933 was largely responsible for the recession being as serious as it was. This monetary view, in turn, came close to being accepted as the orthodox explanation of the depression.[11]

Synthesis

Both the Keynesian and the monetarist explanations of the great depression fit the facts, and both provide answers to the question of why it happened, and how to prevent it from happening again. Inept fiscal and monetary policies both made the great depression severe. If there had been prompt, strong, expansive monetary and fiscal policy, the economy would have suffered a recession but not the trauma it did.

On the question of whether it could happen again, there is agreement that it could not, except, of course, in the event of truly perverse policies. But these are less likely now than they were then. For one thing, we have history to help us avoid its repetition. Taxes would not again be raised in the middle of a depression, nor would attempts be made to balance the budget. The Fed would seek actively to keep the money supply from falling. In addition, the government now has a much larger role in the economy than it did then. The higher level of government spending, which is relatively slow to change, and automatic stabilizers, including the income tax,[12] unemployment insurance, and Social Security, give the economy more stability than it had then.[13]

There is no inherent conflict between the Keynesian and monetarist explanations of the great depression. The *IS-LM* model, augmented by the supply-side analysis of wage and price adjustment in Chapter 7, easily combines both explanations. Why, then, has there been controversy over the causes of the great depression? The reason is that the thirties are seen as the period that set the stage for massive government intervention in the economy. Those opposed to an active role for government have to explain away the debacle of the economy in the thirties. If the depression occurred because of, and not despite, the government (particularly the Fed), the case for an active government role in economic stabilization is weakened. Further, the thirties are a period in which the economy behaved in such an extreme way that competing theories have to be subjected to the test of whether they can explain that

---

[11] Ben Bernanke, in "Nonmonetary Effects of the Financial Crisis in the Propagation of the Great Depression," *American Economic Review,* June 1983, takes issue with the monetary view, arguing instead that the destruction of the financial system made it difficult for borrowers to obtain funds needed for investment.

[12] Recall from Chap. 3 that a proportional income tax reduces the multiplier.

[13] See Martin Baily, "Stabilization Policy and Private Economic Behavior," *Brookings Papers on Economic Activity,* 1978: 1 (Washington, D.C.: The Brookings Institution, 1978).

period. Those are the main reasons the dispute over the causes of the great depression continues more than 50 years after it began.[14]

12-3 THE NEW ECONOMICS

Keynesian economics was rapidly accepted by most macroeconomists, but it affected policy less rapidly. The budget was used in Britain as a countercyclical policy tool in the entire post–World War II period. In the United States, the Employment Act of 1946 imposed on the government the obligation to follow policies that would produce high employment. Nonetheless, it was not until the Kennedy administration in the early 1960s that an administration began to follow avowedly Keynesian policies.

The approach was described as the *New Economics*. The analytical approach consists basically of the tools we have outlined in Chapters 3 through 11. The philosophy characterizing that approach to economics is a mix of activism and optimism. It is well characterized by an excerpt from the 1962 *Economic Report of the President* (page 68)[15]:

Insufficient demand means unemployment, idle capacity, and lost production. Excessive demand means inflation—general increases in prices and money incomes, bringing forth little or no gains in output and real income. The objective of stabilization policies is to minimize these deviations, i.e., to keep over-all demand in step with the basic production potential of the economy.

Stabilization does not mean a mere leveling off of peaks and troughs in production and employment. It does not mean trying to hold over-all demand for goods and services stable. It means minimizing deviations from a rising trend, not from an unchanging average. In a growing economy, demand must grow in order to maintain full employment of labor and full utilization of capacity at stable prices. The economy is not performing satisfactorily unless it is almost continuously setting new records of production, income, and employment. Indeed, unless production grows as fast as its potential, unemployment and idle capacity will also grow. And when the economy starts from a position well below potential, output must for a time grow even faster than potential to achieve full utilization.

---

[14] Among the relevant contributions is Michael Darby, "Three-and-a-Half Million U.S. Employees Have Been Mislaid: Or, an Explanation of Unemployment, 1934–1941," *Journal of Political Economy,* February 1976. Darby argues that unemployment is mismeasured after 1933 because those on government work relief programs are counted as unemployed. Adjusted for those individuals, the unemployment rate falls rapidly from 20.6 percent in 1933 to below 10 percent in 1936. See also Thomas Mayer, "Money and the Great Depression: A Critique of Professor Temin's Thesis," *Explorations in Economic History,* April 1978, and Karl Brunner (ed.), *The Great Depression Revisited* (Boston: Martinus Nijhoff, 1981).

[15] See, too, the history of the New Economics in W. W. Heller, *New Dimensions of Political Economy* (New York: Norton, 1967). Walter Heller, now a professor at the University of Minnesota, was one of the chief architects of the economic policies of the Kennedy-Johnson administration. With him, as members of the Council of Economic Advisers or staff economists, were highly distinguished economists: James Tobin, Kenneth Arrow, Robert Solow, Otto Eckstein, Gardner Ackley, and Arthur Okun. Paul A. Samuelson served as an unofficial adviser.

The contrast between economic policy in the thirties and economic policy in the sixties is marked. In the sixties, policy makers came into a not very difficult economic situation with well-thought-out theories and policies to apply. Those policies were based on the Keynesian analysis that developed in the thirties and out of the experience of the thirties. In the thirties, policy fumbled, and badly, for some way to get the economy moving again. The Roosevelt administration did run budget deficits, but most unwillingly, and it had no concept of the full-employment surplus; the Kennedy-Johnson administration, by contrast, planned a tax cut in 1963–1964 when the budget was in deficit, and sold the policy to a skeptical Congress.

The New Economics emphasized the goal of reattaining full employment after the high unemployment levels of the late 1950s. We briefly review the basic analytical concepts of the New Economics before concluding this section by discussing what was new in the New Economics.

Potential Output and the GNP Gap

To focus attention on the target of full employment and for use as an operating guide to policy, the *Council of Economic Advisers (CEA),* and particularly Arthur Okun, developed and stressed the concept of potential output. Potential output, or full-employment output, measures the level of real GNP the economy can produce with full employment. The full-employment rate of unemployment used in defining potential output in the sixties was about 4 percent.[16] Figure 12-3 shows potential output for the 1956–1971 period.

Along with the concept and measurement of potential output went the notion of the GNP gap. The gap is the difference between actual and potential real output. For the years 1961–1965, actual GNP was below its potential level, and the GNP gap was therefore positive. At the beginning of 1961, the GNP gap was more than 7 percent of GNP. A gap of that magnitude clearly called for expansionary monetary or fiscal policy to raise aggregate demand to a level closer to the economy's potential.

The notions of potential output and the GNP gap seem very simple, but they are important. They dramatize the costs of unemployment in easily understood terms of output lost due to unemployment—and make it easy to understand what alternative target levels of GNP, at which policy makers might aim, would mean for the level of unemployment.

The Full-Employment Budget Surplus

The full-employment budget surplus was discussed in Chapter 3, and we will therefore be brief here. The concept had been introduced before the 1960s,

---

[16] We introduced potential output in Chap. 1. Remember that we pointed out there that new measures of potential output (to be discussed in Chap. 18) take an unemployment rate of as much as 6 percent to represent full employment.

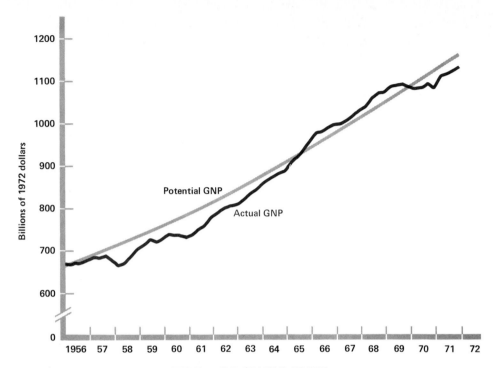

FIGURE 12-3   ACTUAL AND POTENTIAL GNP (BILLIONS OF 1972 DOLLARS) (*Source: The Survey of Current Business*, April 1982 and 1983, and Data Resources, Inc.)

most notably to study fiscal policy in the thirties. The concept is important and useful because it directs attention away from the actual budget, which is a misleading indicator of fiscal policy, toward the full-employment surplus — a more relevant, although still imperfect, indicator of policy.

The New Economists planned to use fiscal policy as the instrument with which to close the GNP gap. It was important for them to get across to Congress and the public the idea of the full-employment surplus because the federal budget was in actual deficit. Any proposals to increase spending or cut taxes would certainly imply a larger deficit. Congress could be relied upon to look with great suspicion on any policy that might increase the budget deficit. By focusing attention on the full-employment budget, the New Economists appropriately succeeded in shifting attention away from the state of the actual budget to concern with how the budget would look at full employment — which had the side benefit of focusing attention on the full-employment issue itself.

Growth

The New Economics emphasized economic growth in two ways. First, there was the need for aggregate demand to grow in order to achieve full employment. In that respect, growth was a matter of achieving full employment and maintaining it. Second, there was an emphasis on achieving a high rate of growth of potential output itself. The emphasis was on investment spending to encourage growth in productive potential. To that end the administration introduced an investment tax credit in 1962.

The Behavior of Money Wages

The New Economics emphasized the behavior of money wages in affecting the rate of inflation. This is in accord with the aggregate demand-supply analysis of Chapter 7, and with the more sophisticated analysis to follow in Chapter 14.

Early in the Kennedy-Johnson years, in 1962, the Council of Economics Advisers set up *guideposts*[17] for the behavior of money wages. The basic guidepost was that money wages should not grow faster than the average rate at which productivity was increasing in the economy. Labor productivity is the ratio of output to labor input.

When productivity is growing, less labor is being used to produce the same amount of goods. Thus if wages are growing as fast as productivity, the labor costs of producing a good are constant. Assuming, as the New Economics did, that prices are set as a markup on labor costs, prices would not rise if wages were rising no faster than productivity.

In setting up the criterion for noninflationary wage increases—that wages should not increase faster than labor productivity—the CEA also suggested that rapid investment could contribute to price stability. The notion was that rapid investment would increase the amount of capital employed in the production of output and would thus increase the productivity of labor. For a given rate of wage increase, this greater productivity would mean less inflation. High investment spending was thus thought helpful in containing inflationary pressures. A similar argument was advanced in the early 1980s by supply-side economists.[18]

---

[17] For an interesting, and sometimes amusing, discussion of the guideposts, see George P. Shultz (who later became famous in other contexts) and Robert Z. Aliber (eds.), *Guidelines* (Chicago: The University of Chicago Press, 1966).

[18] The argument that more rapid productivity growth helps reduce the inflation rate is correct, but it is important to get the orders of magnitude right. Given the growth rate of money, an increase in the growth rate of output results in a lower rate of inflation—because the demand for real balances grows faster when output grows faster. It is unlikely that a 1 percent increase in the growth rate of output would on those grounds reduce the inflation rate by more than 1 percent. Thus increased productivity growth, while of great importance for long-run standards of living (see Chap. 19), would not have large effects on inflation.

What Was New?

What was new about the New Economics? Was the approach to stabilization policy along the lines of fiscal activism, potential output objectives, and the emphasis on the full-employment budget surplus in fact new? The answer here is not simple. It is true that the activism the CEA displayed was unprecedented. But it is true, too, that the tools and concepts the Council used were mainline professional macroeconomics. The idea of active fiscal policy as a countercyclical measure and the notion that there was nothing particularly desirable about a balanced budget were certainly not new.

Even so, the active use of fiscal policy met much resistance in the political process at the time. Herbert Stein, himself chairperson of the CEA under President Nixon, reviews the progress toward the major policy measure of the early sixties, the 1964 tax cut, in his book *The Fiscal Revolution in America*.[19] He shows how the Kennedy administration first had to get accustomed to the idea that, during recession, a move toward an increased budget deficit was not a step toward fiscal irresponsibility. By the same token, Congress had to find its way toward expansionary fiscal policies, away from balanced budgets or tax cuts accompanied by offsetting reductions in public spending. Eventually, many recognized that a measure to expand aggregate demand was necessary to cope with high unemployment.

Thus, what was new about the New Economics was not the analysis, which was standard macroeconomics, but rather the active and successful use of that analysis in the operation of fiscal policy.

The New Economics and the Economy

The most ambitious and successful policy action of the Kennedy-Johnson administration was the tax cut of 1964, which we analyzed in Chapter 5. The tax cut kept the economy growing rapidly through the mid-sixties, thus reducing the unemployment rate. At the same time, as Figure 12-4 shows, the inflation rate stayed below 2.5 percent per year.

Through the middle of the sixties, the economy was behaving as well as it ever has. Productivity growth was high, output was growing fast, unemployment was falling, and the inflation rate was low. It is little wonder that there was considerable optimism about the possibilities of the New Economics.

In the late sixties things began to go wrong. Part of the problem was political. Government spending for the Vietnam war was rising rapidly, but President Johnson was not willing to push for a tax increase to finance the war, fearing that a tax increase would make the war more unpopular. In 1966 and 1967, it was left to monetary policy to fight the increasing expansionary pressure of fiscal policy. Only in 1968 was the Johnson administration willing

---

[19] Chicago: The University of Chicago Press, 1969.

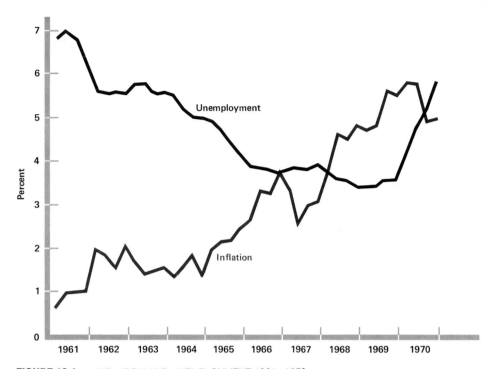

FIGURE 12-4   INFLATION AND UNEMPLOYMENT 1961–1970
(*Source:* Data Resources, Inc.)

to ask Congress for a tax increase to try to contain the expansionary pressure of military spending.

The decision was made to go for a transitory tax increase. The contractionary effect of the tax increase was overestimated, so that by the end of the Johnson administration at the beginning of 1969, the inflation rate was up to more than 5 percent. To be sure, the unemployment rate was below 4 percent, and the economy was still in its longest expansion on record: there was no recession between 1961 and 1969.

The record of the 1960s is one of full employment, expansion, and rising inflation. Keynesian economics, or the New Economics, received the popular credit for the expansion of the mid-sixties following the tax cut. Similarly, it received the blame for the rising inflation, even though many of the economic advisers to the President were urging a tax increase as early as 1966.

The apparent failure of the activist New Economics reopened the question of whether active monetary and fiscal policy could be used successfully to control the economy. We turn now to examine the general principles and problems of stabilization policy.

12-4 ECONOMIC DISTURBANCES

Before identifying in detail the obstacles in the way of successful policy making, we discuss economic disturbances in terms of their sources, persistence, and importance for policy. Disturbances are shifts in aggregate demand or aggregate supply, or shifts in money demand or money supply, that cause output, interest rates, or prices to diverge from their target paths.

FIGURE 12-5   AN AGGREGATE DEMAND DISTURBANCE. The economy is initially in equilibrium at point *E*, with level of output *Y**. An increase in government spending (for example, for defense) shifts the *IS* curve to *IS'*. This disturbance tends to raise the level of output above the full-employment level. Monetary and/or fiscal policy, or even rationing, may be used to try to keep the level of demand in check, shifting the *IS'* curve back to *IS* and/or shifting the *LM* curve up and to the left.

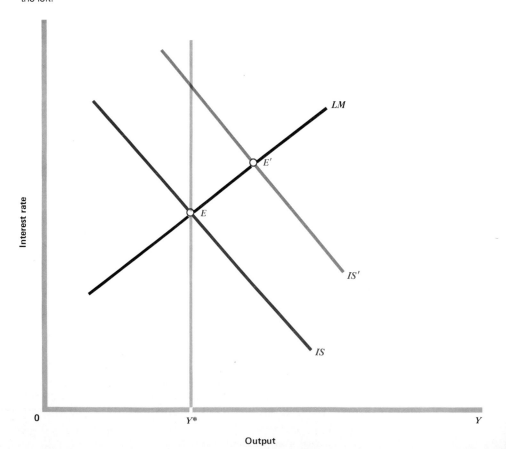

We return to the *IS-LM* model as the framework for the discussion of economic disturbances in this chapter. In Figure 12-5 we show the *IS* and *LM* schedules and also the full-employment level of output, Y^*. The economy is initially at full employment at point *E*. What disturbances might cause the economy to move away from full employment? Obviously, anything that shifts the *IS* and/or *LM* curves would disturb the economy and move it away from *E*.

In terms of overall economic impact, the major disturbances to the economy — the forces moving *IS* and *LM* curves — have typically been wars. The effects of the increases in government spending associated with World War II, the Korean war, and the Vietnam war can be seen in Figure 12-1 in the very low unemployment rates in those periods. Of these, World War II had the largest impact on the economy. At the height of the war, in 1944, federal government spending exceeded 40 percent of GNP.

As shown in Figure 12-5, the increase in government spending would shift the *IS* schedule upward. The aggregate demand curve in Chapter 7 shifts to the right, with both output and prices increasing. To free resources needed for war, the government will both raise taxes and perhaps run a tight monetary policy. But this is not usually enough to prevent wartime inflations.[20]

Changes in government spending or tax policies not connected with wars may also constitute economic disturbances. Government spending or taxes may be increased or reduced for reasons which have to do with the government's view of desirable social policies. Those changes too may affect the level of aggregate demand if not accompanied by appropriate monetary and fiscal policies.

Other economic disturbances that lead to changes in aggregate demand, which originate in the private sector, are shifts in the consumption or investment function. If consumers decide to consume more out of their disposable income at any given level of income, the *IS* curve of Figure 12-5 shifts upward, tending to increase the level of income. If there is no economic explanation for the shift in the consumption function, then it is attributed to a change in the tastes of consumers between consumption and saving. In such a case, we describe the shift as a disturbance.

Similarly, if investment spending increases for no apparent economic reason, then we attribute the increase to an unexplained change in the optimism of investors about the returns from investment. Again, we regard that change in investment behavior as a disturbance to the system. Changes in the optimism of investors are sometimes described as changes in their *animal spirits* — a term that suggests that there may be little rational basis for those

---

[20] Often *rationing* is used to limit private demand in wartime. For instance, in World War II, a system was set up in which investment projects had to be licensed. That system served to reduce the overall rate of private investment and also to direct investment toward areas helpful for the war effort. There was also some rationing of consumption goods, which reduced consumption expenditure as some of the rationed demand spilled over into increased saving rather than being diverted toward other goods. Thus, the aggregate level of consumption spending was reduced by using rationing to reduce the consumption of various goods essential for the war effort (gasoline, tires, meat, shoes, etc.).

spirits.[21] Some shifts in the investment function are caused by new inventions that require large amounts of investment for their successful marketing, such as the development of the railroads in the nineteenth century and the spread of the automobile in the 1920s.

Shifts in the demand for money may affect the interest rate, and thus indirectly affect the rate of investment; they, too, constitute a possible source of private sector economic disturbances.

Among other disturbances are increases in exports, caused by changes in foreigners' demand for our goods, which tend to increase the level of income. Changes in supply conditions, such as the oil price increases of 1973–1974 and 1979–1980 and the oil price decrease of 1985–1986, will affect the level of income. In addition, the behavior of wages may constitute a source of economic disturbances.

Finally, there is the interesting and important possibility that disturbances may be caused by the policy makers themselves. There are two different arguments concerning this possibility. First, since policy making is difficult, it is entirely possible that the attempts of policy makers to stabilize the economy could be counterproductive. Indeed, Friedman and Schwartz's influential view of the causes of the great depression[22] argues that the officials in charge of the Federal Reserve System in the early 1930s did not understand the workings of monetary policy and therefore carried out a policy that made the depression worse rather than better.

The second argument that policy makers themselves may be responsible for economic disturbances arises from the relationship between election results and economic conditions in the period before the election.[23] It appears that incumbents tend to be reelected when economic conditions, primarily the unemployment rate, are improving in the year before the election. Accordingly, it is tempting for incumbents to try to improve economic conditions in the period before the election; their efforts may involve tax reductions or increases in government spending. It is now quite common to talk of the *political business cycle*. The political business cycle consists of economic fluctuations produced by economic policies designed to help win elections.

While some evidence supports the notion of a political business cycle, the argument should be regarded as tentative because the link between economic conditions and election results is not yet firmly established.

We proceed next to discuss econometric models and the factors that make the task of policy makers far more difficult than an overliteral interpretation of the simple *IS-LM* model in Figure 12-5 might suggest.

---

[21] As we noted in Chap. 9, Keynes, in particular, argued that shifts in the investment function were a major cause of fluctuations in the economy. See J. M. Keynes, *The General Theory of Employment, Interest and Money* (New York: Macmillan, 1936), chap. 22.

[22] See Milton Friedman and Anna J. Schwartz, *The Great Contraction* (Princeton, N.J.: Princeton University Press, 1965).

[23] See, for example, Edward R. Tufte, *Political Control of the Economy* (Princeton, N.J.: Princeton University Press, 1978).

12-5 ECONOMETRIC MODELS FOR POLICY MAKING AND FORECASTING

In Figure 12-6 we show the typical situation facing economic policy makers. Something has happened that created a recession. Output is at level Y_0 rather than the full-employment level $Y°$. How should policy makers react if they want to get output back to the full-employment level? The *IS-LM* model gives a number of choices. One possibility is to increase the money stock. Or taxes could be reduced, or government spending increased.

Suppose the decision has been made to attempt to return to full employment at point $E°$, with the interest rate remaining at $i°$. Suppose also that the plan is to do this by increasing government spending and at the same time expanding the money supply. The *IS* curve has to be shifted to *IS'* and the *LM* curve to *LM'*.

Such plans are, however, not detailed enough. The policy makers need to know not only in what direction to shift government spending and the money stock, but also *how much* to change them. If government spending should be increased by $50 billion, it will not do much good to increase it by $5 billion. But if it should be increased by only $5 billion, an increase in government spending of $50 billion will push the economy well beyond the point of full

FIGURE 12-6 POLICIES TO END A RECESSION. The economy is in a recession at point E. Policy makers plan to return to full-employment output at the interest rate i^*, at point E^*. The *IS* curve has to be shifted to *IS'* and the *LM* curve to *LM'*. This requires expansionary fiscal and monetary policy. The precise amounts to increase government spending and the money stock can be calculated from the government spending and monetary policy multipliers.

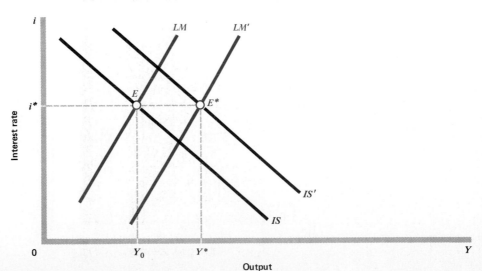

employment and create inflationary pressures. The policy makers have to know not only the medicines to prescribe, but also the right doses.

In other words, they have to know the *multipliers,* associated with monetary and fiscal policy. To calculate these multipliers, they typically rely on *econometric models.* An econometric model is an equation or a set of equations with numerical values for parameters, based on the past behavior of the economy, describing the behavior of some specific sectors of the economy or the economy as a whole.

Figure 12-7 shows estimates of the effects of monetary policy in the DRI (Data Resources, Inc.) model. The monetary policy change permanently increases the amount of unborrowed reserves held by the banks by $1 billion in period zero. The figure shows the resultant changes in GNP in subsequent periods. (The changes in GNP are measured as a percent of GNP.) There is very little change in GNP in period 1, but then the effect builds up, reaching a peak after 2 years before falling again.

FIGURE 12-7   MONETARY POLICY MULTIPLIERS FROM THE DRI MODEL. The figure shows the dynamic multipliers for a one-time increase in the nominal stock of M_1 of 3 percent that occurs during the first four quarters. For each quarter the figure shows the increase in the level of real output relative to the path the economy would otherwise have taken. Thus for the eighth quarter, for example, the 3 percent increase in money implies a rise of real GNP of 3.2 percent. By the eighteenth quarter, output is nearly back to its normal path. (*Source:* Data Resources, Inc.)

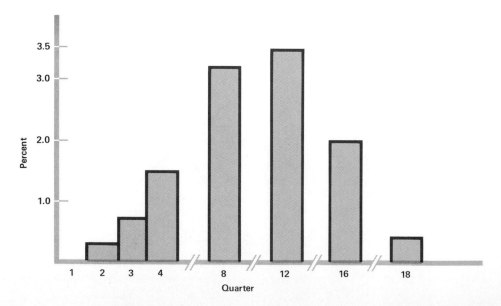

Figure 12-7 presents a *dynamic multiplier*, with the effects of monetary policy on real GNP first building up and then dying away.[24] The monetary policy multiplier in Figure 12-7 seems to be exactly what is needed for policy making. We thus want to look more closely at econometric models.

Econometric models that describe the entire economy are, as we should expect, called *macroeconometric models.*[25] Macroeconometric models differ enormously in size. The smallest model may be a single equation that estimates how the level of real GNP depends on the money stock and fiscal policy variables. By contrast, the WEFA (Wharton Econometric Forecasting Associates, Inc.) model attempts to predict 10,000 variables, among them the level of GNP, the inflation rate, interest rates, and prices and output levels in particular industries.[26]

The Big Models

Many econometric models are owned by corporations, which sell the forecasts and analyses produced by the models. The best known large commercial macroeconometric models are the **DRI** model, the Chase (Chase Econometric Associates Inc.) model, and the **WEFA** model. Customers receive the forecasts of the model for the behavior of the economy over the next few quarters and years.[27] These forecasts are based on assumptions about future economic policy and also about such important factors as future oil prices.

Macroeconometric models are also used by the government. The Federal Reserve Board in Washington uses a model it originally helped develop, now called the **MPS** (MIT-Penn-SSRC) model to predict the effects of different policy choices. The Department of Commerce maintains and uses the **BEA** (Bureau of Economic Analysis) model.

The models mentioned rely for the modeling of aggregate demand on an extended *IS-LM* framework. They estimate equations for the components of aggregate demand, consumption, different categories of investment, exports, and state and local government spending. The consumption function, for instance, would be similar to the sophisticated consumption function we discussed in Chapter 8. In modeling the financial markets, the models will typically include a money demand function similar to that which we presented in Chapter 10. They may also include a money supply *function* like that of Chap-

---

[24] Dynamic multipliers were defined in Chap. 8.

[25] We do not describe the statistical methods of estimating such models. For an introduction to the statistical methods, see Robert S. Pindyck and Daniel L. Rubinfield, *Econometric Models and Economic Forecasts*, 2d ed. (New York: McGraw Hill, 1981).

[26] See Stephen McNees, "The Track Record of Macroeconomic Forecasts," *New England Economic Review*, November/December 1983, and "Which Forecasts Should You Use?" in the same review, July/August 1985.

[27] Customers also typically obtain access to computer programs and data associated with the models.

ter 11, relating the stock of money to the supply of high-powered money. In brief, we can think of the aggregate demand side of most of the larger econometric models as attempts to describe statistically the extended *IS-LM* framework outlined in Chapters 4 and 5 and developed in Chapters 8 through 11.

There are, in addition, many smaller models with much less detail. Among these is the St. Louis model, produced by the St. Louis Federal Reserve Bank, which starts from an equation that links the behavior of nominal GNP to monetary and fiscal policy. It thus leaves out the details of the way in which policy affects the economy, and looks only at the final effects of policy. Four additional equations allow the model to predict the level of real as well as nominal GNP (and thus the GNP deflator and the inflation rate) and also to predict interest rates.

The aggregate supply side of the models typically builds on a Phillips curve linking wage changes to unemployment, and markup pricing, relating prices to wages.

Forecast Accuracy

How accurate are the models? There are many different models, none of them predicting exactly the same set of variables, and none of them predicting better than all the other models on all occasions. There is thus no simple answer to the question of how well econometric models in general predict.

Table 12-3 gives some idea of the accuracy of econometric forecasts. In November and December each year the Federal Reserve Bank of Richmond collects forecasts for the next year from a large number of different forecasters. At the end of 1985, for instance, the Richmond Fed collected 43 forecasts. Table 12-3 shows the median forecasts for the growth rate of real GNP and the inflation rate collected since 1980. We show, in addition, the average error made by the median forecasts over the period 1971–1985.[28] Also, we give what the Richmond Fed describes as typical forecasts for 1986. Since the final data for 1986 will be available only after this book is published, you will have to fill in for yourself in the table how well or badly the forecasters did in 1986.

It is quite clear from Table 12-3 that econometric forecasting is not perfect. A big error was made particularly in 1982. Forecasters did not expect a recession and overpredicted both output and inflation. But typically the forecasters do not make such large errors. For the other years shown, real GNP was generally about 1 percent from the predicted level.

Why do the forecasters make mistakes? One reason is that unexpected

---

[28] Two definitions are needed. First, the *median forecast* for each variable is the middle forecast when the forecasts are lined up in order. Second, the average error in Table 12-3 is the *average absolute error* — the average difference between the forecast and the actual value of the variable, whether positive or negative. For instance, if there are three forecasts, with errors of -3, -1, and 5, the average absolute error is 3 $[= (3 + 1 + 5)/3]$.

TABLE 12-3	ECONOMETRIC FORECASTS*					
	REAL GNP, % CHANGE			INFLATION RATE, GNP DEFLATOR		
Year	Actual	Predicted	Error	Actual	Predicted	Error
1980	−0.3	−0.8	−0.5	9.8	8.2	−1.6
1981	0.9	2.4	1.5	8.9	9.1	0.2
1982	−1.2	2.8	4.0	4.5	7.1	2.6
1983	3.5	2.5	−1.0	3.8	5.1	1.3
1984	6.5	5.2	−1.3	4.1	4.7	0.6
1985	2.3	3.3	1.0	3.3	4.1	0.8
Average error 1971–1985			1.6			1.5
1986	?	2.9		?	3.6	

* These are the median forecasts from those collected.

Source: Federal Reserve Bank of Richmond, *Business Forecasts*, various years.

events happen over the next year; for instance, economic policy may be different from that which the forecasters expected when they made their predictions, or the price of oil may rise — or, as in 1986, fall — unexpectedly. But this is not the only reason. A second reason is that the models themselves are not accurate. That is, even when the actual values of government spending, the money stock, the price of oil, etc., are fed into a model, it does not respond with the actual values of real GNP, or the inflation rate, or the unemployment rate. Why? Because we do not know accurately how the economy works.[29]

With this description of econometric models as background, we are ready to discuss the three handicaps of policy making: lags, expectations, and uncertainty about the effects of policy.

12-6 LAGS IN THE EFFECTS OF POLICY

Suppose that the economy was at full employment and has been affected by an aggregate demand disturbance that reduces the equilibrium level of income below full employment in Figure 12-6 toward point E. Suppose further that there was no advance warning of this disturbance and that, consequently, no

---

[29] Indeed, one of the most useful pieces of statistical information that comes with econometric model estimates is a measure of the confidence that can be attached to estimates of parameters and also multipliers.

policy actions were taken in anticipation of its occurrence. Policy makers now have to decide *whether at all* and *how* to respond to the disturbance.

The first concern—and the first difficulty—should be over the permanence of the disturbance and its subsequent effects. Suppose the disturbance is only transitory, such as a one-period reduction in consumption spending. When the disturbance is transitory so that consumption rapidly reverts to its initial level, the best policy may be to do nothing at all. Provided suppliers or producers do not mistakenly interpret the increase in demand as permanent but, rather, perceive it as transitory, they will absorb it by production and inventory changes rather than capacity adjustments. The disturbance will affect income in this period but will have very little permanent effect. Any policy actions taken to offset the disturbance this period, for example, a tax reduction, will have their impact on spending and income only over time. In later periods, however, the effects of the initial fall in demand on the level of income will be very small, and without the policy action the economy would tend to be very close to full employment. The effects of a tax cut, therefore, would be to raise income in later periods and move it away from the full-employment level. Thus, if the disturbance is temporary and it has no long-lived effects and policy operates with a lag, then the best policy is to do nothing.

Figure 12-8 illustrates the main issue. Assume an aggregate demand disturbance reduces output below potential, starting at time t_0. Without active policy intervention output declines for a while but then recovers and reaches the full-employment level again at time t_2. Consider next the path of GNP under an active stabilization policy, but one that works with the disadvantage of lags. Thus, expansionary policy might be initiated at time t_1 and start taking effect some time after. Output now tends to recover faster as a consequence of the expansion and, because of poor dosage and/or timing, actually overshoots the full-employment level. By time t_3, restrictive policy is initiated, and some time after, output starts turning down toward full employment and may well continue cycling for a while. If this is an accurate description of the potency or scope of stabilization policy, then the question must seriously arise whether it is worth trying to stabilize output or whether the effect of stabilization policy is, in fact, to make things worse. Stabilization policy may actually *destabilize* the economy.

One of the main difficulties of policy making is in establishing whether or not a disturbance is temporary. It was clear enough in the case of World War II that a high level of defense expenditures would be required for some years. However, in the case of the Arab oil embargo of 1973–1974, it was not clear at all how long the embargo would last or whether the high prices for oil that were established in late 1973 would persist. At the time, there were many who argued that the oil cartel would not survive and that oil prices would soon fall—that is, the disturbance was temporary. "Soon" turned out to be 12 years. Let us suppose, however, that it is known that the disturbance will have effects that will last for several quarters, and that the level of income will, without policy, be below the full-employment level for some time. What lags do policy makers encounter?

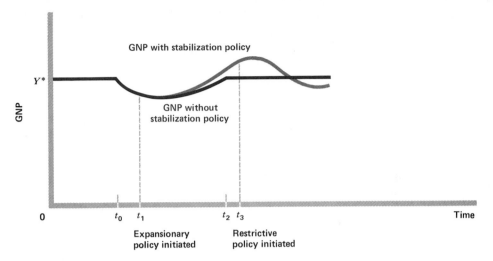

FIGURE 12-8   LAGS AND DESTABILIZING POLICY. A disturbance at time t_0 reduces output below the full-employment level. It takes until t_1 before policy responds, and there is a further lag until the policy starts working. By the time the full effects of the policy are evident, output would already have returned to the full-employment level even without policy. But because a policy action has been taken, output now rises *above* the full-employment level and then fluctuates around Y^*. The lags in policy thus have made policy a source of fluctuations in output that would not otherwise have happened.

We now consider the steps required before a policy can be taken after a disturbance has occurred, and then the process by which that policy action affects the economy. There are delays, or lags, at every stage. It is customary and useful to divide the lags into an *inside* lag, which is the time period it takes to undertake a policy action — such as a tax cut, or an increase in the money supply — and an *outside* lag, which describes the timing of the effects of the policy action on the economy. The inside lag, in turn, is divided into recognition, decision, and action lags.

The Recognition Lag

The *recognition lag* is the period that elapses between the time a disturbance occurs and the time the policy makers recognize that action is required. This lag could, in principle, be *negative* if the disturbance could be predicted and appropriate policy actions considered *before* it even occurs. For example, we know that seasonal factors affect behavior. Thus it is known that at Christmas the demand for currency is high. Rather than allow this to exert a restrictive effect on the money supply, the Fed will accommodate this seasonal demand by an expansion in high-powered money.

In other cases the recognition lag has been positive, so that some time has elapsed between the disturbance and the recognition that active policy was required. This was true, for example, of the 1974–1975 recession. The unemployment rate started increasing very rapidly in the third, and particularly in the fourth, quarter of 1974. It is now clear that expansionary action was required no later than September 1974. Yet, in October 1974, the administration was still calling for a tax *increase* to reduce aggregate demand and inflation. Only in January, in his State of the Union address, did the President call for a tax reduction, which was implemented in the Tax Reduction Act of 1975. Solow and Kareken have studied the history of policy making and have found that on average the recognition lag is about 5 months.[30] That lag was found to be somewhat shorter when the required policy was expansionary and somewhat longer when restrictive policy was required. The speed with which tax cuts follow sharp increases in unemployment was clearly evident in both 1975 and 1980.

The Decision and Action Lags

The recognition lag is the same for monetary and fiscal policy. The Federal Reserve Board, the Treasury, and the Council of Economic Advisers are in constant contact with one another and share their predictions about the future course of the economy. For the *decision lag*—the delay between the recognition of the need for action and a policy decision—by contrast there is a difference between monetary and fiscal policy. The Federal Reserve System's Open Market Committee meets frequently to discuss and decide on policy. Thus, once the need for a policy action has been recognized, the decision lag for monetary policy is short. Further, the *action lag*—the lag between the policy decision and its emplementation—for monetary policy is also short. The major monetary policy actions, we have seen, are open market operations and changes in the discount rate. These policy actions can be undertaken almost as soon as a decision has been made. Thus, under the existing arrangements for the Federal Reserve System, the decision lag for monetary policy is short and the action lag practically zero.

However, fiscal policy actions are less rapid. Once the need for a fiscal policy action has been recognized, the administration has to prepare legislation for that action. Next, the legislation has to be considered and approved by

---

[30] See John Kareken and Robert Solow, "Lags in Monetary Policy," in *Stabilization Policies,* pepared for the Commission on Money and Credit (Englewood Cliffs, N.J.: Prentice-Hall, 1963). See, too, the review of the evidence in Thomas Mayer, *Monetary Policy in the United States* (New York: Random House, 1968), chap. 6, and Michael J. Hamburger, "The Lag in the Effect of Monetary Policy: A Survey of the Recent Literature," Federal Reserve Bank of New York, *Monthly Review,* December 1971. This question has not, so far as we know, been reexamined recently.

both houses of Congress before the policy change can be made. That may be a lengthy process. Even after the legislation has been approved, the policy change has still to be put into effect. If the fiscal policy takes the form of a change in tax rates, it may be some time before the changes in tax rates begin to be reflected in paychecks — that is, there may be an action lag. On occasion, though, as in early 1975 when taxes were reduced, the fiscal decision lag may be short; in 1975 it was about 2 months.

The lengthy legislative process for fiscal policy in the United States has led to repeated suggestions that the President be granted the authority to undertake certain fiscal actions without legislation. One proposal is that the President should be allowed to vary tax rates by limited amounts in either direction without first obtaining specific authorization from Congress but subject to congressional veto.[31] This proposal would reduce the decision lag. Whether such a change is desirable from the economic viewpoint depends obviously on whether the President would, on average, make changes in tax rates that tend to offset disturbances to the economy. Do remember, though, the political business cycle.

Built-in Stabilizers

The existence of the inside lag of policy making focuses attention on the built-in or automatic stabilizers that we discussed in Chapter 3. One of the major benefits of automatic stabilizers is that their inside lag is zero. The most important automatic stabilizer is the income tax. It stabilizes the economy by reducing the multiplier effects of any disturbance to aggregate demand. The multiplier for the effects of changes in autonomous spending on GNP is inversely related to the income tax rate. The higher the tax rate, the smaller the effects of any given change in autonomous demand on GNP. Similarly, unemployment compensation is another automatic stabilizer. When workers become unemployed and reduce their consumption, that reduction in consumption demand tends to have multiplier effects on output. Those multiplier effects are reduced when a worker receives unemployment compensation and disposable income is reduced by less than the loss in earnings.

Figure 12-9 shows the practical importance of automatic stabilizers (and active fiscal policy) in the U.S. economy. The figure shows personal disposable income as a fraction of national income. Personal disposable income, as you will remember from Chapter 2, is the income that actually accrues to households after all taxes and inclusive of all transfers. The figure brings out the fact that during periods of a high GNP gap — the early sixties, the 1969–1971 period, 1974–1975, and 1981–1982 — personal disposable income rises relative to national income. In these periods, transfer payments rise and

---

[31] Report of the Commission on Money and Credit, *Money and Credit — Their Influence on Jobs, Prices and Growth* (Englewood Cliffs, N.J.: Prentice-Hall, 1961), pp. 133–137.

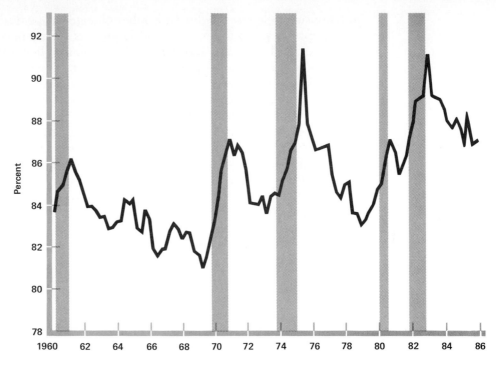

FIGURE 12-9   AUTOMATIC STABILIZERS: THE RATIO OF
PERSONAL DISPOSABLE INCOME TO NATIONAL INCOME.
(*Source:* Data Resources, Inc.)

the growth in income tax collection slows down.[32] In problem 9 we ask you
what the counterpart of the increase in the ratio of personal disposable income
to national income is in a recession. We also ask what ratio you would expect to
decline sharply when the ratio of personal disposable income to national
income rises.

Although built-in stabilizers have desirable effects, they cannot be carried too far without also affecting the overall performance of the economy.
The multiplier could be reduced to 1 by increasing the tax rate to 100 percent,
and that would appear to be a stabilizing influence on the economy. But with
100 percent marginal tax rates, the desire to work, and consequently the level

---

[32] To be precise, the chart reflects both automatic stabilizers and discretionary changes in taxes and transfers.
Thus the increase in the ratio in 1975 reflects not only automatic transfers but also the tax rebate of early 1975.
The data that would separate out the automatic stabilizers are not conveniently available.

of GNP, would be reduced. Thus there are limits on the extent to which automatic stabilizers are desirable.[33] Nonetheless, automatic stabilizers play an important role in the economy; it has been argued that the absence of significant unemployment compensation in the 1930s was one of the major factors that made the great depression so severe, and that the existence of the stabilizers alone makes the recurrence of such a deep depression unlikely.

The Outside Lag

The inside lag of policy is a discrete lag in which policy can have no effect on the economy until it is implemented. The outside lag is generally a distributed lag: once the policy action has been taken, its effects on the economy are spread over time. There is usually a small immediate effect of a policy action, but other effects occur later.

The idea that policy operates on aggregate demand and income with a distributed lag was already shown in Figure 12-7. There we showed the effects of a once-and-for-all increase in bank reserves in period zero. The impact of an increase in bank reserves (corresponding to an open market purchase by the Federal Reserve) is initially very small, and it continues to increase over a long period of time. Thus, if it were necessary to increase the level of employment rapidly to offset a demand disturbance, a large open market purchase would be necessary. But in later quarters, the large initial open market purchase would build up large effects on GNP, and those effects would probably over-correct the unemployment, leading to inflationary pressures. It would then be necessary to reverse the open market purchase and conduct open market sales to avoid the inflationary consequences of the initial open market purchase.

It should thus be clear that when policy acts slowly, with the impacts of policy building up over time, considerable skill is required of policy makers if their own attempts to correct an initially undesirable situation are not to lead to problems that themselves need correcting. Recall also that we have been talking here about the outside lag, and that the policy action we are considering would be taken only 6 months after the initial disturbance if the inside lag is 6 months long.

Why are there such long outside lags? Consider the example of monetary policy. Suppose the Fed conducts an open market purchase. Because aggregate demand depends heavily on lagged values of income, interest rates, and other economic variables, the open market purchase initially has effects mainly on short-term interest rates and not on income. Short-term interest rates, such as the Treasury bill rate, may affect long-term interest rates with a lag. The long-term interest rates, in turn, affect investment with a lag, and also

---

[33] For a discussion of the history of automatic stabilizers, see Herbert Stein, *The Fiscal Revolution in America* (Chicago: The University of Chicago Press, 1969).

affect consumption by affecting the value of wealth.[34] Then when aggregate demand is affected by the initial open market purchase, the increase in aggregate demand itself produces lagged effects on subsequent aggregate demand through the fact that both consumption and investment depend on past values of income. So the effects of an initial open market purchase will be spread through time, as in Figure 12-7.

Monetary versus Fiscal Policy Lags

The discussion of the previous paragraph suggests that fiscal policy and certainly changes in government spending, which act directly on aggregate demand, may affect income more rapidly than monetary policy. This is indeed the case. However, the fact that fiscal policy has a shorter outside lag must not lead us to overlook the fact that it has a considerably longer inside lag. Moreover, the inside lag for government spending is longer than that for taxes because when the government purchases goods and services, it has to decide what goods to buy, have bids for the sale of those goods submitted by the private sector, and then decide on the award of the contracts. In summary, therefore, fiscal policy is attractive because of the short outside lag, but that advantage is more than offset by a potentially long inside lag.

Our analysis of lags indicates clearly one difficulty in undertaking stabilizing short-term policy actions: it takes time to set the policies in action, and then the policies themselves take time to affect the economy. But that is not the only difficulty. Further difficulties considered in Sections 12-7 and 12-8 arise from uncertainty about the exact timing and magnitude of the effects of policy.

12-7 THE ROLE OF EXPECTATIONS

We have discussed the two basic sources of lags in economic behavior in earlier chapters. The first source is the cost of rapid adjustment. For example, in Chapter 9 we showed how the costs of adjusting the actual capital stock to the desired capital stock led to lags in the investment function. The second source of lags is expectations. In this section we focus on expectations, their formation, and the effects they have on policy and its effectiveness.

While it is undoubtedly true that the past behavior of a variable influences expectations about its future behavior, it is also true that consumers and investors will sometimes use more information than is contained in the past behavior of a variable when trying to predict its future behavior.

---

[34] Recall that in Chap. 8 we discussed the life-cycle model of consumption demand, in which consumption is affected by the level of wealth. Part of wealth is the value of stock market assets, which rises when the long-term interest rate falls. Thus, interest rates affect consumption through a wealth effect.

Consider, for example, forecasts of permanent income — long-run average income. In Chapter 8, as in Friedman's original work on the consumption function, permanent income is estimated as an average of income in the recent past. But, as we noted there, individuals take more information into account in forming expectations than just past levels of income. As emphasized by the rational expectations approach, individuals take all economically relevant information into account in forming expectations. Someone who discovers an oil well in the backyard today does not base the estimate of expected income on what he or she earned last year. Or, suppose that you have been estimating the expected rate of inflation as an average of past rates of inflation at a time when the inflation rate is high and a new government is elected on a strictly anti-inflationary platform. You would lower your estimate of the inflation rate; that is, you would use more information in predicting it than is contained solely in its past behavior.

It is, in general, very difficult to incorporate all relevant information that is used by economic agents within a simple econometric model. That means that there will inevitably be errors in what the models predict for the consequences of various policy actions, meaning, in turn, that it is difficult to control the economy precisely.

Expectations and Policy

It is particularly important to consider the effects of a given policy action itself on expectations, since it is possible that a new type of policy will affect the way in which expectations are formed.[35] Suppose that the Federal Reserve System announced a new monetary policy designed to stabilize the average level of income and avoid booms and recessions. The new policy would be to increase the money supply whenever the income level fell. Such a countercyclical rule has implications for expectations. Clearly, it would be inappropriate in the presence of such monetary policy to use an expectations mechanism that implies that an increase in income will persist. The monetary policy rule implies that the money supply should be reduced following an increase in income, and one expects the reduction in money to exert at least a dampening effect on income.

While correct expectations mechanisms must therefore use information about policy responses to disturbances, such care is difficult to apply in practice. Most expectations mechanisms embodied in econometric models of the U.S. economy and used for the assessment of policies assume that expectations affecting consumption and investment spending are based entirely on past values.

---

[35] The interactions of policy and expectations have been the focus of the rational expectations approach to macroeconomics. We have mentioned rational expectations in earlier chapters. Chapter 19 provides a full treatment. For an early statement, see Thomas J. Sargent and Neil Wallace, "Rational Expectations and the Theory of Economic Policy," *Journal of Monetary Economics*, April 1976, and William Fellner, *Towards a Reconstruction of Macroeconomics* (American Enterprise Institute, 1976).

Econometric Policy Evaluation Critique

The preceding example of the effects of a change in policy on expectations is part of a wider *econometric policy evaluation critique* formulated by Robert E. Lucas, of the University of Chicago, intellectual leader of the rational expectations approach to macroeconomics.[36] Lucas argues that existing macroeconometric models cannot be used to study the effects of policy changes *because the way private agents (firms and consumers) respond to changes in income and prices depends on the types of policy being followed.*

For example, suppose there is a change in income this period. How does consumption react? If policy is successful in keeping income always very close to potential, the change in income will be viewed as transitory, and there will be almost no change in consumption. But if policy is such that deviations of output from potential are typically prolonged, the change in income will be regarded as more permanent and the consumption response will be large. The key point is that the consumption response to changes in income depends on the types of policy being followed. Therefore one cannot use a consumption function which does not allow for this change in behavior to examine the effects of policy changes.

Lucas argues that problems of this sort are pervasive in macroeconometric models. He does not argue that it will never be possible to use econometric models to study policy — only that existing models cannot be used for that purpose.

Accordingly, the Lucas critique is not one that rules out the use of econometric models. It suggests rather that very careful modeling of the responses of consumers and firms to changes in income and prices is necessary. For instance, the consumption example above would not be impossible to handle, so long as permanent income were estimated as a weighted average of past incomes that changed appropriately as the behavior of income itself changed with policy.

Summary

This section has made two important points about the role of expectations in explaining the difficulties of policy making. First, the general point is that the difficulties of modeling the way in which expectations are formed will inevitably lead to errors in economists' forecasts of the effects of particular policy actions on the economy. The second point, a particular one, is that expectations themselves are likely to be affected by policy measures, and that failure to take account of the effects of policy on expectations will lead to mistaken predictions of the effects of those policies.

---

[36] See "Econometric Policy Evaluation: A Critique," in R. E. Lucas, Jr., *Studies in Business Cycle Theory* (Cambridge, Mass.: M.I.T. Press, 1981).

12-8 UNCERTAINTY AND ECONOMIC POLICY

So far in this chapter we have described the disturbances that affect the economy, econometric models that are used in policy making, the difficulties of making policy when there are long lags in the effects of policy, and the problem of modeling expectations. We can summarize most of the implied problems for policy making by saying that it is impossible to predict the effects of any given policy action exactly.

How should a policy maker react in the face of these uncertainties? We distinguish between uncertainty about the correct model of the economy and uncertainty about the precise values of the parameters or coefficients within a given model of the economy, even though the distinction is not watertight.

First, there is considerable disagreement and therefore uncertainty about the correct model of the economy, as evidenced by the large number of macroeconometric models. Reasonable economists can and do differ about what theory and empirical evidence suggest are the correct behavioral functions of the economy. Generally, each economist will have reasons for favoring one particular form and will use that form. But, being reasonable, the economist will recognize that the particular formulation being used may not be the correct one, and will thus regard its predictions as subject to a margin of error. In turn, policy makers will know that there are different predictions about the effects of a given policy, and will want to consider the range of predictions that are being made in deciding on policy.

Second, as we noted in Section 12-5, even within the context of a given model there is uncertainty about the values of parameters and multipliers. The statistical evidence does allow us to say something about the likely range of parameters or multipliers,[37] so that at least we can get some idea of the type of errors that could result from a particular policy action.

Uncertainty about the size of the effects that will result from any particular policy action is known as *multiplier uncertainty.* For instance, our best estimate of the multiplier of an increase in government spending might be 1.2. If GNP has to be increased by $60 billion, we would increase government spending by $50 billion. But the statistical evidence might be better interpreted as saying only that we can be quite confident the multiplier is between 0.9 and 1.5. In that case, when we increase government spending by $50 billion, we expect GNP to rise by some amount between $45 and $75 billion.

What is optimal behavior in the face of such multiplier uncertainty? The more precisely policy makers are informed about the relevant parameters, the more activist the policy can afford to be. Conversely, if there is a considerable range of error in the estimate of the relevant parameters — in our example, the

---

[37] We are discussing here confidence intervals about estimates of parameters; see Robert S. Pindyck and Daniel L. Rubinfeld, *Econometric Models and Economic Forecasts,* 2d ed. (New York: McGraw-Hill, 1980), for further discussion. This is the point made in footnote 29.

BOX

12-1

POLICY MAKING UNDER UNCERTAINTY: 1980

In October 1979, in response to the high and rising inflation, the Fed changed its policies with the intention of keeping money growth under control to fight inflation. (This change was discussed in Chapter 11.)

In the beginning of 1980 the inflation news was all bad, as Table 1 shows. From month to month the inflation rate was at an annual rate of about 18 percent. Much of this increase was due to higher oil prices, but the Fed and the administration, nonetheless, were deeply concerned over rising prices. Although a recession had been expected, and would reduce inflation if it happened, the unemployment rate hardly increased in early 1980. At the same time, the demand for loans in the economy was very high; firms and consumers were doing a lot of borrowing despite record high interest rates, which suggested that the demand for investment and con-sumer durables would be high—thus also suggesting that there would not be a recession.

Although interest rates were at record highs, monetary growth data presented a mixed picture. This was a period when the money stock measures were being redefined. $M1$ (there were then two versions) was growing reasonably slowly, while $M2$ was growing more rapidly. Thus judging from interest rates, monetary policy was restrictive, while judging from money growth, it was uncertain what was happening.

In March the administration acted. Worried by the continuing inflation and continuing high level of borrowing, the President announced a program of credit controls. Limits were placed on the amount of loans banks could make, and other steps were taken to reduce the growth of assets that were close substitutes for money, such as money market mutual funds. The growth rate of money ($M1$) had already started falling in March and was negative also for the next 2 months. Interest rates came down sharply in May and June.

The second quarter of 1980 saw the sharpest decline in GNP in a single quarter in the post–World War II period. The unemployment rate increased sharply from March to April and from April to May. The recession that had been widely expected was now fully visible. Indeed, the National Bureau of Economic Research later decided that the recession had begun in January 1980. Thus the credit controls were put in place after the recession had begun.

TABLE 1   ECONOMIC DATA, JANUARY–JUNE 1980*

Month	Inflation rate (CIP), % per annum	Civilian unemployment rate	Money growth rate ($M1B$), % per annum	Money growth rate ($M2$), % per annum	Treasury bill rate
January	18.7	6.2	5.4	7.3	12.0
February	17.8	6.2	10.4	10.0	12.8
March	18.7	6.3	−0.3	5.1	15.5
April	14.4	6.9	−13.2	−2.4	14.0
May	12.5	7.6	−1.2	9.9	9.2
June	14.1	7.5	15.6	19.7	7.0

* Inflation and money growth rates are one-month changes at annual rates.

Source: Economic Report of the President, 1981.

Most likely the credit controls were overkill. The economy was already into a recession when they were imposed. But policy makers and outside observers did not know that then. And the signs in early 1980 were, indeed, very mixed. The problem of policy making is that it cannot be done with the benefit of hindsight. But with the benefit of hindsight we can see that the policy makers in March 1980 were wrong about the current economic situation and the likelihood of recession. Such uncertainties about both the current situation and the future are certain to occur, and to complicate the policy-making task.

multiplier — then policy should be more modest. With poor information, very active policy runs a large danger of introducing unnecessary fluctuations in the economy.

12-9 ACTIVIST POLICY

We started this chapter by asking why there are any fluctuations in the American economy when the policy measures needed to iron out those fluctuations seem to be so simple. The list of difficulties in the way of successful policy making that we have outlined may have raised a different question: Why should one believe that policy can do anything to reduce fluctuations in the economy?

Indeed, considerations of the sort spelled out in the previous four sections have led Milton Friedman and others to argue that there should be no use of active countercyclical monetary policy,[38] and that monetary policy should be confined to making the money supply grow at a constant rate. The precise value of the constant rate of growth of money, Friedman suggests, is less important than the fact that monetary growth be constant and that policy should *not* respond to disturbances. At various times, he has suggested growth rates for money of 2 or 4 or 5 percent. As Friedman has expressed it, "By setting itself a steady course and keeping to it, the monetary authority could make a major contribution to promoting economic stability. By making that course one of steady but moderate growth in the quantity of money, it would make a major contribution to avoidance of either inflation or deflation of prices." [39] Friedman thus advocates a simple monetary rule in which the Fed does not respond to the condition of the economy. Policies that respond to the current or predicted state of the economy are called *activist policies.*

In discussing the desirability of activist monetary and fiscal policy, we want to distinguish between policy actions taken in response to major distur-

---

[38] See Milton Friedman, *A Program for Monetary Stability* (New York: Fordham University Press, 1959).
[39] Milton Friedman, "The Role of Monetary Policy," *American Economic Review,* March 1968.

bances to the economy and *fine tuning*, in which policy variables are continually adjusted in response to small disturbances in the economy. We see no case for arguing that monetary and fiscal policy should not be used actively in the face of major disturbances to the economy. Most of the considerations of the previous sections of this chapter indicate some uncertainty about the effects of policy, but there are still clearly definable circumstances in which there can be no doubt that the appropriate policy is expansionary or contractionary. An administration coming to power in 1933 should not have worried about the uncertainties associated with expansionary policy that we have outlined. The economy does not move from 25 percent unemployment to full employment in a short time (precisely because of those same lags that make policy difficult). Thus, expansionary measures, such as a rapid growth of the money supply, or increased government expenditures, or tax reductions, or all three, would have been appropriate policy since there was no chance they would have an impact only after the economy was at full employment. Similarly, contractionary policies for private demand are called for in wartime. In the fall of 1982, with unemployment rising above 10 percent and the inflation rate falling, expansionary monetary policy was clearly appropriate. In the event of large disturbances in the future, activist monetary and/or fiscal policy should once again be used.[40]

Fine tuning presents more complicated issues. In the case of fiscal policy, the long inside lags make discretionary fine tuning virtually impossible, though automatic stabilizers are in fact fine tuning all the time. But with monetary policy decisions being made frequently, fine tuning of monetary policy is indeed possible. The question then is whether a small increase in the unemployment rate should lead to a small increase in the growth rate of money, or whether policy should not respond until the increase in unemployment becomes large, say more than 1.0 percent.

The problem is that the disturbance that caused the increase in unemployment may be either transitory or permanent. If transitory, nothing should be done. If permanent, policy should react to a small disturbance in a small way. Given uncertainty over the nature of the disturbance, the technically correct response is a small one, between the zero that is appropriate for a transitory shock and the full response that would be appropriate for a permanent disturbance. Accordingly we believe that fine tuning is appropriate provided that policy responses are always kept small in response to small disturbances.

However, we should emphasize that the argument for fine tuning is a controversial one. The major argument against it is that in practice policy makers cannot behave as suggested — making only small adjustments to small disturbances. Rather, it is argued, they tend to try to do too much, if allowed to

---

[40] Interestingly, in the article cited in footnote 39, Friedman argues for the use of active policy in the face of major disturbances.

do anything. Instead of merely trying to offset disturbances, they attempt to keep the economy always at full employment and therefore undertake inappropriate large policy actions in response to small disturbances.

The major lesson of the previous sections is not that policy is impossible, but that policy that is too ambitious in trying to keep the economy always at full employment (with zero inflation) is impossible. The lesson is to proceed with extreme caution, always bearing in mind the possibility that policy itself may be destabilizing. We see no reason why the Federal Reserve System should try to keep the money supply always growing at the same rate; we believe, on the contrary, that the stability of the economy would be improved by its following a careful countercyclical policy. Similarly, if fiscal policy were not subject to a long inside lag, we would believe it possible for cautiously used active fiscal policy to be stabilizing.

Rules versus Discretion

Finally, in this chapter, we want to discuss the issue of "rules versus discretion." The issue is whether the monetary authority and also the fiscal authority should conduct policy in accordance with a preannounced rule that describes precisely how their policy variables will be determined in all future situations, or whether they should be allowed to use their discretion in determining the values of the policy variables at different times.

One example is the constant growth rate rule, say, at 4 percent, for monetary policy. The rule is that no matter what happens, the money supply will be kept growing at 4 percent.[41] Another example would be a rule stating that the money supply growth rate will be increased by 2 percent per year for every 1 percent unemployment in excess of, say, 5 percent. Algebraically, such a rule would be expressed as

$$\frac{\Delta M}{M} = 4.0 + 2(u - 5.0) \tag{1}$$

where the growth rate of money $\Delta M/M$ is at an annual percentage rate, and u is the percentage unemployment rate.

The activist monetary rule of equation (1) is shown in Figure 12-10. On the horizontal axis, we show the unemployment rate, and on the vertical axis, the growth rate of the money stock. At 5 percent unemployment, monetary growth is 4 percent. If unemployment rises above 5 percent, monetary growth is *automatically* increased. Thus, with 7 percent unemployment, monetary growth would be 8 percent. Conversely, if unemployment dropped below 5 percent, monetary growth would be lowered below 4 percent. The rule there-

---

[41] Recall from Chap. 11 that although the monetary authority cannot control the money supply and its growth rate exactly, it is able to control the high-powered money stock with considerable accuracy.

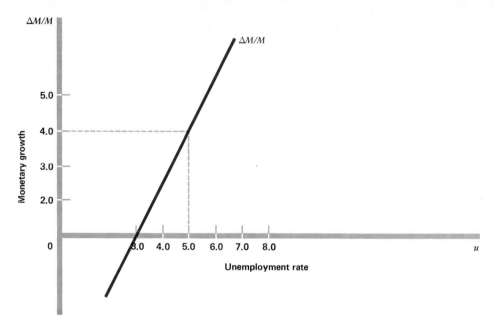

FIGURE 12-10   AN ACTIVIST MONETARY RULE. The figure
describes an activist monetary rule. The growth rate of money is high
when the unemployment rate is high and is low when unemployment is
low. That way monetary policy is expansionary at times of recession
and contractionary in a boom.

fore gears the amount of monetary stimulus to an indicator of the business
cycle. By linking monetary growth to the unemployment rate, an activist,
anticyclical monetary policy is achieved, but this is done without any discretion.

The issue of rules versus discretion has been clouded by the fact that most
proponents of rules have been nonactivist, whose preferred monetary rule is a
constant growth rate rule. Consequently, the argument has tended to center
on whether activist policy is desirable or not. The fundamental point to recognize is that we can design *activist rules*. We can design rules that have countercyclical features without at the same time leaving any discretion in their
actions to policy makers. The point is made by equation (1), which is an activist
rule because it expands money when unemployment is high and reduces it
when unemployment is low. It leaves no room for policy discretion and in this
respect is a rule.

Given that the economy and our knowledge of it are both changing over
time, there is no economic case for stating permanent policy rules that would
tie the hands of the monetary and fiscal authorities permanently. Two practi-

BOX

12-2

DYNAMIC INCONSISTENCY AND
RULES VERSUS DISCRETION

In the last decade economists have developed an intriguing argument in favor of rules rather than discretion. The argument is that policy makers who have discretion will in the end not act consistently, even though it would be better for the economy in the long run if they were consistent.*

How can that be? Here is a noneconomic example. By threatening to punish their children, parents can generally make the children behave better. So long as the children behave well, all is well. But when a child misbehaves, the parent has a problem, since punishing the child is unpleasant for both parent and child. One solution is not to punish but to threaten to punish next time. But if there was no punishment this time, there is unlikely to be punishment next time either, and the threat loses its beneficial effect. The dynamically consistent parent should use punishment each time the child misbehaves, thereby producing better behavior in the long run despite its short-run cost.

What does this have to do with economics? Suppose the inflation rate has risen because of a supply shock. The Fed is considering whether to accommodate it by expanding the money supply or not. If the Fed accommodates, prices will rise more now, but there will be less unemployment. So that seems like a good thing to do. This is the equivalent of not punishing the misbehaving child. But — warn those in favor of rules who worry about dynamic consistency — if the Fed accommodates every inflationary pressure because it fears unemployment, people will soon come to expect it to do that, and they will build an allowance for expected inflation into the wages they set. The Fed will lose whatever reputation it had as an inflation fighter, and the economy will develop an inflationary bias with the inflation rate creeping up over time.

Much better, says the dynamic consistency approach, that the Fed should have a rule that prevents it from making responses that are right from the short-run viewpoint but wrong from the long-run perspective. Those who nonetheless favor discretion for the Fed emphasize the importance of preserving flexibility for monetary policy. To the dynamic inconsistency argument, they counter that as long as the Fed is aware that having a good reputation helps it keep the inflation rate low, it will take any loss of reputation into account when it decides how to respond to particular shocks, and thus will not be dynamically inconsistent.

---

* The basic reference is Finn Kydland and Edward Prescott, "Rules Rather than Discretion; The Inconsistency of Optimal Plans," *Journal of Political Economy*, June 1977. This is very difficult reading.

cal issues then arise in the rules-versus-discretion debate. The first is where the authority to change the rule is located. At one extreme, the growth rate of money could be prescribed by the Constitution. At the other it is left to the Fed or the Fisc (which would be the equivalent fiscal policy making body). In each case policy can be changed, but changing the Constitution takes longer than it takes the Fed to change its policy. In the tradeoff between certainty about future policy and flexibility of policy, activists place a premium on flexibility, and those in favor of rules that are difficult to change place a premium on the fact that the Fed has often made mistakes in the past. Because the financial system responds very quickly to shocks, and is so interconnected, we believe it essential that the Fed have considerable discretion and thus flexibility to respond to disturbances. But that is far from a universal judgment.

The second issue is whether the policy makers should announce in advance the policies they will be following for the foreseeable future. Such announcements are in principle desirable because they aid private individuals to forecast future policy. In fact as we described in Chapter 11, the chairperson of the Fed has been required to announce to Congress the Fed's monetary targets. In practice, however, these announcements have not been a great help because the Fed does not stick to its targets. If the Fed is able by departing from announced policy to keep output close to potential and inflation low, then it helps private individuals forecast the variables in which they are really interested—their future incomes and, in the case of firms, the demand for their goods—rather than those like the money supply that they need know only as an intermediate step in forecasting.

12-10 SUMMARY

1. Despite the apparent simplicity of policies needed to maintain continuous full employment, the historical record of the behavior of unemployment, shown in Figure 12-1, implies that successful stabilization policy is difficult to carry out.

2. The great depression shaped both modern macroeconomics and many of the economy's institutions. The extremely high unemployment and the length of the depression led to the view that the private economy was unstable and that government intervention was needed to maintain high employment levels.

3. Keynesian economics succeeded because it seemed to explain the causes of the great depression—a collapse of investment demand—and because it pointed to expansionary fiscal policy as a means of preventing future depressions.

4. Keynesian views did not much affect economic policy making in the United States until the New Economics of the Kennedy-Johnson administration. The greatest success of the New Economics, was the tax cut of 1964. The New Economics is perceived by the public as having been responsible for increasing inflation during the sixties. As confidence in the New Economics declined, its emphasis on active stabilization policy was reexamined.

5. The potential need for stabilizing policy actions arises from economic disturbances. Some of these disturbances, such as changes in money demand, consumption spending, or investment demand, arise from within the private sector. Others, such as wars, may arise for noneconomic reasons.

6. Inappropriate economic policy may also tend to move the economy away from full employment. Policy may be inappropriate because policy makers make mistakes or because policy is manipulated for political reasons, leading to the political business cycle.

7. Policy makers work with econometric models in predicting the effects of their policy actions. Econometric models are typically statistical descriptions of the types of model we have worked with in earlier chapters. The models do not forecast with perfect accuracy, partly because they cannot forecast policy and disturbances such as changes in the price of oil. But, in addition, their forecasts are inaccurate because we do not have accurate knowledge of the workings of the economy.

8. The three key difficulties of stabilization policy are that (*i*) policy works with lags; (*ii*) the outcome of policy depends very much on private-sector expectations, which are difficult to predict and which may react to policy; and (*iii*) there is uncertainty about both the structure of the economy and shocks that hit the economy.

9. There are clearly occasions on which active monetary and fiscal policy actions should be taken to stabilize the economy. These are situations in which the economy has been affected by major disturbances.

10. Fine tuning — continuous attempts to stabilize the economy in the face of small disturbances — is more controversial. If fine tuning is undertaken, it calls for small policy responses in an attempt to moderate the economy's fluctuations, rather than to remove them entirely. A very active policy in response to small disturbances is likely to destabilize the economy.

11. In the rules-versus-discretion debate, it is important to recognize that activist rules are possible. The two important issues in the debate are how difficult it should be to change policy, and whether policy should be announced as far ahead as possible. There is a tradeoff between the certainty about future policy that comes from rules, and the flexibility of the policy makers in responding to shocks.

KEY TERMS

New Deal	Action lag
New Economics	Outside lag
Economic disturbances	Multiplier uncertainty
Political business cycle	Activist policy
Econometric models	Policy rule
Macroeconometric models	Fine tuning
Inside lag	Rules versus discretion
Recognition lag	Dynamic consistency
Decision lag	

PROBLEMS

1. It is sometimes said that the great depression would have been a severe recession if it had stopped in 1931, but would not have been the calamity it was.
   (a) From Table 12-1 calculate the rate at which GNP was falling from 1929 to 1931.

(b) How does this compare with the rate at which real GNP fell during the 1981–1982 recession?

(c) Do you agree with the first sentence in this question? Explain.

2. Using Table 12-2, explain why concentration on the actual budget deficit might have given a misleading impression of fiscal policy at some stages between 1929 and 1933.

3. In Table 12-1 examine the behavior of the short-term (commercial paper) interest rate and the growth rate of money. Explain why a Keynesian might have thought monetary policy was expansionary during the great depression, while a monetarist would argue that monetary policy was, on the contrary, contractionary.

4. Suppose that GNP is $40 billion below its potential level. It is expected that the next period GNP will be $20 billion below potential, and two periods from now it will be back at its potential level. You are told that the multiplier for government spending is 2 and that the effects of the increased government spending are immediate. What policy actions can be taken to put GNP back on target each period?

5. The basic facts about the path of GNP are as above. But there is now a one-period outside lag for government spending. Decisions to spend today are translated into actual spending only tomorrow. The multiplier for government spending is still 2 in the period that the spending takes place.

(a) What is the best that can be done to keep GNP as close to target as possible each period?

(b) Compare the path of GNP in this question with the path in problem 4, after policy actions have been taken.

6. Life has become more complicated. Government spending works with a distributed lag. Now when $1 billion is spent today, GNP increases by $1 billion this period and $1.5 billion next period.

(a) What happens to the path of GNP if government spending rises enough this period to put GNP back to its potential level this period?

(b) Suppose fiscal policy actions are taken to put GNP at its potential level this period. What fiscal policy will be needed to put GNP on target next period?

(c) Explain why the government has to be so active in keeping GNP on target in this case.

7. Suppose that you knew that the multiplier for government spending was between 1 and 2.5, but that its effects were all over in the period that spending was increased. How would you run fiscal policy if GNP would, without policy, behave as in problem 4?

8. Explain why monetary policy works with a distributed lag, as in Figure 12-7.

9. In Figure 12-9 we show how the ratio of disposable personal income to national income changes between booms and recessions. Go back to Table 2-6 and then explain:

(a) What component of the adjustment between national income and personal income moves with automatic stabilizers to produce the cyclical behavior seen in Figure 12-9?

(b) What other component in that table is likely to fall sharply during recessions?

10. (a) Check the *Economic Report of the President* for 1987 or some other publication (for example, *Survey of Current Business, Economic Indicators*) to see how accurate the typical forecast in Table 12-3 was for 1986.

(b) Explain why econometric forecasts are not totally accurate.

11. Evaluate the argument that monetary policy should be determined by a rule rather than discretion. How about fiscal policy?

12. Evaluate the arguments for a constant growth rate rule for money.

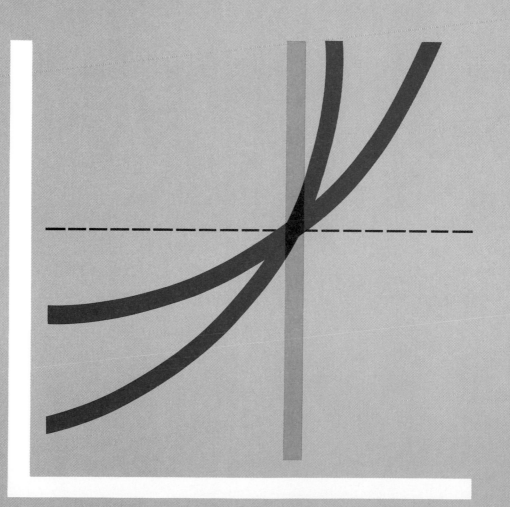

13

AGGREGATE SUPPLY: WAGES, PRICES AND EMPLOYMENT

In this chapter and the next we develop the aggregate supply side of the economy. We show the links between wages, prices, and employment, and the adjustment process to disturbances in aggregate demand — monetary or fiscal policy changes or autonomous changes in spending. The development of the aggregate supply side of the economy also allows us to study how the economy adjusts to *supply shocks*, such as the increases in oil prices in 1973–1974 and 1979–1980, or the decline in oil prices in 1985–1986.

The supply side of the economy is an essential part of the *dynamics* of prices (inflation) and output, that is, of the adjustment of prices and output over time when the economy is hit by a disturbance. Investing time in studying aggregate supply is worthwhile because the theory is needed to understand inflation and, in particular, the policy dilemma that comes from the existence of a short-run tradeoff between inflation and unemployment.

The theory of aggregate supply is one of the least settled areas in macroeconomics. The difficulty arises from the contrast between an idealized world in which output is always at the full employment level and the fact that the labor market in particular seems to adjust slowly to changes in aggregate demand. We start with the frictionless neoclassical model of the labor market to illustrate how the labor market might work in an idealized model. Then in Section 13-2 we present the Phillips curve, which shows the basic fact that wages adjust slowly to changes in aggregate demand. This fact is explained in terms of wage-setting behavior in Section 13-3. In Sections 13-4 and 13-5 we develop a theory of aggregate supply that is consistent with and accounts for the behavior of wages seen in the Phillips curve. We use that theory in Section 13-6 to study the response of the economy to supply shocks.

13-1 THE FRICTIONLESS NEOCLASSICAL MODEL OF THE LABOR MARKET

We have already shown the vertical aggregate supply curve of the classical case that exists when the labor market clears continuously and immediately in response to shocks (Chapter 7). In this section we derive this classical aggregate supply curve starting from microeconomic foundations.

Figure 13-1 presents a microeconomic analysis of the labor market. There is a downward-sloping demand curve for labor, *ND*: the quantity of labor demanded is greater the lower is the real wage. The real wage is the ratio of the wage rate to the price level, or the amount of goods that can be bought with an hour of work. Also shown is an upward-sloping supply curve of labor *NS*, indicating that workers want to supply more hours of work the higher the real wage.

The full derivation of the demand curve for labor in Figure 13-1 is presented in the appendix to this chapter. The demand curve slopes downward because it is assumed that the marginal productivity of labor decreases as more labor is employed. Firms are competitive and are therefore willing to pay a real wage equal to the value of the marginal product of labor. There is a fixed amount of capital. As more labor is added, each new worker has less machinery with which to cooperate than the previous workers, and therefore the amount the new worker adds to output (the marginal product of labor) is lower than the amount added by the previous workers. The marginal productivity of labor is thus declining, and the demand curve slopes downward.

The supply curve of labor is shown as upward-sloping because typically as the wage rises more workers come into the labor force seeking work. But the aggregate supply curve could be vertical (or completely inelastic) if the amount of labor supplied is insensitive to the real wage.[1]

The labor supply and demand curves intersect at point *E*, with a corresponding level of labor input or employment N^* and an equilibrium real wage $(W/P)^*$. N^* is the *full-employment level of employment*. In this idealized fric-

---

[1] If you have studied microeconomics, you have probably seen the "backward-bending" labor supply curve, which is negatively sloped at high wages. That occurs because when the wage rises, individuals can both work less and earn more income. They may choose to respond to higher wages by working less. Although the labor supply curve may well slope backward in the long run (we work fewer hours than our grandparents and have much higher wages than they did) the supply curve of labor *for the economy* in the short run of a few years is positively sloped. That is because as the wage rises, people who were not working decide it is worthwhile to take a job rather than work at home, and they enter the labor force. Further, people already on the job may in the short run want to work longer hours when the real wage rises.

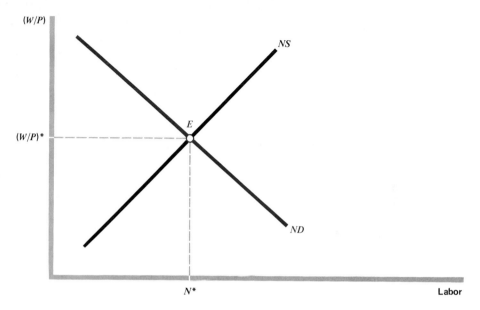

FIGURE 13-1 LABOR MARKET EQUILIBRIUM AND FULL EMPLOY-
MENT. The labor supply curve NS shows the quantity of labor supplied
increasing with the real wage. Along ND a reduction in the real wage
causes an increase in the quantity of labor demanded. The labor market
is in equilibrium at point E.

tionless neoclassical model, everyone is working precisely the amount he or
she wants to at the going wage, $(W/P)^*$ at point E. And firms are hiring
precisely the amount of labor they want at the real wage $(W/P)^*$ at point E.
There is always full employment in the frictionless neoclassical world.[2]

Corresponding to the full-employment level of employment N^* is the
full-employment level of output Y^*. That is the level of output that is produced
using the existing amounts of other factors (the capital stock, land, raw materials) and the full-employment amount of labor N^*.

A Change in the Quantity of Money

In Figure 13-2 we show the labor supply and demand curves with the *nominal*
wage on the vertical axis. The price level is assumed to be at a given level, say

---

[2] In our description here, technology and the stock of capital are given. But these can change and, as a result, the
full-employment level of output will change too. For example, an increase in the capital stock will raise
full-employment output, as does an improvement in technology.

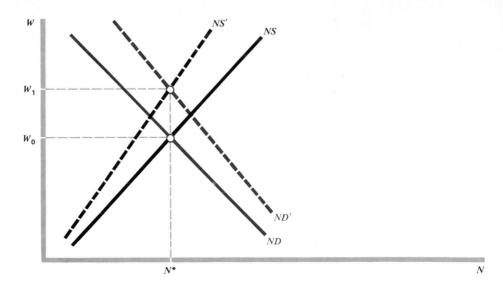

FIGURE 13-2 THE EFFECTS OF A CHANGE IN THE PRICE LEVEL ON THE LABOR MARKET. Labor supply and demand curves NS and ND are shown for a constant price level. An increase in the price level shifts both curves upward in the same proportion, to NS' and ND', respectively. The equilibrium level of employment N^* is unaffected by the change in the price level.

P_0. With a constant price level, a change in the nominal wage is also a change in the real wage, and the labor supply and demand curves thus look exactly as they do in Figure 13-1. The equilibrium nominal wage is W_0.

Now suppose there is an increase in aggregate demand, say because the Fed increases the quantity of money. At the existing price and wage levels the real money stock M/P is higher and interest rates are lower. Hence more goods will be demanded. Suppose that the increase in the demand for goods raises the price level above P_0. Then both the labor demand and supply curves in Figure 13-2 will shift up to ND' and NS', respectively.

The two curves shift upward by exactly the same proportion since, at each level of the nominal wage, the real wage is now lower in the same proportion as the price level has risen. When the two curves shift upward by the same proportion, they intersect at the same level of employment N^*. Thus the level of employment will remain at N^* despite the increase in the price level. The nominal wage rises, in Figure 13-2 to the level W_1, but the real wage remains unchanged. Indeed, any increase in the price level will simply shift both curves by the same vertical distance, leaving the level of employment unaffected. Only when the price level has risen in the same proportion as the money stock, will the economy be back in equilibrium with the same real balances, the same real wage, and the same level of employment. Money is neutral in this frictionless neoclassical world, as we saw at the end of Chapter 7.

Frictional Unemployment and the Natural Rate of Unemployment

Taken literally the frictionless neoclassical model implies that there is no unemployment. But by including frictions, the theory can account for some unemployment of labor. The frictions occur because the labor market is always in a state of flux. Some people are retiring from their jobs, other people are looking for jobs for the first time, some firms are expanding and are hiring new workers, others have lost business and have to contract, firing workers.

Because it takes time for an individual to find the right new job, there will always be some *frictional* unemployment as people search for jobs. Frictional unemployment is the unemployment that exists as a result of individuals shifting between jobs and looking for new jobs.

There is some amount of frictional employment associated with the full-employment level of employment N^* and full-employment level of output Y^*. That amount of unemployment is called the *natural rate.* The natural rate of unemployment is the rate of unemployment arising from labor market frictions that exists when the labor market is in equilibrium.

We do not go into the determinants and estimates of the natural rate of unemployment here, reserving that for Chapter 15. We merely note that the natural rate has been estimated at different times at 4 to 7 percent of the labor force.

The important point is that the existence of some unemployment is not necessarily inconsistent with the neoclassical model of the labor market in which the economy is always at the full employment level of output.

13-2 WAGES, PRICES, AND OUTPUT: THE FACTS

Two major implications of the neoclassical theory of the labor market are at odds with the facts. First, the rate of unemployment fluctuates far more than is consistent with the view that all unemployment is frictional. Figure 13-3 shows the unemployment rate for the period since 1950. It cannot be that the 10 percent unemployment, seen in 1982, is equal to the natural rate. Thus it cannot be that the labor market was always in equilibrium at the full-employment level of employment over the period since 1950. Much less can it be believed that the labor market was at the full-employment level of employment in 1933 when the unemployment rate was 25 percent of the labor force.

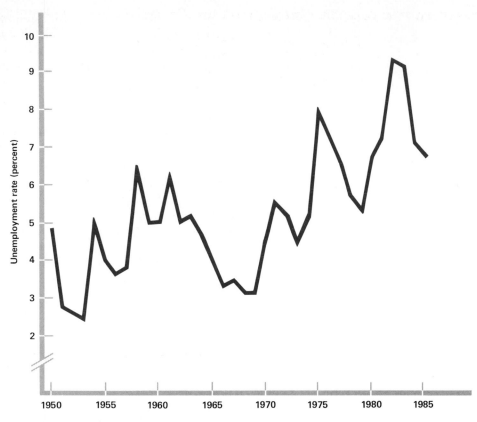

FIGURE 13-3 THE U.S. UNEMPLOYMENT RATE, 1950–1985.
(*Source:* Data Resources, Inc.)

The Phillips Curve

The second fact that is inconsistent with the neoclassical theory is that the wage appears to adjust slowly in response to shifts in aggregate demand. The notion that an increase in aggregate demand will first affect output and employment, and only then wages and prices, is an old one.

The notion is made precise in the *Phillips curve*. In 1958 A. W. Phillips, then a professor at the London School of Economics, published a comprehensive study of wage behavior in the United Kingdom for the years 1861–1957.[3] The main finding is summarized in Figure 13-4, reproduced from his article:

[3] A. W. Phillips, "The Relation between Unemployment and the Rate of Change of Money Wages in the United Kingdom, 1861–1957," *Economica*, November 1958.

The Phillips curve is an inverse relationship between the rate of unemployment and the rate of increase of money wages: The higher the rate of unemployment, the lower the rate of wage inflation. In other words, there is a tradeoff between wage inflation and unemployment.

The Phillips curve shows that the rate of wage inflation decreases with the unemployment rate. Letting W be the wage this period, and W_{-1} the wage last period, the rate of wage inflation gW is defined as

$$gW = \frac{W - W_{-1}}{W_{-1}} \tag{1}$$

With u° representing the natural rate of unemployment we can write the

FIGURE 13-4   THE ORIGINAL PHILLIPS CURVE FOR THE UNITED KINGDOM. (*Source:* A. W. Phillips, "The Relation between Unemployment and the Rate of Change of Money Wages in the United Kingdom, 1861–1957," *Economica*, November 1958.)

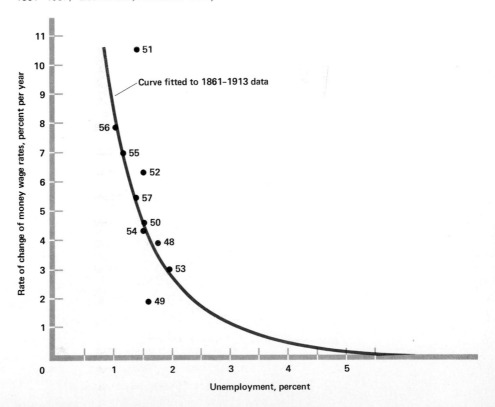

simple Phillips curve as

$$gW = -\epsilon(u - u^*) \qquad (2)$$

This equation states that wages are falling when the unemployment rate exceeds the natural rate, $u > u^*$, and rising when unemployment is below the natural rate.

The Phillips curve implies that wages and prices adjust slowly to changes in aggregate demand. Why? Suppose the economy is in equilibrium with prices stable and unemployment at the natural rate. Now there is an increase in the money stock by say 10 percent. Prices and wages both have to rise by 10 percent for the economy to get back to equilibrium. But the Phillips curve shows that for wages to rise by an extra 10 percent, the unemployment rate will have to fall. That will cause the rate of wage increase to go up. Wages will start rising, prices too will rise, and eventually the economy will return to the full-employment level of output and unemployment. But in the meantime the increase in the money stock caused a reduction in unemployment. This point

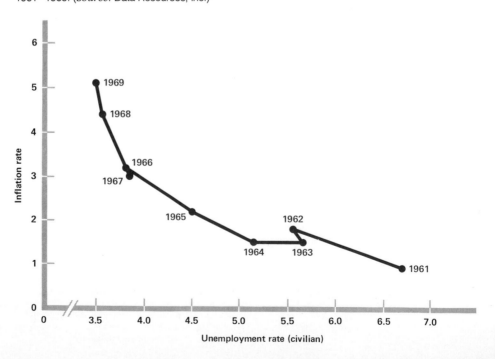

FIGURE 13-5   INFLATION AND UNEMPLOYMENT, UNITED STATES, 1961–1969. (*Source:* Data Resources, Inc.)

can be readily seen by rewriting (2) (using the definition of the rate of wage inflation) to look at the level of wages today relative to the past level:

$$W = W_{-1}[1 - \epsilon(u - u^*)] \tag{2a}$$

For wages to rise above their previous level, unemployment must fall below the natural rate.

Although Phillips' own curve relates the rate of increase of wages or wage inflation to unemployment as in (2) above, the term "Phillips curve" gradually became used to describe either the original Phillips curve *or* a curve relating the rate of increase of *prices*—the rate of inflation—to the unemployment rate. Figure 13-5 shows inflation and unemployment data for the United States in the 1960s, which appear entirely consistent with the Phillips curve.

The Policy Tradeoff

The Phillips curve rapidly became a cornerstone of macroeconomic policy analysis. It suggested that policymakers could choose different combinations of unemployment and rates of inflation. For instance, they could have low unemployment as long as they put up with high inflation — say the situation in the late sixties in Figure 13-5. Or they could maintain low inflation by having high unemployment, as in the early sixties.

But that simple Phillips curve relationship has not held up well to subsequent history, either in Britain or in the United States. Figure 13-6 shows the behavior of inflation and unemployment in the United States over the entire period since 1960. The seventies show no signs of a simple Phillips curve.

The Friedman-Phelps Amendment

Remarkably, the death of the simple Phillips curve was predicted in the late sixties by Professors Milton Friedman then of the University of Chicago and Edmund Phelps of Columbia.[4] Friedman and Phelps argued that the simple Phillips curve would shift over time as workers and firms became used to and began to expect continuing inflation.

On the basis of economic theory[5] they concluded that the notion of a long-run tradeoff between inflation and unemployment was illusory. The Friedman-Phelps proposition is: *In the long run the economy will move to the natural rate of unemployment whatever the rate of change of wages and the inflation rate.*

---

[4] Milton Friedman, "The Role of Monetary Policy," *American Economic Review*, March 1968, and Edmund Phelps, *Inflation Policy and Unemployment Theory*, Norton, 1972.

[5] Remember that at the time they were writing (Phelps first made the argument in the 1960s) the facts appeared to support the Phillips curve as a long-run tradeoff—after all Phillips' own data covered a period of nearly a century.

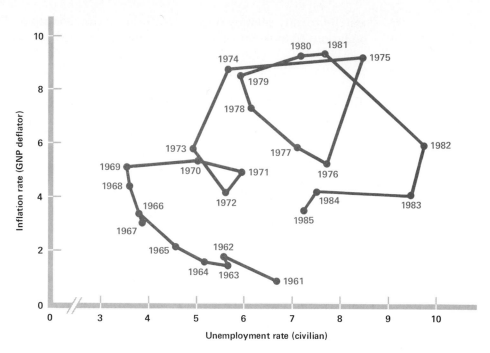

FIGURE 13-6   INFLATION AND UNEMPLOYMENT, UNITED STATES, 1961–1985. (*Source:* Data Resources, Inc.)

The argument was based on the definition of the natural rate of unemployment as the rate of frictional unemployment consistent with the labor market being in equilibrium. As long as unemployment is above the natural rate, more people are looking for jobs than is consistent with equilibrium in the labor market. This excess unemployment should cause the real wage to fall, so that firms want to hire more workers and fewer want to work, reducing the unemployment rate back to the natural rate. Similarly, when unemployment is below the natural rate, there are too few people available for firms to fill jobs as rapidly as they do normally. The real wage should rise, leading firms to want to employ fewer workers and attracting more people into the labor force. The unemployment rate would rise back to the natural level. Thus there is no long-run tradeoff between inflation and unemployment.

Empirical Evidence

Modern empirical analysis broadly supports the Friedman-Phelps view.[6] In the short run an increase in the money stock affects primarily output and has

---

[6] See for instance A. Steven Englander and Cornelis A. Los, "Recovery Without Accelerating Inflation," *Federal Reserve Bank of New York, Review,* Summer 1983.

little effect on inflation or prices or wages. Over longer periods of years, the impact of an increase in money is almost entirely reflected in prices and wages and very little in output. This point is brought out by looking at the estimates of the impact of a monetary expansion as seen by the DRI (Data Resources, Inc.) macroeconometric model for the U.S. economy. Figure 13-7 shows the impact of a 1 percent monetary expansion on output and on the price level for the subsequent 16 quarters or 4 years.[7]

The bars show the percentage difference in output and prices relative to what they would have been in the absence of a monetary expansion. It is clear from the figure that in the first place output expands with practically no impact on prices. Gradually the output expansion builds up and prices, too, start increasing. Only after a year does output start falling back as price increases build up and bring real balances back down. But even after 16 quarters or 4 years, output is still above its initial level and prices have not yet risen by a full percent. In the long run the model has neoclassical properties, but it is appar-

---

[7] See Data Resources *U.S. Review*, April 1983.

FIGURE 13-7   THE IMPACT OF A CHANGE IN THE MONEY STOCK ON THE PRICE LEVEL AND OUTPUT. (*Source:* Data Resources *U.S. Review*, April 1983)

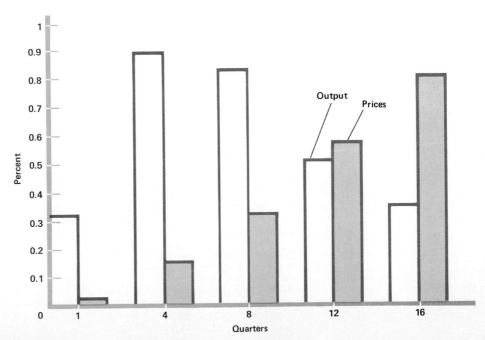

ent that it takes quite a long time before the economy gets there. The exact time shape of response may vary from one model to another. Some will have more rapid price responses and less protracted increases in output, and others will show even longer lags in the adjustment of prices. But virtually all models and studies of the economy agree that the adjustment takes years not weeks.

We explain these results in the next section.

13-3 WHY ARE WAGES STICKY?

The assumption that wages are slow to adjust to shifts in demand is essential in our derivation of an aggregate supply curve that produces a gradual rather than instantaneous adjustment of the economy to disturbances. With gradual adjustment of wages, a monetary or fiscal expansion has an extended effect on output and employment. The key question in the theory of aggregate supply is why the nominal wage adjusts slowly to shifts in demand, or why wages are *sticky*. Wages are sticky, or wage adjustment sluggish, when wages move slowly over time, rather than being fully and immediately flexible so as to assure full employment at every point in time.

To clarify the assumptions that we make about wage stickiness, we translate the Phillips curve in (2) into a relationship between the rate of change of wages gW and the level of employment. But there is a need to distinguish three different employment concepts: (1) actual employment denoted by N, (2) the equilibrium employment level that occurs in a neoclassical labor market, N° (that is, the employment level consistent with unemployment being at the natural rate), and (3) the level of employment, LF, that would exist if there were zero unemployment and everyone was working. Thus LF stands for the total labor force.[8]

With these definitions we can move between the concepts of employment and unemployment. We use the definition of the actual unemployment rate as the fraction of the total labor force (LF) that is not employed:[9]

$$u = \frac{LF - N}{LF} \tag{3}$$

Substituting (3) into (2), we obtain the Phillips curve relationship be-

---

[8] With a positively sloped labor supply curve, the full-employment level of the labor force depends on the real wage. We mean by N° the equilibrium level of N when the labor market is in its neoclassical equilibrium shown in Fig. 13-1, adjusted for frictional unemployment.

[9] Note that the total labor force (LF) exceeds the full-employment level of employment N° because it is normal for some people to be unemployed while they search for jobs. The definition of the natural unemployment rate is $u^\circ = (LF - N^\circ)/LF$, and the actual unemployment rate is $u = (LF - N)/LF$.

tween the level of employment and the rate of change in wages:

$$gW \equiv \frac{W - W_{-1}}{W_{-1}} = -\epsilon\left(\frac{N^* - N}{LF}\right) \qquad (2b)$$

or, rewriting the equation, we show the Phillips curve as a relationship between the wage this period, last period's wage, and the actual level of employment:

$$W = W_{-1}\left[1 + \epsilon\left(\frac{N - N^*}{LF}\right)\right] \qquad (4)$$

Equation (4), the wage-employment relation, WN, is shown in Figure 13-8. The wage this period is equal to the wage that prevailed last period (say, last quarter), but with an adjustment for the level of employment. At full employment $(N = N^*)$ the wage this period is equal to last period's wage. If employment is above the full-employment level, the wage increases above last period's wage. If employment is below the full employment level, the wage this period falls below last period's wage. The extent to which the wage responds to employment depends on the parameter ϵ. If ϵ is large, unemployment has large effects on the wage and the WN line is steep.

FIGURE 13-8   THE WAGE-EMPLOYMENT RELATION. Within a period, the wage increases with the level of employment, as shown by WN. If employment is at its neoclassical equilibrium level, N^*, the wage level in this period is equal to the wage last period.

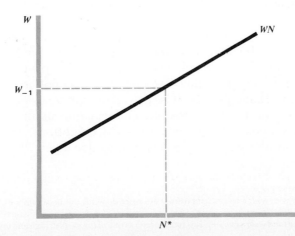

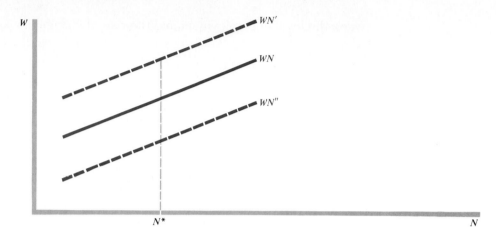

FIGURE 13-9   THE SHIFTING WAGE-EMPLOYMENT RELATION. The
WN curve shifts over time if employment differs from the full-employment level N^*. If N exceeds N^* this period, the *WN* curve will shift
upward to *WN'* next period.

The Phillips curve relationship in (4) also implies that the *WN* relationship
shifts over time, as in Figure 13-9. If there is overemployment this period, the
WN curve will shift upward next period to *WN'*. If there is less than full
employment this period, the *WN* curve will shift downward next period to
WN". Thus changes in aggregate demand that move the rate of unemployment
this period will have effects on wages in subsequent periods. In other words,
the adjustment to a change in employment is dynamic, that is, it takes place
over time.

The central element in any explanation of wage stickiness is the fact that
the labor market involves long-term relations between firms and workers.
Most of the labor force expects to continue in its current job for some time.
Working conditions, including the wage, are renegotiated periodically, but
not frequently. That is because it is costly to negotiate frequently if the wage is
set by negotiation; and costly to obtain information about alternative wages if
the wage is supposed to be set by market conditions. Typically firms and
workers reconsider wages and adjust them once a year.[10]

---

[10] The frequency with which wages (and prices) are reset depends on the stability of the level of output and
prices in the economy. In extreme conditions, such as hyperinflations, wages might be reset daily or weekly. The
need to reset prices and wages frequently is indeed seen as one of the costs of high and unstable rates of inflation.

Wages are usually set in dollar terms in economies with low rates of inflation.[11] Thus the agreement is that the firm will pay the worker so many dollars per hour or per month, for the next quarter or year. Some formal union labor contracts last 2 or 3 years and may fix nominal wages for the period of the contract. Frequently union contracts include separate wage rates for overtime hours, which implies that the wage rate paid by firms is higher the more labor is employed. That is one reason the *WN* curve in Figure 13-8 is positively sloped.

At any moment of time, firms and workers will have agreed, explicitly or implicitly, on the wage schedule that is to be paid to currently employed workers. There will be some base wage, corresponding to a given number of hours of work per week, and depending on the type of job, perhaps a higher wage for overtime. The firm then sets the level of employment each period. If demand is high, employment will be high, and the nominal wage with it.

Now consider how wages adjust when the demand for labor shifts and firms increase hours of work. In the short run, wages rise along the *WN* curve. With demand up, workers will press for an increase in the base wage at the next labor negotiation. However, not all wages are negotiated simultaneously. Rather wage-setting dates are *staggered*, that is, they overlap.[12] Assume that wages for half the labor force are set in January and the other half in July. Suppose the money stock went up in September. When the time comes to renegotiate half the contracts in January, both the firms and the workers negotiating know that other wages will not change for the next 6 months.

Workers do not adjust their base wage all the way to the level that will take the economy to the long-run equilibrium because, if they do, their wages will be very high relative to other wages for the next 6 months. Firms will prefer to employ workers whose wages have not yet risen; there is thus a danger of unemployment to the January wage-setting workers if the renegotiated wages go too high. They are therefore adjusted only part-way toward equilibrium.

Then in July, when the time comes to reset the other half of the wages, those too are not driven all the way to the equilibrium level because the January wages will then be relatively lower. So the July wages will go above the January wages, but still only part way to the full-employment equilibrium base wage.

This process keeps on going, with the supply curve rising from period to period as wages leapfrog each other with first one wage and then another

---

[11] In economies with high inflation, wages are likely to be *indexed* to the price level, that is, adjusted for changes in prices. Even in the United States some long-term labor contracts contain indexing clauses where the wage is increased to compensate for past price increases. The indexing clauses typically adjust wages once a quarter (or once a year) to compensate for price increases in the past quarter (or year).

[12] The adjustment process we present here is based on John Taylor, "Aggregate Dynamics and Staggered Contracts," *Journal of Political Economy*, February 1980.

being renegotiated. The position of the aggregate supply curve in any period will depend on where it was last period, because each unit renegotiating wages has to consider the level of its wage relative to the wages that are not being reset. And the level of the wages that are not being reset is reflected in last period's wage rate. That is why there is a W_{-1} term on the right-hand side of the Phillips curve equation (4).

During this adjustment process, firms will also be resetting prices as wages (and thus firms' costs) change. The process of wage and price adjustment continues until the economy is back at the full-employment equilibrium with the same real balances. The real-world adjustment process is more complicated than the January-July example because wages are not reset quite as regularly as that, and also because not only wage but also price adjustments[13] have to be taken into account. But the January-July example gives the essence of the adjustment process.

This account of slow wage and price adjustment raises at least two serious questions. The first is why firms and workers do not readjust wages more frequently when clearly understandable disturbances affect the economy. If they did, then perhaps they could adjust wages so as to maintain full employment. Recent research emphasizes that comparatively small costs of resetting wages and prices can keep adjustment processes from operating fast.[14] And the problems of coordinating wage and price adjustments to move back rapidly to equilibrium in a large economy where there are many different forces affecting supply and demand in individual markets are also formidable.

The second is why firms and unemployed workers do not get together when there is high unemployment, with the firms giving jobs to the unemployed at wages below those their current workers receive. Such practices are probably bad for the morale of the labor force on the job. But even so this pattern has to a limited extent been seen in the United States in the period since 1982 in the so-called *two-tier* wage system. In this system veterans are on one wage schedule and new employees on a much lower schedule. But — and this is precisely the point of this section — the introduction of the two-tier system did not happen immediately as unemployment developed, but rather took place slowly over a period of years. That pattern is consistent with the sluggish adjustment of wages.

To summarize, the combination of the assumptions that wages are preset and wage adjustments staggered generates the type of gradual wage and

---

[13] For an interesting study of the frequency of price adjustments (for newspapers) see Stephen G. Cecchetti, "Staggered Contracts and the Frequency of Price Adjustment," *Quarterly Journal of Economics*, Supplement, 1985.

[14] These theories are at the frontier of research. For the flavor of the argument, see N. Gregory Mankiw, "Small Menu Costs and Large Business Cycles: A Macroeconomic Model of Monopoly," *Quarterly Journal of Economics*, May 1985.

output adjustment we observe in the real world. That accounts for the dynamics. The upward-sloping aggregate supply curve to which we now turn is accounted for by overtime wages for some workers, and by the fact that wages in those contracts that are renegotiated within the period (such as a quarter) do respond to market conditions.

13-4 THE AGGREGATE SUPPLY CURVE

We derive the aggregate supply curve in four steps. First, we relate output to employment. Second, we relate the prices firms charge to their costs. And, third, we use the Phillips curve relationship between wages and employment. Then we put the three components together to derive an upward-sloping aggregate supply curve, a relationship between the price level and output, of the type used in Chapter 7.

The Production Function

The production function links the level of employment of labor to the level of output. The simplest production function is one in which output is proportional to the input of labor:

$$Y = aN \tag{5}$$

Here Y is the level of output produced, and N is the amount of labor input or employment (measured in hours of work, for example).

The coefficient a is called the input coefficient or *labor productivity*. Labor productivity is the ratio of output to labor input, Y/N, that is, the amount of output produced per unit of labor employed. For instance, if a is equal to 3, then one unit of labor (1 hour of work) will produce three units of output.

The assumption in equation (5) is that the productivity of labor is constant. In fact labor productivity changes over time. It tends to grow over long periods, as workers become better trained, educated, and equipped with more capital. It also changes systematically during the business cycle. Productivity tends to begin to fall before the start of a recession and then to start recovering either during the recession or at the beginning of the recovery. This productivity behavior is explained in Box 13-1.

We simplify by assuming that labor productivity is constant. An important point to notice though is that labor productivity is *not* inversely related to the level of output. The neoclassical demand function for labor shown in Figure 13-1 is built on the assumption that the marginal product of labor decreases as employment increases. If that were so for all levels of output, the average product of labor would also decrease as output increased. But it does not. That

BOX
13-1

THE CYCLICAL BEHAVIOR OF PRODUCTIVITY

In developing the sticky wage macroeconomic model we made a strong assumption about the link between output and employment, namely, $Y = aN$. According to our assumption, labor productivity Y/N is equal to a constant a.

That assumption is readily testable by looking at the data for labor productivity or output per worker, Y/N. The data are shown in Figure 1. It is immediately clear that productivity varies over time — it grows over time, as we shall see in Chapter 18 — but it also moves cyclically.

The figure shows that as or shortly before the economy moves into a recession, productivity declines, while productivity begins to grow again some time after the recession starts. How do we explain these facts, and what implications do they have for our model? Firms maintain long-term relations with their labor force. Part of that long-term relation is that during recessions firms are slow to dismiss personnel, especially highly specialized workers whom the firm does not want to risk losing permanently. This applies also to managers, because even if the firm produces only half the normal level of output, it is difficult to reduce management by half.

Thus employment tends to fluctuate *less* than output or production. During a recession output falls, but employment falls relatively less. Hence productivity — the ratio of output to employment — falls. Conversely, in a recovery production rises, but because the firm has kept on or *hoarded* a lot of the work force, employment increases less. Thus productivity rises in a recovery.

The effects we have just described are reinforced by the fact that the firm bases its hiring and firing on expectations about future production. A firm will hire more workers and incur the expense of increasing employment only if there is an expectation that production and output will

FIGURE 1   THE PRODUCTIVITY OF LABOR, 1960–1985. *Note:* Shaded areas indicate recessions. (*Source:* Data Resources, Inc.)

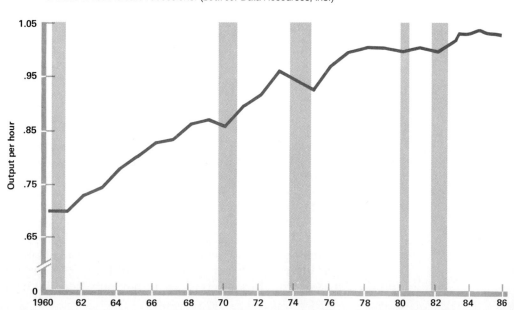

be higher for some time. Otherwise, paying overtime to the existing labor force would be a cheaper solution. Conversely, firms will lay off or dismiss workers only if they believe the decline in demand will last some time. Here then is another source of discrepancy between current employment and current production. Current production may be low but employment high because firms believe demand has declined only transitorily.

By assuming a tight link between output and employment, our model thus simplifies the complex relationships between a firm's production decisions and its employment decisions. For purposes of understanding aggregate supply, the simplification is justifiable, since output and employment do, in practice, move in the same direction, even if not exactly in lockstep.

is one reason the neoclassical analysis is not an accurate description of the behavior of wages and prices over the business cycle.[15]

Costs and Prices

The second step in developing the theory of supply is to link firms' prices to their costs. Labor costs are the main component of costs. The guiding principle here is that a firm will supply output at a price that at least covers its costs. Of course, firms would like to charge far more than cost, but competition from existing firms and firms that might enter the economy to capture some of the profits prevent prices from getting far out of line with costs.

We assume that firms base price on the labor cost of production. Since each unit of labor produces a units of output, the labor cost of production per unit is W/a. For instance if the wage is \$15 per hour and a is 3, then the labor cost is \$5 per unit. The ratio W/a is often called *unit labor cost*.

Firms set price as a *markup, z,* on labor costs:

$$P = \frac{(1 + z)W}{a} \qquad (6)$$

The markup over labor cost covers the cost of other factors of production that the firm uses, such as capital and raw materials, and includes an allowance for

---

[15] A major reason is that the assumption of the neoclassical analysis that capital remains fully employed throughout is not correct. Note from the appendix to this chapter that the diminishing marginal product of labor follows from the assumption that, because the capital stock is fixed in the short run, each succeeding worker has less capital with which to work. However, the use of capital also varies over the cycle, with capital being unemployed in recessions and heavily employed during booms. For instance, factories may run on three shifts a day during booms, using the capital all the time, and only one shift a day during recessions. Data on the use of capital, so-called capacity utilization data are imperfect, but suggest that, if anything, the capital-in-use to labor ratio may be higher during booms than in recessions. In that case neoclassical theory would not predict that the marginal productivity of labor is lower in booms, as it does in Fig. 13-1.

the firm's normal profits. If competition in the industry is less than perfect, then the markup will also include an element of monopoly profit.[16]

Employment and Wages and the Aggregate Supply Curve

The three components of the aggregate supply curve are the production function (5), the price-cost relation (6), and the Phillips curve (4). The price level is proportional to the wage [from equation (6)]. But today's wage is linked through the Phillips curve in (4) to the level of employment and to past wages. We can use that wage equation and replace the wage in (6) to obtain a link between the level of employment and the price level:

$$P = [(1 + z)/a]W_{-1}\left[1 + \epsilon\left(\frac{N - N^*}{LF}\right)\right] \tag{7}$$

which, noting that $P_{-1} = [(1 + z)/a]W_{-1}$ reduces to

$$P = P_{-1}\left[1 + \epsilon\left(\frac{N - N^*}{LF}\right)\right] \tag{7a}$$

Further, the level of output is proportional to employment [from the production function, equation (5)]. Thus we can replace N, N^*, and LF in equation (7a) by Y/a, Y^*/a, and YF/a, respectively, where YF is the level of output that would occur if the entire labor force were employed. Making that change, we obtain

$$P = P_{-1}\left[1 + \epsilon\left(\frac{Y - Y^*}{YF}\right)\right]$$

Finally, defining $\lambda \equiv \epsilon/YF$, we obtain the *aggregate supply curve*

$$P = P_{-1}[1 + \lambda(Y - Y^*)] \tag{8}$$

Figure 13-10 shows the aggregate supply curve implied by equation (6). The supply curve is upward-sloping. Like the WN curve on which it is based, the AS curve shifts over time. If output this period is above the full-employment level Y^*, then next period the AS curve will shift up to AS'. If output this period is below the full-employment level, the AS curve next period will shift down to AS''. Thus the properties of the AS curve are those of the WN curve.

---

[16] Students who have taken microeconomics will realize that in competitive industries price is assumed to be determined by the market, rather than set by firms. That is quite consistent with equation (2), for if the industry were competitive, z would cover only the costs of other factors of production and normal profits, and the price would thus be equal to the competitive price. Equation (2) is slightly more general, because it allows also for price setting by firms in industries that are less than fully competitive.

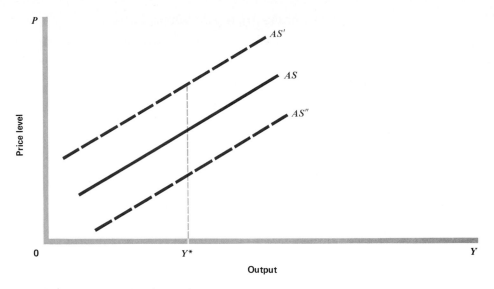

FIGURE 13-10   THE AGGREGATE SUPPLY CURVE. The aggregate supply curve *AS* is derived from the *WN* curve, with the added assumptions that output is proportional to employment, and that prices are set as a markup on labor costs. The *AS* curve, too, shifts over time, depending on the level of output. For instance, if output this period is above the full employment level *Y**, the *AS* curve will shift upward to *AS'* next period.

This is both because the markup is fixed at z and because output is proportional to employment.

The *AS* curve is the aggregate supply curve under conditions where wages are less than fully flexible. Prices increase with the level of output because increased output implies increased employment, reduced unemployment, and therefore increased labor costs. The fact that prices rise with output is entirely a reflection of the adjustments in the labor market where higher employment increases wages.[17] Firms pass on these wage increases by raising prices, and for that reason prices rise with the level of output.

---

[17] Note an important implication of markup pricing in (6). Because firms are assumed to maintain a constant markup of price over cost, the *real wage* does not change with the level of employment in the theory developed in this chapter. Because different theories of aggregate supply have different implications about the cyclical behavior of real wages, that behavior has been studied intensively. For instance, some theories suggest that the level of employment is determined by the neoclassical labor demand curve *ND* in Fig. 13-1. In that case the real wage would be high in recessions and low in booms. Empirical evidence shows however that wages and employment are essentially independent over the cycle. For a study based on data from twelve countries that reaches that conclusion, see P. T. Geary and J. Kennan, "The Employment—Real Wage Relationship: An International Study," *Journal of Political Economy*, August 1982. It is because the data show no clear pattern that we assume in our theoretical development that the real wage is independent of the level of employment.

Properties of the Aggregate Supply Curve

We have now derived the aggregate supply schedule AS used in Chapter 7 and can, with the help of (8), explore its properties more closely. We emphasize three points:

1. The aggregate supply schedule is flatter the smaller the impact of output and employment changes on current wages. If wages respond very little to changes in unemployment, then the AS schedule in Figure 13-10 will be very flat. The coefficient λ in equation (8) captures this employment-wage change linkage.
2. The position of the aggregate supply schedule depends on the past level of prices. The schedule passes through the full employment level of output Y^* at $P = P_{-1}$. For higher output levels there is overemployment, and hence prices today are higher than those last period. Conversely, when unemployment is high, prices today will be below those last period.
3. The aggregate supply schedule shifts over time. If output is maintained above the full employment level Y^*, then overtime wages continue to rise and the wage increases are passed on as increased prices.

Rather than discuss these three points in the abstract, we use the aggregate supply curve to examine the effects of a monetary expansion in Figure 13-11. This will give us a full understanding of both the short-run and long-run implications of the wage-price aggregate supply model.

13-5 THE EFFECTS OF A MONETARY EXPANSION

In Figure 13-11 we show the economy in full-employment equilibrium at point E. The aggregate supply schedule AS is drawn for a given past price level P_{-1}. It passes through the full-employment output level Y^* at the price level P_{-1} because when output is at the full-employment level, there is no tendency for wages to change, and hence costs and prices too are constant from period to period. The aggregate supply schedule is drawn relatively flat, suggesting a small effect of output and employment changes on wages.

Short-Run Effects

Suppose now that the nominal money stock is increased. At each price level real balances are higher, interest rates are lower, and hence the demand for output rises. The AD schedule shifts upward and to the right, to AD'. At the initial price level $P = P_{-1}$ there is now an excess demand for goods. Firms find that their inventories are running down and accordingly hire more labor and raise output until point E', the short-run equilibrium, is reached. Note that at E' both output and prices have risen. A monetary expansion has led to a

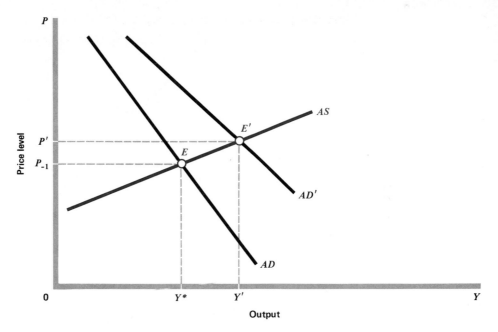

FIGURE 13-11   THE SHORT-RUN EFFECT OF AN INCREASE IN
THE MONEY STOCK. The initial equilibrium at E is disturbed by an increase in the money stock that shifts the aggregate demand curve from
AD to AD'. Short-run equilibrium is at E' where both the price level and
output have increased. Prices are higher because the output expansion
has caused an increase in wages, which are passed on into prices. The
AS schedule is drawn quite flat, reflecting the assumption that wages
are quite sticky.

short-run increase in output. The rise in prices is due to the increase in labor
costs as production and employment rise.

Compare now the short-run result with the Keynesian and classical
models of Chapter 7 and the neoclassical model of this chapter. Our new
equilibrium at E' has a feature of each: output is higher, and prices have risen.
Whether we are more nearly in the classical or Keynesian situation depends
entirely on the slope of the aggregate supply schedule, that is, on the coefficient λ that translates employment changes into wage changes.

Medium-Term Adjustment

The short-run equilibrium at point E' is not the end of the story. At E' output is
above normal. Therefore, from (7) prices *will keep on rising*. Consider now in
Figure 13-12 what happens in the second period. Once we are in the second

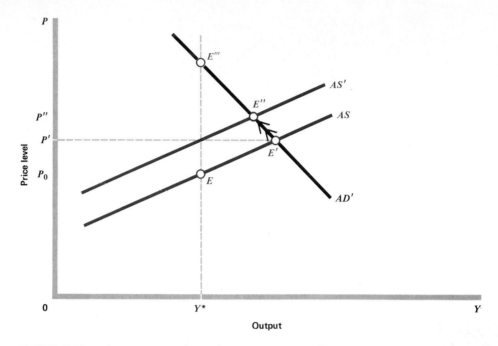

FIGURE 13-12   THE LONGER-TERM EFFECTS OF AN INCREASE IN
THE MONEY STOCK. The increase in the money stock led to a
short-run equilibrium at E'. But because output is above the full-employment level, wages are rising, and the AS curve is shifting upward. In the
next period the AS curve shifts to AS', leading to equilibrium in that
period being at E'', with a higher price level than in the previous period,
but lower output. The adjustment from E to E' reflects cost pressures
that arise in an overemployed economy. Prices continue to rise and
output to fall until the economy reaches E''', at which point prices have
risen in the same proportion as the money stock and output is back at Y^*.

period, looking back, the price in the preceding period was P' at point E'.
Therefore the second-period supply curve passes through the full-employment output level at a price equal to P'. We show this by shifting the aggregate
supply schedule up to AS', reflecting the increase in wages that has taken place
since last period in response to the high level of employment.

With the new aggregate supply schedule AS', and with the aggregate
demand schedule unchanged at the higher level AD', the new equilibrium is at
E''. Comparing E' and E'' we note that output now has fallen compared with
the first period and prices have risen further. The increase in wages has been
passed on by firms as an upward shift of the AS schedule, and the resulting
price increase reduces real balances, raises interest rates, and lowers equilib-

rium income and spending. Thus, starting in the second period, we enter a phase of the adjustment process in which the initial expansion begins to be reversed. We continue this process by looking at the long-term adjustment.

Long-Term Adjustment

As long as output is above normal, employment is above normal, and therefore wages are rising. Because wages are rising, firms experience cost increases, and these are passed on, at each output level, as an upward shift of the aggregate supply schedule. As long as the short- and medium-term equilibrium positions of the economy (points E', E'', etc.) lie to the right of Y^*, the AS schedule is shifting upward and to the left. As a result, output will be declining toward the full-employment level and prices will keep rising. This adjustment is shown in Figure 13-12.

Figure 13-12 shows that the upward-shifting AS schedule gives us a series of equilibrium positions on the AD schedule, starting with E' and moving up toward E'''. During the entire adjustment process, output is above the full-employment level, and prices are rising. But there is a long-run equilibrium at E''' in which the economy has returned to full employment.

Once prices have risen in the same proportion as the nominal money stock, the real money stock M/P is again at the initial level. This happens at E'''. When real balances and therefore interest rates are again at the initial level, so are aggregate demand, output, and employment. In the long run, once wages and prices have had time to adjust fully, the model has the same predictions as the classical case of Chapter 7 and Section 13-1. *The difference is only in the adjustment process.* In the classical case a monetary expansion leads immediately to an equiproportionate rise in prices with no real expansion. Here output and prices *both* rise in the short and medium term, and only in the long run do we reach the classical case. In the short run the predictions of our model more closely resemble the Keynesian case of Chapter 7, and the more slowly that wages adjust to changes in employment, the greater the resemblance.

Because the adjustments of wages and prices are in fact slow, the short- and medium-term adjustments are an important aspect of macroeconomics.

We now conclude the chapter by using the aggregate supply-demand apparatus to study the effects of supply shocks.

13-6 SUPPLY SHOCKS

From the 1930s to the late 1960s, it was generally assumed that movements in output and prices in the economy were caused by shifts in the aggregate demand curve—by changes in monetary and fiscal policy (including wars as fiscal expansions) and investment demand. But the macroeconomic story of the 1970s was largely a story of *supply shocks.*

A supply shock is a disturbance to the economy whose first impact is to shift the aggregate supply curve. The two major supply shocks in the 1970s were the increases in the price of oil in 1973–1974 and 1979–1980. The real price of oil (defined as the world crude oil price deflated by the U.S. GNP deflator) is shown in Figure 13-13. The first OPEC shock, which produced a quadrupling of the real price of oil between 1971 and 1974, helped push the economy into the 1973–1975 recession, up to then the worst recession of the post–World War II period. And the second OPEC price increase, which doubled the price of oil, sharply accelerated the inflation rate. The high inflation led to tough monetary policy to fight inflation in 1980–1982, with the result that the economy went into even deeper recession than in 1973–1975.

These two oil price shock related recessions leave no doubt that supply shocks matter. But the second shock left the oil price so high that many new producers came into the market, the OPEC cartel collapsed, and at the end of 1985 and in early 1986 the price of oil fell back to the level it had been in 1978. That was a favorable oil price shock.

We start examining the effects of supply shocks by incorporating materials prices into the aggregate supply curve.

Incorporating Materials Prices in the Analysis

In equation (6) labor costs (and the markup) were the only determinants of output prices. Materials such as energy or copper or cotton were not explicitly

FIGURE 13-13   THE REAL PRICE OF OIL, 1973–1986.

included. But clearly the manufacturing sector does use these inputs, whose prices have an impact on the prices of final goods.

We incorporate materials prices in our analysis by modifying the price equation to include not only labor costs and the markup, but also *materials prices*, which we denote by P_m:

$$P = \frac{W(1 + z)}{a} + \theta P_m \qquad (9)$$

In (9) the term θ denotes the material requirement per unit output, and hence θP_m is the component of unit costs that comes from materials inputs.

The wage rate, we recall, increases with the level of output. Hence from equation (9) we still get an upward-sloping supply curve. Further, any increase in the price of materials will increase the price level as of a given W. Thus an increase in P_m shifts the AS curve upward, as in Figure 13-14.

We can alternatively write the price equation in terms of the *relative* or *real* price of materials, which we denote by the lowercase p_m. The relative price is given by

$$p_m = \frac{P_m}{P} \qquad (10)$$

Substituting from (10) in (9) gives us a modified equation linking wages and prices:

$$P = \frac{1 + z}{1 - \theta p_m} \frac{W}{a} \qquad 1 > \theta p_m \qquad (11)$$

Equation (11) shows that for given wages, profit margins, and labor productivity, an increase in the real price of commodities will increase prices simply because it raises costs. The impact of a change in real commodity prices therefore is to shift the aggregate supply schedule upward at each level of output, as in Figure 13-14.

An Adverse Supply Shock

An *adverse supply shock* is one that shifts the aggregate supply curve up. Figure 13-14 shows the effects of such a shock. The AS curve shifts upward to AS', and the equilibrium of the economy moves from E to E'. The immediate effect of the supply shock is thus to raise the price level and reduce the level of output. An adverse supply shock is doubly unfortunate: it causes *higher* prices and *lower* output.

There are two points to note about the impact of the supply shock. First, the shock is best thought of as an increase in the price of a raw material used in

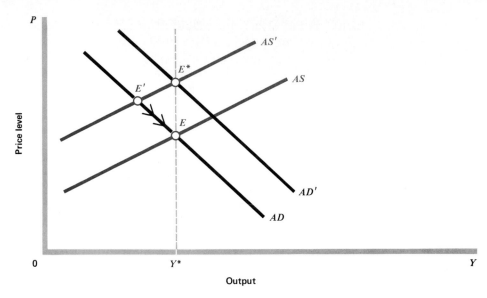

FIGURE 13-14 AN ADVERSE SUPPLY SHOCK. An increase in the real price of oil shifts the aggregate supply schedule upward and to the left, because the cost of production is now higher at each level of output. Because wages do not adjust enough in the short run, the economy moves into an unemployment equilibrium at E'. Prices are higher and output is lower because of the reduction in real balances. Over time, wages decline because of unemployment and the economy returns to the initial equilibrium at E. Accommodating monetary or fiscal policies could shift the AD schedule to AD', reducing the unemployment effects of the supply shock, but increasing its inflationary impact.

production. The AS curve shifts upward because it now costs firms more to produce each unit of output. Second, we are assuming that the supply shock does not affect the level of potential output, which remains at $Y°$.[18]

What happens after the shock has hit? In Figure 13-14, the economy moves, from E' back to E. The unemployment at E' forces wages and thus the price level down. The adjustment is slow because wages are slow to adjust. The adjustment takes place along the AD curve, with wages falling until E is reached.

At E the economy is back at full employment, with the price level the same as it was before the shock. But the nominal wage rate is lower than it was before

---

[18] The increase in the price of oil in the seventies both shifted up the AS curve and reduced the level of potential output because firms reduced their use of oil and could not use capital as efficiently as before. But we are assuming in Fig. 13-14 that the supply shock does not affect $Y°$.

TABLE 13-1	THE 1973–1975 OIL PRICE SHOCK		
		1974	1975
Real fuel price (1973 = 100)		122.6	138.8
GNP deflator (1973 = 100)		108.8	118.9
Real GNP growth (% per year)		−0.6	−1.2
Real wage change* (% per year)		−2.8	−0.8

* Real wage is adjusted hourly earnings in the private nonagricultural sector.

Source: *Economic Report of the President*, 1983.

the shock, because the unemployment in the meantime has forced the wage down. Thus the *real* wage too is lower than it was before the shock: the adverse supply shock reduces the real wage.

1973–1975

Table 13-1 shows data for the 1973–1975 oil price increase.[19] From 1973 to 1974 the oil price increased by 23 percent more than other prices and then increased further in 1975. The GNP deflator increased rapidly in both 1974 and 1975. Real GNP fell, as we should expect from Figure 13-14. And the real wage fell in both years.

Thus the analysis presented in Figure 13-14 describes well the economy's responses to the first OPEC shock.

Accommodation of Supply Shocks

Both fiscal and monetary policy barely responded when the first oil price shock hit the economy at the end of 1973. Because supply shocks were then a new phenomenon, neither economists nor policy makers knew what, if anything, could be done about them. But when the unemployment rate went above the then high level of 8 percent at the end of 1974, both monetary and fiscal policy turned stimulatory in 1975–1976. These policies helped the economy recover from the recession more rapidly than it otherwise would have.

But why not always respond to an adverse supply shock with stimulatory policy? To answer that question, we look at Figure 13-14. If the government

---

[19] In 1973–1974 prices of other raw materials, such as copper, also increased sharply. These increases had the same type of impact as the oil price shock and are not shown separately.

had, at the time of the oil price increase, increased aggregate demand enough, the economy could have moved to E^* rather than E'. Prices would have risen by the full extent of the upward shift in the aggregate supply curve. Money wages would have remained unchanged, and the economy would have stayed at full employment. Of course, the real wage would have been lower, but in the end it is lower anyway.

The monetary and fiscal policies that shift the AD curve to AD' in Figure 13-14 are known as *accommodating* policies. There has been a disturbance that requires a fall in the real wage. Policy is adjusted to make possible, or accommodate, that fall in the real wage *at the existing nominal wage*.

So the question now is why accommodating policies were not undertaken in 1973–1975. The answer is that there is a tradeoff between the inflationary impact of a supply shock and its recessionary effects. The more accommodation there is, the greater the inflationary impact of the shock and the smaller the unemployment impact. The policy mix actually chosen resulted in an intermediate position—some inflation (quite a lot) and some unemployment.

The Effects of a Favorable Oil Shock

The analysis presented in Figure 13-14 shows an adverse supply shock increasing the price level and decreasing GNP, and also decreasing the real wage. A favorable oil price shock should reduce the price level, increase GNP, and raise the real wage. In the mid-eighties the relevant shock is a favorable one.

Table 13-2 presents calculations of the effects of a 20 percent reduction in the price of oil, made using the Federal Reserve Board's macroeconomic model. The model shows that over the 3 years following the price fall, output rises and prices declined relative to the level they would otherwise have had. Note that the effects on output are quite slow, taking well over a year to build

TABLE 13-2	EFFECTS OF A 20 PERCENT OIL PRICE DECLINE			
	Year After Oil Price Fall			
	0	1	2	3
Consumer price index, %	−0.8	−1.0	−1.2	−1.1
Real GNP %	0.1	0.1	0.7	0.9

Source: Board of Governors of the Federal Reserve, FRB Multicountry Model, Version of August 1983, table 18.

up. Note also that there is large immediate impact on prices, as the lower cost of oil immediately feeds through markup pricing into a lower price level.

13-7 SUMMARY

This chapter has covered a lot of hard ground. The major point to be established was that output variations along the short-run aggregate supply schedule are accompanied by only moderate price changes. In the short run, the price level varies little with the level of output. Over time, however, wages, costs, and prices will keep rising if output is above normal and keep falling if output is below normal.

   We summarize the contents of the chapter as:

1. With wages and prices freely flexible, the equilibrium level of employment is determined in the labor market. The labor market is continuously in equilibrium at the full-employment level of employment. Aggregate supply would therefore be the amount of output produced by that amount of labor. Given that the labor market is always in equilibrium, the aggregate supply curve is vertical at the full-employment level of output.
2. The frictions that exist in real-world labor markets as workers enter the labor market and look for jobs, or shift between jobs, mean that there is always some frictional unemployment. The amount of frictional unemployment that exists at the full-employment level of employment is the *natural rate* of unemployment.
3. The labor market does not adjust quickly to disturbances. Rather the adjustment process takes time. The Phillips curve shows that nominal wages change slowly in accordance with the level of employment. Wages rise when employment is high and fall when employment is low.
4. We assume that the productivity of labor is constant over the business cycle, and that prices are based on costs of production. Thus when wages rise because the level of employment is high, prices are increased too.
5. Together the Phillips curve, the assumption that output is proportional to employment, and the proportionality of price to costs imply an upward sloping aggregate supply curve that shifts over time. A shift in the aggregate demand curve increases the price level and output. The increase in output and employment increases wages somewhat in the current period.
6. The full impact of changes in aggregate demand on prices occurs only over the course of time. High levels of employment generate increases in wages that feed into higher prices. As wages adjust, the aggregate supply curve shifts until the economy returns to equilibrium.
7. The aggregate supply curve is derived from the underlying assumptions that wages (and prices) are not adjusted continuously and that they are not all adjusted together. The positive slope of the aggregate supply curve is a result of some wages being adjusted in response to market conditions and of

previously agreed overtime rates coming into effect as employment changes. The slow movement of the supply curve over time is a result of the slow and noncoordinated process by which wages and prices are adjusted.

8. Materials prices, along with wages, are a determinant of costs and prices. Changes in materials prices are passed on as changes in prices and therefore changes in real wages. Materials price changes have been an important source of aggregate supply shocks.

9. Supply shocks, such as a material price increase, pose a difficult problem for macroeconomic policy. They can be accommodated through an expansionary aggregate demand policy with the effect of increased prices but stable output. Alternatively, they can be offset so that prices remain stable because of deflationary aggregate demand policy, but then output falls.

KEY TERMS

Frictionless neoclassical model	Unit labor cost
Frictional unemployment	Markup
Natural rate of unemployment	Sticky wages
Phillips curve	Adverse supply shock
Labor productivity	Accommodation of supply shocks

PROBLEMS

1. In the frictionless neoclassical model, assume that labor becomes more productive, with the labor demand curve shifting upward and to the right.
   (a) What is the effect of this change on the full-employment levels of employment and output?
   (b) What is the effect on the full-employment real wage?
   (c) How would your answers to (a) and (b) be affected if the labor supply curve were vertical?

2. What is the effect of an increase in the productivity of labor on the equilibrium price level in the frictionless neoclassical model? (Recall from Chapter 7 the type of aggregate supply curve implied in this case.)

3. Using Figures 13-11 and 13-12, analyze the effects of a reduction in the money stock on the price level and on output when the aggregate supply curve is positively sloped and wages adjust slowly over time.

4. In problem 3, what happens to the level of real balances as a result of the reduction in the nominal money stock?

5. Suppose that the productivity of labor rises, that is, that the coefficient a in equation (1) increases. What are the short- and long-run impacts on prices, output, and the real wage? Compare your answer here with the answers to problems 1 and 2 above.

6. Discuss the short-run and long-run adjustments to an increase in government spending using diagrams similar to Figures 13-11 and 13-12.

7. Suppose the economy is in a recession. How can monetary and fiscal policies speed up the recovery? What would happen in the absence of these policies?

8. The government increases income taxes. What are the effects on output, prices, and interest rates (a) in the short run and (b) in the long run?
9. Discuss why wages move only sluggishly.
10. Use the aggregate supply and demand framework to show the effect of a decline in the real price of materials. Show the effects (a) in the short run and (b) in the long run.
11. Suppose a policy could be found to shift the AS curve down.
    (a) What are the effects?
    (b) Why do you think there is great interest in such policies? [In Chapter 14 we discuss TIP (tax-based incentive programs) that are intended to shift the AS schedule down.]
12. Suppose that an increase in materials prices is accompanied by a fall in the level of potential output. There is no change in monetary or fiscal policy, and so the AD curve does not shift.
    (a) What is the long-run effect of the disturbance on prices and output? Compare the effect with the case in the text where potential output does not fall.
    (b) Assume the upward shift of the AS schedule leads initially to a decline in output below the new potential level. Then show the adjustment process by which output and prices reach the new long-run equilibrium.

APPENDIX: THE NEOCLASSICAL MODEL OF THE LABOR MARKET

The frictionless classical model is an idealized case where wages and prices are *fully* flexible, where there are no costs either to workers in finding jobs or to firms in increasing or reducing their labor force, and where firms behave competitively and expect to sell all they produce at prevailing prices. That case both serves as a benchmark for the discussion of more realistic cases and also allows us to introduce such useful concepts as the production function and the demand for labor. Throughout, we assume that labor is the only *variable* factor of production in the short run and that the capital stock is given.

The Production Function

A production function provides a relation between the quantity of factor inputs, such as the amount of labor used, and the maximum quantity of output that can be produced using those inputs. The relation reflects only technical efficiency. In equation (A1) we write the production function

$$Y = F(N, \ . \ . \ .) \tag{A1}$$

where Y denotes real output, N is labor input, and the dots denote other cooperating factors (capital, for example) that are in short-run fixed supply. The production function is shown in Figure 13-A1. The production function exhibits *diminishing returns* to labor, which means that the increase in output resulting from the employment of one more unit of labor declines as the amount of labor used increases.

Diminishing returns are shown in the production function by the fact that it is not a straight line through the origin (constant returns) or an upward-curling line (increasing returns). Diminishing returns are explained by the fact that as employment increases and other inputs remain constant, each laborer on the job has fewer machines with which to work and therefore becomes less productive. Thus, increases in the amount of labor progressively reduce the addition to output that further employment can bring. An increase in the labor force will always raise output,

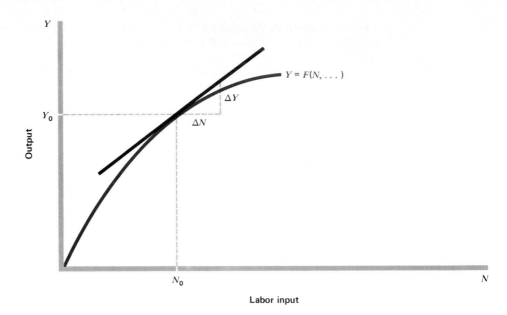

FIGURE 13-A1 THE PRODUCTION FUNCTION AND THE MARGINAL PRODUCT OF LABOR. The production function links the amount of output produced to the level of labor input, given other factors of production such as capital. The schedule shows diminishing returns. Successive increases in labor yield less and less extra output. The marginal product of labor is shown by the slope of the production function, $\Delta Y/\Delta N$, that is, the increase in output per unit increase in employment. The flattening of the slope shows that the marginal product of labor is declining.

but progressively less so as employment expands. The marginal contribution of increased employment is indicated by the slope of the production function, $\Delta Y/\Delta N$. It is readily seen that the slope flattens out as we increase employment, thus showing that increasing employment makes a diminishing, but still positive, contribution to output.

Labor Demand

From the production function we proceed to the demand for labor. We are asking how much labor a firm would want to hire. The rule of thumb is to hire additional labor and expand production as long as doing so increases profits. A firm will hire additional workers as long as they will bring in more in revenue than they cost in wages.

The contribution to output of additional labor is called the *marginal product of labor*. It is equal, in Figure 13-A1, to the slope of the production function. The marginal product, as we have seen, is both positive — additional labor is productive — and diminishing, which means that additional employment becomes progressively less productive. *A firm will employ additional labor as long as the marginal product of labor, MPN for short, exceeds the cost of additional labor.* The cost of additional labor is given by the real wage, that is, the nominal wage divided by the price level. The real wage measures the amount of real output the firm has to pay each worker. Since hiring one more worker results in an output increase of *MPN* and a cost to the firm of the real wage, firms will hire additional labor if the *MPN* exceeds the real wage. This point is formalized in Figure 13-A2, which looks at the labor market.

The downward-sloping schedule in Figure 13-A2 is the demand for labor schedule, which is the *MPN* schedule; firms hire labor up to the point at which the *MPN* is equal to the real wage. The *MPN* schedule shows the contribution to output of additional employment. It follows from our reasoning that the *MPN* is positive but that additional employment reduces it, so that the *MPN* schedule is negatively sloped.

Now consider a firm that currently employs a labor force, N_1, and assume the real wage is $(W/P)_0$, where W is the money wage and P the price of output. At an employment level N_1 in Figure 13-A2, the firm is clearly employing too much labor since the real wage exceeds the *MPN* at that level of employment. What would happen if the firm should reduce employment by one unit? The reduction in employment would decrease output by the *MPN*, and therefore reduce revenue to the firm. On the other side of the calculation, we have the reduction in the wage bill. Per unit reduction in employment, the wage bill would fall at the rate of the real wage $(W/P)_0$. The

FIGURE 13-A2   THE OPTIMAL EMPLOYMENT CHOICE FOR A
GIVEN REAL WAGE. The marginal product of labor *MPN* is a declining
function of the level of employment because of diminishing returns.
Given a real wage $(W/P)_0$, the optimal employment choice is N_0. At N_1
the marginal product of labor is less than the real wage, so that the firm
would save by reducing employment. Conversely, at N_2 the marginal
product exceeds the real wage, so that the firm would gain by hiring an
additional worker.

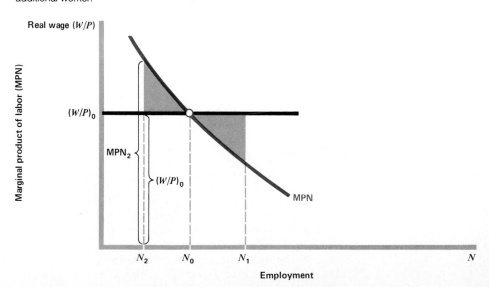

net benefit of a reduction in the employment level is thus equal to the vertical excess of the real wage over the MPN in Figure 13-A2. It is apparent that at the level of employment N_1, the excess is quite sizable, and it pays the firm to reduce the employment level. Indeed, it pays to reduce employment until the firm gets to point N_0. Only at that point does the cost of additional labor — the real wage — exactly balance the benefit in the form of increased output.

The same argument applies to the employment level N_2. Here employment is insufficient because the contribution to output of additional employment, MPN_2, exceeds the cost of additional employment, and it therefore pays to expand the level of employment. It is readily seen that with a real wage $(W/P)_0$, the firm's profits are maximized when employment is N_0. In general, given *any* real wage, the firm's demand for labor is shown by the MPN curve.

The firm's optimal employment position is formalized in equation (A2). At the optimal employment level the marginal product of labor (which is a declining function of employment) $MPN(N)$ is equal to the real wage:

$$MPN(N) = \frac{W}{P} \tag{A2}$$

FIGURE 13-A3   EQUILIBRIUM IN THE LABOR MARKET. The labor supply curve is NS. The demand for labor is the marginal product schedule MPN. Labor market equilibrium obtains at a real wage $(W/P)_0$. At that real wage the demand for labor equals the quantity of labor supplied. At a lower real wage there is an excess demand for labor; at a higher real wage there is an excess supply or unemployment.

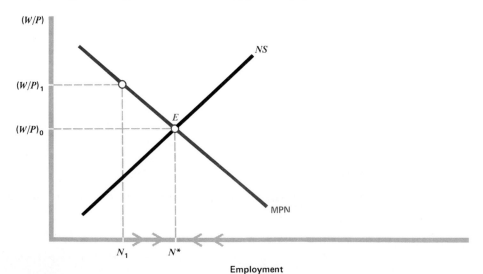

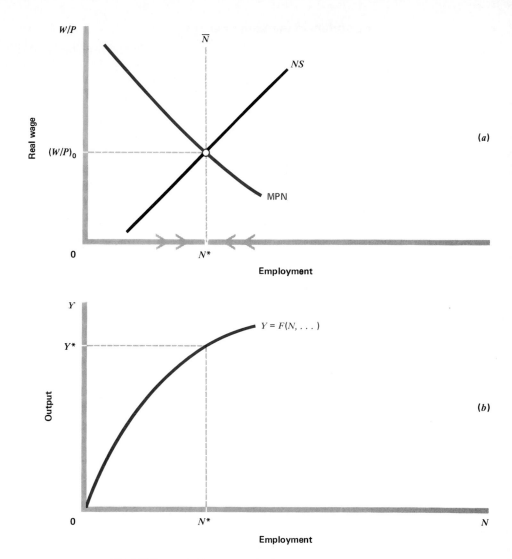

FIGURE 13-A4   EQUILIBRIUM IN THE LABOR MARKET AND
FULL-EMPLOYMENT OUTPUT. Part *(a)* of the diagram repeats the
labor market equilibrium of Figure 13-A3. Part *(b)* shows the production
function. The equilibrium employment level N^*, also the full-employment
level, leads to an output Y^*, which is the full-employment level of output.

Equilibrium in the Labor Market

We have now developed the relation between output and employment (the production function) and the optimal employment choice for a given real wage that is implied by the demand for labor. It remains to consider the determination of the real wage as part of labor market equilibrium. What we have not yet dealt with is the supply of labor.

We assume that labor supply increases with the real wage (W/P). The labor supply curve, NS, intersects the labor demand curve, MPN, at E. The equilibrium real wage is $(W/P)_0$, and the equilibrium level of employment is N^*.

How would the labor market get to that equilibrium? Suppose that the real wage fell whenever there was an excess supply of labor and that it rose whenever there was an excess demand. In terms of Figure 13-A3 this would mean that the real wage would decline whenever it was above $(W/P)_0$. At $(W/P)_1$, for example, labor demand is only N_1 and thus falls short of the labor supply. This would put downward pressure on the real wage, cause the real wage to fall, and make it profitable to expand employment. Exactly the reverse argument holds for real wages lower than $(W/P)_0$, where there is an excess demand for labor.

From Figure 13-A3 we see that adjustment of the real wage would bring the labor market into full-employment equilibrium at a real wage $(W/P)_0$ and an employment level equal to N^*. Figure 13-A4 summarizes the complete equilibrium in the labor market and the corresponding level of *full-employment output* Y^*, which is the level of output associated with employment equal to the given labor supply.

INFLATION AND UNEMPLOYMENT

I know of no example of a country that has cured substantial inflation without going through a transitional period of slow growth and unemployment.
Milton Friedman, *Bright Promises, Dismal Performance*[1]

The 1981–1982 recession was a painful experience for many. . . . The protracted recession was an unexpected and unwanted part of the economy's transition to lower inflation.

Economic Report of the President, 1985

From the late 1950s through the end of the 1970s the inflation rate in the United States increased in every successive business cycle. During a recession inflation would fall below its previous trend, but in the following recovery it would rise again and before long exceed its past level. Figure 14-1 shows that pattern of an ever-increasing inflation rate from just above 2 percent in the early 1950s to well above 10 percent in 1979–1980. In late 1979 the Fed

---

[1] New York: Harcourt, Brace, Jovanovich, 1983, p. 202.

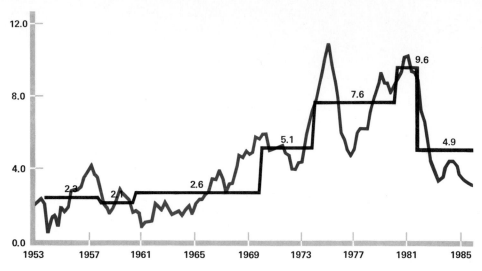

FIGURE 14-1 CYCLICAL AVERAGE INFLATION RATES.
(GNP deflator, peak to peak, last cycle from 1981:3 to 1986:1.)

made a dramatic decision: monetary policy was to be changed decisively to stop inflation from rising and to force it back down to the level of the 1950s.

The decision was dramatic because there was little disagreement among economists of widely different macroeconomic persuasions that the move toward tight money would cause a recession along with a reduction in the inflation rate. Most economists shared Friedman's view, quoted above, that disinflation would bring a recession; the claim in the 1985 *Economic Report of the President* that the recession was an unexpected part of the disinflationary process is simply not accurate.

There was indeed a sharp disinflation in 1982, as Figure 14-2 shows. There was also a major recession, with the economy reaching the highest level of unemployment since the end of the great depression, 10.6 percent, at the end of 1982. Figure 14-2 also shows the rapid improvement in economic performance that came after the recession, as unemployment fell but inflation did not increase. In the second half of the 1980s, the question is whether the economy has finally broken the inflationary bias of the sixties and seventies, and moved into a long period of prosperity with low inflation.

In this chapter we address the problem of inflation and unemployment, extending the analysis of Chapter 13 that focused on the determinants of the price level, to examine the inflation rate. We develop the short- and long-run aggregate supply curves, emphasizing the role of inflationary expectations in shifting the supply curve, and we extend the aggregate demand curve to take account of ongoing inflation.

A key question is: Why is it apparently inevitable that inflation stabilization should bring about unemployment and recession? The distinction between the short- and long-run aggregate supply curves is essential here. In the short run inflation cannot be reduced without creating a recession; in the long run, though, there is no tradeoff between inflation and unemployment.

We develop the analysis of the determination of output and inflation in Sections 14-1 to 14-6. This material includes the analysis of adjustments to changes in money growth and to fiscal policy changes. The chapter concludes with an important application of the dynamic model, the examination of alternative strategies for reducing inflation.

14-1 INFLATION, EXPECTATIONS, AND THE AGGREGATE SUPPLY CURVE

The aggregate supply curve in Chapter 13 shows the price level at which firms are willing to produce and sell different levels of output. The aggregate supply curve is

$$P = P_{-1}[1 + \lambda(Y - Y^\circ)] \tag{1}$$

FIGURE 14-2   INFLATION AND UNEMPLOYMENT, 1980–1985.
(*Source:* Data Resources, Inc.)

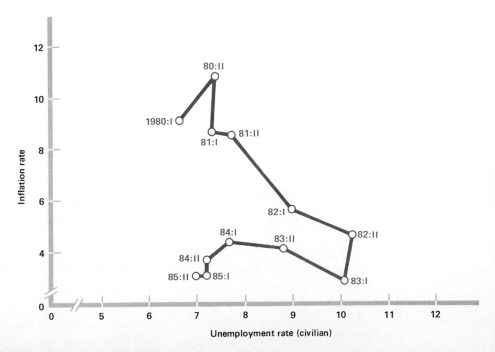

where P is the price level, Y the level of output, and Y^* the full-employment level of output.

Recall now that the aggregate supply curve builds on three foundations:

- The Phillips curve, which shows that wages increase more rapidly the lower the level of unemployment
- The relationship between the unemployment rate and the level of output, with output being higher the lower the unemployment rate
- The assumption of *markup pricing*, that firms' prices are based on labor costs, being higher the higher the wage

The Phillips curve in turn is the result of market pressures on wages. When the unemployment rate is low, firms find it difficult to obtain the labor they demand and accordingly offer higher wages to attract workers. Thus wages rise more rapidly when unemployment is low. When the unemployment rate is high, jobs are difficult to find and firms can fill any vacancies they might have without raising wages — indeed wages may even be falling as workers compete for scarce jobs.

In this chapter we develop the aggregate supply curve in two directions. First, we modify it to take account of *expected inflation:* firms and workers take account of expected increases in the price level when they are fixing wages. And second, we transform the aggregate supply curve into a relationship between output and the *inflation rate* rather than the price level. That way we can use the aggregate supply curve to model ongoing inflation, that is, continuing changes in the price level.

Wage Setting and Expected Inflation

In setting wages, firms and workers react to conditions in the labor market. Thus when output and employment are high, wages tend to rise fast. When output and employment are low, wages do not rise fast and may even fall. The *wage*-Phillips curve summarizes the link between wage inflation and the output gap. Let $gW = (W - W_{-1})/W_{-1}$ be the rate of wage inflation. Then we can write the wage-Phillips curve as

$$gW = \lambda(Y - Y^*) \tag{2}$$

which states that the rate of wage increase is larger the higher the level of output.

Friedman and Phelps pointed out[2] one major flaw in the wage-Phillips curve, equation (1): it ignores the effects of expected inflation on wage setting.

---

[2] See footnote 4 in Chap. 13. Another flaw that we have already seen in Chap. 13 is that the simple aggregate supply curve omits changes in the prices of factors of production other than labor, such as raw materials. We will leave those factors out here too.

Workers are interested in *real* wages, the amount of goods they can buy with their wages, not *nominal* wages, the dollar value of wages. And firms, too, are concerned with the *real* wage, the dollar wage relative to the price at which they can sell their output.

It is clear that workers, who are concerned with the real wage they receive, will want the nominal wage to fully reflect inflation that they expect during the period between the time the wage is fixed and the time the wage is actually paid. In other words, quite independent of the effects of the level of employment on wage bargaining, workers will want compensation for expected inflation.

But what about the other side? Why do firms agree to raise wages more rapidly when they expect higher prices? The reason is that they can afford to pay higher nominal wages if they will be able to sell their goods at higher prices. And if all prices are rising, each firm can expect to be able to sell its output for a higher price because the prices of competing goods are increasing. Indeed, when wages and prices are rising at the same rate, both firms and workers are in the same position as they would be if there were no inflation and the real wage were constant.

When inflation is expected, the wage-Phillips curve becomes

$$gW = \pi^e + \lambda(Y - Y^*) \tag{3}$$

Here π^e is the expected inflation rate. Equation (3) is called the *expectations-augmented* wage-Phillips curve, that is, it is the original Phillips curve augmented or adjusted to take account of expected inflation. At any given level of output, wages rise more the higher the expected rate of inflation: indeed, the assumption is that nominal wages rise 1 percent faster for each extra 1 percent of inflation that is expected.

The Aggregate Supply Curve

The next step is to transform the expectations-augmented wage-Phillips curve into a relationship between the inflation rate and the level of output, which depends on the expected rate of inflation. Once again we assume that firms maintain a constant markup of prices over wages. But that implies that the rate of increase of prices will be equal to the rate of increase in wages. We already denoted the rate of wage increase by gW and now denote the rate of increase of prices or the rate of inflation as $\pi = (P - P_{-1})/P_{-1}$. With this notation the statement that inflation is equal to the rate of wage increase becomes

$$\pi = gW \tag{4}$$

Substituting the rate of wage increase equation (3) in (4) yields the *dynamic aggregate supply curve*:

$$\pi = \pi^e + \lambda(Y - Y^*) \tag{5}$$

Equation (5) is one of the two building blocks of a model of the inflation process. It is the *expectations-augmented supply curve,* which we use in the remainder of this chapter to study the behavior of output and inflation. The fundamental difference from the aggregate supply curve of Chapter 13 is the inclusion of the expected inflation rate. In addition, because equation (5) deals with the inflation rate rather than the price level, it is a convenient form of the supply curve for studying ongoing inflation.

14-2 SHORT- AND LONG-RUN AGGREGATE SUPPLY CURVES

Expectations-augmented aggregate supply curves are shown in Figure 14-3. There is an aggregate supply curve corresponding to each expected rate of inflation. For example, on *SAS* the expected inflation rate is 5 percent, as can be seen from the fact that when $Y = Y^*$, at point A on *SAS*, the inflation rate on the vertical axis is 5 percent. [Note from equation (5) that when $Y = Y^*$, $\pi = \pi^e$.] The short-run aggregate supply curve shows the relationship between the inflation rate and the level of output when the expected rate of inflation is

FIGURE 14-3   THE SHORT-RUN AGGREGATE SUPPLY CURVE.
The expected inflation rate is constant on a short-run aggregate supply curve: it is 5 percent on *SAS,* 10 percent on *SAS'.* Each short-run aggregate supply curve is shown quite flat, reflecting the fact that, in the short run, it takes a large change in output to generate a given change in inflation.

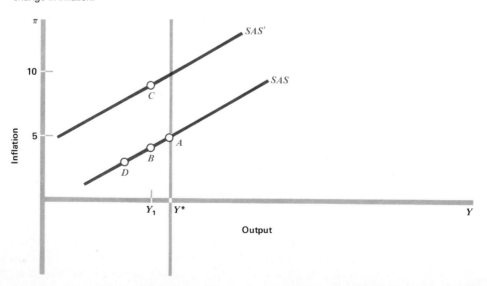

held constant. The curves are called short-run because it is assumed that the expected rate of inflation is constant (or at least does not change much) in the short run of a few months or as much as a year.

Given the expected inflation rate, the short-run aggregate supply curve shows the inflation rate rising with the level of output: the higher the level of output, the higher the rate of inflation. This is a reflection of the effect of higher output levels on the rate of increase of wages and, through higher wages, on the rate of increase of prices.

The higher the expected inflation rate, the higher the aggregate supply curve. Thus on SAS', the expected inflation rate is 10 percent. And for any expected inflation rate, there is a corresponding short-run aggregate supply curve, parallel to SAS and SAS'.

On each short-run aggregate supply curve there is a tradeoff between inflation and output. To reduce the inflation rate it is necessary to reduce the level of output, producing a recession, forcing the rate of wage increase down through unemployment, and thus achieving a lower inflation rate.

We show the short-run aggregate supply curves in Figure 14-3 as quite flat, reflecting the evidence that in the short run — up to a year or even two — it takes a large recession to bring about a substantial reduction in the inflation rate. That was the choice made for example in the United States in 1982 and 1983 when the inflation rate was reduced.

Changes in the Expected Inflation Rate

Each aggregate supply curve is drawn for a given expected rate of inflation. As the expected rate of inflation changes, the economy moves from one short-run aggregate supply curve to another. That means that the combination of the level of output and inflation rate that occurs depends on the expected inflation rate. For instance, the level of output of Y_1 in Figure 14-3 would be consistent with a low inflation rate at point B on SAS and a higher inflation rate at point C on SAS'.

If the economy moves from B to C as a result of an increase in expected inflation, we would find inflation rising without any increase in output. Going further, it is possible even for the inflation rate to increase and output to fall as the economy moves from one short-run aggregate supply curve to another. In these cases the usual tradeoff between inflation and output — more inflation produces higher output — totally disappears.

Changes in the expected rate of inflation help explain why the simple Phillips curve relationship seen in Figure 13-5 for 1961 – 1969 seemed to break down later (as seen in Figure 13-6). Through the end of the 1960s, there was relatively little awareness of inflation, and the economy was basically moving along an SAS curve. When at the end of the sixties, people in the United States began to expect inflation to continue, the short-run aggregate supply curve began to shift, generating higher inflation at each given output level. The Friedman-Phelps analysis thus can explain why the simple Phillips

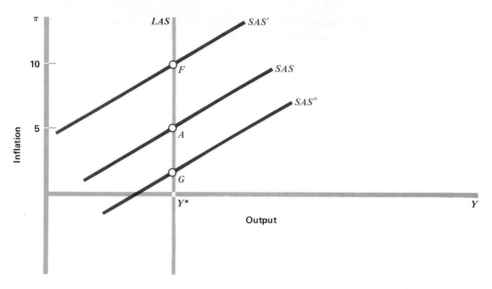

FIGURE 14-4   SHORT- and LONG-RUN AGGREGATE SUPPLY
CURVES. The long-run aggregate supply curve joins points on short-run
aggregate supply curves at which expected inflation is equal to actual
inflation. It is thus the vertical line *LAS*, at the level of output *Y**.

curve of the sixties seemed to break down in the seventies — and recall that
their analysis was made before the Phillips curve began to shift.

The conclusion of this section is the most important lesson economists and
economic policy makers learned in the last 20 years. *The short-run aggregate
supply curve shifts with the expected rate of inflation. The inflation rate corresponding to any given level of output therefore changes over time as the expected
inflation rate changes. The higher the expected inflation rate, the higher the
inflation rate corresponding to a given level of output.* That is why it is possible
for the inflation rate and the unemployment rate to increase together, or for
the inflation rate to rise while the level of output falls.

The Vertical Long-Run Aggregate Supply Curve

On each short-run aggregate supply curve, the expected inflation rate is constant and, except at points such as *A* where $Y = Y^*$, will turn out to be different
from the actual inflation rate. For instance, at point *D* on *SAS* in Figure 14-3
the expected inflation rate is 5 percent, but the actual inflation rate is only 3
percent.

If the inflation rate remains constant for any long period, firms and
workers will expect that rate to continue, and the expected inflation rate will

become equal to the actual rate. The assumption that $\pi = \pi^e$ distinguishes the *long-run* from the short-run aggregate supply curve. The long-run aggregate supply curve describes the relationship between inflation and output when actual and expected inflation are equal.

With the actual and expected inflation rates equal $(\pi = \pi^e)$, the aggregate supply curve (5) shows that

$$Y = Y^\circ$$

(6)

The long-run aggregate supply curve *LAS* in Figure 14-4 is a vertical line, joining points on short-run aggregate supply curves at which the actual and expected inflation rates are equal.

The meaning of the vertical long-run aggregate supply curve is that *in the long-run the level of output is independent of the inflation rate*. Note the important contrast between the short and the long run: in the short run, with a given expected rate of inflation, higher inflation rates are accompanied by higher output; in the long run, with the expected rate of inflation equal to the actual rate, the level of output is independent of the inflation rate.

14-3 THE ROLE OF EXPECTED INFLATION

Many of the controversies in macroeconomics are connected with the inclusion of expected inflation in the aggregate supply function. We therefore expand the discussion of the expectations-augmented Phillips curve in this section. There are three key questions. First, what exactly is the process by which expected inflation comes to be reflected in wages? Second, is it clearly *expected* inflation rather than compensation for *past* inflation that shifts the short-run aggregate supply curve? And third, what determines expected inflation?

Wage Adjustment

Wages are generally set before the work is done. Further, these are typically nominal, or dollar, wages. In some cases, particularly where there are union contracts, wages will be set for as much as 3 years ahead. In other cases, wages are adjusted once a year in an annual salary review.

It is in the adjustment of these wages that expected inflation makes its way into the wage. Wages will adjust both because prices are higher at the time the contract is negotiated than they were last time the wage was set and because inflation is expected between the time the wage is negotiated and the time it will actually be paid. Thus as a process of inflation gets under way, wages fixed in each successive period are higher than they would otherwise have been.

Because some wages are preset for 1 or 2 years or even more, it takes time for expectations of inflation to work their way into wage adjustments. For instance, if a new policy that will produce higher inflation comes into effect in 1988, it may take until 1991 before all the wages that will eventually be affected by that new policy are fully adjusted. And indeed, as we described in Chapter 13, if all wages are not adjusted at the same time, it may take much longer for all wages to come into line with a higher inflation rate, because the wage that is set in one firm or union or industry depends on the wages set elsewhere in the economy, not all of which are adjusting to the new conditions simultaneously.

Compensation for Past Inflation or Expected Inflation

We have described the adjustment for inflation in the expectations-augmented Phillips curve or aggregate supply curve as being for expected inflation. Another interpretation is that wage agreements compensate workers not only for expected inflation but also to some extent for past inflation.

The argument here is that when the inflation rate rises, workers who lost out because their real wages were low, want compensation for the losses. Note that this argument implies that compensation would be only for unexpected inflation, or inflation that was not taken into account when the previous contracts were negotiated.

In practice, at low inflation rates, an adjustment for expected inflation is very hard to distinguish from compensation for past inflation. If prices went up 10 percent last year, the firm is quite likely to raise wages this year. That may just be compensation for last year's inflation, or it may be compensation paid in advance for the inflation expected to take place during the coming year. Thus, it is very difficult to determine whether it is expected inflation or recent inflation that is represented by the π^e term in the expectations-augmented aggregate supply curve.

The confusion between whether it is compensation for past inflation or for expected inflation is illustrated by those contracts that contain formal *index* clauses, which adjust wages for inflation. These are called *COLA*, or cost-of-living adjustments, which are contained in about 60 percent of union contracts.[3] The typical COLA clause adjusts the wage once a year, or once every 3 months, by an amount that depends on the rate of inflation since the last adjustment. For instance, if the inflation rate in the last year was 8 percent, the wage rate may go up by 6 percent.

Now, is this compensation for past inflation or for future inflation? Be-

---

[3] Union membership in the United States has been steadily declining, to the point where in 1986 only 18 percent of the labor force belongs to unions. Union contracts play a more important role in wage determination than the 18 percent figure suggests (1) because there is some unionization in firms employing more than 50 percent of the labor force, so that, when setting wages for their workers, those firms have to pay attention to the wages unionized workers are receiving and (2) because many firms desiring to keep unions out of their plants have to match or better the terms of union contracts so that their workers will not want to unionize. On these issues, see Richard Freeman and James Medoff, *What Do Unions Do?* (New York: Basic Books, 1984).

cause it is based on the past inflation rate, it looks like compensation for past inflation. But the wage that is to be paid is that for the *coming* year. So maybe it is compensation in advance for inflation in the coming year.

Why does it matter whether wage adjustments for inflation respond to yesterday's actual inflation or tomorrow's expected inflation? The difference is very important because the explanation has different implications for how quickly it takes for the inflation rate to change. If wages for next year reflect last year's inflation and prices are based on wages, as they are, then inflation today will reflect yesterday's inflation and inflation rates will change only gradually. If it is only expected inflation that matters for wage setting, then perhaps a radical change in policy that changes expectations can also change the inflation rate quickly.

Determinants of Expected Inflation

The question of whether it is compensation for past inflation or future inflation that affects wages is further complicated when we consider how people form their expectations of inflation.

ADAPTIVE EXPECTATIONS

One hypothesis that was used in the fifties and sixties, and that still commands some support, is that expectations are *adaptive*, based on the past behavior of inflation. Thus under adaptive expectations the rate of inflation expected for next year might be the rate of inflation last year. Under this simplest adaptive expectations assumption, we would have

$$\pi^e = \pi_{-1}$$

(7)

Of course, the adaptive expectations assumption could be more complicated, for instance, if the expected inflation rate is the average of the last 3 years' inflation.

Note that if expectations are adaptive, it becomes virtually impossible to tell whether the π^e term in the aggregate supply curve represents expected inflation or compensation for past inflation. If $\pi^e = \pi_{-1}$, there is no difference between past inflation and expected inflation.

RATIONAL EXPECTATIONS

The rational expectations view is more general, arguing that for the determinants of expected inflation there can be no formula that is independent of the actual behavior of inflation. The rational expectations hypothesis is the assumption that people base their expectations of inflation (or any other economic variable) on all the information economically available about the future behavior of that variable.

The rational expectations approach to macroeconomics, associated primarily with the names of Robert Lucas of the University of Chicago and Thomas Sargent of the University of Minnesota, has been extremely influential. As we shall see in Chapter 18, the approach developed by Lucas, Sargent, and others involves much more than just a theory of expectations. For now, though, we concentrate on the expectations part of the theory.

The rational expectations hypothesis implies that people do not make systematic mistakes in forming their expectations. Systematic mistakes—for instance, always underpredicting inflation—are easily spotted. According to the rational expectations hypothesis, people correct such mistakes and change the way they form expectations accordingly. On average, according to rational expectations, expectations are correct because people understand the environment in which they operate. Of course people make mistakes from time to time, but they do not make *systematic* mistakes.

For much of this chapter we work with the simple adaptive expectations assumption (7) that the expected inflation rate is equal to the lagged inflation rate. The aggregate supply curve is thus[4]

$$\pi = \pi_{-1} + \lambda(Y - Y^*) \tag{8}$$

We use the aggregate supply curve (8), together with an aggregate demand curve to be introduced in the next section, to study the dynamic adjustment of the economy to changes in policy. By way of contrast, we also use the rational expectations assumption and show just how radical are its implications.

14-4 DYNAMIC AGGREGATE DEMAND

The aggregate demand curve in Chapter 13 represents combinations of the *price level* and level of output at which the goods and assets markets are simultaneously in equilibrium. In this chapter, where we are studying continuing inflation, we work with an aggregate demand curve that shows the relationship between the level of output and the *inflation rate*. The dynamic aggregate demand curve shows the relationship between the rate of inflation and the rate of change of aggregate demand.

The dynamic aggregate demand curve used in this chapter, and which is derived in the appendix, is

$$Y = Y_{-1} + \varphi(m - \pi) + \sigma f \tag{9}$$

---

[4] Recall that with the assumption $\pi^e = \pi_{-1}$ in (8) we cannot distinguish the view that the π^e term represents expected inflation from the alternative view that it represents compensation for past inflation.

In (9), m is the growth rate of the nominal money stock. Thus $(m - \pi)$ is the rate of change of real balances: when m exceeds π, the money stock is increasing faster than prices so real balances (M/P) are increasing. The other term, σf, denotes the impact on the increase of demand of a fiscal expansion.

The curve is most simply understood as saying that the *change* in aggregate demand $(Y - Y_{-1})$ is determined by the growth rate of real balances and by fiscal expansion. The higher the level of real balances, the lower the interest rate and the higher the level of aggregate demand; therefore, the more rapidly are real balances growing, the more rapidly is the interest rate falling, and the more rapidly is aggregate demand increasing. By the same line of argument an *increase* in government spending or a *cut* in taxes means an expansionary fiscal policy and hence an increase in demand over the previous period's level.

In the appendix to this chapter we show that the aggregate demand curve (9) is a simplified version of the aggregate demand curve obtained by using the full *IS-LM* model. The simplificaton is that we omit the expected rate of inflation that affects aggregate demand.[5] To start, we concentrate on presenting the aggregate demand schedule diagrammatically. For simplicity, we therefore suppress the term relating to fiscal policy changes. We return to fiscal policy changes later in the chapter.

In Figure 14-5 we plot the dynamic aggregate demand schedule (9), *DAD*. The shape of that schedule is most clearly seen by rewriting equation (9) as[6]

$$\pi = m - \frac{1}{\varphi}(Y - Y_{-1}) \tag{10}$$

The schedule is drawn for a given growth rate of money and is downward sloping. Given the growth rate of money, a lower rate of inflation implies that real balances are higher and thus the interest rate is lower, and aggregate demand is higher. The negative slope results from this connection between lower inflation, implying higher growth in real balances, and hence higher spending.

The position of the aggregate demand curve depends on the level of output last period. The higher the level of output last period, the higher the inflation rate corresponding to any given level of current output on the aggregate demand curve.

A change in the growth rate of money will shift the aggregate demand

---

[5] The expected rate of inflation enters because investment is affected by the *real* interest rate, whereas the demand for money is affected by the nominal interest rate. Thus when we say above that increases in real balances reduce interest rates, we should, to be more precise, say that while they reduce the nominal interest rate, whether they also reduce the real interest rate depends on how the expected inflation rate is changing.
[6] As noted above we are now assuming $f = 0$ so that there is no fiscal policy change in the current period.

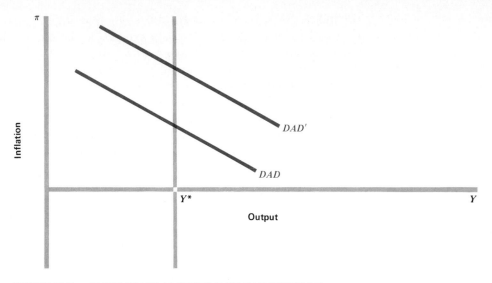

FIGURE 14-5   THE DYNAMIC AGGREGATE DEMAND SCHEDULE.
The dynamic aggregate demand curve is downward-sloping and drawn
for a given rate of growth of money and lagged output level. The growth
rate of money is higher on *DAD'* than on *DAD*.

curve. As we see from equation (10), a change in the growth rate of money
shifts the *DAD* curve vertically by precisely the same amount as the growth
rate of money changes. Thus the dynamic aggregate demand curve *DAD'* in
Figure 14-5 lies above *DAD* by the same distance as the growth rate of money
has increased between *DAD* and *DAD'*.

14-5 DETERMINING THE INFLATION RATE AND OUTPUT LEVEL

The inflation rate and level of output are determined by aggregate demand
and supply. Figure 14-6 shows the intersection of the upward-sloping aggregate supply curve and the downward-sloping aggregate demand curve at point
E. The inflation rate this period is π_0, and the level of output is Y_0.

   The current rate of inflation and the level of output clearly depend on the
positions of the aggregate supply and demand curves. Thus changes in any of
the variables that shift the aggregate supply and demand curves will affect the
current inflation and output levels.

The Inflation Rate and Output in the Short Run

Any upward shift in the aggregate demand curve causes an increase in both the rate of inflation and the level of output, as can be seen in the shift from E to E_1 when the DAD curve shifts upward to DAD'. Such a shift would be caused by an increase in the growth rate of money. It could also be caused by an increase in government spending or reduction in taxes, though we do not explicitly include those variables in the aggregate demand curve (8).[7] In addition, the position of the aggregate demand curve depends on the level of output last period. The higher the level of output last period (Y_{-1}) the higher the aggregate demand curve.

Given that an increase in the growth rate of money shifts the aggregate demand curve up by exactly the same amount as the growth rate of money rises, we see in Figure 14-6 that an increase in the growth rate of money causes both output and inflation to rise, but that the increase in inflation is less than

---

[7] Recall also that changes in expected inflation will shift the aggregate demand curve.

FIGURE 14-6   INFLATION AND OUTPUT IN THE SHORT-RUN. In the short run inflation and output are determined by the intersection of the aggregate supply and demand curves at point E. An upward shift of the aggregate demand curve raises both output and inflation. An upward shift of the aggregate supply curve increases the inflation rate while reducing the level of output.

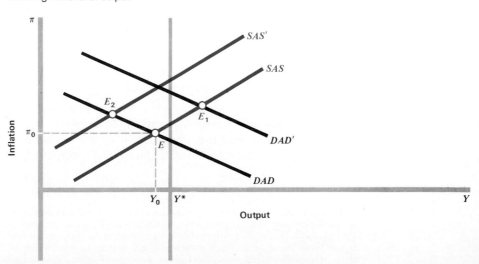

the increase in the growth rate of money. Thus in the short run a 1 percent increase in money growth produces a less than 1 percent increase in inflation, because some of the effects of the increase in the money stock show up in producing higher output. This is exactly the same conclusion as we reached in Chapter 13, when we showed that in the short run an increase in the money stock causes both the price level and the level of output to increase.

Shifts in the aggregate supply curve also affect the rate of inflation and the level of output. An upward shift of the aggregate supply curve such as the shift from SAS to SAS', moves the equilibrium from E to E_2, raising the inflation rate and reducing the level of output. An increase in the expected rate of inflation would cause an upward shift such as that from SAS to SAS'. The reason is that the higher expected rate of inflation produces more rapid rises in wages that cause more rapid inflation.

Summarizing, we see that in the short run:

- An increase in the growth rate of money causes higher inflation and higher output, but inflation rises less than the growth rate of money.

- An increase in the expected rate of inflation causes higher inflation and lower output.

We also note, and leave to you to show, that the factors we have omitted here from the aggregate supply and demand curves change the inflation rate and output in the short run:

- A supply shock that shifts the aggregate supply curve upward causes higher inflation and lower output.

- An increase in expected inflation shifts the aggregate demand curve upward and to the right.[8] To understand this point note from the appendix that the analysis in the text has omitted changes in inflationary expectations as another determinant of dynamic aggregate demand.

The Inflation Rate and Output in the Long Run

From the short run, we move to the hypothetical longest run, in which the growth rate of money is and will continue to be constant, in which expectations have adjusted to actual inflation, and in which output and inflation are constant. Such a situation is called a *steady state*, obviously because nothing is

---

[8] When we include inflation in the aggregate demand curve, an increase in expected inflation causes both the aggregate supply and demand curves to rise, certainly increasing the inflation rate, but producing an uncertain effect on output. The net effect on output depends on whether the aggregate demand or supply curve moves up more. Typically the aggregate supply curve would shift up more, implying higher inflation and lower output — which corresponds with the conclusion reached above when we omit expected inflation from the aggregate demand curve.

changing. Returning to the aggregate demand equation,

$$\pi = m - \frac{1}{\varphi}(Y - Y_{-1}) \tag{10}$$

we recognize that with output constant $(Y = Y_{-1})$, the inflation rate is equal to the growth rate of money. Thus, *in the steady state, the inflation rate is determined solely by the growth rate of money.*

On the aggregate supply side,

$$\pi = \pi^e + \lambda(Y - Y^*) \tag{5}$$

We set $\pi = \pi^e$ and recognize that output is at its potential level Y^*. Thus *in the steady state output is at its full-employment level.*

In the steady state, then, we have very simple relationships: the growth rate of money determines the inflation rate and output is at its potential level.

We want now to consider the real world importance of these steady-state relationships. The first thing to notice is that the economy never reaches a steady state. There are always disturbances affecting aggregate supply and demand: changes in expectations, or in the labor force, or in the prices of other factors of production, or in methods of production on the aggregate supply side; changes in fiscal policy, or in consumer tastes, or in monetary policy, on the aggregate demand side. Thus in practice the economy will not ever reach a steady state: as it starts on the route toward a steady state, some shock or disturbance will come along to bump it off that route onto another path.

The steady-state relationships are useful, though, in indicating the long-run average behavior of the economy. Over long periods, we can expect the economy on average to behave as if the steady-state relationships hold. On average, we expect output to be at its potential level.[9] And on average, we expect the inflation rate to be determined by the growth rate of money. We take up the long-run relationship between inflation and output in more detail in the next chapter.

14-6 DYNAMIC ADJUSTMENT OF OUTPUT AND INFLATION

Many factors drive the inflation rate and the level of output in the short run, whereas in the steady state output is at its full-employment level and inflation is determined by the growth rate of money. In this section we ask how the economy moves toward the long-run equilibrium when a shock or disturbance

---

[9] Indeed, some economists define the natural rate of unemployment as the long-run average rate of unemployment. In that case by definition the unemployment rate is on average over long periods equal to the natural rate, to which the level of potential output corresponds.

affects aggregate supply or demand. To be specific, we examine the dynamic effects — that is, the effects that take place over time — of a change in the growth rate of money. We summarize here our two building blocks:

Dynamic aggregate supply: $\qquad\qquad \pi = \pi_{-1} + \lambda(Y - Y^*) \qquad\qquad$ (8)

Dynamic aggregate demand: $\qquad \pi = m - \dfrac{1}{\varphi}(Y - Y_{-1}) \qquad\qquad$ (10)

Note that we have made the adaptive expectations assumption that expected inflation is equal to last period's inflation rate.

In Figure 14-7, the economy is initially at point E, with output at its

FIGURE 14-7 ADJUSTMENT TO A CHANGE IN THE GROWTH RATE OF MONEY. The increased growth rate of money shifts the aggregate demand curve up, from DAD_0 to DAD_1, raising the inflation rate and output. These changes in turn cause both the supply and demand curves to shift upward in the next period, raising the inflation rate. The process continues until the economy reaches the new steady state.

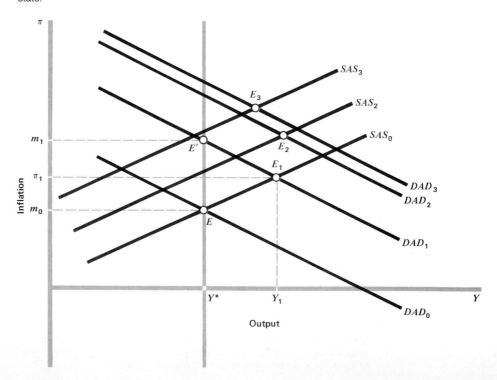

potential level Y° and with inflation equal to the growth rate of money m_0, implying an initial inflation rate $\pi_0 = m_0$. Now suppose the growth rate of money increases, to a new higher level m_1. Refer to the period in which the growth rate of money changes as period 1.

The immediate short-run effect is for the inflation rate and output both to rise, to π_1 and Y_1, respectively. But those changes in turn set off further changes. On the aggregate supply side, the increase in inflation causes expected inflation to increase, with the SAS curve shifting up to SAS_2. The new aggregate supply curve intersects the Y° line at precisely the same rate of inflation as occurred in period 1, i.e., at π_1. The aggregate demand curve also shifts upward, because the level of output was higher last period. On the new aggregate demand curve, the rate of inflation is equal to m_1 at the level of output Y_1 [from equation (9)].

The period 2 equilibrium is at point E_2. Because both the aggregate supply and aggregate demand curves have shifted upward, the inflation rate in period 2, π_2, is certainly higher than π_1. However, it is not clear whether the level of output in period 2, Y_2, is higher or lower than Y_1. That depends on whether the aggregate demand or supply curve shifted more from period 1 to period 2.[10]

In Figure 14-7 we show output higher in period 2 than in period 1. The process now continues, with the aggregate supply and demand curves moving yet further upward. We show the third-period equilibrium E_3 with a higher inflation rate and lower level of output than in the previous period.

It is not worth following the shifts of the aggregate supply and demand curves during the adjustment process in much further detail. Figure 14-8 shows the pattern of adjustment as the economy moves from E_1, the first-period equilibrium, to the eventual steady-state equilibrium at E'. So as to keep the diagram clear, we do not include the shifting supply and demand curves that underlie the pattern of adjustment shown. And we have, for convenience, smoothed the time path of adjustment. The first few points that we traced in Figure 14-7, E_1, E_2, and E_3, are also shown in Figure 14-8.

Stagflation

Two special features of the adjustment process can be seen in Figure 14-8. First, there are times at which output decreases while the inflation rate increases. For instance, between E_2 and E_3 in Figures 14-7 and 14-8, the inflation rate increases while output decreases. This inverse relationship between the rate of inflation and output is a result of the shifts of the aggregate supply curve caused by changes in expected inflation.

The inverse relationship between the rate of inflation and output is im-

---

[10] If $1 > \lambda\varphi$, then output rises in period 2 relative to period 1. If φ is small, the aggregate demand curve moves up a great deal, thereby tending to cause output in period 2 to be higher than Y_1.

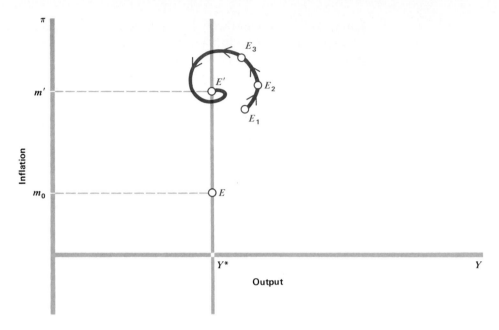

FIGURE 14-8   THE FULL ADJUSTMENT PATH. The full adjustment path moves from E_1 to E', but with fluctuations. During the adjustment process there are periods in which output is falling while inflation is rising.

portant, for it often occurs in practice and is widely believed not to be consistent with accepted macroeconomics. This is *stagflation*. Stagflation occurs when inflation rises while output is either falling or at least not rising.

If one ignores the role of expected inflation in the Phillips curve, it is easy to conclude that periods in which output and inflation move in opposite directions — equivalently that increases in both inflation and unemployment at the same time — are impossible. Indeed, it is not only changes in expectations, but any supply shock, such as an increase in oil prices, that shifts the aggregate supply curve that can produce stagflation. Nonetheless, during periods of stagflation, such as 1973–1974 and 1980, there are articles in the newspapers that the laws of economics are not working as they should because inflation is high or rising even as output is falling.

Overshooting

The most striking feature of Figure 14-8 is that the economy does not move directly to a new higher inflation rate following the increase in the growth rate of money. Rather, given the adaptive expectations assumption we are making, the level of output at some stages falls below Y^*. Similarly the inflation rate is sometimes above its long-run level m_1. In Figure 14-8 the economy fluctuates around the new long-run equilibrium at E'.

There is one more major lesson from this section. It is that the details of the adjustment process depend on the formation of expectations. Since the shifts in the supply curve are determined by shifting expectations, that point is easy to see in a general way. We make the point more specifically now, though, by replacing the adaptive expectations assumption by rational expectations.

Perfect Foresight Expectations

When there is no uncertainty, the rational expectations assumption is equivalent to the assumption of perfect foresight, namely, that firms and individuals correctly predict what will happen when policy changes. In that case we write

$$\pi^e = \pi \tag{11}$$

Under rational expectations, and without uncertainty, we assume that people understand how the economy works and have enough information to figure out what the inflation rate will be.

Substituting the perfect foresight assumption into the aggregate supply curve (5), we obtain

$$Y = Y^* \tag{12}$$

This is a radical result, for it means that, under perfect foresight, the economy is always at potential output. It is as if under rational expectations the long-run results take place in the short run.

How can that be? The underlying assumption of the Phillips curve mechanism that includes expected inflation is that firms and workers are trying to set wages at the level such that there will be full employment. In the Friedman-Phelps version of the Phillips curve, the only reason they might not achieve that is errors in expectations. If by assumption we remove errors in expectations, the economy will then always be at full employment.

Expected and Unexpected Changes in Monetary Policy

The timing of policy actions and the formation of expectations becomes very important under rational expectations. The Friedman-Phelps Phillips curve assumes that wages are set before the period begins. That would mean that wages cannot react to changes in the growth rate of money that are made after wages are set. So the rational expectations assumption would leave open the possibility that an *unexpected* change in monetary policy could affect output.

The logic of rational expectations implies that people base their expectations of inflation on the policies they believe the government is following.

Suppose the growth rate of money has been m_0 for a long time. Then we will have under rational expectations $\pi^e = m_0$, as long as m_0 is the expected growth rate of money.

Then if the Fed unexpectedly changes the growth rate of money to m_1, the initial impact will be exactly as in Figure 14-7, with the economy moving to point E_1, because the terms of wage contracts have not yet been changed. But one period later the adjustment under rational expectations will be very different from that in Figure 14-7. Namely, if everyone believes the Fed has indeed changed the growth rate of money, then the aggregate supply curve will move up by just that amount necessary for the economy to go back immediately to full employment, at Y^*.[11] One period later the economy will be in the steady state with output equal to Y^* and inflation equal to m_1.

The rational expectations assumption thus implies that monetary policy will not have real effects unless changes in monetary policy are unexpected. This remarkable conclusion is examined further in Chapter 18, where we discuss the rational expectations–equilibrium approach to macroeconomics at length.

At this point we should note that the issue of how π^e gets into the aggregate supply function is clearly crucial. If instead of expected inflation, the π^e term reflects compensation for past inflation, or if it takes a period of years for changed inflation rates to be reflected in labor contracts, then the adjustment pattern seen in Figures 14-7 and 14-8 is more representative of what will happen than is the rapid adjustment that takes place under rational expectations.

Summary

1. If inflationary expectations are based on last period's inflation rate — or in general are adaptive, based on past inflation — an increase in the growth rate of money increases both the inflation rate and the level of output in the short run. Both the inflation rate and the level of output continue to fluctuate thereafter, tending eventually to move to the long-run equilibrium of the economy.
2. In the adjustment process to a change in the growth rate of money, there are stages at which inflation and output move in opposite directions. This is because the aggregate supply curve is shifting. Stagflation occurs when output is falling while inflation stays high or rises.
3. Adjustment patterns are radically different under rational expectations. A fully expected change in the growth rate of money does not affect the level

---

[11] Using the aggregate supply and demand equations, it can be shown that the period 1 inflation rate under the perfect foresight assumption is given by the expression:

$$\pi_1 = \frac{m_0 + \lambda \Phi m_1}{1 + \lambda \varphi}$$

of output at all, and only affects inflation. Even if the change in money growth was not expected, output is affected only until expectations adjust to the new growth rate of money. The question of how expectations translate into wages now becomes crucial to the dynamics. If it takes time for changed expectations to affect wages, then even with rational expectations, the adjustment process to a change in the growth rate of money will be lengthy.

14-7 THE ADJUSTMENT TO A FISCAL EXPANSION

In this section we consider how inflation and output respond to a permanent fiscal expansion. We saw in Chapter 13 that a sustained fiscal expansion leads to a cumulative increase in prices and a decline in the real money stock that raises interest rates until crowding out returns the economy to the initial equilibrium. We now establish exactly the same result in the dynamic framework.

Since we now focus on a fiscal expansion we return to (9) above and rewrite the equation, moving the inflation rate to the left-hand side:

$$\pi = m - \frac{1}{\varphi}(Y - Y_{-1}) + \frac{\sigma}{\varphi}f \qquad (10a)$$

This equation differs from (10) only in that it includes the current fiscal expansion as an extra term on the right-hand side of the equation. Given output and given the growth rate of money, a fiscal expansion ($f > 0$) will increase the rate of inflation or shift the aggregate demand schedule upward and to the right. Conversely, a current fiscal contraction ($f < 0$) shifts the aggregate demand schedule downward and to the left.

Suppose now that we have a given growth rate of money m_0 and that the economy is an initial steady state such that $Y = Y^*$ and $\pi = \pi^e = m$. Now a permanent fiscal expansion takes place. That means in the current period f in (10a) is positive and for every period after it is zero because government spending now remains constant at the higher level. In Figure 14-9 we show the fiscal expansion as the rightward shift of the aggregate demand schedule from DAD to DAD_1. In the short-run the economy moves to point E_1. Output unambiguously expands and inflation rises.

The subsequent adjustment process can be understood from (10a). Note that in the second period $f = 0$. Hence the aggregate demand schedule will shift downward to DAD_2. Because Y_1 exceeds Y^*, DAD_2 lies above DAD. On the supply side, using (8) the aggregate supply curve shifts upward to SAS_2. The new equilibrium, in period 2, already involves a return of output toward full employment. Inflation may be higher or lower than in period 1, depending on the relative shifts of the two schedules. This process continues over time, with the demand curve shifting inward and the aggregate supply curve shifting

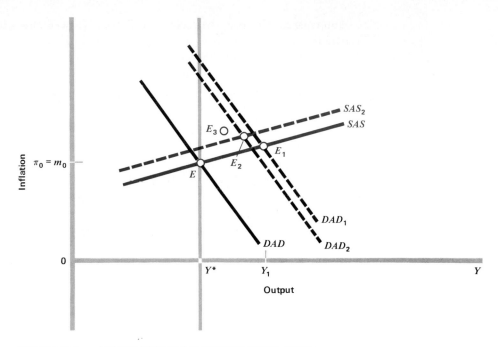

FIGURE 14-9   ADJUSTMENT TO A SUSTAINED FISCAL EXPAN-
SION. Starting from the steady state at E, a fiscal expansion shifts
aggregate demand to DAD_1 so that in the short run the economy
moves to E_1. In the subsequent adjustment the aggregate demand
schedule shifts back while the aggregate supply schedule shifts up and
to the left as inflationary expectations increase. The economy thus
suffers stagflation along a path shown by points E_2 and E_3.

upward and to the left. The economy returns to full employment and then
overshoots, as in Figure 14-8.

But there is an important difference. In this case the growth rate of money
is not changed and hence, in the long run, we return to the initial rate of
inflation $\pi = m_0$. The typical path of the adjustment to a sustained fiscal expansion would then look like that shown in Figure 14-10. In the transition
period inflation will have been higher than the growth rate of money and, as a
result, real balances decline, interest rates rise, and real spending declines.
The fact that the economy returns to full-employment output, with government spending higher, means that private demand has been crowded out.
Once again we note the stagflation syndrome. After the initial expansion, at
point E_1 output is falling, but inflation is increasing. Thus fiscal expansion, just
as much as increased monetary growth, cannot *permanently* raise output
above normal. Of course, output will be above normal for a time, and that may

be enough of a motive, at the right time, for a government to implement a fiscal expansion.

14-8 ALTERNATIVE STRATEGIES TO REDUCE INFLATION

Suppose the inflation rate in the economy is 10 percent, and the government decides to fight high inflation to try to get down to inflation rates of around 2 to 3 percent. This is the decision that was made in the United States in 1979, and it took effect most seriously in 1982. By the mid-eighties the inflation rate was down to the 3 to 4 percent range. In the meantime the economy went through two recessions, in 1980 and again in 1981–1982.

The key question for any government contemplating disinflation is how to disinflate as cheaply as possible — that is, with as small a recession as possible. In this section we consider alternative strategies for disinflation. The basic method of disinflation should be clear from the previous section: it is to reduce the growth rate of aggregate demand, shifting the *DAD* curve downward. In the model we are using, that can be done by cutting back on money growth

FIGURE 14-10   THE SMOOTHED ADJUSTMENT PATH FOR A SUSTAINED FISCAL EXPANSION. The smoothed adjustment path shows that following an initial expansion to point E_1, inflation rises further, but output falls. In the long run, following a period of unemployment, output returns to full employment Y^* and inflation to the level determined by the rate of money growth m_0.

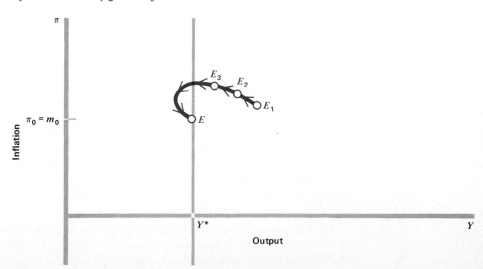

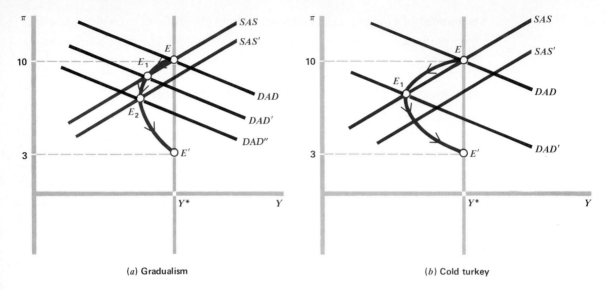

(a) Gradualism   (b) Cold turkey

FIGURE 14-11   ALTERNATIVE DISINFLATION STRATEGIES. In panel
(a) policy reduces the inflation rate gradually from 10 to 3 percent,
seeking to keep output from falling much below the potential level. In
panel (b), by contrast, the decision is made to try to end the inflation
rapidly, by starting with a large cut in the growth rate of money that
produces much lower inflation, at the cost of a large recession.

and, in the short run, by using fiscal policy. In this section we consider only
monetary policy.

Gradualism

Figure 14-11 shows the choices. A policy of gradualism (in the left panel)
attempts a slow and steady return to low inflation. The gradualist policy in
Figure 14-11a begins with a small reduction in the money growth rate that
shifts the aggregate demand curve down from DAD to DAD', moving the
economy a little way along the short-run aggregate supply curve SAS, from E
to E_1. In response to the lower inflation at E_1, the short-run aggregate supply
curve shifts downward to SAS'. A further small cut in money growth moves the
economy to E_2, the aggregate supply curve shifts down again, and the process
continues.

Eventually output returns to its potential level at point E', at a lower
inflation rate. There is no massive recession during the adjustment process,
although unemployment is above normal throughout.

Cold Turkey

The right panel of Figure 14-11 shows the alternative. *The cold turkey strategy tries to cut the inflation rate fast.* The strategy starts with an immediate sharp cutback in money growth shifting the aggregate demand curve from *DAD* to *DAD'*, moving the economy from *E* to *E*₁. There is a large recession, but because the aggregate supply curve is relatively flat, the reduction in inflation is small to begin with.

By creating a larger fall in the inflation rate than when gradualism is used, the cold turkey strategy causes the short-run supply curve to move down faster than it does in Figure 14-11*a*. The cold turkey strategy keeps up the pressure by holding the rate of money growth low. Eventually the rate of inflation falls enough that output and employment begin to grow again. The economy returns to point *E'* with full employment and a lower rate of inflation.

Gradualism versus Cold Turkey

Figure 14-12 presents the gradualist and cold turkey strategies in an alternative form. In the gradualist strategy the growth rate of money is initially reduced only slightly, and the economy never strays very far from the natural rate of unemployment. But the inflation rate comes down only slowly. The

FIGURE 14-12   COLD-TURKEY VERSUS GRADUALISM. This is an alternative way of comparing the two strategies. Cold turkey (colored curves) cuts the growth rate of money sharply, producing a massive but shorter recession. The gradualist strategy (black curves) produces much less unemployment, but also a much less rapid reduction in the inflation rate.

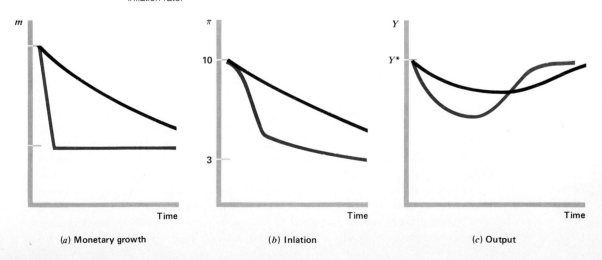

(*a*) Monetary growth   (*b*) Inlation   (*c*) Output

cold turkey strategy, by contrast, starts with a massive cut in the growth rate of money and a large recession. The recession is much worse than it ever is in the gradualist strategy, but the reduction in inflation is more rapid.

Which strategy should be chosen? Is moderate unemployment with higher inflation preferable to high unemployment with lower inflation? We cannot answer that before discussing the costs of inflation and unemployment in Chapter 15. U.S. policy makers in 1981 – 1982 chose a policy closer to cold turkey than to gradualism.

Credibility

The cold turkey strategy has one major point in its favor. It is clear in the case of cold turkey that a decisive policy change has been made, and that policy has the firm aim of driving down the inflation rate. The gradualist strategy, which takes a long time to be implemented, is more likely to be abandoned if it seems to be producing more unemployment than expected, or if the policy-making team changes.

Thus people forming their expectations rationally will be more likely to believe policy has changed under the cold turkey strategy than under gradualism. A belief that policy has changed will by itself drive down the expected rate of inflation and for that reason cause the short-run Phillips curve to shift down. A credible policy is one that the public believes will be kept up and succeed. The cold turkey policy gets a *credibility bonus* that gradualism does not.

Credibility and Rapid Deflation

Throughout the period of deflation, starting with the Fed's change in policy in October 1979, there has been strong emphasis on the credibility of policy. Some proponents of rational expectations even believed that if policy could only be made credible, it would be possible to disinflate practically without causing any recession at all.

The argument went like this. The expectations-augmented aggregate supply curve, equation (5), is

$$\pi = \pi^e + \lambda(Y - Y^*) \tag{5}$$

If policy is credible, people immediately adjust their expectations of inflation to the new policy, with its lower rate of growth of money. Thus the short-run aggregate supply curve will move down immediately when the new policy is announced. Accordingly, it is possible to move immediately from point E in Figure 14-8 to E'. In brief, the argument is that if policy is credible and if expectations are rational, the economy can move to a new long-run equilibrium immediately when there is a change in policy.

The experience of the United States in the early 1980s, seen in Figure 14-2, and even more the experience of Britain in the same period when the

Thatcher government was pursuing a resolute anti-inflationary policy that led to a 13 percent unemployment rate, casts doubt on this optimistic scenario. The reason the extreme credibility – rational expectations argument does not work is that it is not enough for people to believe a new policy will reduce the inflation rate. The expectations must also be incorporated into wage and other long-term contracts. The economy at any time has an overhang of past contracts, embodying past expectations, and it takes time for those to be renegotiated. Thus a rapid return to lower inflation in economies experiencing inflation rates in the 10 to 20 percent range is unlikely.

It is easiest to change the inflation rate when there are no long-term contracts in the economy. There will be few contracts of that kind if inflation is high and variable, for instance in a hyperinflation. Under such conditions no one will want to sign agreements in nominal terms because they will be gambling too much on the future behavior of the price level. Long-term contracts disappear, and wages and prices are frequently reset. A credible policy will have rapid effects. But such rapid success cannot be expected in an economy where the structure of contracts has not yet been destroyed by extreme inflation.

It remains true, though, that whatever the structure of contracts, the more credible a policy that aims to disinflate the economy is, the more successful that policy will be.[12]

Is There a Better Way?

The treatments for the inflation disease summarized in Figure 14-11 are painful and have led to a search for better ways. In this section we briefly describe two other anti-inflationary policies, incomes policy and tax incentive plans.

INCOMES POLICY (OR WAGE AND PRICE CONTROLS)

Inflation stabilization takes time and involves unemployment because that is what is needed to get the rate of wage change down. Incomes policies try to short-circuit that slow process by getting the rate of wage change down fast, either by law (wage-price controls) or by persuasion. *Incomes policies* are policies that attempt to reduce the rate of wage and price increases by direct action. Either wages and prices are controlled, or the government tries to persuade labor leaders and business to raise wages and prices more slowly than they otherwise would. Incomes policies, if successful, shift the short-run aggregate supply curve down.

Wage and price controls are typically used in wartime in many countries and were used in the United States in the period 1971–1974. The 1971 controls were imposed in an effort to break the back of an inflation that for 2

---

[12] The credibility issue is treated in several interesting papers in "Anti-inflation Policies and the Problem of Credibility," *American Economic Review* (Papers and Proceedings), May 1982.

BOX

14-1

DISINFLATION AND THE SACRIFICE RATIO

Given that it is not in practice possible to reduce the inflation rate without a recession, the question arises, How much output is lost through different methods of disinflation, such as cold turkey and gradualism? Discussion of the costs of disinflation makes extensive use of the concept of the *sacrifice ratio*. The sacrifice ratio is the ratio of the cumulative percentage loss of GNP (as a result of a disinflation policy) to the reduction in inflation that is actually achieved.

Thus, suppose a policy reduces the inflation rate from 10 to 4 percent over a 3-year period, at the cost of levels of output that are 10 percent below potential in the first year, 8 percent below potential in the second year, and 6 percent below potential in the third year. The total loss of GNP is 24 percent (10 + 8 + 6), the reduction in inflation is 6 percent (10 − 4), and the sacrifice ratio is 4.

Before the disinflation of the 1980s, economists estimated sacrifice ratios that would apply if a disinflation program were undertaken. Estimates ranged between 5 and 10. In Table 1 we show the elements needed to calculate the sacrifice ratio, based on U.S. Department of Commerce estimates of the level of output at full employment.

Taking the accumulated output loss as 23.9 percent of a year's potential GNP and the reduction in inflation as 6.4 percent (from 9.7 to 3.3 percent), the sacrifice ratio is 3.7. This is a low number relative to previous estimates, but clearly in line with them. The calculation is only an estimate both because we do not know potential output for sure and because the 3.3 percent inflation rate we assume may be below the new long-run level since complete adjustment has not yet occurred. The estimate may underestimate the true cost of disinflation because events favorable for disinflation, such as declining oil prices and the strong dollar, have influenced the path of actual inflation.

We can also use our theory of the aggregate supply curve to calculate sacrifice ratios. Suppose first that expectations were rational, and that all it took to reduce the inflation rate was an announcement that the growth rate of money would be reduced next year. Then according to the simplest rational expectations view, and if the announcement was believed, the sacrifice ratio would be zero, because the inflation rate would fall without a recession.

TABLE 1 ACTUAL AND POTENTIAL OUTPUT, AND INFLATION, 1980–1985

Year	Actual/Potential GNP, %	Output loss, %	Inflation, %
1980	97.4	2.6	9.0
1981	96.9	3.1	9.7
1982	92.4	7.6	6.4
1983	93.7	6.3	3.8
1984	97.8	2.2	4.1
1985	97.9	2.1	3.3
	Total	23.9	

Notes: (1) Inflation rate is for GNP deflator. (2) Potential GNP series is calculated for unemployment rate of 6%. This series is reported in the *Survey of Current Business*, March 1986, p. 13.

Alternatively, suppose that aggregate supply curve (8), based on adaptive expectations, applies:

$$\pi = \pi_{-1} + \lambda(Y - Y^*) \tag{8}$$

This has a very strong implication. Namely, to reduce the inflation rate by 1 percent, over any length of time, costs $1/\lambda$ units of GNP. It is clear that to reduce the inflation rate in one period by 1 percent costs $1/\lambda$ of GNP. Now suppose we did it in two steps: 0.5 percent in each of 2 years. In the first year, the output loss would be $0.5/\lambda$; the loss in the second year would also be $0.5/\lambda$. The total would again be $1/\lambda$. The same conclusion would be reached however long the period over which the adjustment was spread.

The conclusion is that, with the adaptive expectations, and given certain other conditions, the sacrifice ratio is independent of how rapidly the inflation rate is reduced. That does not mean of course that it does not matter whether a government undertakes a cold turkey or a gradualist policy. It may be that a short, very deep recession (cold turkey) has greater costs than a long period of only slightly greater than usual unemployment (gradualism).

The analysis also makes the role of credibility clear: to the extent that expectations of inflation can be reduced by announcements about policy, the sacrifice ratio is reduced — in the extreme (but unrealistic) simplest rational expectations case it is theoretically even possible to disinflate with no output cost at all.

years had shown little sign of responding to restrictive monetary and fiscal policy. The controls began with a 90-day wage-price *freeze.* For 3 months firms were forbidden to raise prices or pay higher wages. The freeze applied to the prices of most goods, with some exceptions, for example, for agricultural goods.

A wage-price freeze certainly brings the inflation rate down. So why not get rid of inflation that way? The reason is that wages and prices have to change if resources are to be allocated efficiently in the economy. Anti-inflationary policy has to try to reduce the average rate of price increase without interfering with the role of prices in allocating resources.

Over a short period, misallocations of resources from frozen wages and prices will be small and not costly. But if wages and prices are kept fixed for a long time, shortages of labor and particular goods will develop. The problem then is to find a way out of controls that does not reignite inflation. The United States did not avoid that problem when, after many policy shifts, controls were lifted in 1973 – 1974 — at the time the oil price shock hit the economy.

One reason incomes policies have rarely been successful is that they are not combined with appropriate aggregate demand policies.[13] Incomes poli-

---

[13] For a careful account of wage and price controls see Hugh Rockoff, *Drastic Measures, A History of Wage and Price Controls in the United States* (London: Cambridge University Press, 1984). See, too, Robert Russell, *Can Chronic Inflation be Cured?* E. S. Woodward Lectures, Department of Economics, University of British Columbia, 1982.

cies, or wage and price controls aim to move the aggregate supply curve down, thereby reducing the inflation rate. So long as the aggregate demand curve moves down at the same time, the inflation rate will fall and can stay low. But if there is no accompanying change in the aggregate demand curve, the wage and price controls will only build up inflationary pressures that will eventually explode.

An interesting recent development is the use of wage and price controls as part of a complete package of economic policy measures taken to end extremely high inflation episodes. In 1985 in Argentina and Israel, and in 1986 in Brazil, policy packages were put into effect to reduce the inflation rate from several hundred percent per year to low double-digit per annum figures. In each case the policy measures involved cuts in the budget deficit and measures to control monetary growth. They also involved as central parts of the package controls on wages and prices. All three programs showed early signs of success. Whether they will ultimately succeed remains to be seen, but their initial success does suggest an important potential role for wage and price controls in rapidly ending inflation, *provided, of course, that the accompanying aggregate demand reduction measures are taken.*

TIP

Tax incentive plans (TIP) to reduce the inflation rate encourage workers and firms to keep wage and price increases low by providing tax incentives to do so.[14]

For instance, TIP might set a baseline rate of wage increase of 5 percent. Any firm that pays a higher rate of wage increase to its employees has its taxes increased. Any firm paying a lower rate of wage increase receives a tax break. Or the penalties and rewards might be placed directly on the workers. Any worker receiving an increase in excess of 5 percent would have his or her tax rate increased, and so forth.

The major problem with TIP is that it would be very difficult to administer.[15] The aim is to discourage wage or price increases that are being made only to compensate for inflation. We would not, for instance, want to penalize a worker who has a large wage increase because of having worked hard and having been promoted. But how can the law discriminate between these two cases? If the law says anyone who is promoted is not penalized for receiving a rate of wage increase above the baseline rate, firms and workers who find it in their joint interest to raise the wage will do so by promoting people.

Both incomes policies and TIP run into the same difficulty. The difficulty is that relative wages and prices in the economy do have to change if the price

---

[14] The *Brookings Papers on Economic Activity*, 2: 1978, contains several articles and discussions of TIP.

[15] TIP has not been implemented, though the Carter administration did in 1978 propose a form of TIP that the Congress rejected.

mechanism is to work. Policies that operate directly on wages and prices have to try to prevent the overall price level from rising while relative prices are permitted to change. This is either impossible or extremely difficult over any extended period.

Is There Hope?

The disinflation that started in the United States at the beginning of the eighties was still operating successfully in 1986. The inflation rate had come down and stayed down. In part this was a result of the fall in the price of oil. But it was also a result of a cautious monetary policy, for at no stage during the disinflation process was aggregate demand allowed to grow very rapidly. Even after 3 years of recovery, by the middle of 1986, the unemployment rate was still hovering around 7 percent, above the full-employment unemployment rate. Restrictive, nonaccommodating policies can continue to keep the inflation rate low, even in the face of inflationary shocks that will inevitably hit the economy from time to time.

14-9 SUMMARY

1. The aggregate supply and demand curves introduced in this chapter differ from those of Chapter 13 by showing the relationship between output and the inflation rate rather than output and the price level.
2. The aggregate supply curve is modified further to include expected inflation. Wages increase more rapidly when inflation is expected, thus shifting the aggregate supply curve upward. Expected inflation enters prices through wages, which are changed as new wage terms are set. Thus the process through which a change in the expected inflation rate works its way into the aggregate supply curve may be quite slow.
3. The short-run aggregate supply curve, with constant expected rate of inflation, is positively sloped, and quite flat, because in the short run changes in output do not cause large changes in prices. In the short run there is a tradeoff between inflation and output. The long-run aggregate supply curve, with the actual and expected inflation rates equal, is vertical: there is no long-run tradeoff between inflation and output.
4. Under adaptive expectations, expected inflation is based on the recent behavior of the inflation rate. For most of the chapter we make the particular adaptive expectations assumption that the expected inflation rate is equal to last period's inflation rate. Under rational expectations, there is no simple formula for determining expectations. Rather people are assumed to form expectations using all the information that is available about the determinants of the inflation rate. Whereas under adaptive expectations a change in policy would not affect expectations until the actual inflation rate

is affected, under rational expectations people knowing that policy will change will adjust their expectations immediately.

5. The dynamic aggregate demand curve is a negatively sloped relationship between the inflation rate and the level of output. Its position is determined by the growth rate of money, and by last period's level of output. The basic relationship follows from the link between aggregate demand and real balances: the more rapidly are real balances growing, the more rapidly is aggregate demand increasing. The dynamic aggregate demand curve is also shifted by changes in the aggregate demand curve and by fiscal policy changes.

6. The inflation rate and level of output are determined by the intersection of the aggregate supply and demand curves. In the short run changes in the growth rate of money affect both output and inflation. In the long run a change in the growth rate of money affects only the inflation rate.

7. During the adjustment process to a change in the growth rate of money, assuming adaptive expectations, there are periods of stagflation during which inflation is increasing while output falls. Typically, there is also overshooting of the new inflation rate, in the sense that on average during the adjustment process the increase in the inflation rate exceeds the increase in the growth rate of money.

8. The adjustment pattern is much more rapid under rational expectations. If the change in the growth rate of money is anticipated, then only the inflation rate changes when the money growth rate changes. If the change in monetary policy is unexpected, it does affect both the level of output and the inflation rate in the short run, but output returns to its potential level as soon as the new policy is understood.

9. There are two basic strategies to reduce the inflation rate. The gradualist strategy aims to bring the inflation rate down slowly, thereby avoiding any large recession. The cold turkey strategy cuts the growth rate of money by a large amount up front, thereby trying to reduce inflation fast at the cost of a larger recession. The cold turkey strategy may gain from a credibility bonus in that the government reduces expected inflation more rapidly by demonstrating its willingness to pay the price of disinflation.

KEY TERMS

Expectations-augmented aggregate
  supply curve
Short-run aggregate supply curve
Long-run aggregate supply curve
Adaptive expectations
Rational expectations
Stagflation
Overshooting

Gradualism
Cold turkey
Credibility
Sacrifice ratio
Incomes policies
Wage and price controls
TIP

PROBLEMS

1. Explain why the expected rate of inflation affects the position of the expectations-augmented aggregate supply curve.
2. (a) Define the long-run aggregate supply curve.
   (b) Explain why the expectations-augmented long-run supply curve is vertical.
   (c) Does the economy ever reach the long run?
3. In Figures 14-7 and 14-8 we show how the economy reaches a higher rate of inflation. Starting at a steady state with 10 percent inflation, show how inflation would shift back to 4 percent if the growth rate of money were reduced immediately to 4 percent.
4. Consider the adjustment to a *transitory* fiscal expansion. For one period only government spending increases. In the next period it falls back to the initial level. Use (8) and (10a) to trace the adjustment path of inflation and of output. (*Note:* This is different from the analysis of Section 14-7. Here we have $f > 0$ in period 1 and $f < 0$ in period 2.)
5. Using the assumptions $\pi^e = \pi_{-1}$, $\lambda = 0.4$, and $\phi = 0.5$, and starting from a steady state with money growth equal to the inflation rate equal to 4 percent, calculate the inflation rate and output in the first three periods following an increase in the growth rate of money to 8 percent.
6. Suppose that in problem 5, expectations are rational instead of adaptive:
   (a) Suppose the change in money growth was announced before it happens, and everyone believes it will take place. What happens to inflation and output?
   (b) Suppose that money growth is unexpectedly increased from 4 percent to 8 percent in period 1, but that people believe from period 2 on that money growth will be 8 percent. Calculate the inflation rate in period 1 and in subsequent periods.
7. Calculate the sacrifice ratio using the assumptions of problem 5. Confirm that the sacrifice ratio is greater the flatter the aggregate supply curve.
8. Consider an economy that experiences an adverse supply shock. We can model this by introducing in (8) a one-time shock which we denote by x:

$$\pi = \pi_{-1} + \lambda(Y - Y^*) + x$$

The term x is positive during the supply shock. Show the adjustment process to such a disturbance.
9. The economy finds itself in a recession as a result of an adverse supply shock. Show that both a fiscal expansion or increased monetary growth can speed the return of the economy to full employment.
10. Suppose that a new policy mix of fiscal expansion and a permanent reduction in money growth goes into effect.
    (a) What are the long-run effects on output and inflation?
    (b) How does the fiscal expansion affect the adjustment relative to that you discussed in answering problem 3?

APPENDIX: DYNAMIC AGGREGATE DEMAND

In the text we use the simplified dynamic aggregate demand curve

$$Y = Y_{-1} + \varphi(m - \pi) \tag{A1}$$

In (A1), m is the growth rate of the nominal money stock. In this appendix we derive the dynamic aggregate demand curve carefully from the *IS-LM* model of aggregate demand and show exactly where (A1) simplifies matters.

To derive the aggregate demand curve we return to the goods market equilibrium condition

$$Y = \overline{\alpha}(\overline{A} - br) \tag{A2}$$

where $\overline{A}$ denotes autonomous spending, $\overline{\alpha}$ is the multiplier, and r denotes the *real* rate of interest. Recall that investment demand is determined by the *real* and not the nominal interest rate.

Recognizing that the real interest rate is equal to the nominal interest rate i minus the expected rate of inflation, we rewrite (A2) as

$$Y = \overline{\alpha}(\overline{A} - bi + b\pi^e) \tag{A3}$$

In this form we recognize that goods market equilibrium depends on both the nominal interest rate *and* the expected inflation rate. Given the nominal interest rate, an increase in the expected rate of inflation increases aggregate demand — because it implies a lower real interest rate and larger investment demand.

Now we bring in the asset markets, by rewriting the condition that the supply of real balances is equal to the demand. Putting the interest rate on the left-hand side, as we did in equation (4) of Chapter 5,

$$i = \frac{1}{h}\left(kY - \frac{M}{P}\right) \tag{A4}$$

Substituting (A4) into (A3), we find that the level of output at which both the goods and assets markets are in equilibrium can be written as

$$Y = \overline{\alpha}\left(\overline{A} - \frac{b}{h}\left(kY - \frac{M}{P}\right) + b\pi^e\right)$$

or

$$Y = \gamma\left(\overline{A} + \frac{b}{h}\frac{M}{P} + b\pi^e\right) \tag{A5}$$

where

$$\gamma = \frac{\overline{\alpha}}{1 + (\overline{\alpha}bk/h)}$$

The aggregate demand curve (A5) shows that the *level* of aggregate demand is determined by autonomous demand (including fiscal policy), real balances, and the expected inflation rate. An increase in any of these three factors will increase the level of aggregate demand. Note that the only difference between the aggregate demand curve here and in the previous chapter is that we are now including the expected inflation rate — and that it enters because, given the nominal interest rate, a higher expected rate of inflation means a lower real interest rate.

It follows that the *change* in aggregate demand is determined by *changes* in autonomous demand, real balances, and the expected inflation rate. Assuming that the only change in autonomous demand comes from fiscal policy, we write

$$\Delta Y = \sigma f + \varphi(m - \pi) + \eta(\Delta \pi^e) \qquad \text{(A6)}$$

where Δ indicates the change in a variable and f is the *change* in fiscal policy.

As described in the text, the term $(m - \pi)$ is the change in real balances, the difference between the growth rate of money and the rate of inflation: when money is growing faster than prices, real balances are increasing, and when money is growing more slowly than prices, real balances are decreasing.

Rewriting (A6) by recognizing that $\Delta Y = Y - Y_{-1}$,

$$Y = Y_{-1} + \sigma f + \varphi(m - \pi) + \eta(\Delta \pi^e) \qquad \text{(A7)}$$

Equation (A7) is the complete aggregate demand relationship between the level of output and the inflation rate. Given last period's income, expectations, the change in fiscal policy, and the growth rate of money, higher inflation rates imply lower aggregate demand.

In the text we simplify by omitting the change in expected inflation, $\Delta \pi^e$.

15

THE TRADEOFFS BETWEEN INFLATION AND UNEMPLOYMENT

In 1982 the U.S. unemployment rate reached its highest level since the great depression of the 1930s. More than 1 person in 10 in the labor force was unemployed. Where only 2 years before the public had declared inflation to be the major problem of the nation, now unemployment became the chief issue. By 1986, after 3 years of expansion with low inflation, neither inflation nor unemployment was perceived as a major issue, just as had been the case in the very stable period of the 1960s.

Figure 15-1 shows the public's perceptions of inflation and unemployment as the chief problems facing the nation. The figure reports the results of a Gallup poll where a sample of people were questioned on what they regarded as the country's major problem. The figure shows the percentages of those who answered "inflation" and those who answered "unemployment." The figure makes two points. First, economic problems bother people. For most of the seventies inflation and/or unemployment were thought by a large majority of the public to be the most serious problems facing the nation — and there were many other possibilities, like nuclear war, pollution, and crime, to worry them. Second, high inflation rates make people worry about inflation and high unemployment rates make people worry about unemployment.[1]

---

[1] More careful study of the data shows that while a *high* inflation rate causes people to worry about inflation, their concern about unemployment is affected more by *rising* than by *high* unemployment.

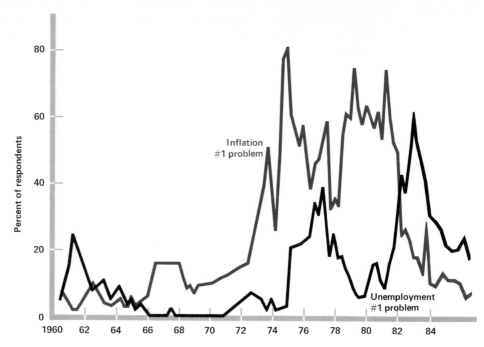

FIGURE 15-1   INFLATION AND UNEMPLOYMENT AS THE
NATION'S MOST IMPORTANT PROBLEM — THE GALLUP REPORT.
(*Source: The Gallup Opinion Index*, June 1979, and the *Gallup
Report*, various issues.)

In most of this chapter we take a careful look at the costs of both inflation
and unemployment. We also take up a second issue. As the discussion of
alternative disinflation strategies at the end of Chapter 14 showed, it is necessary to go through a period of higher unemployment to reduce the inflation
rate significantly. Even though there is no long-run tradeoff between inflation
and unemployment, there is a short-run tradeoff with which policy makers
have to deal. How should they weigh the relative costs of producing a recession versus continuing with higher inflation?[2] And how do they in practice deal
with the tradeoff? One answer is given by the theory of the *political business
cycle*, described at the end of the chapter. According to political business cycle
theory, policy makers choose the timing of policy moves to produce the infla-

---

[2] The need to weigh the costs of temporarily higher unemployment against the benefit of a reduction in the
inflation rate is emphasized in Edmund Phelps, *Inflation Policy and Unemployment Theory. The Cost Benefit
Approach to Monetary Planning* (New York: Norton 1972). See also Arthur Okun, in J. Pechman (ed.), *Economics
for Policy Making* (Washington, D.C.: The Brookings Institution, 1983).

tion and unemployment results to come out just right at the time of elections. Of course the inflation (or the recession to stop it) will come later, after the election.

We start with a discussion of unemployment. The main point of the discussion is to distinguish between *cyclical* and *structural* unemployment and to develop the concept of the natural rate of unemployment. The discussion proceeds from there to the costs of inflation and to the cost-benefit analysis of inflation stabilization.

15-1 THE ANATOMY OF UNEMPLOYMENT

An unemployed person is defined as one who is out of work *and* who (1) has actively looked for work during the previous 4 weeks, or (2) is waiting to be recalled to a job after having been laid off, or (3) is waiting to report to a new job within 4 weeks. The requirement of having looked for a job in the past 4 weeks is included to try to ensure that the person is actively interested in a job, and not merely expressing an interest if a job should happen to show up.

In April 1983, 10.1 percent of the total or 10.4 percent of the civilian labor force (excluding resident armed forces) were unemployed. Table 15-1 presents some details of unemployment rates at that time and 3 years later, in April 1986, for different groups in the population. In April 1986 the overall civilian unemployment rate was 7.1 percent.

The table reveals extraordinary differences in the unemployment rates for the four groups. In 1983 nearly one in every two black teenagers was unemployed, but "only" one in five white teenagers, and fewer than one in ten white adults. By 1986 unemployment rates were lower, but the racial and age differences were still extremely large. These differences in group unemployment rates are an important part of understanding unemployment in the United States, as we shall see shortly. But before that we want to make the

TABLE 15-1	UNEMPLOYMENT RATES BY AGE AND RACE (Percentage of Group Unemployed)					
	APRIL 1983			APRIL 1986		
	Black	White	Total	Black	White	Total
16–19 years	47.8	20.3	23.4	42.6	16.4	19.6
20 years and older	18.4	7.9	9.2	12.6	5.3	6.1

Source: Employment and Earnings, May 1983 and May 1986.

distinction between the part of unemployment that is cyclical and the part that is called noncyclical, or structural.

Table 15-2 shows data for three different periods—1978:IV, a time when unemployment was at the lowest level in the last 10 years, 1983:I, when unemployment was at the highest level since the 1930s, and 1986:I, when unemployment again was low. The data bring out two important contrasts. In all periods unemployment rates for teenagers are much higher than they are for people 20 years and older. Second, unemployment rates for whites are much lower than they are for blacks.

The unemployment rate in the first row of Table 15-2 corresponds, roughly, to structural unemployment. *Structural unemployment* is the unemployment that exists when the economy is at full employment. Structural unemployment corresponds to the *natural rate of unemployment.* Structural unemployment results from the structure of the labor market—from the nature of jobs in the economy and from the labor force participation patterns of workers. We discuss the determinants of structural unemployment in more detail below when we examine the natural rate of unemployment. *Cyclical unemployment* is unemployment in excess of structural unemployment; it occurs when output is below its full-employment level.

Characteristics of U.S. Unemployment

The anatomy of unemployment is built around three central facts of U.S. unemployment behavior:

1. There are substantial flows of individuals in and out of unemployment each month, and most people who become unemployed in any given month remain unemployed for only a short time.
2. Much of U.S. unemployment is constituted of people who will be unemployed for quite a long time.
3. There is considerable variation of unemployment rates across different groups in the labor force (as can be seen in Tables 15-1 and 15-2).

The first and second facts may seem contradictory. A numerical example should make it clear that there is no necessary contradiction. Suppose that the labor force consists of 100 (million) people and that five people become unemployed each month. Suppose that four of those people are unemployed for precisely 1 month, and one person will be unemployed for 6 months. Suppose also that the economy is in a steady state, so that this situation has repeated itself every month for years.

We ask first how many people are unemployed at any one time, say, September 30. There will be five people who became unemployed September 1, one person who became unemployed August 1 (and who has been unemployed for 2 months), and so on, back to the person who became unemployed April 1, and whose 6 months of unemployment will end the next day, on

TABLE 15-2   SELECTED UNEMPLOYMENT INDICATORS
             (Percentage of Group Unemployed)

| | | 20 YEARS+ | | | | Black |
	Total	Men	Women	16–19 years	White	and other
1978:IV	5.9	4.1	5.7	16.3	5.1	11.5
1983:I	10.4	9.7	8.9	22.8	9.1	18.5
1986:I	7.1	6.0	6.5	18.5	5.9	13.1

Source: *Employment and Earnings*, 1979, 1983, 1986.

October 1. In total, there will be ten people unemployed, so the unemployment rate is 10 percent. Of the ten, six will suffer a 6-month spell of unemployment before they again become employed. This is consistent with the second fact. But remember that we started with five people becoming unemployed each month, four of whom remain unemployed for only a month. And that is consistent with the first fact, that most people who become unemployed within a given month remain so for only a short time. We return to this example later in this section.

The third fact, variation of unemployment rates across different groups in the labor force, can be examined using the relationship between the overall unemployment rate u and the unemployment rates u_i of groups within the labor force. The overall rate is a weighted average of the unemployment rates of the groups:

$$u = w_1 u_1 + w_2 u_2 + \cdots + w_n u_n \tag{1}$$

The weights w_i are the fraction of the civilian labor force that falls within the specific group, say, black teenagers.

Equation (1) makes it clear that the overall unemployment rate either could be made up of unemployment rates that are much the same for different groups in the labor force or could conceal dramatic differences in unemployment rates among groups categorized, say, by age, race, and sex. Fact 3 is that the aggregate rate does conceal substantial differences in unemployment rates. For instance, in April 1986, the aggregate unemployment rate averaged 7.0 percent: white unemployment was 6.1 percent, and nonwhite unemployment was 13.6 percent. In terms of equation (1), we have

$$7.0\% = (0.88)6.1\% + (0.12)13.6\% \tag{1a}$$

where the shares of the two groups in the labor force are 88 percent and 12 percent, respectively.

We now turn to a more detailed examination of the three central facts about the anatomy of unemployment.

Flows In and Out of Unemployment

Figure 15-2 shows how people enter and leave the *unemployment pool.* A person may become unemployed for one of four reasons: (1) The person may be a new entrant into the labor force, looking for work for the first time, or else be a reentrant—someone returning to the labor force after not having looked for work for more than 4 weeks. (2) A person may quit a job in order to look for other employment and register as unemployed while searching. (3) The person may be laid off. The definition of *layoff* is a suspension without pay lasting or expected to last more than 7 consecutive days, initiated by the employer "without prejudice to the worker." The latter qualification means that the worker was not fired but rather will return to the old job if demand for the firm's product recovers. A firm will typically adjust to a decline in product demand by laying off some labor. A firm may also rotate layoffs among its labor force so that the individual laid-off worker may expect a

FIGURE 15-2   FLOWS IN AND OUT OF THE UNEMPLOYMENT POOL.

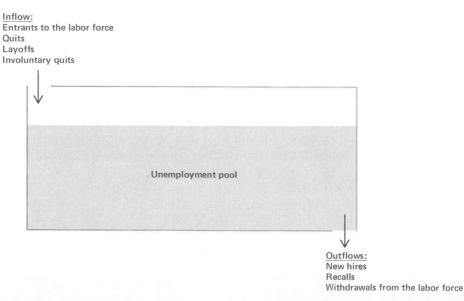

Inflow:
Entrants to the labor force
Quits
Layoffs
Involuntary quits

Unemployment pool

Outflows:
New hires
Recalls
Withdrawals from the labor force

TABLE 15-3	LABOR TURNOVER RATES IN MANUFACTURING IN 1981 (Per 100 Employees, Average of Monthly Data)					
ACCESSIONS			SEPARATIONS			
Total	New hires	Recalls	Total	Quits	Layoffs	Other
3.2	2.0	1.0	3.6	1.3	1.6	0.7

Note: Components do not add to totals due to averaging and rounding. "Other" includes involuntary separations.
Source: Employment and Earnings, March 1982.

recall even before product demand has fully recovered. In manufacturing, it appears that over 75 percent of laid-off workers return to jobs with their original employers.[3] (4) A worker may lose a job to which there is no hope of returning, either because of being fired or because the firm closes down. This last way of becoming unemployed is referred to as *involuntary quits*.

These sources of inflow into the pool of unemployment have a counter-part in the outflow from the unemployment pool. There are essentially three ways of moving out of the pool of unemployment. (1) A person may be hired into a new job. (2) Someone laid off may be recalled. (3) An unemployed person may stop looking for a job and thus, by definition, leave the labor force. Such a person may plan to look for a job again soon.

Table 15-3 shows the average of monthly flows in 1981 into and out of employment. These data, which unfortunately are no longer collected, show the movement, or *turnover*, in the labor market by splitting net employment changes into the different components. They support our conclusion about large flows in and out of the pool of unemployment.

Research has concentrated on the flows into and out of unemployment.[4] The research starts from the recognition that the flows are large relative to the average level of unemployment. A first way of looking at the flows in and out of unemployment is by obtaining direct estimates of the rate at which the labor force turns over in manufacturing establishments. *Accessions* are names added to the payroll of a company in a given month. Thus, in 1981, manufacturing

---

[3] See Martin Feldstein, "Temporary Layoffs in the Theory of Unemployment," *Journal of Political Economy*, October 1976.

[4] Robert E. Hall, "Why Is the Unemployment Rate So High at Full Employment?" *Brookings Papers on Economic Activity*. 3:1970 (Washington, D.C.: The Brookings Institution); Stephen T. Marston, "Employment Instability and High Unemployment Rates," *Brookings Papers on Economic Activity*, 1:1976 (ibid.); and Kim B. Clark and Lawrence H. Summers, "Labor Market Dynamics and Unemployment: A Reconsideration," *Brookings Papers on Economic Activity*, 1:1979 (ibid.).

companies on average added 3.2 names to their payrolls per 100 employees. *Separations* are names removed from the payrolls during the month. In 1981 manufacturing companies each month on average removed 3.6 names from their payrolls per 100 employees. Note first that the levels of accessions and separations (per 100 employees) are consistently high, each above 3 percent *per month*. Second, note that even though the unemployment rate was at 7.6 percent, accessions were equal to 3.2 percent of the manufacturing work force. Firms were hiring new people and calling back workers who had earlier been laid off, despite the high unemployment rate. Perhaps even more surprising, 1.3 percent of the workers in manufacturing quit their jobs voluntarily. Table 15-3 presents a remarkable picture of movement in the labor force. People are taking *and* leaving jobs, even during times of high unemployment.

Duration of Unemployment

A second way of looking at flows in and out of unemployment is to consider the *duration of spells of unemployment.* A spell of unemployment is defined as a period in which an individual remains continuously unemployed. Given the unemployment rate, the shorter the average spell of unemployment — the time the individual is unemployed — the larger the flows. For instance, in the example at the beginning of this section we had a 10 percent unemployment rate with five people becoming unemployed each month. We could also have a 10 percent unemployment rate if ten people became unemployed each month and each one remained unemployed for exactly 1 month. In the earlier example, the average spell is longer than a month since four out of five spells end in a month, but one out of five lasts 6 months. (The average spell is thus 2 months.) The shorter the average duration, the larger the flows of labor through the unemployment pool, given the overall unemployment rate.

As Table 15-4 shows, in 1974, a year in which unemployment was 5.6 percent, or about the natural rate, 60 percent of all spells ended within a month, and the average completed spell of unemployment lasted less than 2 months. Again, the suggestion is one of considerable movement of labor in and out of unemployment. We should note, though, one perhaps surprising feature, which is that almost half the spells of unemployment ended in withdrawal from the labor force, rather than in employment in a new job. Indeed, the distinction between being unemployed and being out of the labor force is not a very sharp one, and individuals move quite easily in both directions — between being unemployed (meaning essentially that they looked for a job in the past 4 weeks) and being out of the labor force.

Now that we have a picture of the labor market as being in a constant state of movement, we can ask about the factors changing the rate of unemployment and those determining the overall level of unemployment. Figure 15-2 makes it clear that unemployment increases when the flow into unemployment exceeds that out of the pool. Thus, increases in quits and layoffs increase unemployment, as does an increase in the flow of new entrants into the labor market,

TABLE 15-4   CHARACTERISTICS OF COMPLETED SPELLS OF UNEMPLOYMENT, BY DEMOGRAPHIC GROUP, 1974, AND FOR ALL GROUPS, 1969 AND 1975

	1974					1969	1975
	MALES		FEMALES			All groups	All groups
Characteristic	16–19	20 and over	16–19	20 and over	All groups		
Proportion of spells ending within one month	0.71	0.47	0.70	0.60	0.60	0.79	0.55
Mean duration of a completed spell (months)	1.57	2.42	1.57	1.91	1.94	1.42	2.22
Proportion of spells ending in withdrawal from the labor force	0.46	0.26	0.58	0.55	0.45	0.44	0.46

Source: Kim B. Clark and Lawrence H. Summers, "Labor Market Dynamics and Unemployment: A Reconsideration," *Brookings Papers on Economic Activity*, 1:1979 (Washington, D.C.: The Brookings Institution, 1979). Copyright © 1979 by the Brookings Institution, Washington, D.C.

since new entrants typically take time to find a job once they decide to become employed. Unemployment is reduced by increases in hiring rates and by unemployed workers leaving the labor force.

Table 15-5 provides some information about the breakdown of the reasons for unemployment. The categories in this table show the importance of variations in the rate of job loss, as well as the reentry rate, in affecting the overall rate of unemployment. When unemployment was very high, as in

TABLE 15-5   UNEMPLOYMENT BY REASON FOR UNEMPLOYMENT (Percentage of Unemployed Persons)

	JOB LOSERS				
	Layoff	Other	Job leavers	Reentrants	New entrants
1983:I	19.2	38.3	8.8	22.9	10.7
1986:I	17.0	36.2	12.1	26.4	12.5

Source: Employment and Earnings, 1983, 1986.

1983, job loss was by far the most important reason for unemployment. The data also show the importance of the reentrant category, which is consistent with the earlier comment that flows both from unemployment to "out of the labor force" and in the reverse direction are large.

The Unemployment Rate and the Time Unemployed

We turn now to the second fact to be established in this section. We noted earlier that the average duration of a spell of unemployment is quite short — under 2 months — and that most spells of unemployment end within a month. But as the example with which we started this section showed, it is still possible that much of unemployment can be traced to people who are unemployed for long spells. Indeed, given the fact that a spell of unemployment ends when someone either withdraws from the labor force or finds a job, it is possible for a person to have several spells of unemployment within the year and not actually work at all that year.

Table 15-6 provides information about the proportion of unemployment that consists of people who are unemployed for different lengths of time within the year.[5] In 1974, only 4.2 percent of total unemployment within the year was accounted for by people who were unemployed for 1 to 4 weeks,

---

[5] The *total* amount of time unemployed (over all spells of unemployment) is counted for an individual who experiences more than one spell of unemployment.

TABLE 15-6   PERCENTAGE OF UNEMPLOYMENT ACCOUNTED FOR BY TERM UNEMPLOYED
(Per Unemployed Person)

All groups	1974	1975
Weeks of unemployment		
1–4 weeks	4.2	2.6
5–14 weeks	22.4	15.6
15–26 weeks	31.7	27.0
27–39 weeks	21.1	22.3
40 weeks or more	20.7	32.5
	100.0	100.0

Source: Adapted from Kim B. Clark and Lawrence H. Summers, "Labor Market Dynamics and Unemployment: A Reconsideration," *Brookings Papers on Economic Activity*, 1:1979 (Washington, D.C.: The Brookings Institution, 1979). Copyright © 1979 by The Brookings Institution, Washington, D.C.

even though most spells of unemployment ended within a month. Nearly 42 percent of unemployment (the sum of the last two rows in Table 15-6) was accounted for by people who were unemployed for 27 or more weeks, or more than 6 months.

If instead of looking at unemployment we looked at nonemployment data—adding together the time individuals are unemployed and the time they are not in the labor force—we would find long-term *nonemployment* to be even more important than long-term unemployment. For instance, in 1974, over 50 percent of total time not employed of all individuals taken together could be attributed to those not employed for 40 or more weeks.

These data establish that despite the substantial flows in and out of unemployment, much of aggregate unemployment is accounted for by people who remain unemployed for a substantial time. Thus, if one believes that unemployment is a more serious problem when it affects only a few people intensely, rather than many people a little, these data suggest that unemployment is a more severe problem than the aggregate unemployment rate indicates.[6] The next set of data we review, those on the distribution of unemployment by age, race, and sex groups, supports that view.

The Distribution of Unemployment

The third important fact about the anatomy of unemployment is that unemployment is distributed very unevenly across the population. Tables 15-1 and 15-2 already showed unemployment rates by age, sex, and race categories. The message from the data is clear. First, there are some differences in unemployment rates between males and females, given age and race. However, these differences are relatively small. Second, nonwhite unemployment is substantially higher than white unemployment, with the unemployment rate for black teenagers (not shown in the table) being twice the corresponding rate for white teenagers. In fact, in all age and sex groups, black unemployment rates are at least 1½ times as large as white unemployment rates. And third, unemployment rates fall as age rises.[7]

The difference between the unemployment behavior of teenagers and that of adult workers is evident in Table 15-7. Here we observe that older workers suffered unemployment primarily as a consequence of job losses. Teenagers, by contrast, were either entering the labor force looking for a job or reentering after a period out of the labor market.

---

[6] This finding applies to teenagers as much as to older workers. For example, 54 percent of total male teenage unemployment is accounted for by people unemployed more than 6 months of the year. See Kim B. Clark and Lawrence H. Summers, "The Dynamics of Youth Unemployment," in Richard B. Freeman and David A. Wise (eds.), *The Youth Labor Market Problem: Its Nature, Causes, and Consequences* (Chicago: University of Chicago Press, 1982).

[7] For details see *Monthly Labor Review*, which regularly gives unemployment data by age, sex, and race.

TABLE 15-7   DIFFERENCES BETWEEN TEENAGE AND ADULT UNEMPLOYMENT: REASONS FOR UNEMPLOYMENT (Percentage of Group Unemployed, April 1986)

	Job losers	Job leavers	Reentrants	New entrants
16–19 years	21.9	5.4	25.7	47.0
20 years+				
Men	80.1	5.4	12.8	1.9
Women	52.8	10.0	31.3	6.0

Source: Employment and Earnings.

The duration of unemployment differs across groups in the labor force, lengthening particularly with age.[8] Table 15-4 also shows data on the proportion of spells of unemployment ending in withdrawal from the labor force. Spells of unemployment are more likely to end in withdrawal from the labor force among young males than among older males; this difference does not exist between younger and older females.

Despite the greater movement of the young workers among jobs, unemployment, and being out of the labor force, a significant part of teenage unemployment is accounted for by long-term unemployment, just as it is for older workers.[9]

The evidence tells an unambiguous story. Unemployment is much higher among the young than among the older. But the nature of the unemployment is different. The young tend to be unemployed more often and for short spells, whereas older workers are unemployed less often but for longer periods. It should also be noted that about half the teenage unemployed are, in fact, at school and looking for part-time work.

We have now reviewed the three central facts about U.S. unemployment experience:

• There are substantial flows through the pool of unemployment each month.

---

[8] *Technical note:* If you consult one of the sources of labor market data, such as *Monthly Labor Review* or *Employment and Earnings,* you will find figures on the duration of unemployment by characteristic, along with overall rates of unemployment. These duration data refer to the length of time the individual has been unemployed to date, *not* to the length of a *completed spell* of unemployment. Going back to our example at the beginning of this section, the duration data in the oficial sources would show five people who have been unemployed 1 month, one person unemployed 2 months, and one each unemployed for 3, 4, 5, and 6 months. The average duration would be computed as $[(5 \times 1) + (1 \times 2) + (1 \times 3) + \cdots + (1 \times 6)]/10 = 2.5$ months. The average duration computed as in Table 15.4 would be 2 months $= [(4 \times 1) + (1 \times 6)]/5$. Of course, the duration as reported in the official sources would increase together with the duration of completed spells. Thus the comparative duration rates shown in the official sources agree fully with the statements here, and are well worth examining.

[9] See footnote 6.

- Nonetheless, most unemployment is accounted for by people who will be unemployed for several months during the year.
- There are substantial variations in unemployment rates across different labor force groups.

We turn next to the natural rate of unemployment.

15-2 THE NATURAL RATE OF UNEMPLOYMENT

The *natural rate of unemployment* is also called the full-employment level of unemployment, or the long-run equilibrium level of unemployment, or the structural unemployment rate. In this section, we discuss the determinants of the natural rate of unemployment, then examine estimates of changes in the natural rate since the fifties, then consider proposals for reducing it.

Figure 15-2 points to the factors causing the unemployment rate to change. Increases in the rate of entry to the labor force, or quits, or layoffs, or involuntary quits cause the unemployment rate to rise. Increases in hiring, or recalls, or withdrawals from the labor force cause the unemployment rate to fall. Each of these factors is in part determined by economic variables, such as the level of aggregate demand and the actual and expected real wage rate. When aggregate demand rises (at a given real wage), firms increase their hiring. When aggregate demand falls, firms lay off workers. Thus there is an immediate link between the factors emphasized in Figure 15-2 and aggregate demand. However, it should be noted that the relationship between aggregate demand and the variables affecting the rate of unemployment is not unambiguous. For instance, an increase in the demand for labor increases quits at the same time as it reduces layoffs. A person thinking of leaving a job to search for another would be more likely to quit when the job market is good and demand is high than when there is heavy unemployment and the prospects of finding a good job quickly are low. In fact, it can be seen from Table 15-5 that quits and layoffs move in the opposite direction.

When the unemployment rate is constant, flows in and out of unemployment just balance each other. These flows can match at any level of unemployment. The *natural rate of unemployment*, however, is that rate of unemployment at which flows in and out of unemployment just balance,[10] *and* at which expectations of firms and workers as to the behavior of prices and wages are correct.

The determinants of the natural rate of unemployment can be thought of in terms of the duration and frequency of unemployment. The *duration* of unemployment is the average length of time a person remains unemployed.

---

[10] We should recognize that when the labor force is growing and the unemployment rate is constant, the pool of unemployed grows over time. For example, with a labor force of 90 million and 5 percent unemployment, total unemployment is 4.5 million people. With a labor force of 100 million and 5 percent unemployment, there are 5 million unemployed, and the unemployment pool has grown by a half-million people.

The duration depends on (1) the organization of the labor market, in regard to the presence or absence of employment agencies, youth employment services, etc.; (2) the demographic makeup of the labor force, as discussed above; (3) the ability and desire of the unemployed to keep looking for a better job; and (4) the availability and types of jobs. If all jobs are the same, an unemployed person will take the first one offered. If some jobs are better than others, it is worthwhile searching and waiting for a good one. If it is very expensive to remain unemployed, say, because there are no unemployment benefits, an unemployed person is more likely to accept a job offer than to continue looking for a better one. If unemployment benefits are high, then it may be worthwhile for the unemployed person to continue looking for a better job rather than to accept a poor job when one is offered.

The behavior of workers who have been laid off is also important when considering the duration of unemployment. Typically, a worker who has been laid off returns to the original job and does not search for another job. The reason is quite simple: a worker who has been with a firm for a long time has special expertise in the way that firm works which makes that worker valuable to that firm but is not of great benefit to another employer. In addition, the worker may have built up seniority rights, including a pension. That means that such an individual could not expect to find as good a job if he or she searched for a new one. The best course of action may be to wait to be recalled, particularly if the individual is eligible for unemployment benefits while waiting.

Frequency of Unemployment

The *frequency of unemployment* is the average number of times, per period, that workers become unemployed. There are two basic determinants of the frequency of unemployment. The first is the variability of the demand for labor across different firms in the economy. Even when aggregate demand is constant, some firms are growing and some are contracting. The contracting firms lose labor and the growing firms hire more labor. The greater this variability of the demand for labor across different firms, the higher the unemployment rate. Further, the variability of aggregate demand itself will affect the variability of the demand for labor. The second determinant is the rate at which new workers enter the labor force: The more rapidly new workers enter the labor force — the faster the growth rate of the labor force — the higher the natural rate of unemployment.

The four factors affecting duration and the two factors affecting frequency of unemployment are the basic determinants of the natural rate of unemployment.

You should note that the factors determining the level of the natural rate of unemployment are not immutable. The structure of the labor market and the labor force can change. The willingness of workers to remain unemployed while looking for, or waiting for, a new job can change. The variability of the demand for labor by different firms can shift. As Edmund Phelps has noted, the natural rate is not "an intertemporal constant, something like the speed of light, independent of everything under the sun." [11] Indeed, the natural rate is difficult to measure, and estimates of it have changed over the past few years from about 4 percent in the 1960s to around 6 or even 7 percent in the 1980s.

Estimates of the Natural Rate of Unemployment

Estimates of the natural rate of unemployment typically try to adjust for changes in the composition of the labor force, and perhaps for changes in the natural rate of unemployment of the various groups in the labor force. We can write an equation very similar to equation (1) for the natural rate $\bar{u}$:

$$\bar{u} = w_1\bar{u}_1 + w_2\bar{u}_2 + \cdots + w_n\bar{u}_n \tag{2}$$

Equation (2) says that the natural rate is the weighted average of the natural rates of unemployment of the subgroups in the labor force.

Estimates of the natural rate generally start from some period when the labor market was thought to be in equilibrium and when the aggregate unemployment rate and the unemployment rates of the groups in equation (2) were at their natural levels. This period is usually taken to be the mid-1950s, and the aggregate natural rate for that period is assumed to be 4 percent. The natural rate estimated for each group will differ from 4 percent: for teenagers it will be much higher, for prime-age males it will be lower, and so on.

The first adjustment made to the 4 percent rate follows from the fact that the composition of the labor force has been changing since the mid-1950s. The weight of teenagers and women in the labor force has been rising. Holding the $\bar{u}_i$ constant, the changing composition of the labor force is taken into account by changing the weights w_i in equation (2) to reflect the current composition of the labor force rather than that of the mid-fifties. The result is a rise in the natural rate.

The second adjustment that is typically undertaken is to assume that the natural rate for each group may depend on the relative size of that group in the labor force, that is, on the weight w_i. The idea here is that one type of labor is not a perfect substitute for another and that the more of some type of labor there is, the higher the unemployment rate for that group.[12] There are other estimates of the natural rate; they differ in their method of calculation, but

[11] See E. Phelps, "Economic Policy and Unemployment in the Sixties," *Public Interest*, Winter 1974.

[12] For details of the method of adjustment, see Peter K. Clark, "Potential GNP in the United States, 1948–1980," in *U.S. Productive Capacity: Estimating the Utilization Gap*, Working paper 23 (St. Louis: Washington University, Center for the Study of American Business, 1977).

they all include adjustments for the composition of the labor force, and they all show the natural rate rising substantially since the fifties.[13]

In Figure 15-3 we show annual data for the actual unemployment rate. We also show an estimate of the natural rate of unemployment as a shaded range. The natural rate rose from 3.5 to 4.5 percent in the 1950s and 1960s, to 4.5 to 5.5 percent in the early 1970s, to a yet higher range of 5.5 to 6.5 percent in the 1980s. The natural rate is drawn as a range rather than as a precise number to reflect the fact that there is very considerable uncertainty surrounding the estimates. For example, in 1986 many observers felt that the U.S. economy was substantially at full employment, even though the unemployment rate was slightly above 7 percent. For others a much lower benchmark of perhaps 5.5 percent represented full employment, and accordingly they felt that there was room for expansion.

Until recently there was an official full-employment/unemployment rate estimate. In the 1960s it was 4 percent. Adjustments for changes in the composition of the labor force raised the estimate to 4.9 percent in the early 1970s. By that standard 1973 would represent a year of full employment. A range of estimates, as we have drawn in Figure 15-3, is inadequate for some purposes: for example, some assumption has to be made about the natural rate of unemployment to calculate the full- or high-employment surplus. For these practical purposes, and without much conviction, the provisional benchmark now is 6 percent unemployment.[14]

The Rising Natural Rate of Unemployment

What can be the meaning of a 6 percent estimated natural rate when the actual unemployment rate has only rarely been that low since 1973? The experience of the great depression tells us that the actual unemployment rate can be below the full-employment rate for a long period. But there is a serious problem with continuing rises in the estimated natural rate.

The problem is that estimates of the natural rate based on the changing demographic structure of the labor force typically produce only about a 1 percent increase in the natural rate over the past 20 years. However, the estimated natural rate has risen by 2 to 3 percent. One possible explanation of the difference is that extended periods of high unemployment raise the natural rate, making it difficult to return to previously low levels of unemployment.[15]

---

[13] See, for instance, George L. Perry, "Potential Output and Productivity," *Brookings Papers on Economic Activity,* 1977:1 (Washington, D.C.: The Brookings Institution, 1977), and Jeffrey Perloff and Michael Wachter, "A Production Function — Nonaccelerating Inflation Approach to Potential Output," in Karl Brunner and Allan Meltzer (eds.), *Carnegie-Rochester Conference Series,* vol. 10 (Amsterdam: North-Holland, 1979).

[14] Thomas M. Holloway, "The Cyclically Adjusted Federal Budget and Federal Debt: Revised and Updated Estimates," *Survey of Current Business,* March 1986.

[15] See James Tobin, "Stabilization Policy Ten Years After," *Brookings Papers on Economic Activity I,* 1980. Olivier Blanchard and Lawrence Summers, "Hysteresis in the Unemployment Rate," *NBER Macroeconomics Annual, 1986.*

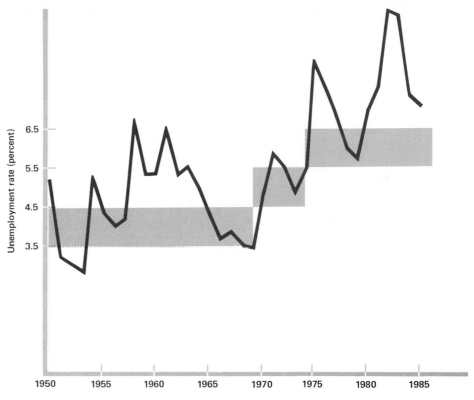

FIGURE 15-3 ACTUAL UNEMPLOYMENT AND THE NATURAL
RATE OF UNEMPLOYMENT. (*Source:* Data Resources, Inc.)

A related difficulty is that it is hard to believe that normal frictional
unemployment — people being between jobs, newcomers, and reentrants
searching for new jobs — can amount to as much as 7 percent of the total labor
force. After a burst of research in the 1970s on these topics, there was relatively little advance in the first half of the eighties. Now, new theoretical
developments are coming rapidly. A particularly interesting possibility is *efficiency wage theory,* which argues that many firms may pay above-market
clearing wages in order to obtain the loyalty of the work force or to provide
workers with the incentive to work hard to avoid being fired. With the real
wage set high, there will tend to be excess unemployment. We take up efficiency wage theory in Chapter 18.

Reducing the Natural Rate of Unemployment

Discussion of methods for reducing the natural rate of unemployment tends to
focus on the high unemployment rates of teenagers, and on the very high

TABLE 15-8	UNEMPLOYED PERSONS BY REASON FOR UNEMPLOYMENT BY SEX AND AGE, MAY 1986 (In Percent)			
	Males, 20+	Females, 20+	Both sexes, 16–19	Total
Total unemployed (percentage distribution)	100	100	100	100
Job losers	67.8	42.1	14.0	46.2
Job leavers	11.5	11.7	8.4	10.0
Reentrants	16.6	38.6	30.6	29.6
New entrants	4.0	7.7	46.9	14.2

Source: *Employment and Earnings,* June 1986.

proportion of total unemployment accounted for by the long-term unemployed.[16]

We start with teenage unemployment. We have pointed out earlier that teenagers are unemployed more frequently than others. Reasons for their unemployment may be examined with the help of Table 15-8. It can be seen that many of the unemployed teenagers are new entrants to the labor force, and also that more teenagers than adult males are reentrants to the labor force. The unemployment among teenagers could be reduced if the length of time teenagers take to find a first job were reduced. In order to reduce delays in the finding of jobs, it has been suggested that a Youth Employment Service be set up to help those who leave school locate jobs.

One of the main reasons teenagers enter and leave the labor force often is that the jobs they hold when they are working are not particularly attractive. It is a matter of some controversy as to how to improve existing jobs. Martin Feldstein has suggested that part of the reason jobs are unappealing is that the minimum wage is too high to make it worthwhile for employers to spend more money training the labor they hire in order to make their employees more skilled in their line of work.[17] He points to the apprentice system in other countries, in which young workers either receive very low pay or else pay to get jobs while they are learning skills. He argues that a reduction in the minimum wage would help make such on-the-job training more attractive to employers in the United States. He also suggests that there should be a system of scholarships for this type of training, since he doubts that a lower minimum

[16] See the *Economic Report of the President,* 1983, Chap. 2.
[17] Martin Feldstein, "The Economics of the New Unemployment," *Public Interest,* 33, Fall 1973.

wage by itself would be sufficient to encourage the right amount of on-the-job training. Similarly, there might be a case for the payment of wage subsidies to encourage firms to hire teenagers who might otherwise be unemployed.

Since 1981 the minimum wage has not been increased. It has thus fallen relative to the market wage. Even so, there has been no marked effect on relative teenage unemployment rates.

TARGETED PROGRAMS

In 1983 the administration introduced a program to deal specifically with youth unemployment. This was a "summer special," reducing the minimum wage by 25 percent during the May 1 – September 30 period. This program, being geared with its timing to favor the hiring of young people, not only would provide increased summer employment, but also would go further by providing teenagers access to jobs and therefore better long-run chances in the labor market.[18]

Other measures included tax credits that acted as an incentive for firms to employ teenagers from economically disadvantaged groups during the summer. Under this program employers could hire eligible young people and pay them the minimum wage, but at a cost to the firm of only 50 cents per hour. Each of the programs was *targeted* to cope specifically with the program of youth employment.

THE SECONDARY LABOR MARKET

Peter Doeringer and Michael Piore[19] doubt that measures such as reducing the minimum wage will do much to improve the nature of jobs in what they call the *secondary labor market.* They suggest that there are a host of noneconomic factors affecting the kinds of jobs that are typically available in the economy. The major economic variables they cite as determining the nature of jobs are the stability and level of aggregate demand. They argue that the instability of aggregate demand is the major reason firms rely on temporary labor and subcontracting to meet high levels of demand. If demand were maintained at a high *and* stable level, firms would have more incentive to create good stable jobs for their entire work force.

When we move away from teenage unemployment to other categories of unemployment, it is clear from Table 15-8 that reentry rates into the labor

---

[18] In the problem set we ask you to discuss whether this program is just a way of cheating young people out of their summer income. For a review of the effects of minimum wage legislation see J. P. Martin, "Effects of the Minimum Wage on the Youth Labor Market in North America and France," *Occasional Papers*, OECD, June 1983.

[19] Peter B. Doeringer and Michael J. Piore, "Unemployment and the 'Dual Labor Market,'" *Public Interest*, 38, Winter 1975. See, too, Robert Ullrich and Rand Araskog (eds.) *The American Work Force: Labor and Employment in the 1980s* (Auburn House Publishing Co., 1984).

force are much higher for all categories other than mature males. This suggests that these other groups, too, move in and out of the labor force frequently. Thus the same policies that might increase the stability of teenage employment should be expected to work for these groups. These would include policies to provide such workers with more training, perhaps in government training schemes. There have been many such programs, the success of which is difficult to evaluate. They would also include attempts to create "job banks" which would make it possible to match the characteristics of available jobs with those of workers looking for jobs. Better day-care facilities would also contribute to more stable labor market participation.

Unemployment Benefits

We come next to the implication of unemployment benefits for unemployment. Table 15-9 shows an index of relative family incomes for families that differ in unemployment experience and the number of family members working. Incomes are measured relative to the median income of families in which both the husband and wife work and which suffered no unemployment during the year. For example, suppose only the husband works. When he is working, the family earns 79 percent of the amount earned by a family in which both husband and wife work. If he becomes unemployed, for less than 26 weeks, his family earns 52 percent of the amount earned by the family with both partners at work. In this case, the family receives 66 percent $[=(52/79) \times 100$ percent] of its normal income when the worker in the family loses his job.

Note that as long as unemployment does not last more than 26 weeks, almost half of income is maintained even when the family suffers some unemployment. But, of course, disposable income falls dramatically when the family's worker(s) is unemployed for a long period.

The effects of changes in unemployment benefits, and in the tax treatment of benefits, on the unemployment rate remains an important current research

TABLE 15-9   UNEMPLOYMENT AND RELATIVE MEDIAN FAMILY INCOMES IN 1981

Normal work status	DURATION OF UNEMPLOYMENT		
	None	Less than 26 weeks	More than 26 weeks
Husband and wife both work	100	73	57
Only husband works	79	52	32
Only wife works	60	48	35

Source: Economic Report of the President, 1983, p. 30.

issue.[20] Researchers focus on the role of the *replacement ratio* in determining how likely workers are to become unemployed, and how long they remain unemployed. The replacement ratio is the ratio of after-tax income while unemployed to after-tax income while employed.

Unemployment benefits add in three separate ways to the *measured* rate of unemployment. First the presence of unemployment benefits allows longer job search. A high level of unemployment benefits makes it less urgent for an unemployed person to obtain a job: the higher the replacement ratio, the less urgent the need to take a job. Feldstein and Poterba[21] have shown that high replacement ratios significantly affect the reservation wage, the wage at which a person receiving unemployment is willing to take a new job.

The issue of the effect of unemployment compensation on unemployment rates is particularly live in Europe. Many observers of the very high levels of European unemployment see a major explanation in the fact that replacement ratios there are so high. Patrick Minford argues:[22]

> The picture presented . . . is a grim one from the point of view of incentives to participate in employment. The replacement ratios are such that, should a person "work the system," incentives to have a job are, on the whole, rather small for a family man.

The second channel through which unemployment benefits raise the *measured* unemployment rate is through *reporting effects.* To collect unemployment benefits people have to be "in the labor force," looking for work even if they do not really want a job. They therefore get counted as unemployed. In the absence of unemployment benefits some people might not be in the labor force, and hence measured unemployment rates would be lower. A 1978 estimate suggests that elimination of unemployment insurance would have reduced the unemployment rate by more than one-half percentage point below the 6 percent level of that year. The employment ratio would have risen by one-half percentage point, and the nonparticipation rate would have increased by more than a full percentage point.[23]

The third channel is *employment stability.* With unemployment insurance, the consequences of being in and out of jobs are less severe, and accordingly, workers and firms do not find it as much in their interest to create highly

---

[20] Until 1978 unemployment benefits were exempt from federal income tax. Since then they have been taxed if family income is above a certain level.

[21] M. Feldstein and J. Poterba, "Unemployment Insurance and Reservation Wages," *Journal of Public Economics,* February–March 1984.

[22] See Patrick Minford, *Unemployment, Causes and Cures* (Oxford: Blackwell, 1985), p. 39.

[23] See K. Clark and L. Summers, "Unemployment Insurance and Labor Market Transitions," in M. Bailey (ed.), *Workers, Jobs and Inflation* (Washington, D.C.: The Brookings Institution, 1982), pp. 314–315.

stable employment. Further, the fact that a laid-off worker will not suffer a large loss from being unemployed makes it more attractive for an employer to lay off workers temporarily than to attempt to keep them on the job.[24]

There seems to be little doubt that unemployment compensation does add to the natural rate of unemployment. This does not imply, though, that unemployment compensation should be abolished. Individuals need time to do some searching if the economy is to allocate people efficiently among jobs. It would not make sense to put a skilled worker in an unskilled job the moment she loses her previous job, just because the worker cannot afford to search. Thus even from the viewpoint of economic efficiency, zero is not the ideal level of unemployment benefits. Beyond that, society may be willing to give up some efficiency so that the unemployed can maintain a minimal standard of living. What is appropriate is a scheme that will create less incentive for firms to lay off labor while at the same time ensuring that the unemployed are not exposed to economic distress.[25] This is obviously difficult to carry off.

It has become fashionable to argue that unemployment does not present a serious social problem because the unemployed choose to be unemployed and live off unemployment compensation. This argument is wrong in assuming that all unemployed people are covered by unemployment benefits. In fact, insured unemployment is less than two-thirds of total unemployment.

15-3 THE COSTS OF UNEMPLOYMENT

The costs of unemployment are so obvious that this section might seem superfluous. Society on the whole loses from unemployment because total output is below its potential level. The unemployed as individuals suffer both from their income loss while unemployed and from the low level of self-esteem that long periods of unemployment cause.[26]

This section provides some estimates of the costs of foregone output resulting from unemployment, and clarifies some of the issues connected with the costs of unemployment and the potential benefits from reducing unemployment. We distinguish between cyclical unemployment, associated with short-run deviations of the unemployment rate from the natural rate, and "permanent," or structural, unemployment that exists at the natural rate.

---

[24] An important issue here concerns *experience rating*. If the unemployment benefit scheme could be designed in such a way that firms that lay off workers end up having to pay the full cost of doing so, then there is no benefit to the firm of using layoffs in the way described in the text. Experience rating is used to some extent in the United States, but it is estimated that 30 percent of all layoffs are the result of imperfect experience rating. See Robert H. Topel, ''On Layoffs and Unemployment Insurance,'' *American Economic Review*, September 1983.

[25] Experience rating is one such mechanism.

[26] See Robert J. Gordon, ''The Welfare Cost of Higher Unemployment,'' *Brookings Papers on Economic Activity*, 1:1973 (Washington, D.C.: The Brookings Institution, 1973).

The Costs of Cyclical Unemployment

We now discuss the costs that arise from cyclical unemployment. The problem here is to identify the costs to society of the output forgone because the economy is not operating at full employment. A first measure of the cost is provided by a calculation using Okun's law.

In Chapter 1 we saw the link between unemployment and the GNP gap summarized in Okun's law. According to the law a one percentage point reduction in the unemployment rate translates, approximately, into a 2.2 percentage point increase in real GNP.

Consider now how the relationship can be used to estimate the amount of output loss owed to excess unemployment or the gain in output that could be realized by an expansion in output. Table 15-10 shows the actual rate of unemployment and the value of output lost (in 1982 dollars) from 1983 to 1985 owing to excess unemployment over and above 6 percent. Thus in 1985, for example, the output loss is $94.2 billion = (2.2 × 1.2 × 3,570) obtained from a 1.2 percentage point excess unemployment rate and a $3,570 billion real GNP.

Table 15-10 invites the question of why policy makers should have tolerated such high unemployment, given the staggering costs as reflected in these estimates of output lost because of unemployment.

Other Costs and Benefits

Are there any other costs of unemployment or, for that matter, offsetting benefits? It is possible to imagine offsetting benefits. We do not discuss here the benefit arising from a temporary reduction in the inflation rate accompanying a temporary increase in unemployment, but rather focus on the costs of unemployment taken by itself. A possible offsetting benefit occurs because the unemployed are not working and have more leisure. However, the value that can be placed on that leisure is small. In the first place, much of it is unwanted leisure.

Second, there is a fairly subtle issue that we shall have to explore. If people are free to set their hours of work, they would work up to the point at

TABLE 15-10   THE OUTPUT COSTS OF UNEMPLOYMENT

	1983	1984	1985
Unemployment rate, %	9.6	7.5	7.2
Output loss, (billions of 1982 $s)	259.6	115.2	94.2

Source: Data Resources, Inc.

which the marginal value of leisure to themselves was equal to the marginal return from working an extra hour. We would then be able to conclude that if their workday were slightly reduced, the overall loss to them would be extremely small. The reason is that they acquire extra leisure from working less, at the cost of having less income. But they were previously at the point where the marginal value of leisure was equal to the after-tax marginal wage, so that the benefit of the increased leisure almost exactly offsets the private loss of income. However, the net marginal wage is less than the value of the marginal product of an employed person to the economy. The major reason is that society taxes the income of the employed person, so that society as a whole takes a share of the marginal product of the employed person. When the employed people in our example stop working, they lose for themselves only the *net* of tax wage they have been receiving. But society also loses the taxes they have been paying. The unemployed value their leisure at the net of tax wage, and that value is smaller than the value of their marginal product for society as a whole. Therefore, the value of increased leisure provides only a partial offset to the Okun's law estimate of the cost of cyclical unemployment.

Note that we do not count both the individual's personal loss of income and the Okun's law estimate of forgone output as part of the cost of unemployment. The reason is that Okun's law estimate implicitly includes the individual's own loss of income — it estimates the total loss of output to the economy as a whole as a result of the reduction of employment. That loss could in principle be distributed across different people in the economy in many different ways. For instance, one could imagine that the unemployed continue to receive benefit payments totaling close to their previous income while employed, with the benefit payments financed through taxes on working individuals. In that case, the unemployed would not suffer an income loss from being unemployed, but society would still lose from the reduction in total output available.

However, the effects of an increase in unemployment are, in fact, borne heavily by the unemployed themselves. There is thus an extra cost to society of unemployment that is very difficult to quantify. The cost arises from the uneven distribution of the burden of unemployment across the population. Unemployment tends to be concentrated among the poor, and that makes the distributional aspect of unemployment a serious matter. It is not one we can easily quantify, but it should not be overlooked. Further, there are many reports of the adverse psychic effects of unemployment that, again, are not easy to quantify but should not be ignored.[27]

"Structural" Unemployment

The benefits of reducing the natural rate of unemployment are more difficult to estimate than the costs of cyclical unemployment. It is clear that the Okun's

---

[27] See Harry Maurer, *Not Working* (New York: Holt, Rinehart and Winston, 1979), and Kay L. Schlozman and Sidney Verba, *Injury to Insult* (Cambridge, Mass.: Harvard University Press, 1979).

law estimate of a 2.5 percent change in output resulting from a change of one percentage point in the unemployment rate is not appropriate here. The reason is that the increase in output associated with cyclical changes in unemployment results in part from the fact that the labor put back to work in the short run is able to use capital that has not been fully utilized when unemployment was high. However, in the long run, which is relevant when considering a reduction in the natural rate of unemployment, it would be necessary to invest to provide for the capital with which the newly employed would work. The Okun 2.5:1 ratio is therefore too high for the long-run benefits of reducing the natural rate of unemployment. One estimate of benefit is that a reduction of one percentage point in the natural unemployment rate would increase long-run output by only 0.76 percent.[28]

The available estimates of the social benefits of a reduction in long-run unemployment cannot be narrowed down to very solid numbers. Even more difficult is the estimate of an "optimal" long-run unemployment rate. Here we ask the question whether any — and, if so, how much — unemployment is desirable in the long run. A first guess at the answer to that question is that all unemployment is wasteful, since the unemployed labor could usefully be employed. However, that answer is not right. Those people who are unemployed in order to look for a better job are performing a valuable service not only for themselves. They are also performing a service for society by attempting to put themselves into a position in which they earn the most and are the most valuable.

Because the composition of demand shifts over time, we can expect always to have some firms expanding and some contracting. This is true even with a stable level of aggregate demand. Those who lose their jobs will be unemployed, and they benefit both society and themselves by not taking the very first job that comes along, but rather searching for the optimal employment. Accordingly, we can conclude that some unemployment is a good thing in an economy in which the composition of demand changes over time. It is one thing to recognize this and quite another to pin down the optimal rate of unemployment numerically.

15-4 THE COSTS OF INFLATION

The costs of inflation are much less obvious than those of unemployment. There is no direct loss of output from inflation, as there is from unemployment. In studying the costs of inflation, we again want to distinguish the short run from the long run. In the case of inflation, though, the relevant distinction is between inflation that is *perfectly anticipated,* and taken into account in economic transactions, and *imperfectly anticipated,* or unexpected. We start with

---

[28] See Robert J. Gordon, cited in footnote 26. Can you see how a number like this would emerge if the economy's production function is Cobb-Douglas with a labor share of about ¾? See Chap. 19 where we discuss the link between employment growth and output.

perfectly anticipated inflation because that case provides a useful bench mark against which to judge unanticipated inflation.

Perfectly Anticipated Inflation

Suppose that an economy has been experiencing a given rate of inflation, say, 5 percent, for a long time, and that it is correctly anticipated that the rate of inflation will continue to be 5 percent. In such an economy, all contracts would build in the expected 5 percent inflation. Borrowers and lenders will both know and agree that the dollars in which a loan will be repaid will be worth less than the dollars which are given up by the lender when making the loan. Nominal interest rates would be 5 percent higher than they would be in the absence of inflation. Long-term wage contracts will increase wages at 5 percent per year to take account of the inflation, and then build in whatever changes in real wages are agreed to. Long-term leases will take account of the inflation. In brief, any contracts in which the passage of time is involved will take the inflation into account. In that category we include the tax laws, which we are assuming would be indexed. The tax brackets themselves would be increased at the rate of 5 percent per year.[29] Inflation has no real costs in such an economy, except for a minor qualification.

That qualification arises because the interest rate that is paid on money might not adjust to the inflation rate. No interest is paid on currency — notes and coins — throughout the world, and no interest is paid on demand deposits in many countries. It is very difficult to pay interest on currency, so that it is likely that the interest rate on currency will continue to be zero, independent of the perfectly anticipated inflation rate. It is reasonable to expect that in a fully anticipated inflation, interest would be paid even on demand deposits, and the interest rate paid on demand deposits would adjust to the inflation rate. If so, the only cost of perfectly anticipated inflation is that the inflation makes it more costly to hold currency.

The cost to the individual of holding currency is the interest forgone by not holding an interest-bearing asset. When the inflation rate rises, the nominal interest rate rises, the interest lost by holding currency increases, and the cost of holding currency therefore increases. Accordingly, the demand for currency falls. In practice, this means that individuals economize on the use of currency by carrying less in their wallets and making more trips to the bank to cash smaller checks than they did before. The costs of these trips to the bank are often described as the "shoeleather" costs of inflation. They are related to the amount by which the demand for currency is reduced by an increase in the anticipated inflation rate, and they are small.

We should add that throughout this discussion, we are assuming inflation

---

[29] The taxation of interest would have to be on the *real* (after-inflation) return on assets for the tax system to be properly indexed.

rates that are not too high effectively to disrupt the payments system. This disruption was a real problem in some instances of hyperinflation, but it need not concern us here. We are abstracting, too, from the cost of "menu change." This cost arises simply from the fact that with inflation—as opposed to price stability—people have to devote real resources to marking up prices and changing pay telephones and vending machines as well as cash registers. These costs are there, but one cannot get too excited about them. On balance, the costs of fully anticipated inflation are small.

The notion that the costs of fully anticipated inflation are small does not square well with the strong aversion to inflation reflected in policy making and politics. The most important reason for that aversion is probably that inflations in the United States have not been steady, and that the inflationary experience of the United States is one of imperfectly anticipated inflation, the costs of which are substantially different from those discussed in this section.

There is a further line of argument that explains the public aversion to inflation, even of the fully anticipated, steady kind. The arguments are that it is a mirage to believe that policy makers could and would maintain a steady inflation rate at any level other than zero and that policy makers are reluctant to use restrictive policy to compensate for transitory increases in the inflation rate. Rather than maintain a constant rate of inflation in the face of inflation shocks, the authorities would accommodate these shocks and therefore validate them. Any inflationary shock would add to the inflation rate rather than being compensated by restrictive policy. In this manner, inflation, far from being constant, would, in fact, be rising as policy makers validate any and every disturbance rather than use policy to rigidly enforce the inflation target. Zero inflation, it is argued, is the only target that can be defended without this risk.[30]

Although there are many examples of countries with long inflationary histories, there does not appear to be any tendency for the inflation rate of those countries to increase over time. The argument thus seems weak. However, it is true that the inflation rate has been more stable in countries with low rates of inflation than in countries with inflation rates that are on average higher, which is some evidence in support of the notion.

Imperfectly Anticipated Inflation

The idyllic scenario of full adjustment to inflation drawn here does not describe economies that we know. Modern economies include a variety of institutional features representing different degrees of adjustment to inflation. Economies with long inflationary histories, such as those of Brazil and Israel,

---

[30] See William J. Fellner, introductory essay in William J. Fellner (ed.), *Contemporary Economic Problems* (Washington, D.C.: American Enterprise Institute, 1973).

have made substantial adjustments to inflation through the use of indexing.[31] Others in which inflation has been episodic, such as the U.S. economy, have made only small adjustments for inflation.

One of the important effects of inflation is to change the real value of assets fixed in nominal terms. A tripling of the price level, such as the United States experienced in the period from 1966 to 1986, cuts the purchasing power of all claims or assets fixed in money terms to one-third. Thus, someone who bought a 20-year government bond in 1966 and expected to receive a principal of, say, $100 in constant purchasing power at the 1986 maturity date actually winds up with a $100 principal that has purchasing power of $33 in 1960 dollars. The more than tripling of the price level has transferred wealth from creditors—holders of bonds—to debtors. This effect operates with respect to all assets fixed in nominal terms, in particular, money, bonds, savings accounts, insurance contracts, and some pensions. Obviously, it is an extremely important effect since it can wipe out the purchasing power of a lifetime's saving that is supposed to finance retirement consumption. In 1985 the total value of assets fixed in nominal terms held by households was about $4 trillion, or about $17,000 per head. An increase of one percentage point in the price level would reduce the real value of these assets by $40 billion, or an amount equal to 1 percent of GNP.

Those figures by themselves seem to explain the public concern over inflation. There appears to be a lot riding on each percentage-point change in the price level. That impression is slightly misleading. Many individuals are both debtors and creditors in nominal assets. Almost everyone has some money and is thus a creditor in nominal terms. Many of the middle class own housing, financed through mortgages whose value is fixed in nominal terms. Such individuals benefit from inflation because it reduces the real value of their mortgage. Other individuals have borrowed in nominal terms to buy consumer durables, such as cars, and to that extent have their real indebtedness reduced by inflation.

Table 15-11 shows the net position of different sectors in the economy in terms of the amounts of nominal assets they own or owe. In other words, the table shows the net debtor or creditor status in terms of nominal or "monetary" assets and liabilities.[32] The household sector shows up as a net monetary creditor, with the government the offsetting major monetary debtor. Nonfinancial corporations are to a large extent monetary debtors reflecting their debt-financed capital structure. Similarly, financial corporations are net monetary debtors. For example, the banks' net debtor position is reflected by their

---

[31] In 1985 and 1986 Israel and Brazil, respectively, undertook major stabilization programs to reduce inflation. Many economists in both countries blamed indexing for the inflationary momentum that had made it difficult to stop inflation earlier. Accordingly, the stabilization packages reduced the extent of indexing in the economies.
[32] Table 15-11 is an updated version of a similar table in G. L. Bach and James B. Stephenson, "Inflation and the Distribution of Wealth," *Review of Economics and Statistics*, February 1974.

TABLE 15-11   NET DEBTOR OR CREDITOR STATUS
IN NOMINAL ASSETS OF MAJOR ECONOMIC SECTORS
(In Billions of Dollars)

	1960	1970	1985
Households	+350	+696	+1,550
Unincorporated businesses	−23	−108	−90
Nonfinancial corporations	−57	−172	−997
Financial corporations	+24	−18	−466
Governments	−250	−341	−1,476

Note: A plus sign indicates a net monetary creditor.
Source: Federal Reserve Flow-of-Funds Accounts, Assets and Liabilities Outstanding.

liabilities in the form of debt and deposits, while their assets include some real assets like land and structures.

The important point about Table 15-11 is the recognition that a change in the price level brings about a major *redistribution of wealth* between sectors. Thus an inflation rate of 5 percent in 1985 would have resulted in a transfer of $75 billion from the household sector to the government. Obviously, we must be careful in assessing the implications of that statement. A redistribution of wealth from corporations to the household sector, for example, means that as a household the average person has gained, but as an owner of a corporate stock, the average household has lost. This singles out transfers between the government and the private sector as particularly important because here the offset is much less immediate.

Much the same problems of redistribution arise with deflation or falling prices. Thus, from 1929 to 1933, the consumer price index fell by almost 25 percent, and that decline meant an extremely large increase in the real value of liabilities, in particular, the real debt of farmers. Inflation redistributes wealth within society from creditors to debtors, and deflation redistributes wealth from debtors to creditors.

We must go beyond Table 15-11 in two respects. First, that table really indicates the vulnerability of different sectors to inflation. It does not tell us to what extent inflation was anticipated when the contracts behind the figures in Table 15-11 were drawn. The 10 percent inflation referred to above might have been correctly anticipated, so that the wealth transfers occurring as a result of the inflation would not cause any surprises. Second, the gains and losses from these wealth transfers basically cancel out over the economy as a whole. When the government gains from inflation, the private sector may have to pay lower taxes later. When the corporate sector gains from inflation, owners of corporations benefit at the expense of others. If we really did not care about the distribution of wealth among individuals, the costs of unanticipated inflation would be neglible. Included in the individuals of the previous sentence are those belonging to different generations, since the current owners of the national debt might be harmed by inflation — to the benefit of future taxpayers.

The costs of unanticipated inflation are thus largely distributional costs. There is some evidence[33] that the old are more vulnerable to inflation than the young in that they own more nominal assets. Offsetting this, however, is the fact that Social Security benefits are indexed, so that a substantial part of the wealth of those about to retire is protected from unanticipated inflation. There appears to be little evidence supporting the view that the poor suffer unduly from unanticipated inflation.

Inflation redistributes wealth between debtors and creditors because changes in the price level change the purchasing power of assets fixed in money terms. There is room, too, for inflation to affect income positions by changing the distribution of income. A popular line of argument has always been that inflation benefits capitalists or recipients of profit income at the expense of wage earners. Unanticipated inflation, it is argued, means that prices rise faster than wages and therefore allow profits to expand.[34] For the United States in the postwar period, there is no persuasive evidence to this effect. There is evidence that the real return on common stocks — that is, the real value of dividends and capital gains on equity — is reduced by unanticipated inflation. Thus, equity holders appear to be adversely affected by unanticipated inflation.[35]

The last important distributional effect of inflation concerns the real value of tax liabilities. A failure to index the tax structure implies that inflation moves the public into higher tax brackets and thus raises the real value of its tax payments or reduces real disposable income. Inflation acts as though Congress had voted an increase in tax schedules. Tax brackets in the United States have been indexed since 1985.

The fact that unanticipated inflation acts mainly to redistribute wealth, the net effects of which redistribution should be close to zero, has led to some questioning of the reasons for public concern over inflation. The gainers, it seems, do not shout as loudly as the losers. Since some of the gainers (future

---

[33] See Bach and Stephenson, cited in footnote 32.

[34] Louis De Alessi, "Do Business Firms Gain from Inflation? Reprise," *Journal of Business*, April 1975. See also Nancy Jianakoplos, "Are You Protected from Inflation?" Federal Reserve Bank of St. Louis, *Review*, January 1977.

[35] See Charles R. Nelson, "Inflation and Rates of Return on Common Stocks," *Journal of Finance*, May 1976. See also Franco Modigliani and Richard Cohn, "Inflation, Rational Valuation and the Market," *Financial Analysts Journal*, March–April 1979, for a controversial view of the reasons why inflation affects the stock market.

taxpayers) have yet to be born, this is hardly surprising. There is also a notion that the average wage earner is subject to an illusion when both the nominal wage and the price level increase. Wage earners are thought to attribute increases in nominal wages to their own merit rather than to inflation, while the general inflation of prices is seen as causing an unwarranted reduction in the real wage they would otherwise have received. It is hard to know how to test the validity of this argument. Nonetheless, it does appear that the redistributive effects of unanticipated inflation are large, and that, accordingly, some parts of the population could be seriously affected by it.

15-5 INFLATION, INTEREST RATES, AND WAGE INDEXATION

In this section we look at two kinds of contracts that are especially affected by inflation. These are long-term loan contracts and wage contracts. In each case payments are fixed in nominal terms over some length of time ahead. But the future price level is not known ahead of time, and hence the *real* value of the payments can turn out to be very different from what borrowers and lenders, or workers and firms, had anticipated.

Inflation and Interest Rates

One of the areas where inflation plays an important role is the capital market. Here borrowers and lenders make loan contracts that specify fixed dollar payments. For example, a firm may sell 20-year bonds in the capital markets at an interest rate of 10 percent per year. Whether the real interest rate on the bonds turns out to be high or low depends on what the inflation rate will be over the next 20 years. The borrower and lender will each have some idea of what inflation will be. They may even agree, but they may also turn out to be wrong. Inflation has major effects particularly in the area of home financing, where loans are made for 25 to 35 years.

Inflation and Housing

Investment in housing is one of the areas where errors in inflation expectations can bring about large redistributions between borrowers and lenders. The typical household buys a home by borrowing from a bank or savings and loan institution. The mortgage — this is the term for the home loan — used to be a fixed nominal interest rate loan for a duration of 25 or 30 years. The interest payments are deductible in calculating federal income taxes, and accordingly, the effective cost of the loan is less than the actual interest by an amount that depends on the household's marginal tax rate. Suppose the marginal tax rate is 30 percent; then the nominal interest cost is 70 percent of the actual mortgage rate.

TABLE 15-12   HOME PRICE INFLATION AND MORTGAGE RATES (Average Percentage Rate per Year)

	Home price inflation rate	Mortgage rate	After-tax real differential*
1963–1982	5.76	5.89	1.64
1973–1982	8.36	7.60	2.86
1977–1982	9.0	9.02	2.87
1981–1982	5.19	14.70	−5.10
1982–1985	10.37	12.18	1.84

* The differential is calculated as the difference between the home price inflation and 0.7 times the mortgage rate.

Source: Economic Report of the President, 1983, updated.

Now consider the economics of investing in a home, comparing the interest cost with the capital gains that arise from inflation. With inflation, the value of the home rises over time. Therefore if the interest cost falls short of the capital gains, investing in a house is a good idea, even leaving aside noneconomic considerations of owning versus renting.

Consider, for example, someone buying a home in 1963. At that time the mortgage rate was 5.89 percent for a long-term loan. Looking now at the 1963–1985 period, we see that housing prices increased roughly at the same rate as the mortgage rate. Without including the tax deductions for interest payments, the borrower in 1962 over the next 20 years paid *real* interest of essentially zero because the rate of inflation of housing prices was almost equal to the interest rate. When the interest deductibility is figured in, capital gains exceed the tax-adjusted interest cost, as the last columns of Table 15-12 show. This is even more the case for an investment starting in the 1970s and especially in the late 1970s. Nominal interest rates are higher, but the rate of increase of housing prices is higher too. The differential including the tax treatment now makes the purchase of a house especially favorable because the after-tax interest cost rises much less than the capital gains. But housing is not a sure bet. For example, someone who bought in 1981 with a high 14.7 percent mortgage rate and had to sell in 1982 would have lost 5 percent, even taking into account tax treatment of the loan.[36]

Uncertainty about the outlook for inflation was one of the reasons why a new financial instrument made its appearance: *the adjustable-rate mortgage.*

---

[36] For a further discussion see L. Summers, "Inflation, the Stock Market and Owner-Occupied Housing," *American Economic Review*, May 1981.

These are long-term loans with an interest rate that is periodically (every year, for example) adjusted in line with prevailing short-term interest rates. To the extent that nominal interest rates roughly reflect inflation trends, adjustable-rate mortgages reduce the effects of inflation on the long-term costs of financing home purchases. There will not be large unanticipated capital gains, nor will there be persistent capital losses.

Indexation of Wages

In Chapter 14 we discussed the role of automatic cost of living adjustment (COLA) provisions in wage contracts. COLA provisions link increases in money wages to increases in the price level. The adjustment may be complete — 100 percent indexation — or only partial. Partial indexation takes one of two forms. There may be a *threshold* or a *cap.* A threshold specifies a minimum increase in the price level before indexation comes into play. This implies that small price increases are not compensated, while larger ones are. A cap puts a limit on the extent to which price increases are compensated, say, 10 percent per year. COLA clauses are designed to allow workers to recover purchasing power lost through price increases.

WHY INDEXATION?

Indexation in some form is a quite common feature of labor markets in many countries. Indexation strikes a balance between the advantages of long-term wage contracts and the interests of workers and firms in not having *real* wages get too far out of line. Bargaining for wages is costly because workers (unions) and the firm have to devote time and effort to arrive at a settlement and often work is disrupted through strikes. It is in the common interest of workers and firms therefore to hold to a minimum the number of times these negotiations take place.

Thus wages are not negotiated once a week or once a month, but rather they are negotiated in the form of 2- or 3-year contracts. But over the term of these contracts the evolution of prices — consumer prices and the prices at which firms sell their output — is not known with certainty. Therefore real wages paid by firms or received by workers are not known even if money wages are. To remedy this uncertainty, some provision is made to adjust wages for inflation. Broadly, there are two possibilities. One is to index wages to the CPI and in periodic reviews, say, quarterly, increase wages by the increase in prices over the period. The other is to schedule periodic, preannounced wage increases based on the expected rate of price increase. If inflation were known with certainty, the two methods would come to the same thing. But since inflation can differ from expectations, there will be discrepancies. Prefixed wage increases may turn out to be high or low relative to actual inflation. On that account indexation on the basis of actual inflation offers greater assurance of stable real wages for workers than do scheduled increases.

SUPPLY SHOCKS AND INDEXATION

Suppose real material prices increase, and firms pass these cost increases on into higher prices of final goods. Consumer prices will rise, and under a system of 100 percent indexation, wages would rise. This leads to further price and material costs, and wage increases. Indexation here leads to an inflation spiral that would be avoided under a system of prefixed wage increases because then real wages could fall as a consequence of higher material prices.

The example makes it clear that we must distinguish two possibilities in considering the effects of wage indexing, monetary disturbances and real disturbances. In the case of a monetary disturbance (a shift in the *LM* schedule), there is a "pure" inflation disturbance, and firms can afford to pay the same real wages and therefore would not mind 100 percent indexation. In the case of adverse real disturbances, however, real wages must fall, and full indexation is entirely the wrong system because it stands in the way of downward real wage flexibility.

From the two cases it is apparent that neither completely prefixed wage increases nor complete indexation is likely to be optimal. The best arrangement will depend on the relative importance of monetary and real shocks. Countries that had practiced 100 percent indexation—for example, Italy and Brazil—found in the 1970s that it was difficult to adjust to real shocks and that the indexation led to a wage-price spiral that pushed up inflation with great speed.

WAGE INDEXATION IN THE UNITED STATES

In the U.S. economy more than 50 percent of workers who are covered in major collective bargaining agreements have contract provisions for automatic cost-of-living adjustments. Table 15-13 shows that these provisions were much more common after 1973 than before. The increase in the level and variability of the rate of inflation is the explanation. As inflation recedes in the eighties, the percentage of clauses with COLA's should again fall.

Table 15-13 might give the impression that indexation is a very common feature of the U.S. labor market. But that is not the case once we note that major bargaining agreements cover only a small part of the labor force. In 1985 about 10 million workers of a total labor force pool of 110 million were covered by COLA provisions.

The role of indexation is further limited because 100 percent indexation is not the rule. For example, a common rule adjusts the wage by $0.01 per hour for each 0.2 percent, increase in the CPI. With an hourly wage of $10 and an inflation rate of 5 percent, the adjustment is $0.25 (= $0.01 × 5 percent/0.2) per hour, or 2.5 percent (= $0.25/$10). Under this rule, indexation compensates for just 50 percent of the inflation.

We noted above that a system of 100 percent indexation is difficult to manage when there are supply shocks such as occurred in the 1970s. The U.S.

TABLE 15-13	INFLATION AND COLA PROVISIONS (In Percent)	
Rate	Average inflation rate	Workers with COLA coverage*
1963–1972	3.5	26.7
1973–1982	8.2	54.6
1983–1985	3.5	55.4

* Percentage of all workers covered in major collective bargaining agreements.
Source: Monthly Labor Review, various issues, and Data Resources, Inc.

system is clearly very far from full indexation. Some observers see in this fact the reason that the U.S. economy more easily adjusted to the oil shocks than did countries in Europe where full indexation is more common.[37]

15-6 THE POLITICAL ECONOMY OF INFLATION AND UNEMPLOYMENT

We have seen the costs of unemployment and the problems that arise from inflation. The final question is how policy makers strike a balance, deciding how much unemployment to live with and how much inflation to accept. It is clear from the outset that the best of all worlds is one without either inflation or excess unemployment. But disturbances in the economy do occur, and in the absence of full wage-price flexibility, it will not be possible to restore full employment with stable prices instantly. Policy makers therefore face a trade-off: Should they try to maintain the economy close to or at full employment, even if that involves risks of inflation bursts when shocks do occur? Or should they opt for policies that are much less accommodating and therefore involve larger swings in unemployment but more stable prices?

Alternative Policy Paths

What should be done when a disturbance, say a supply shock, creates both high unemployment and inflation? Should the return to full employment be rapid, even at the cost of high inflation? Or should stopping inflation be the first priority even if that means an extended period of unemployment? Policy makers must reach these decisions. Even if their control of the economy is not perfect, for the reasons discussed in Chapter 12, there is still a need to set policy instruments to move the economy in the desired direction.

---

[37] See Michael Bruno and Jeffrey Sachs, *The Economics of Worldwide Stagflation* (Cambridge, Mass.: Harvard University Press, 1985).

Figure 15-4 shows a long-run Phillips curve *LPC*, which indicates that in the long run there is no tradeoff between inflation and unemployment. Suppose now that as a consequence of a disturbance, say, an oil shock, the economy finds itself at point *A* with high inflation and high unemployment. We show two possible adjustment paths. The solid path shows higher inflation rates in the transition and corresponds to a policy choice of rapid restoration of low unemployment levels and then a long period of decelerating inflation. An alternative is the dashed path along which there is an immediate reduction in inflation. Along this path inflation is falling, but the cost is that the reduction in unemployment is more gradual.

Figure 15-4 makes the point that policy makers do not choose between inflation and unemployment, but rather between *adjustment paths* that differ in the inflation-unemployment mix. The solid path corresponds to the gradualist disinflation policy in Chapter 14; the broken-line path is more like the cold-turkey policy.

FIGURE 15-4   ALTERNATIVE PATHS OF INFLATION AND UNEMPLOYMENT. A disturbance moves the economy to point *A* where there is high inflation and high unemployment. There are alternative strategies for returning to full employment. The upper path emphasizes a rapid elimination of unemployment, the lower path a more rapid disinflation.

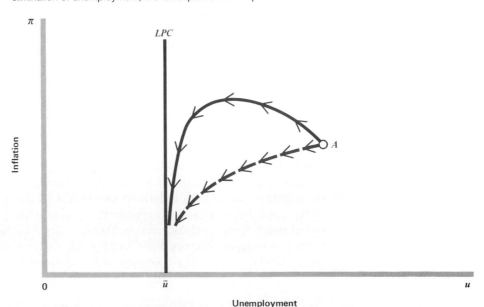

The Extended Phillips Curve

To see more precisely the options open to policy makers, we look at the expectations-augmented Phillips curve of Chapter 14, expressed now in terms of unemployment rather than output:

$$\pi = \pi^e - \epsilon(u - \bar{u}) \tag{3}$$

where, as a reminder, π denotes the inflation rate and π^e the trend or expected inflation rate. In this form the Phillips curve states that inflation will decline relative to the previous trend if the actual unemployment rate exceeds the natural rate $\bar{u}$. But often it is argued that the rate of inflation depends not only on the expected inflation rate π^e and on the *level* of the unemployment rate but also on the *change* in the unemployment rate. The argument is that at the same level of the unemployment rate, inflation will be different depending whether unemployment is rapidly falling or sharply increasing. Suppose the unemployment rate is 8 percent, and there are two possibilities. In one case unemployment is declining by 2 percent per year; in another it is not declining at all. We would expect higher inflationary pressure or less rapidly falling inflation in the former case than in the latter.

This extension is shown in equation (4), where we add another term $\beta(u - u_{-1})$ to the Phillips curve. The coefficient β measures the extent to which changing unemployment $(u - u_{-1})$ affects inflation. The larger is β, the more important is the effect of changing unemployment on the inflation rate. In this extended form high unemployment still exerts dampening effects on inflation, but they are now modified by the change in unemployment effect.

$$\pi = \pi^e - \epsilon(u - \bar{u}) - \beta(u - u_{-1}) \tag{4}$$

Equation (4) is immediately useful for policy decisions because it suggests that there is a concrete tradeoff. The more rapid the reduction in unemployment, the less disinflation is achieved at each unemployment level. Even if unemployment is very high, inflation falls little if the economy is moving too rapidly out of the recession. Conversely, a slow recovery reinforces the inflation dampening effects of high unemployment.

Okun's Law Again

We saw Okun's law as a link between the unemployment rate and the GNP gap. Now we look at a different version of the same law that links the behavior of real output growth and changes in unemployment over time. In this alternative form the "law" draws attention to the fact that over time the labor force grows and unemployment would rise unless real output, and with it employment, grows sufficiently fast. In fact, just to keep unemployment constant, output must grow to compensate for the increasing labor force and the reduction in labor requirements that come from productivity growth.

In this growth form, Okun's law establishes a simple numerical link between the growth rate of output and the change in unemployment. The law states that the unemployment rate declines by $0.4(=1/2.5)$ percentage points for every 1 percentage point of annual real GNP growth above trend. Thus if output grows 3 percentage points above trend, the unemployment rate declines by 1.2 percentage points $(= 0.4 \times 3)$, but if output growth were, say, 2 percent below trend, unemployment would rise by 0.8 percentage points. The trend growth rate of output, discussed further in Chapter 19, is between 2.5 and 2.9 percent in the 1980s. For concreteness we assume it is 2.7 percent, and we denote actual output growth by gy. With this assumption Okun's law linking real growth and the change in unemployment reads as follows:

$$u = u_{-1} - 0.4 \, (gy - 2.7) \tag{5}$$

From (5) unemployment exceeds or falls short of last period's unemployment as the growth rate of output, gy, exceeds or falls short of trend growth. Every extra point of output growth buys a reduction of unemployment of 0.4 percent, or every 2.5 percent extra growth, sustained for a year, reduces unemployment by a whole percentage point.

Once again it is necessary to emphasize that Okun's law summarizes an empirical relation between growth and unemployment, not an immutable law. In particular, the numerical estimates of trend growth and the growth-unemployment linkage have changed over time. But even with that qualification in mind, the relation is an extremely useful tool for macroeconomic planning.

The Policy Tradeoff

We can now return to the policy problem posed in Figure 15-4. The problem is to reduce unemployment but at the same time produce a long-run reduction in inflation. Okun's law suggests that reducing unemployment requires a sustained high-growth strategy. But the extended Phillips curve in equation (4) shows that a strategy of rapidly reducing unemployment will tend to increase the inflation rate. There is a choice to be made between a *high-growth recovery* that rapidly reduces unemployment and a *slow-growth recovery* that cuts into inflation, but at the cost of sustained high unemployment.[38]

Okun's law and the extended Phillips curve have another implication. High unemployment exerts a strong dampening effect on inflation, making

---

[38] We can derive the exact tradeoff by substituting $u - u_{-1}$ from equation (5) into equation (4) to obtain $\pi = \pi^e - \epsilon(u - \bar{u}) + 0.4\beta(gy - 2.7)$. This equation shows that inflation is higher, given π^e and u, the higher the growth rate of output. To achieve a reduction in inflation below trend, growth must be sufficiently slow, the more so the lower the level of the unemployment rate.

deceleration possible even in the presence of rapidly falling unemployment. But following such a strategy over time, the level of the unemployment rate declines, and hence the dampening effects on inflation become smaller. To achieve continuing deceleration of inflation, growth of output and the decline in unemployment must slow down. The second implication of the combined tools — Okun's law and the extended Phillips curve — is that growth can be fast at high rates of unemployment without reigniting inflation.

What Do Policy Makers Do?

We have now seen the menu of growth-unemployment-inflation from which policy makers must choose their path. How do they decide, and what typically is the choice? There are two ways of thinking about this problem. One is to assume that policy makers act in the interest of society. They form estimates of the social costs associated with alternative paths of inflation and unemployment and choose the one that minimizes the total cost of stabilization to society. This is the approach a benevolent dictator would choose.

In a democracy, policy makers respond to the electorate and choose policies that will maximize their chances of being kept in office. This may or may not result in policy makers choosing the socially optimal path. This second approach has given rise to an extensive literature in economics and political science that is classified as the political business cycle.

THE POLITICAL BUSINESS CYCLE

Policy makers who hold office in a democracy choose policies that contribute to their reelection. It is therefore important for them to determine the issues that voters are concerned with, their relative importance, and the ease and degree of risk or certainty with which macroeconomic policy can be used to help secure reelection. The theory of the *political business cycle* predicts that the path of the macroeconomy mirrors the timetable of the election cycle. We now review the building blocks of that theory.[39]

We have already discussed the first building block: the tradeoffs from which a policy maker can choose. There are two more building blocks: first, how do voters rate the issues — inflation versus unemployment — and second, what is the optimal timing to influence election results?[40]

---

[39] See Bruno Frey, *Modern Political Economy* (New York: Wiley, 1978), Edward Tufte, *Political Control of the Economy* (Princeton, N.J.: Princeton University Press, 1978), and D. Golden and James Poterba. "The Price of Popularity: The Political Business Cycle Reexamined," *American Journal of Political Science*, November 1980. For a critical view, see K. Alec Chrystal and David A. Peel, "What Can Economics Learn from Political Science, and Vice Versa," *American Economic Review*, May 1986.

[40] On the general topic see Herbert Stein, *Presidential Economics* (New York: Simon and Schuster, 1984).

OPINION POLLS

Voters are concerned with both inflation and unemployment. Figure 15-1 shows responses to the Gallup opinion poll. In virtually every poll between 1973 and 1983, more than 50 percent of the respondents rated either inflation or unemployment as the most serious problem facing the country. The same pattern emerges from almost all public opinion polls.

There is an important further lesson to be drawn from opinion polls: the public is concerned less with the level of unemployment than with the direction of change. *Rising* unemployment brings about sharply increased concern over unemployment. Concern over inflation depends on the expectation of rising inflation, as well as on the level of inflation.

The evidence is thus that voters worry about both the *level* and the *rate of change* of the inflation and unemployment rates. For instance, the public is less worried about a high but *falling* unemployment rate than it is about a medium but constant unemployment rate. These facts will influence the types of policies politicians will choose.

THE TIMING ISSUE

The policy maker wants to be sure that at election time the economy is pointed in the right direction to yield a maximum of voter approval. The inflation rate and unemployment rate should be falling if possible — and should not be too high if that can be managed. The problem is how to use the period from inauguration to election to bring the economy into just the right position.

The answer of the political business cycle hypothesis is that politicians will use restraint early in an administration, raising unemployment but reducing inflation. The need for restraint can often be blamed on a previous administration. But as the election approaches, expansion takes over to assure that falling unemployment brings voter approval even while the level of unemployment still checks inflation. In this hypothesis then there is a systematic cycle in unemployment, rising in the first part of a presidential term and declining in the second. There is a matching cycle, of course, in the policy instruments. Thus in the first part of the term, fiscal policy would tighten to create slack and disinflation; in the second part, expansion takes over to reduce unemployment.

The empirical evidence on the political business cycle remains mixed. The U.S. data do not show a clear pattern over the 4-year presidential cycle in the United States, as the theory would lead us to expect.[41] Every now and then, though, as in 1969–1972 and 1981–1984, the facts seem in accord with the theory.

In any event, there are factors that work against the political business cycle. One is that the President cannot use the business cycle fully because of

---

[41] See Golden and Poterba cited in footnote 39.

midterm congressional elections. The second is that a President cannot indulge too openly in staging recession and recoveries timed solely with a view to the election. There are risks to being caught in a cynical application of macroeconomic policies. Third, large macroshocks — oil shocks and wars — may on occasion overshadow the election cycling. Fourth, the executive does not control the full range of instruments. Specifically the Fed, in principle at least, is independent and therefore need not accommodate an attempt to move the economy in an election cycle. In fact, though, the Fed, has not always spoiled the game.[42] At least on one occasion, in 1972, the Fed very obviously provided expansion just at the right time. Fifth, if expectations are rational, then monetary-policy expansions staged just for the elections will have only small real effects and will mainly produce inflation. Fiscal expansions could still have real effects even if perfectly anticipated.

Thus we should not be surprised that the electoral cycle is not completely regular. Nonetheless, the hypothesis should not be entirely dismissed. For instance, other things being equal, we should be surprised to see an administration staging a recession in an election year to sharply reduce the inflation rate — with the falls in inflation to come only later. On occasion, for instance 1984 in the United States, a perfect electoral cycle seemed to be in action. On other occasions noneconomic issues may take precedence.

15-8 SUMMARY

1. The anatomy of unemployment in the United States reveals frequent and short spells of unemployment. Nonetheless, a substantial fraction of U.S. unemployment is accounted for by those who are unemployed for a large portion of the time.

2. There are significant differences in unemployment rates across age groups and race. Unemployment among black teenagers is highest, and that of white adults is lowest. The young and minorities have significantly higher unemployment rates than middle-aged whites.

3. The concept of the natural or structural rate of unemployment singles out that part of unemployment which would exist even at full employment. The unemployment arises in part because of the high frequency of job changes, in particular for teenagers. The high frequency of teenage unemployment is explained partly by the poor quality of jobs available to people without training. The natural rate of unemployment is hard to conceptualize and even harder to measure. The consensus is to estimate it around 6 percent, up from the 4 percent of the mid-fifties.

4. Policies to reduce the natural rate of unemployment involve labor market

---

[42] L. Laney and T. Willett, "Presidential Politics, Budget Deficits, and Monetary Policy in the United States, 1960–76," *Public Choice*, 1, 1983.

and aggregate demand policies. The economy needs a stable, high level of aggregate demand. Disincentives to employment and training, such as minimum wages, and incentives to extended job search, such as untaxed unemployment benefits, also tend to raise the natural rate.

5. The cost of unemployment is the psychic and financial distress of the unemployed as well as the loss of output. The loss of output is little compensated for by the unemployed's enjoying leisure. For one thing, a large part of unemployment is involuntary. For another, the social product of labor exceeds the wage rate because of income taxes.

6. The economy can adjust to perfectly anticipated inflation by moving to a system of indexed taxes and to nominal interest rates that reflect the expected rate of inflation. In the absence of regulations that prevent these adjustments (such as usury laws or interest rate ceilings), there are no important costs to perfectly anticipated inflation. The only costs are those of changing price tags periodically and the cost of suboptimal holdings of currency.

7. Imperfectly anticipated inflation has important redistributive effects among sectors. Unanticipated inflation benefits monetary debtors and hurts monetary creditors. The government gains real tax revenue, and the real value of government debt declines.

8. In the U.S. housing market, unanticipated increases of inflation, combined with the tax deductibility of interest, made housing a particularly good investment over the 1960–1980 period.

9. In the U.S. economy, wage indexation is neither very widespread nor complete. This absence of strong indexation probably eased the adjustment to supply shocks.

10. Stabilization policy involves choosing an optimal path of inflation and unemployment. The choice is between more or less rapid paths of recovery. The more rapid path reduces unemployment rapidly but does so without making large inroads on inflation. To reduce inflation quickly, unemployment must be high and/or recovery slow.

11. The political business cycle hypothesis emphasizes the direction of change of the economy. For incumbents to win an election, the unemployment rate should be falling and the inflation rate not worsening.

KEY TERMS

Unemployment pool	Costs of cyclical unemployment
Layoffs	Okun's law
Involuntary quits	Anticipated inflation
Accessions	Redistribution of wealth
Separations	Indexation
Duration of spells of unemployment	COLA
Natural rate of unemployment	Extended Phillips curve
Frequency of unemployment	Political business cycle
Targeted programs	

PROBLEMS

1. Discuss strategies whereby the government (federal, state, or local) could reduce unemployment in or among (a) depressed industries, (b) unskilled workers, (c) depressed geographical regions, (d) teenagers. Include comments on the *type* of unemployment you would expect in these various groups (that is, relative durations of unemployment spells).

2. Discuss how the following changes would affect the natural or structural rate of unemployment. Comment also on the side effects of these changes.
   (a) Elimination of unions
   (b) Increased participation of women in the labor market
   (c) Larger fluctuations in the *level* of aggregate demand
   (d) An increase in unemployment benefits
   (e) Elimination of minimum wages
   (f) Larger fluctuations in the *composition* of aggregate demand

3. Discuss the differences in unemployment between adults and teenagers. What does this imply about the types of jobs (on average) the different groups are getting?

4. Some people say that inflation can be reduced in the long run without an increase in unemployment, and so we should reduce inflation to zero. Others say a steady rate of inflation at, say, 4 percent is not so bad, and that should be our goal. Evaluate these two arguments and describe what, in your opinion, are good long-run goals for inflation and unemployment. How would these be achieved?

5. The following information is to be used for calculations of the unemployment rate. There are two major groups, adults and teenagers. Teenagers account for 10 percent of the labor force and adults for 90 percent. Adults are divided into men and women. Women account for 35 percent of the adult labor force. The following table shows the unemployment rates for the groups.

Group	Unemployment rate, u, %
Teenagers	19
Adults	
Men	6
Women	7

   (a) How do the numbers in this table compare (roughly) with the numbers for the U.S. economy?
   (b) Calculate the aggregate unemployment rate.
   (c) Assume the unemployment rate for teenagers rises from 19 to 29 percent. What is the effect on female unemployment? (Assume 60 percent of the teenagers are males.) What is the effect on the aggregate unemployment rate?
   (d) Assume the share of women in the adult labor force increases to 40 percent. What is the effect on the adult unemployment rate? What is the effect on the aggregate unemployment rate?
   (e) Relate your answers to methods of estimating the natural rate of unemployment.

6. Use the *Economic Report of the President* to find the unemployment data for the years 1975, 1979, and 1986. Use, as labor force groups, males and females, 16 to 19 years of age and 20 and older (that is, four groups). Calculate what 1975 and 1986 unemployment would have been if each group in 1975 and 1986 had the unemployment rate of the group in 1979. What does the answer tell you?

7. In the *Economic Report of the President,* you will find data on the duration of unemployment. Compare the distribution of unemployment by duration in 1982 and 1986. What relationship do you find between duration and the overall unemployment rate?

8. (a) What are the economic costs of inflation? Distinguish between anticipated and unanticipated inflation.

   (b) Do you think anything is missing from the list of costs of inflation that economists present? If so, what?

9. A reduction in minimum wages during summer months reduces the cost of labor to firms, but it also reduces the income per hour that a teenager receives.

   (a) Who benefits from the measure? Firms who have access to cheaper labor, teenagers who otherwise would not have a job, or both?

   (b) Who "pays" for the program? Teenagers who would have a job anyway but who now receive less pay than they would have, and/or other workers who are displaced by the cheaper labor on reduced minimum wages? Spell out what you think is the answer to these questions and decide whether you think the program is a good idea.

10. Evaluate the following argument that attempts to dispose of the notion of the political business cycle. "The public is too sophisticated to think that it makes much difference which party is running the economy. Both the Democrats and Republicans want the economy to boom, and want to keep inflation low. Both have access to the best economists available. Why would anyone think economic performance would be different with one party than with the other?"

BUDGET DEFICITS AND THE PUBLIC DEBT

In 1985–1986 the United States had to confront a major budget crisis. Budget deficits that followed income tax cuts in the early 1980s were rapidly adding to the national debt, which was growing fast as a percentage of GNP. A political stalemate on how to bring the deficits under control threatened potentially explosive growth in the national, or public, debt.

Until the mid-1970s the public debt had been declining steadily relative to GNP. From a level of more than 100 percent in the immediate post-World War II period the debt-GNP ratio fell to less than 25 percent in 1974. But after then debt grew relative to GNP—and that growth accelerated sharply with the large budget deficits of the period after 1982. Figure 16-1, which shows the public debt as a percentage of GNP, highlights the sharp increase in the debt-to-income ratio since 1975.

This rapid growth of the public debt was at the center of budget debates in 1985–1986. Without measures to bring the deficits under control there seemed to be a real prospect that the ratio of debt to income would continue to rise rapidly. President Reagan opposed increases in taxes or cuts in defense spending, while the Congress opposed cuts in social expenditures. The country faced the risk of huge deficits—$200 billion a year—as far as the eye could see. The deficits would have to be financed, implying a mounting public debt.

The 1985 Gramm-Rudman-Hollings Act brought the prospect of reduced deficits, which are reflected in the turnaround of the debt-income ratio in the late 1980s shown by the dashed lines in Figure 16-1. If deficits are in fact brought under control as planned, the debt-income ratio will begin to decline at the end of this decade: the greater the cuts in budget deficits, the more rapid the turnaround in the debt-income ratio.

The budget discussion brought to the fore important macroeconomic issues, which are treated in this chapter. Some people feared that the deficits and growing debt would eventually cause inflation or financial instability, or force a large tax increase, and/or crowd out investment spending. In this chapter we investigate the consequences of deficits and the existence and size of the national debt. We discuss the historical record of the federal budget, how deficits are financed, and what are the implications of deficit finance. Two questions are particularly important in discussing the public debt. One is whether the public debt represents a burden on future generations. The other

FIGURE 16-1   THE RATIO OF PUBLIC DEBT TO GNP. (*Source:* Congressional Budget Office, *The Fiscal and Budget Outlook,* February 1986.)

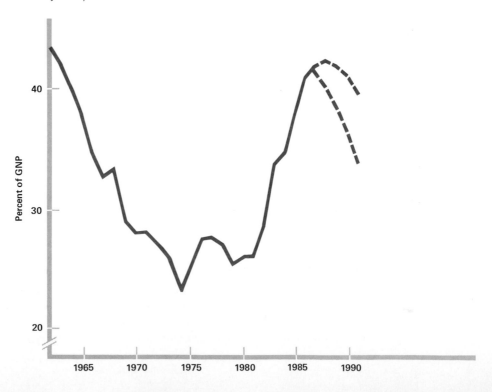

is whether the public debt represents net wealth for the economy, and if so, what are the implications for the effects of deficit finance.

In this chapter we focus on budget deficits and public debt. The next chapter deals with the link between budget deficits, money, and inflation. We start our discussion by examining the financing of budget deficits. From there we proceed to the causes of recent U.S. deficits. In the following sections we look at the impact of deficit finance and issues connected with the public debt. The chapter concludes with a discussion of the size of government.

16-1 THE MECHANICS OF FINANCING THE BUDGET

In this section we examine how the federal government finances its spending. We are particularly interested in the relationship between the federal government's deficit and changes in the stocks of money and government debt.

How does the government pay for its spending? Directly, it pays for most of its spending with checks, drawn on a Federal Reserve bank. Aside from the fact that the checks are drawn on a bank in which private individuals do not have accounts, payments made by the government look much like check payments made by anyone else. Like an individual, the federal government must have funds in the accounts on which it writes checks. So the question of how the federal government finances its spending is the same as the question of how it makes sure that it has funds in the bank accounts (at the Federal Reserve System) on which it writes its checks.

The Treasury is the agency of the federal government that collects government receipts and makes payments for the government. The government's accounts at the Federal Reserve System are held and operated by the Treasury. The Treasury receives the bulk of its receipts from taxes.

How does the Treasury make payments when its tax receipts are insufficient to cover its expenditures, in other words, when there is a budget deficit? The answer is that it has to borrow. In describing how the Treasury borrows to finance its deficit, we shall step back a moment from the particular institutional arrangements of the U.S. economy and talk in general terms of a treasury financing its budget deficit by borrowing either from the public or from its central bank. We shall talk as if the Treasury can borrow directly from the central bank by selling it securities. Alternatively, it can sell securities (debt) to the public.[1]

Debt-Financed Deficits

When the Treasury finances its deficit by borrowing from the private sector, it is engaged in debt financing. In this case the Treasury sells Treasury bonds or

---

[1] Foreign central banks, financial institutions, and individuals buy some U.S. Treasury securities and thus help finance the deficit. We treat sales of securities to foreigners as sales to the public.

bills to the private sector. Individuals and firms (including banks) pay for the securities with checks. The checks are deposited either in Treasury accounts at private banks ("tax and loan accounts") or at the central bank. The funds can then be spent by the Treasury in the same way as tax receipts.

Money-Financed Deficits

When the Treasury borrows from the central bank to finance its deficit, it is engaged in money financing. In the case of money financing, the central bank purchases some of the debt of the Treasury.

There is a major difference between the Treasury's borrowing from the public and its borrowing from the central bank. When the central bank buys Treasury debt, it pays for the debt by giving the Treasury a check on the central bank — that is, by creating high-powered money. When the Treasury spends the deposit it has received at the central bank in exchange for its debt, it leaves the private sector with larger holdings of high-powered money. By contrast, when the Treasury borrows from the public, it receives and then spends high-powered money, thus leaving the amount of high-powered money in the hands of the public unchanged — except for a brief transition period between the sale of securities and expenditures by the Treasury. Since the stock of high-powered money is an important macroeconomic variable, the distinction between selling debt to the public and selling it to the central bank is essential.

The distinction between money and debt financing can be further clarified by noting that Treasury sales of securities to the central bank are referred to as *monetizing the debt,* meaning that the central bank creates (high-powered) money to finance the debt purchase. Yet another way of looking at the difference between sales to (borrowing from) the central bank and sales to the public is to ask, What is the net change in the private sector's portfolio after the Treasury has made and financed its expenditures? Consider first the case of borrowing from the public, or selling debt to the public. In this case, the public

FIGURE 16-2   BUDGET DEFICITS AND THEIR FINANCING.

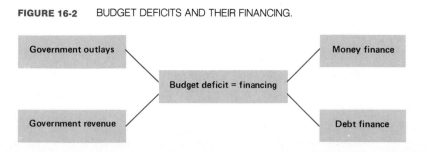

holds more debt, having bought the Treasury offering, and holds an un-changed quantity of high-powered money, since the Treasury spends the money it obtains from the debt sale to cover its deficit. Consider next the case where the deficit is financed by sale of debt to the central bank. Here, the private sector's debt holding is unchanged, while its holding of high-powered money is increased. The reason is that Treasury expenditures were financed by the creation of high-powered money by the central bank.

The government deficit can thus be financed in two ways: by selling debt to the private sector and by borrowing from the central bank. The main relationships are summarized in the flowchart in Figure 16-2. The budget deficit is equal to the difference between total outlays and total revenues. The two forms of financing are the sale of debt — government bonds or Treasury bills — and the creation of high-powered money.[2] (Sometimes economists speak loosely and describe money finance of the deficit as the printing of money to finance the deficit.) Of course, the government may have a surplus rather than a deficit. In that case, instead of selling bonds or increasing the amount of high-powered money, the government is retiring debt (reducing the outstanding stock of government bonds) or reducing the supply of high-powered money.

Alternatively, we can show how the government finances its deficit by using an equation. Let ΔB_p be the value of sales of government bonds to the private sector and ΔB_f be the value of sales of bonds to the central bank. Let H be the stock of high-powered money, and recall that BD is the budget deficit, measured in *real* terms. P is the price level. We have just seen that[3]

$$P \cdot BD = \Delta B_f + \Delta B_p \approx \Delta H + \Delta B_p \qquad (1)$$

Equation (1) is called the government's budget constraint. It states that the nominal budget deficit is financed by borrowing either from the central bank (ΔB_f) or from the private sector (ΔB_p). The change in the central bank's holdings of Treasury debts causes a corresponding change in high-powered money (ΔH), so that we can say that the budget deficit is financed either by selling debt to the public or by increasing the stock of high-powered money. It is in this sense that the central bank "monetizes" the debt.[4]

---

[2] In addition the government can finance its spending by selling off some of its assets, such as land or buildings or companies that it owns. For instance, in Britain the telephone company was originally government-owned but was sold to the private sector in 1984.

[3] As we saw in Chap. 10 the stock of high-powered money may change for reasons other than open market operations. For that reason we use the symbol for "approximately equal to" ($\approx$) in equation (1). The change in the central bank's holdings of government bonds is only approximately equal to the change in high-powered money.

[4] Note that the government budget constraint, equation (1), also shows that for a given value of the deficit, changes in the stock of high-powered money are matched by offsetting changes in the public's holdings of government debt. A positive ΔH matched by a negative ΔB_p is nothing other than an open market purchase.

The view that the deficit is financed either by selling debt to the public or by increasing the stock of high-powered money looks at the government sector as a whole, including, or "consolidating," the central bank with the Treasury in the government sector. When one thinks of the government sector as a whole, relative to the private sector, the transactions in which the central bank buys debt from the Treasury or lends to the Treasury are seen as mere bookkeeping entries within the government sector.

The Fed and the Treasury

In many countries it is useful to think of the government sector as a whole, without bothering to distinguish between the actions of the Treasury and the central bank. However, in the United States the Fed retains considerable power and independence. Indeed, the Fed does not generally buy debt directly from the Treasury, and so it does not directly finance the deficit in the way just described. The great bulk of Fed purchases of debt are made directly from the public. However, that should be thought of as only an institutional detail. For although the Fed by and large does not buy directly from the Treasury, it can do so indirectly by buying securities from the public. Suppose that the Fed is conducting open market purchases at the same time as the Treasury is selling debt to the public. The net effect of the combined Treasury sale of debt and Fed open market purchase is that the Fed ends up holding more Treasury debt, which is precisely what would happen if it bought directly from the Treasury.

In the United States the Fed is largely responsible for the division of the total deficit, BD in equation (1), between the change in high-powered money and the change in government debt held by the private sector. There is no necessary association between the size of the government deficit in the United States and increases in the stock of high-powered money. If the Fed does not choose to conduct open market purchases when the Treasury is borrowing, the stock of high-powered money is not affected by the Treasury's deficit.

Nonetheless, there have been occasions in the past when there was a more or less automatic association between Fed open market purchases and Treasury borrowing. This link was most direct when the Fed was committed to maintaining constant the nominal interest rates on government bonds, in the period from 1941 to 1951. An increase in the government deficit tends to increase the nominal interest rate. If the Fed were committed to maintaining constant the nominal interest rate, an increase in the deficit would force it to conduct an open market purchase to keep the nominal interest rate from rising. Thus there would be a link between Treasury borrowing and Fed open market purchases.

The Fed's commitment to maintain constant nominal interest rates on government bonds ended formally in 1951 in the "Accord" between the Fed and the Treasury. Even though, after 1951, the Fed had no formal commitment to maintain constant nominal interest rates, its long-time policy of having target nominal interest rates — which could change from time to time — also led to an association between deficits and Fed open market purchases. Given the Fed's target interest rates, Treasury borrowing which would have led to interest rate increases triggered Fed open market purchases to keep the interest rate from rising above its target level. Thus, for much of the fifties and sixties, there was a link between increased Treasury borrowing and Fed open market purchases.

Once the Fed targets strictly a monetary aggregate rather than interest rates, there is no longer any *automatic* link between budget deficits and the monetary base. In the 1979 – 1982 period the Federal Reserve emphasized monetary targets, and even though budget deficits pushed interest rates extremely high, there was no automatic response of monetizing the deficits. Whereas interest rate targets would have led to a huge expansion in the money stock, the emphasis on monetary targets prevented a highly inflationary monetary accommodation of the deficit. We return to this issue in Chapter 17, where we discuss the evidence on the deficit-money link as part of our discussion of links between budget deficits and inflation.

Deficits and the National Debt

It follows from equation (1) that when the budget is not balanced, the Treasury changes the net amount of claims on it held by the private sector and the Fed. Those claims are the securities the Treasury sells to the private sector and (indirectly) the Fed, and they represent claims for future interest payments. The total stock of government bonds (or claims on the government) outstanding constitutes the *national,* or *public,* debt. When the budget is in deficit, the national debt increases — the stock of claims against the Treasury increases. When the budget is in surplus, the national debt decreases. The Treasury takes in more taxes than it pays out, and it can use the excess to retire (or buy back) previously issued debt.

The national debt is a direct consequence of past deficits in the federal budget. The national debt increases when there is a budget deficit and decreases when the budget is in surplus. The Treasury sells securities more or less continuously. There is, for instance, a weekly Treasury bill auction, at which prospective buyers of Treasury bills (lenders to the federal government) submit sealed bids specifying how much they are prepared to lend at different interest rates. The Treasury sells the amount of Treasury bills it has offered at the auction to the bidders who offer the highest prices, or the lowest interest rates.[5] Longer-term debt issues are less frequent. Issues of Treasury

---

[5] Technically, no interest is paid on Treasury bills. Instead, a Treasury bill is a promise by the Treasury to pay a given amount on a given date, say, $100 on June 30. Before June 30, the Treasury bill sells for a discount at less than $100, with the discount implying a rate of interest. For instance, if the Treasury bill just described sold for $97.50 on January 1, the holder of the bill for 6 months would earn a little more than 5 percent per annum, or 2.5 percent for 6 months.

debt are not all made for the purpose of financing the budget deficit. Most debt issues are made to refinance parts of the national debt that are maturing. For example, 6 months after a 180-day Treasury bill is issued, the Treasury has to pay the face amount of the Treasury bill to the holder. Typically, the Treasury obtains the funds to make those payments by further borrowing. The process by which the Treasury (with the help and advice of the Fed) finances and refinances the national debt is known as *debt management*. Only part of debt management is concerned with financing the current budget deficit. Most of it is concerned with the consequences of past budget deficits.

We have discussed in this section the financing of budget deficits. The same principles apply in the case of a budget surplus. When the government has an excess of tax revenues over outlays, there is a surplus. Rather than having to borrow, the Treasury is in a position to *retire debt*. Practically, what happens is the following. The excess of tax receipts over outlays means that the government's tax and loan accounts and accounts at the Fed are building up. The Treasury responds by not renewing maturing debt, but rather by paying off bonds or Treasury bills that are coming due. Thus the stock of public debt outstanding declines.

Summary

1. Federal government spending is financed through taxes and through borrowing, which is necessary when the budget is in deficit.
2. Borrowing may be from the private sector or indirectly from the Federal Reserve System.
3. Lending by the Fed to the Treasury changes the stock of high-powered money, whereas lending by the private sector to the Treasury does not affect the stock of high-powered money.
4. The stock of claims held by the Fed and the private sector against the Treasury — the national debt — changes with the budget deficit. The national debt increases when there is a budget deficit and decreases when there is a budget surplus.
5. Because the deficit can be financed in two ways, there is no *necessary* connection between the budget deficit and changes in the stock of high-powered money. Equation (1), the government budget constraint, says only that the *sum* of changes in the stock of debt and changes in high-powered money is approximately equal to the budget deficit.

16-2 THE SIZE AND DETERMINANTS OF DEFICITS

Figure 16-3 shows the budget surplus of the federal government as a fraction of GNP. Throughout the period the surplus fluctuates with the business cycle, but there is also a definite trend of a decreasing surplus or increasing deficit.

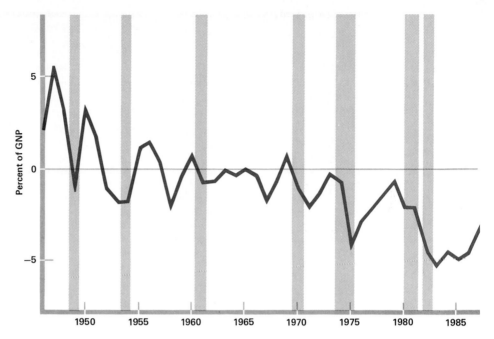

FIGURE 16-3   THE BUDGET SURPLUS AS A FRACTION OF GNP.
(*Source:* Data Resources Inc.)

Whereas deficits and surpluses alternate up to the end of the 1960s, there has been a deficit in every year since 1970. In the 1980s the deficit reaches its highest levels for the entire period.

Table 16-1 shows the averages of the budget deficit as a fraction of GNP in successive 5-year periods. The table highlights the high and persistent deficits in the 1970s and the 1980s, with no major change anticipated before the end of the 1980s. Underlying the behavior of the deficit are changes in government outlays and/or revenues. We now look at the more or less automatic effects on the budget of cyclical fluctuations, inflation, and growth. In the next section we turn to consider the tax and spending changes that produced the shift toward persistent deficits.

The Business Cycle and Deficits

The distinction in Table 16-1 between the actual and the *structural* deficit is widely used. The structural deficit, or the full-employment or high-employment or cyclically adjusted deficit, is the deficit calculated as if the economy

TABLE 16-1	FEDERAL BUDGET DEFICITS, 1955–1989 (Percent of GNP)				
Period	Actual	Structural	Period	Actual	Structural
1955–1959	−0.1	−0.9	1975–1979	2.3	1.5
1960–1964	0.2	−0.9	1980–1984	3.8	1.7
1965–1969	0.9	1.1	1985–1989*	4.1	3.2
1970–1974	1.2	0.9			

* Projection by the Congressional Budget Office. The structural budget for the 1970s and 1980s is based on a 6 percent unemployment rate benchmark.
Source: Data Resources Inc., Congressional Budget Office, *The Economic Outlook,* February 1984, and *The Economic and Budget Outlook: Fiscal Years 1987–1991,* February 1986.

were at a full- or high-employment level, typically 6 percent unemployment. The actual deficit differs from the structural deficit by a cyclical component, which is that part of the deficit that occurs purely because the economy is not currently at the high-employment level of output. Table 16-1 shows that over the 1980–1984 period, most of the budget deficit was a result of cyclical effects: the actual deficit was 3.8 percent of GNP, but only 1.7 percent of that deficit was structural. The forecast for 1985–1989 shows a large structural deficit of 3.2 percent of GNP, the largest over the entire period.

The difference between the structural and actual deficits occurs because government revenues and government spending both respond systematically to the business cycle. *Given tax rates,* increases in the level of income produce larger revenues for the government. And because the government pays unemployment benefits, its spending rises when the economy goes into recession.

The impact of booms and recessions on the budget is quite apparent in Figure 16-3, for example, in the recession of 1975. We now look at quantitative estimates of the impact of the business cycle on the budget. The estimate we report serves as a rough rule of thumb, and as such is well worth knowing.[6]

Each percentage point increase in the unemployment rate increases the budget deficit by about $25 to $30 billion. At the 1985 level of GNP this amounts to about 0.7 percent of GNP.

The size of this effect makes it clear that a major recession, with an increase in unemployment from 6 to 11 percent would give rise to a cyclical increase in the budget deficit amounting to more than 3 percent of GNP.

---

[6] See T. Holloway, "The Economy and the Federal Budget: Guide to the Automatic Effects," *Survey of Current Business,* July 1984, and T. Holloway, "The Cyclically Adjusted Federal Budget and Federal Debt: Revised and Updated Estimates," *Survey of Current Business,* March 1986.

Fiscal Drag, Bracket Creep, and Deficits

When nominal income increases, because of growth and inflation, tax collection rises. First, higher real income, with unchanged tax rates, means more taxes will be collected. But there is another effect that stems from progressive income taxes. If taxes are progressive, meaning that taxes are a higher proportion of income the higher the level of income, the share of taxes in GNP will rise as real income increases. In addition, if taxes are not adjusted for inflation, rising prices which increase nominal income will also raise taxes as people move into higher tax brackets.

The effect of nominal income growth on tax collection and the budget is called *fiscal drag*. The term is suggestive of the fact that with rising incomes the government's tax take increases and thus exerts a potentially depressing effect on aggregate demand and perhaps also on aggregate supply.

It is interesting to note that the impact of progressive taxation on tax collection can come from both a rise in real income and from the effect of inflation in raising nominal income and thus bringing a person into a higher tax bracket. We refer to increases in real tax collection arising simply from inflation as *bracket creep*. Bracket creep occurs when inflation interacts with progressive taxation of nominal income to move people over time automatically into higher income tax brackets.

How does bracket creep work? With progressive income taxes, the higher the income, the larger the share of income on which taxes are paid. Table 16-2 illustrates this. We compare two people, both in the same year. One earns $20,000, and the other earns $40,000. With progressive taxation, the person earning $40,000 pays a larger *share* of income in taxes than the other person. Thus the $20,000 earner pays 35 percent of income in taxes ($7,000), while the $40,000 earner pays 50 percent of income in taxes ($20,000).

So far we have been comparing two people at the same time. Now suppose we compare one person at two different times, with two different price levels. Initially the person earns $20,000, with the price level equal to 100. After-tax real income is $13,000. Now the price level doubles to 200, while pretax real income remains constant. That means pretax nominal income rises from

TABLE 16-2	EFFECTS OF INFLATION ON AFTER-TAX INCOME			
Price level	Pretax income, nominal	Taxes, nominal	After-tax income, nominal	After-tax income, real
100	$20,000	$ 7,000	$13,000	$13,000
200	40,000	20,000	20,000	10,000

$20,000 to $40,000. Before taxes, the person has the same real income with $40,000 now that was had with $20,000 when the price level was at 100. But because of progressive taxation, the after-tax income situations are different. Now taxes take 50 percent of the person's income, leaving only $20,000 nominal income worth only $10,000 in real terms. Thus the share of income taken by the government has risen as a result of the inflation.

How important is bracket creep in practice? The Congressional Budget Office estimated that over the period 1983–1985, bracket creep would generate between 0.6 and 1.2 percent of GNP in extra government revenue. Bracket creep is a potentially important source of government revenue, especially when the inflation rate is high.

Bracket creep can be avoided by *indexing* tax brackets. *Tax brackets are indexed when nominal (dollar) tax brackets specified in the tax system are automatically adjusted in proportion to the price level.* In Table 16-2 example, tax bracket indexation would ensure that when the price level rises to 200 from 100, the individual pays $14,000 in taxes and not $20,000. Indexation thus removes the effects of inflation in creating fiscal drag.

Indexation of personal taxes was introduced in the United States in 1985. Indeed, that indexation is in part responsible for the high deficits projected through the end of the decade. Many people were surprised that Congress introduced tax bracket indexation because bracket creep was such a convenient way for Congress to raise revenue. Tax rates did not have to be raised *explicitly;* rather, as prices went up, so did the share of taxes in GNP, without anyone having to vote for higher taxes.

Estimated Fiscal Drag

A recent estimate of fiscal drag is as follows:[7] *Each $100 billion increase in nominal GNP reduces the deficit by about $34 to $38 billion.* At the 1985 level of income this means that a 2.5 percent increase in nominal GNP reduces the budget deficit by just under 1 percent of GNP. Note that this estimate is, through Okun's law, consistent with the earlier estimate that a change of one percentage point in the unemployment rate affects the budget deficit by about 0.7 percent of GNP.

We thus note that income growth is a safe way of reducing budget deficits over time. Steady growth in nominal GNP, given constant tax rates and government spending that is not growing too fast, will mean that any deficit will come to be wiped out after a while. But the qualifications matter. Income growth will help wipe out deficits over time only if the government does not cut tax rates and if government outlays do not increase fast. One possible cause of increasing government outlays arises from a growing national debt, on

---

[7] See T. Holloway, "The Economy and the Federal Budget: Guide to the Automatic Effects," referred to in the previous footnote. Note that the Holloway estimates are from 1984, before tax indexation went into effect. Tax bracket indexation must somewhat reduce the size of fiscal drag.

which interest has to be paid. Rising interest payments can produce larger deficits, which increase the debt further, increasing interest payments even more. We discuss the potential instability of debt finance later in the chapter. Rising interest payments are one cause of the deficits of the later 1980s. So are the cuts in tax rates in the early 1980s that prevented fiscal drag from working in the usual way.

We turn now to a closer look at the government's outlays and receipts.

16-3 FEDERAL GOVERNMENT RECEIPTS AND OUTLAYS

In this section we review the facts about the composition and trend of government spending and revenues. The main question is why the U.S. deficit reached such high levels in the mid-1980s.

Outlays

Table 16-3 shows the outlays of the federal government over the past 20 years. The table introduces some special terminology. There is a distinction between *mandatory* and *discretionary* outlays. The former are outlays that the government is committed to make under existing laws. These payments have to be made under *entitlement programs,* where the law specifies that a person meeting certain requirements is automatically entitled to receive payments. Mandatory spending includes, for example, Medicaid or Social Security. Discre-

TABLE 16-3	FEDERAL GOVERNMENT OUTLAYS (Percent of GNP, Fiscal Year, and Unified Budget)				
	1965–1969	1970–1974	1975–1979	1980–1984	1985
National defense	8.6	6.8	5.1	5.7	6.4
Entitlements and other mandatory spending	5.7	8.1	10.2	11.1	11.2
Nondefense discretionary spending	4.9	4.6	5.5	5.1	4.4
Net interest	1.3	1.4	1.9	2.6	3.3
Total outlays*	19.3	19.7	21.3	23.2	24.0

* The table omits a peculiar negative outlay item called "offsetting receipts." This reflects federal revenues from Medicaid, federal contributions to retirement funds, and receipts from federally controlled land and offshore territories. These offsetting receipts amount to somewhat over 1.2 percent and account for the difference between the sum of the first four items in each column and the "total outlays" amount.

Source: Congressional Budget Office, *The Economic and Budget Outlook*, February 1986.

tionary spending, by contrast, is governed by the Congressional appropriation process and includes, for example, defense expenditures, outlays for the administration of justice, and foreign aid.

Three points in Table 16-3 are of particular interest. First, over the past 20 years, defense expenditures have declined significantly as a fraction of income. Second, entitlements programs have nearly doubled. This reflects a growing involvement of the government in social programs. Third, interest payments by the government have become an important part of government outlays. Their share in total outlays has more than doubled over the past 20 years.

For macroeconomic purposes there is an important distinction between the government's purchases of goods and services, and transfer payments. The former are a component of aggregate demand — the G term in Chapter 3 — whereas the latter affect aggregate demand indirectly, via changes in disposable income. The increased share of transfers in total government spending is brought out in Figure 16-4. By 1985 only a third of federal government

FIGURE 16-4   FEDERAL GOVERNMENT OUTLAYS AS A FRACTION OF GNP. (*Source:* Data Resources Inc.)

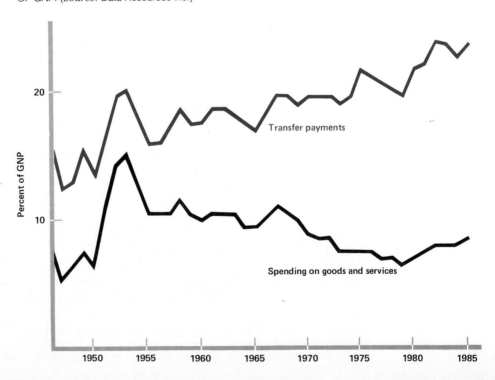

outlays (less than 10 percent of GNP) represented spending on goods and services, while transfer payments accounted for two-thirds.

Receipts

The federal government receives most of its revenue from tax collection. The sources of revenue, and the total, are shown in Table 16-4. Each of the revenue sources is self-explanatory, except perhaps for social insurance taxes. These are taxes on wages paid by employers and by wage earners.

First, note from Table 16-4 that total revenue as a share of GNP has changed very little over the past 20 years. Second, we observe a shift in the sources of revenue. Social Security taxes and contributions are becoming an increasing source of revenue, while corporate income taxes are declining. However, the 1986 tax reform act will substantially increase the share of corporate taxes while reducing the share of individual income taxes. Third, there is a remarkable stability of the revenue from the personal income tax. The decline in 1985 compared with the 1980–1984 period is a reflection of the tax rate cuts during the first Reagan administration.

The Deficit Problem

In Table 16-5 we combine outlays, revenues, and the deficit. The table shows strikingly that rising outlays rather than falling taxes are responsible for the growing deficits. Revenue, as we saw above, remains steady, but outlays have sharply increased. An important part of that increase results from payments of interest on the national debt. We now focus on the interaction between deficits and rising interest payments.

TABLE 16-4   SOURCES OF FEDERAL REVENUE (Percent of GNP, Period Average)

	1965–1969	1970–1974	1975–1979	1980–1984	1985
Individual income tax	8.0	8.4	8.2	9.0	8.5
Corporate income tax	3.9	2.8	2.7	1.7	1.6
Social insurance taxes and contributions	3.8	4.8	5.5	6.2	6.7
Other*	2.7	2.4	1.9	2.2	1.8
Total revenue	18.4	18.4	18.3	19.1	18.6

* This entry lumps together excise or sales taxes, estate and gift taxes, customs duties, and miscellaneous receipts.
Source: Congressional Budget Office, *The Economic and Budget Outlook*, February 1986.

BOX

16-1

STATE AND LOCAL GOVERNMENT SPENDING AND FINANCING

Most state and local government spending is on purchases of goods and services and constitutes an important component of aggregate demand. In fact, state and local governments purchase more goods and services than the federal government does. In 1986, state and local governments spent nearly $500 billion on goods and services, compared with $360 billion for the federal government. The rapid increase in state and local government purchases relative to federal purchases of goods and services began in the late sixties.

Table 1 shows some details of the composition of outlays and receipts of the state and local government sector. The goods and services that state and local governments buy are typically education, highways, hospitals, fire protection, garbage removal, and police protection. State and local governments spend relatively small amounts on transfer payments. With regard to interest payments, state and local governments actually, on balance, receive more interest than they pay out. This is a result of the budget surpluses they have been running which have enabled them, taken together, to purchase federal securities. Although many state and local governments run deficits and have to borrow, thus accounting for the existence of state and local government securities, others run surpluses and purchase securities.

The major sources of state and local government revenues are indirect taxes, primarily the sales tax. Other large sources of funds are state income taxes, property taxes, and grants-in-aid from the federal government.

State and local government financing differs from federal financing mainly in that the state and local governments cannot borrow from the Fed. Thus, when a state or local government runs a deficit, it has to borrow by selling securities to the private sector.

Two major questions arise in connection with the role of state and local governments in the economy. The first concerns the determinants of state and local government spending. In large part, this is determined through the political process. After rising rapidly in the sixties, and less rapidly in the seventies, the share of state and local government spending in GNP began to decline in the eighties, reflecting the political tide of opposition to big government.

The second question concerns the effects of state and local government spending on the economy. Here the analysis of federal government spending and taxing presented in earlier chapters is relevant. There are multiplier effects for changes in state and local spending, just as there are for changes in federal spending.

TABLE 1   COMPOSITION OF OUTLAYS AND RECEIPTS OF STATE AND LOCAL GOVERNMENTS, 1985 (Percent of Total)

Outlays	100.0
Purchases of goods and services	89.1
Transfers to persons	19.1
Net interest and subsidies	−8.1
Receipts	100.0
Personal tax and montax payments	24.7
Indirect business taxes and property taxes	47.2
Federal grants in aid	15.6
Other	12.5

Source: Data Resources Inc.

TABLE 16-5	THE FEDERAL BUDGET: OUTLAYS, REVENUES, AND THE DEFICIT (Percent of GNP, Period Averages, and Unified Budget)				
	1965–1969	1970–1974	1975–1979	1980–1984	1985
Outlays	19.3	19.7	21.3	23.2	24.0
Revenues	18.4	18.4	18.3	19.1	18.6
Deficit	0.9	1.2	3.0	4.2	5.4
Memo: interest payments	1.3	1.4	1.9	2.6	3.3

Source: See Table 16-4.

Interest Payments and Deficits

It is useful to distinguish between two components of the budget deficit: the *primary or noninterest deficit* and interest payments on the public debt.

$$\text{Total deficit} = \text{primary deficit} + \text{interest payments} \qquad (2)$$

The primary deficit (or surplus) represents all government outlays, except interest payments, less all government revenue.

$$\text{Primary deficit} = \text{noninterest outlays} - \text{total revenue} \qquad (3)$$

The distinction between the two components highlights the role of the public debt in the budget. Interest has to be paid when there is debt outstanding. The overall budget will be in deficit unless the interest payments on the debt are more than matched by a primary surplus. Table 16-6 shows the total deficit and the two components.

Consider first the period 1960–1964: here the interest payments amount to 1.2 percent of GNP, but the total or overall budget shows a deficit of only 0.2 percent. The reason is that the budget excepting interest shows a surplus of 1 percent. By contrast in 1980–1984 interest payments amount to 2.6 percent of GNP, and the overall budget deficit is equal to more than four percent of GNP. The noninterest budget in this period is in deficit and thus adds to the interest payments in creating a huge deficit.

Table 16-6 draws attention to a key problem in deficit financing. *If there is a primary deficit in the budget, then the total budget deficit will keep growing as the debt grows because of the deficit, and interest payments rise because the debt is growing.* The problem is exactly the same for an individual as for a country: someone who is spending more than he or she earns, and borrowing to cover the difference, will find a need to borrow more and more each year just because the interest on past borrowings keeps rising. This potential instability

TABLE 16-6   COMPOSITION OF THE BUDGET DEFICIT (Percent of GNP, Unified Budget, and Fiscal Years)

	Total deficit	Primary deficit	Interest payments
1960–1964	0.2	−1.0	1.2
1965–1969	0.9	−0.4	1.3
1970–1974	1.2	−0.2	1.4
1975–1979	3.0	1.1	1.9
1980–1984	4.2	1.6	2.6
1985	5.4	2.1	3.3

Source: Data Resources Inc. and Congressional Budget Office.

of debt finance is studied in more detail in the next section and in the appendix to this chapter.

The United States in the mid-1980s faced the dilemma that unless budget deficits were brought under control, the public debt would explode. That meant that either the government had to collect more in taxes or else spending had to be cut. Interestingly, if tax rates had not been so drastically cut in the early 1980s there would not have been any dramatic deficit problem. It is worth looking therefore at the tax cut issue.

Supply-Side Economics, Tax Rates, and Deficits

In 1981–1983 tax rates were cut by 30 percent in a three-stage process known as the Kemp-Roth tax cuts. If those cuts had not been made, income taxes would have risen as a share of GNP and the budget deficit would not have risen so rapidly.

No political candidate or officeholder is in favor of deficits. How, then, did the tax cuts of 1980–1983 pass when they resulted in such large deficits? There are two explanations. The first is that supply-side economists argued that the tax cuts would produce *more*, not less, revenue for the government. The other is an argument of political economy that says that Congress will spend whatever revenue it receives and that therefore the only way to get it to cut spending is to cut its revenues. We take up the two arguments in turn.

Tax Cuts and Government Revenue

Much of the controversy surrounding the tax cuts centered on a highly unusual proposition advanced by supply-side economists: a *cut* in income tax rates will *raise* tax revenues. The idea was highly controversial because it had until then been accepted that lower tax rates usually mean lower government revenues. For example, we saw in Chapter 3 that a tax cut would increase the budget deficit, even when we took into account the expansion in output induced by lower taxes.

But the supply-side economists, some of whom were installed in the U.S. Treasury by the Reagan administration, were certainly not thinking in terms of the simple Keynesian analysis of Chapter 3. Rather they were concentrating on the *incentive effects* of tax cuts. Take the income tax as an example. Anyone who is taxed, say at a 25 percent marginal rate, on income earned receives only 75 percent of the wage for working an extra hour. Supply-siders argued that a cut in income taxes, say from 25 to 15 percent, would encourage such a person to work harder. For instance, suppose the wage rate is $10 per hour. Before the tax cut a person working 1 extra hour earns, after tax, $7.50; after the tax cut the same extra hour brings in $8.50. Surely, supply-siders argued, such a person would want to work more hours.

Up to this point the analysis is relatively uncontroversial. There is some question whether cuts in tax rates encourage people to work more, because conflicting effects are operating. The cut in the tax rate raises the after-tax wage and therefore makes work more desirable, relative to leisure. But with a higher after-tax wage, a worker needs to work less to support the same standard of living. Perhaps when the after-tax wage rises, the response is to work less, earn more income, and have more leisure. For example, suppose someone is working 40 hours at an after-tax wage of $7.50, earning $300 per week. Now the after-tax wage rises to $8.50. By working 38 hours, the worker earns $323 per week—income and leisure have both risen.[8] However, empirical evidence, discussed in Chapter 19, suggests that a given worker will work more when the after-tax wage rises. Further, there is an unambiguous increase in the number of people working when wages rise—people who used to stay home now enter the labor force to find work. So on balance a cut in tax rates will increase output through supply-side incentive effects.

But the supply-side claim was stronger than a claim that a cut in income tax rates would motivate people to work more. The supply-side claim was that, despite the cut in the tax rate, total tax revenue would rise because a lot more work would be done. To see the point, we use the simple formula

$$\text{Income tax revenue} = \text{income tax rate} \times \text{income} \qquad (4)$$

The supply-side claim was that when the tax rate fell, income would rise enough that total income tax revenue would increase. For instance, suppose the tax rate was cut from 20 to 15 percent. Suppose income was originally

---

[8] If you have taken a course in microeconomics, you will recognize that the substitution effect of the increase in the after-tax wage causes the worker to work more, while the income effect reduces work. The net effect is therefore ambiguous.

BOX
16-2

THE LAFFER CURVE

Arthur Laffer, of Pepperdine University, is among the best known of the supply-side economists. Figure 1 shows the *Laffer curve,* relating tax revenues to the tax rate. The curve shows total tax revenue first increasing as the tax rate rises and then eventually decreasing.

The argument supporting the shape of the curve is as follows. Assume that we are discussing the income tax rate. When the tax rate is zero, government tax revenue is certainly zero. Hence we have point A on the curve. Further, suppose the tax rate were 100 percent. Then the government would be taking all the income that people earn. There would be no point in working if the government took all earnings, and so income in that case too would be zero. Then tax revenue would also be zero. Accordingly, point B is also a point on the Laffer curve.

Between A and B, though, the government certainly takes in some revenue from taxes. Thus we expect the curve to start to rise from point A as the tax rate is increased from zero to some very small rate, such as 3 percent. Eventually, though, the curve has to come back down to B. Thus at some point it will turn around — perhaps at a tax rate of 60 percent, as shown in Figure 1. Point C is the dividing line: at tax rates below 60 percent, any increase in the tax rate *raises* total tax revenue. At tax rates above 60 percent, any increase in the tax rate *reduces* total revenue. Looking at the same relationship in the opposite direction, we find that at any tax rate above 60 percent a *cut* in the tax rate will *increase* total tax revenue.

Supply-siders were thus arguing in 1981 that the American economy was to be right of the point where the Laffer curve turns down — say, at some point such as D. There was no evidence to support this assertion, and it does not appear to have been right. But it is a theoretical possibility.

Supply-siders made a similar claim about the effects of cuts in taxes on saving. When tax rates on saving are cut, the after-tax rate of return rises. For instance, suppose someone is earning 9 percent before tax on savings. The tax rate is 25 percent, implying an after-tax rate of return on savings of 6.75 percent ($= 0.75 \times 9$ percent). Now suppose the tax rate is cut to 20 percent. The after-tax rate of return rises to 7.2 ($= 0.8 \times 9$ percent). Surely, supply-siders

FIGURE 1   THE LAFFER CURVE.

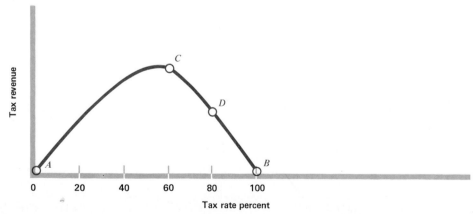

argued, such a person will save more.* Then there will be more investment, a larger capital stock, and higher output. With output higher, total tax revenue could be higher despite the cut in the tax rate.

Whatever the theoretical possibilities, the Kemp-Roth tax cuts did not lead to an increase in government revenue. Even if we concentrate on the full-employment budget, we do not see an increase in government revenue resulting from the tax cuts. This excessively optimistic element in supply-side economics was never believed by any but a small minority of economists, and it is now totally dismissed.† The emphasis on the role of incentives, though, is a valuable component of supply-side analysis and is discussed further in Chapter 19.

---

* There are conflicting income and substitution effects at work in this case, too, and the theoretical effect of the cut in the tax rate on saving is uncertain.

† On the supply-side story, see Jude Wanniski, *The Way the World Works* (New York: Touchstone, 1978); Paul Craig Roberts *The Supply-Side Revolution,* Harvard University Press, 1984; and Richard H. Fink (ed.) *Supply-Side Economics* (University Publications of America, 1982). For a critical view, see Robert Lekachman, *Greed Is Not Enough: Reganomics* (New York: Pantheon, 1982).

---

equal to $2 trillion. Taxes would thus be $400 billion to begin with. With a tax rate of 15 percent, income would have to rise to $2,667 billion for total revenue from the income tax to increase. It is rare, indeed, that income rises by one-third within a short time—but that is the size of the increase that would be needed if taxes were cut by one-quarter, as in the example of this paragraph. Thus this supply-side claim was implausible.

Tax Cuts and Government Spending

Quite another motive than supply-side arguments also led the Reagan administration to cut tax rates, despite the high deficits that would probably result over the next few years. That was the argument that the only way to get Congress to cut government spending is to reduce the revenue it receives.

The administration believed that unless tax rates were cut, and tax revenues reduced, the Congress would continue to spend. One of the major aims of the Reagan administration was to cut government spending, and so it was willing to have deficits for some time to put pressure on the Congress to reduce spending.

Gramm-Rudman-Hollings Act

There was a stalemate between Congress and the President on the budget in 1985. The President insisted on maintaining the tax rate cuts of the early 1980s. He was adamantly opposed to higher taxes, insisting that expenditure cuts, outside the defense area, were the only acceptable means to eliminate the deficit. But cutting nondefense spending, as is clear from Table 16-3, meant cutting social programs. This in turn was difficult for Congress to accept, and it certainly seemed impossible to put together an assortment of budget cuts that would fill the budget gap.

A decisive change in the budget outlook occurred in late 1985. Faced with the risk of an unending string of deficits and a mounting public debt, Congress passed the Balanced Budget and Emergency Deficit Control Act, better known as the Gramm-Rudman-Hollings Act (GRH) named after the sponsors of the legislation.

The special feature of the GRH Act is to mandate a phasing out of deficits by imposing a declining schedule of maximum deficits for the period 1986 to 1990, leading up to a balanced budget in 1991. The act requires the President each year to submit budget proposals not exceeding the maximum deficit limit for that year. If the proposals are not acceptable to Congress and hence not enacted in legislation, or if Congress fails to enact a deficit reduction program acceptable to the President, *automatic deficit reduction* takes place.[9]

The deficit reduction is achieved by automatic, roughly across-the-board cuts in spending on all programs with the following exceptions: Social Security benefits, interest on the public debt, certain specified welfare programs, and nondefense spending already obligated. The important feature of this across-the-board approach is that it falls on defense as well as on social programs. The only override on these cuts can come from a Presidential decision to invoke national security to exempt defense spending from the cuts.

The across-the-board cuts were the Congressional response to a political stalemate where nobody was willing to cut preferred programs and the President was unwilling to see increased taxes cover the deficits. But GRH turned out to be unconstitutional. Even so, there is little doubt that Congress will find one way or another — perhaps a son of GRH — to significantly reduce deficits. Few believe that taxes will be raised during the Reagan administration, but some economists argue that an eventual solution to the budget problem will include higher taxes.

16-4 DEBT-FINANCED DEFICITS

This is the section where we discuss the consequences of deficits. We concentrate here on debt-financed deficits and leave money financing for the next chapter. We draw a distinction between transitory and persistent deficits.

---

[9] See J. Wakefield "Reducing the Federal Deficit: An Update," *Survey of Current Business,* February 1986, for a detailed discussion of the budget process under GRH. See also Henry Aaron *et al., Economic Choices 1986* (Washington, D.C.: The Brookings Institution, 1986).

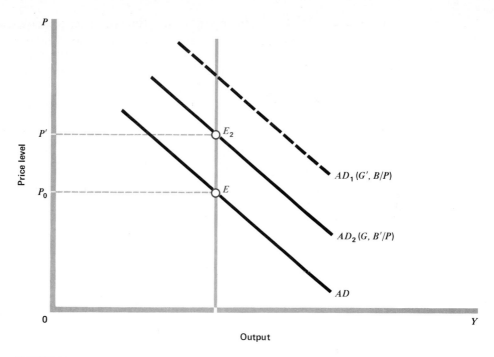

FIGURE 16-5 A TRANSITORY, DEBT-FINANCED DEFICIT. A cut in
taxes shifts the aggregate demand curve from AD to AD_1. In the short
run, aggregate demand expands. Because the deficit is transitory, the
tax cut is later reversed. The rise in public debt that financed the
transitory deficit raises the wealth of the debt holders. Once the deficit
has returned to normal, the effect of increased debt outstanding implies
higher aggregate demand. AD_1 shifts back only to AD_2 rather than to
AD. There is a permanent increase in the price level and, given nominal
money, a rise in interest rates.

A Debt-Financed, Transitory Deficit

Figure 16-5 presents the aggregate demand and supply diagram. We consider
the effects of a tax cut. The tax cut is temporary, and the budget deficit is
financed by selling debt to the private sector.

   The initial effect of the cut in taxes is to shift the aggregate demand curve
out from AD to AD_1. Because the private sector is buying bonds during the
period of the deficit, it ends up holding a higher stock of government bonds.
What effect does that higher stock of government debt held by the private
sector have on aggregate demand?

   Suppose that individuals holding government bonds regard those bonds
as part of their wealth. Thus it would seem that, given the level of income,

aggregate demand should rise when the stock of government bonds rises, because individuals holding those bonds have higher wealth. The higher wealth increases consumption demand.[10] Accordingly, the aggregate demand curve would shift out to the right as a result of the increase in privately held wealth. Hence, we show the final aggregate demand curve — after government spending has returned to its original level — at AD_2 above the initial AD curve. The difference between the two aggregate demand schedules AD and AD_2 arises from the higher stock of government bonds B', compared with $\bar{B}$ on the initial aggregate demand curve. Since the effects of the higher wealth on consumption demand are likely to be small, we show the final aggregate demand curve AD_2 below the aggregate demand curve AD_1.

There are two complications to this analysis. The first is that the existence of the higher stock of debt raises the amount of interest payments in the federal budget. If the budget was originally balanced at point E, it may not be balanced at E_2. Of course, since the price level at E_2 is higher than at E, bracket creep may have balanced the budget. If it has not, then further financing of the deficit would have to be undertaken, and that would have subsequent effects on the equilibrium.

Are Bonds Wealth?: The Barro-Ricardo Problem

The second complication is related to the first. It is possible that individuals in the economy calculate their wealth taking into account the tax payments they will have to make in the future. Suppose that everyone believed that the national debt would eventually be paid off. Then everyone would know that at some point in the future the federal government would have to run a surplus. Individuals might think the federal government would at some future date have to raise taxes in order to pay off the debt. In this case an increase in the debt would increase their wealth and at the same time suggest to them that their taxes would be higher in the future. The net effect on aggregate demand might then be zero. The issue raised by this argument is sometimes posed by the question, Are government bonds wealth?

The question whether government bonds are net wealth goes back at least to the classical English economist David Ricardo. It has been given prominence in the work of the new classical economists, in particular Robert Barro.[11] Hence it is known as the *Barro-Ricardo equivalence proposition.* The proposition is that debt finance by bond issue merely postpones taxation, and therefore, in many instances is strictly equivalent to current taxation.

The strict Barro-Ricardo proposition that government bonds are not net wealth turns on the argument that people realize their bonds will have to be

---

[10] Recall the discussion of wealth as a factor in consumption spending in Chap. 8.
[11] See Robert Barro, "Are Government Bonds Net Wealth?," *Journal of Political Economy,* December 1974. A recent theoretical challenge to the Barro-Ricardo view is Olivier Blanchard's "Debt, Deficits and Finite Horizons," *Journal of Political Economy,* April 1985.

paid off with future increases in taxes. (Incidentally, after raising this as a theoretical possibility, Ricardo rejected its practical significance.) If so, an increase in the budget deficit unaccompanied by cuts in government spending should lead to an increase in saving that precisely matches the deficit.

When the government reduces taxes to run a deficit, the public recognizes their taxes will be higher in the future. Their permanent income is thus unaffected by the government's switch from taxes today to taxes tomorrow. Their consumption is accordingly also unchanged. Since the tax cut increased disposable income, but consumption has not risen, saving must rise. The Barro-Ricardo proposition thus implies that a cut in current taxes that carries with it an implied increase in future taxes should lead to an increase in saving. The failure of the U.S. saving rate to rise with the tax cuts of 1981–1983 and higher deficits is one piece of evidence against the proposition.

Less casual empirical research continues in an attempt to settle the issue of whether the debt is wealth.[12] The issue is not yet closed. The theoretical arguments are not conclusive, and it is difficult to isolate the effects of changes in debt on consumption demand in empirical studies. We believe the evidence to date is on balance unfavorable to the Barro-Ricardo proposition, but recognize that the issue has not yet been decisively settled.

Money and Debt Financing

There is one important difference between debt financing and money financing of a given short-run budget deficit. Money financing of the deficit tends to reduce the interest rate in the short run compared with debt financing. That is because money financing increases the nominal money stock (shifting upward the *LM* curve in the *IS-LM* model), whereas debt financing does not. In the short run, then, debt financing reduces the level of investment compared with money financing. That is an issue connected with the crowding-out question.

We want also to compare the effects on the price level of money and debt financing of a temporary increase in government spending. The price level is higher with money financing than with debt financing. There are two reasons. First, money financing increases the money stock, and debt financing does not. The higher the money stock, the greater the aggregate demand at any given price level. Second, we attributed a price level rise in the case of debt financing to the wealth effect of a greater stock of debt on consumption. While there is some argument about whether bonds are wealth, there is no question that money is wealth. So the wealth effect on consumption is larger in the case of

---

[12] Intensive empirical work on this issue is taking place. For examples and reviews see David Aschauer, "Fiscal Policy and Aggregate Demand," *American Economic Review,* March 1985; Roger Kormendi, "Government Debt, Government Spending and Private Sector Behavior," *American Economic Review,* December 1983; James Barth, George Iden, and Frank Russek, "Do Federal Deficits Really Matter?," *Contemporary Policy Issues,* Fall 1984; John Tatom, "Two Views of the Effects of Government Budget Deficits in the 1980s," Federal Reserve Bank of St. Louis, *Review,* October 1985.

money financing than debt financing. That, too, means that aggregate demand at any given price level will be higher with money than with debt financing.

We now summarize the effects of a temporary budget deficit financed by debt creation. Such financing probably increases aggregate demand, but because of the possible effects of anticipated future tax liabilities on consumption, that is not certain. Debt financing, starting from a balanced budget and if not compensated for by higher taxes or reductions in other transfer payments, leads to a permanent deficit in the budget because interest has to be paid on the debt. Debt financing raises the interest rate[13] and reduces investment in the short run as compared with the effects of money financing.

Debt-Financed Persistent Deficits

We turn now to a persistent real deficit. Suppose, to begin with, that the economy is not growing. Then any attempt to run a permanent primary deficit, financed by debt, will fail. For as the debt accumulates over time, interest payments on the debt increase, and keep on increasing. Thus attempts to finance a given primary deficit purely through debt financing cannot be viable in the long run in an economy that is not growing.

Debt, Growth, and Instability

The impossibility of running a permanent debt-financed primary deficit in a nongrowing economy is a dramatic conclusion, which certainly seems to justify concern over the massive deficits the U.S. economy faces for the next decade. It is therefore worth emphasizing what the problem is, and also showing why the problem is less serious in a growing economy.

Suppose the economy is not growing and the government is running a budget deficit. It can finance the deficit by issuing debt. But next period it has to pay interest on all the debt that existed in the past, *and also on the new debt that it issued to cover last period's deficit.* How can it pay this interest? One way is to borrow some more. But then next period the interest needed to service the debt is even larger, and hence even more debt needs to be issued, and so on. This is the potential instability referred to in the previous section.

The national debt in the United States has typically risen year after year for the past 50 years. Does that mean the government budget is bound to get out of hand, with interest payments rising so high that taxes have to keep rising, until eventually something terrible will happen? The answer is no, because the economy has been growing.

---

[13] On the link between deficits and interest rates see Gerald Dwyer, "Federal Deficits, Interest Rates and Monetary Policy," *Journal of Money, Credit and Banking,* November 1985; Gregory Hoelscher, "New Evidence on Deficits and Interest Rates," *Journal of Money, Credit and Banking,* February 1986; and Michael Hutchinson and David Pyle, "The Real Interest Rate/Budget Deficit Link," Federal Reserve Bank of San Francisco, *Review,* Fall 1984.

Figure 16-6 shows the U.S. public debt as a fraction of GNP for a long stretch of time, starting in the early nineteenth century. The most striking fact is that the debt rises sharply as a result of large wartime deficits. Then, in each postwar period it declines. Over most of the period from World War II to 1974 the debt-income ratio was falling even though the debt itself was rising as the result of budget deficits. How could this happen? The answer is that the ratio of debt to GNP falls when nominal GNP grows more rapidly than the debt.

To see this point it is useful to look separately at the numerator and denominator of the debt-GNP ratio. The numerator, the debt, grows because of deficits. The denominator, nominal GNP, grows as a result of both inflation and real GNP growth. If the debt is growing more rapidly than GNP, the debt-GNP ratio is rising. If the debt is growing less rapidly than GNP, the debt-GNP ratio is falling.

Consider two examples. First, the stock of debt is $500 billion, and the debt-financed budget is $20 billion. Therefore the growth rate of debt is 4 percent [= (20/500 × 100) percent]. Suppose inflation is 3 percent and real growth 4 percent, and therefore nominal GNP growth is equal to 7 percent. With nominal income growth exceeding debt growth, the debt-GNP ratio decreases. Alternatively, suppose the stock of debt is $1,500 billion and the deficit is $200 billion. The debt is growing at 13.33 percent. Suppose inflation is 5 percent and real growth 4 percent, so that GNP growth is 9 percent. With debt growing faster than income, the debt-to-income ratio is rising.

Why is it useful to look at the ratio of debt to income rather than at the absolute value of the debt? The reason is that GNP is a measure of the size of the economy, and the debt-GNP ratio is thus a measure of the magnitude of the debt relative to the size of the economy. A national debt of $2 trillion would

FIGURE 16-6   THE U.S. DEBT-INCOME RATIO IN HISTORICAL PERSPECTIVE.
(*Source:* Congressional Budget Office, from material cited in
James R. Barth and Stephen O. Morrell, "A Primer on Budget Deficits,"
Economic Review, Federal Reserve Bank of Atlanta, August 1982.)

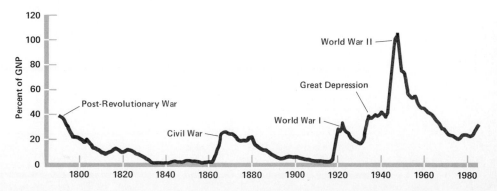

have been overwhelming in 1929 when U.S. GNP was about $100 billion — even if the interest rate had been only 1 percent, the government would have had to raise 20 percent of GNP in taxes to pay interest on the debt. But when GNP is more than $4 trillion, a $2 trillion debt is not so overwhelming.

We can formalize this discussion by writing the equation for the debt-income ratio and considering explicitly how it changes over time. We define the following symbols:

r = real or inflation adjusted interest rate

x = noninterest or primary budget surplus measured as a fraction of nominal income

y = growth rate of real GNP

b = debt-income ratio

In the appendix we show the debt-income ratio is rising over time if

$$b(r - y) - x > 0$$

The evolution of the debt-income ratio depends on the relationship between the real interest rate and the growth rate of output, and the noninterest budget surplus. The higher the interest rate and the lower the growth rate of output, the more likely the debt-income ratio is to be rising. A large noninterest surplus tends to make the debt-income ratio fall. Table 16-7 summarizes the conditions derived in the appendix that determine whether the debt-GNP ratio is rising or falling.

The table brings out why over the 1950s and 1960s the debt-income ratio was falling. The real interest rate was practically zero, output grew steadily, and the noninterest budget was in surplus or near balance. In these circumstances debt grows less rapidly than nominal income and hence the debt-income ratio fell. By contrast, in the 1980s the opposite is the case. Real interests are very high, growth is sluggish, and the noninterest budget is in deficit. As a result the debt-income ratio is rising. In a period of slow growth and high real interest rates deficits therefore translate into a rapidly rising debt-income ratio.

TABLE 16-7	DETERMINANTS OF THE DEBT-INCOME RATIO		
	$b(r - y) - x > 0$	$b(r - y) - x = 0$	$b(r - y) - x < 0$
Debt-income ratio is:	Rising	Constant	Falling

What would happen if the deficit were too large, so that debt grows relative to income seemingly without bounds? Such a process can really not go on forever. Ultimately the public debt totally overshadows and displaces other assets, and crowding out becomes so pervasive that the public comes to expect *some* action to balance the budget. This might involve inflation,[14] special taxes, or cuts in government spending to balance the budget.

How does inflation help solve the deficit problem? First, the inflation tax can make some small contribution to financing the deficit. But more importantly, a large *unanticipated* inflation will reduce the real value of the outstanding stock of government debt. The national debt in most countries is *nominal,* meaning that the government is obliged to pay only a certain number of dollars to the holders of the debt. A policy that raises the price level thus reduces the real value of the payments the government is obliged to make. The debt can therefore virtually be wiped out by a large enough unanticipated inflation — so long as the debt is a nominal debt.

It is important to have some perspective on the relevance of these extreme conditions to the world today. The United States in the mid-1980s was not close to facing a massive debt crisis in which the national debt was so large as to overshadow other macroeconomic problems and in which the government could not finance its deficit by borrowing from the public. But it did face the prospect of a rapid rise in the ratio of debt to income, back toward the levels it had been in the 1950s. That prospect was sufficient to make the political system respond with the Gramm-Rudman-Hollings bill as a way to bring deficits down to lower levels within a short time.

There are, though, a number of countries even today where many years of deficits have cumulated into a large public debt that ultimately becomes unmanageable. Often that outcome is clearly visible ahead of time, but on occasion a sharp increase in real interest rates together with a major loss in tax revenues, perhaps because of a world recession, can suddenly make the debt problem much more immediate. In particular, that problem faced many developing countries that had borrowed abroad during the seventies and in 1980 – 1981 when the real interest rate was still low. When the real interest rate rose, their heavy indebtedness meant that they had to make large interest payments to foreigners, which for many of the countries was extremely difficult to do. The result was the world debt crisis of 1982 – 1986.

16-5 THE BURDEN OF THE DEBT

As deficits continue, the national debt piles up. The U.S. national debt now exceeds $1.5 trillion, an amount that is enough to get anyone worried. In per

---

[14] See T. Sargent and N. Wallace, "Some Unpleasant Monetarist Arithmetic," *Federal Reserve Bank of Minnesota, Quarterly Review,* Fall 1981. As the title suggests, the treatment is technical. The main point the authors make is that debt problems ultimately become inflation problems. We return to this issue in Chap. 17.

capita terms, the national debt now exceeds $6,000 per person in the United States. That seems to be a heavy debt for each individual to bear. It is the notion that every person in the country has a large debt that makes the existence of the debt seem so serious.

However, we should realize that corresponding to the debt that individuals each have as their share of the national debt, there are Treasury bonds and bills that every person on average has. By and large, we owe the national debt to ourselves. Each individual shares in the public debt, but many individuals own claims on the government that are the other side of the national debt. If there is a debt for individuals taken together, it arises from prospective taxes to pay off the debt. The taxes that different individuals would pay to retire the debt would also vary among the population. To a first approximation, one could think of the liability that the debt represents as canceling out the asset that the debt represents to the individuals who hold claims on the government.

You will recognize that we are now discussing the question of whether the debt is counted as part of wealth for the population as a whole. Earlier, we started from the view that the government bonds and Treasury bills that individuals hold are part of their wealth. We then asked whether the possibility that all individuals consider the future tax liabilities connected with the hypothetical paying off of the debt at some future date meant that on balance the debt was not part of the wealth. In this section we started from the other side: we first talked of the national debt as a debt and then pointed out that there were assets held by individuals corresponding to that debt. We pointed out earlier that it was not yet certain whether individuals taken together in fact count the national debt as a part of wealth. There certainly does not seem to be any argument that the liability represented by some possible paying off of the debt at some unknown future time outweighs the value of the assets that individuals hold at present. At this level, then, there is no persuasive argument that the debt is a burden in the sense that the economy as a whole regards the national debt as a reduction in its wealth.

The only factor ignored in the previous paragraph is that part of the debt is owned by foreigners. In that case, for the U.S. economy as a whole, part of the asset represented by the debt is held by foreigners, while the future tax liability accrues entirely to residents. Then that part of the debt held by foreigners represents a net reduction in the wealth of U.S. residents.

Although the debt is not a burden in the fairly crude sense in which one asks whether individuals regard themselves as being poorer because of the existence of the debt (leaving aside the part of the debt owned by foreigners), there are more sophisticated senses in which it might be a burden. The most important sense in which there is a possible burden arises from the potential long-run effects of the debt on the capital stock. We saw earlier that debt financing increases the interest rate and reduces investment.[15] That would

---

[15] Recall that the real interest rate will not rise when the debt increases if individuals do not regard the debt as net wealth.

mean that the capital stock would be lower with debt financing than other-wise. If individuals regard the debt as part of their wealth, then they tend to increase their consumption at a given level of income, which results in a smaller proportion of GNP being invested, in a lower capital stock, and thus lower output. This is a real burden.

Further, the debt might be a burden because debt servicing in the long run could require higher tax rates. If those tax rates have adverse effects on the amount of work that individuals do, then real output would be reduced.

Thus, if the debt is a burden, it is a burden for reasons very different from those suggested by the statement that every person in the United States has a debt of $6,000 as a share of the national debt. The major possible source of burden arises from the possible effects of the national debt on the capital stock.

Government Assets

It is important to recognize that the government has assets as well as debts. Imagine a government that runs a deficit, borrowing from the public, to add to the capital stock. For example the government builds roads, post offices, or universities. The real capital acquired by the government should be treated as an offset against the debt issued. But in public discussions it is often forgotten that government spending is not all consumption or transfers.

Professor Robert Eisner of Northwestern University has strongly empha-sized this point in presenting government balance sheets in which both gov-ernment debts and assets are listed.[16] For example in 1980 the federal govern-ment owned tangible assets (valued at replacement cost) of $730 billion, but had net debts of only $447 billion. Thus the government had a net worth of $279 billion. Net worth here means that if the government were, so to speak, sold off, someone could walk away with a net profit.

There are serious issues of how to value government assets. No question, the government can sell outright a school or a post office, a jet fighter or an offshore oil lease. But if it does not plan to do so, and if — as in the case of a jet fighter — it rather will likely have to continue to spend large amounts to keep the asset operating, it is not entirely clear whether that item should count as a government asset in calculating the government's net worth. Whatever the details, though, Eisner's calculations drive home one message: concentrating on only government debt rather than all its potential sources of future income and outlays in analyzing its financial position is likely to be misleading.

The Budget Deficits of the 1980s

The U.S. budget deficits of the 1980s were not, however, a result of a large increase in government spending on capital goods, like roads and schools.

---

[16] See Robert Eisner, *How Real is the Federal Deficit?* (New York: Free Press, 1986); and Robert Eisner and Paul Pieper, "A New View of Federal Debt and Deficits," *American Economic Review,* March 1984.

These deficits will increase the burden on future generations. They have been accompanied by very large deficits in the U.S. current account, and thus by borrowing from foreigners. And on the domestic side, the deficits have not been matched nearly one-for-one by an increase in saving. On the contrary, they were matched primarily by higher consumption spending.

Simplifying somewhat, we can say that the government offered consumers lower present taxes, financing the deficit by borrowing abroad. Someone will ultimately have to pay the taxes that finance the interest on these loans from abroad. In this respect the U.S. is no different from many less developed countries, such as Mexico or Brazil, that have incurred a public debt by borrowing abroad.

The U.S. economy in the early 1980s was, in fact, saving little, and spending more than its available income by borrowing abroad. This pattern is apparent from Table 16-8 which reports the shares of private saving, investment, and external borrowing in income.

Since the U.S. economy did not increase its investment when the deficit increased, there is no prospect that the federal deficit will somehow generate extra earnings in the economy to pay the interest on the debt. Accordingly, a growing external debt burden is clearly on the horizon. This is part of the case for deficit correction that led to the GRH bill.

Optimal Deficits

Figure 16-6 shows how the national debt has typically increased during wartime and then declined as a percentage of GNP in peacetime. This seems like a sensible way for the debt to behave, reflecting large wartime deficits and peacetime surpluses or peacetime deficits that are small enough for the debt-to-income ratio to decline.

Is it possible to go beyond the general good sense of this behavior to something more specific, to ask about optimal behavior of the budget deficit over time? If the Barro-Ricardo hypothesis that current and future taxation

TABLE 16-8   PRIVATE SAVING, INVESTMENT, AND FOREIGN LENDING, UNITED STATES (Percent of Net National Income)

	Private saving	Net investment	Foreign lending
1961–1970	9.2	7.6	0.6
1971–1980	9.7	7.4	0.3
1981–1985	8.6	5.2	−1.3

Source: B. Bosworth, "Fiscal Fitness: Deficit Reduction and the Economy," *The Brookings Review*, Winter/Spring 1986.

have the same effects on current behavior was correct, then it would not at all matter how budgets were financed. If a government ran a large deficit in wartime, people would recognize that meant higher taxation in the future and would consume the same amount as if they were taxed during the war.

There are in fact two main theories of optimal deficit finance. Their prescriptions depend on the assumed reason that the timing of taxes matters.

MINIMIZING INTERTEMPORAL TAX DISTORTIONS

One theory, developed by Finn Kydland of Carnegie-Mellon University and Edward Prescott of the University of Minnesota,[17] focuses on tax distortions, or *tax wedges*. These distortions occur because taxes create a difference between the market price of commodities and their value to consumers and producers. For instance, the income tax means that workers, who take home only an after-tax wage, place a lower value on their work than the employer, who has to pay a pretax wage.

In order to minimize these distortions over time, Kydland and Prescott show that tax *rates* should be kept constant. To see why, suppose that on the contrary taxes were high during war and low during peace. Then according to this theory, which is a supply-side theory, individuals would work less during the war and more during peace. Rather than have labor supply moving perversely in that way, Kydland and Prescott show that under their assumptions tax rates should be kept constant.

The government budget constraint says that the present value of government spending has to be equal to the present value of taxes. If tax rates are constant, deficits will be high when government spending is *temporarily* high and surpluses will occur when government spending is temporarily low. The reason is that on average the budget has to be balanced. If tax rates are kept constant, then revenues will change relatively little. Government spending can fluctuate more, and when it is high there will be a deficit.

This tax-smoothing argument indeed suggests that the typical pattern of large wartime deficits is the correct one.

INTERGENERATIONAL FAIRNESS

In discussing the burden of the national debt, we showed that when Barro-Ricardo equivalence does not hold, the national debt creates a burden on future generations by reducing their capital stock. That would mean that a government that runs a deficit and creates a larger debt shifts some of the burden of current government spending to future generations.

In that case, the criterion on which decisions on budget deficits have to

---

[17] "A Competitive Theory of Fluctuations and the Feasibility and Desirability of Stabilization Policy," in Stanley Fischer (ed.), *Rational Expectations and Economic Policy,* University of Chicago Press, 1980.

be made is one of intergenerational fairness. For instance, when a country is in a war, it might be thought fair that future generations should share the economic burden with those facing the burdens of both fighting and economic hardship. By that criterion, too, deficit finance would probably be widely agreed as justified in wartime.

Of course, there is no hard-and-fast economic principle that describes what is fair and not fair in allocating burdens over time. Nonetheless politicians and the average person probably have little trouble basing their decisions on their views about the fair sharing of burdens across generations.

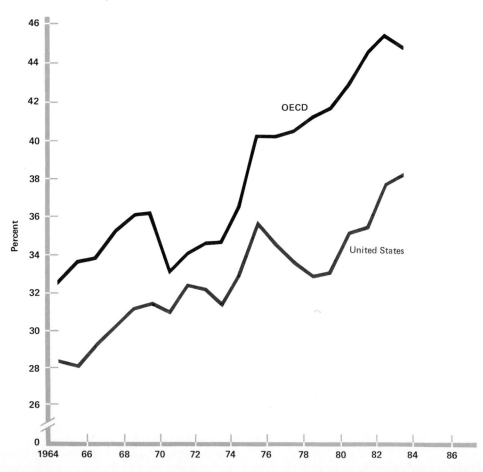

FIGURE 16-7   THE SHARE OF GOVERNMENT OUTLAYS IN GNP: THE UNITED STATES AND THE OECD. (*Source:* OECD *Economic Outlook,* June 1986.)

16-6 THE SIZE OF GOVERNMENT CONTROVERSY

There has been a worldwide trend over the last 25 years toward an increased share of government in GNP. Figure 16-7 shows the share of government outlays (all levels of government) in GNP for the United States and for the group of industrialized countries. In 1980 the share was significantly higher than it had been in 1960 in the United States, and even more so abroad. This increase reflects in large measure the broadening of government social programs, especially the growth of transfer programs discussed above. Since 1981 growth in spending has been under sharp attack.

A vocal part of the electorate and the government argues that much of government spending is wasteful, that the tax burden is excessive, and that the role of government in the economy should be reduced. In the United States the response to the growth of government has been a tax revolt, leading to limitations on taxes in several states, and an attempt to secure a constitutional amendment that would both prevent government spending from rising and require budgets to be balanced, or almost so. The balanced budget amendment has had the support of the Reagan administration, despite the administration's introducing extremely unbalanced budgets.

A Constitutional Amendment

In 1982 a Senate resolution, supported by the administration, proposed a constitutional amendment from which we quote here:

> SECTION 1. Prior to each fiscal year, the Congress shall adopt a statement of receipts and outlays for that year in which total outlays are no greater than total receipts. The Congress may amend such statement provided revised outlays are no greater than revised receipts. Whenever three-fifths of the whole number of both Houses shall deem it necessary, Congress in such statement may provide for a specific excess of outlays over receipts by a vote directed solely to that subject. The Congress and the President shall, pursuant to legislation or through exercise of their powers under the first and second articles, ensure that actual outlays do not exceed the outlays set forth in such statement.

> SECTION 2. Total receipts for any fiscal year set forth in the statement adopted pursuant to this article shall not increase by a rate greater than the rate of increase in national income in the year or years ending not less than six months nor more than twelve months before such fiscal year, unless a majority of the whole number of both Houses of Congress shall have passed a bill directed solely to approving specific additional receipts and such bill has become law.

The Balanced Budget

The constitutional amendment has two main sets of provisions. First, it essentially requires a balanced budget. It thus limits the government's ability to run deficits. Under the proposed amendment, unbalancing of the budget requires a three-fifths majority of the Congress. The presumption will be that the budget should be balanced, even in a recession. Fiscal policy thus loses flexibility to deal with the business cycle. By requiring annual budget balance, the amendment ensures that even automatic stabilizers are neutralized — for if the budget is going into deficit because of automatic stabilizers, it takes a three-fifths majority to permit that deficit. Otherwise taxes have to be raised or other spending cut. This feature of the amendment is widely believed to be a setback.

But even if there are economic disadvantages to a balanced budget the proposal remains politically alive and attractive. In a recent review of the politics of the balanced budget Alan Blinder and Douglas Holtz-Eakin note:[18]

> Like wage-price controls, balancing the federal government budget has long enjoyed greater popularity with the public than with economists. A poll taken after a decade of the Great Depression showed that 61 percent of the populace was willing to cut federal spending immediately by enough to balance the budget, while only 17 percent were opposed. Nor has this idea's popularity declined over time.

The Size of Government

The second set of provisions, and the more significant, deals with the size of government. Government spending is to be reduced to 20 percent of GNP. Only real growth of the economy will permit government spending to increase. The balanced budget amendment would make the 1960–1985 pattern of a growing share of government in GNP impossible.[19]

How large should the government be? That is, of course, a difficult question. Clearly, some government programs are widely regarded as desirable: for instance, few dispute the need for an adequate national defense. Other programs, such as the Social Security program, also command wide assent, though just how large such programs should be is controversial.

But there is no simple test that will tell us whether we get our money's worth from government spending in general. There have been a number of studies of particular government programs showing that they work less effectively than was originally expected, perhaps very badly, and arguing that it would be better if the programs were abandoned and the problem left to the free market to handle. Even the Social Security system and the food stamp program have received substantial criticism. The approach that looks at individual programs to examine their success and suggest changes is clearly the most careful way to evaluate government spending.

---

[18] See Alan Blinder and Douglas Holtz-Eakin, "Public Opinion and the Balanced Budget," *American Economic Review*, May 1984. See, too, Herbert Stein *Presidential Economics* (New York: Simon and Schuster, 1984).

[19] See the study by the Congressional Budget Office, *Balancing the Federal Budget and Limiting Federal Spending: Constitutional and Statutory Approaches*, September 1982.

The evaluation of individual programs has also to take into account the costs of financing such programs. Raising taxes creates disincentives to work and save that are properly counted as part of the cost of government spending. There is no getting away from the fact that resources are not free (except perhaps in a recession) and that resources that are used by the government could also have been used in other ways by the private sector.

There is no reason to think that a careful analysis of the costs and benefits of government programs would conclude that the share of government in GNP should be some fixed number, such as 20 percent. Richer societies may want to spend a greater share of GNP through the government, to finance programs that provide support for the poor. Or richer societies may feel that there are so many good opportunities in the private economy that people should look after themselves.

In practice, of course, the issue of how much government spending there should be is handled by the political process. In the 1930s and in the 1960s the rules and traditions of fiscal policy were changed by activist government policy in pursuit of full employment and widening social objectives. Today there is a widespread sentiment that things have gone too far and need to be brought under control by a return to "sound fiscal policy." We have seen that long-run control of deficits is, indeed, necessary for macroeconomic stability. The rest of the fiscal revolt reflects a disagreement in society on how best to use resources.[20]

16-7 SUMMARY

1. Federal government expenditures are financed through taxes and borrowing. The borrowing takes place directly from the public, and maybe indirectly from the Fed.
2. Under present institutional arrangements, there is no necessary link between Treasury borrowing and changes in the stock of high-powered money. Federal Reserve financing of the deficit increases the stock of high-powered money.
3. When the Fed tries to control the level of interest rates, it creates an automatic link between Treasury borrowing and the creation of high-powered money.
4. Federal government receipts come chiefly from the individual income tax and social insurance taxes and contributions. The share of the last category has increased rapidly in the postwar period, especially since the 1960s.

---

[20] These issues are in no way special to the United States. In fact they are being debated in all industrial countries. See Peter Saunders and Friedrich Klau, "The Role of the Public Sector," *OECD Economic Studies*, Spring 1985, for a comprehensive review.

5. Federal government expenditures are chiefly on defense and transfer payments to individuals. The share of defense in federal expenditure has fallen over the past 25 years, while the share of transfers has risen.

6. A temporary increase in government spending or cut in taxes financed by debt will raise the price level and increase the interest rate.

7. The Barro-Ricardo equivalence proposition notes that debt represents future taxes. Accordingly it asserts that debt-financed tax cuts will not have any effect on aggregate demand.

8. The debt-income ratio rises if the growth rate of debt—determined by interest payments and the primary deficit—exceeds the growth rate of nominal income.

9. Debt financing of a permanent increase in government spending is not viable if the economy is not growing. The interest payments on the debt would continually increase, making for a rising deficit that has to be funded by ever-increasing borrowing. In a growing economy, small deficits can be run permanently without causing the debt-GNP ratio to rise.

10. The major sense in which the national debt may be a burden is that it may lead to a decline in the capital stock in the long run.

11. The balance sheet of the government shows as an offset to the public debt government real assets.

12. The U.S. deficits of the 1980s have consumption as their primary counterpart, and they are financed by external borrowing. They accordingly represent exactly the kind of deficit that does give rise to a debt burden.

13. The increase in government spending in the 1960–1985 period led to the imposition of limits on taxes and spending in several states and a proposed constitutional amendment in the United States to require a balanced budget and limits on government spending as a share of GNP.

KEY TERMS

Public debt	Debt-income ratio
Debt finance	Laffer curve
Entitlement spending	Gramm-Rudman-Hollings
Discretionary spending	Barro-Ricardo equivalence
Bracket creep	Primary deficit
Tax indexation	Noninterest deficit
Transfers	Burden of the debt

PROBLEMS

1. What effect does a federal government surplus have on the stock of money and the stock of debt? Explain in detail the mechanics of how the stocks of money and bonds are affected.

2. Suppose the Treasury issues $1 billion in Treasury bills which are bought by the public. Then the Fed conducts open market purchase of $300 million. Effectively, how has the debt been financed?

3. Under what circumstances are fiscal and monetary policy related rather than existing as two completely independent instruments in the hands of the government?

4. Trace the path the economy follows when there is a permanent increase in government spending that is financed by borrowing from the public. Assume the economy is growing. Evaluate the argument that the budget should be balanced every period.

5. Analyze the difference in the impact on the interest rate, investment, and the price level of a temporary change in government spending, financed by borrowing.

6. What would be the bracket creep effect of inflation on real income taxes if income taxation was (a) regressive, (b) proportional, (c) indexed?

7. Suppose the real interest rate is 3 percent, output growth is 7 percent, the debt-income ratio is 50 percent, and the primary budget shows a deficit of 7 percent of GNP. Will the debt-income ratio increase or fall?

8. Explain in words why a high growth rate of output will tend, other things being equal, to reduce the debt-income ratio. How does your answer help explain Figure 16-6?

9. A government increases spending by building a dam. The spending is financed by issuing debt. Does the debt issue create a debt burden? Would your answer differ if the government had bought a fleet of automobiles for the Pentagon?

10. The Kemp-Roth tax cuts of the early 1980s cut government receipts collection from an average of 19.7 percent of GNP in 1980–1982 to only 18.6 percent in 1985. Are these tax cuts the main explanation for the budget deficit problem of the 1980s?

11. "The unsustainable deficits of the 1980s urgently call for a new approach to fiscal policy. Budgets need to be balanced year by year so that today's taxpayers pay the full bill of what they want the government to do for them." Comment on this statement.

12. "The United States faces a fiscal crisis because mounting deficits are driving the debt-income ratio far beyond the range that this country has experienced. From these high debt levels there is no return except by years of high taxes to pay off the debt." Comment on this statement.

APPENDIX: THE POTENTIAL INSTABILITY OF DEBT-FINANCE

In this appendix we develop a framework to assess the instability problem associated with debt finance. We focus on the debt-income ratio and ask under what conditions the debt-income ratio will rise over time. Instability arises if the debt-income ratio rises year after year without limits.[21]

---

[21] The discussion of debt-income ratios draws on James Tobin, "Budget Deficits, Federal Debt and Inflation in the Short and Long Run," in The Conference Board, *Toward a Reconstruction of Federal Budgeting*, 1982; Robert Eisner and Paul Pieper, "A New View of the Federal Debt and Budget Deficits," *American Economic Review*, March 1984; Willem Buiter, "A Guide to Public Sector Debt and Deficits," *Economic Policy*, November 1985; and Congressional Budget Office, *The Economic Outlook*, February 1984.

The derivation uses definitions, addition and subtraction and avoids calculus. Its main purpose is for you to see where Table 16-7 comes from.

B = nominal stock of debt outstanding
i = nominal interest rate
r = real interest rate
P = price level
Y = level of real output
x = noninterest or primary budget surplus (relative to income)
b = debt-income ratio
y = growth rate of output

The debt-income ratio is defined as the ratio of debt outstanding relative to nominal GNP:

$$\text{Debt-income ratio} = b \equiv \frac{B}{PY} \tag{A1}$$

The increase in debt from one year to the next is the result of the budget deficit. It therefore is equal to interest payments, which are equal to the debt outstanding times the interest rate, iB, less the noninterest surplus, xPY:

$$B_{t+1} - B_t \equiv \Delta B = iB_t - xP_tY_t \tag{A2}$$

Over time the debt-income ratio changes by Δb. From equation (A1) the change over time can be calculated as

$$\Delta b = \frac{B_{t+1}}{P_{t+1}Y_{t+1}} - \frac{B_t}{P_tY_t} = \frac{B_t + \Delta B}{P_tY_t(1 + y)(1 + \pi)} - b_t \tag{A3}$$

where we have simply used the definitions of the growth rate $Y_{t+1} \equiv Y_t(1 + y)$ and inflation rate $P_{t+1} \equiv P_t(1 + \pi)$ and (A1). Note that the growth rate of nominal income appears in (A3) as the term $(1 + y)(1 + \pi)$. To simplify notation we use the definition $q \equiv 1/(1 + y)(1 + \pi)$ to denote the reciprocal of the growth rate of nominal income.

Equation (A3) can be simplified to the following form:

$$\Delta b = b\left[\frac{1 + \Delta B/B}{(1 + y)(1 + \pi)} - 1\right] = qb\left[\left(1 + \frac{\Delta B}{B}\right) - (1 + y)(1 + \pi)\right] \tag{A3a}$$

which states that if the growth rate of debt $(1 + \Delta B/B)$ exceeds the growth rate of nominal income $(1 + y)(1 + \pi)$ the debt-income ratio must increase.

Our next task is to relate the change in the debt-income ratio to interest rates and the primary budget. For that purpose we go back to (A3). Substituting the expression for the change in nominal debt from (A2) into (A3) yields

$$\Delta b = qb[(1 + i) - (1 + y)(1 + \pi)] - qx \tag{A4}$$

Using the approximation $(1 + y)(1 + \pi) \simeq 1 + y + \pi$ and the definition of the real interest rate, $r = i - \pi$, we get the final form of the equation:[22]

$$\Delta b = q[(r - y)b - x] \tag{A5}$$

This equation states that the debt-income ratio will be rising if the expression in square brackets is positive. The expression *must* be positive if the real interest rate exceeds the growth rate *and* there is a noninterest deficit ($x < 0$). It must be falling if the real interest rate is less than the growth rate *and* there is a noninterest surplus. In between there are different possibilities. The important point to recognize is that a shift in the economy toward high real interest rate and low growth rates, combined with a noninterest deficit cannot but cause the debt-income ratio to be rising.

---

[22] The approximation $(1 + y)(1 + \pi) \simeq 1 + y + \pi$ neglects the term $y\pi$. If both the growth rate of output and the inflation rate are small fractions, say 0.05 and 0.11, the product is only a small quantity and can be ignored. But if inflation is large, say 500 percent the interaction term $y\pi$ cannot be neglected.

MONEY, DEFICITS, AND INFLATION

In this chapter we concentrate on the role of money growth in generating inflation and influencing interest rates and output. We take up four main topics. First, we examine the monetarist proposition that inflation is a monetary phenomenon, which means that inflation is entirely, or at least primarily, due to excessive money growth. Second, we study the linkages among interest rates, inflation, and money growth. The question is whether increased money growth raises or lowers interest rates. Third, we look at the links between budget deficits and money growth, asking whether or under what circumstances budget deficits generate money growth. Finally, we briefly describe hyperinflations and the role of money growth in them.

We establish a few important, basic results in this chapter. The most important is that really high inflation is indeed primarily a monetary phenomenon in the sense that inflation could not continue without continued money growth. But typically in conditions of high inflation there are also high budget deficits underlying the rapid money growth. Such was the case for instance in the hyperinflations in 1984–1985 in Argentina, Bolivia, Brazil, or Israel. Similarly in conditions of high inflation nominal interest rates become very high as expected inflation becomes incorporated in nominal rates.

The real world application and significance of these results is quite striking and can be seen in many high inflation countries around the world. However, when inflation rates are lower, in the single-digit or low-double-digit range, real disturbances like supply shocks may well be playing a relatively larger role, and the simple results isolating the role of money become less dominant. Similarly, the role of the deficit in causing money growth becomes less definite: for instance, there was no acceleration in money growth in the United States in the early 1980s despite growing budget deficits.

We start out in Section 17-1 with the linkages between money growth and inflation. This section develops material covered in Chapter 14. Then we discuss evidence on the links between money and inflation, and between inflation and interest rates. In the third section we analyze the relationship between budget deficits and money growth in the U.S. economy. We conclude with a discussion of hyperinflation.

17-1 MONEY AND INFLATION

In this section we develop Chapter 14's analysis of the dynamics of inflation to show exactly the role played by money growth. Our task is to make sense of the monetarist claim that inflation is always and everywhere a monetary phenomenon.

To obtain a firm understanding of these points a double distinction has to be kept in mind. The first is between the short run and the long run. The second is the distinction between monetary and other disturbances (fiscal, for example, or oil shocks) to the economy.

Monetarists tend to concentrate on the long run and on economies where changes in money growth are the primary disturbances. Not surprisingly they tend to be right, *for this special case,* when they argue that money explains most of what is happening to inflation. But as one moves away from the long run and from monetary disturbances, toward short-run inflation determination and alternative shocks, it becomes necessary to be much more eclectic. In the short run, disturbances other than changes in the money stock affect inflation and, conversely, changes in the money stock do have real effects. Even if the disturbances are purely monetary it will still generally take a while before they are fully reflected in inflation and only in inflation.

A key point in the distinction between the short run and the long run and in determining the dynamics of inflation is the role of expectations. Increased money growth will have real effects as long as inflationary expectations have not fully adapted. Milton Friedman has put this point as follows:[1]

> Monetarist analysis goes on to say that any changes in the nominal quantity of money that are anticipated in advance will be fully embedded in inflationary and other expectations, but that unanticipated changes in the quantity of money will not be. An unanticipated increase or decrease in the quantity of money tends to affect total nominal spending some six to nine months later in countries like the United States, Japan or Great Britain. The initial effect is primarily on output

---

[1] See Milton Friedman, ''Monetarism in Rhetoric and Practice,'' Bank of Japan *Monetary and Economic Studies,* October 1983, p. 2.

rather than on prices. Prices tend to be affected only some 18 months to two years later. This does not mean that there is no further effect on real quantities. On the contrary, the delayed impact on prices means an overshooting of output—up or down depending on the initial stimulus—which will then require an overshooting in the opposite direction to allow the price level to reach its appropriate level. As a result the cyclical reaction pattern in both output and prices tends to last for a considerable period—years, not months. . . .

We formalize these ideas by drawing on the model of Chapter 14. While using exactly the same model, we shift the exposition a little to focus on dynamics. Our task is to highlight a number of relationships involving money, interest rates, and inflation.

The Model

The starting point is the aggregate demand equation derived in Chapter 14. Aggregate demand and output will rise whenever real balances are increasing. Conversely, when real balances are falling, so, too, are aggregate demand and output.[2] We write this relation in equation (1) using the notation $\Delta Y = Y - Y_{-1}$, m = growth rate of money, π = inflation rate:

$$\Delta Y = f(m - \pi) \qquad (1)$$

Assume now a given growth rate of money, m_0. In Figure 17-1a we show the schedule $\pi = m_0$ along which output is neither rising nor falling. Now we consider how output is changing at different points in Figure 17-1a. For points above the $\pi = m_0$ schedule, inflation exceeds the given growth rate of money. Hence real balances are falling and so, according to equation (1), is output. This is indicated by the arrow showing falling output. Conversely, below the schedule inflation is less than money growth, and hence real balances are increasing, interest rates are falling, and demand and output are growing.

The second relationship is the aggregate supply curve

$$\pi = \pi^e + \lambda(Y - Y^*) \qquad (2a)$$

In equation (2a) Y^* is the full-employment level of output, assumed in this section to be constant. For most of this section we make the simplest adaptive expectations assumption, that inflation expectations are given by last period's

---

[2] In the appendix to Chap. 14 we developed the aggregate demand curve taking account of the role of inflationary expectations in determining the real interest rate. In that case there is an additional term in the aggregate demand relationship equation (1). Under the assumption to be made for much of this section that $\pi^e = \pi_{-1}$, i.e., that the expected inflation rate is equal to last period's inflation rate, current aggregate demand increases with the lagged inflation rate. In order to simplify, we do not include this term on the aggregate demand side in this section. The omission does not affect the general results obtained except possibly if the expectations effect on aggregate demand were very large.

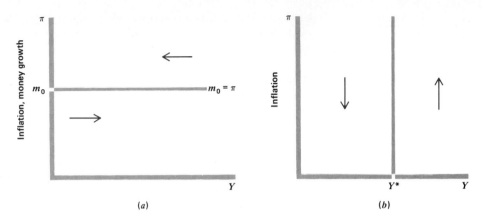

FIGURE 17-1   THE DYNAMICS OF INFLATION AND OUTPUT. The panel (*a*) shows the response of output to real balances. When inflation exceeds the growth rate of money, real balances are falling and hence demand and output are declining. Conversely, when inflation falls short of money growth, output is rising. The panel (*b*) shows that at output levels above Y^* inflation rises and at output levels below Y^* inflation declines.

inflation rate, $\pi^e = \pi_{-1}$.[3] Making that substitution in equation (2*a*), the change in inflation over time, denoted by $\Delta\pi = \pi - \pi_{-1}$ depends on the output gap and is given by

$$\Delta\pi = \lambda(Y - Y^*) \tag{2}$$

---

[3] We discuss behavior under rational expectations of inflation later in this section.

TABLE 17-1   THE DETERMINANTS OF OUTPUT AND INFLATION

	$m > \pi$	$m < \pi$
$Y > Y^*$	I	II
	Y is ↑	Y is ↓
	π is ↑	π is ↑
$Y < Y^*$	III	IV
	Y is ↑	Y is ↓
	π is ↓	π is ↓

Focusing again on dynamics, in Figure 17-1*b* we show the arrows that indicate the direction in which inflation is moving. When output is below the full-employment level, inflation is falling, and when output is above the full-employment level, inflation is rising.

Table 17-1 and Figure 17-2 combine the information in the two parts of Figure 17-1. The table shows the direction in which output and inflation are moving in each of the four regions in Figure 17-2. We use the arrows to show the combined movement or the path of inflation and output at each point.

Suppose the economy is at point *A* in region I. Because output is above the full-employment level, inflation is rising. But inflation is below money growth. Therefore real balances are increasing, and hence demand and output are rising. Thus at point *A* output is rising as is inflation so that the economy moves in a northeastward direction. We can establish the direction of movement at points *B*, *C*, and *D* in a similar fashion. Note that point *E* is the only point in the diagram where *both* output and inflation are constant. This is the long-run equilibrium to which the economy ultimately converges.

In Figure 17-2 we complete the model by bringing in the *IS* schedule. On the vertical axis we show in the lower diagram the *real* or *inflation-adjusted* interest rate. Real aggregate demand, as we saw in previous chapters, depends on the real interest rate. A higher real interest rate lowers aggregate demand and hence reduces equilibrium output as shown by the *IS* schedule. The lower part of Figure 17-2 helps us track the real interest rate in the adjustment process. For each level of output in the upper part we can find the corresponding equilibrium real interest rate on the *IS* schedule. Thus we can follow output, inflation, and the real interest rate all at the same time.

In Figure 17-2 we show a typical adjustment path starting at point *A*. The corresponding point is also labeled *A* in the lower part of Figure 17-2. At *A* inflation is rising because of overemployment. But because inflation is low relative to money growth, real balances are rising and hence demand and output are growing. The economy thus moves in a northeasterly direction. The driving force is the increasing level of real balances, which reduces interest rates and pushes up demand and output. Over time, as the economy cycles back to point *E*, the real interest rate first declines and then, as the economy enters region II, starts rising. The interest rate overshoots the long-run equilibrium level r^* (several times) before it ultimately settles at r^*.

An Increase in Money Growth

We now use this framework to examine once more the effects of a sustained increase in money growth. The conclusions are, of course, the same as those in Chapter 14. We start in long-run equilibrium at point *E* in Figure 17-3, where money growth is initially m_0. The inflation rate is equal to the growth rate of money, and output is at its full-employment level. Now the growth rate of money is permanently raised to m'. The new $\pi = m'$ schedule lies above the previous one (which is not drawn to avoid cluttering up the diagram). The

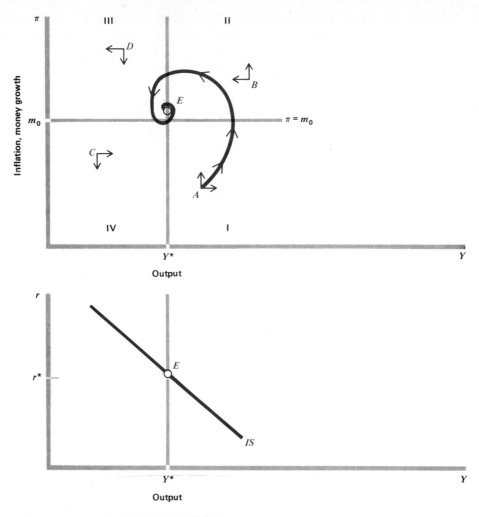

FIGURE 17-2   THE ADJUSTMENT PROCESS. The upper panel
combines the information in Figure 17-1 to show how output and
inflation evolve over time. The long-run equlibrium is at point E where
inflation equals money growth and output is at the full-employment level.
The lower panel shows the real rate of interest corresponding to each
level of output along the IS curve. For example, if the economy is at
point A in the upper panel, point A on the IS curve gives the corresponding real interest rate. The long-run equilibrium real interest rate is r^*.

arrows in each region show the direction in which inflation and output are
moving. The path starting at E shows the evolution of the economy.

At point E the growth rate of money m' now exceeds the initial inflation
rate $\pi = m_0$. As a result, the real money stock is increasing. Interest rates are
pushed down, and thus aggregate demand and output will be rising. At the
very beginning of the adjustment process the economy therefore moves hori-

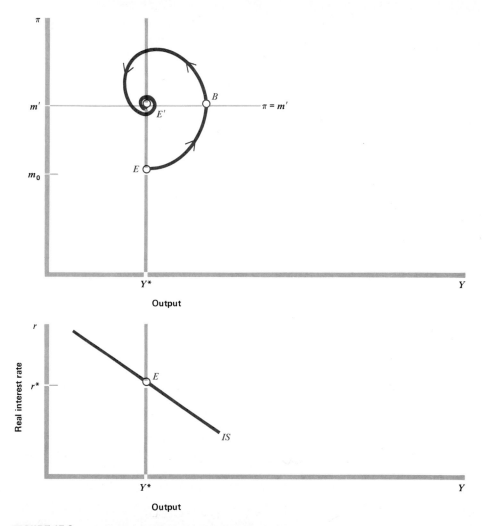

FIGURE 17-3 THE ADJUSTMENT TO AN INCREASE IN MONEY GROWTH. A sustained increase in money growth from m_0 to m' leads the economy along a path from E to E'. Output first expands, and inflation gradually builds up. In the long run, inflation rises to equal the growth rate of money. The economy returns to full employment at the real interest rate r^*.

zontally to the right with output rising. But the moment output starts exceeding the full-employment level, inflation increases. Now the path starts pointing in a northeasterly direction with rising output, because inflation remains low relative to money growth, and with inflation rising.

Over time the economy moves to point B. Here real balances are constant because now inflation has risen to the level of money growth. But output is above the full-employment level. Therefore inflation is still increasing, and the economy is thus pushed into region II. We do not describe the whole path, but it is apparent that the economy will cycle its way gradually to point E'.

Rational Expectations

The exact details of the adjustment path shown in Figure 17-3 depend on the assumptions about expectations. But the general pattern—that increased monetary growth first raises output and ultimately is fully reflected in higher inflation—is valid for (almost) any assumption about expectations.

Only in a world of complete flexibility of wages and prices combined with rational expectations would the adjustment occur instantly without any dynamics whatsoever. In that case, if a change in the growth rate of money is expected, π^e in equation (2a) will be equal to m' at the time the growth rate of money changes, and output will remain at its full-employment level throughout.[4]

Once we move away from that extreme case—which requires both rational expectations and full flexibility of prices and wages—the pattern of adjustment is that shown in Figure 17-3. Alternative assumptions about expectations and the adjustment of wages and prices will primarily influence the speed of adjustment and the movement of nominal interest rates, but it will generally imply a slow adjustment pattern of the type seen in Figure 17-3.

Before going further we want to summarize the main results so far. There are four characteristics of the adjustment process and the new long-run equilibrium that are important to retain:

- A sustained increase in the growth rate of money will, in the long run when all adjustments have taken place, lead to an equal increase in the rate of inflation. If money growth rises by 5 percent, so, too, ultimately will the inflation rate.

- A sustained change in money growth will have no long-run effects on the level of output. Thus there is no long-run tradeoff between inflation and output.

- In the short run, during the adjustment process, increased monetary growth will affect the real interest rate, aggregate demand, and output. Specifically, in the initial stages there will be an expansion in output while inflation builds up.

- In the short run increased money growth will reduce the real interest rate. But in the long run, after all adjustments have taken place, the real interest rate will return to its initial level.

---

[4] Remarkably, in this case the inflation rate would generally start to rise before the growth rate of money increases: that is because people expecting there to be inflation in the future reduce the quantity of real balances demanded and the price level therefore starts moving up.

We ask you in Problem 1 at the end of the chapter to demonstrate the corresponding results for a sustained reduction in the growth rate of money. To complete our analysis, we now turn to the behavior of real balances and the nominal interest rate.

The Fisher Equation

We have noted at various points in this book the relationship between nominal interest rates, real rates, and the expected rate of inflation. The (expected) real rate of interest is the nominal rate less the expected rate of inflation:

$$r^e = i - \pi^e \tag{3}$$

Equation (3) is the Fisher equation, so named after Irving Fisher (1867 – 1947), the most famous American economist of the first third of this century, who drew attention to the inflation – interest rate linkage.[5]

The Fisher equation immediately draws attention to a very important finding about money growth, inflation, and interest rates. We saw above that in the long run the real interest rate returns to the full-employment level r°, and that actual and expected inflation converge. Using these two facts ($r^e = r^\circ$, $\pi^e = \pi$) we write the long-run relationship as

$$i = r^\circ + \pi \tag{4}$$

With r° constant, equation (4) implies a central result: *In the long run when all adjustments have occurred, an increase in inflation is reflected fully in nominal interest rates.* Nominal interest rates rise one-for-one with the increase in inflation. The reason we have such a strong inflation – nominal interest rate link is that in the long run the real interest rate is unaffected by purely monetary disturbances.

Of course, we already saw in Figure 17-3 that the constancy of the real interest rate holds only in long-run equilibrium. During the adjustment process the real interest rate does change, and hence changes in the nominal interest rate reflect both changes in real rates and changes in inflationary expectations.

Alternative Expectations Assumptions

The way in which expectations of inflation are formed will influence the adjustment path of the interest rate, real and nominal, to a change in money growth, though not the long-run implication of the Fisher equation. Depend-

---

[5] See Irving Fisher, *The Rate of Interest*, New York, Macmillan, 1907. Fisher taught at Yale and was an effective and sophisticated developer of the quantity theory of money. He had other interests too; he was the inventor of the card index file still used for keeping addresses, and was a health food enthusiast who wrote several books on the subject. Fisher was an early, if long forgotten, discoverer of the Phillips curve. See the reprinted version of his 1926 article "A Statistical Relation between Unemployment and Price Changes," under the heading "Lost and Found," *Journal of Political Economy*, March/April 1973, pp. 496 – 502.

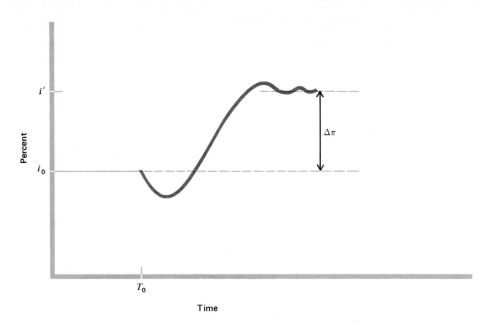

FIGURE 17-4   THE FISHER EFFECT. A sustained increase in money
growth leads first to a reduction in nominal interest rates. Then, as
output and inflation both increase, the interest rate gradually rises. In the
long run it increases by the same amount as money growth and inflation.

ing on expectations, there are different paths for interest rates. The nominal
rate may start out rising or it may first decline and then later rise.

Figure 17-4 shows a possible pattern, which has received considerable
attention in empirical work. In response to increased growth in nominal
money, at time T_0 the real money stock grows and initially pushes down the
nominal interest rate. Then, as output rises and with it inflation, the nominal
interest rate is pushed up until, ultimately, after some cycling it has increased
by the full increase in money growth and inflation.

The declining phase of the nominal interest rate path is called the *liquidity
effect* to denote the impact of increased real balances (liquidity) on the interest
rate. The phase of increasing nominal interest rates just after the bottom is
reached is called the *income effect.* In this phase increasing nominal income
pushes up interest rates by increasing the quantity of real balances demanded.
The long-run effect is called the *Fisher effect,* or *expectations effect,* to represent the impact of an increase in inflationary expectations, at a constant real
interest rate, on the nominal interest rate. These names are suggestive of the
three phases of adjustment as the economy is initially surprised by increased
money growth and gradually adjusts to it.[6]

---

[6] For an extensive discussion see Milton Friedman and Anna Schwartz, *Monetary Trends in the United States and
the United Kingdom,* National Bureau of Economic Research, 1982, Chap. 10.

Real Balances and Inflation

In Figure 17-5 we present the demand for real balances as a function of the nominal interest rate. We now study the effect of a sustained change in the growth rate of money on the long-run equilibrium level of real balances.

For that purpose we simply combine two of our results. We saw that a sustained change in monetary growth changes, in the long run, the rate of inflation and the nominal interest rate in the same direction and by the same amount. A 3 percentage point increase in money growth raises the nominal interest rate by three percentage points in the long run. We therefore conclude from Figure 17-5 that *a sustained increase in money growth and in inflation ultimately leads to a reduction in the real money stock.*

This is a very important result that might seem a bit puzzling: increased *nominal* money growth reduces the long-run *real* money stock. Conversely, reduced nominal money growth raises the long-run real money stock. The reason is that higher inflation raises the nominal interest rate and hence raises the opportunity cost of holding money. Hence money holders will reduce the amount of real balances they choose to hold. This reduction in real balances is an important part of the adjustment process to an increase in money growth. It

FIGURE 17-5   THE DEMAND FOR REAL BALANCES. An increase in inflation and accordingly in the nominal interest rate will reduce the equilibrium stock of real balances. As the interest rate increases in long-run equilibrium from i_0 to i', real balances decline from E to E'.

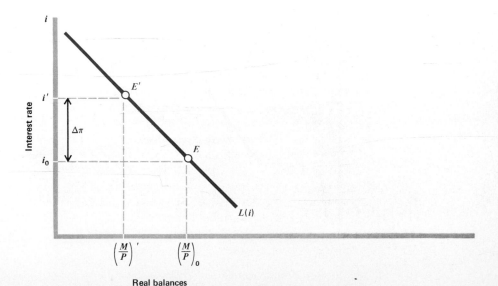

Real balances

means that, *on average, in the adjustment period to an increase in money growth, prices must rise faster than money.*

Figure 17-6, which shows the time paths of inflation and money growth, helps explain the adjustment of real balances. At time T_0 money growth rises from m_0 to m'. At the very beginning, as we saw in Figure 17-3, nothing happens to inflation. Inflation builds up gradually until, with overshooting and cycling, it settles down at the higher level m'. In the phase up to time T_1 money growth exceeds inflation and real balances are rising. Then in the following phase real balances are falling as the inflation rate exceeds money growth. The diagram is drawn to show that in the phase of decline, real balances fall more than they rise in the initial phase. This is the phase in which the economy adjusts in a major way to increased money growth as rising output and expectations push up the rate of inflation.

Alternative Expectations Assumptions

Once again, the long-run reduction in real balances in response to higher money growth is a general result. A sustained increase in money growth, *must*

FIGURE 17-6 MONEY GROWTH AND INFLATION. An increase in money growth from m_0 to m' only gradually translates into increased inflation. In the adjustment process prices rise cumulatively more than money as shown by the overshooting of inflation. This implies that real balances will be reduced in the long run.

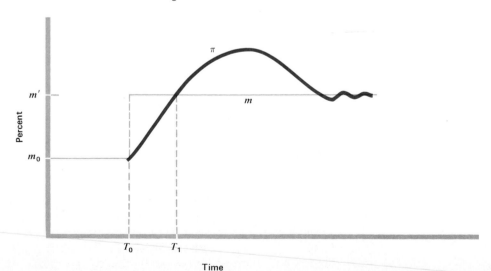

in the long run reduce the equilibrium level of real balances. The particulars of how expectations are formed determines the particular details of the path.

In the extreme case of full wage-price flexibility and rational expectations there would be an instant adjustment. The announcement of increased money growth would lead to an instant recognition that the opportunity cost of holding money is increased. The public would try to shift out of money because it is now expected to be more expensive to hold. But, of course, the economy in the aggregate cannot get rid of the existing nominal money stock. People trying to spend fast to get rid of their real balances would cause prices to jump, thereby reducing real balances to the lower desired level. Following the jump, prices and money would start rising at the long-run equilibrium rate m' and the nominal interest rate would have increased to i'. All adjustments would occur literally in no time.

This full flexibility of wages and prices – rational expectations case may sound implausible, but it serves as a useful benchmark for comparison. On one side there is a world with only gradual adjustment of inflation and inflationary expectations. In that world increased money growth takes time to find itself translated fully into inflation and interest rates, as described by Friedman in the quote above. In the other world all adjustments are instant.

How exactly the real world adjustment takes place depends in good part on people's experience with inflation. In economies where inflation is the number one issue — because of a hyperinflation — it takes very little time for adjustment to occur, as we will see later in this chapter. But in the U.S. economy where inflation never became a complete way of life, the path of Figure 17-3 is a lot more likely.

17-2 EMPIRICAL EVIDENCE

We now turn to evidence on the links between money growth and inflation and between money growth and interest rates.

The Money-Inflation Link

To start we note the often-made statement that inflation is a monetary phenomenon. The claim that inflation is a monetary phenomenon means that sustained high rates of money growth produce high inflation and that low rates of money growth will eventually produce low rates of inflation. Further, the statement that inflation is a monetary phenomenon means that high rates of inflation cannot long continue without high rates of money growth. The view that inflation is a monetary phenomenon is the implication of the quantity theory of money and is the backbone of monetarist macroeconomics.

In Figure 17-7 we present U.S. data on the relationship between money and inflation over long periods. We see that the inflation rate and the growth ·

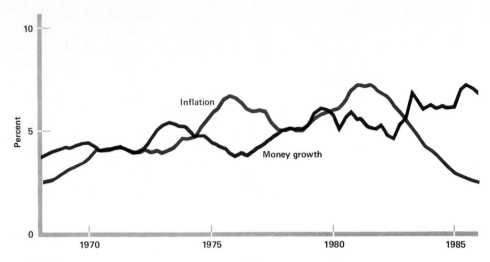

FIGURE 17-7   MONEY GROWTH AND INFLATION. Inflation (GNP deflator) and money growth (M_1) are shown as the average growth rate over the past 3 years. The money growth is shown with a 2-year lag. See text. (*Source:* Data Resources Inc.)

rate of money have, more or less, moved together over the period since 1965 in the United States. The inflation rate and the rate of money growth in the figure are each average rates over the past 3 years. To take account of lags in the effect of money growth on inflation, the money growth rate is lagged 2 years. For example, the data for 1985:1 appearing in the figure show the average inflation rate over period 1982:1 to 1985:1 and the average money growth rate for 1980:1 to 1983:1. The existence of a lag is not in doubt, in fact the theory developed above already leads us to expect such a lag. But the exact timing—a year, 18 months, 2 years or even more—is not certain at all. Indeed, because the effects of changes in money growth depend on how far in advance the money growth was expected, the lags will not be the same in all cases where the growth rate of money changes.

Although the relationship in Figure 17-7 is clearly positive, it is also obvious that the link between inflation and money growth is not precise. This is clear, for example in 1985–1986. Money growth had not decelerated significantly; on the contrary it had increased somewhat, but inflation steadily declined until mid-1986. Thus even with 3-year averages the money-inflation link is far from tight.

We expect to find a link between inflation and money growth because we showed earlier that in the steady state the inflation rate is determined by money growth. The aggregate demand curve was

$$\pi = m - \frac{1}{\varphi}(Y - Y_{-1}) \tag{5}$$

With $Y = Y_{-1} = Y^{\circ}$, that is with constant output, the inflation rate is equal to the growth rate of money. That is the basis for the view that inflation is in the long run a monetary phenomenon. We now want to expand the model slightly to recognize the growth of full-employment output over time. Suppose that output, instead of being constant, grows in the long run at the growth rate of potential output, g°. In the United States g° has been about 3 percent per annum. Some money growth is needed just to meet the increasing demand for real balances arising from growing income. Accordingly, the money growth rate will exceed the inflation rate in the long run.

The difference between money growth and inflation arises from the amount of money growth needed to meet the demand increases resulting from steadily rising income. How much money growth is that? Suppose the income elasticity of money demand is 0.7. Then for every 1 percent that income rises, the demand for real balances rises 0.7 percent. The 3 percent growth in potential output thus increases the demand for real balances by 2.1 percent a year.

If real money demand is rising — say, at the rate of 2.1 percent per year — as a result of income growth, then monetary equilibrium requires that the real money supply increase at the same rate. The growth rate of the real money stock is just the difference between the growth rate of the nominal money stock and the rate of inflation. For instance, if the nominal money stock is increasing at 10 percent and the rate of inflation is 7.9 percent, the real money stock is increasing at 2.1 percent per year.

If the real money supply has to be growing at 2.1 percent per year to maintain monetary equilibrium, then the rate of inflation has to be 2.1 percent less than the rate of money growth, or, in symbols, $\pi = m - 2.1$

More generally, with g° as the growth rate of potential output and η as the income elasticity of the demand for real balances, the long-run relationship among the inflation rate, the growth rate of money, and the growth rate of output is

$$\pi = m - \eta g^{\circ} \tag{6}$$

Changes in Velocity and Inflation

Table 17-2 shows the inflation rate, the growth rate of $M1$, and the growth rate of real GNP for six countries over the period 1955–1984. According to equation (6), we should find that

$$\pi - (m - \eta g^{\circ}) = 0 \tag{6a}$$

TABLE 17-2   MONEY GROWTH AND INFLATION, 1955–1984

Country	(1) Inflation rate (CPI), π	(2) Growth rate of M1, m	(3) Growth rate of real GNP (or GDP), g^*	(4) $\pi - (m - g^*)$	(5) $\pi - (m - 0.7g^*)$
Canada	5.1	8.3	4.1	0.9	−0.3
Germany	3.5	8.3	4.0	−0.8	−2.0
Italy	8.4	15.3	4.2	−2.7	−4.0
Japan	5.7	12.5	6.8	0.0	−2.0
United Kingdom	7.4	7.7	2.3	2.0	1.3
United States	4.8	5.0	3.2	3.0	2.0

Source: International Financial Statistics.

In column (4) of Table 17-2 we calculate $\pi - (m - g^*)$, an amount which should be zero if the income elasticity of money demand is unity. Column (5) shows a similar calculation, assuming the income elasticity of money demand is 0.7.

Whichever estimate of the income elasticity of demand for money is used, the inflation experienced by the countries does not exactly match that predicted by equation (6). In the United Kingdom and the United States, inflation has been, on average, faster than predicted. In Italy, and, depending on the correct income elasticity, perhaps Japan and Germany, inflation has been, on average, slower than predicted by equation (6).

The deviations of the inflation rate from the quantity theory predictions in Table 17-2 are a result of shifts in the demand for money over the last 30 years. In particular, the downward shifts of the demand function for $M1$ in the United States have reduced the amount of real balances individuals want to hold. If M/P demand falls, then P will rise, in the adjustment process, faster than M. That is why the inflation rate has exceeded the rate we would predict from knowledge of the growth rate of $M1$ and the growth rate of income.

Is Inflation a Monetary Phenomenon in the Long Run?

The answer to the question whether inflation is a monetary phenomenon in the long run is yes. No major inflation can take place without rapid money growth, and rapid money growth will cause rapid inflation. Further, any policy that determinedly keeps the growth rate of money low will lead eventually to a low rate of inflation.

But at the same time the long-run link between money growth and inflation is not precise, as the data of Table 17-2 show. There are two reasons for that. First, increases in output increase the demand for real balances and reduce the inflation rate corresponding to a given rate of money growth. And second, financial institutions change, the definition of money changes, and the demand for money may shift over time. Those are the reasons that the United States, which has the lowest average growth rate of M1 in Table 17-2, does not have the lowest average inflation rate.

The role of money growth in determining inflation is well summarized in a passage from the *1986 Economic Report of the President* (p. 27):

> There is a well-established causal link between money growth and inflation over the long run that has been supported by empirical evidence for the United States as well as many other countries. The exact nature of this relationship varies with time and institutions, but the long-run relationship between appropriately defined money growth and inflation is difficult to refute. . . .
>
> With a lag of 1 to 2 years, most significant slowdowns in money growth are also reflected in subsequent movements in the inflation rate. There are, however, several periods, notably the period since 1982, when the inflation rate has diverged from the trend rate of money growth. . . .
>
> There are several reasons why the inflation rate may not track money growth closely in the short run. The short-run impact of a change in money growth may differ, depending on the state of inflation expectations. If, for example, an increase in money growth occurs when current inflation rates are already high, or when monetary or fiscal actions are already perceived as inflationary, the rise in money growth is likely to show up in the inflation rate more quickly. The immediate effect of a given change in money growth also depends on whether it is perceived as permanent or just a temporary deviation from a long-term policy path. An acceleration of money growth that is perceived to be a permanent move toward a more inflationary policy is likely to translate more immediately into a higher inflation rate.

Those other causes of inflation in the short run will shift the aggregate supply or demand curves and cause changes in both output and inflation. In the 1970s, the major other cause of inflation was supply shocks, particularly the oil price increases of 1973–1974 and 1979–1980 that shifted the aggregate supply curve upward, causing more rapid inflation and recessions. In the 1980s there were large changes in fiscal policy in the United States: fiscal expansion through large tax cuts in 1982 and 1983 caused the aggregate demand curve to shift upward, slightly offsetting the effects of tight money in shifting the aggregate demand curve downward.

Inflation and Interest Rates

The Fisher equation asserts a positive link between nominal interest rates and inflation. With the real interest rate approximately constant in the long run, and with expectations of inflation adjusting to actual inflation, the nominal interest rate adjusts to the prevailing rate of inflation.

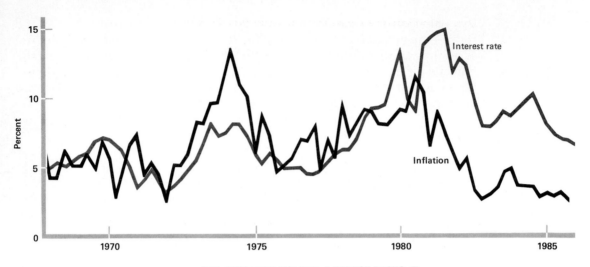

FIGURE 17-8   INFLATION AND NOMINAL INTEREST RATES. The
interest rate is the yield on 3-month Treasury bills. The inflation rate is the
rate of inflation of the GNP deflator over the following quarter. (*Source:*
Data Resources Inc.)

Figure 17-8 shows quarterly averages of the nominal interest rate on
3-month Treasury bills and the rate of inflation over the period for which the
bills are outstanding. The *realized* real interest rate then is the difference
between the nominal interest rate and the actual rate of inflation or, in symbols,

$$r = i - \pi \tag{7}$$

We do not have data on expected inflation and hence can reliably report only
realized *actual* rates rather than expected real rates of interest. But in the short
term, with inflation quite predictable there are no big discrepancies between
expected and actual real rates.

Note from Figure 17-8 that in the 1970s there were several episodes of
negative real rates, particularly in 1974–1975 when inflation increased
sharply and exceeded the interest rate by a significant margin. By contrast, in
the period since 1980 the real rate of interest has been *persistently* positive,
and by a good margin. This is a quite new experience if we look back only a few
years, but it certainly has precedents in U.S. experience in the past 100 years
where real interest rates were significantly positive in several decades. Table
17-3 shows the real rate of return on Treasury bills or their equivalent over
different periods.

Clearly there have been decades with positive and even high real interest
rates. But the average real rate has been low for well over a half-century.

TABLE 17-3 THE REAL INTEREST RATE, UNITED STATES, 1860–1979 (Average Annual Percent)			
Period	Rate	Period	Rate
1860–1869	1.5	1920–1929	6.0
1870–1879	9.8	1930–1939	3.6
1880–1889	7.2	1940–1949	−4.6
1890–1891	4.2	1950–1959	0.4
1900–1909	2.3	1960–1969	2.1
1910–1919	−3.6	1970–1979	−0.2

Source: Lawrence Summers, "The Non-Adjustment of Nominal Interest Rates: A Study of the Fisher Effect," in J. Tobin (ed.), *Macroeconomics, Prices and Quantities* (Washington, D.C.: The Brookings Institution, 1983).

Imagine an investor who put money into Treasury bills in the mid-1920s and reinvested (tax free) all the earnings every time the bills matured. The real return over the period 1925–1985 would have been barely positive, just 0.3 percent.[7]

Table 17-4 shows international evidence on the interest rate–inflation link. The table conveys clearly the notion of a positive relationship between the nominal interest rate and inflation. The link is especially clear for a country like Brazil, which had both exceptionally high inflation rates and also extremely high interest rates. If that were not the case, real interest rates would be spectacularly negative.

The evidence we have seen does tend to show that inflation and interest rates move together, within a country over time and across countries. But the evidence does not support a very strict Fisher equation. Year-to-year changes in inflation are not reflected one for one in nominal interest rates. The real rate does move, and hence the Fisher equation is primarily a guide to interest rates when inflationary disturbances are large relative to all other factors determining interest rates.

17-3 DEFICITS, MONEY GROWTH, AND THE INFLATION TAX

We have seen that a sustained increase in money growth ultimately translates into increased inflation. But that still leaves the question of what determines the money growth rate. A frequent argument is that money growth is the result

---

[7] See Roger G. Ibbotson and Rex A. Sinquefield, *Stocks, Bonds, Bills and Inflation: The Past and the Future* (Charlottesville, Virginia: Financial Analysts Research Foundation, 1982), updated to 1985 by the authors.

TABLE 17-4	INTEREST RATES AND EXPECTED INFLATION, 1984*	
Country	Interest rate % per annum	Average inflation rate, 1980–1984
Australia	12.2	8.7
Brazil	215.3†	132.5
Canada	11.1	8.3
France	11.7	10.5
Germany	5.5	4.3
Italy	17.3	14.9
Switzerland	4.7‡	4.5
United Kingdom	9.3	7.2
United States	9.6	6.0

* Interest rates are short-term market rates except as noted. The expected inflation rate is assumed to be the average of inflation rates over the previous 4 years.
† Bank rate.
‡ Government bond yield.
Source: International Financial Statistics.

of government budget deficits. In this section we examine several possible relationships between the budget deficit and inflation.

The Government's Budget Constraint

The Federal government as a whole, consisting of the Treasury plus the Fed, can finance its budget deficit in two ways. It can either sell bonds or "print money." By printing money we mean that the Fed increases the stock of high-powered money, typically through open market purchases that buy up part of the debt that the Treasury is selling.

The government budget constraint,[8] used in Chapter 16, is

$$\text{Budget deficit} = \text{sales of bonds} + \text{increase in money base} \qquad (8)$$

There are two types of possible links between budget deficits and money growth. First, in the short run, an increase in the deficit caused by expansion-

---

[8] We show here the government's *flow* or year-by-year budget constraint. In addition, the government faces a stock budget constraint which says that the present value of all its future outlays has to be equal to the present value of all its future receipts. Technically, the stock budget constraint can be obtained by integrating the year-by-year flow constraints.

ary fiscal policy will tend to raise nominal and real interest rates. If the Fed is targeting interest rates in any way, it may increase the growth rate of money in an attempt to keep the interest rate from rising. Second, the government may deliberately over the long term be increasing the stock of money as a means of obtaining government revenue.

In the remainder of this section we examine first the short-run links between money and deficits that come from central bank policy and then the use of money printing as a means of financing government budgets. Finally, we link the short- and long-run aspects.

The Fed's Dilemma

The Fed is said to monetize deficits whenever it purchases a part of the debt sold by the Treasury to finance the deficit. In the United States the monetary authorities enjoy independence from the Treasury and therefore can choose whether to monetize or not.[9]

The Fed typically faces a dilemma in deciding whether to monetize a deficit. If it does not finance the deficit, the fiscal expansion, not accompanied by accommodating monetary policy, raises interest rates and thus crowds out private expenditure. There is accordingly a temptation for the Fed to prevent crowding out by buying securities, thereby increasing the money supply and hence allowing an expansion in income without a rise in interest rates.

But such a policy of accommodation or monetization runs a risk. If the monetization leads to excessive money growth, then the policy ultimately will feed inflation. Eventually higher aggregate demand will raise the real interest rate; crowding out will in any event occur, and thus the policy fails in its objective of preventing crowding out, but it does have a cost in terms of higher inflation.

Much discussion of Fed policy centers on this question: Should the Fed control monetary aggregate or interest rates? In the context of an increase in budget deficits the answer must often be that the Fed should *not* accommodate, that is, it should let the interest rate increase and keep the growth rate of money constant. If the economy is close to full-employment, an accommodating policy would simply feed inflation. An unwise fiscal expansion would be made even more potent by fueling it with a monetary expansion.

There are other circumstances, though, where the risks of igniting inflation are much more remote. Certainly in a deep recession there is no reason to shy away from accommodating a fiscal expansion with higher money growth.

---

[9] In other countries the central bank may enjoy much less independence; for instance, it might be under the control of the Treasury, and then it may simply be ordered to finance part or all of the deficit by creating high-powered money.

In any particular case, the Fed has to judge whether monetary policy should be accommodating or whether, rather, to stay with an unchanged monetary target or even offset a fiscal expansion by a tightening of monetary policy. To make that decision, the Fed must decide on the relative weight it attaches to inflation and to unemployment whenever expansionary policy threatens to cause inflation.

The U.S. Evidence

A number of studies have tried to determine how the Fed in practice reacts to deficits. The question here is whether there is a systematic link between monetary policy and the budget. Specifically, does the Fed allow money growth to rise when the budget deficit increases?

Figure 17-9 shows a scatter diagram of the change in the growth rate of the monetary base[10] and of the change in the cyclically adjusted budget (expressed as a percent of GNP). There is no very clear pattern of accommodation. Nor does a diagram relating money growth to the *level* of the deficit show a closer relationship.

The empirical evidence on this question thus remains open. There is some evidence that the Fed does react in the direction of accommodation, monetizing deficits at least in part. But the evidence is not conclusive because it is difficult to know whether the Fed is reacting to the deficit itself or rather to other macroeconomic variables, specifically unemployment and the rate of inflation.[11]

The question of accommodation and the monetary-fiscal policy mix was certainly a major issue in the discussion leading up to the Gramm-Rudman-Hollings deficit control legislation of 1985. Fiscal and monetary policy combined in the early eighties to take real interest rates to exceptionally high levels. As a result the dollar remained very strong, hurting U.S. trade and hurting debtors, both here and in the developing countries. The Fed was seen in a very unusual position: holding out on monetary accommodation, it raised the economic and political cost of an excessive fiscal expansion. It thus made the economy experience a "lopsided" recovery in which imports increased and exports fell. Chairman Volcker of the Fed explicitly held out the promise of easier money to continue the recovery if the Congress and the administration would cut the budget deficit.

---

[10] The monetary base is the relevant aggregate because, as noted in Chap. 16, the deficit can be financed either by the sale of bonds or by the creation of high-powered money (or monetary base).

[11] See Alan Blinder, "Issues in the Coordination of Monetary and Fiscal Policy," Federal Reserve Bank of Kansas City *Monetary Policy Issues in the 1980s*, 1983; and "On the Monetization of Deficits," in Laurence Meyer, *The Economic Consequences of Government Deficits* (Kluwer-Nijhoff, 1983); Gerarld Dwyer, "Federal Deficits, Interest Rates and Monetary Policy," *Journal of Money, Credit and Banking*, November 1985; and Douglas Joines, "Deficits and Money Growth in the United States: 1872–1983," *Journal of Monetary Economics*, November 1985.

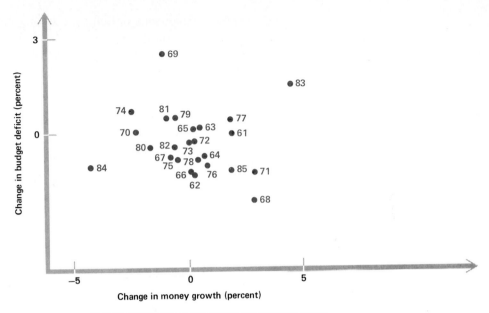

FIGURE 17-9   BUDGET DEFICITS AND MONEY ACCOMMODATION.
The diagram shows the change in the cyclically adjusted budget
expressed as a fraction of GNP and the change in the growth rate of
high-powered money. (*Source:* DRI, Inc.)

Of course, strict monetarists saw the role of the Fed as already accommodating massively, following its "usual" pattern of responding to high interest
rates with acceleration of money growth. Rather than regarding the high
interest rates as evidence of Fed tightness, they saw high levels of money
growth and regarded that as accommodation. Thus some viewed the Fed's
response to deficits as leading inevitably to higher inflation.

The Inflation Tax

In discussing monetization of deficits in the United States we paid no attention
to the fact that financing government spending through the creation of high-
powered money is an alternative to explicit taxation. Governments can — and
some do — obtain significant amounts of resources year after year by printing
money, that is, by increasing high-powered money. This source of revenue is
sometimes known as seigniorage, which means the government's ability to
raise revenue through its right to create money.

When the government finances a deficit by creating money, it in effect keeps printing money, period after period, which it uses to pay for the goods and services it buys. This money is absorbed by the public. But why would the public choose to increase its holdings of nominal money balances period after period?

The only reason, real income growth aside, that the public would be adding to its holdings of nominal money balances is to offset the effects of inflation. Assuming there is no real income growth, in the long run the public will hold a constant level of *real* balances. But if prices are rising, the purchasing power of a given stock of *nominal balances* is falling. To maintain the real value of its money balances constant, the public has to be adding to its stock of nominal balances, exactly at the rate that will offset the effects of inflation.

When the public is adding to its stock of nominal balances in order to offset the effects of inflation on holdings of real balances, it is using part of its income to increase holdings of nominal money. For instance, suppose someone has an income of $20,000 (nominal) this year. Over the course of the year, inflation reduces the value of that person's real balances. He or she therefore has to add, say, $300, to a bank account just to maintain the real value of his or her money holdings constant. That $300 is not available for spending. The person seems to be saving $300 in the form of money holdings, but in fact in real terms is not increasing his or her wealth by adding the $300 to nominal balances. All that person is doing is preventing his or her wealth from falling as a result of inflation.

Inflation acts just like a tax because people are forced to spend less than their income and pay the difference to the government in exchange for extra money.[12] The government thus can spend more resources, and the public less just as if the government had raised taxes to finance extra spending. When the government finances its deficit by issuing money, which the public adds to its holdings of nominal balances to maintain the real value of money balances constant, we say the government is financing itself through the inflation tax.[13]

How much revenue can the government collect through the inflation tax? The amount of revenue produced is the product of the tax rate (the inflation rate) and the object of taxation (the real monetary base). When real output is constant, inflation tax revenue is given by

$$\text{Inflation tax revenue} = \text{inflation rate} \times \text{real money base} \qquad (9)$$

---

[12] There is one complication in this analysis. As noted above, the amount that is received by the government is the increase in the stock of *high-powered* money, because the Fed is buying Treasury debt with high-powered money. But the public is increasing its holdings of both bank deposits and currency, and thus part of the increase in the public's holdings of money does not go to the government to finance the deficit. This complication in no way changes the essence of the analysis.

[13] Inflation is often referred to as the "cruelest tax." This does not refer to the above analysis of the inflation tax, but rather to the redistribution of wealth and income associated with unanticipated inflation, discussed in Chap. 15.

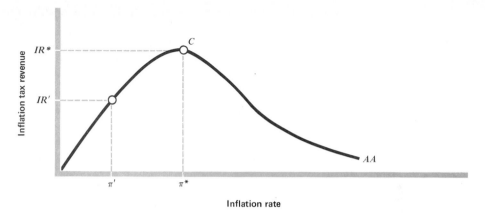

FIGURE 17-10   THE INFLATION TAX. At a zero inflation rate, the inflation tax revenue is zero. As the inflation rate rises, the government receives more revenue from inflation, up to point C, where the tax revenue reaches its maximum of IR^*. The corresponding inflation rate is π^*. Beyond point C the demand for real balances is falling so much as the inflation rate increases that total tax revenues decline.

The amount of revenue the government can raise through the inflation tax is shown by the curve AA in Figure 7-10. When the inflation rate is zero, the government gets no revenue from inflation.[14] As the inflation rate rises, the amount of inflation tax received by the government increases. But, of course, as the inflation rate rises, people reduce their real holdings of the money base — because the base is becoming increasingly costly to hold. Individuals hold less currency, and banks hold as little excess reserves as possible. Eventually the real monetary base falls so much that the total amount of inflation tax revenue received by the government falls. That happens starting at point C. This means there is a maximum amount of revenue the government can raise through the inflation tax: it is shown as amount IR^* in Figure 17-10. There is a corresponding inflation rate, denoted π^*, the steady-state inflation rate at which the inflation tax is at its maximum.

We can now look back to Figure 17-3 to study the long-run effects of money-financed deficits. We start at point E. Now the government cuts taxes and finances the deficit by printing money. We assume that the deficit is equal to amount IR' in Figure 17-10, and thus it can be financed entirely through the inflation tax. Now money growth has been permanently increased, and infla-

---

[14] When the economy is growing, the government obtains some revenue from seigniorage even if there is no inflation. That is because when the demand for real monetary base is growing, the government can create some base without producing inflation.

tion will in the long run move to the rate π', corresponding to the inflation tax revenue IR'.

In the long run the economy reaches point E'. In that equilibrium expectations have fully adjusted to the inflation, and output is at the full-employment level. Inflation equals the growth rate of money,[15] and the inflation rate depends on the deficit size. The larger the deficit, the higher the inflation rate. Figure 17-10 raises the question of what happens if the government tries to finance a deficit larger than IR° by printing money. That cannot be done. We take up that issue in the following section, on hyperinflations.

Inflation Tax Revenue

How much revenue can governments in practice obtain from the printing of money? The amount is quite small in developed economies in which the real money base is small relative to the size of the economy. For instance, in the United States the base is slightly above 5 percent of GNP even with the current low rates of inflation. At a 10 percent inflation rate the government would, from equation (9), be collecting about 0.5 percent of GNP in inflation tax revenue. That is not a trivial amount, but it is not a major source of government revenue either.[16] It is hard to believe that the inflation rate in the United States is set with the revenue aspects of inflation as the main criterion. Rather the Fed and the administration choose policies to influence the inflation rate on the basis of an analysis of the costs and benefits of inflation along the lines of Chapter 16.

In countries where the banking system is less developed and where people therefore hold large amounts of currency, the government obtains more revenue from inflation and is more likely to give high weight to the revenue aspects of inflation in setting policy. There have been cases where the government obtains as much as 10 percent of GNP in revenue from the creation of the money base. And, as we see in the next section, in conditions of high inflation where the conventional tax system breaks down, the inflation tax revenue may be the government's last resort to keep paying its bills.

Unpleasant Monetarist Arithmetic

In a well-known article, Thomas Sargent and Neil Wallace of the University of Minnesota have pointed to an important implication of the government bud-

---

[15] Except for an adjustment that takes acount of growth in real output.

[16] A measure of seigniorage different from the value of the printing of high-powered money is sometimes used in the United States. It is the value of the interest payments the Fed earns on its portfolio. Since the Fed's securities were obtained through open market purchases that increased the high-powered money stock, this is a measure of how much interest the Treasury saves (since the Fed pays its profits to the Treasury) as a result of *previous* Fed money printing. The printing of high-powered money is a measure of the current command over resources obtained as a result of money printing this period.

get constraint, equation (7).[17] Specifically, *debt-financing of a deficit may in the long run be more inflationary than money financing.*

The argument turns on the fact that when a government finances a current deficit through debt, it incurs the obligation to pay interest on that debt in future. Recall Chapter 16's distinction between the primary, noninterest deficit and the total budget deficit:

$$\text{Total deficit} \equiv \text{primary deficit} + \text{interest payments} \qquad (10)$$

Combining equation (10) with equation (8), we obtain

$$\text{Bond sales} + \text{money base creation} \equiv \text{primary deficit} + \text{interest payments} \qquad (11)$$

Consider now the choice between debt financing (bond sales) and money financing of a given deficit. If money financing is used, interest payments will be no larger in the future than they are now. But if the government turns to debt financing, it will have a larger deficit in the future. That in turn will have to be financed, either through money finance or debt finance.

Now imagine the following circumstances. The government has a given national debt today. The primary deficits today and in the future are, by assumption, given at some constant level, for example, the primary deficit may be zero. The government is considering whether to finance its current deficit by borrowing or by printing money. If it finances by borrowing, it intends to stop borrowing and switch to money financing in 5 years.

Under which alternative will the inflation rate ultimately be higher? The answer can be worked out from the following considerations. If the government starts money financing today, it will have to create money at a rate that finances the interest payments on the *existing* national debt. But if it waits 5 years to start money financing, it will have to create money at a rate that finances the interest payments on the national debt that will exist 5 years from now. Because interest on the debt will have accumulated in the meantime, the debt will be larger 5 years from now, therefore so will the inflation rate.

This example shows that, because of the accumulation of interest, short-run debt financing that ends in money financing will generally ultimately be more inflationary than immediate money financing of a given deficit.

The arithmetic is unpleasant for monetarists because it suggests that budget deficits may have more to do with the eventual inflation rate than the current growth rate of money.

The main question raised by this example is whether the government is eventually forced into money financing of a given deficit or whether it can

---

[17] "Some Unpleasant Monetarist Arithmetic," Federal Reserve Bank of Minneapolis, *Quarterly Review*, Fall 1981.

continue debt finance forever. That depends on the relationship between the growth rate of output and the real interest rate. As we saw in Chapter 16, if the real interest rate is above the growth rate of output, and given a zero primary deficit, debt financing cannot continue forever, because the debt becomes a larger and larger part of GNP and interest payments keep mounting up. At some point, in that case, the government will have to turn to money financing. The turn to money financing will both provide some revenue, and, if the debt is nominal, perhaps reduce the value of the outstanding debt through unanticipated inflation.

If the real interest rate is below the growth rate of output, with a zero primary deficit, then the government can continue debt financing without the debt-GNP ratio rising. In that case debt finance is viable for the long term, and the hard choice posed by the Sargent-Wallace example can be avoided. Note also though that the tight link examined by Sargent and Wallace takes future primary deficits as given. If the government is willing to raise taxes at some future date to pay higher interest bills, there is no necessary link between current deficits and future money growth.

The Sargent-Wallace analysis does make clear why permanent deficits cause concern. If the national debt is growing relative to GNP, then ultimately the government will have to raise taxes or raise the inflation rate to meet its debt obligations. That is the long-run threat that leads people to worry about deficits. But the long run in this case may be decades away.

There is a further important point. The Sargent-Wallace concern is about *primary* deficits: if the total deficit is constant as a percentage of GNP, then ultimately the debt-GNP ratio will stabilize provided the economy is growing at all. For instance, a statement that the deficit in the United States would be 5 percent of GNP forever would not mean that the debt would explode as a percentage of GNP. Rather if the deficit were financed through debt, the debt-GNP ratio would eventually reach a steady state.[18] The explanation is that when the deficit is measured to *include* interest payments, a statement that the deficit will be constant forever means that behind the scenes the primary deficit or surplus is being adjusted to ensure that interest payments are being made without the debt-GNP ratio exploding.

---

[18] This is a fairly technical but important point. If the total deficit is kept at a constant ratio to GNP, say 5 percent, that means that behind the scenes increasing interest payments are being met by higher taxes or lower government spending. Suppose that the debt-GNP ratio is denoted b, that GNP is growing at a real rate y, and that the total deficit as a percentage of GNP is denoted td. In steady state debt is being issued at just the rate that keeps the debt-GNP ratio constant. That means that in steady state $td = y \cdot b$. Then the steady-state debt-GNP ratio is just equal to td/y. For instance, if the deficit is 5 percent of GNP forever, and the growth rate of GNP is 4 percent, then the debt-GNP ratio will be 1.25, or 125 percent in steady state. At that point interest payments are a constant proportion of GNP.

17-4 HYPERINFLATION

Large budget deficits are inevitably part of the extreme inflations of 50 to 100 or even 500 percent per year that took place in the mid-80s in Latin America and Israel. They are also part of the even more extreme cases of *hyperinflation.* Although there is no precise definition of the rate of inflation that deserves the star ranking of hyper- rather than high inflation, a working definition takes 1,000 percent per annum as the rate that marks a hyperinflation.

In a hyperinflationary economy, inflation is so pervasive and such a problem that it completely dominates daily economic life. People spend significant amounts of resources minimizing the inflationary damage: they have to shop often, to get to the stores before the prices go up; their main concern in saving or investing is how to protect themselves against inflation; they reduce holdings of real balances to a remarkable extent to avoid the inflation tax, but have to compensate by going to the bank more often, daily or hourly instead of weekly, for example, to get currency.

The classic hyperinflations have taken place in the aftermath of wars. The most famous of all — though not the most rapid — was the German hyperinflation of 1922–1923. The average inflation rate during the hyperinflation was 322 percent *per month.* The highest rate of inflation was in October 1923, just before the end of the hyperinflation, when prices rose by over 29,000 percent.[19] In dollars that means that something that cost $1 at the beginning of the month would have cost $290 at the end of the month. The most rapid hyperinflation was that in Hungary at the end of World War II: the *average* rate of inflation from August 1945 to July 1946 was 19,800 percent per month, and the maximum monthly rate was 41.9 quadrillion percent.[20]

Keynes, in a masterful description of the hyperinflation process in Austria after World War I tells of how people would order two beers at a time because they grew stale at a rate slower than the price was rising.[21] This and similar stories appear in all hyperinflations. They include the woman who carried her (almost worthless) currency in a basket and found that when she set it down for a moment, the basket was stolen but the money left behind. And, it was said, it was cheaper to take a taxi than a bus because in the taxi you pay at the end of the ride and in the bus at the beginning.

[19] Data based on C. L. Holtferich, *Die Deutsche Inflation, 1914–1923* (New York: Walter de Gruyter, 1980).
[20] At least, so we think. The price level rose 41.9×10^{15} percent in July 1946. Data are from Phillip Cagan, "The Monetary Dynamics of Hyperinflation," in Milton Friedman (ed.), *Studies in the Quantity Theory of Money* (Chicago: University of Chicago Press, 1956). This classic paper contains data on seven hyperinflations.
[21] John Maynard Keynes, *A Tract on Monetary Reform* (New York: Macmillan, 1923). This remains one of the most readable accounts of inflation. See also Thomas William Guttmann and Patricia Meehan, *The Great Inflation* (Gordon and Cremonsi, 1975); and Leland Yeager and associates, *Experiences with Stopping Inflation* (Washington, D.C.: American Enterprise Institute, 1981).

Hyperinflationary economies are typically marked by widespread indexing, more to the foreign exchange rate than to the price level. That is because it becomes difficult to keep measuring prices on a current basis, when they change so fast. So prices might be specified in terms of dollars, and the actual amount of the local currency (marks in the German case) that has to be paid in each transaction is calculated from the dollar price and the exchange rate. Wages are paid very often, at the end of the German hyperinflation several times a day.

Deficits and Hyperinflation

The hyperinflationary economies all suffered from large budget deficits and from rapid money printing. In several cases the origin of the budget deficit was wartime spending, which generated large national debts and also destroyed the tax-gathering apparatus of the country.

But there is a two-way interaction between budget deficits and inflation. Large budget deficits can lead to rapid inflation by causing governments to print money to finance the deficit. In turn, high inflation increases the measured deficit. There are two main mechanisms whereby inflation increases budget deficits.

THE TAX-COLLECTION SYSTEM

As the inflation rate rises, the real revenue raised from taxation falls. The reason is that there are lags in both the calculation and payment of taxes. Suppose, to take an extreme example, that people pay taxes on April 15 on the income they earned the previous year. Consider someone who earned $50,000 last year, who has a tax bill of $10,000 due on April 15. If prices have in the meantime gone up by a factor of 10, as they might in a hyperinflation, the real value of the taxes is only one-tenth of what it should be. The budget deficit can rapidly get out of hand.

In principle the tax system can be indexed to adjust for the inflation. But that is difficult, especially for business taxation, and in any event even indexing lags behind. For example, if the monthly rate of inflation is 20 percent (equivalent to an annual rate of nearly 800 percent), then even if the amount that has to be paid is fixed according to the most recent price index, and if it takes a month to collect taxes, inflation causes the government to lose 20 percent of the value of its taxes.

NOMINAL INTEREST AND THE BUDGET DEFICIT

Nominal interest rates rise with the inflation rate and increase the measured budget deficit. To make this point we repeat equation (10):

$$\text{Total deficit} \equiv \text{primary deficit} + \text{interest payments} \qquad (10)$$

Suppose now that the government debt is at the relatively low level of just 20 percent of GNP. With an interest rate of, say, 10 percent, total interest payments are 2 percent of GNP (10 percent interest rate × 20 percent of GNP debt). Let the inflation rate rise by 90 percent, with the real interest rate remaining unchanged, so that the nominal interest rate goes up to 100 percent. Then total interest payments amount to 20 percent of GNP (100 percent interest rate × 20 percent of GNP debt), and the budget deficit measured as in (10) rises by no less than 18 percent of GNP. The data in this example are essentially those of Mexico in 1986, where the budget deficit during the inflation looked very large, despite the noninterest part of the budget being in surplus.

The problem here is that the conventional way of measuring the deficit includes *nominal* interest on the debt. This can give a distorted impression of the size of the deficit, because in fact the government is paying the high interest to offset the effect of inflation in reducing the value of its outstanding debt. We should recognize that at the same time as the government has to pay high interest, it also receives revenue from the decline in the value of its outstanding debt, owing to inflation. And indeed, in the 1970s many economists began to calculate inflation-corrected budget deficits that took account of the government's gain from inflation because the value of its debt fell.

The inflation-corrected budget deficit calculates the budget deficit taking into account the effect of inflation in reducing the outstanding value of the government's debt.

We return to the previous example for an illustrative calculation. Suppose the real interest rate is 5 percent, and that the primary deficit is zero. Then, with a debt-GNP ratio of 20 percent, the budget deficit at a zero inflation rate is only 1 percent of GNP. When the inflation rate hits 95 percent, with a nominal interest rate of 100 percent, the calculated nominal deficit becomes 20 percent of GNP. But the inflation-corrected deficit is still only 1 percent of GNP, as long as the real interest rate remains at 5 percent.

Although the principle of the calculation of inflation-corrected deficits is clear, there is some controversy about whether they should be used. The question that should be asked is whether the private sector wants to maintain the value of the debt-to-GNP ratio. If so, it will willingly finance the apparently increased nominal deficit by purchases of bonds — people need to step up bond purchases precisely because the real value of their existing bonds is being reduced through inflation. If on the other hand the inflation rate is high as a result of unexpectedly high printing of money, then the inflation-corrected deficit does not give a good measure of the extent to which people are willing to continue financing the existing deficit at the existing real interest rate by purchasing bonds.

The Inflation Tax and Accelerating Hyperinflation

Rates of money growth are also very high during hyperinflations, of the same order of magnitude as the inflation rate.[22] The high rates of money growth originate in attempts to finance government spending.

But as the inflations progress, and the tax collection system breaks down, the government reaches a point where it tries to raise more through money printing than the maximum amount IR^* that it can in Figure 17-10. It can succeed in raising more than IR^* *temporarily*, by printing money even faster than people expected. That increased money growth causes the inflation rate to increase. And as the government continues to try to spend more than IR^*, it continues driving up the inflation rate. The amount of real money base that people hold becomes smaller and smaller, as they try to flee the inflation tax, and the government prints even more rapidly to try to finance its expenditure. In the end the process will break down.

Stopping Hyperinflations

All hyperinflations come to an end. The dislocation of the economy becomes too great for the public to bear, and the government finds a way of reforming its budget process. Often a new money is introduced, and the tax system is reformed. Typically, too, the exchange rate of the new money is pegged to that of a foreign currency, to provide an anchor for prices and expectations. Frequently there are unsuccessful attempts at stabilization before the final success.

The presence of so many destabilizing factors in inflation, particularly the collapse of the tax system as the inflation proceeds, together with an economy that is extremely dislocated by inflation, raises a fascinating possibility. A coordinated attack on inflation may stop the inflation with relatively little unemployment cost. This approach was used in Argentina and Israel in 1985, and Brazil in 1986, when the governments froze wages and prices. That stopped the inflation at a single blow. They also fixed their exchange rates, and there were significant changes in fiscal policy, to put the budget closer to long-run balances. In each case there was little increase in unemployment. Despite the early encouraging signs, the ultimate success of these stabilization programs remains to be established.

One more important feature of the stabilizations should be brought out. *Money growth rates following stabilization are very high.* Why? Because as people expect less inflation, nominal interest rates decline, and the demand for real balances rises. With the demand for real balances increasing, the government can create more money without creating inflation. Thus at the

---

[22] On average, though, the growth rate of money is below the inflation rate. That is because people are reducing their holdings of real balances during hyperinflation: if M/P is falling, then P has on average to be growing faster than M.

beginning of a successful stabilization there may be a bonus for the government: it can temporarily finance part of the deficit through the printing of money, without renewing inflation. But it certainly cannot do so for very long periods without reigniting inflation.

SUMMARY

1. A sustained monetary expansion typically expands output in the short run. In the long run higher money growth is translated fully into inflation. Real interest rates and output return to the full-employment level. Only under rational expectations and with full wage and price flexibility does a monetary expansion translate instantly into a more rapid rate of inflation with no impact on output.

2. A sustained change in money growth ultimately raises the nominal interest rate by the same amount. This positive association between inflation and nominal interest rates is called the Fisher effect.

3. In the short run increased money growth will lead to lower nominal interest rates if expectations adjust slowly. This is called the liquidity effect.

4. A sustained monetary expansion ultimately raises nominal interest rates and hence reduces the demand for real balances. That means that prices must on average rise faster than money in the transition to the new long-run equilibrium.

5. In the U.S. economy, broad trends in money growth and in inflation do coincide. Money growth does affect inflation, but the effects occur with a lag that is not very precise. In the short term, inflation is affected by other than monetary shocks, for example fiscal policy changes and supply shocks.

6. Nominal interest rates tend to reflect the rate of inflation in the U.S. economy. But the real interest rate is definitely not constant. In the early 1980s the real rate increased sharply compared with the levels of the 1970s and long-term average rates.

7. When fiscal policy turns expansionary, the Fed has to decide whether to monetize the deficit, printing money to prevent a rise in interest rate and crowding out, to keep the growth rate of money constant, or even to tighten montary policy. If it monetizes the deficit, it runs the risk of increasing the inflation rate. The evidence on deficit monetization in the U.S. remains ambiguous.

8. Inflation is a tax on real balances. To keep constant the purchasing power of holdings of money in the face of rising prices, a person has to add to nominal balances. In this fashion resources are transferred from money holders to money issuers, specifically the government.

9. A decision to finance a deficit through bond sales today may mean a higher inflation rate in the future if the government eventually has to finance the

deficit through money printing. That is because the interest payments on the debt accumulate to increase future deficits, given a fixed primary deficit. This tradeoff exists when the interest rate exceeds the growth rate of output.

10. Hyperinflations have generally taken place in the aftermaths of wars. Large deficits are typical in hyperinflations. Governments can use the inflation tax to finance deficits to a limited extent. But if too large a deficit has to be financed, inflation explodes.

11. There is a two-way interaction between inflation and budget deficits. Higher inflation rates raise the deficit by reducing the real value of tax collection. Higher nominal interest rates raise the measured deficit by increasing the value of nominal interest payments in the budget. The inflation-corrected deficit adjusts for this latter effect.

12. Money growth rates are very high following a successful inflation stabilization, as people increase their holdings of real balances.

KEY TERMS

Fisher effect
Liquidity effect
Expectations effect
Monetization of deficits

Hyperinflation
Inflation tax
Seigniorage
Inflation-corrected deficit

PROBLEMS

1. (a) Show graphically the effects of a reduction in the growth rate of money on output and inflation.
   (b) Show also how the real interest rate adjusts over time. Be specific about the expectations assumption you are using.
2. In the above example show how the nominal interest rate adjusts to lower inflation.
3. We stated in the text that under rational expectations and with full price and wage flexibility, the inflation rate rises immediately to its new steady-state level when the growth rate of money increases. We also stated that real balance holdings decline when the expected inflation rate rises. How can the level of real balances fall under rational expectations if the inflation rate is equal to the growth rate of money? (*Hint:* with prices fully flexible, they can change all at once when new information becomes available.)
4. (a) Study the growth rate of money and the inflation rate in the last 5 years in the tables on the inside covers of the book. How closely are they linked?
   (b) Calculate the real rate of interest on Treasury bills during the last 2 years and compare with the historical average.
   (c) What is the explanation for the high levels of real rates in the early 1980s relative to the historical average?
5. Suppose the ratio of money base to GNP is 10 percent. The government is considering raising the inflation rate from the current 0 to 10 per annum and believes it will obtain an

increase in government revenue of 1 percent of GNP by doing so. Explain why that calculation overestimates the inflation tax the government will receive at a 10 percent inflation rate.

6. During 1981 – 1986 the U.S. government has added massively to the national debt. (a) Explain why you might worry that this is inflationary. (b) Explain whether you actually worry that the high deficits of the early eighties will lead to high inflation later.

7. At the height of the German hyperinflation, the government was covering only 1 percent of its spending with taxes. (a) What happened to the rest? (b) How could the German government possibly finance the remaining 99 percent of its spending? Refer to Figure 17-10.

8. (a) If the debt-GNP ratio is 30 percent, the nominal interest rate is 12 percent, the inflation rate is 7 percent, and the total budget deficit is 4 percent of GNP, calculate the inflation-adjusted deficit.

   (b) Suppose you were to discover in an inflationary economy that the inflation-corrected budget was in surplus. Explain why in that case the government might be able to sustain a low inflation rate if it could only find a way of getting the rate down to start with.

   (c) Then explain why governments in the mid-80s used wage and price controls in trying to stop high inflations.

9. Explain how, following the end of hyperinflation, it was possible for the nominal money stock in Germany to increase by a factor of nearly 20 without restarting the inflation.

10. Why do budget deficits create such alarm? Distinguish the short from the long run in developing your answer.

MACROECONOMICS: THE INTERACTION OF EVENTS AND IDEAS

The ideas of economists and political philosophers, both when they are right and when they are wrong, are more powerful than is commonly understood. Indeed, the world is ruled by little else.

John Maynard Keynes, 1936

As an advice-giving profession we are in way over our heads.

Robert E. Lucas, Jr., 1980[1]

Macroeconomics, more than microeconomics, seems to be subject to changing fashions and beliefs. As late as 1971 President Nixon announced, "I am a Keynesian." Within the next decade, monetarism, rational expectations, supply-side economics, and Reaganomics all, at one time or another, were confidently prescribed as the solution for the economy's problems. And during that same period, none of the different approaches delivered what it promised.

In this chapter we describe the major currents of thought in macroeconomics since the 1960s, when the monetarist challenge to mainstream Keynesian economics first gathered strength. Because policy and ideas are

---

[1] The quotes are from J. M. Keynes, *The General Theory of Employment, Interest and Money* (London: Macmillan, 1936), p. 383; and Robert E. Lucas, "Rules, Discretion, and the Role of the Economic Adviser," in his book *Studies in Business Cycle Theory* (Cambridge, Mass.: MIT Press, 1981).

intertwined, in discussing the main macroeconomic currents, we refer also to economic events of the time. We show how theories influence policies, and how the results of policies influence views about theory.

The success of Keynesian economics was itself the result of the great depression, from which it showed the way out. Support for Keynesian economics or the New Economics (described in Chapter 12) strengthened after the successful 1964 tax cut. Support weakened as inflation worsened in the second half of the sixties. Monetarism promised to deal with inflation — but the 1969–1971 failure of slower money growth to stem inflation weakened support for monetarism. In the early eighties supply-side economists promised that disinflation was possible without unemployment. The 1981–1982 recession punctured that hope. But supply-side economics made a partial comeback because the recovery from that deep recession was extremely rapid.

Any student may wonder about a field where opinions and policy prescriptions change so often. And you should worry, too, about the differences in views among macroeconomists at a given time. For instance, what should you conclude about budget deficits when one group of economists claims deficits have no real effects and another group blames them for high real interest rates and the large trade deficit?

There certainly are disagreements among economists. But it is also true that those disagreements, and the distinguishing features of different points of view, are systematically exaggerated by the media. Macroeconomic controversies are always in the newspapers because macroeconomics concerns some of the most important issues of daily life — whether jobs are hard or easy to find, whether prices are rising slowly or fast, whether living standards will rise fast or hardly at all. The disagreements are systematically exaggerated because disagreements are news.

Behind the rapidly changing macroeconomic fashions of the media is a more balanced macroeconomic analysis that addresses current economic problems while at the same time weighing carefully the evidence that leads to changes — mostly small, but sometimes, as when the aggregate supply side was remodeled to include expected inflation, large — in macroeconomic theories.

We start the chapter by providing the necessary background of economic events from the sixties to the mid-eighties. In Section 18-2 we describe monetarism. The radical rational expectations – equilibrium approach to macroeconomics is described in detail in Section 18-3. We then go on to supply-side economics and Reaganomics, ending by discussing how to make sense of the different views and approaches.

18-1 THE ECONOMY: 1969–1986

The sixties was a period of generally rising inflation and falling unemployment. It was also a period of rapid growth of real GNP. Table 18-1 presents data on

TABLE 18-1	COMPARATIVE ECONOMIC PERFORMANCE, 1961–1968, 1969–1982, AND 1982–1985, %			
	Growth rate of real GNP	Unemployment rate	Inflation (CPI)	Money growth ($M1$)
1961–1968	4.9	4.8	2.2	4.3
1969–1982	2.3	6.4	7.5	6.4
1982–1985	4.1	8.0	3.7	9.1

comparative economic performance in the sixties, in the period 1969–1982, and in the period 1982–1985. Growth in the sixties was substantially higher, and inflation and unemployment were lower, than in subsequent years. In the period since 1982 growth was higher and inflation lower than in the seventies. Be warned, though, that the last 3 years started at the bottom of a deep recession and that the average growth rate of real GNP for the eighties is likely to be less than 4 percent; the unemployment rate for the eighties will probably average less than 8 percent, though it is unlikely to go below 6 percent. However, it is reasonable to expect inflation to be lower in the eighties than it was in the seventies.

To set the background for the discussion of developments in macroeconomics, we now describe the behavior of the economy since 1969 in more detail. Figure 18-1 shows the unemployment and inflation rates over the period since 1969. Figure 18-2 shows the growth rate of $M1$ and the high-employment surplus (as a percent of potential GNP) for the period. There were four recessions (shaded) during this period, in contrast with none during the previous 8 years.[2] The 1973–1975 and 1981–1982 recessions were the deepest since World War II.

The period opened with restrictive monetary and fiscal policies designed to reduce the inflation rate below the 5 percent level it had reached at the end of 1968. The restrictive policies were kept in place for more than 2 years. But when the inflation rate proved resistant to conventional aggregate demand policies, the Nixon administration turned in 1971 to wage and price controls, aiming to bring the inflation rate down rapidly through direct measures.

From 1971 to 1973 the economy boomed, with the encouragement of expansionary monetary and fiscal policies. During 1973 food and raw materials prices rose sharply, and then at the end of 1973, the first oil price shock hit the economy. The rapid rises in food and raw materials—particularly oil—prices constituted the first serious supply shock to hit the economy in the

---

[2] Some economists argue that the period 1980–1982 should count as one long recession rather than two recessions interrupted by a recovery. In support of this argument, note that the decline in unemployment following the 1980 recession was very small.

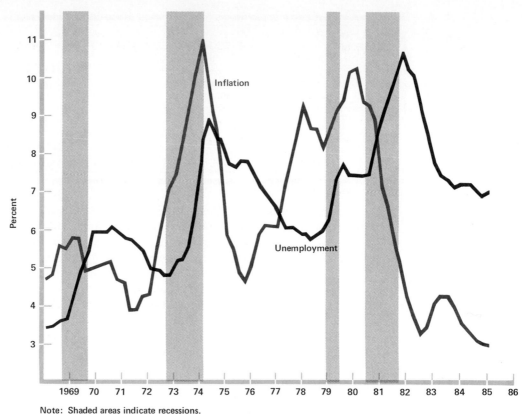

Note: Shaded areas indicate recessions.

FIGURE 18-1   INFLATION AND UNEMPLOYMENT, 1969–1986.
(*Source:* Data Resources, Inc.)

post-World War II period. Policy makers and economists were perplexed about how to respond to the shock. The high inflation rate seemed to call for restrictive monetary and fiscal policy, but the supply shock was reducing output; so perhaps policy should have been expansionary or at least accommodating of the shock. In any event, monetary policy became restrictive to fight the inflation. As late as the end of 1974, with the recession well under way, the administration was still considering a tax *increase* to fight the inflation. By early 1975, though, fiscal policy became expansionary; consumers were given a tax rebate on their 1974 taxes, and the investment tax credit was increased.

The 1973–1975 recession reduced the inflation rate. Consumer prices rose less than 5 percent during 1976. From the low-inflation/high-unemployment situation at the beginning of 1975, the economy grew rapidly. The growth rate of GNP was 5 percent per year or more in each year from 1976 to 1978. This was a strong recovery from the recession as can be seen in the rapidly falling unemployment rate from 1975 to 1979 in Figure 18-1. The only fly in the ointment—and it was no small fly—was the rising inflation rate. In 1979 a second oil price shock caused the inflation rate to rise sharply again.

In response to the high inflation, the Fed in October 1979 adopted its new monetary policy, which was henceforth to concentrate on keeping the growth rate of money under control and on target. Exceptionally high inflation at the beginning of 1980 led the Fed and the administration to panic and impose credit controls in March 1980, probably after a recession had already begun (see Box 12-1: "Policy Making under Uncertainty: 1980").

The Reagan administration took office in 1981 with a commitment to sharply reducing taxes and the size of the government, while also building up national defense. Its major fiscal move was the phased-in 3-year Kemp-Roth tax cut. Government revenues as a percentage of GNP fell, but spending did not. The result was a large increase in the full-employment deficit, which can

FIGURE 18-2   MONEY GROWTH AND THE HIGH-EMPLOYMENT SURPLUS (PERCENTAGE OF GNP). (*Source:* Data Resources, Inc., Bureau of Economic Analysis.)

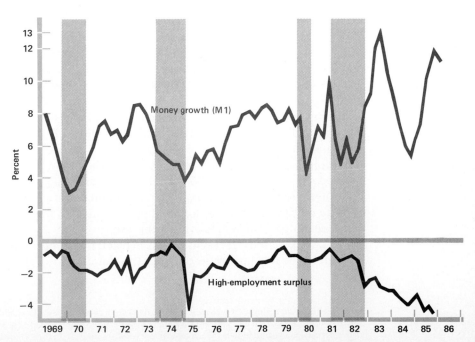

TABLE 18-2	BUDGET AND TRADE DEFICITS (% OF GNP), AND THE REAL INTEREST AND EXCHANGE RATES, 1980–1985				
	Actual deficit	Full-employment deficit	Trade deficit	Real interest rate	Real exchange rate
1980	2.2	1.3	−0.3	3.4	89.5
1981	2.1	0.9	−0.4	6.0	100.6
1982	4.6	1.8	0.0	5.9	109.9
1983	5.3	2.8	1.1	5.7	112.7
1984	4.6	3.7	2.5	8.2	118.2
1985	4.9	4.2	2.6	5.9	121.3

Notes:
1. Actual and trade deficits are percent of actual GNP; full-employment deficit is percent of potential GNP calculated at 6 percent unemployment rate.
2. Actual and trade deficits are from *Economic Report of the President*, 1986; full-employment deficit is from "The Cyclically Adjusted Federal Budget and Federal Debt," *Survey of Current Business*, March 1986, p. 17.
3. Real interest rate is nominal rate on 3-year Treasury bonds (*Economic Report*, 1986, p. 332) minus expected inflation calculated as average inflation rate of GNP deflator for last year, current year, and next year (assuming 3.6 percent for 1986).
4. Real exchange rate is index, with 1980–1982 = 100, from *World Financial Markets*, Morgan Guaranty.

be seen in Figure 18-2. With the Fed still attempting to control money growth to reduce inflation, a second recession began in the middle of 1981 and continued to the end of 1982. Measured by the unemployment it created, this was the worst recession since the great depression. In the fall of 1982 the Fed in effect abandoned its money targeting procedures, permitting very rapid growth in money to try to fight the deepening recession and high interest rates (see Figure 18-3).

The economy began to recover at the end of 1982. Real GNP growth was exceptionally rapid during 1983 and into 1984. The rapid decline in unemployment from 1983 to 1985 seen in Figure 18-1 reflects that GNP growth.[3] Inflation continued to fall despite the falling unemployment. But growth slowed substantially in 1985 and 1986, as can be seen in Figure 18-3 where the unemployment rate was essentially unchanged over that period. By the middle of 1986 the unemployment rate seemed to be stuck at around 7 percent, accompanied by a low inflation rate.

The first half of the eighties was marked by exceptionally high real interest rates and foreign trade deficits; the data are in Table 18-2, which also

---

[3] The decline in unemployment in the 1983–1984 recovery was even faster than would have been expected on the basis of Okun's law. Okun's law estimates in the sixties implied that it would take 3 percent of GNP growth above normal for a year to reduce the unemployment rate by 1 percent; in the 1983–1984 recovery, the ratio was closer to 2 percent of above-normal GNP growth to reduce the unemployment rate by 1 percent.

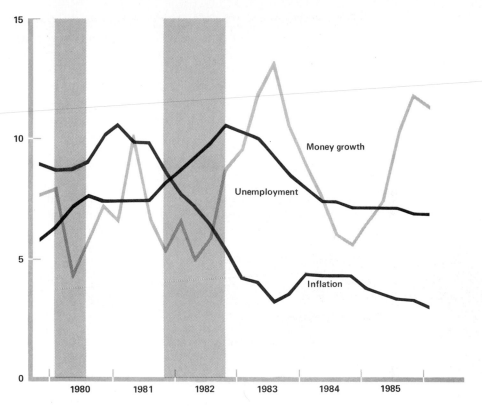

FIGURE 18-3   INFLATION, UNEMPLOYMENT, AND MONEY
GROWTH, 1979–1986. Inflation rate is of GNP deflator; money growth
is of $M1$, each for the given quarter over same quarter a year before.
(*Source:* Data Resources, Inc.)

presents an index of the dollar exchange rate. The cause of both the high real
interest rate and the trade deficit became the subject of dispute. One view,
consistent with the *IS-LM* model and the extended version that includes foreign trade (developed in Chapter 6) is that both high interest rates and a
foreign trade deficit are implied by the policy mix of exceptionally easy fiscal
policy and tight monetary policy. It has also been argued though that the fiscal
deficit has nothing to do with either the real interest rate or the trade deficit.
On the trade deficit the argument goes as follows: the U.S. economy became a
more attractive place in which to invest, foreigners therefore bought American assets, raising the value of the dollar, which made importing cheaper and
exporting more difficult (because foreigners had to pay more for American
goods), thereby creating a trade deficit.

At the end of 1985 and early in 1986 the third oil shock since 1973 struck.

This one was favorable, with oil prices declining sharply. The favorable shock came at just the right time for an economic recovery that was running out of steam. In the middle of 1986 the question is whether the favorable supply shock and good economic policy can combine to produce continuing growth while maintaining the success that has been achieved on the inflation front.

The poor economic performance of the 1969–1982 period and the improvements since raise interesting and important questions. Why was performance so disappointing in the seventies? Are supply shocks mainly to blame? If so, are there better ways of dealing with them? Does part of the blame go to excessively expansionary monetary policy? The low growth of the seventies and stalled growth in 1985 raise the essential issue: Is there any way to get the economy moving again at high growth rates?

In searching for answers to these questions, macroeconomics developed and moved away from the New Economics of the sixties. The emphasis in 1969 was on monetarism, which promised control of inflation by controlling the money supply.

18-2 MONETARISM

Milton Friedman and monetarism are almost synonymous. Monetarism appears, however, in many shades and covers quite a spectrum from a hard monetarism, beyond the Friedman variety, to eclectic Keynesianism. In that spectrum one would include Karl Brunner of the University of Rochester, Allan Meltzer and Bennett McCallum of Carnegie-Mellon, Thomas Mayer of the University of California at Davis, Phillip Cagan of Columbia University, David Laidler and Michael Parkin of the University of Western Ontario, and William Poole of Brown University, to name only some of the most prominent. Monetarism is not confined to academic economists. Indeed, the Federal Reserve Bank of St. Louis has long been a haven of a monetarist perspective on macroeconomics, and so have congressional committees. If monetarism admits of some diversity, it nevertheless comes down to the proposition that money is extremely important for macroeconomics, that money is more important than other things such as fiscal policy, and, in some variants, that money is virtually all that matters.

We define monetarism by describing Friedman's views, but we should warn you that in so doing we overemphasize Friedman's role in developing and sustaining monetarism. Friedman's views on macroeconomics have been laid out in a series of scholarly articles, books, and popular writings.[4] Outstanding among his publications is *A Monetary History of the United States, 1867–1960*, written jointly with Anna J. Schwartz of the National Bureau of

---

[4] In addition to the books referred to earlier see *The Optimum Quantity of Money* (Chicago: Aldine, 1969); *A Program for Monetary Stability* (New York: Fordham University Press, 1959); and *Monetary Trends in the United States and the United Kingdom* (Chicago: University of Chicago Press, 1982).

Economic Research. We have already noted the influential monetary explanation of the great depression in *Monetary History*. More generally, *Monetary History* is an absorbing book that skillfully relates the behavior of the economy to the behavior of the stock of money.

What are the main features of monetarism?

Emphasis on the Stock of Money

Monetarism emphasizes the importance of behavior of the money stock in determining (1) the rate of inflation in the long run and (2) the behavior of real GNP in the short run. Friedman has said:[5]

> I regard the description of our position as "money is all that matters for changes in *nominal* income and for *short-run* changes in real income" as an exaggeration but one that gives the right flavor of our conclusions.

The view that the behavior of the money stock is crucial for determining the rate of inflation in the long run is consistent with the analysis of Chapter 14, as we noted there. The view that the behavior of the money stock — by which Friedman usually means the *growth rate* of the money stock — is of primary importance in determining the behavior of nominal and real GNP in the short run is not one we have accepted. Our treatment has given emphasis to *both* monetary and fiscal variables in determining the short-run behavior of nominal and real GNP. But there is no doubt that monetary variables play an important role in determining nominal and real GNP in the short run.

An important part of monetarism is the insistence that changes in the growth rate of money — accelerations and decelerations — account for changes in real activity. Instability in monetary growth is mirrored in variability in economic activity. Thus Friedman argues:[6]

> Why should we be concerned about these gyrations in monetary growth? Because they exert an important influence on the future course of the economy. Erratic monetary growth almost always produces erratic economic growth.

Monetarists point to a number of economic expansions and recessions as being caused by monetary accelerations and decelerations. These would certainly include the 1966 slowdown of economic activity in response to the credit crunch, the failure of the 1968 tax surcharge because it was swamped by expansionary monetary policy, and the 1970, 1980, and 1981–1982 recessions.

---

[5] "A Theoretical Framework for Monetary Analysis," *Journal of Political Economy*, March/April 1970, p. 217.
[6] "Irresponsible Monetary Policy," *Newsweek*, Jan. 10, 1972. Reprinted in Friedman's collection of public policy essays, *There's No Such Thing as a Free Lunch* (La Salle, Ill.: Open Court Publishing, 1975), p. 73.

Friedman's view of the primary importance of money is based in part on his careful historical studies, in which he was able to relate the booms and recessions of U.S. economic history to the behavior of the money stock. In general, it appeared that increases of the growth rate of money produced booms and inflations, and decreases in the money stock produced recessions and sometimes deflations.

Long and Variable Lags

Monetarism has emphasized that although the growth rate of money is of prime importance in determining the behavior of GNP, the effects of changes in the growth rate of money on the subsequent behavior of GNP occur with long and variable lags. On average, it takes a long time for a change in the growth rate of money to affect GNP, and so the lag is long. In addition, the time it takes for this change to affect GNP varies from one historical episode to another — the lags are variable. These arguments are based on empirical and not theoretical evidence. Friedman estimates the lags may be as short as 6 months and as long as 2 years.

The Monetary Rule

Combining the preceding arguments, Friedman argues against the use of active monetary policy. He suggests that because the behavior of the money stock is of critical importance for the behavior of real and nominal GNP, and because money operates with a long and variable lag, monetary policy should not attempt to "fine-tune" the economy. The active use of monetary policy might actually destabilize the economy, because an action taken in 1987, say, might affect the economy at any of various future dates, such as in 1988 or 1989. By 1989, the action taken in 1987 might be inappropriate for the stabilization of GNP. Besides, there is no certainty that the policy will take effect in 1989 rather than 1988. For example, suppose that the economy is currently in a recession, and that the money supply is increased rapidly today to increase the growth rate of real GNP. Today's increase in the growth rate of money might affect GNP within 6 months, and achieve its purpose. However, it might work only in 2 years, by which time GNP might well already have increased without the aid of the monetary policy action. And if the expansionary monetary policy affects an economy by then close to full employment, inflation will result.[7]

Thus monetarists argue that although monetary policy has powerful effects on GNP, it should not be actively used lest it destabilize the economy.

---

[7] For a concise statement, see Milton Friedman, "The Case for a Monetary Rule," *Newsweek*, Feb. 7, 1972. Reprinted in Milton Friedman, *Bright Promises, Dismal Performance* (New York: Harcourt, Brace, Jovanovich, 1983), pp. 225–227. See too his article "The Role of Monetary Policy," *American Economic Review*, March 1968.

Accordingly, their view is that the money supply should be kept growing at a constant rate, to minimize the potential damage that inappropriate policy can cause.[8]

The Unimportance of Interest Rates

In the *IS-LM* model changes in the money stock affect the economy primarily by changing interest rates, which, in turn, affect aggregate demand and thus GNP. When interest rates are low, monetary policy seems to be expansionary, encouraging investment and thus producing a high level of aggregate demand. Similarly, high interest rates seem to indicate contractionary policy. Since the Fed can control the level of interest rates, and since interest rates provide a guide to the effects of monetary policy on the economy, it seems perfectly sensible for the Fed to carry out monetary policy by controlling interest rates. Through the 1950s and most of the 1960s, the Fed did carry out its monetary policy by attempting to set the level of interest rates.

Friedman and monetarism brought two serious criticisms of the Fed procedure of attempting to set interest rates as the basis for the conduct of monetary policy. The first is that the behavior of nominal interest rates is not a good guide to the direction—whether expansionary or contractionary—of monetary policy. The *real* interest rate, the nominal interest rate minus the expected rate of inflation, is the rate relevant to determining the level of investment. But a high nominal interest rate, together with a high expected rate of inflation, means a low real rate of interest. Thus monetary policy might be quite expansionary in its effects on investment spending even when nominal interest rates are high. Consequently, Friedman and other monetarists argue that the Fed should not concentrate on the behavior of nominal interest rates in the conduct of monetary policy.

The second criticism is that the Fed's attempts to control nominal interest rates might be destabilizing. Suppose the Fed decides that monetary policy should be expansionary and that the interest rate should be lowered. To achieve these goals the Fed buys bonds in the open market, increasing the money supply. The expansionary monetary policy itself tends to raise the inflation rate. It thus tends to raise the nominal interest rate as investors adjust their expectation of inflation in response to the behavior of the actual inflation rate. But then the Fed would have to engage in a further open market purchase in an attempt to keep the nominal interest rate low. And that would lead to further inflation, further increases in nominal interest rates, and further open market purchases. The end result is that an attempt to keep nominal interest rates low may lead to increasing inflation. Therefore, Friedman argues, the

---

[8] In Chap. 12 we discussed the case for a monetary rule that arises from the problem of dynamic inconsistency. This argument was not typically made by monetarists; rather it is an argument of the seventies more closely associated with the rational expectations-equilibrium approach to macroeconomics.

Fed should not pay attention to the behavior of nominal interest rates in the conduct of monetary policy, and should, rather, keep the money supply growing at a constant rate.[9]

Each of these arguments on the dangers of conducting monetary policy by reference to nominal interest rates is important. It is indeed correct that real, and not nominal, interest rates provide the appropriate measure of the effects of monetary policy on aggregate demand. It is also true that the Fed could, by attempting to keep nominal interest rates low forever, destabilize the economy. However, once the latter danger has been pointed out, the probability that the Fed will destabilize the economy by operating with reference to interest rates is reduced. The use of interest rates as a guide to the direction of monetary policy does not mean that the Fed has to attempt to keep the interest rate fixed forever at some level. Instead, it may aim each month or quarter for an interest rate target that it regards as appropriate for the current and predicted economic situation.

The monetarist case for concentrating on the behavior of the money stock in the conduct of monetary policy is a strong, but not conclusive, one. The major weakness in the argument is that the demand for real balances may shift over time, as it has done since 1973 (see Chapter 10). The problem of shifts in the demand-for-money function became particularly acute in the early eighties, following the change in Federal Reserve monetary policy in October 1979. The policy change was intended to place more emphasis on keeping the growth rate of money under control. But at the same time there were extensive reforms of the monetary system, which, as we discussed in Chapter 10, shifted the demand function for (and definitions of) money. With a shifting demand function it became unclear what the right rate of growth of money was to keep the economy on track. At the end of 1982 the Fed announced it was temporarily abandoning its $M1$ money growth rate targets, until the shifts in the demand function for money were completed.

Indeed, without taking changes in the behavior of velocity into account, the behavior of inflation seen in Table 18-1 is hard to explain. Note that in the period 1982–1985 the growth rate of money was higher than in the earlier two periods, but nonetheless the inflation rate fell considerably. The explanation is that velocity was decreasing over this period, partly because nominal interest rates were declining, partly because of changes in the monetary system.

Because of shifts in the demand for money, the behavior of the money stock is not a perfect guide to the conduct of monetary policy. Neither is the behavior of nominal interest rates. However, the behavior of the nominal money stock and the behavior of nominal interest rates *both* provide some information about the direction in which monetary policy is pushing the econ-

---

[9] The details of the argument are spelled out in Friedman's "The Role of Monetary Policy," *American Economic Review*, March 1968.

omy, imperfect as each measure is. Accordingly, the Fed should pay attention to the behavior of both interest rates and the quantity of money in the conduct of its monetary policy.[10]

The Importance of Fiscal Policy

Friedman has frequently, if tongue in cheek, said that fiscal policy is very important. Although we noted earlier that he argues fiscal policy itself is not important for the behavior of GNP, he does contend that it is of vital importance in setting the size of government and the role of government in the economy. Friedman is an opponent of big government. He has made the interesting argument that government spending increases to match the revenues available. The government will spend the full tax collection — and some more. Accordingly, he is in favor of tax cuts as a way of reducing government spending. This argument was probably influential in the Reagan administration's 1981 decision to pass tax cuts well before it had figured out how to cut government spending.

Friedman stands out in arguing that fiscal policy does not have strong effects on the economy except to the extent that it affects the behavior of money. Thus he has remarked:[11]

> To have a significant impact on the economy, a tax increase must somehow affect monetary policy — the quantity of money and its rate of growth. . . .
> The level of taxes is important — because it affects how much of our resources we use through the government and how much we use as individuals. It is not important as a sensitive and powerful device to control the short-run course of income and prices.

The Inherent Stability of the Private Sector

The final aspect of monetarism we consider here is the monetarist view that the economy, left to itself, is more stable than when the government manages it with discretionary policy and that the major cause of economic fluctuations lies in inappropriate government actions. This view is quite fundamental to the monetarist position. It is because the point is so fundamental that a major stage in the acceptance of monetarism occurred when Friedman and Schwartz published their *Monetary History of the United States.* In it they provided evidence for the view that the great depression was the result of bad monetary policy rather than private sector instability, arising, say, from autonomous shifts in consumption or investment demand.

---

[10] The argument is worked out in Benjamin M. Friedman, "Targets, Instruments, and Indicators of Monetary Policy," *Journal of Monetary Economics,* October 1975.
[11] Milton Friedman, "Higher Taxes? No," *Newsweek,* Jan. 23, 1967. Reprinted in *There's No Such Thing as A Free Lunch,* op. cit., p. 89.

Summary: We Are All Monetarists

From the viewpoint of the conduct of economic policy, the major monetarist themes are (1) an emphasis on the growth rate of the money stock, (2) arguments against fine tuning and in favor of a monetary rule, and (3) a greater weight that monetarists, as compared, for example, with Keynesians, place on the costs of inflation relative to those of unemployment.

Although we describe these as the major monetarist propositions relating to policy,[12] it is not true that macroeconomists can be neatly divided into groups, some subscribing to the monetarist religion and the others to their faiths. Most of the arguments advanced by Friedman and his associates are technical and susceptible to economic analysis and the application of empirical evidence. Many of those propositions are now widely accepted and are no longer particularly associated with monetarism. As Franco Modigliani has remarked, "We are all monetarists now." He adds that we are monetarists in the sense that all (or most) macroeconomists believe in the importance of money.

Much of the analysis of this book would, in the past, have been considered monetarist. For example, we have assumed the long-run Phillips curve is vertical, a proposition that was originally associated with monetarism. We have laid considerable stress on the behavior of the money stock and have emphasized that fiscal policy affects long-run inflation to the extent that it affects the long-run growth rate of money. Older readers will doubtless detect other places at which we appear monetarist to their eyes. That is all to the good. If economists did not modify their analyses in the light of new theories and evidence, the field would be barren.

Friedman and his associates indeed changed macroeconomics. The forceful and persuasive way in which they emphasized the role of money changed the views of most economists on the importance of monetary policy. It is always possible that those views would have changed anyway, in the light of the increasing inflation of the sixties and seventies. The fact remains, however, that it was Friedman, and not someone else, who hammered away at the importance of money.

Monetarism and the Economy

Over the period since World War II there has been an increasing emphasis on limiting money growth as an essential ingredient in controlling inflation. In 1975 the United States adopted money growth targets for one or more monetary aggregates ($M1$, $M2$, high-powered money, etc.). All major nations now

---

[12] For a range of views on monetarism in addition to the references in Chap. 16 see Franco Modigliani, "The Monetarist Controversy," *American Economic Review*, March 1977; Thomas Mayer, *The Structure of Monetarism* (New York: Norton, 1978); D. Batten and C. Stone, "Are Monetarists an Endangered Species?", Federal Reserve Bank of St. Louis, *Review*, May 1983; and J. H. McCulloch, *Money and Inflation* (New York: Academic Press, 1982).

have such targets.[13] The adoption of money targets is a result of the monetarist emphasis on the importance of money. Thus monetarism has certainly had an impact on the way in which monetary policy is carried out.

Of course, having a target and hitting it are not the same thing. No central bank is so committed to its money target that it wants to hit it regardless of what else is happening in the economy. As we saw in the case of the United States in Chapter 11, when interest rates start rising rapidly, the central bank typically compromises on its money target, letting the money stock go above target to avoid interest rates rising too far. Despite such compromises, the central bank does try to adhere to its targets unless there is a compelling reason not to. By announcing the targets, the central bank also takes on the responsibility of explaining why it departs from those targets when it does.

Beyond the general monetarist influence visible in the adoption of money targets, there have been several policy episodes that are more narrowly monetarist. Among these are the period 1969–1971 in the United States, when policy aimed to reduce the inflation rate of 5 percent inherited from the Johnson administration, by gradually slowing the money growth rate; the policies of the Thatcher government in Britain from 1979, which attempted to reduce the inflation rate; and the Fed's adoption of a new monetary policy in 1979.

The Fed's monetarism lasted until 1982, when it explicitly announced that it was temporarily exceeding its money targets in light of the increased demand for money at that time. Figure 18-3 shows the extremely high rates of money growth in 1983 and again in 1985. Monetarists argue that the Fed never (not even from 1979 to 1982) seriously adopted monetarist policies:[14]

> Insofar as U.S. policy can ever be said to have been monetarist, it was so solely in rhetoric, never in performance. Since the Fed adopted temporarily the rhetoric of monetarism in 1979, monetary growth has been more unstable than in any other postwar period of comparable length. That hardly constitutes a monetarist policy. . . .

The record seen in Figures 18-2 and 18-3 makes it hard to disagree with this view.

Even monetarists have always insisted that inflation cannot be ended without recession. This viewpoint is widely accepted and was borne out by the most recent disinflation, the attempt at which started in 1979. It took two recessions and 3 years until the rate of inflation came down—but when it started falling, it came down fast. Figure 18-3 shows the course of inflation and unemployment during disinflation in the United States.

---

[13] Data are published in the OECD's *Economic Outlook,* which appears twice a year.
[14] Letter from Milton Friedman to the *Wall Street Journal,* Dec. 18, 1985.

The picture is complicated by the second oil shock at the end of 1979 and beginning of 1980 and by the brief recession at the beginning of 1980. The complication is that at the beginning of 1980[15] the oil shock produced extremely high inflation of the consumer price index, which led to the credit controls and sharp contraction of the money supply in the first half of 1980. The recession was so sharp that the Fed immediately switched gears and briefly raised money growth. After that turbulence, the growth rate of money was again reduced. Ignoring these jiggles, the overall picture is clear: money growth was on average kept well below the inflation rate, reducing real balances until the 1981–1982 recession took place. That caused unemployment, and the inflation rate fell dramatically.

Although both monetarists and Keynesians relied on much the same analysis to explain why disinflation could not come cheaply—the aggregate supply-demand analysis of Chapter 14—that explanation left many economists dissatisfied. They worried that the slow adjustment of wages and prices assumed in those models lacked a firm theoretical basis. Early in the 1970s, a radical new development in macroeconomics seemed to promise improved understanding of the effects of policy measures on the economy. This was the rational expectations–equilibrium approach.

18-3 THE RATIONAL EXPECTATIONS–EQUILIBRIUM APPROACH

The failure to reduce inflation in the 1970s and the apparent inability of macro policy to achieve its goals led to a reconsideration of the premises of modern macroeconomics. The reconsideration places great emphasis on expectations, on the credibility of policies, and on the limited scope for discretionary stabilization policies. These are among the hallmarks of what is called the *rational expectations approach* to macroeconomics. Among the leading members of the school are Robert Lucas of the University of Chicago, and Edward Prescott, Thomas Sargent, and Neil Wallace of the University of Minnesota.[16]

The rational expectations approach acquired that name because the assumption of rational expectations in the context of the expectations-augmented aggregate supply curve of Chapter 14 has such striking implications.

---

[15] This inflation does not show up however in the GNP deflator inflation rate seen in Fig. 18-3.

[16] For an introduction see Thomas Sargent and Neil Wallace, "Rational Expectations and the Theory of Economic Policy," *Journal of Monetary Economics*, April 1976. See also Robert Lucas, "Understanding Business Cycles," in Robert E. Lucas (ed.), *Studies in Business Cycle Theory*, MIT Press, 1981; Bennett McCallum, "Macroeconomics after a Decade of Rational Expectations: Some Critical Issues," in Federal Reserve Bank of Richmond, *Economic Review*, November/December 1982; Arthur Okun, "Rational-Expectations-with-Misperceptions as a Theory of the Business Cycle," *Journal of Money, Credit and Banking*, November 1980, part 2. Two textbooks review the tools and propositions. These are Steven Sheffrin, *Rational Expectations* (London: Cambridge University Press, 1983), and David Begg, *The Rational Expectations Revolution in Macroeconomics* (Baltimore: Johns Hopkins University Press, 1983).

Recall that in Chapter 14 we defined the rational expectations hypothesis as assuming *individuals form expectations using information efficiently and do not make systematic mistakes in expectations.*

We saw in Chapter 14 that rational expectations applied to the expectations-augmented aggregate supply curve implied that an expected reduction in the growth rate of money would reduce the inflation rate without causing a recession. We also noted in the same context that only unexpected changes in monetary policy would have real effects, and we discussed the important role of credibility of the intentions of policy makers.

But the group known as the rational expectations school has a broader aim. The rational expectations – equilibrium approach aims to build all of macroeconomics on sound microeconomic foundations, in which individuals maximize utility, firms maximize profits, and markets are in equilibrium. The emphasis on markets being in equilibrium is far more fundamental than just the rational expectations assumption. It is for that reason that we add "equilibrium" in referring to the approach as the rational expectations – equilibrium approach.

In the remainder of this section we briefly take up the rational expectations part of the approach. In the next section we turn to the equilibrium approach.

Rational Expectations As a Theory of Expectations

The assumption that expectations are rational, based on the efficient use of information, and not systematically incorrect, is made on occasion by almost all macroeconomists. Its use does not automatically qualify the user as a member of the rational expectations – equilibrium school.

The question of whether individuals make systematic mistakes in expectations is an empirical one. Indeed, there is some evidence that individuals do make systematic mistakes.[17] At the level of individual firms forecasting sales, some firms seem to be perpetual optimists, others perpetual pessimists. It has to be recognized that firms or individuals may make mistakes in expectations for long periods. In normal times, they may use simple rules of thumb for forecasting. Nonetheless, the rational expectations approach suggests that if forecast errors are expensive to the forecaster, any systematic errors will eventually be corrected by the people making them.

Beyond that, rational expectations as a theory of expectations implies that policy cannot rely for its effectiveness on systematic misunderstandings by the public. For instance, if at first the public does not understand that countercyclical tax changes are transitory, those changes will have powerful effects on

---

[17] See Michael C. Lovell, "Tests of the Rational Expectations Hypothesis," *American Economic Review*, March 1986. See, too, the challenging paper by Amos Tversky and Daniel Kahneman, "Judgment Under Uncertainty: Heuristics and Biases," *Science*, 185, pp. 1124–1131, 1984.

the economy. But as people begin to realize that tax changes are reversed as the economy reaches full employment, such a policy comes to have less powerful effects because the tax changes are understood to be transitory. The expectations part of rational expectations suggests that it is best, in formulating policy, to assume that the public will soon understand how a particular policy is working. It also implies that any policy which works for some time only because the public does not correctly anticipate its effects is doomed to eventual failure.

18-4 THE EQUILIBRIUM APPROACH

The equilibrium component of the rational expectations–equilibrium approach is also known as the *new classical macroeconomics*. The approach accepts as its basic challenge the need to explain the fluctuations in output and employment that take place in the business cycle.

Money and Business Cycles

The early work in this area was done by Robert Lucas. Lucas saw the Phillips curve, the tradeoff between inflation and unemployment, as the central empirical fact that had to be explained. And he aimed to explain it in a model in which prices can move to make supply equal to demand.[18]

Why is the Phillips curve a central problem for an equilibrium approach to macroeconomics? Recall that we showed in Chapter 7 that when prices are flexible, an increase in the money stock is fully neutral, raising prices but not output. If prices are not assumed to be sticky — and the equilibrium approach assumes prices are free to move to clear markets — it is necessary to explain why an increase in the money stock that raises prices apparently is accompanied also by higher output. Equivalently, it has to be explained why it appears impossible to reduce the inflation rate without creating a recession.

Lucas focused on the tradeoff between output (rather than unemployment) and inflation. The explanation assumed that individuals have imperfect information about the current price level and thus mistake movements in *absolute* prices for *relative* price changes.

The model starts from the supply of a particular good, call it good i; quantity supplied increases with the *relative* price of that good. This is simple microeconomics. The aggregate price level (P_t) is not known at the time suppliers have to decide how much to produce and sell. Instead suppliers base their output decisions on the estimated or expected aggregate price level, P_t^e.

---

[18] The most influential single article is Robert E. Lucas, "Some International Evidence on Output-Inflation Tradeoffs," *American Economic Review*, September 1973.

The price of the particular good i is P_{it}. The supply curve of good i is

$$Y_{it} = f \frac{P_{it}}{P_t^e} \tag{1}$$

Y_{it} is the output of the ith good.

In a competitive market each supplier knows the price in his or her market. But because information is imperfect, all suppliers know only P_{it} in their individual market, not any other prices or the aggregate price level. On the basis of P_{it} and the price level they expected, P_t^e, they have to make a best estimate of the actual relative price of good i, that is, of P_{it}/P_t.

Individuals know that there are two types of shocks in the economy. Some shocks are *relative,* or specific to individual markets. These relative shocks sum to zero across the markets, some markets having higher than average demand, others having less than average. There are also *aggregate* shocks, which raise quantity demanded at a given price in every market. An unexpected increase in the money stock is one such shock.

Consider the supplier who has some expectation of the aggregate price level, P_t^e and who now learns the relative price in the market. Suppose the relative price is high. The supplier has to decide whether that is because there has been an increase in demand in all markets, raising the aggregate price level, or just in his or her market, raising the relative price. If the high price in market i is a result of a shock to the money stock that affects all markets, the supplier will not want to raise output. If the shock is specific to market i, the supplier will want to raise output.

The key result that Lucas establishes is this: the rational calculation is to assume that when price in market i is high, that is partly because the aggregate price level is high and partly because there has been a relative shock in market i. The statistically best guess that individuals in the market can make assigns responsibility for the high price between its two possible sources. That means that when seeing a price that, relative to the expected aggregate price level, seems high, a supplier will react to the higher price by producing more — though the reaction is less than if the supplier was certain the relative price in his or her market was high.

The next step is to look at all markets together. If there has been no shock to the money supply, the relative shocks will cancel out in their total effects on output. Output will be higher than average in some markets, lower than average in others. But if there has been an unexpected increase in the money stock, output will on average be higher than normal — because everyone partly mistook the increase in aggregate demand as a shift in relative demand and produced more than average. Adding up output across markets, total production will be higher when the money stock has unexpectedly increased. And on average prices will be higher, because demand in each market was greater.

Lucas thus succeeded in producing a Phillips curve type of tradeoff in which a higher average price level would be accompanied by higher output. This is remarkable, but so is the accompanying implication, that *only unexpected changes in the money stock affect output.*[19] If the changes had been expected, suppliers in individual markets could have figured out the effects on the aggregate price level, taken them into account, and would not have increased production in response to a higher price level.

The Lucas demonstration of a possible Phillips curve based on incomplete information attracted much attention, particularly the demonstration that with regard to monetary policy, only unexpected changes in the stock of money affect the price level. Under these circumstance, there appears to be no role for monetary policy to systematically affect output or unemployment. Any systematic policy, such as increased monetary expansion in a recession (remember that recessions are possible as a result of surprises) would be predicted by market participants, and wages and prices would be set accordingly.[20] Unless the Fed had better information, or shorter reaction lags than the market, it could not, according to this theory, have a systematic *real* effect.

Empirical Testing

The proposition that only monetary *surprises* affect output has been the subject of intense empirical research. Early work by Robert Barro[21] appeared to support the proposition. Later research by, among others, Frederic Mishkin and Robert Gordon cast substantial doubt on the early findings.[22] The later results suggest that both expected and unexpected changes in the money stock affect output. By this stage, the evidence does not support the strong implication of the market clearing approach that only unanticipated changes in the money stock affect output. Accordingly, the evidence also does not support the view that systematic monetary policy does not affect the behavior of output.

Equilibrium Real Business Cycles

The weakness of the empirical evidence for the view that only unanticipated money affects real output led to two reactions. Some economists believed that

---

[19] We have already seen a result like this in Chap. 14, but we did not there use the microeconomic underpinnings that Lucas provides.

[20] You might wonder at this stage whether the equilibrium approach does not also imply that the economy should return immediately to equilibrium following a shock. We show below that is not necessarily the case.

[21] Robert J. Barro, "Unanticipated Money, Output, and the Price Level in the United States," *Journal of Political Economy,* August 1978.

[22] Frederic Mishkin, "Does Anticipated Monetary Policy Matter? An Econometric Investigation," *Journal of Political Economy,* February 1982 (this is difficult reading); and Robert Gordon, "Price Inertia and Policy Ineffectiveness in the United States, 1890–1980," *Journal of Political Economy,* December 1982.

better explanations would have to be found for the role of money in the business cycle. Others questioned the evidence linking money with the business cycle at all.

In particular, economists working on the equilibrium approach developed *equilibrium real business cycle* theory, the view that fluctuations in output and employment are the result of a variety of real shocks hitting the economy. They explained the apparent link between money and output as a result of the money stock accommodating movements in output. Thus money could be correlated with changes in output, but would not necessarily cause them.[23]

With monetary causes of the business cycle assumed out of the way, real business cycle theory is left with two tasks. The first is to explain the *shocks* or *disturbances* that hit the economy, causing fluctuations in the first place. The second is to explain the *propagation mechanisms.* A propagation mechanism is the means through which a disturbance is spread through the economy. In particular, the aim is to explain why shocks to the economy seem to have long-lived effects.

Propagation Mechanism

Many of the mechanisms that real business cycle theory relies on to explain why a shock to the economy affects output for several years have already been discussed. Among these are inventory adjustments and changes in investment caused by shifts in profitability. These are part of anyone's theory of the business cycle.

The one mechanism that is most associated with equilibrium business cycles though is *the intertemporal substitution of leisure.* Any theory of the business cycle has to explain why people work more at some times than at others; during booms employment is high and jobs are easy to find; during recessions people work less.

A simple equilibrium explanation would be that people work more in booms because wages are higher. That way they would voluntarily be supplying more labor in response to a higher wage. (Remember that the equilibrium approach requires people to be on their supply-and-demand curves at all times.) However, the facts are not strongly in favor of that argument because the real wage changes very little over the business cycle. People are thus not obviously working more in response to higher wages.

The Keynesian or monetarist approaches explain these movements in output by saying that the demand for labor shifts as aggregate demand shifts, and that people may be unemployed in recessions because they cannot get

---

[23] This view is developed in a technically very advanced paper by Robert King and Charles Plosser, "Money, Credit and Prices in a Real Business Cycle Model," *American Economic Review,* June 1984. A nontechnical review is in Carl Walsh, "New Views of the Business Cycle," Federal Reserve Bank of Philadelphia *Business Review,* January–February 1986.

work despite their willingness to work at the going wage.[24] But the equilibrium approach constrains itself to assume markets are in equilibrium. The explanation for the large movements in output with small movements in wages is the following: that there is a large elasticity of labor supply in response to temporary changes in the wage. Or, as the argument is put, people are willing to substitute leisure intertemporally.

The argument is that people care very little about when in any given period of a year or two they work. Suppose that within a 2-year period they plan to work 4,000 hours at the going wage (50 weeks each year for 40 hours a week). If wages are equal in the 2 years, they would work 2,000 hours each year. But if wages were just 2 percent higher in one year than the other, they might prefer to work, say, 2,200 hours in one year, forgoing vacations, and working overtime, and 1,800 hours in the other. That way they work the same total amount and earn more total income.

This intertemporal substitution of leisure is clearly capable of generating large movements in the amount of work done in response to small shifts in wages — and thus could account for large output effects in the cycle accompanied by small changes in wages. However, there has not been strong empirical support for this view either.

Similar intertemporal substitution arguments have been advanced to explain fluctuations in consumption over the course of the business cycle. In this case the real interest rate is assumed to move, with individuals reducing current levels of consumption when the interest rate is high in order to take advantage of the higher rate of return on saving.

Disturbances

The most important disturbances isolated by equilibrium business cycle theorists are shocks to *productivity,* or supply shocks, and shocks to *government spending.*

A productivity shock raises output as of a given level of input. Good weather and new methods of production are examples. Suppose there is a temporary favorable productivity shock this period. Then individuals will want to work harder to take advantage of the higher productivity. In working more this period they raise output. They will also invest more, thus spreading the productivity shock into future periods by raising the stock of capital. If the intertemporal substitution of leisure effect is strong, even a small productivity shock could have a relatively large effect on output.

---

[24] In some versions of the Keynesian model, including that of Keynes in the *General Theory,* it is assumed that output is determined by the demand for labor curve (see the neoclassical labor demand curve in the appendix to Chap. 13). That implies the real wage would be higher in recessions than in booms — firms hire more labor in booms because it is profitable to do so. Since the real wage does not move much in the cycle, this explanation, too, cannot be correct. In the model developed in Chaps. 13 and 14, the real wage is constant as a result of markup pricing, and employment changes with aggregate demand. Constancy of the real wage is a reasonable approximation to actual wage behavior.

Increased government spending is another type of shock. To provide the extra goods the government needs, individuals will work harder if the real wage rises, and save more if the real interest rate rises. Thus we should expect an increase in government spending to raise the real interest rate and the real wage.[25]

There is less certainty in the real business cycle approach about the effects of a cut in taxes than about the effects of an increase in government spending. As we discussed in Chapter 17, the Ricardian view is that individuals recognize that a cut in taxes today is just an increase in taxes tomorrow, and that they therefore should not increase consumption when taxes are cut.

Summary

The equilibrium real business cycle approach is still a subject of intense research. Its goal of building macroeconomics on sound microeconomic foundations is surely widely shared. There is no doubt too that some of the mechanisms, such as inventory accumulation and investment dynamics, that underlie its explanation of the dynamics of the business cycle, will form part of future business cycle models. But there is room to doubt that the attempt to build business cycle models in which there is no role for monetary factors will be ultimately successful.

18-5 THE RATIONAL EXPECTATIONS–EQUILIBRIUM APPROACH TO POLICY

The rational expectations approach has led to a sophisticated view of policy making. The rational expectations approach emphasizes that economic agents do not react mechanically to every policy change. Rather, they try to figure out what the policy change means for the behavior of the economy, and for future changes in policy. And they behave accordingly. For instance, as we noted in Chapter 8, economic agents adjust their consumption more in response to a permanent income tax cut than to a transitory tax cut of the same size.

Credibility

The approach leads naturally to the emphasis on the credibility of policy makers to which we have referred above. Individuals' reactions to policy decisions depend so much on their interpretations of what future policy decisions are implied that believability of policy becomes crucial.

---

[25] Note that increased government spending raises the real interest rate in the *IS-LM* model, too, though there the crowding out is more of investment than consumption.

Suppose the Fed announces a reduction in the growth rate of money. If people believe the Fed, the rate of wage increase will slow and the Fed will be able to reduce the growth rate of money without any significant output cost. Suppose they do not believe the Fed. Then it is faced with the decision of whether to do what it said and create a recession, or not to do it, thereby avoiding the recession but losing credibility.

Indeed, it is even possible to see how under rational expectations individuals' beliefs can be self-justifying. Suppose the Fed announces that it will reduce money growth. Suppose people believe it and wage increases slow. Then the Fed will do it, and the expectations were right. Suppose they do not believe the Fed and wages go on rising as before. Then if the Fed fears a recession, it will not cut the growth rate of money. The people were right again. This example illustrates the value of credibility.[26]

Institutional Reform

The approach leads also to an emphasis on institutional changes as ways of altering the behavior of the economy. Members of the rational expectations school are less interested in what policy should be *now* than they are in ways of making it possible for policy to operate better in general. The quote from Lucas at the beginning of this chapter shows a general attitude toward attempts to predict the effects of a particular policy action. Members of the rational expectations school doubt that we know enough to predict how the public will respond in the short run to a particular policy change, because the response depends on how the policy measure affects expectations. But in the long run the public will catch on to the effects of any policy change, and it thus becomes possible to predict the long-run effects of long-run policy changes. A member of the rational expectations school might support a constitutional amendment to balance the budget, in part because a constitutional amendment should have a very strong predictable effect on expectations.

Similarly, a rational expectations economist confronted with the inflationary experience of the seventies would argue that the best way to change the behavior of the Fed is to change the institutional environment in which it works. Accordingly, such an economist is likely to support a monetary rule for the Fed, for example, requiring the money supply to grow at 4 percent per year.[27]

---

[26] The development of the rational expectations approach to policy has led to much game theoretical (the mathematical theory of games) research on policy, like the above example.

[27] You might wonder why members of the rational expectations school should care at all about monetary policy if they believe that (1) only unexpected changes in money affect real output, and (2) the public's expectations eventually catch up with reality. The two assumptions (1) and (2) seem to suggest that whatever the Fed is doing, it will eventually have no effect on real output. However, the strong form of rational expectations does not argue that monetary policy is irrelevant to the behavior of *prices.* Thus members of the rational expectations school concerned about keeping inflation low can logically be in favor of a monetary rule that will prevent the average rate of growth of money from becoming high.

The Rational Expectations – Equilibrium Approach, Monetarism, and the Mainstream

There is considerable overlap between the policy views of monetarists and those of members of the rational expectations school. The similarity extends to the usually conservative views of policy held by members of both groups. But there are important differences between the monetarist and rational expectations approaches to macroeconomics. Monetarists are willing to assume that expectations may be systematically wrong and that markets are very slow to clear, whereas a member of the rational expectations school would not make such assumptions. Monetarism can be viewed as operating within the same framework and model as Keynesianism, while disagreeing over the relative importance of monetary and fiscal policy. The rational expectations school believes that the standard framework is fundamentally flawed and thus has developed the market clearing approach, which argues that imperfect information is responsible for the business cycle. It is thus a more radical attack on standard macroeconomics than is monetarism.

Where will the rational expectations – equilibrium alternative to conventional macroeconomics lead? It has already had a substantial influence on the way macroeconomists think. First, rational expectations is widely used as a theory of expectations. Second, the sophisticated view of policy, in which responses to policy depend on the public's analysis of what policy measures will do to current and future behavior of the economy, is widely adopted. The equilibrium approach, however, is more controversial than other components of the rational expectations view, and it seems to be inconsistent with the slow reaction of the economy to policy measures.[28]

18-6 SUPPLY-SIDE ECONOMICS

Supply-side economics was all the rage in the United States in 1981, the first year of the Reagan administration. And so-called supply-siders still run a very active publicity machine, proclaiming the correctness of their views in the press (particularly the *Wall Street Journal*) and in books.[29]

Supply-side economists lay heavy stress on the incentive effects of taxation in determining the behavior of the economy. Beyond that broad agreement there are really two separate supply-side groups. The mainstream group includes economists such as Martin Feldstein of Harvard, President of the National Bureau of Economic Research, and from 1982 to 1984, Chairman of the Council of Economic Advisers, and Michael Boskin of Stanford University.

---

[28] See the discussion in the special issue of the *Journal of Money, Credit and Banking*, November 1980.

[29] Paul Craig Roberts, *The Supply-Side Revolution* (Cambridge, Mass.: Harvard University Press, 1984), presents an insider's view of the supply-side impact on U.S. economic policy in the first Reagan administration. Various arguments of the supply-side case are brought together in the collection edited by Richard Fink, *Supply Side Economics* (University Publications of American 1982).

This group stresses the importance of tax incentives in promoting growth, by affecting saving and investment. Similarly, it analyzes the effects of tax changes on labor supply, the effects of social security on saving and on retirement decisions, and a host of other important issues.

The mainstream group has been presenting the results of its research in scholarly journals for many years and is influential and active within the economics profession. There are few economists who believe incentives are unimportant. Indeed it was the New Economics that was sufficiently concerned about growth in 1962 to introduce investment incentives through the investment tax credit.

But it was the radical fringe of the supply-side group that received most of the publicity.[30] This group made exaggerated claims for the effects of tax cuts on savings, investment, and labor supply and for the effects of tax cuts on total government revenue from taxation. Among the leaders of the radical fringe are Arthur Laffer, whose curve was described in Chapter 17, and George Gilder, whose radical supply-side book *Wealth and Poverty*[31] was on the best-seller list in 1981. Radical supply-siders were installed in the Treasury. Congressman Jack Kemp was the congressional leader of the supply side. The radical fringe argued (1) that tax rate reductions would have such powerful effects on work effort that total tax revenues would rise, and (2) that the supply-side effects of the tax cuts would have a powerful effect in reducing inflation by increasing the growth rate of output.

In 1981 the Reagan administration presented an optimistic scenario for growth with low inflation that was supposedly justified by supply-side considerations. Tax rates were to be cut significantly but, it was claimed, the rapid increase in growth would keep the budget close to balance. That at least was the public claim.[32]

Radical supply-side economics was thus an essential part of the rhetoric supporting *Reaganomics.* There is no precise definition of Reaganomics, other than that it is the economic policies pursued by President Reagan, especially in 1981–1982. The most important factor in these policies was the President's determination to cut taxes. This was done in the belief that the government was too large and that government spending could be cut by denying tax revenue to the Congress to spend. Arguments by supply-siders that tax cuts would rapidly increase economic growth and reduce inflation were certainly welcome, but it is quite likely that President Reagan would have proceeded

---

[30] The distinction between mainstream and radical groups is drawn by Harold McClure and Thomas Willett in "Understanding the Supply Siders," in W. C. Stubblebine and T. D. Willett (eds.), *Reaganomics A Midterm Report* (Institute of Contemporary Studies, 1983). See this paper and a paper by Richard Rahn in the same volume for more details on supply-side economics and for lists of the players in the two groups.

[31] New York: Basic Books, 1981.

[32] In his memoirs, David Stockman, President Reagan's first Director of the Office of Management and Budget, revealed that the administration did not believe its own forecasts. See *The Triumph of Politics* (New York: Harper & Row, 1986).

with his policies even had he known they would result in massive budget deficits, so long as they would reduce the size of government.

Supply-side predictions were criticized at the time by mainstream macroeconomists. The evidence is that tax reductions do affect incentives and that tax cuts would increase output.[33] But there is no evidence that the incentives would be so strong as to result in higher government revenue after a tax cut. Similarly, an increase in the growth rate of output will contribute to reducing the inflation rate — but the effects are unlikely to be powerful.

The events of the 2 years following the Reagan tax cuts do not support the views of the radical supply-siders. Inflation was indeed reduced, but the reduction was a result of tight monetary policy and not of expansionary fiscal policy. Output fell rapidly; it did not increase. These events led to the departure of the radical supply-siders from responsible policy-making positions, but did not slow down their claims that supply-side economics (of the radical branch) was the solution for the economy's problem.

The extremely rapid recovery from the recession that took place in 1983 and 1984 refueled the claims of supply-siders that incentives were crucial to growth. An alternative explanation is that the rapid growth of the money stock seen in Figure 18-3 and the large increases in the full-employment deficit seen in Figure 18-2 are mainly responsible for the rapid growth.

An interesting sidelight on supply-side economics comes from considering the relationship between supply-side economics and monetarism. Both approaches are often associated with conservative political positions. But the two groups of economists are critical of each other, and competed for influence in the Reagan administration. In their policy positions, favoring tax cuts in almost all circumstances and believing also that the Fed should allow rapid money growth to foster rapid output growth, the supply-siders are closer to Keynesianism than monetarism.

18-7 RECENT APPROACHES

Under the challenge of the rational expectations–equilibrium approach, there has been substantial research since 1973 attempting to explain why wages and prices are sticky. We have already mentioned several of the new approaches, but draw them together here for review.

Relative Wages, Wage Contracts, and Rational Expectations

The strongest form of the rational expectations–equilibrium approach assumes markets clear every period and attributes the effects of monetary policy

---

[33] Some of the evidence is examined in Chap. 19. The effects of cuts in tax rates on tax revenue were discussed in Chap. 17.

to imperfect information. That model has not been empirically successful. There are, however, models that use rational expectations as a theory of expectations but also recognize economic institutions such as long-term labor contracts and the importance to one group of workers of the wages received by others.[34] Relatively simple amendments to the basic Lucas imperfect information Phillips curve have gone far in removing some of the least-plausible implications of the strong form of rational expectations – equilibrium theory.

Suppose we have 2-year labor contracts and that half the contracts in the economy come up for renewal every year. Suppose further that we start from price stability and that an unanticipated decline in the money stock occurs. If all wages and prices were instantaneously flexible, they would immediately decline in proportion to the fall in money, and no real effects would arise. This does not occur, however, if we have long-term contracts that fix nominal wages. With a lowering in the money stock, there is potentially a decline in employment. Unemployed workers whose wages come up for renewal now have the choice of reducing their wages enough to become employed. If they do so, the price level will fall because the average wage has fallen. But when the price level falls, the real wage being paid to workers on existing contracts rises (the nominal wage they receive is fixed, and the price level has fallen), and some of them lose their jobs.

In addition, workers may be concerned that their *relative* wages not fall. If those whose contracts come up for renewal now accept cuts in wages large enough to keep them fully employed, their wages will not have to fall relative to those whose wages were negotiated earlier. Workers may be willing to accept some unemployment if they can keep their wages in line with those of others. If so, current wages will be set somewhere in between the full-employment level and the level of wages on contracts still running. That means wages do *not* adjust immediately to money changes; that is, wages are less than fully flexible. It takes some time until the whole wage structure adjusts. The fact that we have long-term nonsynchronized wage setting, and that relative wages matter, directly implies the possibility of extended periods of wage stickiness and unemployment.

The model is thus able to explain simultaneous wage inflation and unemployment. Suppose there is a contraction in demand, as we have just discussed, and that labor knows that policy will be expansionary in the future. Then those whose wages are currently up for renegotiation recognize that if they set too low a wage, they will be out of line with the wages that will be set next year by a group that will then be facing strong demand. Accordingly, even with the possibility of current unemployment, the prospect of expansionary aggregate

---

[34] The discussion here follows a paper by John Taylor, "Staggered Wage Setting in a Macro-Model," *American Economic Review,* May 1979. For a careful, advanced introduction see D. Begg, *The Rational Expectations Revolution in Macroeconomics* (Baltimore: Johns Hopkins University Press, 1983).

BOX

18-1

DISEQUILIBRIUM ECONOMICS AND POST-KEYNESIAN ECONOMICS

In the main text we have developed the history of ideas as running from Keynesian economics to monetarism and the rational expectations – equilibrium challenge, with supply-side economics as a flashy sideshow. However, two other strands of macroeconomics are sufficiently distinct and fruitful to deserve attention.

THE DISEQUILIBRIUM APPROACH

As early as the 1950s economists recognized the implications of disequilibrium in one market for supply or demand in other markets. If workers cannot sell all the labor they wish at the going wage, and cannot borrow, how will this affect their consumption decision? If they cannot buy all the goods they wish at the going prices, how does this affect their supply of labor or their demands for money and other assets. If firms cannot sell at the going price all the output they would like to produce, how does this affect their demand for labor?

The disequilibrium approach answers these questions by constructing a model of the economy that explicitly takes into account the *quantity constraints* on the decisions which households and firms face. Quantity constraints are present when households or firms cannot at the going wages or prices buy or sell all the quantities they wish. Central to the approach is the assumption that wages and prices do not move rapidly, leaving markets in disequilibrium, which gives rise to quantity adjustments. These quantity adjustments in different markets are interdependent through the quantity constraints under which households and firms make their optimal decisions.*

The most interesting contribution of the disequilibrium approach so far has been to influence empirical work. For example, studies of consumption pay close attention to the role of income and wealth, reflecting the possibility that individuals cannot borrow against future income so that *liquidity constraints* affect spending behavior. In studies of the labor market the approach suggests the important distinction between "high-wage" or classical unemployment on one side and Keynesian or "lack of demand" unemployment on the other (see Section 18-8).

POST-KEYNESIAN ECONOMICS

Post-Keynesians are a diverse group of economists who share the belief that modern macroeconomics leaves aside or explicitly assumes away many of the most central elements of Keynes' *General Theory*.†

Five elements of this approach stand out distinctly. First, adjustment, just as in the disequilibrium approach, takes place primarily through quantity adjustment, not price changes. Indeed, price changes where they occur are often seen as disequilibrating. Second, the distribution of income between profits and wages plays a central role in affecting consumption and investment decision. Third, expectations (Keynes' animal spirits), together with profits, are the chief determinant of investment plans. Fourth, institutional features — credit constraints on households and self-finance by firms, as well as the financial structure involving credit creation in a pyramid —

---

* The early reference is D. Patinkin, *Money, Interest and Prices* (New York: Row, Peterson, 1956), chap. 13. The complete working out of these ideas can be found in R. Barro and H. Grossman, *Money, Employment and Inflation* (London: Cambridge University Press, 1976); and E. Malinvaud, *The Theory of Unemployment Reconsidered* (Oxford: Basil Blackwell, 1977), and *Profitability and Unemployment* (Oxford: Basil Blackwell, 1981).

† For an introduction see A. Eichner (ed.), *A Guide to Post-Keynesian Economics* (White Plains, N.Y.: M. E. Sharpe, 1979), and the essays on post-Keynesian economics in the *American Economic Review*, May 1980.

interact in shaping the business cycle and on occasion financial crises. Finally, unlike in classical macroeconomics, the focus of post-Keynesian economics is to explain why the economy does not work well.

Post-Keynesian economics remains an eclectic collection of ideas, not a systematic challenge, as, for example, the rational expectations hypothesis. It has influenced economists in their research program. But the deliberate downplaying, indeed rejection, of individual rationality and maximization as a basis of behavior by firms and households has kept the approach at odds with the mainstream of the profession that has been attempting to bring macroeconomics into closer touch with microeconomics.

demand policies in the future will make current economic slack less effective in dampening wage and price inflation. Rational expectations enter here in that the groups currently setting their wages look ahead and ask themselves what will be the macroeconomic environment in which other groups set their wages next period. If the policy setting next period is expected to be expansionary, this fact will already be anticipated in this year's wages.[35]

The relative wage model, combined with rational expectations, thus has two important features: first, wages are sticky downward in the face of unemployment; and second, wage inflation may persist in the face of unemployment. The extent of persistence is determined by, among other things, the degree to which the policy setting is accommodative or not.

Efficiency Wages

As we have noted, the basic question to answer is why wages and prices do not move quickly to clear markets when there is unemployment. *Efficiency wage theory argues that wages are not cut because doing so reduces a firm's profits.*[36]

There are several explanations for this assumption. The simplest occurs in very poor countries where individuals cannot feed themselves adequately unless they receive a reasonable wage. Cutting wages in such a country would reduce the physical ability of the workers to perform their tasks. Even if there were substantial unemployment, it would not pay an employer to cut wages because doing so would reduce profits as the efficiency of workers fell owing to poor nutrition.

---

[35] Similar implications follow if workers are concerned about the real wages they will be receiving in future years, rather than relative wages.

[36] See Janet Yellen, "Efficiency Wage Models of Unemployment," in *American Economic Review*, May 1984. For a more extensive examination, see Lawrence Katz, "Efficiency Wage Theories: A Partial Evaluation," in *NBER Macroeconomics Annual* (Cambridge, Mass.: MIT Press, 1986). See, too, Assar Lindbeck and Dennis Snower, "Explanations of Unemployment," *Oxford Review of Economic Policy*, no. 2, 1985, and, by the same authors, "Wage Setting, Unemployment and Insider–Outsider Relations," *American Economic Review*, May 1986.

Physical efficiency is not the problem in developed countries. One efficiency wage explanation is that it is often difficult to observe the amount of effort put out by workers. To give the right incentive to work, there has to be a benefit to having this particular job. To create the benefit, so that the worker really wants to keep the job, the firm pays above-market wages. Then anyone who is found not be working hard pays the price by being fired and going back into the labor market to look for a lower-paid job.

This view suggests that there may be two types of jobs — high-paying desirable jobs that are difficult to find because the wage is above the market equilibrium wage and other jobs where firms can easily observe the workers' effort and where jobs are easy to find, at a lower wage. That description brings to mind such jobs as driving a cab, in which there are almost always available positions, even when there is unemployment.[37]

Alternatively, there may simply be a social custom that wages are not cut. If workers whose wages are cut regard that as unfair and reduce their work effort in response, then wage cutting will not take place. This fairness argument is not fully satisfactory, because there is no explanation of how the custom developed, but it, too, is plausible.

Small Menu Costs

There is a puzzling aspect of business cycle theories based on the assumption that wages are slow to adjust. Unemployment is a very serious problem, creating large costs for the society. Changing a wage or price is a relatively simple and apparently cheap matter. The payroll has to be reprogrammed, or a new price tag has to be put on. The puzzle is why these apparently small costs stand in the way of adjusting prices so as to get rid of unemployment.

A very recent development is the so-called small menu cost approach, which argues that small costs of changing prices can have large effects.[38] The argument is technical, but asserts that when firms set prices optimally, they lose very little by meeting increases or decreases in demand by producing more or less without changing prices.[39] Then if there is some small cost for the firm of changing its prices or wages, a small shift in demand will not trigger a price or wage change. But if firms do not change prices in response to shifts in demand, then the economy exhibits price (and/or wage) stickiness. The authors in this area show that extremely small costs of changing prices can

---

[37] Sometimes the two types of jobs are described as primary and secondary, primary jobs being the better ones. This is the so-called *dual-labor market hypothesis*.

[38] The simplest such model is N. Gregory Mankiw, "Small Menu Costs and Large Business Cycles: A Macroeconomic Model of Monopoly," *Quarterly Journal of Economics*, May 1985. A more extensive model is developed in George Akerlof and Janet Yellen, "A Near-Rational Model of the Business Cycle, with Wage and Price Inertia," *Quarterly Journal of Economics*, supplement, 1985.

[39] An essential assumption is that the firm *sets* prices or wages; this means the firm cannot be perfectly competitive, taking the price or wage as given by the market.

generate enough wage and price stickiness to give changes in the money stock substantial real effects.

Profit Sharing

Another response to the macroeconomic difficulties of the seventies and the continuing problems of European economies, to which we turn below, has been the *profit-sharing* proposal of Professor Martin Weitzman of MIT.[40] The proposal is that workers take part of their pay as a share of profits rather than as a fixed wage.

By taking part of their pay as a share of profits, workers would cut the base wage firms would have to pay. This would tend to encourage employment. In effect, profit sharing makes the wage more flexible.[41] Weitzman argues that the Japanese have essentially a profit-sharing scheme. Japanese workers receive a substantial part of their income (often around one-third) in the form of a bonus. If their company has a good year, the bonus will be higher; if it has a bad year, the bonus can be cut. And of course the Japanese have by far the lowest unemployment rate of any of the major economies.

Weitzman suggests that similar benefits could flow from the adoption of profit sharing in other economies. He recommends that governments provide tax subsidies for profit sharing. The scheme will not get off the ground otherwise, he argues, because there is no benefit to one company of introducing profit sharing unless other firms do it too. The benefits come from both lower unemployment and greater macroeconomic stability that would occur if the scheme were implemented on a major scale.

The profit-sharing proposal has attracted considerable attention, especially in Europe. The British government in 1986 announced it would promote wage-sharing. Critics question whether workers would want to receive part of their income as an uncertain amount of profits rather than a known wage. In response Weitzman contends that employment would be more stable for most people than it is now — when the prospect of unemployment certainly creates uncertainty about income for those in serious danger of losing their job.

18-8 EUROPEAN UNEMPLOYMENT

The theme of this chapter is the interaction of events and ideas. Events in Europe have differed from those in the United States, leading to consideration of different economic problems there. The striking European problem is the

---

[40] Martin Weitzman, *The Share Economy* (Cambridge, Mass.: Harvard University Press, 1984).
[41] Weitzman prefers to emphasize the effect of profit sharing on increasing employment because of a lower base wage, rather than the flexibility of the real wage that it creates.

TABLE 18-3	COMPARATIVE UNEMPLOYMENT RATES, %				
	U.S.	Japan	Germany	France	U.K.
1960–1966	5.1	1.3	0.7	1.2	1.4
1967–1973	4.5	1.2	1.0	2.4	2.4
1974–1980	6.8	1.9	3.5	4.8	4.7
1981–1984	8.5	2.5	7.8	8.3	11.7
1985	7.1	2.6	8.6	10.1	13.2

Sources: OECD *Historical Statistics*, 1960–1980, and OECD *Economic Outlook*, no. 39, May 1986.

rising unemployment rate. In the fifties and sixties European unemployment was well below U.S. rates. In the seventies European unemployment began to reach U.S. levels. Now it is well above the U.S. level. Table 18-3 presents the information.

The overall picture of an inexorable rise in European unemployment rates is remarkable. So are some of the details, for instance that the unemployment rate in France has risen every single year since 1973. The British unemployment rate in particular is remarkably high.

Such a prolonged increase in unemployment, to such high levels, calls for an explanation. The argument in Europe was over whether excessively high real wages or insufficient aggregate demand was the chief source of the problem. Figure 18-4 helps sort out the issues. The figure shows the labor demand schedule — the marginal product of labor (MPN) — with the real wage on the vertical axis and N as the full-employment labor supply. The full-employment real wage is $(w/P)_0$.

One interpretation of the unemployment problem of the early 1980s was that the economy was at a point such as A at a real wage $(w/P)'$. At point A firms hire only an amount of labor N' which falls short of full employment because the real wage is too high. The economy suffers from *classical*, or *real wage, unemployment*. The cure is either a reduction in the real wage to $(w/P)_0$ or else productivity growth or increased investment that shifts the *MPN* schedule out and to the right and thus reduces unemployment.

An alternative interpretation is that the economy was at a point such as A'. Again there is unemployment, but this time the real wage is not the problem. Firms are not willing to hire more workers than N' because they cannot sell the output. Aggregate demand is insufficient to absorb more output than is produced by an employment level N'. Therefore firms do not hire more workers, and accordingly, there is *Keynesian unemployment*. The cure, in this case, is not a cut in real wages but rather an expansion in aggregate demand through monetary or fiscal stimulus.

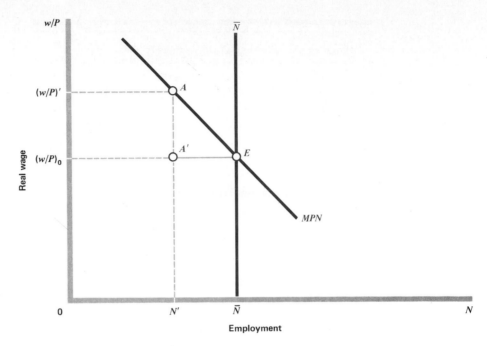

FIGURE 18-4   CLASSICAL OR KEYNESIAN UNEMPLOYMENT? The
schedule *MPN* is the marginal product of labor or the demand curve for
labor. The full-employment labor supply is $\overline{NN}$. At a real wage $(w/P)'$
there is "high real wage" unemployment because firms only want to hire
a labor force of N', which falls short of the supply $\overline{N}$. But it is also
possible that even at the lower wage $(w/P)_0$ firms only want to hire N'
of labor because they cannot sell the output that would be produced by
a larger labor force. The question is to know whether the unemployment
results from high real wages, as at point A, or from insufficient
aggregate demand, as at point A'.

In both cases there is unemployment. In both cases it is unprofitable for
firms to hire more labor than N'. In one case the problem is that labor is too
expensive; in the other there is no market for the increased output. But it is
essential to identify what kind of unemployment the economy faces before
designing policy action. Because we do not know the equilibrium real wage,
there is no direct way to decide whether unemployment is Keynesian or
classical.

In all likelihood in the early eighties, there was some classical unemployment in Europe, because real wages had not adjusted enough in response to
the increased price of oil and reduced productivity growth. But in addition a
dose of Keynesian unemployment was superimposed between 1980 and

1982, so that the economy was to the left of point A. In that case expansionary aggregate demand policies would go some way toward reducing unemployment, but there was also a need to cut labor costs relative to labor productivity.

There is also a question of why, if the real wage is too high, the existence of massive unemployment has not driven it down. The argument that has been advanced here distinguishes between insiders and outsiders in a firm. The wage is set between the firm and those working inside it. There is no easy way for the outsiders — the unemployed — to affect the wage. These theories do not explain, however, why other firms are not set up to hire the unemployed at low wages.

The European unemployment problem is becoming so severe and prolonged that the influence of that event will almost certainly substantially change theories of unemployment in the next few years. One possible change may be that the natural rate of unemployment will come to be seen as being heavily influenced by the recent behavior of unemployment, with high unemployment driving the natural rate up.[42]

18-9 WHERE DOES IT ALL LEAD?

At the start of this chapter we asked why macroeconomics suffers from such rapidly changing opinions. The answer is that it does not. There has been an evolution from simple Keynesianism toward a more sophisticated approach, not a series of rapidly changing beliefs. Macroeconomics has evolved, and it now gives more weight to monetary factors and to aggregate supply, emphasizing the roles of both expectations and labor market institutions. The recent work reviewed in Section 18-7 does not lead to a significantly different overall view of the economy — rather it should be viewed as attempting to develop microeconomic foundations for existing macroeconomics.

The rational expectations – equilibrium approach does pose a more radical challenge to the standard way of viewing the economy, and it has already had a major impact on mainstream macroeconomics. As of now, it remains far from a major empirical success, though it has more theoretical appeal. Whether it will lead to the replacement of current mainstream macroeconomics with a new standard model remains to be seen — and time and evidence will determine that.

If there haven't in fact been frequent changes of opinion in macroeconomics, why does it still seem that way? Because macroeconomic issues are important, macroeconomics is both news and politically useful. Politicians look for economists with the arguments to support their positions. For instance, supply-side economists had an influential role in the Reagan adminis-

---

[42] A theory of this type is developed in Olivier Blanchard and Lawrence Summers, "Hysteresis and the European Unemployment Problem," *NBER Macroeconomics Annual* (Cambridge, Mass.: MIT Press, 1986).

tration because the President wanted to cut taxes and needed professional support. No matter that the radical supply-side arguments were accepted by only a very small part of the profession: they provided at least some intellectual support for a policy that was based more on the President's ideology than on a detailed analysis of the potential effects of the tax cuts.

It is hoped that careful study will cumulate over the years to improved knowledge. Opinions, of course, change as new evidence accumulates, but genuine revolutions in thinking are rare. There was a Keynesian revolution in the thirties and a significant shift toward monetarism in the fifties and sixties — which was easily accommodated by expanding the Keynesian framework. There may be a rational expectations revolution in progress. Even if it succeeds, it will build in much of the existing structure of macroeconomics. And even if it does not radically reshape macroeconomics, it will, nonetheless, make for serious changes in understanding of the formation of expectations and the operation of economic policy. It has, in addition, spurred new work on the microfoundations of wage and price determination.

There was never a radical supply-side revolution.

The hope is that study of existing macroeconomics combined with the right degree of skepticism and questioning will make it possible for you to reach your own conclusions when the next brand of economics hits the headlines.

18-10 SUMMARY

1. Economic performance in the United States (and other countries) was much worse from 1969 to 1982 than during the sixties. There were four recessions in the latter period and none in the 1961–1969 period. The poor economic performance led to a search for explanations and cures. Since 1982 the inflation rate has declined substantially.

2. Monetarism lays heavy stress on the money stock as determining the level of output in the short run and the inflation rate in the long run. The essential step in the advance of monetarism was the Friedman-Schwartz analysis of the great depression as having been significantly worsened by extremely poor monetary policy.

3. Monetarists generally view the money supply as having powerful, but not easily predictable, effects on the economy. Money works with long and variable lags. For that reason monetarists favor a monetary rule. Monetarists argue that interest rates are a poor guide to the direction of monetary policy. They also believe that the private economy is inherently stable.

4. Monetarism's influence on economic policy can be seen in the adoption of money targeting in major countries. Monetarism has also been influential in several policy episodes in which tight money was used to bring down

the inflation rate. This takes a long time and works by creating a recession that puts pressure on wages and prices.

5. The rational expectations – equilibrium approach to macroeconomics has two components. The first is a theory of expectations, arguing that people form expectations using all available information and do not make systematic mistakes. The second is the equilibrium approach. This assumes that markets are in equilibrium each period and attributes deviations of output from normal levels to imperfect information.

6. The equilibrium approach implies that monetary policy can affect real output only by creating surprises. Early empirical evidence supported this view, but later evidence is less favorable.

7. Equilibrium real business cycle theory denies any causal role for money in the business cycle. Rather the cycle is seen as resulting from real shocks hitting the economy, being then distributed through the economy and also into future periods by a variety of propagation mechanisms. The main real shocks are to productivity and government spending. The main propagation mechanism is intertemporal substitution of leisure and consumption. More standard mechanisms, such as inventory accumulation and investment in physical capital, also play a role.

8. The rational expectations approach to policy making emphasizes the credibility of policies as an important factor determining their success or failure. The approach views institutional reform as the main way to get better policy.

9. Supply-side economics focuses on the incentive effects of taxation. There are two groups — mainstream and radical. The radical group attracted much attention at the time the new Reagan fiscal policy was going into effect in 1981. They argued that incentive effects of taxes were powerful enough that tax cuts would not cause a major budget deficit and would have a powerful supply-side effect on inflation. Neither argument was supported by later events. Mainstream supply siders continue to be influential in both policy making and economics.

10. A synthesis combines rational expectations assumptions with institutional features of the economy, such as long-term labor contracts. This can explain the slow adjustment of the economy to changes in monetary policy.

11. Efficiency wage theories explain wage stickiness as a result of losses in productivity that would occur if firms cut wages. In combination with small menu costs, efficiency wage theory can produce sticky wages and prices.

12. Profit sharing has been suggested as a means of increasing the level and stability of employment. The proposal has received attention especially in Europe, where unemployment has continued rising over 15 years. Explanations for European unemployment focus on high real wages and on inadequate demand.

KEY TERMS

Monetary rule

Rational expectations – equilibrium approach

Credibility

Imperfect information

Real business cycles

Propagation mechanism

Intertemporal substitution of leisure

Supply-side economics

Reaganomics

Efficiency wage

Small menu costs

Profit-sharing

PROBLEMS

1. Figure 18-3 shows the growth rate of money for the 1979 – 1986 period. To what extent do those data justify the view that inflation is caused by money growth? (Explain your answer.)

2. Using the *IS-LM* model, examine the effects of a combination of tight money and easy fiscal policy on the real interest rate. To what extent is that analysis supported by the data in Table 18-2?

3. (a) In what ways is monetarism closer to Keynesianism than to the rational expectations – equilibrium approach?

   (b) In what ways is monetarism closer to the rational expectations – equilibrium approach than to Keynesianism?

4. Distinguish and define the two components of the rational expectations – equilibrium approach to macroeconomics.

5. Suppose that people did not believe the Fed was serious about stopping inflation in 1979, and 1980, and 1981. Can you then reconcile the 1981 – 1982 recession with the rational expectations approach? Explain.

6. (a) Explain why, in the aggregate supply and demand model of Chapter 14, more work is done in booms than recessions.

   (b) Contrast this with the real business cycle explanation.

7. Supply-side economics points, appropriately, to the importance of incentives in determining economic behavior. Why then have mainstream macroeconomists generally been critical of radical supply-side economics?

8. (a) Why according to efficiency wage theory are employers reluctant to cut wages?

   (b) Suppose there were always some jobs available at a low enough wage. Could efficiency wages still help explain why high unemployment can continue for year after year?

9. (a) Explain the idea of profit sharing.

   (b) In what ways could profit sharing improve macroeconomic performance?

10. (a) Check a source such as the *Economic Report of the President* to find out whether the European unemployment picture has improved at all since 1985.

    (b) Why is high European unemployment a challenge for economics to explain?

11. Evaluate the quote of Keynes with which this chapter begins.

12. In the introduction we note contradictory views on the budget deficit. One group of economists believes that large deficits cause high real interest rates and a balance of trade deficit. Another group believes that the budget deficit has no real effects. Going back to Chapter 17, trace the key point that leads to this difference of opinion. What is your opinion of this issue in light of Chapter 17?

LONG-TERM GROWTH AND PRODUCTIVITY

In this chapter we turn our attention away from short-run problems of the business cycle to look at where the economy has been and may be heading in the long term. Figure 19-1 shows real GNP since 1889. Over long periods output shows roughly steady growth. The business cycle appears as short-run fluctuations around the trend path of output.

From 1889 to 1986 real GNP grew at an average annual rate of 3.2 percent in the United States. At that rate of growth, real GNP doubles every 22 years. As Table 19-1 shows, *per capita* real GNP grew at the slower rate of 1.8 percent, doubling every 39 years. At that rate, a 20-year-old college student could anticipate per capita GNP doubling before she reached retirement. The difference between the growth rate of total real GNP and that of per capita real GNP is the result of population growth, which averaged 1.4 percent per annum over the period.

To analyze the long-run behavior of the economy we focus on *trend*, or *potential output*. The major questions we pose are, What determines the *growth rate* of potential output? Why does output grow over time and how

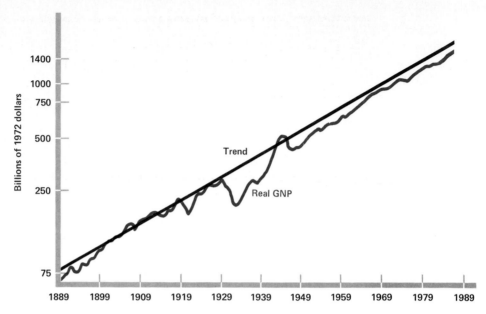

FIGURE 19-1   REAL GNP IN THE UNITED STATES, 1989–1986
(billions of 1972 dollars). (*Source:* Data Resources, Inc., and *Historical Statistics of the United States.*)

fast? Will growth in the future be as high as it has been in the past? Will the economy keep on a trend of rising output per capita, as it has been in the past century?

In discussing the growth of potential output we are also posing the question, What are future levels of output likely to be? Even small differences in the growth rate of potential output cumulate over time to the large differences

TABLE 19-1	AVERAGE ANNUAL GROWTH RATES, 1889–1986			
	1889–1986		1966–1986	
	GNP	GNP per capita	GNP	GNP per capita
GNP growth, % per year	3.2	1.8	2.6	1.6

Source: U.S. Department of Commerce, *Long-term Economic Growth, 1860–1970,* 1973 *Economic Report of the President,* and estimates by the authors.

TABLE 19-2   COMPARATIVE PER CAPITA INCOME LEVELS ($U.S. in 1983)

	U.S	Japan	Korea	Brazil	Mexico
Per capita income (1984 $)	15,390	10,630	2,110	1,720	2,040
Growth rate of per capita income 1965–1984 (% per year)	1.7	4.7	6.6	4.6	2.9

Source: World Bank, *World Development Report 1986.*

in the level of per capita GNP and hence in the standard of living. With a growth rate of per capita income of 2 percent per year it takes 35 years for per capita GNP to double. But if the growth rate is only 1.0 percent, it takes 70 years to achieve a doubling of output per head. The growth rate of potential output is thus of central importance. If two economies start off with the same level of per capita real GNP, an economy growing at 2 percent per capita will have double the per capita GNP of one growing at 1 percent within 70 years. Whatever the shortcomings of real GNP as a measure of welfare, the residents of the faster growing country will be materially much better off as time goes on.

The question of comparing income levels is addressed in Table 19-2 in terms of an international perspective.[1] Table 19-2 shows data for the United States, Japan, and several developing countries. Using the United States as the benchmark, the first row shows the respective countries' income levels. The second row shows growth rates of per capita income.

It is interesting to note from Table 19-2 that U.S. *growth* in per capita income is much lower than that of the other countries, but that its *level* of per capita income is much higher. But if Korea, for example, maintains a high growth rate long enough it will ultimately catch up with and even surpass the U.S. level of income. Using the growth rates in Table 19-2, we can calculate that it would take 42 years to get there. That may seem to be a long period, but it might be instructive to think of Japan in the post-World War II period. In the past 40 years U.S. real income per capita only doubled but that of Japan increased by a factor of more than 10. In that perspective many of the newly industrialized countries in Asia and Latin America may well get within the

---

[1] For historical international comparisons see Angus Maddison, *Phases of Capitalist Development* (London: Oxford University Press, 1982). The difficulties with comparing incomes across countries and a methodology for these comparisons are presented in Irving Kravis et al., *World Product and Income* (Baltimore, Md.: Johns Hopkins University Press, 1982).

reach of the old and established nations like the United Kingdom, Germany, or even the U.S. within the next 30 to 50 years.

Because future per capita GNP levels are so sensitive to the growth rate of potential output, it is worth worrying about changes of even ¹/₁₀ of 1 percent in the long-run growth rate of output. To answer questions about the growth rate of potential output, we go back to fundamentals. With output at the full-employment level, and hence the available factor supplies fully utilized, there are only two possible sources of growth. *Factor supplies may grow, or the productivity of factors of production may increase.* This, in turn, raises the questions of what determines the growth of factor supplies and their productivity, and what the quantitative link is between growth in factor supplies and productivity, and output growth.

There are two complementary approaches to these questions. One is *growth theory*, which models the interactions among factor supplies, output growth, saving, and investment in the process of growth. The other is *growth accounting*, which attempts to quantify the contribution of different determinants of output growth. The two approaches draw on a common analytical framework which we now outline.

19-1 SOURCES OF GROWTH IN REAL INCOME

In this section we use the production function to study the *sources of growth*. We show that growth in labor, growth in capital, and improved technical efficiency are the three sources of growth.

The Production Function

In earlier chapters we introduced the concept of a production function. The *production function* links the amount of output produced in an economy to the inputs of factors of production and to the state of technical knowledge. Equation (1) represents the production function in symbols:

$$Y = AF(K, N) \tag{1}$$

where K and N denote the inputs of capital and labor and A denotes the state of technology. The production function $AF(K, N)$ in (1) states that the output produced depends on factor inputs K and N and on the state of technology. Increases in factor inputs and improved technology lead to an increase in output supply.

The next step is to make these links more precise by looking at an expression for the growth rate of output. In equation (2) (which is derived in the appendix) we show the determinants of output growth.[2]

---

[2] Equation (2) applies when there are *constant returns to scale* in production; that is, increases in both inputs, in the same proportion, increase output in that proportion.

$$\Delta Y/Y = (1 - \theta) \times \Delta N/N + \theta \times \Delta K/K + \Delta A/A$$

$$\begin{array}{c} \text{Output} \\ \text{growth} \end{array} = \begin{array}{c} \text{labor} \\ \text{share} \end{array} \times \begin{array}{c} \text{labor} \\ \text{growth} \end{array} + \begin{array}{c} \text{capital} \\ \text{share} \end{array} \times \begin{array}{c} \text{capital} \\ \text{growth} \end{array} + \begin{array}{c} \text{technical} \\ \text{progress} \end{array} \qquad (2)$$

where $(1 - \theta)$ and θ are weights equal to the income shares of labor and of capital in production.

Equation (2) summarizes the contributions of growth of inputs and of improved productivity to growth of output:

1. The contribution of the growth of factor inputs is seen in the first two terms. Labor and capital each contribute an amount equal to their individual growth rate *multiplied by the share of that input in income.*
2. The rate of improvement of technology, called *technical progress* or the *growth of total factor productivity,* is the third term in equation (2). The growth rate of total factor productivity is the amount by which output would be increasing as a result of improvements in methods of production, with all inputs unchanged. In other words, there is growth in total factor productivity when we get more output from the same factors of production.[3]

EXAMPLE

Suppose the income share of capital is 0.25 and that of labor is 0.75. These values correspond approximately to the actual values for the U.S. economy. Furthermore, let labor force growth be 1.2 percent and growth of the capital stock 3 percent, and suppose technical progress increases at the rate of 1.5 percent. What is the growth rate of full-employment output? Applying equation (2) we obtain a growth rate of $\Delta Y/Y = 3.15$ percent ($= 0.75 \times 1.2$ percent $+ 0.25 \times 3$ percent $+ 1.5$ percent).

An important point to note in equation (2) is that the growth rates of capital and labor are weighted by the respective income shares. The reason for these weights is that the importance of a 1 percent change in capital or labor to production differs, and that difference in importance is measured by their relative income shares. Specifically, if labor has a larger share than capital, output rises more when labor increases by, say, 10 percent than if capital increases by 10 percent.

Returning to our example, if labor alone grows by 1 percent, output will grow by 0.75 percent, using the 0.75 income share for labor. If capital alone grows by 1 percent, output will grow by only 0.25 percent, reflecting the smaller importance of capital in production. But if each grows by 1 percent, so does output.

---

[3] There is a distinction between *labor productivity* and total factor productivity. Labor productivity is just the ratio of output to labor input, Y/N. Labor productivity certainly grows as a result of technical progress, but it also grows because of the accumulation of capital per worker.

This point — that growth in inputs is weighted by factor shares — turns out to be quite critical when we ask how much extra growth we get by raising the rate of growth of the capital stock, say by supply-side policies. Suppose in the example above, with everything else the same, capital growth had been twice as high, 6 percent instead of 3 percent. Doing the calculations with the help of equation (2), we find that output growth would increase to 3.9 percent, rising by less than a percentage point even though capital growth rises by three percentage points.

19-2 EMPIRICAL ESTIMATES OF THE SOURCES OF GROWTH

The previous section prepares us for an analysis of empirical studies that deal with sources of growth. Equation (2) suggests that the growth in output can be explained by growth in factor inputs, weighted by their shares in income, and by technical progress. An early and famous study by Robert Solow of MIT dealt with the period 1909–1949 in the United States.[4] Solow's surprising conclusion was that over 80 percent of the growth in output per labor hour over that period was due to technical progress, that is, to factors other than growth in the input of capital per labor hour. Specifically, Solow estimated for the United States an equation similar to equation (2) that identifies capital and labor growth along with technical progress as the sources of output growth. Of the average annual growth of total GNP of 2.9 percent per year over that period, he concluded that 0.32 percent was attributable to capital accumulation, 1.09 percent per annum was due to the increases in the input of labor, and the remaining 1.49 percent was due to technical progress. Per capita output grew at 1.81 percent, with 1.49 percent of that increase resulting from technical progress.

The very large part of the growth contribution that is taken up by "technical progress" makes that term really a catchall for omitted factors and poor measurement of the capital and labor inputs. Further work therefore turned quite naturally to explore this residual, that is, growth not explained by capital accumulation or increased labor input.

Perhaps the most comprehensive of the subsequent studies is that by Edward Denison.[5] Using data for the period 1929–1982, Denison attributed 1.9 percent of the 2.9 percent annual rate of increase in real output to increased factor inputs. Output per labor hour grew at the rate of 1.58 percent,

---

[4] "Technical Change and the Aggregate Production Function," *Review of Economics and Statistics,* August 1957.

[5] *Accounting for United States Economic Growth 1929–1969* (Washington, D.C.: The Brookings Institution, 1974). See also E. Denison's *Accounting for Slower Economic Growth: The United States in the 1970s* (ibid., 1980), and *Trends in American Economic Growth, 1929–1982* (Washington, D.C.: The Brookings Institution, 1985).

of which 1.02 percent was due to technical progress. Denison's findings thus support Solow's estimate that most of the growth in output per labor hour is due to technical progress. Table 19-3 shows a breakdown of the increased factor inputs.

Technical progress explains one-third of the growth in output, with growth in total factor inputs accounting for the other two-thirds of growth. Consider now the breakdown between the various components of increased factor use. Here increases in the labor force get a very large credit for their contribution to growth. Why? Because labor grows very fast? The answer is provided by equation (2), which suggests that labor's growth rate has a relatively large weight mainly because labor's share of income is relatively large. The counterpart is obviously the relatively low share of capital. As noted above, even if capital and labor grew at the same rate, the fact that they have different shares in income—labor having a share of about 75 percent and capital having a share of about 25 percent—implies that labor would be credited with a larger contribution toward growth.

Next we look at the various sources of increased factor productivity or increased output per unit factor input. Here the striking fact is the importance of advances in knowledge that account for almost two-thirds of the contribution of technical progress toward growth. Two other sources of increased factor productivity are worth recording. One is the increase in productivity that stems from improved resource allocation. Here we can think of people leaving low-paying jobs or low-income areas and moving to better jobs or locations, thus contributing to increased output or income growth. An important element is relocation from farms to cities.

TABLE 19-3	SOURCES OF GROWTH OF TOTAL NATIONAL INCOME, 1929–1982
Source of growth	Growth rate, percent per annum
Total factor input 　Labor: 1.34 　Capital: 0.56	1.90
Output per unit of input 　Knowledge: 0.66 　Resource allocation: 0.23 　Economies of scale: 0.26 　Other; −0.13	1.02
National income	2.92

Source: E. Denison, *Trends in American Economic Growth, 1929–1982*, (Washington, D.C.: The Brookings Institution, 1985), table 8-1.

The remaining significant part of technical progress is *economies of scale*. This is a bit troublesome because we assumed away economies of scale in deriving equation (2). In deriving that equation, we explicitly assumed constant returns to scale, but we find now that more than 10 percent of the average annual growth in income is due to an expanding scale of operation. As the scale of operation of the economy expands, fewer inputs are required per unit output, presumably because we can avail ourselves of techniques that are economically inefficient at a small-scale level but yield factor savings at a larger scale of production.

The major significance of Denison's work, and the work in this area of others, including Nobel laureate Simon Kuznets (1901–1985) and J. W. Kendrick, is to point out that there is no single critical source of real income growth. The early finding by Solow that growth in the capital stock makes a minor, though not negligible, contribution to growth stands up well to the test of later research. Capital investment is certainly necessary — particularly because some technological improvements require the use of new types of machines — but it is clear that other sources of growth can make an important contribution. Furthermore, since for most purposes we are interested in output per head, we have to recognize that we are left with only technical progress and growth in capital to achieve increased output per head. Here we have to ask, What are the components of technical progress? *Advances in knowledge stand out as a major source and point to the roles of research, education, and training as important sources of growth.*[6]

The Decline in Growth

We saw in Table 19-1 the decline in U.S. output growth in the 1970s. The decline in growth was not limited to the United States. In the 1970s trend growth rates of output declined throughout the industrialized world. Pinpointing the exact source of the decline remains a controversial issue, but the growth accounting framework of equation (2) provides some help. We can rewrite that equation, taking employment growth to the left-hand side, to obtain an equation that gives the determinants of the growth in output per head, $\Delta Y/Y - \Delta N/N$:

$$\frac{\Delta Y}{Y} - \frac{\Delta N}{N} = \theta \left(\frac{\Delta K}{K} - \frac{\Delta N}{N} \right) + \frac{\Delta A}{A} \tag{2a}$$

The equation states that output per head grows either because capital per head increases or because total factor productivity rises.

---

[6] A collection of useful papers on the sources of growth are contained in Edmund Phelps (ed.), *The Goal of Economics Growth* (New York: Norton, 1969), and Dennis C. Mueller (ed.), *The Political Economy of Growth* (New Haven, Conn.: Yale University Press, 1983).

TABLE 19-4	THE DECLINE IN GROWTH OF OUTPUT PER PERSON EMPLOYED (Percent per Year)		
	U.S.	Japan	Germany
1960–1973	2.0	8.4	4.2
1973–1983	0.4	2.8	2.3

Source: OECD *Historical Statistics 1960–83.*

Table 19-4 compares the sources of growth over the 1960–1973 period with those of the more recent 1973–1982 period of slowdown. The data are presented for the United States, Japan, and Germany. In each case there is a large reduction in the growth of output per hour of labor. The growth reduction, in each case, is a reflection of reduced capital accumulation and of reduced total factor productivity growth.

In the case of the United States there are estimates for the sources of the decline in output per person employed. Where output per person employed had grown at the rate of 2.3 percent per year in the 1948–1973 period it declined to only 0.4 percent in the 1973–1983 period. The decline in the growth of output per person employed was not due to a reduction in capital formation. Capital accumulation followed much the same pattern as in the earlier period, but output per unit of input or total factor productivity turned from 1.5 percent per year to −0.27. In Table 19-3 we saw that total factor productivity accounted for one-third of the growth in output and two-thirds in growth of output per unit of labor. It thus was *the* source of growth and, accordingly, its disappearance in the last decade brought with it a sharp downturn in potential output growth.

A negative number here is, of course, surprising. The explanation includes a worsened age-skill mix of the population and costs of "nuisance" outputs such as investment in pollution abatement and crime prevention. The category "advances in knowledge" shows a negative growth contribution.[7] A particularly important source of negative growth in total factor productivity was regulation.

In an international comparison of the sources of the growth slowdown conducted by J. W. Kendrick, government regulation appears uniformly as a negative contribution to growth.[8] In comparing the two periods, regulation is

---

[7] For detailed accounting of the decline in growth see Denison, op. cit., and J. W. Kendrick, "The Implications of Growth Accounting Models" in C. Hulten and I. Sawhill (eds.), *The Legacy of Reaganomics* (Washington, D.C.: Urban Institute Press, 1984).

[8] See J. W. Kendrick, "International Comparisons of Recent Productivity Trends," in W. Fellner (ed.), *Contemporary Economic Problems* (Washington, D.C.: American Enterprise Institute, 1981).

one of the items responsible for the reduced growth in the 1970s. Interestingly, increased regulation accounts for a much smaller cost in terms of reduced growth in the United States, where regulation is a big issue, than in Japan.

In principle, government regulation could be a source of increased efficiency and therefore of growth. But in none of the nine countries and two subperiods studied by Kendrick is this the case. Government regulation, from this account, appears harmful to growth. But in interpreting that finding we must bear in mind that the regulation, which reduced pollution, brought improvements in the quality of the environment. These improvements make us better off but do not show up in GNP.

19-3 OUTPUT GROWTH AND SUPPLY-SIDE ECONOMICS

In the early 1980s, partly as a result of disappointment with slow growth and generally poor macroeconomic performance, *supply-side economics* (discussed in Chapter 18) attracted much attention. We now concentrate on the solid aspect, which argues that the level and/or the growth rate of output could be significantly increased through policies designed to promote greater efficiency, reduced regulation, greater willingness to work, and greater willingness to save and invest.[9]

In discussing full-employment output in earlier chapters we took the labor supply to be given and independent of the real wage, and similarly, we assumed a given stock of capital. But the basic premise of supply-side economics is that capital and labor supplies are not given, independent of incentives to work, save, and invest. On the contrary, it is argued that the labor-leisure choice is strongly affected by the *after-tax* real wage and that the willingness to save and invest is likewise affected by the *after-tax* rates of return on assets. This perspective directs attention to fiscal policy as influencing factor supplies and hence the level and rate of increase of output.

Labor Supply

Households have to choose how much labor to supply. In practice that means choosing how many members of the family work and for how many hours per week or month. At first sight there appears to be little choice since the typical job comes with a given number of working hours per week. But that is not quite the case once we take into account the possibility that more than one

---

[9] On supply-side economics see particularly Barry Bosworth, *Tax Incentives and Economic Growth* (Washington, D.C.: The Brookings Institution, 1984), Charles Hulten and Isabel Sawhill (eds.), *The Legacy of Reaganomics*, (The Urban Institute, 1984), Laurence Meyer (ed.), *The Supply Side Effects of Economic Policy* (Federal Reserve Bank of St. Louis, 1981), and Martin Feldstein, "Supply Side Economics: Old Truths and New Claims," *American Economic Review*, May 1986.

family member might work or the possibilities of working overtime hours or holding part-time jobs. Households' labor supply can thus vary in response to incentives.

The main determinant of labor supply is the after-tax real wage. Suppose it rises. Then some family members who had preferred to stay home may now be tempted into the labor force. But for those already working, the real wage increase has ambiguous effects on labor supply. The *income effect* of the wage increase tends to reduce labor supply because it is now possible to work less and earn more. But because every hour of leisure is now more costly, the *substitution effect* tends to increase labor supply. The outcome of conflicting income and substitution effects is thus a matter for empirical study. In addition, of course, higher participation in the labor force will tend to increase labor supply when the after-tax real wage rises.

Empirical Evidence

Jerry Hausman of MIT has shown in a number of studies that the household labor supply increases *significantly* in response to increased after-tax real wages.[10] This implies that changes in the tax structure that increase the after-tax real wage would increase labor supply and output. Hausman finds that the progressivity of income taxes reduces labor supply by someone already working. The magnitude of the effect can be judged from the following experiment. Suppose the progressive income tax structure were eliminated and replaced by a flat 15 percent income tax which would lead to the same amount of revenue. What would happen to labor supply? Hausman estimates that total labor supply would rise by 5 percent. With an income share of 0.75, a 5 percent growth in labor supply would increase the level of full-employment output by 3.75 percent. This is certainly a nonnegligible gain, although the policy experiment — the move to a flat income tax — is far more radical than the 1986 tax reform.

Supply of Capital

The supply of capital represents the cumulation of past investment. The capital stock grows if additions to the stock more than offset the depreciation due to wear and tear and to obsolescence.

A supply-side point of view emphasizes the links between saving and investment. Recall that when the goods market clears and when net exports are zero, investment minus saving equals the budget surplus, or

$$I = S + (T - G) \tag{3}$$

---

[10] See J. Hausman, "Labor Supply and the Natural Unemployment Rate," in L. Meyer, *The Supply Side Effects* op. cit., and Hank Aaron and Joe Pechman (eds.), *How Taxes Affect Economic Behavior* (Washington, D.C.: The Brookings Institution, 1981).

Equation (3) shows that to raise investment, and thus growth of the capital stock, we require increased saving or reduced government budget deficits. Supply-side economics has focused on the incentives to save and invest. Supply-side economists argue that regulation has reduced the productivity of investment and that corporate and personal income taxes further reduce the rate of return eventually received by the savers who provide the funds needed to finance investment. If savers receive a lower rate of return as a result of taxation, say the supply-siders, they reduce saving, and therefore capital accumulation is reduced.

For instance, consider an investment that yields 12 percent per year in real terms. That is, someone who undertakes the investment, costing $100 in year 1, earns $12 per year in real terms forever after (net of labor and material costs). If the income tax rate is 40 percent, the saver can at most earn, after tax, 60 percent of 12 percent, or 7.2 percent. As a result of taxation, the return to saving is substantially reduced. Accordingly, claim supply-siders, the higher the tax rate, the less saving there will be.[11]

What supply-side policies increase the yield on saving? There are a variety of means of exempting the return on saving from taxation. For instance, an individual can contribute up to $2,000 per year to an IRA (individual retirement account). The amount contributed is not counted as income for federal tax purposes, and the interest is not taxed either. There are other such tax-free means of saving. There is also considerable support for the use of a *consumption tax* rather than the income tax. A consumption tax levies taxes only on consumption spending, not on income. Since the difference between income and consumption is saving, a consumption tax effectively exempts any amount that is saved from being taxed in the year it is earned, and thereby encourages saving.

There is considerable disagreement on the issue of the response of saving to changes in its return. The contention that increased after-rax rates of return to saving will *strongly* raise saving does not have much support. Once again we have two opposing effects: With increased interest rates, less saving is needed to ensure a given future income, say, for retirement. This effect (actually an income effect) reduces saving. At the same time a dollar saved today yields increased future wealth and consumption and would therefore lead households to postpone consumption and increase saving (this is the substitution effect). The balance of effects is theoretically uncertain.

The empirical evidence does not settle the issue of whether changes in the after-tax rate of return affect the rate of saving.[12] Therefore policies that

---

[11] See M. Boskin, "Economic Growth and Productivity," in M. Boskin (ed.), *The Economy in the 1980s: A Program for Growth and Stability* (San Francisco: Institute for Contemporary Studies, 1980); the *Economic Report of the President,* 1982 and 1983; and especially, Michael K. Evans, *The Truth about Supply-Side Economics* (New York: Basic Books, 1983).

[12] Gerald A. Carlino, in "Interest Rate Effects and Intertemporal Consumption," *Journal of Monetary Economics,* March 1982, reviews and extends the (ambiguous) evidence. See, too, Larry Kotlikoff, "Taxation and Savings: A Neoclassical Perspective," *Journal of Economic Literature,* December 1984.

reduce taxes on saving as a means of generating more saving, capital formation, and growth have an uncertain effect on the economy.

Another line of argument questions the quantitative importance of policies to promote saving. We note from the growth equation (2a) that growth in capital receives a very small weight in determining output growth. Even if policies led to a 10 percent rise in the capital-labor ratio, output per head would only increase by 2.5 percent. But to achieve a 10 percent rise in the capital-labor ratio, say, over 10 years, net investment as a share of GNP would have to double.[13]

Regulation

Government regulation involves a tradeoff. Government regulations serve some social purpose (the environment, safety, conservation), but they also involve costs to firms that have to abide by them. Regulation therefore reduces business profitability. Policy makers are keenly aware that the tradeoff exists and therefore, rightly, focus on inefficient regulation and particularly costly (nonmarket) regulation as requiring review. That process has been under way for some time, but it would be a mistake to expect major growth in output from reduced regulation.

Budget Deficits and Growth

In equation (3) we showed that private investment and capital formation will be higher when saving is higher and the government budget deficit is smaller.[14] Government budget deficits thus imply, other things equal, a reduction in full-employment output growth. Government budget deficits absorb private saving—households buy government securities rather than the stocks or bonds that firms issue to finance their investment. Therefore funds are diverted from growth toward other purposes. It is clear that if the only objective is to promote growth, the government should balance the budget or even run a surplus to free resources for investment. However, there is a tradeoff between growth and the social objectives that may lie behind a budget deficit.

---

[13] Suppose the capital stock is equal to 3 times output. Then a 10 percent increase in capital represents an amount equal to 30 percent of GNP or, over a 10-year period, an increase in net investment of 3 percent of GNP. Net investment is now between 2 and 5 percent of GNP. The increase therefore would imply doubling the share of net investment in GNP.

[14] We implicitly assume that all investment is undertaken by the private sector, not by the government. But in many countries government investment is a large part of total investment. Larry Kotlikoff, "The Economic Impact of Deficit Financing," IMF *Staff Papers*, November 1984, shows particularly strong adverse effects of budget deficits on longterm growth.

Evaluating Supply-Side Economics and Growth Incentives

The emphasis on increasing incentives to work, save, and invest is the valid core of supply-side economics. There are two questions here. The first is, Will the proposed policies work, that is, increase future potential output? The second question is, If the policies do work, how far should we go in creating incentives to increase future potential output?

Policies to increase the labor supply by reducing taxes and policies to increase investment by reducing government budget deficits and by providing investment subsidies would be effective in increasing potential output today and in the future. Thus supply-side policies are available. But we can also go overboard on such policies. If we are reducing government budget deficits while reducing other taxes, we are also reducing government spending. We could reduce government spending by getting rid of the armed forces. But most people would think it better to have higher taxes and some armed forces than lower taxes and no armed forces. And similarly, the government provides many useful services through its welfare programs — services that most people prefer to have — rather than aiming purely to maximize the level of investment.

Further, given government spending, and at full employment, increases in saving imply reductions in consumption. Thus in supply-side economics we are trading off current consumption for future consumption. We are trading off the consumption of those now alive for the consumption of their children and children who come later yet. This process also can go too far. In the extreme, we (society) would not want to force the current generation to consume at a bare survival level just so their grandchildren can sit around their pools doing very little work while automated factories made possible by a huge volume of past investment produce a high level of output. Somewhere between not saving now and saving almost all of output, there is an optimal amount of saving to be done.

It is no easy task for society to decide what that optimal amount of saving is. Those who will be consuming in the future are not here to vote, because they have not yet been born. And those who are around now will have different views. Some may ask, as reportedly has Joan Robinson (1905–1984), the famous English economist, "What did posterity ever do for us?" Others may feel it is the duty of the parents to sacrifice for their children's sake. Ultimately the policy decisions that affect growth are settled politically.

19-4 MEASURING POTENTIAL OUTPUT

When policy makers decide to use monetary or fiscal policy to bring the economy closer to full employment, they need to know where to aim. If the full-employment unemployment rate were 6 percent, it would not make much sense to use expansionary fiscal policies at a 5.5 percent unemployment rate. Thus we need measures of the full-employment unemployment rate and the corresponding level of *potential output* or *full-employment output.* The concept draws on the ideas of growth accounting to construct a GNP series that can serve as a benchmark for policy planning.

There are two approaches to constructing a series for potential output. Both approaches use the production function of equation (1) as a conceptual framework, but they use it differently.

1. Data on capital, labor, and material inputs are used to estimate the production function. Then estimates of the high-employment factor supplies are inserted to calculate what potential output is. This point is expanded upon below.
2. The alternative approach does not attempt to identify the separate contributions to output of capital, labor, and other factors, but rather focuses on employment and labor productivity.

We start by sketching the second approach.

The Traditional Approach to Estimating Potential Output

The basic equation of the traditional approach uses as a starting point an identity that relates output to employment and to labor productivity, or output per hour of labor:

$$\text{Output} = \text{output per hour of labor} \times \text{total labor hours} \qquad (4)$$

or, in fewer words, output = productivity × hours. To move from here to potential output we need estimates of (1) the *high-employment* level of labor productivity and (2) the *high-employment* total labor hours. Because both labor hours and productivity vary over time and cyclically, the problem is to determine the high-employment value of each and to guess their future course.[15]

HIGH-EMPLOYMENT LABOR HOURS

Consider first the calculation involved in finding the high-employment number of work hours. This is the product of hours worked per person employed and the number of persons employed. The number of persons employed is a

---

[15] See A. M. Okun, "Potential GNP: Its Measurement and Significance," reprinted in his book *The Political Economy of Prosperity* (New York: Norton, 1970); and G. Perry, "Potential Output: Recent Issues and Present Trends," in *U.S. Productive Capacity* (St. Louis, Mo.: Center for the Study of American Business, Washington University, 1977).

function of the employment rate, the labor force, and the labor force participation rate in the population. Say the working age population is 200 million people, of whom 60 percent are in the labor force, of which, in turn, at full-employment 95 percent are employed, each of whom works for 2,000 hours per year. Then total high-employment work hours are 228,000 million hours. Equation (5) shows the formula

$$
\begin{array}{l}
\text{Total high-} \\
\text{employment} \\
\text{hours}
\end{array} =
\begin{array}{l}
\text{hours} \\
\text{per} \\
\text{worker}
\end{array} \times
\begin{array}{l}
\text{employment} \\
\text{ratio}
\end{array} \times
\begin{array}{l}
\text{labor force} \\
\text{participation} \\
\text{ratio}
\end{array} \times
\begin{array}{l}
\text{working} \\
\text{age} \\
\text{population}
\end{array}
\qquad (5)
$$

where each of the ratios on the right-hand side is evaluated at the high-employment level.

Equation (5) is interesting because it points to a number of different factors influencing labor hours. Among the factors, for example, is the sex and age composition of the labor force, which has a strong influence on the participation rate. But institutional factors and tax incentives, as we saw above, also influence the fraction of the population that is in the labor force. Shifts over time in the underlying determinants will change the labor force participation rate and hence, given the other determinants, total hours and potential output.

The employment ratio, or 1 minus the unemployment rate, is one of the determinants of high-employment hours. Here an estimate must be made of what is the high-employment rate of unemployment. The unemployment rate, as we saw in Chapter 15, is a weighted average of the unemployment rates of different groups — experienced workers and young people, men and women, each of which has different unemployment characteristics. The aggregate unemployment rate is therefore affected by shifts in the age-sex composition of the labor force. Young people, for example, have a higher full-employment unemployment rate. Therefore an increase in the proportion of young people in the labor force, as a consequence of the baby boom, would raise the aggregate full-employment unemployment rate.

The number of hours per workweek changes over time. The tendency has been toward a reduction. At the same time, because different sectors of the economy (manufacturing, services, construction) have slightly different workweeks, the economywide average is also influenced by the trend changes in the composition of output. Because the workweek is strongly influenced by cyclical factors, the trend and cyclical factors need to be disentangled here too.

PRODUCTIVITY

The second determinant of high-employment output in equation (4) is labor productivity. In Table 19-4 we saw the determinants of labor productivity, or output per hour. These include not only increases in capital per work hour, but also changes in the quality of labor, in knowledge, and in the regulatory

TABLE 19-5	GROWTH RATES OF ACTUAL AND POTENTIAL OUTPUT (Percent per Year)	
	1955–1970	1970–1985
Actual output	3.25	2.64
Potential output	3.22	2.85

Source: See footnote 16.

environment. As we have seen, productivity growth has not been constant in the past. It changes over time and very significantly over the business cycle. Once again it is necessary to disentangle the trend, change in trend, and cyclical factors to find out what the behavior of cyclically adjusted or high-employment productivity is.

THE HIGH-EMPLOYMENT BENCHMARK

The most difficult point in estimating potential output arises when we have to specify the benchmark unemployment rate that corresponds to full employment.

Estimates of potential output were published by the Council of Economic Advisers through 1981 and are still published by the U.S. Department of Commerce. The full-employment rate of unemployment was taken to be 4.0 percent in 1955, rising to 4.9 percent in 1973. The increase represents shifts in the composition of the labor force that we discussed above. Further shifts in the composition of the labor force raised official estimates of the high-employment level to above 6 percent in the late 1970s and the 1980s.

Figure 19-2 shows actual and potential output.[16] The trend growth rate of potential output has declined. Table 19-5 shows the growth rates of actual and potential output over the past 30 years. The large deterioration in performance in the past 15 years reflects the deterioration in productivity performance which we have already discussed.

UNCERTAINTY ABOUT POTENTIAL OUTPUT AND PRODUCTIVITY GROWTH

The low growth rate of output and the high unemployment rates of the last decade have created considerable uncertainty about both the full-employ-

---

[16] The potential output series is obtained by using for the period 1955–1973 the old series reported in the *Survey of Current Business,* November 1980 and April 1983, and from 1984 to 1986 the series using a bench mark of 6 percent unemployment reported in the March 1986 issue.

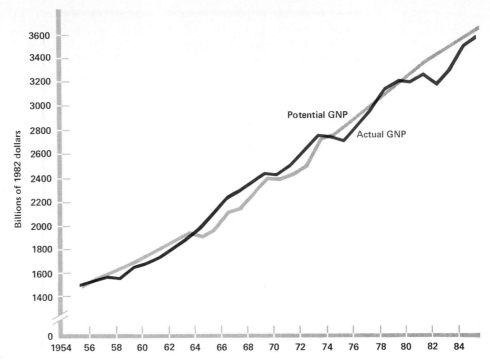

FIGURE 19-2 ACTUAL AND POTENTIAL OUTPUT, 1955–1986 (billions of 1982 dollars). (*Source: Survey of Current Business,* various issues.)

ment unemployment rate (and thus about potential output) and the growth rate of potential output. In response to the uncertainty, the Council of Economic Advisors stopped publishing calculations of potential output in 1982.

The reason for uncertainty is that since 1973, the unemployment rate has not been as low as 5 percent, the number then used by the U.S. Department of Commerce in its *Survey of Current Business.* Since that time, the unemployment rate went below 6 percent only in 1978 and 1979. Even then the lowest civilian unemployment rate was 5.6 percent. It seems almost certain that full employment corresponds more realistically to a benchmark rate of about 6 percent, and many argue for an even higher rate. The 6 percent rate underlies the potential output measures in Figure 19-2 for the period after 1973.

Despite the uncertainties about both the benchmark unemployment rate and the growth rate of potential output, we should note that we are talking about a relatively narrow range of unemployment rates. There is no doubt that the full-employment rate of unemployment is far below the 10 percent ranges of 1982–1983, and estimates above 7 percent are rare indeed. Estimates of the growth rate of potential output are more uncertain — but those estimates are of less immediate relevance to stabilization policy. The concept of potential output is still a highly useful one in understanding both the current state of the economy and the budget — since estimates of the high-employment budget depend on the estimate of full-employment output.[17]

The Production Function Approach

An alternative to equation (5) is to attempt directly to estimate the production function relation between output and the inputs of capital, labor, and materials. Once estimates of the relation between output and the inputs are obtained, the level of high-employment output can be calculated by using a high-employment series for capital and labor and a measure of the use of materials.

The production function approach attracted interest in part because it seemed a way of finding out just how important the energy shocks of the 1970s were in reducing the level or growth rate of potential output. The energy shocks were prime suspects in the search for an explanation of lower productivity growth because productivity growth fell most dramatically after the first oil shock in 1973. By using an explicit production function framework, an estimate can be obtained of the effect of increased energy prices on energy use and hence on output. This approach has turned out to be controversial. The reason is that the production function approach suggests a very significant decline in real potential output in response to increased energy costs.[18]

One study finds that a 10 percent rise in the real price of energy reduces output in the short run by 0.89 percent and in the long run by 1.22 percent. In the period 1974–1982 the real price of energy increased by 68 percent, which implies a reduction of potential output of about 8 percent.[19] For many observers this estimate of the role of energy is far too high. There is no question that energy does matter, but the precise estimate remains a subject of further research.

---

[17] The late William Fellner sharply questioned the entire idea of potential output. He argued that the notion of potential output is not useful because it seems to imply that only demand variables (reflected in the unemployment rate) determine the economy's potential output. But, said Fellner, supply-side variables also matter. See William Fellner, *The High Employment Budget and Potential Output* (Washington, D.C.: American Enterprise Institute, 1982).

[18] See J. Tatom, "Potential Output and the Recent Productivity Decline," Federal Reserve Bank of St. Louis *Review*, January 1982; J. Tatom, "Investment and the New Energy Regime," in Board of Governors of the Federal Reserve, *Public Policy and Capital Formation*, Washington, D.C. 1981; and J. Perloff and M. Wachter, "A Production Function-Nonaccelerating Inflation Approach to Potential Output," in K. Brunner and A. Meltzer (eds.), *Carnegie-Rochester Conference Series*, vol. 10 (Amsterdam: North-Holland, Publishing Company, 1979).

[19] This is the estimate provided in Tatom, "Potential Output," op. cit., p. 7. See, however, the discussion in Dension, "Explanations of Declining Productivity," op. cit.

If the oil price increase of the 1970s reduced potential output, what are the effects of the oil price decline in the 1980s and especially in 1986. It remains to be seen whether the reduced real price of oil brings with it a significant increase in the economy's supply potential as we would expect from a favorable supply shock. But at least it can be asserted that the favorable inflation effects will create a better macroeconomic environment.

Conclusion

We use measures of potential output to judge fiscal policies and to plan stabilization policies. The measures of potential output we have are far from perfect. They attempt to estimate from the actual behavior of output, productivity, and employment what would be the behavior of output along a full-employment path. But because of the difficulties discussed above, the measures of potential output are subject to a wide margin of error. In the recent past, potential output measures have been revised almost each year, and occasionally by large amounts, and in 1982–1983 they were no longer made public by the Council of Economic Advisers.

The disappearance of a well-defined and easy-to-measure potential output series is very disturbing, given how central it is to many policy questions. But two points need to be made. The first is that the *theoretical concept* of full-employment output — even if that output is responsive to supply-side policies — remains entirely intact. The second is that controversies surrounding the *measurement* of potential output are in part a reflection of the puzzles about productivity growth in the 1970s. If and when these puzzles are better understood, potential output measures will again become more widely used.

19-5 GROWTH THEORY

We turn now from empirical issues and the historical record to the theory of economic growth. The theory of economic growth asks what factors determine the full-employment rate of output over time. Growth theory is important because it both helps explain growth rates and helps explain why per capita income levels differ among countries. One of the central results of growth theory, for example, is the proposition that between two countries with the same technology and saving rates the one that has the higher rate of population growth will eventually have lower per capita income.

We have already examined the sources of growth in equation (2), where we showed that full-employment output growth depends on the growth in factor inputs and on technical progress. In this section we pursue the issue further to ask what determines the growth of factor supplies and what is the link to long-run per capita incomes or standards of living.

We take a rather simple formulation here by assuming a given and constant rate of labor force growth, $\Delta N/N \equiv n$, and also that there is no technical progress, $\Delta A/A = 0$.[20] With these assumptions the only variable element left in equation (2) is the growth rate of capital.

Capital growth is determined by saving, which, in turn, depends on income. Income or output, in turn, depends on capital. We are thus set with an interdependent system in which capital growth depends, via saving and income, on the capital stock. We now study the short-run behavior, the adjustment process, and the long-run equilibrium of that interdependent system.

Steady State

We start by discussing the steady state of the economy. Here we ask whether in an economy with population growth and saving, and therefore growth in the capital stock, we reach a point where output per head and capital per head become constant. In such a steady state, current saving and additions to the capital stock would be just enough to equip new entrants into the labor force with the same amount of capital as the average worker uses.

The idea of a steady state is this: If capital per head is unchanging, given technology, so is output per head. But for capital *per head* to remain unchanging even though population is growing, capital must grow at just the right rate, namely, at the same rate as population. More formally, if output per head is to remain constant, output and population must grow at the same rates, or $\Delta Y/Y = \Delta N/N = n$. Therefore, from equation (2a), setting productivity growth and growth in output per capita equal to zero, we have $0 = \Delta K/K - n$, or

$$\frac{\Delta K}{K} = n$$

(6)

Equation (6) states that in the steady state the growth rate of the capital stock is equal to the growth rate of population. Equivalently, in the steady state the amount of capital per head is constant.

We now show the steady state graphically in Figure 19-3. We put output per head on the vertical axis and capital per head on the horizontal axis. The production function, which is central to understanding growth, exhibits diminishing returns to capital. As capital per head increases, so that workers use increasing amounts of machinery, output per head increases, but at a diminishing rate. Thus an increase in the capital-labor ratio is productive, but there are diminishing returns. In steady state, the economy settles down to a fixed capital-labor ratio $(K/N)^\circ$. The production function shows the corresponding amount of output per head $(Y/N)^\circ$.

---

[20] For further simplicity we also assume that the entire population works, so that the labor force and the population are the same.

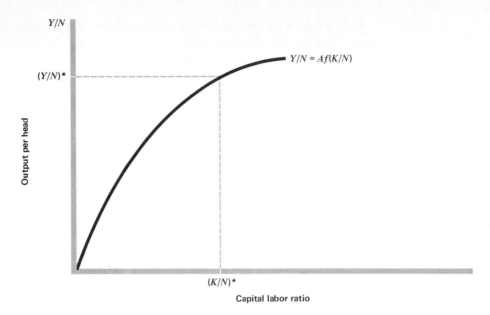

FIGURE 19-3   OUTPUT PER HEAD AND THE CAPITAL-LABOR
RATIO. The production function shows output per head as a function of
the amount of capital per head, or the capital-labor ratio. The higher the
capital-labor ratio, the higher is output per head. But the increment to
output from raising the capital-labor ratio grows progressively smaller as
the capital-labor ratio rises.

Saving and Growth

We gain insight by examining the link between saving and the growth in
capital. We are assuming there is no government. Accordingly, investment, or
the gross increase in capital, is equal to saving. To obtain the increase in the
capital stock, however, we have to deduct depreciation. Therefore the net
addition to the capital stock is equal to saving less depreciation.

$$\Delta K = \text{saving} - \text{depreciation} \qquad (7)$$

Two assumptions take us from (6) and (7) to a complete description of the
steady state. In (7) we need to specify saving behavior and to make an assumption about depreciation. We assume first that saving is a constant fraction s of
income Y. Second, depreciation is at a constant rate of d percent of the capital
stock. Concretely, we might assume that people save $s = 15$ percent of their
income and that depreciation is at a rate of 10 percent per year so that every
year 10 percent of the capital stock needs to be replaced to offset wear and
tear.

Substituting these assumptions in equation (7) yields

$$\Delta K = sY - dK \qquad (7a)$$

or placing the right-hand side in equation (6), we arrive at the following result that describes the steady state:[21]

$$sY = (n + d)K \qquad (6a)$$

Equation (6a) states that in the steady state, saving (sY) is just sufficient to provide for enough investment to offset depreciation (dK) *and* to equip new members of the labor force with capital (nK). If saving were larger than this amount, net investment would be sufficiently large to make capital per head grow, leading to rising income per head. Conversely, if not enough were saved, capital per head would be falling and with it income per head.

The Growth Process

We next study the adjustment process that leads the economy from some initial capital-labor ratio over time to the steady state. The critical element in this transition process is the rate of saving and investment compared with the ratio of depreciation, and population growth.

NOTATION

The argument is made easier by a bit of new notation. We define the amount of output per head as $x = Y/N$ and the amount of capital per head, or the capital-labor ratio, as $k = K/N$. This is simply notation and in no way changes our model.

$$k \equiv \text{capital-labor ratio} = \frac{K}{N} \qquad x \equiv \text{output per head} = \frac{Y}{N} \qquad (8)$$

Thus in terms of Figure 19-3 the vertical axis is labeled x and the horizontal axis k.

CAPITAL ACCUMULATION

We now turn to the transition to the steady state. Note from equation (2) that output per head will grow if capital per head grows and that capital per head will grow if saving is *more than sufficient* to cover depreciation of the capital

---

[21] Placing equation (7a) in equation (6) yields $(sY - dK)/K = n$. By multiplying both sides by K and collecting terms, we obtain $sY = (n + d)K$.

stock and also to equip new members of the population with capital. This can be formalized by writing the change in the capital-labor ratio as follows:[22]

$$\Delta k = sx - (n + d)k \qquad (9)$$

The growth process can now be studied with the help of equation (6a) and Figure 19-4. Here we reproduce the production function from Figure 19-3, writing output per capita as a function of the capital-labor ratio.

We have added the savings function, which, for each capital-labor ratio, is simply the fraction s of output. Thus, for any capital-labor ratio, say, k_0, the corresponding point of the saving schedule tells us the amount of saving per head, sx_0, that will be forthcoming at that capital-labor ratio.

We know that all saving is invested, so that gross investment or gross additions to the capital stock, in per capita terms, are equal to sx, given a capital-labor ratio of k_0. We know, too, from equation (9) that the increase in the capital-labor ratio falls short of that gross addition for two reasons:

- Depreciation reduces the capital-labor ratio, and part of gross investment must be devoted to offsetting depreciation. In particular, if the depreciation rate is d, an amount dk is required as a depreciation allowance. For example, if the depreciation rate is 10 percent and the capital-labor ratio is 10 machines per person, each year the equivalent of 1 machine would depreciate and would have to be replaced; that is, 10 percent times 10 machines equals 1 machine that has to be replaced.

- Growth in the labor force implies that with a given stock of capital, the capital-labor ratio would be declining. To maintain the amount of capital per head constant, we have to add enough machines to the stock of capital to make up for the growth in population; that is, we need to invest at the rate nk.

It follows that we can write the investment required to maintain constant the capital-labor ratio in the face of depreciation and labor force growth as $(n + d)k$. When saving and hence gross investment are larger than $(n + d)k$, the stock of capital per head is increasing. If saving and gross investment are less, then we are not making up for depreciation and population growth, and accordingly, capital per head is falling. We can therefore think of the term $(n + d)k$ as the investment requirement that will maintain constant capital per head and therefore, from Figure 19-3, output per head.

In Figure 19-4 we show this investment requirement as a positively sloped schedule. It tells us how much investment we would require at each

---

[22] The percentage growth rate of the capital-labor ratio is equal to the difference between the growth rate of capital and the growth rate of labor, or $\Delta k/k = \Delta K/K - n$. Now using equation (7a) to replace ΔK, we have $\dfrac{\Delta k}{k} = \dfrac{sY}{K} - d - n = \dfrac{s(Y/N)}{K/N} - (d + n) = \dfrac{sx}{k} - (d + n)$. Multiplying both sides by k yields equation (9) in the text.

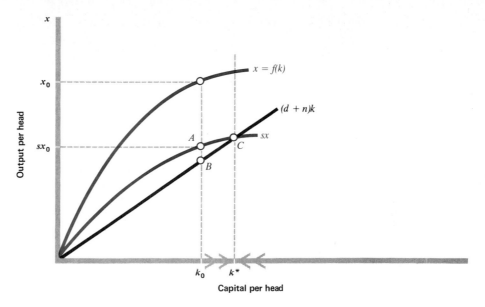

FIGURE 19-4   SAVING, INVESTMENT, AND CAPITAL ACCUMULA-
TION. The saving function shows at each capital-labor ratio the part of
income that is saved, sx. The straight line $(d + n)k$ shows the
investment requirement. At low capital-labor ratios, saving exceeds the
investment requirement, and hence output per head grows. Conversely
at high capital-labor ratios, saving is less than the investment requirement, and capital per head is falling. The steady-state capital-labor is k^*,
where saving is just sufficient to maintain the capital-labor ratio constant.

capital-labor ratio just in order to keep that ratio constant. It is positively
sloped because the higher the capital-labor ratio, the larger the amount of
investment that is required to maintain that capital-labor ratio. Thus, with the
depreciation rate of 10 percent and a growth rate of population of 1 percent,
we would require an investment of 1.1 machines per head per year at a
capital-labor ratio of 10 machines per head to maintain the capital-labor ratio
constant. If the capital-labor ratio were 100 machines per head, the required
investment would be 11 machines (=100 machines per head times 11 percent).

We have seen that the saving schedule tells us the amount of saving and
gross investment associated with each capital-labor ratio. Thus, at a capital-
labor ratio of k_0 in Figure 19-4, saving is sx_0 at point A. The investment
requirement to maintain constant the capital-labor ratio at k_0 is equal to
$(n + d)k_0$ at point B. Clearly, saving exceeds the investment requirement.
More is added to the capital stock than is required to maintain constant the

capital-labor ratio. Accordingly, the capital-labor ratio grows. Not surprisingly, the increase in the capital-labor ratio is equal to actual saving or investment less the investment requirement and is thus given by the vertical distance AB.

In the next period, capital per head will be higher. Thus on the horizontal axis we draw an arrow showing k increasing. You recognize the line of argument we are taking. From Figure 19-4 it is clear that with a somewhat higher capital-labor ratio, the discrepancy between saving and the investment requirement becomes smaller. Therefore the increase in the capital-labor ratio becomes smaller. However, the capital-labor ratio still increases, as indicated by the arrows.

The adjustment process comes to a halt at point C. Here we have reached a capital-labor ratio k° for which saving and investment associated with that capital-labor ratio exactly match the investment requirement. Given the exact matching of actual and required investment, the capital-labor ratio neither rises nor falls. We have reached the steady state.

We can make the same argument by starting with an initial capital-labor ratio in excess of k°. From Figure 19-4 we note that for high capital-labor ratios, the investment requirement is in excess of saving and investment. Accordingly, not enough is added to the capital stock to maintain the capital-labor ratio constant in the face of population growth and depreciation. Thus, the capital-labor ratio falls until we get to k°, the steady-state capital-labor ratio.

To review our progress so far:

- To maintain the capital-labor ratio constant, saving and investment have to be sufficient to make up for the reduction in capital per head that arises from population growth and depreciation.

- With saving a constant fraction s of output, we established that the capital-labor ratio moves to a steady-state level k° at which output and therefore saving (investment) are just sufficient to maintain constant the capital-labor ratio.

- The convergence to a steady-state capital-labor ratio k° is ensured by the fact that, at low levels of the capital-labor ratio, saving (investment) exceeds the investment required to maintain capital per head and therefore causes the capital-labor ratio to rise. Conversely, at high capital-labor ratios, saving (investment) falls short of the investment requirement, and thus the ratio declines.

Now we turn to a more detailed study of the steady-state equilibrium and the adjustment process. We note that the steady-state level of capital per head is constant, and thus the steady-state level of output per head is also constant. The steady state is reached when all variables, in per capita terms, are constant. This means that in the steady state, output, capital, and labor all grow at the same rate. They all grow at a rate equal to the rate of population growth.

Note particularly that the steady-state growth rate is equal to the rate of population growth and therefore is *not* influenced by the saving rate. (Recall that we are assuming no technical progress.) To explore this property of the steady state in more detail, we investigate the effects of a change in the saving rate.

A Change in the Saving Rate

Why should the long-run growth rate be independent of the saving rate? If people save 10 percent of their income as opposed to 5 percent, should we not expect this to make a difference to the growth rate of output? Is it not true that an economy in which 10 percent of income is set aside for additions to the capital stock is one in which capital and therefore output grow faster than in an economy in which only 5 percent of income is saved?

We show here that an increase in the saving rate does the following: In the short run, it raises the growth rate of output. It does not affect the *long-run growth rate* of output, but it raises the long-run level of capital and output per head.

Consider Figure 19-5 with an initial steady-state equilibrium at point C, where saving precisely matches the investment requirement. At point C, ex-

FIGURE 19-5   AN INCREASE IN THE SAVING RATE. An increase in the saving rate implies that at each capital-labor ratio a larger fraction of output is saved. The saving schedule shifts upward to $s'x$. At the initial steady state, saving now exceeds the investment requirement, and hence the capital-labor ratio rises until point C' is reached. An increase in the saving rate raises steady-state per capita income. The growth rate rises only in the transition from C to C'.

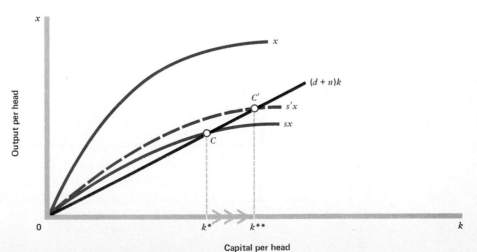

Capital per head

actly enough output is saved to maintain the stock of capital per head constant in the face of depreciation and labor force growth. Next consider an increase in the saving rate. For some reason, people want to save a larger fraction of income. The increased saving rate is reflected in an upward shift of the saving schedule. At each level of the capital-labor ratio, and hence at each level of output, saving is larger.

At point C, where we initially had a steady-state equilibrium, saving has now risen relative to the investment requirement, and as a consequence, more

FIGURE 19-6 (a) THE TIME PATH OF PER CAPITA INCOME. A rise in the saving rate leads to a rising capital-labor ratio and therefore to increasing output per head until a new steady state is reached. (b) THE TIME PATH OF THE GROWTH RATE OF OUTPUT. An increase in the saving rate raises investment above the investment requirement and thus leads to capital accumulation. Output growth transitorily rises and then falls back to the growth rate of population.

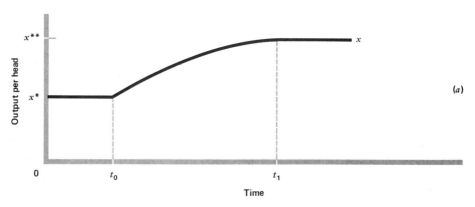

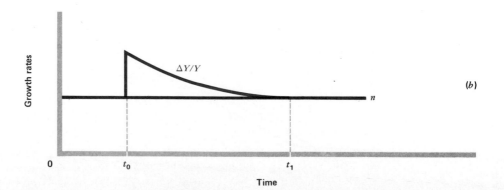

is saved than is required to maintain capital per head constant. Enough is saved to allow the capital stock per head to increase.

It is apparent from Figure 19-5 that the capital stock per head will keep rising until we reach point C'. At C', the higher amount of saving is just enough to maintain the higher stock of capital. At point C', both capital per head and output per head have risen. Saving has increased as has the investment requirement. We have seen, therefore, that an increase in the saving rate will in the long run raise only the level of output and capital per head, and not the growth rate of output per head.

The transition process, however, involves an effect of the saving rate on the growth rate of output and the growth rate of output per head. In the transition from k^* to k^{**}, the increase in the saving rate raises the growth rate of output. This follows simply from the fact that the capital-labor ratio rises from k^* at the initial steady state to k^{**} in the new steady state. The only way to achieve an increase in the capital-labor ratio is for the capital stock to grow faster than the labor force (and depreciation). This is precisely what happens in the transition process where increased saving per head, owing to the higher saving rate, raises investment and capital growth over and above the investment requirement and thus allows the capital-labor ratio to rise.

In summary, the long-run effect of an increase in the saving rate is to raise the level of output and capital per head but to leave the growth rate of output and capital unaffected. In the transition period, the rates of growth of output and capital increase relative to the steady state. In the short run, therefore, an increase in the saving rate means faster growth, as we would expect.

Figure 19-6 summarizes these two results. Figure 19-6a shows the level of per capita output. Starting from an initial long-run equilibrium at time t_0, the increase in the saving rate causes saving and investment to increase, the stock of capital per head grows, and so does output per head. The process will continue at a diminishing rate. In Figure 19-6b we focus on the growth rate of output and capital. The growth rate of output is equal to the growth rate of population in the initial steady state. The increase in the saving rate immediately raises the growth rate of output because it implies a faster growth in capital and therefore in output. As capital accumulates, the growth rate decreases, falling back toward the level of population growth.

Population Growth

The preceding discussion of saving and the influence of the saving rate on steady-state capital and output makes it easy to discuss the effects of increased population growth. The question we ask is, What happens when the population growth rate increases from n to n' and remains at that higher level indefinitely? We will show that such an increase in the rate of population growth will *raise* the growth rate of output and *lower* the level of output per head.

The argument can be conveniently followed in Figure 19-7. Here we show the initial steady-state equilibrium at point C. The increase in the growth

BOX

19-1

THE LIMITS OF GROWTH

The record of growth since 1889 reviewed in Table 19-1 is impressive indeed. Per capita GNP in the United States has been doubling in less than 40 years over a period of nearly a century. And the growth certainly goes back further than that. The question of the limits to growth is whether limited resources and the pressure of population on scarce land and food will ultimately bring the growth process to a dramatic halt. Are growing economies headed toward stagnation or even disaster?

The disaster scenario is a simple one. First, only so much oil, coal, copper, and other raw materials are in the earth. One day they will all be used up. Then what do we do? The "one day" seemed to come very close in the early seventies when many experts were predicting we would run out of oil by the year 2020. Second, there is the problem of an ever-growing population. The world, being of finite size, cannot accommodate an ever-growing population. Unless we can colonize other planets, population growth has to decline. In particular, there is the problem of food. Can we grow enough food to feed the nearly 6 billion people (compared with a current 4.5 billion) expected to be alive at the turn of the century? If not, will world population be forced down through starvation, as Malthus long ago predicted?*

The standard retort of the growth-oriented economist is to point out that all the concerns we have today about the limits to growth were equally valid a century ago. Indeed, in 1865 the famous English economist W. S. Jevons wrote a book about the impending exhaustion of Britain's coal resources — coal that is still being mined today.† The experience after the oil price shock in 1973 was that price changes can cause massive conservation of resources, and thus there is reason to hope that most *exhaustible* resources — resources present on earth in limited quantities — will be around for a long time, albeit with rising relative prices.

A more important challenge to the limits set by exhaustible resources is technical progress. Much technical progress takes the form of inventions and processes that save on scarce resources used up in production. The expectation or hope is that the same technical progress that has proved an important source of real growth in the last century will help overcome the effects of the reduced availability of raw materials.

Of course there is no assurance that the right technical progress will come along to bail us out when coal or oil run short in supply. Perhaps we should not bank on technical progress, innovation, and ingenuity to help us out. At the same time, it would surely be irresponsible to dismiss entirely the extraordinary record of technical progress that has contributed around one-half of the average growth in real income. Public policy directed at encouraging research and development could help ensure continued technical progress.

The idea of a convergence in per capita incomes among different countries has been suggested by William Baumol.‡ Studying the long-term behavior of productivity growth, he finds that industrial countries, and even the newly industrializing countries, tend to converge over time in their levels of per capita income. This convergence occurs because growth rates of productivity slow down as differences in per capita incomes narrow. The countries that lag in terms of development tend to experience higher growth rates of productivity until they have caught up, and the countries that are ahead in terms of the level of productivity have lower growth in productivity.

---

* Thomas Malthus, *The Principle of Population* (Homewood, Ill.: Richard D. Irwin, Inc., reprint).

† W. S. Jevons, *The Coal Question*, 1885 (New York: Augustus M. Kelly Publishers, 1965, reprint).

‡ William Baumol, "Productivity Growth, Convergence and Welfare: What the Long Run Data Show," C. V. Starr Center for Applied Economics, New York University, August 1985.

The catching up hypothesis seems to be particularly applicable to Japan in the postwar period, but also to the *newly industrialized countries,* or *NICs,* like Korea or Brazil. These countries have shown particularly high growth rates in the 1960s and 1970s. But the debt crisis of the 1980s, particularly affecting countries in Latin America, may well have imposed at least a temporary slowdown if not a stop to this rapid growth pattern.

rate of population means that, at each level of the capital-labor ratio, it takes a larger amount of investment just to maintain the capital-labor ratio constant. Suppose we had 10 machines per head. Initially, the growth rate of population is 1 percent and depreciation is 10 percent, so that we require per year 11 percent times 10 machines, or 1.1 machine, just to offset population growth and depreciation and thus maintain capital per head constant. To maintain the capital-labor ratio constant in the face of higher growth rate of population, say, 2 percent, requires a higher level of investment, namely, 12 percent as op-

FIGURE 19-7   AN INCREASE IN THE POPULATION GROWTH RATE REDUCES PER CAPITA INCOME. Increased population growth raises the investment requirement, rotating the schedule upward to $(d + n')k$. At point C saving is insufficient to maintain capital per head constant in face of the more rapidly growing population. Capital and output per head decline until a new steady state at C' is reached.

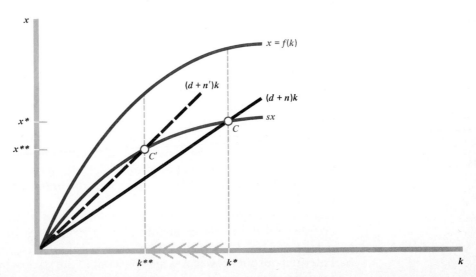

posed to 11 percent. This is reflected in Figure 19-7 by an upward rotation of the investment requirement schedule.

It is clear from the preceding argument that we are no longer in steady-state equilibrium at point C. The investment that was initially just sufficient to keep the capital-labor ratio constant will no longer be sufficient in the face of higher population growth. At the initial equilibrium, the higher population growth with unchanged saving and investment means that capital does not grow fast enough to keep up with labor force growth and depreciation. Capital per head declines. In fact, capital per head will keep declining until we reach the new steady-state equilibrium at point C'. Here the capital-labor ratio has declined sufficiently for saving to match the investment requirement. It is true, too, that, corresponding to the lower capital-labor ratio, we have a decline in output per head. Output per head declines from $x°$ to $x°°$.

The decline in output per head as a consequence of increased population growth points to the problem faced by many developing countries. Fast growth in population, given the saving rate, means low levels of income per head. Indeed, in poor countries one can trace poverty, or low income per head, to the very high rate of population growth. With high population growth, saving will typically be too small to allow capital to rise relative to labor and thus to build up the capital-labor ratio to achieve a satisfactory level of income per head. In those circumstances, and barring other considerations, a reduction in the rate of population growth appears to be a way of achieving higher levels of steady-state per capita income and thus an escape from poverty.

19-6 SUMMARY

1. A production function links factor inputs and technology to the level of output. Growth of output, changes in technology aside, is a weighted average of input growth with the weights equal to income shares. The production function directs attention to factor inputs and technological change as sources of output growth.
2. Growth theory studies the determinants of intermediate-run and long-run growth in output.
3. In U.S. history over the 1929–1969 period, growth in factor inputs and technical progress each accounted for roughly one-half of the average growth rate of 3.4 percent of output. Growth in the stock of knowledge, along with growth in labor input, was the most important source of growth.
4. Per capita output grows faster, the more rapidly the capital stock increases and the faster is technical progress. In U.S. history since 1889, output per head has grown at an average rate of 1.8 percent.
5. Potential output grew at nearly 4 percent in the sixties, but its growth rate has fallen to less than 3 percent since then. The fall is in large part due to the decline in productivity growth. The prospects for a return to the high

productivity growth rates of the 1948–1973 period are slim, but some improvement from the poor performance of the late seventies is likely.

6. Supply-side economics proposes to raise the level and growth rate of full-employment output by creating improved incentives for work, saving, and investment and by reducing regulation. Empirical research suggests that incentives would be successful on the labor supply side, and that reduced government deficits would stimulate investment.

7. Potential output or full-employment output is estimated as the product of the high-employment level of work hours and high-employment productivity. Important changes in the labor market and the puzzling reduction in productivity growth have led to questions about the appropriateness of the traditional potential output concept and measure.

8. Production function estimates of potential output show a very important role for energy. According to these estimates, a doubling of energy prices would lead to a fall in potential output of about 12 percent. These numbers are very large and remain the topic of research.

9. The concept of steady-state equilibrium points (in the absence of technical change) to the conditions required for output per head to be constant. With a growing population, saving must be just sufficient to provide new members of the population with the economywide amount of capital per head.

10. The steady-state level of income is determined by the saving rate and by population growth. In the absence of technical change, the steady-state growth rate of output is equal to the rate of population growth. An increase in the growth rate of population raises the steady-state growth rate of total output and lowers the level of steady-state output per head.

11. An increase in the saving rate transitorily raises the growth rate of output. In the new steady state, the growth rate remains unchanged, but the level of output per head is increased.

12. With technical change, per capita output in the steady state grows at the rate of technical progress. Total output grows at the sum of the rates of technical progress and population growth.

13. Potential limits to growth pose a serious question about continued increases in real per capita income or even the maintenance of current consumption standards. The historical record is one of technological progress that offsets limitational factors and scarce resources. There is no certainty that this offset will continue, but so far it has done so. Public policy to encourage research and development can make a contribution in that direction.

KEY TERMS

Potential output
Production function
Growth accounting

Growth of total factor productivity
Supply-side economics
Steady state

Sources of growth
Labor productivity
Technical progress

Limits of growth
Catching-up hypothesis

PROBLEMS

1. Which of the following government activities have effects on the long-term growth rate? Explain how they can do so. (a) Monetary policy, (b) labor market policies, (c) educational and research programs, (d) fiscal policy, (e) population control programs.

2. Discuss the role of government policy in raising (a) the supply of labor and (b) the supply of capital. How successful can such policies be?

3. Discuss why the 5.0 percent full-employment benchmark may no longer be a sensible basis for potential output calculations. What do you think should be done: abandon the potential output concept, or assume some new benchmark?

4. Since 1973, the growth rate of productivity has sharply declined in most industrialized countries. List several of the factors that are responsible for this decline and discuss why the decline in productivity growth is an important issue.

5. Suppose the share of capital in income is 0.4 and the share of labor is 0.6. Capital grows by 6 percent, and labor supply declines by 2 percent. What happens to output?

6. An earthquake destroys one-quarter of the capital stock. Discuss in the context of the growth model the adjustment process of the economy, and show, using Figure 19-4, what happens to growth.

7. (a) In the absence of technical progress, what happens to output per head and total output over time? Why?

   (b) What is the long-run effect of the saving rate on the *level* of output per capita? On *growth* of output per capita?

8. Evaluate this statement: "The saving rate cannot affect the growth of output in the economy. That is determined by the growth of labor input and by technical progress."

9. Suppose we assume a production function of the form

$$Y = AF(K, N, Z)$$

where Z is a measure of the natural resources going into production. Assume this production function obeys constant returns to scale and diminishing returns to each factor [like equation (1)].

   (a) What will happen to output per head if capital and labor grow together but resources are fixed?

   (b) What if Z is fixed but there is technical progress?

   (c) Interpret these results in terms of the limits to growth.

10. Use the model of long-run growth to incorporate the government. Assume that an income tax at the rate t is levied and that, accordingly, saving per head is equal to $s(1 - t)x$. The government spends the tax revenue on public consumption.

    (a) Use Figure 19-4 to explore the impact of an increase in the tax rate on the steady-state output level and capital per head.

    (b) Draw a chart of the time path of capital per head, output per head, and the growth rate of output.

(c) Discuss the statement: "To raise the growth rate of output, the public sector has to run a budget surplus to free resources for investment."

11. Use Figure 19-4 to explore the impact of a *once-and-for-all* improvement in technology.
    (a) How does technical progress affect the level of output per head as of a given capital-labor ratio?
    (b) Show the new steady-state equilibrium. Has saving changed? Is income per head higher? Has the capital stock per head increased?
    (c) Show the time path of the adjustment to the new steady state. Does technical progress transitorily raise the ratio of investment to capital?

12. Discuss the statement: "The lower the level of income, the higher the growth rate of output."

13. Explain the catching-up hypothesis that asserts that productivity growth is lower the higher the level of per capita income. What factors do you think are responsible for this observed pattern?

APPENDIX: PROPERTIES OF THE PRODUCTION FUNCTION

In this appendix we briefly show how the fundamental growth equation (2a) is obtained. The material is presented for completeness; it is not essential to an understanding of the text.

We start with a production function that exhibits constant returns: increasing *all* inputs in the same proportion raises output in that same proportion. Thus if we double all inputs, output will double. With that property the change in output due to technical progress and to changes in inputs can be written as

$$\Delta Y = F(K, N) \, \Delta A + MPK \, \Delta K + MPN \, \Delta N \qquad \text{(A1)}$$

where MPK and MPN are the marginal products of capital and labor, respectively. We remember that the marginal product of a factor tells us the contribution to output made by employing one extra unit of the factor. Dividing both sides of the equation by $Y = AF(K, N)$ yields the expression

$$\frac{\Delta Y}{Y} = \frac{\Delta A}{A} + \frac{MPK}{Y} \, \Delta K + \frac{MPN}{Y} \, \Delta N \qquad \text{(A2)}$$

Equation (A2) further simplifies by multiplying and dividing the second term on the right-hand side by K and the third term by N.

$$\frac{\Delta Y}{Y} = \frac{\Delta A}{A} + \left(K \frac{MPK}{Y} \right) \frac{\Delta K}{K} + \left(N \frac{MPN}{Y} \right) \frac{\Delta N}{N} \qquad \text{(A3)}$$

We now argue that the terms in parentheses are the income shares of capital and labor. In a competitive market factors are paid their marginal product. Thus the term $N(MPN/Y) = wN/Y$, where w is the real wage. The right-hand side is recognized as the ratio of labor income to total income or the share of labor in income. Similarly, the term $K(MPK/Y)$ is the share of capital in income. With constant returns and competition, factor payments exhaust the total product. Therefore the shares of capital and labor sum to unity. Denoting the share of capital in income by θ and the labor share by $1 - \theta$, we arrive at equation (2a) in the text.

We note a further property of the constant returns production function. When returns to scale are constant, we can write the production function as follows:

$$Y = AF(K, N) = NAf\left(\frac{K}{N}\right)$$

(A4)

or using the notation $x = Y/N$ and $k = K/N$,

$$x = Af(k)$$

(A5)

This is the form used in the growth theory section of the text, where output per head is a function of the capital-labor ratio.

MONEY, PRICES, AND EXCHANGE RATES

In this chapter open economy issues are once again at the center of the discussion. The major change is that where in Chapter 6 we assumed that the price level was constant, we now extend the analysis to take account of changes in the price level. The central message is that short-run results remain much the same. The open economy *IS-LM* model of Chapter 6 is a sturdy workhorse for macroeconomic discussion even in an economy in which prices are flexible.[1]

We start the chapter by discussing how adjustment to balance of payments problems takes place in an economy with fixed exchange rates. Although exchange rates among the major countries have been freely flexible since 1973, the discussion remains relevant both because some smaller countries do still operate with fixed exchange rates[2] and because the adjustment mechanisms that operate under fixed exchange rates increase understanding of the operation of the flexible exchange rate system. We then discuss the

---

[1] This chapter uses and extends concepts already introduced in Chap. 6. You should go back to briefly refresh your understanding of the main concepts before going on.

[2] Also some not-so-small countries: exchange rates in the European Monetary System, which includes Germany, France, and Italy, and which Britain is thinking of joining, are held fixed for long periods of time and only occasionally adjusted.

monetary approach to the balance of payments, which argues that balance of payments problems are a result of too rapid money growth.

We then switch back in Section 20-3 to consider the adjustment process under flexible exchange rates when prices are flexible. This section generalizes Chapter 6's *IS-LM* discussion of adjustment in a flexible exchange rate system with a constant price level. In the remainder of the chapter we take up aspects of the behavior of the current flexible exchange rate system: interest rate linkages among different countries; the effects of exchange rate changes on trade flows; and the interdependence among countries' economic policies that exists even in the world of flexible exchange rates.

20-1 POLICY CONFLICTS AND ADJUSTMENT UNDER FIXED EXCHANGE RATES

In this first section we discuss adjustment to external imbalances under fixed exchange rates. The discussion is relevant today for those economies that keep their exchange rate fixed to that of another country. It is also relevant in considering adjustment under a system of fixed exchange rates, such as the Bretton Woods system that operated from the end of World War II to 1973, or the gold standard of the nineteenth and first third of the twentieth century.

Adjustment to a balance of payments problem can be achieved in two ways. One way is by changing economic policy. The second way is through *automatic* adjustment mechanisms. The automatic mechanisms are two: payments imbalances affect the money supply and hence spending, and unemployment affects wages and prices and thereby competitiveness. Policy measures by contrast include not only monetary and fiscal policy but also tariffs or devaluation.

The Role of Prices in the Open Economy

We start the analysis by bringing prices explicitly into the model. In Chapter 6 we assumed that the price level was constant. With fixed prices and a given exchange rate the *real* exchange rate was also fixed. Recall the definition of the real exchange rate:

$$R = \frac{eP_f}{P} \tag{1}$$

Here e is the exchange rate, P_f the foreign price level, and P the domestic price level. We now abandon the assumption of a fixed domestic price level, but for the time being take the exchange rate and foreign prices as given.

In this section we develop the model of aggregate demand and supply in Chapters 13 and 14 taking account of international linkages. We start by reviewing the main points. Aggregate demand depends on the level of prices. A higher level of prices implies lower real balances, higher interest rates, and lower spending. In an open economy, the relation is slightly more complicated because now an increase in our prices reduces demand for our goods for two reasons. The first is the familiar higher interest rate channel summarized above. The second is that an increase in our prices makes our goods less competitive with foreign-produced goods. When the prices of goods produced at home rise, and given the exchange rate, our goods become more expensive for foreigners to buy, and their goods become *relatively* cheaper for us to buy. An increase in our prices is thus an increase in the *relative price* of the goods we produce, and shifts demand away from our goods toward imports, as well as reducing exports.

In summary, then, an increase in our price level reduces the demand for our goods both by increasing the interest rate (and reducing investment demand) and by reducing net exports — by making the goods we produce relatively more expensive than foreign-produced goods. In Figure 20-1 we show the downward-sloping demand schedule for our goods, AD. Demand is equal, as before, to aggregate spending by domestic residents, plus net exports, $AD \equiv A + NX$.

The demand for domestic goods, AD, is drawn for a given level of foreign prices, a given nominal money supply, and given fiscal policy. Remember, too, that the exchange rate is fixed. An increase in the nominal money stock shifts the schedule upward, as does expansionary fiscal policy. We show, too, the short-run aggregate supply schedule AS and the full-employment level of output Y^*. Initial equilibrium is at point E, where we have unemployment.

Next we look at the trade balance equilibrium schedule, $NX = 0$. An increase in our income raises imports and worsens the trade balance. To restore trade balance equilibrium, domestic prices would have to be lower. This would make the home country more competitive, raise exports, and reduce imports. Thus, we show the trade balance equilibrium schedule as downward-sloping.[3] We assume that it is steeper than the demand schedule for domestic goods. The schedule is drawn for a given level of prices abroad. The short-run equilibrium at point E is one where the home country has a trade deficit. Our prices are too high or our income is too high to have exports balance imports. To achieve trade balance equilibrium, we would have to become more competitive, thus exporting more and importing less. Alternatively, we could reduce our level of income in order to reduce import spending.

Financing and Adjustment

What does a country with a current account deficit, like that at E in Figure 20-1, do? In a fixed exchange rate system, it is possible for the central bank to

---

[3] We assume that a decline in prices improves the trade balance. This requires that exports and imports are sufficiently responsive to prices. There is a possibility that a reduction in our price level (which reduces the prices of our exports) lowers our revenue from exports — because the increased sales are not sufficient to compensate for the lower prices. We assume that this possibility does not occur. We shall assume, too, that import spending does not depend on the interest rate.

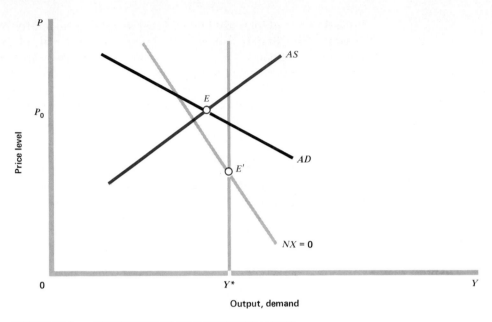

FIGURE 20-1   OPEN ECONOMY EQUILIBRIUM WITH PRICE
ADJUSTMENT. Net exports and the demand for domestic goods
depend on the relative price of our goods. Demand for domestic goods
also depends on the price level because this affects the real money
supply and hence interest rates. AD is the aggregate demand
schedule. It is downward-sloping because a reduction in our prices
raises the real money stock, lowering interest rates, and because lower
prices for our goods increase our international competitiveness. The
trade balance equilibrium schedule is also downward-sloping, reflecting
the increased competitiveness that we derive from a lower relative price
of our goods. Macroeconomic equilibrium obtains at E, where
aggregate demand equals aggregate supply. This need not be a point
of full employment and external balance, which obtain at E'.

use its reserves to finance temporary imbalances of payments—that is, to
meet the excess demand for foreign currency at the existing exchange rate
arising from balance of payments deficits. Other ways of financing temporary
payments imbalances are also available. A country experiencing balance of
payments difficulties can borrow foreign currencies abroad. The borrowing
may be undertaken either by the government (usually the central bank) or by
private individuals. Although borrowing may be undertaken to finance both
current and capital account deficits, we concentrate in this section on the
current account.

A current account deficit cannot be financed by borrowing from abroad
without raising the question of how the borrowing will be repaid. If the coun-

terpart of the current account deficit is productive domestic investment, there need be little concern about repaying. The investment will pay off in terms of increased output, some of which may be exported or which may replace goods that previously were imported. The investment would thus yield the foreign exchange earnings with which to *service* (make payments on) the debt. However, problems may well arise in repaying the foreign debt if borrowing is used to finance consumption spending.

The Adjustment Process

Maintaining and financing current account deficits indefinitely or for very long periods of time is impossible. The economy has to find some way of *adjusting* the deficit. That can happen automatically or through policy. We examine first the important automatic adjustment mechanisms.

Automatic Adjustment

First we look at the aggregate demand side. We remember that there is a link between the central bank's holdings of foreign exchange and the domestic money supply, assuming now no sterilization, as defined in Chapter 11. When the central bank pegs the exchange rate, selling foreign exchange, it reduces domestic high-powered money and therefore the money stock. This is exactly what happens in the case of a deficit. Thus the trade deficit at point E implies that the central bank is pegging the exchange rate, selling foreign exchange to keep the exchange rate from depreciating, and reducing the domestic money stock. It follows immediately that over time the aggregate demand schedule (which is drawn for a given money supply) will be shifting downward and to the left.

On the aggregate supply side, we remember that unemployment leads to a decline in wages and costs, which is reflected in a downward-shifting aggregate supply schedule. Over time, therefore, the short-run equilibrium point E in Figure 20-1 moves downward as both demand and supply schedules shift (not shown). The points of short-run equilibrium move in the direction of point E', and the process will continue until that point is reached. (The approach may be cyclical, but that is not of major interest here.)

Once point E' is reached, we have achieved long-run equilibrium. Because the trade balance is in equilibrium, there is no pressure on the exchange rate and therefore no need for exchange market intervention. Accordingly, there is no influence from the trade balance on the money supply and thereby on aggregate demand. On the supply side, we have reached full employment. Therefore wages and costs are constant, so that the supply schedule is not shifting. At point E' we have a combination of relative price, demand, and employment that gives both internal and external balance. The adjustment of the level of prices ensures that we can—in the long run—have both full employment and trade balance equilibrium.

The adjustment process we have just described is called the *classical adjustment process.* It relies on price adjustments and an adjustment in the money supply based on the trade balance. The adjustment process "works" in the sense that it moves the economy to a long-run equilibrium of internal and external balance. However, the mechanism is far from attractive. There is no good case for a protracted recession simply to achieve a cut in prices. The alternative to waiting for the automatic adjustment mechanisms to work is to make policy changes that move the economy more rapidly towards balance.

Policy Conflicts and the Choice of Policies

In considering policies to adjust the balance of payments problem at point E in Figure 20-1, the government has also to take account of its internal economic problem. At point E there is not only a deficit in the balance of payments but also unemployment. The government wants to achieve not only *external balance* (in the balance of payments) but also *internal balance.* Internal balance means that output is at the full-employment level Y°. External balance occurs when the trade balance is zero.

The interesting and important point about internal and external balance is that there is sometimes a policy conflict between the solutions to the two problems. It can happen that policies to improve the external balance will worsen internal balance. For instance, a current account deficit can be reduced through restrictive domestic policy that reduces the levels of income and imports. But such policies will increase the rate of unemployment, which would not help internal balance from a point such as E in Figure 20-1. This can create a problem for policy makers.

The policy problem is illustrated in Figure 20-2. We can break up the diagram into four regions corresponding to booms and recessions, surpluses and deficits. Two of the regions do not present problems: corrective policies bring us closer to both internal and external balance. This is the case for regions I and III. In region I, for example, we have unemployment and a surplus. Expansionary fiscal policy would reduce both unemployment and the deficit. Similarly, in region III a contractionary monetary or fiscal policy will help correct the problem of overemployment and external deficit. But in the other two regions there are policy dilemmas.

Policy Dilemmas

At point A, the economy is in a position of recession and deficit. Here we have to choose whether we want to use tight policies to achieve trade balance equilibrium or expansionary policies to achieve full employment. Not only are we unable to reach both targets simultaneously by manipulating aggregate demand, but any attempt to reach one target gets us further away from the other. Such a situation is called a *policy dilemma*, and it can always arise when there are more targets of policy than instruments with which to move the

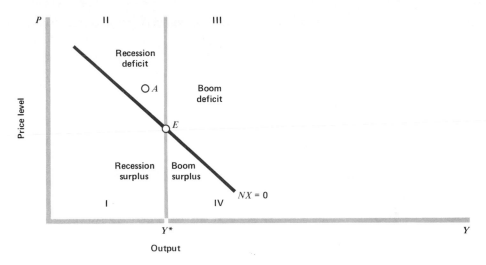

FIGURE 20-2 POLICY DILEMMAS In regions I and III monetary or fiscal policy can move the economy toward internal and external balance. In regions II and IV there is a policy dilemma. For example, in region II unemployment calls for expansion but the deficit calls for contraction.

economy toward its targets. In our case we have only one policy instrument—aggregate demand policies—but we have two independent targets—external and internal balance.

The policy dilemma can be solved by finding another policy instrument to cope with the multiple targets. What is needed is some policy that shifts the trade balance schedule to the right so that, at any given price level, trade is balanced at a higher level of income. An obvious policy would be to cut down on imports at each level of income. Such a policy would reduce import spending at each level of income and thus shift the trade balance schedule to the right.

How can we cut import spending? We can use any of a number of tools, among them tariffs and exchange rate changes. Tariffs are taxes on imported goods. A tariff raises the cost of imports to domestic residents and thereby diverts demand away from imports to domestic goods. A 10 percent tariff on imported shoes, for instance, makes imported shoes more expensive relative to domestically made shoes and shifts demand to locally made shoes. A devaluation, as we shall see, achieves the same effect by raising import prices relative to the prices of domestically made goods. In summary, if we have a trade deficit at full employment, we require a policy that directly affects the trade balance so as to give us trade balance equilibrium at full employment.

The Use of Expenditure Switching/Reducing Policies

The argument of the previous subsection needs to be spelled out in more detail to focus attention on a subtle and important point: Policies to shift spending from imports to domestic goods generally also affect aggregate demand in the goods market. Accordingly, policies to shift the $NX = 0$ line generally have to be accompanied by policies that adjust aggregate demand.

The important point is: In general it is necessary to combine both *expenditure switching policies*, which shift demand between domestic and imported goods, and *expenditure reducing* (or *expenditure increasing*) *policies*, to cope with the targets of internal and external balance. This point is of general importance and continues to apply when we take account of capital flows and other phenomena omitted in this section.

One method of adjusting a current account deficit is through the imposition of tariffs. However, tariffs cannot be freely used to adjust the balance of trade, partly because there are international organizations and agreements such as GATT (General Agreement on Tariffs and Trade) and the IMF (International Monetary Fund) that outlaw, or at least frown on, the use of tariffs. Tariffs have generally fallen in the post-World War II period as the industrialized world has moved to desirably freer trade between countries.

Another way of adjusting a current account deficit is to use a restrictive domestic policy. These are expenditure reducing policies. In this regard, it is worth repeating that a trade deficit reflects an excess of expenditure by domestic residents and the government over income. In Chapter 2 we showed that

$$NX \equiv Y - (C + I + G) \tag{2}$$

where NX is the trade surplus and I is actual investment. Thus, a balance of trade deficit can be reduced by reducing spending $(C + I + G)$ relative to income (Y). The trade deficit can be eliminated by reducing aggregate demand, by reducing C, or G, or I, by using restrictive monetary and/or fiscal policy.

Devaluation

The unemployment that typically accompanies adjustment through recession and the desirability of free trade, which argues against the use of tariffs, both suggest that an alternative policy for reconciling internal and external balance be considered. The major policy instrument for dealing with payments deficits in the dilemma situation is *devaluation*—which usually has to be combined with restrictive monetary and/or fiscal policy. A devaluation, as we noted in Chapter 6, is an increase in the domestic currency price of foreign exchange. Given the nominal prices in two countries, devaluation increases the relative price of imported goods in the devaluing country and reduces the relative price of exports from the devaluing country. Devaluation is primarily an expenditure switching policy.

How does a devaluation assist in achieving internal and external balance? Let us take first a special case of a country that has been in full employment with balance of trade equilibrium, at point E in Figure 20-3. Now let there be an exogenous decline in export earnings, so that the $NX = 0$ schedule shifts to the left to $NX' = 0$. At the given exchange rate the foreign demand for domestic goods is assumed to decline. In the absence of domestic policy intervention, and with fixed rates, output would decline. The AD schedule moves to the left as a result of the fall in exports, and the resultant income decline to point E' lowers prices and imports, but not enough to make up for the loss of export revenue. The net effects are therefore unemployment and a trade deficit.

Next, we ask how the home country can adjust to the loss of export markets. One possibility is to go through an adjustment process of declining domestic wages and prices as the high unemployment slowly reduces wages or slows down their rate of increase. This is the automatic process described earlier. Such an adjustment would, over time, lower domestic costs and prices as compared with the prices of foreign goods. The home country would gain in competitiveness in world markets and thus restore export earnings and em-

FIGURE 20-3   A LOSS OF EXPORT REVENUE. The economy starts in full equilibrium at point E. An export loss shifts the $NX = 0$ and AD schedules to the left. The new short-run equilibrium is at point E' with unemployment and a deficit.

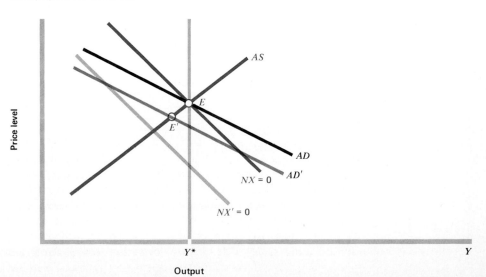

BOX

20-1

MEXICO: EXTERNAL DEBT, OIL, AND ADJUSTMENT PROBLEMS

In the short run, payments deficits can be financed by borrowing abroad. In the long run, they require adjustment. But politically there is never a good time for adjustment — and that is often how extreme policy difficulties arise. Mexico is a case in point.

Mexico is an oil-exporting country. It discovered and began to exploit its large oil reserves in the 1970s, when oil prices skyrocketed. Mexico enjoyed a large increase in export revenues. Even so, its domestic spending increased so fast that Mexico ran big trade deficits. These deficits were financed by borrowing abroad. Foreign banks were willing to lend to Mexico because it was oil-rich and its prospects looked good for being able to pay interest on the debt and repay the amounts borrowed. By 1982 the Mexican external debt had reached $82 billion, about 50 percent of GNP.

Mexican external balance problems came to the fore in 1982. Real interest rates in the world market increased sharply in 1981. That meant Mexico had to pay more interest on every dollar of its debt. At the same time oil prices started to fall. Losses of export revenues and higher interest bills led to a loss of confidence in the Mexican currency, which resulted in massive capital outflows. The government financed these outflows by borrowing dollars abroad to defend the exchange rate from collapse.

By 1982 Mexico entered into deep debt difficulties. External borrowing became impossible. At the same time Mexico was not earning enough dollars to pay interest on the debt. In August 1982, Mexico had to enter a moratorium — telling its creditors that it could not pay the full amounts due and that debts would have to be serviced (interest paid and debt rolled over) on an adjusted basis. Since that time, extensive adjustment and sharply falling oil prices have put Mexico into even further economic difficulties. Table 1 shows the extent of adjustment.

Note that the trade balance after 1982 shows a large surplus. The surplus was achieved by cutting spending and by a real depreciation of the peso. But even this large surplus was not enough to pay all the interest on the accumulated debt. The extent of adjustment shows in the sharp decline in real wages. Real wage reduction is the counterpart of a gain in competitiveness (a depreciation of the real exchange rate) which is the instrument for improving the external balance.

Even Table 1 understates the full extent of Mexico's difficulties, for at the end of 1985 the price of oil collapsed, falling below $15 per barrel. By the middle of 1986 it seemed that Mexico would have to undertake even further adjustment.

TABLE 1   MEXICO'S EXTERNAL BALANCE ADJUSTMENT

	1980–1982	1983	1984	1985
External debt ($U.S. billion)	75	94	97	97
Trade balance ($U.S. billion)	−0.3	13.8	12.8	8.4
Oil price ($/barrel)	34	29	27	26
Real wage*	100	77	71	71

* Index 1980–1982.

ployment. This is a feasible adjustment process, and, indeed, is the process that would occur by itself, given enough time.

An alternative solution is to recognize that in order to restore full employment and export earnings, the home country must become more competitive in the prices charged for exports and imports. To restore competitiveness, domestic costs and prices have to decline *relative* to foreign prices. That adjustment can occur in two ways: (1) through a decline in domestic costs and prices at a given exchange rate and (2) through a depreciation of the exchange rate with unchanged domestic costs and prices.

The latter strategy has the obvious advantage that it does not require a protracted recession to reduce domestic costs. The adjustment is done by a stroke of the pen—a devaluation of the currency. Why would a devaluation achieve the adjustment? *Given* prices of foreign goods in terms of foreign currency (for example, the mark prices of German goods), a devaluation raises the relative price of foreign goods. The effect is to induce an increased demand for American goods and a reduction in demand for imports in the United States.

The case we have just considered is special, however, in one important respect. The economy was initially in balance of trade equilibrium at full employment. The disturbance of the economy took place in the trade account. Accordingly, if we could move the $NX' = 0$ locus back to the full-employment level of income—as we could with a devaluation—both internal and external balance would be attained. Put differently, the reason there was an internal balance problem of unemployment in Figure 20-3 was the reduction in exports and consequent external balance problem. Both problems could thus be cured through devaluation.

In general, though, we cannot secure both external and internal balance following a disturbance by using just one instrument of policy. A general rule of policy making is that we need to use as many policy instruments as we have policy targets. Thus if the disturbance causes a trade deficit, it will, in general, not be enough just to have a devaluation.

Finally, a comment on the role of the exchange rate in a fixed rate system: In the fixed rate system, the exchange rate is an *instrument of policy.* The central bank can change the exchange rate for policy purposes, devaluing when the current account looks as though it will be in for a prolonged deficit. In a system of clean floating, by contrast, the exchange rate moves freely to equilibrate the balance of payments. In a system of dirty floating, the central bank attempts to manipulate the exchange rate while not committing itself to any given rate. The dirty floating system is thus intermediate between a fixed rate system and a clean floating system.

20-2 THE MONETARY APPROACH TO THE BALANCE OF PAYMENTS

It is frequently suggested that external balance problems are monetary in nature. In this section we take up the question of the role of monetary considerations in explaining balance of payments problems. In particular, we consider the claim that balance of payments deficits are a reflection of an excessive money supply.

There is a simple first answer to that claim. It is obviously true that, for any given balance of payments deficit, a sufficient contraction of the money stock will restore external balance. The reason is that a monetary contraction, by raising interest rates and reducing spending, generates a contraction in economic activity, a decline in income, and therefore a decline in imports. It is equally true that this result could be achieved by tight fiscal policy, and so there is nothing especially monetary about this interpretation of remedies for external imbalance.

A more sophisticated interpretation of the problem recognizes the link, between the balance of payments deficit, foreign exchange market intervention, and the money supply. The automatic mechanism is for a sale of foreign exchange—as arises in the case of deficits—to be reflected in an equal reduction in the stock of high-powered money. The central bank merely sells one asset (foreign exchange) and buys another (high-powered money). This process will automatically lead to a decline in the stock of money in deficit countries and an increase in the money stock in surplus countries. Given that the money supply is thus linked to the external balance, it is obvious that this adjustment process must ultimately lead to the right money stock so that external payments are in balance. This is the adjustment process discussed above.

Sterilization

The only way the adjustment process can be suspended is through *sterilization operations.* We discussed this in Chapter 11 on the money supply. There we noted that central banks frequently offset, or sterilize, the impact of foreign exchange market intervention on the money supply through open market operations. Thus, a deficit country that is selling foreign exchange and correspondingly reducing its money supply may offset this reduction by open market purchases of bonds that restore the money supply.

TABLE 20-1	BALANCE SHEET OF THE MONETARY AUTHORITIES
Assets	Liabilities
Net foreign assets (*NFA*) Domestic credit (*DC*)	High-powered money (*H*)

Such a practice suspends the automatic adjustment mechanism. Persistent external deficits are possible because the link between the external imbalance and the equilibrating changes in the money stock is broken. It is in this sense that persistent external deficits are a monetary phenomenon: by sterilizing, the central bank actively maintains the stock of money too high for external balance.

The Monetary Approach and the IMF

The emphasis on monetary considerations in the interpretation of external balance problems is called the *monetary approach to the balance of payments.*[4] The monetary approach has been used extensively by the IMF in its analysis and design of economic policies for countries in balance of payments trouble. We give the flavor of the approach by describing typical IMF procedure in analyzing a balance of payments problem.

We start with the balance sheet of the monetary authority, typically the central bank, as in Table 20-1. The monetary authority's liabilities are high-powered money. But on the asset side it can hold both foreign assets—including foreign exchange reserves, gold, and claims on other central banks or governments—and domestic assets, or *domestic credit.* Domestic credit consists of the monetary authority's holdings of claims on the public sector—government debt—and on the private sector—usually loans to banks.

From the balance sheet identity, we have

$$\Delta NFA = \Delta H - \Delta DC \qquad (3)$$

where ΔNFA denotes the change in net foreign assets, ΔH the change in high-powered money, and ΔDC the change in domestic credit. In words, the change in the central bank's holdings of foreign assets is equal to the change in the stock of high-powered money minus the change in domestic credit.

The important point about equation (3) is that ΔNFA is the balance of payments: recall from Chapter 6 that official reserve transactions, which is all that ΔNFA is, are equal to the balance of payments.

The first step in developing a monetary approach–type stabilization policy package is to decide on a balance of payments target, ΔNFA^*. The IMF asks how much of a deficit the country can afford and then suggests policies to make the projected deficit no larger. The target is based largely on the availability of loans and credit from abroad and the possibility of drawing down existing reserves.

The next step is to ask how much the demand for money in the country will increase. The planned changes in the stock of high-powered money ΔH^* will

---

[4] For a collection of essays on this topic, see Jacob Frenkel and Harry G. Johnson (eds.), *The Monetary Approach to the Balance of Payments* (London: Allen & Unwin, 1976). See also *The Monetary Approach to the Balance of Payments* (Washington, D.C.: International Monetary Fund, 1977).

have to be just sufficient to produce, via the money multiplier process, the right increases in the stock of money to meet the expected increase in demand. Then, given ΔNFA^* and ΔH^*, equation (3) tells the monetary authority how much domestic credit it can extend consistent with its balance of payments target and expected growth in money demand. Typically, a stabilization plan drawn up by the IMF will include a suggested limit on the expansion of domestic credit.

The limit provides a *ceiling on domestic credit expansion*. The adoption of such a ceiling helps the central bank avoid the temptation of expanding its loans to the government or private sector in the face of rising interest rates or government budget deficits.

How Does It Work?

The simplicity of equation (3) raises an obvious question. Since all it takes to improve the balance of payments is a reduction in the rate of domestic credit expansion, why not balance payments immediately and always? To answer this question, we need to understand the channels through which the curtailment of domestic credit improves the balance of payments.

Controlling domestic credit means operating a tight monetary policy. Consider an economy that is growing and has some inflation, so that demand for nominal balances is rising. If domestic credit expansion is slowed, an excess demand for money develops. This, in turn, causes interest rates to rise and spending to decline. The increase in interest rates leads to a balance of payments improvement. That is, the monetary approach as used by the IMF relies on restrictive monetary policy to control the balance of payments. There is, though, a subtle difference between domestic credit ceilings and ordinary tight money. In an open economy with fixed exchange rates, the money stock is endogenous. The central bank cannot control the money stock, since it has to meet whatever demand arises for foreign currency. But it can make "money" tight by reducing the growth of domestic credit. That will imply that the only source of money growth becomes an increase in foreign exchange reserves or foreign borrowing. The economy has to go through enough of a recession or rise in interest rates to generate a balance of payments surplus.

The use of domestic credit ceilings is a crude policy to improve the balance of payments. But the simplicity of the conceptual framework, and the apparent definiteness of the policy recommendations to which it leads, frequently makes it the best policy tool available, particularly if dramatic action is needed and the credibility of the government's policies need to be restored.

The Monetary Approach and Depreciation

Proponents of the monetary approach have argued that depreciation of the exchange rate cannot improve the balance of payments except in the short run. The argument is that in the short run the depreciation does improve a country's competitive position and that this very fact gives rise to a trade surplus and therefore to an increase in the money stock. Over the course of time, the rising money supply raises aggregate demand and therefore prices until the economy returns to full employment and external balance. Devaluation thus exerts only a transitory effect on the economy which lasts as long as prices and the money supply have not yet increased to match fully the higher import prices.

The analysis of the monetary approach is entirely correct in its insistence on a longer-run perspective in which, under fixed exchange rates, prices and the money stock adjust and the economy achieves internal and external balance. It is also correct in arguing that monetary or domestic credit restraint will improve the balance of payments. But this mechanism is not painless, since the tight money policy produced by slow domestic credit growth typically produces a recession.

The approach is misdirected when it suggests that exchange rate policy cannot, even in the short run, affect a country's competitive position. More importantly, exchange rate changes frequently occur from a position of deficit and unemployment. In that case, a depreciation moves the economy toward equilibrium. It eases the adjustment mechanisms by achieving an increase in competitiveness through an increase in import prices rather than through a recession-induced decline in domestic prices.

Summary

1. Once we allow for price flexibility with fixed exchange rates, we use the analytical apparatus of Chapter 13. Price flexibility ultimately leads an economy to full employment with balanced trade. The mechanism involves changes in the domestic money supply which occur as the central bank keeps selling foreign exchange to domestic residents in exchange for domestic currency (essentially an open market sale of foreign currency). The falling money stock reduces our prices and therefore improves the balance of trade. Policy can be used actively to bring about adjustments without relying on this automatic and slow-moving mechanism.
2. Because trade does not necessarily balance in short-run equilibrium, there may be a *policy dilemma* in attempting both to move income to the potential output level and to balance trade. Increasing the level of income to move it closer to potential may well worsen the trade balance. The use of *expenditure switching* policies, which change the relative prices of domestic and imported goods, combined with *expenditure reducing* policies, can move the economy to full employment with balanced trade.
3. The monetary approach to the balance of payments emphasizes the central bank's balance sheet identity, equation (3), which shows that sufficient contraction of domestic credit will improve the balance of payments. This improvement comes about through higher interest rates and lower domestic income. We should also note that the link between the balance of

payments and the domestic stock of money, which is central to the monetary approach, may be broken through sterilization operations by the central bank.

20-3 FLEXIBLE EXCHANGE RATES, MONEY, AND PRICES

We now return to a flexible exchange rate world. We once again assume, just as in the Mundell-Flemming model of Chapter 6, that capital is perfectly mobile. The only difference with the earlier treatment is that now prices, too, are allowed to change. Our question now is how output, the exchange rate, and prices respond to monetary and fiscal policy and how that response evolves over time. The starting point is a discussion of the adjustment of prices and the exchange rate to the state of the economy.

The Adjustment Process

Figure 20-4 shows the interest rate and output. Full employment is shown by the vertical line Y^*. The assumption of perfect international capital mobility is reflected in the horizontal BB schedule. Only at an interest rate $i = i_f$, will the balance of payments be in equilibrium. If the interest rate were higher, there would be net inflows of capital. Conversely, with a domestic interest lower, capital would flow out and the balance of payments would turn to deficit.

We make two strategic assumptions to describe the adjustment process: First, whenever output exceeds full employment, prices are rising. Conversely, when output is below potential, prices are falling. Second, we assume that capital is highly mobile. That implies we are always moving toward the BB schedule in Figure 20-4 because our interest rate cannot diverge far from that in the rest of the world. Decline in interest rates, say, because of a monetary expansion, leads to depreciation and an increase in net exports, income, money demand, and interest rates, moving us back toward BB. Conversely, a tightening in money or a fiscal expansion leads to a tendency for interest rates to rise. In response, capital flows in, and the currency appreciates. There is a loss in competitiveness and a fall in net exports, income, and money demand, and so the pressure on interest rates to rise is offset.

With these assumptions we can study the adjustment process in terms of Figure 20-4. Anywhere to the right of Y^*, prices are rising and to the left prices are falling. Points above BB lead to capital inflows and appreciation; points below, to capital outflows and depreciation. Moreover, with capital mobility that is extremely high, the exchange rate will adjust very rapidly so that we are practically always on the BB schedule.

A Monetary Expansion: Short- and Long-Run Effects

We saw earlier that with given prices a monetary expansion, under flexible rates and perfect capital mobility, leads to depreciation and increased in-

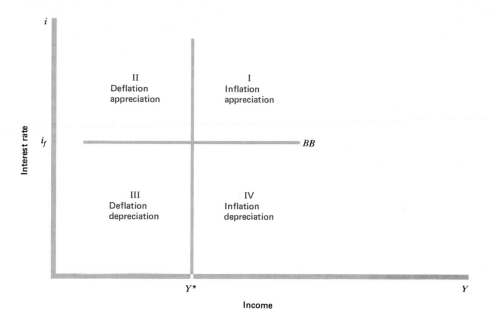

FIGURE 20-4   ADJUSTMENT OF EXCHANGE RATES AND PRICES.
Prices move in response to the deviation of the economy from full
employment. When output is above potential, prices are rising (regions I
and IV), and they are falling at output levels below potential (regions II
and III). With capital highly mobile the balance of payments is sensitive to
interest rates. If our interest rate falls below the world level, capital tends
to flow out, and that leads to a deficit and depreciation of the exchange
rate (regions III and IV). Conversely, a rise in interest rates leads to
capital inflows, a surplus, and appreciation (regions I and II).

come. We ask how that result is modified once we take adjustments in prices
into account. We will show that the output adjustment is now only transitory.
In the long run a monetary expansion leads to exchange depreciation and to
higher prices with no change in competitiveness. Figure 20-5 helps make
these points.

In Figure 20-5 we start at an initial equilibrium with full employment,
payments balance, monetary equilibrium, and equilibrium in the domestic
goods market. All this occurs at point E. Now a monetary expansion takes place
and shifts the LM schedule to LM'. The new goods and money market equilibrium at E' involves an interest rate below the world level, and therefore the
exchange rate immediately depreciates, raising home competitiveness and
thus shifting the IS schedule to IS'. The economy moves rapidly from E via E' to
E''. Output has risen, the exchange rate has depreciated, and the economy has
thereby gained in external competitiveness. But that is not the end of the story.

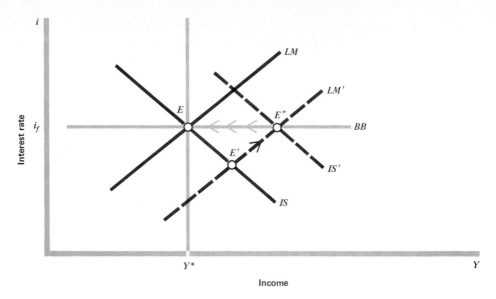

FIGURE 20-5 THE SHORT- AND LONG-RUN EFFECTS OF A MONETARY EXPANSION. The economy is in initial equilibrium at E when a monetary expansion shifts the LM schedule to LM'. The goods and money market equilibrium at E' involves an interest rate below the world level. Capital outflows now lead to immediate exchange depreciation, and therefore the IS schedule shifts to IS'. The economy thus moves rapidly from E to E''. But at E'' there is overemployment, and hence prices are rising. Rising prices reduce real balances and shift the LM schedule back toward E. As real balances decline, interest rates tend to rise, drawing in capital and leading to appreciation, which shifts the IS' schedule back toward E. In the long run, output returns to normal, and money, prices, and the exchange rate all rise in the same proportion.

At E'' output is above the full-employment level. Prices are therefore rising, and that implies real balances are falling. As the real money stock M/P declines because of rising prices, the LM schedule starts shifting to the left. Interest rates tend to rise, capital tends to flow in, and the resulting appreciation leads now to a decline in competitiveness that also shifts the IS schedule back toward the initial equilibrium. Both the IS and LM schedules thus move back toward point E. The process continues until point E is reached again.

What adjustments have taken place once the economy is back to point E? At point E interest rates have returned to their initial level and so have relative prices eP_f/P. In moving from E to E' the exchange rate depreciated immediately, ahead of the rise in prices. But when prices increased and real balances fell, some of that depreciation was reversed. Over the whole adjustment process, prices and exchange rates rose in the same proportion, leaving relative prices eP_f/P and therefore aggregate demand unchanged. In the long run money was therefore *entirely neutral*. Table 20-2 summarizes these results. Neutrality of money means, in terms of the second row of the table, that nominal money, prices, and the exchange rate all increase in the same proportion so that real money and relative prices are unchanged.

Exchange Rate Overshooting

The analysis of monetary policy under flexible exchange rates given above leads to an important insight about the adjustment process. The important feature of the adjustment process is that *exchange rates and prices do not move at the same rate*. When a monetary expansion pushes down interest rates, the exchange rate adjusts immediately, but prices adjust only gradually. Monetary expansion therefore leads in the short run to an immediate and abrupt change in relative prices and competitiveness.

Figure 20-6 shows time paths of nominal money, the exchange rate, and the price level implied by the analysis of Figure 20-5. For each of these variables we show an index that is initially equal to 100. The economy starts at long-run equilibrium. Then, at time T_0, the money stock is increased by 50 percent. Thus the money stock rises from 100 to 150 and stays at that higher level as shown by the solid schedule. The exchange rate immediately depreciates. In fact the exchange rate index rises by more than money, say, from the initial level of 100 at point A to a new level of 170 at point A'. Prices by contrast do not move rapidly.

Following the impact effect at time T_0, further adjustments take place. Because the gain in competitiveness at time T_0 has raised output above potential, there is now inflation. Prices are rising, and at the same time the exchange rate is appreciating, thus undoing part of the initial, sharp depreciation. Over time, prices rise to match the increase in money, and the exchange rate will also match the higher level of money and prices. In the long run, real variables are unchanged. The adjustment pattern for the exchange rate seen in Figure 20-6 involves *overshooting*. The exchange rate overshoots its new equilibrium

TABLE 20-2 THE SHORT- AND LONG-RUN EFFECTS OF A MONETARY EXPANSION

	M/P	e	P	eP_f/P	Y
Short run	+	+	0	+	+
Long run	0	+	+	0	0

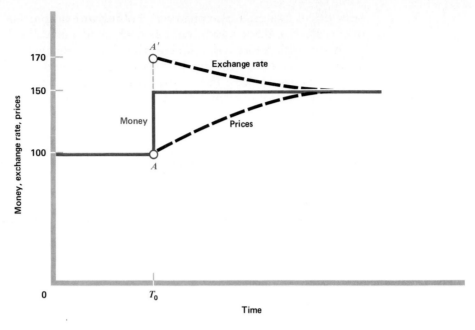

FIGURE 20-6 EXCHANGE RATE OVERSHOOTING. The diagram
shows an index for prices, money, and the exchange rate. Initially the
economy is in full equilibrium, and the value of each index is chosen as
100. A permanent increase in the money stock of 50 percent takes
place at time T_0, as shown by the solid schedule. The exchange rate
immediately depreciates from A to A', more than the increase in money.
Prices adjust only gradually. In the short run, the relative price of
imports, eP_f/P, thus increases sharply. That gain in competitiveness
causes a transitory income expansion. But over time prices rise and the
exchange rate appreciates somewhat, undoing the initial overshooting.
In the long run, nominal money, the exchange rate, and prices all rise in
the same proportion (50 percent, from 100 to 150), and real balances
and the relative price of imports are therefore unchanged.

level when, in response to a disturbance, at first it moves *beyond* the equilibrium it ultimately will reach and then gradually returns to the long-run equilibrium. **Overshooting means that changes in monetary policy produce large
changes in exchange rates.**

Figure 20-7 shows an index of the DM (deutsche mark)/$ exchange rate
for the period since 1979. We notice the sharp depreciation of the DM or
appreciation of the dollar from 1979 to the beginning of 1985, and the
subsequent reversal, which continued well into 1986. We also show an index
of the relative price, eP_f/P, using consumer prices in Germany and the United

States. The diagram shows clearly that along with an appreciating dollar there occurs a loss in U.S. competitiveness as eP_f/P declines. The dollar appreciation is partly explained by the shift toward tight money in the United States, starting in late 1979. Our model predicts that, in the case of tight money and easy fiscal policy, there would be an immediate appreciation of the dollar. Moreover, in the short run, prices would respond relatively little, and therefore competitiveness would immediately decline, almost one for one with the appreciation. The episode supports strongly the notion that under flexible exchange rates monetary policy has powerful effects on the exchange rate, competitiveness, and net exports.

FIGURE 20-7   THE EXCHANGE RATE AND RELATIVE PRICES:
GERMANY–UNITED STATES (index: 1980 = 100).

These effects are so strong that they have become a source of major concern. Those who believe that exchange rate overshooting introduces an undesirable instability into the economy argue that governments should intervene in foreign exchange markets to avoid large, excessive exchange rate fluctuations. The sharp dollar appreciation of 1980 – 1985 strongly reinforced the call for such intervention. In 1985 the major countries agreed in principle that they would intervene to try to prevent exchange rate instability.

Purchasing Power Parity

The long-run neutrality of money discussed above illustrates the potential role of exchange rates in offsetting the effects of changes in the price level at home and abroad on the terms of trade. In the preceding analysis, the exchange rate rose by precisely the right amount to offset the effects of domestic inflation on the terms of trade. That is, the exchange depreciation maintained the *purchasing power* of our goods in terms of foreign goods between the initial and the final equilibrium positions.

An important view of the determinants of the exchange rate is the theory that exchange rates move primarily as a result of differences in price level behavior between the two countries in such a way as to maintain the terms of trade constant. This is the *purchasing power parity* (PPP) theory. The theory argues that exchange rate movements primarily reflect divergent rates of inflation. Examining the terms of trade, eP_f/P, the theory maintains the following: When P_f and/or P change, e changes in such a way as to maintain eP_f/P constant.

PPP is a plausible description of the trend behavior of exchange rates, especially when inflation differentials between countries are large. In particular, we have seen that the PPP relationship does hold in the face of an increase in the money stock. If price level movements are caused by monetary changes — as they are likely to be if the inflation rate is high — then we should expect PPP relationships to hold in the long term.

But qualifications are necessary. First, even a monetary disturbance affects the terms of trade in the short run. Exchange rates tend to move quite rapidly relative to prices, and thus in the short term of a quarter or a year, we should not be at all surprised to see substantial deviations of exchange rates from the rates implied by PPP. And indeed, the terms of trade do move in the short run, as we already saw above.

The second important qualification concerns the role of nonmonetary disturbances in affecting exchange rates. For example, we saw that an increase in exports improves our terms of trade or leads to currency appreciation at unchanged domestic prices. Or if we look at an increase in potential output as another example, we will find that the equilibrium terms of trade worsen. To absorb the increased output, demand must rise, implying a decline in the relative price of our goods. Thus, it is apparent that, over time, adjustments to *real* disturbances will affect the *equilibrium* terms of trade. In the longer run,

BOX
20-2

THE STRONG DOLLAR: 1980–1985

In the period 1980–1985 the dollar appreciated strongly in world currency markets. The explanation for the dollar appreciation must be seen in tight monetary and expansionary fiscal policy followed in the United States beginning in 1981.* The effects of the strong dollar were felt in a loss of competitiveness and a large increase in imports. The United States was becoming a net debtor.

Table 1 shows some of the data. The real exchange rate ($R = eP_f/P$) appreciated more than 30 percent. Net exports declined from plus 1.2 percent of GNP in 1980 to -2.0 percent in 1985.

TABLE 1 EFFECTS OF THE STRONG DOLLAR	1980	1981	1982	1983	1984	1985
Real exchange rate (index 1980–1982 = 100)	111	100	91	88	82	78
Net exports (percent of GNP)	1.2	1.1	0.8	−0.2	−1.7	−2.0
Import penetration, %						
Capital goods	14.6	17.0	19.7	24.6	29.6	29.2
Consumer goods	6.9	7.4	7.7	8.7	10.7	10.8
Net investment position ($U.S. billion)	106	141	147	106	28	−60

Source: *Federal Reserve Bulletin* and Morgan Guaranty.

The effects of the real appreciation can be seen in the change in import penetration. *Import penetration* is defined as the fraction of domestic spending that is met by imports. In the 1980–1985 period import penetration in the area of capital goods (investment goods) doubled: in that area nearly 30 cents of every dollar spent is on imports. Even in the area of consumer goods, import penetration rose sharply. Whereas in 1980 less than 7 cents of every dollar spent on consumer goods was for imports, by 1985 nearly 11 cents per dollar was on imports. This is an extraordinary change. Businesses responded to the import invasion by calling for protection from foreign producers through tariffs or quotas.

The costs of the external deficit show up in a declining net foreign asset position. To finance the external deficit, the United States is selling assets. In 1980–1983 the country was still a net creditor in the world, having more foreign assets than foreigner-owned U.S. assets. But by 1985 foreigners owned more U.S. assets than the United States owned abroad. The U.S. had rapidly become a net debtor nation, to the same total extent as Mexico or Brazil.

The rapid accumulation of external debts is a warning signal that the external balance needs adjustment. And indeed, the decline in the dollar in 1985–1986, provides the hope that adjustment will take place in the second half of the eighties.

---

* See Martin Feldstein, "The Budget Deficit and the Dollar," in *NBER Macroeconomics Annual*, 1986.

exchange rates and prices do *not* necessarily move together, as they do in a world where all disturbances are monetary. On the contrary, we may have important changes in relative prices. Such changes run counter to the purchasing power parity view of exchange rates.

Figure 20-8 shows the level of prices in the United Kingdom compared with the United States. The index P_{UK}/P_{US} measures the relative prices. It rises when inflation in the United Kingdom exceeds that in the United States. It remains flat when inflation rates are the same. We also show an index of the exchange rate, measuring the price of a dollar in pound sterling.

Strict PPP theory would argue that the exchange rate index and the relative price level should move in line. But that clearly is *not* the case. For example, in 1976, the exchange rate depreciated more than relative prices changed. Conversely, in 1980–1981, relatively high inflation in the United Kingdom was not at all matched by depreciation. Thus in the short run, and over longer periods, exchange rates can diverge from the evolution of relative prices. "Real" factors, such as a change in fiscal policy, discovery of North Sea oil, or supertight money, have short-run effects on the exchange rate, and some can even change long-run relative prices.

As an empirical matter, PPP views of exchange rates work well when, as frequently happens, inflation differences predominate. Thus PPP is an impor-

FIGURE 20-8   PURCHASING POWER PARITY? RELATIVE PRICES AND THE EXCHANGE RATE. UK/US 1973–1985 (index: 1973–1975 = 100).

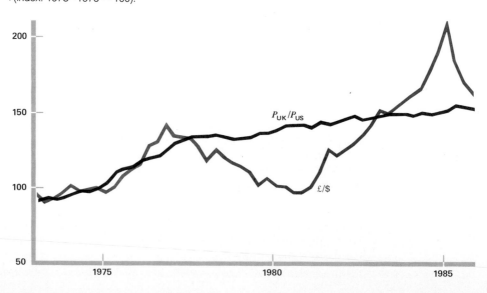

tant explanation of some large exchange rate movements, particularly in hyperinflations. But not all exchange rate changes are caused by monetary disturbances, and PPP does not provide a good explanation for the short-run behavior of exchange rates.

Summary

In this section we allowed for price flexibility as well as exchange rate flexibility. We assumed that the price level increases when output is above the full-employment level and that the exchange rate appreciates when the interest rate is above the world level, and there is therefore a capital inflow. The examination of monetary disturbances under flexible prices and exchange rates gave us the following results:

1. Price level and exchange rate adjustments affect the level of income and the interest rate. An increasing price level reduces real balances, tending to increase the interest rate. Changes in the price level and the exchange rate also affect the terms of trade and thus influence the demand for our goods.
2. A monetary expansion in the long run increases the price level and the exchange rate, keeping real balances and the terms of trade constant. In the short run, though, the monetary expansion increases the level of output and reduces the interest rate, depreciating the exchange rate. The exchange rate overshoots its new equilibrium level.
3. Purchasing power parity theory argues that exchange rate changes are, in practice, caused by divergences in inflation rates between countries, with the exchange rate changing in a way that maintains the terms of trade constant. This theory is a good predictor of the behavior of the exchange rate over long periods when disturbances are caused mainly by monetary factors, such as in hyperinflations. But in the short-run, monetary disturbances are not neutral, and even in the long run the exchange rate can change as a result of real disturbances. Examples include changes in technology in different countries, shifts in export demand, and shifts in potential output.

We have now completed the core of this chapter. The remaining sections take up a number of issues that extend the basic analysis.

20-4 INTEREST DIFFERENTIALS AND EXCHANGE RATE EXPECTATIONS

A cornerstone of our theoretical model of exchange rate determination was international capital mobility. In particular, we argued that, with capital markets sufficiently integrated, we would expect interest rates to be equated across countries. How does this assumption stand up to the facts? In Figure 20-9 we show the U.S. interest rates on certificates of deposit (CDs) and an

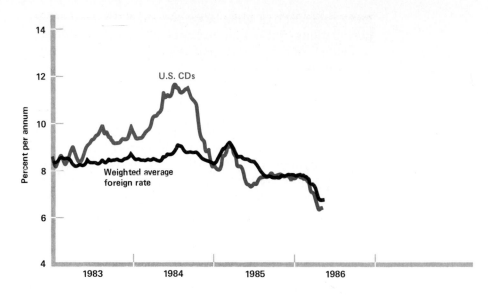

FIGURE 20-9   THE INTEREST RATE ON U.S. CERTIFICATES OF
DEPOSIT AND FOREIGN INTEREST RATES. (*Source:* Board of
Governors of the Federal Reserve, *Selected Interest Rates and
Exchange Rates.*)

average of interest rates in major industrialized countries over the period
1983–1986. It is quite apparent from the chart that these rates are certainly
not equalized. Thus, in 1984, the interest differential reached nearly four
percentage points. How do we square these facts with our theory?

Exchange Rate Expectations

Our theoretical analysis was based on the assumption that capital flows internationally in response to nominal interest differentials. For example, if domestic interest rates were 10 percent and foreign rates 6 percent, we would,
according to the earlier sections, expect a capital inflow.

However, such a theory is incomplete in a world where exchange rates
can, do, and are expected to change. For example, consider a situation where
the deutsche mark is expected to appreciate by 5 percent over the next year
relative to the dollar. Suppose the interest rate in Germany is 6 percent.
Anyone buying German bonds will earn a return in deutsche marks of 6
percent. Suppose now that the U.S. interest rate is 10 percent. A German
investing in the United States for a year will, at the beginning of the year,
exchange deutsche marks for dollars and then earn 10 percent on dollars. At

				Adjusted interest differential,
Case	Domestic interest rate i	Foreign interest rate i_f	Depreciation $\Delta e/e$	$i - i_f - \Delta e/e$
1	10	5	0	5
2	10	15	−5	0
3	10	15	−2	−3
4	10	15	−10	5

TABLE 20-3   INTEREST RATES AND EXCHANGE DEPRECIATION (In Percentages)

the end of the year, she will want to change the dollars back into deutsche marks to spend in Germany. But she expects that by the end of the year, each dollar will be worth 5 percent less in terms of deutsche marks, as a result of the expected depreciation. Therefore, in terms of marks, she will expect to earn only 5 percent (10 percent minus 5 percent) by investing in American bonds, whereas she earns 6 percent by investing in German bonds. The natural preference will be to invest in German bonds.[5]

It is clear, therefore, that we must extend our discussion of interest rate equalization to incorporate expectations of exchange rate changes. Table 20-3 gives some combinations of the domestic interest rate i, the foreign interest rate i_f, and exchange rate changes $\Delta e/e$. Suppose we want to know the return, in terms of domestic currency, of investments here compared with those abroad. For domestic investments we look at the interest rate i. For foreign investments, we look at the interest rate i_f *and* at the exchange depreciation. Suppose foreign interest rates were 5 percent and exchange rates did not change. This occurs in case 1, and the *adjusted* interest differential $(i - i_f - \Delta e/e)$ is 5 percent in favor of the home country. In case 2 interest rates abroad are high (15 percent), but our currency appreciates at the rate of 5 percent or the foreign currency depreciates by that amount. Here the depreciation exactly offsets the higher foreign interest rates, and the adjusted differential is zero—what would be gained in interest is lost through the foreign depreciation. Cases 3 and 4 show circumstances where the foreign depreciation falls short of, and exceeds, the interest differential, respectively. In cases 1 and 4, we would want to invest in the home country; in case 2 we are indifferent; and case 3 favors the foreign country.

---

[5] You should confirm that an American who expects the dollar to depreciate by 5 percent would, given the 6 and 10 percent interest rates, also prefer to buy German bonds.

The trouble, of course, is that we do not know ahead of time how the exchange rate will move. We know the interest rates on, say, 3-month Treasury bills in the United States and the United Kingdom, so that we can compute the interest differential, but we do not know whether the pound will appreciate or depreciate over the next 3 months. Even if we somehow knew the direction, we would certainly not know the precise amount.

Investors then have to form *expectations* about the behavior of the exchange rate; that is, in deciding whether to invest at home or abroad, they have to make forecasts of the future behavior of the exchange rate. Given these forecasts, we would expect that, in a world of high capital mobility, the interest differentials, *adjusted for expected depreciation*, should be negligible. That means that a country that is certain to depreciate will have interest rates above the world level, and conversely, a country that is expected to appreciate will have interest rates below the world level.

The introduction of exchange rate expectations modifies our equation for the balance of payments. Now capital flows are governed by the difference between our interest rate and the foreign rate adjusted for depreciation, $i - i_f - \Delta e/e$. An increase in foreign interest rates or an expectation of depreciation, given our interest rates, would lead to a capital outflow. Conversely, a rise in our rates or an expectation of appreciation would bring about a capital outflow. We thus write the balance of payments as

$$BP = NX\left(Y, \frac{eP_f}{P}\right) + CF\left(i - i_f - \frac{\Delta e}{e}\right) \qquad (4)$$

The adjustment for exchange rate expectations thus accounts for international differences in interest rates. These differences are affected by differences in inflation rates and are reflected in trend movements of the exchange rate. High-inflation countries have high interest rates and depreciating currencies. We thus have an international extension of the Fisher equation discussed in Chapter 17. The international extension relies on PPP to argue that inflation differentials internationally are matched by depreciation. Our long-term relation then is

$$\text{Inflation differential} \simeq \text{interest differential} \simeq \text{depreciation rate} \qquad (5)$$

(The $\simeq$ sign means "approximately equal to.") The relation is only approximate because, as we have seen, exchange rates can move independently of prices and also because obstacles to capital flows may create long-term interest differentials.

There is another respect in which the introduction of exchange rate expectations is important, and that concerns speculative capital flows and their impact on macroeconomic equilibrium. The point is made with the help of Figure 20-10. Here the *BB* schedule is drawn for a given foreign interest rate

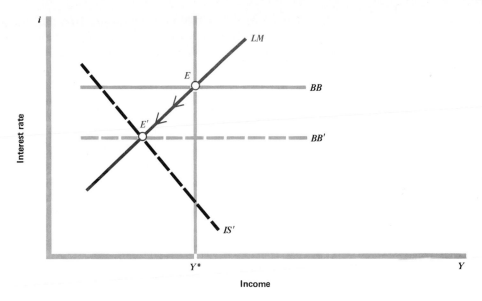

FIGURE 20-10   RESPONSE TO AN EXPECTED APPRECIATION OF
THE CURRENCY. The initial equilibrium at E is disturbed by the
expectation that the home currency will appreciate. The BB schedule
shifts down to BB', reflecting the fact that people are willing to hold
domestic assets at a reduced interest rate since they are compensated
for the differential by anticipated appreciation. At E there is now a
capital inflow that leads to exchange appreciation. The IS schedule (not
drawn) shifts to IS', and the economy moves into a recession. The
capital inflow has brought about a loss of trade competitiveness and
thus unemployment at point E'.

and a given expected rate of change for the exchange rate, say, zero. Suppose
that we start in full equilibrium at point E and that the market develops the
expectation that the home currency will appreciate. This implies that even
with a lower home interest rate, domestic assets are attractive, and so the BB
schedule shifts downward by the amount of expected appreciation.

Point E is no longer an equilibrium, given the shift of the BB schedule to
BB', but rather a position of surplus with large-scale capital inflows motivated
by the anticipation of appreciation. (This might well describe the case of the
United Kingdom in 1979 after awareness of British oil discoveries spread in
the market.) The surplus caused the exchange rate to start appreciating, and
we move in a southwesterly direction, as indicated by the arrow. The speculative attack causes appreciation, a loss in competitiveness, and, consequently,
falling output and employment.

This analysis confirms that exchange rate expectations, though their impact on capital flows and thus on actual exchange rates, are a potential source of disturbance to macroeconomic equilibrium.

20-5 EXCHANGE RATE CHANGES AND TRADE ADJUSTMENT: TWO EMPIRICAL ISSUES

In this section we take up two important empirical issues related to the possibilities for adjusting current account imbalances by changes in the exchange rate. The first possibility is that wages and prices may respond to movements in the exchange rate in a way that makes it impossible or at least difficult to change relative prices through changes in the exchange rate. This issue is particularly important if formal wage indexation arrangements link wage behavior to import prices and thus to the exchange rate.

The second issue we consider is whether changes in relative prices, assuming that they are possible, will affect the current account in the direction we have so far assumed. The assumption, so far, has been that a decline in the relative price of our goods improves the current account. But the possibility arises that at least in the short run there might be a perverse reaction. With import prices rising, for example, import demand may not decline sufficiently to compensate for higher prices, and thus total import spending (price times quantity) may actually increase. We turn our attention now to these two issues.

Exchange Rates and Relative Price Adjustment

In studying the flexible wage-price model, we assumed that wages and prices adjust to achieve full employment. Now we consider as an alternative the possibility that prices are based on labor cost or wages and that wages are inflexible in real terms. Suppose that labor wants to maintain the purchasing power of wages or to keep real wages constant. In such a world, changes in the cost of living would lead to changes in money wages, in labor cost, and therefore in prices, which in turn feed back into wages. Two points emerge from this description. The first is that in such a world, we may not be able to get to full employment. Labor may set the real wage too high, and at least in the intermediate run, the full-employment level of output cannot be sustained. The second point is that a process in which changes in prices feed back into wages and from there into prices is one of a *wage-price spiral* that may produce considerable volatility in the price level. Small disturbances can set off quite large changes in the price level.

Suppose, first, that the real wage is fixed in terms of the consumer price index that includes both domestic goods and imports so that changes in the consumer price index are fully passed on into wages. Assume further that changes in wages are fully passed on into increased domestic prices.

Starting from an initial equilibrium, there is now an exchange depreciation brought about by some short-term, reversible disturbance. The depreciation raises import prices and thereby has a direct effect on consumer prices and wages. To maintain the purchasing power of their wages, workers increase money wages and firms pass on the wage increase into higher prices. Where are we after the process ends? Real wages are constant, which means wages and the price level (a weighted average of the prices of domestic and imported goods) have risen in the same proportion; wage increases have been fully passed on, which means that real wages *in terms of domestic output* are also unchanged. The two results imply that relative prices are unchanged, or that the exchange depreciation is fully matched by domestic inflation.

Of course, this is not really the end because we have to ask how the higher price level affects the macroeconomic equilibrium. To the extent that lower real balances lower aggregate demand, we would have a reduction in employment. To round out our story, we can imagine that the central bank steps in to prevent unemployment by raising the money stock. If nominal money rises in proportion to the price increase, then the full-employment equilibrium, at the same terms of trade, is reestablished but, of course, at a higher level of wages and prices. This is an economy where there is very little stability in the price level because the slightest change in exchange rate expectations leads to actual exchange rate movements that are fully *validated* by domestic wage, price, and monetary developments.

A second context in which the idea of *sticky real wages* (wages that are difficult to change) is important is that of real disturbances. Suppose our export demand declines permanently because of, say, the introduction of superior technology abroad. To return to full employment, the relative price of our goods must fall so as to encourage foreign demand. But how can the relative price fall? In Section 20-3, we argued that the exchange rate will depreciate, thereby raising import prices relative to domestic prices and restoring our competitiveness. In the present context we have to recognize that import price increases would be immediately matched by wage increases and that these wage increases would be fully passed on into price increases. Relative prices cannot change. The consequence would, of course, be protracted unemployment. Unemployment would continue until the *real* wage declines.

The empirical question, then, is, How flexible are real wages? That is, to an important extent, a question of institutional arrangements. In small open economies with substantial cost-of-living indexation in wage agreements, it may indeed be very difficult to change real wages and relative prices through exchange rate changes.

Relative Prices and the Trade Balance: The J Curve

We come now to the second issue, the effect of changes in relative prices on the trade balance and the possibility that a depreciation *worsens* the trade balance. To make this point, we write out the trade balance, measured in terms of domestic goods, as

$$NX = X - \frac{eP_f}{P}Q \tag{6}$$

where X denotes the foreign demand for our goods or exports and Q denotes our own import quantity. The term $(eP_f/P)Q$ thus measures the *value* of our imports in terms of domestic goods.

Suppose that we now have an exchange depreciation and that in the first instance, domestic and foreign prices, P and P_f, are unchanged. Then the relative price of imports, eP_f/P, rises. This leads to two effects. First, if the physical *volume* of imports does not change, their *value* measured in domestic currency unambiguously increases because of the higher price. With unchanged physical import volume, Q, higher prices mean increased import spending and thus a worsening of the trade balance. This is the source for the potentially perverse response of the trade balance to exchange depreciation. However, there is an adjustment that runs in the opposite direction. The increased relative price of imports makes us more competitive and shifts demand in volume terms toward domestic goods. This *volume effect* of substitution in response to changed relative prices shows up in equation (6) in the form of increased export volume, X, and reduced import volume, Q. The volume effects thus ambiguously improve the trade balance.

The question, then, is whether the volume effects on imports and exports are sufficiently strong to outweigh the price effect, that is, whether depreciation raises or lowers net exports. The empirical evidence on this question is quite strong and shows the following result: *The short-term volume effects, say, within a year, are quite small and thus do not outweigh the price effect.*[6] *The long-term volume effects, by contrast, are quite substantial, and certainly enough to make the trade balance respond in the normal fashion to a relative price change.*

Where does this asymmetry come from, and what does it imply about trade adjustment to relative prices? First, the low short-term and high longer-term volume effects result from the time consumers and producers take to adjust to changes in relative prices. Some of these adjustments may be instantaneous, but it is clear that tourism patterns, for example, may take 6 months to a year to adjust and that relocation of production internationally, in response to changes in relative costs and prices, may take years. A case in point is increased foreign direct investment in the United States—say, Toyota moving from Japan to California. In the long term, such direct investment leads to

---

[6] See Michael C. Deppler and Duncan M. Ripley, "The World Trade Model: Merchandise Trade," *IMF Staff Papers,* March 1978; Duncan M. Ripley, "The World Model of Merchandise Trade: Simulation Applications," *IMF Staff Papers,* June 1980; and "Issues in the Assessment of the Exchange Rates of Industrial Countries," *IMF Occasional Paper No. 29,* July 1984.

reduced imports by the United States, and thus to an improved trade balance, but such an adjustment takes years, not weeks or months.

The lag in the adjustment of trade flows to changes in relative prices is thus quite plausible. The next question is, What do these lags imply about the impact of relative price changes on the trade balance? Suppose that at a particular time, starting with a deficit, we have a depreciation that raises the relative price of imports. The short-term effects result primarily from increased import prices with very little offsetting volume effects. Therefore, the trade balance initially worsens. Over time, as trade volume adjusts to the changed relative prices, exports rise and import volume progressively declines. The volume effects come to dominate, and in the long run, the trade balance shows an improvement. This pattern of adjustment is referred to as the *J-curve effect*, because diagrammatically the response of the trade balance looks like a J.

The J-curve effect could be seen in 1986 in the United States. Despite a rapid depreciation of the dollar starting in February 1985, the current account continued to worsen for the next year. But that depreciation should be expected to affect the current account with a lag, so that lower current account deficits can be anticipated at the end of 1986 and in later years.

The medium-term problem of sticky real wages and the J-curve effect are important qualifications to the macroeconomics of flexible rates as spelled out in Section 20-3. They imply that flexible exchange rates do not provide for instant, costless flexibility of relative prices and trade flows. At the same time, these considerations provide important clues for the interpretation of macroeconomic experiences across countries, particularly in showing why depreciations typically do not lead to improvements in the current account in the short term.

20-6 EXCHANGE RATE FLUCTUATIONS AND INTERDEPENDENCE

In the 1960s there was growing dissatisfaction with fixed exchange rates. The Bretton Woods system was called a crisis system because from time to time exchange rates would get out of line and expectations of exchange rate changes would mobilize massive capital flows that often precipitated the exchange rate changes that speculators expected. Is the flexible rate system of the 1970s and 1980s better? Is it less crisis-prone, and does it provide a better framework for macroeconomic stability? Before providing an answer, we look briefly at how flexibly the system has, in fact, operated.

Dirty Floating and Intervention

Under *fully* flexible exchange rates the government takes no action in the foreign exchange market. Far from buying or selling foreign exchange at a fixed price, the government does not conduct *any* foreign exchange transactions. It stays out of the foreign exchange market, whatever happens to the exchange rate. Such a system is almost unheard of, although the United States did behave that way briefly in 1981–1982. More commonly, governments intervene in the foreign exchange market to a lesser or greater extent. Foreign exchange market *intervention* occurs when a government buys or sells foreign exchange in an attempt to influence the exchange rate. The extent to which governments intervene varies substantially. They may only try to offset short-term fluctuations and buy or sell foreign exchange to maintain "orderly markets." But they also may try to keep an overvalued exchange rate from depreciating or an undervalued exchange rate from appreciating. *Dirty floating* (as opposed to clean) is the practice of using substantial intervention to try to maintain an exchange rate against the pressure of market forces.

During the 1973–1986 period, exchange market intervention has been of the decidedly dirty variety. Governments have intervened on a very large scale. This leads naturally to the question of why a government should try to resist market forces, to prevent an appreciation or a depreciation of the currency.

Why Governments Intervene

Central banks intervene to affect exchange rates for several reasons. Probably the main reason is the belief that many capital flows represent merely unstable expectations and that the induced movements in exchange rates move production in the economy in an unnecessarily erratic fashion. The second reason for the intervention is a cental bank's attempt to move the real exchange rate in order to affect trade flows. The third reason arises from the effects of the exchange rate on domestic inflation. Central banks sometimes intervene in the exchange market to prevent the exchange rate from depreciating, with the aim of preventing a depreciation-induced increase in the inflation rate.

Should central banks intervene in the exchange market? The basic argument for such intervention is that it is possible for intervention to smooth out fluctuations in exchange rates. At one extreme, the argument would assert that any movements in exchange rates produce unnecessary fluctuations in the domestic economy and that exchange rates therefore ought to be fixed. This is the basic argument for dirty floating. The only—and overwhelming—objection to the argument that the central bank should smooth out fluctuations is that there is no simple way of telling an erratic movement from a trend movement. How can we tell whether a current appreciation in the exchange rate is merely the result of a disturbance which will soon reverse itself, rather than the beginning of a trend movement in the exchange rate? There is no way of telling at the time a change occurs, although with the benefit of hindsight one can see which exchange rate movements were later reversed.

There is one circumstance under which central bank intervention might be desirable. It is clear from our earlier analysis that one of the key determinants of exchange rate behavior consists of expectations of economic policy. It may sometimes be possible to make it clear that there has been a change in policy only by intervening in the foreign exchange market. This is a case of putting your money where your mouth is.

Should Governments Intervene?

There is disagreement on whether governments should intervene in the foreign exchange market. The United States, for example, in 1981–1982 strongly refused consideration of any kind of intervention. The reason was that policy makers in the United States, unlike those in Europe, believed the market knows better than policy makers what level the exchange rate should be. But there is another and more interesting disagreement: it concerns the effectiveness of intervention. Does it make any difference to the exchange rate if the Bundesbank sells $1 billion from its reserves?

To judge the effectiveness of intervention we must make a distinction between *sterilized* and *nonsterilized intervention.* In the case of sterilized intervention a central bank, say, buys foreign exchange, issuing domestic money. But then the increase in home money is reversed by an open market sale of securities. In the sterilized intervention case, therefore, the home money supply is kept unchanged. By contrast in the case of nonsterilization, there is a change in the money stock equal to the amount of intervention.

Thus nonsterilized intervention results in a change in the money stock. It is widely agreed that nonsterilized intervention, because it changes the money supply, will affect exchange rates. There is widespread skepticism, however, about the effectiveness of sterilized intervention. In 1978–1979 the U.S. dollar was depreciating in currency markets even though there was intervention on a massive scale. But that intervention was carefully sterilized. Only in late 1979, when the dollar depreciation had come to alarm the Fed, did a change in policy take place. Monetary policy was tightened, and immediately the dollar depreciation was stopped and soon massively reversed.

That episode strongly suggests the effectiveness of nonsterilized intervention and of intervention that is backed by credible policies. The earlier failure of sterilized intervention suggested that only unsterilized intervention could affect the exchange rate. But a more recent episode gives cause for rethinking that issue.

The very large appreciation of the dollar from 1980 to 1985, described in Figure 20-7 and in Box 20-2, was a major concern to policy makers in the United States, Europe, and Japan.[7] Many policy makers thought that the markets had pushed the dollar too high, and that only speculative forces were

---

[7] See Federal Reserve Bank of Kansas City, "The U.S. Dollar—Recent Development, Outlook and Policy Options," 1985, which includes a discussion of many of the issues raised by the strong dollar, intervention, and coordination. See also Jeffrey Frankel, "Six Possible Meanings of Over-valuation: The 1981–85 Dollar," *Essays in International Finance* (Princeton, N.J.: Princeton, December 1985), and the Symposium in the Brookings Papers on Economic Activity, I, 1986.

keeping it up. In September 1985 the finance ministers of the Group of Five (the United States, Japan, Germany, France, and the United Kingdom) announced their view that the dollar was too high, and their central banks went into action to sell dollars to drive the rate down. The dollar responded quickly, suggesting that concerted action can affect the exchange rate even if there is no obvious change in monetary policy. Such action is certainly not guaranteed to work, but could work if there is widespread speculation in the markets about the future course of policy and if announcements and intervention suggest that future policy will try to move the exchange rate in a particular direction.

Interdependence

It used to be argued that under flexible exchange rates countries can pursue their own national economic policies—monetary and fiscal policy and the inflation rate—without having to worry about the balance of payments. That is certainly correct, but it is also misleading. There are important linkages between countries *whatever the exchange rate regime.*

These *spillover,* or *interdependence,* effects have been at the center of the discussion about flexible exchange rates. The effects of the tight U.S. monetary policies in 1980–1982 created problems for all industrialized countries. The reason is clear from our models: As the United States tightens monetary policy, our interest rates rise, and that attracts capital flows from abroad. The dollar appreciates, and foreign currencies depreciate. Table 20-4 shows the effects on other countries.

The U.S. appreciation implies a loss in competitiveness. World demand shifts from U.S. goods to those produced by our competitors. Therefore, at home, output and employment decline. Abroad, our competitors benefit from the depreciation of their currency. They become more competitive, and therefore output and employment abroad expand. Our monetary tightening

TABLE 20-4	MONETARY AND FISCAL POLICY EFFECTS WITH INTERDEPENDENCE			
	U.S. MONETARY EXPANSION		U.S. FISCAL EXPANSION	
	U.S.	Rest of the world	U.S.	Rest of the world
Exchange rate	$ depreciates		$ appreciates	
Output	+	−	+	+
Inflation	+	−	−	+

thus tends to promote employment gains abroad, which come, of course, at the expense of our own employment.

There are also spillover effects through prices. When our currency appreciates, import prices in dollars fall. Therefore our inflation tends to decline quite rapidly when there is a sharp dollar appreciation. But abroad the opposite occurs. Their currency depreciates, and therefore prices in foreign currency tend to increase. Inflation abroad thus rises. Foreigners might welcome an increase in employment as a side effect of our monetary policy, but they certainly can do without the inflation that comes from currency depreciation.

In the same way our fiscal policies exert effects abroad. A U.S. fiscal expansion such as in the 1980–1985 period will lead to dollar appreciation and a loss in competitiveness. The direct increase in our spending and the deterioration in our competitiveness are the channels through which our expansion is shared abroad. When the United States has a fiscal expansion, the rest of the world shares via increased exports. Table 20-4 summarizes these interdependence effects.[8]

Table 20-4 also shows the effects of monetary and fiscal policy on inflation. Because fiscal expansion leads to appreciation, the decline in import prices helps reduce inflation on the expanding country. But abroad import prices will rise, and that means inflation will be increased. These impacts of exchange rate movements on inflation were important factors in changing inflation rates in industrial countries in the 1980–1985 period.

Policy makers abroad therefore must decide whether to accept the higher employment-higher inflation effects of our policies or whether they should change their own policies. If inflation is already a problem abroad, or if the rest of the world is highly averse to inflation, then the policy response abroad to this *imported inflation* may well be to tighten money. A monetary contraction abroad, matching our own, ensures that exchange rates will not move or at least will move less. But it also means that our own tight money and recession become the world's tight money and a world recession. This was substantially what happened in the worldwide recession of 1981–1982.

Policy Synchronization

The large changes in exchange rates that arise when policies are not fully synchronized between countries pose a major threat to a world of free trade. When import prices fall by 20 or 30 percent because of a currency appreciation, large shifts in demand will occur. Domestic workers become unemployed, and they have no trouble seeing that it is foreigners who gain the jobs they just lost. Accordingly, there will be pressure for protection — tariffs or

---

[8] We showed before that in a country that takes foreign interest rates and income as given a fiscal expansion leads to *full* crowding out. Table 20-4 shows that once interactions with the rest of the world are taken into account, there is a world expansion. We do not prove this result here. For a demonstration see Robert Mundell, *International Economics* (New York: Macmillan, 1968).

quotas — to keep out imports that are "artificially cheap" due to the currency appreciation. In the United States repeated calls for protection in the automobile industry, in steel, and in many other industries reflect in large part the side effects of a dollar that appreciated sharply in response to tight money.

On the question of independence or interdependence under flexible exchange rates, the experience of the last 14 years offers a quite unambiguous answer. Under flexible exchange rates there is as much or more interdependence as there is under fixed rates. Moreover, because exchange rates are so flexible and so ready to respond to policies (good or bad), macroeconomic management does not become easier. Further, to the extent that exchange rate overshooting causes sharp changes in competitiveness, it leads to protectionist sentiment.

On all counts then, flexible rates are far from being a perfect system. But there is no better system. Therefore we can ask only whether through international coordination of interests and policies, we can make the system work better than it has in the recent past. In 1985 and 1986 the leaders of the major industrial countries recognized their independence and agreed to work toward more coordinated policies. But there were as yet no major institutional changes that would provide a mechanism to ensure that coordination would take place.

20-7 SUMMARY

1. External imbalances can be financed in the short-term. In the long run they call for adjustment.

2. Adjustment of the external balance calls for expenditure reducing and expenditure switching policies. The former change the level of spending, the latter affect the composition of spending between domestic goods and imports and exports.

3. Under fixed exchange rates, the automatic adjustment mechanism works via prices and money. Unemployment leads to a decline in prices, a gain in competitiveness, increased net exports, and a gain in employment. Money responds to trade imbalances, affecting the level of interest rates, spending, and hence the payments deficit.

4. The monetary approach to the balance of payments draws attention to the fact that a payments deficit always is a reflection of a monetary disequilibrium and always is self-correcting. But the correction mechanism, because it involves unemployment, may be excessively painful compared with policy actions such as devaluation.

5. Exchange rate overshooting results from the rapid response of exchange rates to monetary policy and the sluggish adjustment of prices. A monetary expansion will lead to an immediate depreciation but only a gradual

increase in prices. Exchange rate overshooting implies that real exchange rates are highly volatile.

6. Purchasing Power Parity (PPP) refers to the long-run tendency of exchange rates to offset divergent trends in national price levels. The currency of the country with the higher rate of inflation would tend to be depreciating at a rate equal to the inflation differential. If exchange rates follow PPP, then nominal exchange rate movements have no effects on competitiveness. In the short run, exchange rates certainly do not follow a PPP pattern.

7. Capital moves internationally in response to yield differentials taking into account anticipated exchange rate movements. Interest rates in a country with a depreciating currency have to be sufficiently high to compensate asset holders for the depreciation of the assets.

8. Changes in nominal exchange rates will affect relative prices only if there are no offsetting changes in wages and prices. The real exchange rate $R = eP_f/P$ can change only as a result of nominal exchange rate movements if P_f/P does not move in a fully offsetting manner. Among industrialized countries stickiness of wages and prices assures that real exchange rates change when nominal rates do.

9. If trade flows respond only gradually to a change in the real exchange rate, we observe a J-curve pattern. A real depreciation will worsen the trade balance in the short run, but then gradually improve it in later years.

10. Governments can intervene in exchange markets to limit the impact of exchange rate fluctuations, stemming from asset market disturbances, on output and prices. But intervention is very problematic when the authorities cannot determine whether the exchange rate is moving on account of fundamentals or noise.

11. Even under flexible exchange rates economies are closely tied to one another. A monetary expansion at home will lead to unemployment and disinflation abroad. A fiscal expansion will cause an expansion abroad along with inflation. These interdependence effects make a case for coordinating policies.

KEY TERMS

Real exchange rate
Expenditure switching
Expenditure reducing policies
Policy dilemmas
Monetary approach
Sterilization
Devaluation

Exchange rate overshooting
Exchange rate expectations
Purchasing power parity
J curve
Intervention
Dirty float
Interdependence

PROBLEM

1. It is sometimes said that a central bank is a necessary condition for a balance of payments deficit. What is the explanation for this argument?

2. Use the central bank balance sheet to show how a balance of payments deficit affects the stock of high-powered money under fixed exchange rates. Show, too, how sterilization operations work.

3. Consider a country that is in a position of full employment and balanced trade. Which of the following types of disturbance can be remedied with standard aggregate demand tools of stabilization? Indicate in each case the impact on external and internal balance as well as the appropriate policy response.
   (a) A loss of export markets
   (b) A reduction in saving and a corresponding increase in demand for domestic goods
   (c) An increase in government spending
   (d) A shift in demand from imports to domestic goods
   (e) A reduction in imports with a corresponding increase in saving

4. Discuss the manner in which income, price adjustments, and money supply adjustments interact in leading the economy ultimately to full employment and external balance. Choose as an example the case where a country experiences a permanent increase in exports.

5. In relation to external imbalance, a distinction is frequently made between imbalances that should be "financed" and those that should be "adjusted." Give examples of disturbances that give rise, respectively, to imbalances that require adjustment and those that should more appropriately be financed.

6. Consider a world with some capital mobility: The home country's capital account improves as domestic interest rates rise relative to the world rate of interest. Initially, the home country is in internal and external balance. (Draw the *IS, LM,* and *BB* schedules.) Assume now an increase in the rate of interest abroad.
   (a) Show the effect of the foreign interest rate increase on the *BB* schedule.
   (b) What policy response would immediately restore internal and external balance?
   (c) If the authorities took no action, what would be the adjustment process along the lines described by the "monetary approach to the balance of payments"? (You may refer here to your answer to problem 4.)

7. Suppose in year 1 we have price levels $P = 100$ and $P_f = 100$. Suppose next that in year 2 the respective price levels are $P_2 = 180$ and $P_{2f} = 130$. Let the exchange rate initially be $2/£.
   (a) If there were no real disturbances between year 1 and year 2, what would be the equilibrium exchange rate in year 2?
   (b) If the real exchange rate, eP_f/P had deteriorated between years 1 and 2 by 50 percent, what would the exchange rate be in year 2?

8. Explain why an expansionary fiscal policy reduces foreign income less than direct intervention by the central bank in the foreign exchange markets to depreciate the exchange rate.

9. Assume that capital is perfectly mobile, the price level is fixed, and the exchange rate is flexible. Now let the government increase purchases. Explain first why the equilibrium levels of output and the interest rate are unaffected. Then show whether the current account improves or worsens as a result of the increased government purchases of goods and services.

10. Assume that there is perfect mobility of capital. How does the imposition of a tariff affect the exchange rate, output, and the current account? (*Hint:* Given the exchange rate, the tariff reduces our demand for imports.)

11. Explain how and why monetary policy retains its effectiveness when there is perfect mobility of capital.

12. Consult the *Wall Street Journal* or some other newspaper which has foreign exchange rates listed on its financial pages. For some countries, such as Britain and Germany, you should find future prices listed. This is the price to be paid today to receive one unit of the foreign currency in the future. A 30-day future price for the pound sterling, say, is the price paid today to receive 1 pound 30 days from now. Explain why the future prices are not generally equal to the spot prices — the price paid today to receive the foreign currency today. See whether you can explain the difference between the relationship of spot and future prices for the pound and deutsche mark, respectively.

13. Assume you expect the pound to depreciate by 6 percent over the next year. Assume that the U.S. interest rate is 4 percent. What interest rate would be needed on pound securities — such as government bonds — for you to be willing to buy those securities with your dollars today, and then sell them in a year in exchange for dollars? Can you relate your answer to this question to your answer to problem 12?

14. What considerations are relevant for a country deciding whether to borrow abroad to finance a balance of trade deficit, or to adjust?

15. Explain the purchasing power parity theory of the long-run behavior of the exchange rate. Indicate whether there are any circumstances under which you would not expect the PPP relationship to hold.

INDEX

Aaron, Hank, 707n.
Accelerator model of investment, 313–316
  cost of capital effects and, 315–316
  defined, 307n., 313
  empirical results, 314–316
  sales and profits as determinants of
    investment, 316
Accessions, 543–544
Accommodation of supply shocks, 489–490
Accounting identity, 64
Ackley, Gardner, 426n.
Action lag, 442–443
Activism, 451–456
  of the CEA, 430
  defined, 451
  expectations and, 21–22
  fine tuning, 452–453
  Friedman on, 451
  monetarism and, 20–21
  money and inflation and, 20
  rules versus discretion, 453–456
  uncertainty and, 449–451
Actual aggregate demand, 67
Adaptive expectations, 509
Adjustable rate mortgages (ARMs), 323n.,
  568–569
Adjustment paths, 572
Adjustments:
  balance of payments, under fixed
    exchange rates, 734–743
  classical, 737–738
  to a fiscal expansion, 521–523
  in the *IS-LM* model, 281–284
  to a monetary disturbance, 210–212
  to a monetary expansion, 482–485
  to money and prices, under flexible
    exchange rates, 748–757
  of output and inflation (*see* Inflation and
    unemployment, dynamic
    adjustment of output and)

Adjustments (*Cont.*):
  to a real disturbance, 205–206
    adjustment process, 207, 209
    fiscal policy and, 209–210
Adverse supply shock, 487–489
Aggregate consumption and saving, 265
Aggregate demand:
  aggregate supply and, 22–25, 219–224
  components of (*see* Components of
    demand)
  consumption function and (*see*
    Consumption function and
    aggregate demand)
  curve (*see* Aggregate demand curve)
  defined, 22–24, 65
  equilibrium output and, 65–69
    actual aggregate demand and, 67
    aggregate demand, 65
    defined, 65, 68–69
    inventories and, 67–68
    national income identity and, 66–68
    planned aggregate demand and, 67–68
  inflation and, 15
  interest rates and, 116–125
  monetarism and, 20–21
Aggregate demand curve, 226–238
  change in price level and, 226
  classical case (fiscal policy), 235
  crowding out and, 235–238
  defined, 222–223
  derivation of, 227
  dynamic, 510–512, 533–535
  effect of a fiscal expansion on, 230–231
  effect of a monetary expansion on, 232
  graphical analysis of, 23–25
  Keynesian case, 234–235
  properties of, 228–232
  slope of, 228–230
Aggregate demand schedule (*see*
  Aggregate demand curve)

Aggregate supply, 243–247, 461–462, 491–492
  aggregate demand and, 22–25, 219–224
  classical theory of, 243–244
  curve (*see* Aggregate supply curve)
  defined, 23
  frictionless model (*see* Frictionless neoclassical model of the labor market)
  imperfect information–market clearing approach, 245–246
    search and, 246–247
  modern Keynesian approaches, 244–245
  real business cycle theory and, 247
  sticky wages (*see* Sticky wages)
  supply shocks (*see* Supply shocks)
  wages, prices, and output, 465–472
    Friedman-Phelps amendment, 469–472
    Phillips curve, 466–469
    policy tradeoff, 469
Aggregate supply curve, 477–482
  classical, 224–225
  costs and prices, 479–480
  defined, 23, 223–224
  dynamic, 503–504
  effects of a monetary expansion on, 482–485
  employment, wages and, 480–481
  expectations-augmented, 503–504
  factor markets and, 224
  graphical analysis of, 23–25
  inflation, expectations and, 501–507
  Keynesian, 224, 225
  long-run, 506–507
  production function, 477, 479
  properties of, 482
  shape of, 24
  short-run, 504–506
  slope of, 221–222
Aggregate supply schedule (*see* Aggregate supply curve)
Akerlof, George, 689n.
Aliber, Robert Z., 429n.
Ando, Albert, 258n., 267n.
"Animal spirits," 317, 433–434
Anticipated inflation, 561–567
Appreciation, currency, 186
Arrow, Kenneth, 426n.
Aschauer, David A., 278n., 605n.
Asset price of housing, 321
  rate of investment and, 321–322

Assets:
  bonds, 126
  equities or stocks, 126–127
  government, 611
  life-cycle theory of consumption and saving and, 262
  money, 126
  real, 127
  speculative demand for money and, 352–354
Assets markets (see *LM* curve, assets markets and)
Auerbach, Alan, 310n.
Automatic stabilizers, 88
Autonomous spending, 64
  multiplier and (*see* Multiplier)
Average cash balance, 344n.

Bach, G. L., 564n., 566n.
Bads, 38–39
Baily, Martin, 425n.
Balance of payments, 180–187
  adjustment to, under fixed exchange rates, 734–743
  capital account segment of, 181
  capital flows and, 197–198
  current account segment of, 180–181
  defined, 180, 181
  fixed exchange rates and, 182–183
  flexible exchange rates and, 184–185
  intervention and, 183–184
  making international payments, 181
  monetary approach to (*see* Monetary approach to balance of payments)
  overall, 181
  reserves and, 183
  surpluses and deficits, 181–185
  terminology, 185–186
Balanced budget amendment, 615–616
Balanced budget multiplier, 97–98, 108–110
Bank credit, 386n.
Bank deposits, multiple expansion of, 385–386, 413–414
Barro, Robert, 21, 241, 278, 349n., 604, 678n., 687n.
Barro-Ricardo equivalence proposition, 278–279, 604–605
Barter economy, 339
Barth, James, 605n.
Base drift, 403–406
Base-weighted price index, 62
Batten, D., 672n.

Baumol, William, 343*n*., 346, 726
Begg, David, 674*n*., 686*n*.
Beggar-thy-neighbor policy, 212
Bequests, 267
Bernanke, Ben, 316*n*., 425*n*.
Bilateral exchange rates, 187
Blanchard, Olivier, 552*n*., 604*n*., 693*n*.
Blinder, Alan, 405*n*., 616, 644*n*.
Bonds, 125–127
  coupon, 139
  coupon rate of, 329*n*.
  defined, 125, 126
  interest rates, present value, and
    discounting, 329–332
  open market operations and, 142–143
  perpetuity, 139
  as wealth, 604–605
  yield on, 330
  (*See also* Budget deficits, debt-financed)
Boskin, Michael, 278*n*., 683*n*., 708*n*.
Bossons, John, 267*n*.
Bosworth, Barry, 318–319, 612*n*., 706*n*.
Bracket creep, 591–592
Bretton Woods system, 734, 765
Broaddus, Alfred, 402*n*., 404*n*.
Broker's fee, 343
Brown, E. Cary, 421*n*.
Brumberg, Richard, 258*n*.
Brunner, Karl, 241, 407*n*., 426*n*., 552*n*.,
  666
Bruno, Michael, 571*n*.
Bryant, Ralph C., 399*n*.
Budget deficits, 581–621
  actual and full-employment, 102–103,
    589–590
  automatic reduction of, 602
  Barro-Ricardo equivalence proposition
    and, 278–279, 604–605
  bracket creep and, 591–592
  burden of, 609–614
  business cycle and, 589–590
  debt-financed, 602–609
    bonds as wealth, 604–605
    debt, growth, and instability,
      597–598, 606–609, 619–621
    defined, 583–584
    money-financed compared to,
      584–586, 605–606
    persistent deficits, 606
    transitory deficit, 603–604
    unpleasant monetarist arithmetic,
      648–650
  debt-income ratio, 607–609, 619–621
  defined, 56, 92

Budget deficits (*Cont.*):
  discretionary versus mandatory
    spending and, 593–594
  entitlement programs and, 593, 594
  fiscal drag and, 591–593
  government spending and revenues
    and, 593–602
    deficit problem, 595
    Gramm-Rudman-Hollings Act and,
      92, 582, 601–602
    interest payments and, 597–598
    Laffer curve and, 600–601
    outlays, 593–595
    receipts, 595
    state and local governments, 596
    supply-side economics and, 598
    tax cuts and revenues, 598–601
    tax cuts and spending, 601
  hyperinflation and, 652–653
  inflation-corrected, 653
  mechanics of, 583–588
  monetizing, 160
  money, inflation and (*see* Money and
    inflation, deficits and)
  money-financed, 584–586, 605–606
  national debt and, 587–588, 609–614
  national income accounting and, 93–95
  of the 1980s, 611–612
  nominal interest rates and, 652–653
  noninterest, 597–598
  optimal, 612–614
  as percent of GNP, 607–608
  primary, 597–598
  relationship between the Fed and the
    Treasury and, 381
  size and determinants of, 588–593
  size of government controversy, 615–617
  structural, 589–590
  supply-side economics and, 709
  unemployment rate and, 590
Budget surplus, 92–104
  balanced budget multiplier and, 97–98,
    108–110
  defined, 92
  effects of government purchases and tax
    changes on, 95–98
  full employment, 99–104
  national income accounting and, 93–95
Buiter, Willem, 619*n*.
Bureau of Economic Analysis (BEA), 12,
  13*n*., 36, 37
Business cycles:
  budget deficits and, 589–590
  control of (*see* Stabilization policy)

Business cycles (*Cont.*):
  defined, 10
  equilibrium real, 678–679
    propagation mechanisms of, 679–680
  inventories in, 293–296
  money and, 676–678
  output gap and, 10–13
  political (*see* Political business cycles)
  real, 247
Business fixed investment, alternative
    approaches, 311–317
  accelerator model of investment,
    313–316
  "animal spirits" and, 317
  business investment decision, 311–313
  discounted cash flow analysis, 311–313
    interest rates, present values and,
    329–332
  fluctuation of, 316–317
  sales and profits as determinants of,
    316
  timing of, 317
  uncertain expectations and, 317
Business fixed investment, neoclassical
    approach, 296–311
  Cobb-Douglas production function and,
    299
  component of GNP and, 291–292
  desired capital stock and (*see* Desired
    capital stock)
  marginal product of capital (*see*
    Marginal product of capital)
  1982–1985 boom in, 318–319
  real rate of interest and, 303–304
  rental cost of capital and (*see* Rental
    cost of capital)
  return to capital and, 299–300

Cagan, Phillip, 364, 651*n.*, 666
Capital:
  accumulation of, 719–723
  balance of payments and, 181
  full employment of, 11*n.*
  growth in real GNP and, 7
  marginal productivity of (*see* Marginal
    productivity of capital)
  rental cost of (*see* Rental cost of capital)
  supply of, and supply-side economics,
    707–709
Capital account segment of balance of
    payments, 181
Capital consumption allowance, 33
Capital gains, 126
Capital mobility and the policy mix,
    195–201

Capital mobility and the policy mix (*Cont.*):
  balance of payments and capital flows,
    197–198
  capital market integration and, 195–197
  internal and external balance, 198–199
  perfect, 201–212
    under fixed exchange rates, 201–204
    under flexibility exchange rates,
    204–212
  policy mix, 200–201
Carlino, Gerald A., 278*n.*, 708*n.*
Carson, Carol S., 36*n.*
Carter, Jimmy, 8
Catching-up hypothesis, 726–727
Cecchetti, Stephen G., 476*n.*
Certificates of deposit (CDs), 337
Checkable deposits, 334–336
Chirinko, Robert S., 310*n.*
Chrystal, K. Alec, 575*n.*
Clark, Kim B., 543*n.*, 545*n.*, 546*n.*,
    547*n.*, 557*n.*
Clark, Peter K., 316*n.*, 551*n.*
Classical case, 146–147
  aggregate supply curve, 224–225
  crowding out and, 158–159
  fiscal expansion and, 235
    crowding out and, 235–238
  IS-LM model and, 175
  monetary expansion under, 238–240
  quantity theory of money and, 360–361
Clean floating, 184
Cobb-Douglas production function, 299
Cohn, Richard, 566*n.*
Cold turkey strategy, 525
  credibility bonus of, 526
  gradualism versus, 525–526
Competitive depreciation, 212
Components of demand, 48–52
  consumption, 49
  final sales, 52
  government, 49–50
  investment, 50–51
  net exports, 51–52
Composition of output, 161–165
Constant dollar GNP (*see* Real GNP)
Constant dollars, 34
Consumer durables, 51
Consumer price index (CPI), 15, 41, 42, 61
Consumption:
  as component of demand, 49
  consumption-income relationship, 72–73
  dynamics of, 270–272
  of the elderly, 267
  international differences in saving rates,
    276–277

Consumption (*Cont.*):
  IS–LM framework and, 279–284
    dynamics of adjustment, 281–284
    policy implications, 284
    wealth and, 280–281
  life-cycle theory of (*see* Life cycle theory of consumption and saving)
  permanent-income theory of (*see* Permanent-income theory of consumption)
  savings and, 70–73
    interest rates and, 277–278
    tax cuts, Barro-Ricardo hypothesis and, 278–279
Consumption function and aggregate demand, 69–78, 253
  budget constraint, 70
  consumption-income relationship, 72, 253–256
  defined, 69–70
  equilibrium income and output, 74–76
    formula for, 76–77
  marginal propensity to consume, 70
  marginal propensity to save, 70
  planned investment, 73–74, 77
  puzzle of, 257, 259, 266
  regression line of, 253–256
  saving and investment, 77–78
  savings function, 70–73
  wealth and, 280–281
Consumption tax, 708
Contractions (*see* Recessions)
Contracts, 244–245
Cornell, B., 394n.
Cost-of-living adjustments (COLA), 508, 569–571
Council of Economic Advisers (CEA), 15, 241
  activism of, 430
  guideposts of, 429
  members of, 426n.
  potential output and, 427
Countercyclical policy, 20
  (*See also* Stabilization policy)
Coupon bonds, 139
Credibility, 526
  rapid deflation and, 526–527
  rational expectations equilibrium approach and, 681–682
Credit crunch, 325
Credit rationing, 405
Crowding out, 153–161
  budget deficits and, 160
  classical case and, 158–159, 235–238
  defined, 153

Crowding out (*Cont.*):
  demand for money and, 334
  dynamics of adjustment, 156
  extent of, 157
  full, 235–238
  increase in government spending, 155–156
  likelihood of, 159–160
  liquidity trap, 157–158
  monetary accommodation and, 160, 161
  monetizing budget deficits and, 160
Currency, 186, 334–336
Currency-deposit ratio, 371–372, 382
  adjustment process and, 386
Current account segment of balance of payments, 180–181
Current dollar GNP (*see* Nominal GNP)
Current dollars, 34
Current output, 32
Current-weighted price index, 62
Cyclical unemployment, 540
  costs of, 559
Cyclically adjusted surplus, 99

Danziger, Sheldon, 267
Darby, Michael, 426n.
David, Paul, 277n.
De Alessi, Louis, 566n.
Debt-financed budget deficits (*see* Budget deficits, debt-financed)
Debt-income ratio, 607–609, 619–621
Debt management, 588
Decision lag, 442–443
Deflation, 526–527
Demand (*see* Aggregate demand)
Demand for money, 129–130, 333–368
  components of (*see* Money stock, components of)
  defined, 129
  elasticities, 347–348
  empirical evidence on, 354–359
    empirical results, 355–357
    income elasticity and, 354–359
    interest elasticity and, 354–359
    lagged adjustment, 354–355
    level of prices and, 357
    long-run elasticity, 356
    money demand instability, 357–359
    shifting money demand curve and, 357–359
    short-run elasticity, 355–356
  functions of money, 339–340
  high inflation and, 364
  income elasticity of, 130, 347–348, 354–359
  income velocity of money and, 361–363

Demand for money (*Cont.*):
  integer constraints, 348–349
  interest elasticity of, 130, 347, 354–359
  money illusion, 334
  nominal, 128–129
  payment period, 349
  precautionary, 350–352
  properties of, 346–347
  real, 128–129
  real balances and, 333–334, 348
  speculative, 352–354
  square-root formula for, 346–347
  transactions (*see* Transactions demand
      for money)
Demand for real balances, 128
  described, 333–334
  money market and, 129–130
  when prices double, 348
  (*See also* Demand for money)
Demand for real bond holdings, 128–129
Denison, E., 702–704, 705*n*.
Denison's law of savings, 277
Depository Institutions Decontrol Act,
      372*n*., 382*n*.
Deppler, Michael C., 764*n*.
Depreciation:
  competitive, 212
  currency, 186
  as deduction from GNP, 33
  expected, 760
  monetary approach and, 746–747
Desired capital stock, 296–297, 302, 306
  Cobb-Douglas production function, 299
  defined, 296
  dynamic behavior and, 309
  effects of fiscal and monetary policy on,
      306
  expected output and, 300–301
  gradual adjustment hypothesis, 307–309
  to investment from, 307
  marginal productivity of capital and,
      297–300
  real interest rates and, 303–304
Devaluation, 740–743
  defined, 186
Diminishing returns, 493
Dirty (managed) floating, 184–185, 766
Discount rate, 18, 379–380
  equilibrium in the money market and
      changes in, 389–391
Discounted cash flow analysis, 311–312
  interest rates, present values and,
      329–332
Discrete lag, 445

Discretionary outlays, 593–594
Disequilibrium economics, 687
Disinflation:
  recession and, 499, 500
    (*See also* Inflation and
      unemployment)
  sacrifice ratio and, 528–529
Disintermediation, 324–326
Disposable personal income, 47–48
  government sector and, 83–85
Dissaving, 260–262
Distributed lag, 283, 445
Disturbances, 680–681
  adjustments to (*see* Adjustments)
  economic (*see* Economic disturbances)
  propagation mechanisms of, 679–680
  response to (*see* Stabilization policy)
  (*See also* Supply shocks)
Dividends, 46, 126
Doeringer, Peter, 555
Domestic credit, 745–746
  ceiling on, 746
Domestic spending and spending on
      domestic goods, 189–192
Dornbusch, Rudiger, 267*n*.
Dual-labor market hypothesis, 689*n*.
Durable goods, 51
Dwyer, Gerald, 606*n*., 644*n*.
Dynamic aggregate demand curve,
      510–512
  derivation of, 533–535
Dynamic aggregate supply curve, 503–504
Dynamic behavior, 309
Dynamic inconsistency, 455
Dynamic multiplier, 283–284
  econometric models and, 436–437

Eckstein, Otto, 426*n*.
Econometric models for policy making and
      forecasting, 435–439
  defined, 417, 436
  forecast accuracy of, 438–439
  macroeconomic models, 437–438
  major, 437–438
  multipliers and, 436–437
Econometric policy evaluation critique,
      448
Economic disturbances, 432–434
  defined, 434
  other, 433–434
  political business cycle and, 434
  transitory, 439–442
    recognition lag and, 441–442
  wars as, 433

Economies of scale:
  in cash management, 347
  technical progress and, 704
Economy, U.S., 1969–1986, 660–666
  decline in growth of, 704–706
Education, 50
Effective exchange rate, 187–188
Efficiency, growth in real GNP and, 7–8
Efficiency wage theory, 245, 553, 688–689
Eichner, A., 687n.
Einzig, Paul, 340n.
Eisner, Robert, 39, 40, 301n., 611, 619n.
Elderly, consumption of the, 267
Employment:
  aggregate supply curve and, 480–481
  full, 11n., 462–463
  unemployment and, 8
Employment stability and unemployment
  benefits, 557–558
Endogenous money stock, 204
Englander, A. Steven, 470n.
Entitlement programs, 593, 594
Equilibrium approach to macroeconomics
    (see Rational expectations–equilibrium
    approach, equilibrium component of)
Equilibrium income:
  government sector and, 83–91
  interest rates and, 173–174
  output and, 68–69
Equilibrium output (see Aggregate
    demand, equilibrium output and)
Equilibrium real business cycle theory,
    678–679
  disturbances and, 680–681
  propagation mechanisms of, 679–680
Equities, 126–127
European unemployment, 690–693
Evans, Michael K., 708n.
Excess demand for goods, 123, 124
Excess demand for money, 134–135
Excess reserves, 383–385
Excess sensitivity and liquid constraints,
    274–275
Excess supply of goods, 123, 124
Excess supply of money, 134–135
Exchange rate expectations, 758–762
Exchange rate overshooting, 751–754
Exchange rates:
  fixed (see Fixed exchange rates)
  flexible (see Flexible exchange rates)
  fluctuations in, 765–770
    dirty floating and intervention, 765–766
    government intervention and,
      766–768

Exchange rates (*Cont*.):
    interdependence and, 768–769
    policy synchronization and, 769–770
  measures of, 187–189
  real, 188–189, 734
  relative price adjustment and,
    762–763
    trade balance and, 763–765
  terminology of, 185–186
Expansion, 10, 11, 15
Expectations-augmented Phillips curve,
    503–510
  changes in expected inflation rate,
    505–506
  compensation for past inflation or
    expected inflation, 508–509
  determinants of expected inflation,
    509–510
  long-run, 506–507
  short-run, 504–506
  wage adjustment, 507–508
  (*See also* Rational
    expectations–equilibrium approach)
Expectations effect, 632
Expenditure reducing policies, 740
Expenditure switching policies, 740
Experience rating, 558n.
External balance, 198–199, 738

Factor cost, 32, 44
Factor markets, aggregate supply curve
    and, 224
Factor shares in national income, 44–45
Falk, B., 394n.
Fan versus the band, 403–406
Federal Deposit Insurance Corporation
    (FDIC), 385, 421
Federal funds rate, 383
Federal Reserve System (Fed), 13, 21,
    130, 421
  balance sheet of, 377–379
  dilemma over monetizing deficits,
    643–645
  discount rate, 18
  econometric models used by, 437,
    438
  Great Depression and, 423–425
  instruments of monetary policy, 18
  money supply and (*see* Money supply
    and the Fed)
  open market operations (*see* Open
    market operations)
  policy making under uncertainty,
    450–451

Federal Reserve System (Fed) (*Cont.*):
  Treasury Department and, 380
    financing federal deficits, 381,
      586–587
  (*See also* Monetary policy)
Feldstein, Martin, 4, 316*n*., 543*n*., 554*n*.,
  557, 683, 706*n*., 755*n*.
Fellner, William J., 447, 563*n*., 705*n*.
Final goods and services, 31, 32
Final sales, 52
Financial assets, 126–127
Fine tuning, 452–453
Fink, Richard, 683*n*.
Fiscal drag, 591
  estimated, 592–593
Fiscal expansion:
  adjustment to, 521–523
  under classical conditions, 235
    crowding out and, 235–238
  effect of, on the aggregate demand
    curve, 230–231
  Keynesian case and, 234–235
  perfect capital mobility under fixed
    exchange rates, 204
Fiscal policy:
  active, 91
  composition of output and, 161–165
  crowding out and (*see* Crowding out)
  defined, 84
  desired capital stock and, 306
  expansion (*see* Fiscal expansion)
  income velocity of money and, 361
  instruments of, 18
  interest rates, 175–176
  in the *IS-LM* mode, 153–154
  lags and, 446
  monetarism and, 671
  monetary policy and (*see* Monetary–
    fiscal policy mix)
  in the Mundell-Fleming model, 208–210
  uncertainties of, 18
  (*See also* Government sector)
Fiscal policy multiplier, 174
Fiscalists, 20
  (*See also* Keynesian economics)
Fischer, Stanley, 267*n*., 613*n*., 648*n*.,
  686*n*.
Fisher, Irving, 241, 242, 631
Fisher effect, 632
Fisher equation, 631
Fixed exchange rates, 182–183, 734–743
  defined, 182
  financing and adjustment, 735–737
    automatic adjustment, 737–738

Fixed exchange rates, financing and
  adjustment (*Cont.*):
    devaluation, 740–743
    expenditure switching/reducing, 740
    in Mexico, 742
    policy conflicts and the choice of
      policy, 738
    policy dilemma, 738–739
  perfect capital mobility under, 201–204
    endogenous money stock, 204
    fiscal expansion, 204
    monetary expansion, 203
  role of prices in the open economy,
    734–735
Flavin, Marjorie, 273, 275
Fleming, Marcus, 204
Flexible exchange rates, 184
  clean floating, 184
  managed (dirty) floating, 184–185, 766
  money and prices and, 748–757
    adjustment process, 748
    exchange rate overshooting, 751–754
    monetary expansion, short- and long-
      run effects, 748–751
    purchasing power parity, 754–757
    strong dollar, 1980–1985, 755
  perfect capital mobility and (*see*
    Mundell-Fleming model)
  (*See also* Exchange rates, fluctuations
    in)
Floating exchange rates (*see* Flexible
  exchange rates)
Floating rate mortgages, 323*n*., 568–569
Flow supply curve, 321
Foreign exchange market intervention, 379
Foreign trade, 179–218
  balance of payments and (*see* Balance of
    payments)
  capital mobility (*see* Capital mobility
    and the policy mix)
  domestic spending and spending on
    domestic goods, 189–192
  exchange rates and (*see* Exchange rates)
  goods market equilibrium and, 192
  identities concerning, 55–56
  marginal propensity to import, 191–192
Freeman, Richard B., 508*n*., 547*n*.
Frenkel, Jacob, 204*n*., 745*n*.
Frey, Bruno, 575*n*.
Frictional unemployment, 465
Frictionless neoclassical model of the labor
  market, 462–465
  change in the quantity of money,
    463–465

Frictionless neoclassical model of the labor market (*Cont*.):
  equilibrium in the labor market, 462–463, 497–498
  frictional and natural rate of unemployment, 465
  labor demand, 462–463, 494–496
  production function, 493–494
Friedman, Benjamin M., 671*n*.
Friedman, Milton, 4, 5, 20, 364, 385*n*., 402*n*., 434*n*., 447, 632*n*., 651*n*.
  on activism, 451, 452*n*.
  Great Depression and, 419*n*., 420*n*., 421*n*., 424–425
  on inflation and unemployment, 499, 500
  on inflationary expectations, 624–625
  permanent-income theory of consumption and, 258, 266–273
  on the quantity theory of money, 241–243
  (*See also* Monetarism)
Friedman-Phelps amendment to the Phillips curve, 469–472, 502–503, 505–506, 519
Full crowding out, 235–238
Full employment, 11*n*.
Full-employment budget deficit, 102–103
Full-employment budget surplus, 99–104
  New Economics and, 427–428
  trends in, 101–104
Full-employment level of employment, 462–463
Full employment level of unemployment (*see* Natural rate of unemployment)
Full-employment output (*see* Potential output)

Geary, P. T., 481*n*.
Gilbert, R. Alton, 402*n*.
Gilder, George, 684
Gold, 421
Golden, D., 575*n*., 576*n*.
Goldfeld, Stephen, 355–359, 362
Goodfriend, Marvin, 402*n*., 404*n*.
Goods market equilibrium:
  adjustment toward, 139–142
  foreign trade and, 192
  money market equilibrium and, 136–139
  schedule, 114, 117
  (See also *IS* curve, goods market and)
Gordon, Robert J., 358*n*., 419*n*., 558*n*., 561*n*., 678
Government expenditures, 50

Government purchases:
  as component of demand, 49–50
  defined, 50
  effects of a change in, 86–88
    on the budget surplus, 95–98
    crowding out and, 155–156
  full crowding out and, 236–237
  as supply shock, 681
Government sector:
  budget and, 92–104
  budget constraints, 585
    money, inflation and, 642–643
  budget deficits and (*see* Budget deficits, government spending and revenues and)
  equilibrium income and, 83–91
  identities concerning, 55–56
  monetarism versus activism over, 21
  new classical macroeconomists and, 22
  size of government controversy, 615–617
    balanced budget and, 615–616
    constitutional amendment and, 615
Gradual adjustment hypothesis, 307–309
Gradualism, 524
  cold turkey versus, 525–526
Gramm-Rudman-Hollings Act, 92, 582, 601–602, 644
Great Depression, 4, 126, 417–426
  economic policy during, 420–421
  expansionary aggregate demand and, 22
  Fed and, 423–425
  fiscal policy during, 420, 423–426
  institutional change during, 421–422
  international aspects of, 422
  Keynesian explanation of, 423–424
  monetarist explanation of, 424–425
  statistics on, 417–419
  stock market crash and, 417, 419
  synthesis of opinions on, 425–426
  unemployment during, 8
Gross domestic product (GDP), 33
Gross domestic purchases, 52
Gross National Product (GNP), 5–7
  calculation of, 31–35
    current output, 32
    factor cost, 32
    final goods, 32
    intermediate goods, 32
    market prices, 32–33
    in a simple economy, 31, 34–35
    value added, 32
  components of demand (*see* Components of demand)

Gross National Product (GNP) (*Cont.*):
  defined, 5, 30, 31
  deflator, 15*n.*, 41, 42
  deriving national income from, 43–44
  GNP gap, 427
  gross domestic product, 33
  net national product, 33
  in 1985, 31
  nominal (*see* Nominal GNP)
  problems with measurement of, 36–40
    badly measured outputs, 38–39
    estimates, 37
    quality changes, 39–40
    revisions, 37
    total incomes system of accounts, 39
    underground economy, 36
  real (*see* Real GNP)
Gross private domestic investment, 50–51
Grossman, H., 687*n.*
Growth:
  New Economics and, 429
  Okun's law, 15, 559–561, 573–574,
    664*n.*
  productivity and (*see* Long-term growth
    and productivity)
  real GNP and, 7–8
  unemployment and, 8–9, 13–15
Growth of total factor productivity, 701
Growth accounting, 700
Guideposts, money wage, 429
Gutman, Peter M., 36*n.*
Guttmann, Thomas William, 651*n.*

Haberler, Gottfried, 422*n.*
Hall, Robert E., 273
Hamburger, Michael, 359*n.*, 442*n.*
Hausman, Jerry, 707
Hayashi, Fumio, 275*n.*
Heller, Walter W., 426*n.*
Hetzel, Robert L., 364*n.*
Hicks, J. R., 114*n.*
High-employment labor hours, 711–712
  benchmark, 713
  productivity and, 712–713
  uncertainty about, 713–715
High-employment surplus, 99
High-growth recovery, 574
High-powered money, 377–382
  creation of, 377
  defined, 372
  discount rate and, 379–380
  effects of an increase in, 388–390
  Fed balance sheet and, 377–379
  financing federal deficits and, 381

High-powered money (*Cont.*):
  foreign exchange market intervention
    and, 379
  inflation tax and, 645–648
  money multiplier and (*see* Money
    multiplier)
  open market purchases, 377–378
  sterilization and, 379
  stock of, 377–382
  supply and demand for, 373
  targeting, 407
  Treasury and, 380–381
Hoelscher, Gregory, 606*n.*
Holloway, Thomas M., 100*n.*, 590*n.*, 592*n.*
Holtferich, C. L., 651*n.*
Holtz-Eakin, Douglas, 616
Housing investment (*see* Residential
  investment)
Hulten, C., 705*n.*
Human capital, 50
Hutchinson, Michael, 606*n.*
Hyperinflation, 364, 651–655
  classic, 651
  deficits and, 652–653
  defined, 364, 651
  inflation tax and, 654
  nominal interest and, 652–653
  stopping, 654–655
  tax-collection system and, 652

Ibbotson, Roger G., 641*n.*
Iden, George, 605*n.*
Identities, 54*n.*
Illegal economy, 36
Illiquidity, 350–352
Imperfect information, 245–246
Imperfectly anticipated inflation, 561,
  563–567
Incentive effects of tax cuts, 599
Income:
  dynamic multiplier of, 283–284
  flow of, 29–30
  labor, 258–259
  lifetime, 259–260
  national (*see* National income)
  sources of growth in real, 700–706
Income-consumption relationship, 72–73
Income effect, 632
  supply-side economics and, 707
Income elasticity of money demand, 130,
  347–348, 354–359
Income velocity of money, 359–365
  defined, 359–360
  demand for money and, 361–363

Income velocity of money (*Cont.*):
  fiscal policy and, 361
  inflation and, 637–638
  in practice, 363–365
  quantity theory of money and, 360–361
  velocity puzzle, 363–365
Incomes policy (wage and price controls), 527–530
Indexation of tax brackets, 592
Indexation of wages, 508, 569–571
  COLA and, 569–571
  reason for, 569
  supply shocks and, 570
  in the U.S., 570–571
Inflation:
  aggregate demand and, 15
  costs of, 16–17, 561–567
  defined, 15
  disinflation (*see* Disinflation)
  expectations of, 502–510
    adaptive, 509
    changes in, 505–506
    compensation for past inflation or, 508–509
    Friedman on, 624–625
    long-run, 506–507
    rational, 509–510
    short-run, 504–505
    wage adjustment, 507–508
    wage setting and, 502–503
  fluctuations in, 16
  hyperinflation, 364
  imperfectly anticipated, 561, 563–567
  interest rates and, 567
    housing and, 567–569
    indexation of wages and, 569–571
  money and (*see* Money and inflation)
  money demand and, 364
  nominal GNP and, 7
  perfectly anticipated, 561–563
  Phillips curve and (*see* Phillips curve)
  as a political issue, 8, 13
  redistribution of wealth and, 565–567
  stagflation, 517–518
  steady state and, 514–515
  strategies to reduce, 523–531
    cold turkey, 525–526
    credibility and, 526–527
    gradualism, 524–526
    incomes policy (wage and price controls), 527–530
    rapid deflation, 526–527
    restrictive, nonaccommodating policies and, 531

Inflation, strategies to reduce (*Cont.*):
    sacrifice ratio and, 528–529
    tax incentive plans (TIP), 530–531
    tradeoffs between unemployment and (*see* Inflation-unemployment tradeoffs)
  unpopularity of, 8
Inflation and unemployment, 499–535
  aggregate supply curve and, 501–507
    changes in the expected inflation rate, 505–506
    short-run, 504–506
    vertical long-run, 506–507
    wage setting and expected inflation, 502–504
  dynamic adjustment of output and, 515–521
    expected and unexpected changes in monetary policy, 519–520
    overshooting, 518–519
    perfect foresight expectations, 519
    stagflation, 517–518
  dynamic aggregate demand and, 510–512
    derivation of, 533–535
  expected inflation and (*see* Inflation, expectations of)
  growth and, 8–9
  output level and, 512–515
    long-run, 514–515
    short-run, 513–514
  reduction of inflation (*see* Inflation, strategies to reduce)
  stabilization policy and, 18–20
  tradeoffs between (*see* Inflation-unemployment tradeoffs)
  (*See also* Money and inflation)
Inflation tax, 645–648
  accelerating hyperinflation and, 654
  nominal balances of money and, 646
  revenue, 648
Inflation-unemployment tradeoffs, 415–416, 537–539, 571–580
  alternative policy paths, 571–572
  Okun's law and, 573–574
  opinion polls and, 576
  Phillips curve and, 17–18, 469
    extended, 573
  policy tradeoff, 574–575
  political business cycle and, 575
  timing issue, 576–577
Inside lag, 441–443
Institutional reform, 682–683

Instruments of monetary control, 387
Integer constraints, 348–349
Interbank deposits, 383n.
Interdependence and exchange rates,
      768–769
Interest adjustment, 46
Interest differentials, 757–762
Interest elasticity of money demand, 130,
      347, 354–359
Interest forgone:
   reserve requirements and, 383–384
   transactions demand for money and,
      342–346
Interest rates:
   aggregate demand and, 116–125
   composition of output and, 161–165
   consumption, saving and, 277–278
   discount rate and, 380n.
   discounted cash flow analysis and,
      311–313, 329–332
   equilibrium income and, 173–174
   fiscal policy and, 175–176
   inflation and, 567
      empirical evidence on, 639–641
      housing and, 567–569
      indexation of wages and, 569–571
   investment and, 115
   monetarism and, 669–671
   money stock and (*see* Money stock and
      interest rate targets)
   mortgages and, 323–324, 567–569
   1982–1985 investment boom and,
      318–319
   nominal (*see* Nominal interest rates)
   pegging, 392
   present values and, 329–332
   real (*see* Real interest rates)
   rental cost of capital and, 303–304
   simultaneous equilibrium and, 136–139
      adjustment toward, 139–142
   on Treasury bills, 111–112, 587n.,
      640–641
Intergenerational fairness, 613–614
Intermediate goods, 32
Intermediate targets, 406–408
Internal balance, 198–199, 738
International differences in savings rates,
      276–277
International Monetary Fund (IMF), 740,
      745–746
Intertemporal substitution of leisure,
      679–680
Intervention, foreign exchange, 183–185
   clean or dirty floating and, 184–185, 766
   defined, 183, 766

Intervention, foreign exchange (*Cont*.):
   fixed exchange rates and, 182–183
   flexible exchange rates and, 184
   government, 766–768
   market, 379
   sterilized, 378, 744–745, 767
Inventories, 292
Inventory cycle, 69n., 294–296
Inventory investment, 54, 292–296
   business cycle and, 293–296
   as component of GNP, 291–292
   inventory cycle and, 294–296
   inventory-sales ratio, 292–293
   unintended, 67–68
      anticipated versus, 293–296
Inventory-theoretic approach to demand
      for money, 343–346
Investment, 50–51
   defined, 50, 290
   from desired capital stock to, 307
   gross private domestic, 50–51, 290
   interest rates and, 115
   net, 51, 290–291
   1980–1984 policy mix and, 171–172
   planned, 73–74, 77
   savings and, 55–57, 77–78
   timing of, and the investment tax credit,
      309–311
Investment demand schedule, 115–116
Investment friction, 73
Investment spending, 53, 289–332
   business fixed investment (*see* Business
      fixed investment, alternative
      approaches; Business fixed
      investment, neoclassical approach)
   components of, as percentage of GNP,
      291–292
   defined, 290
   from desired capital stock to, 307
   fluctuations of, 316–317
   inventory (*see* Inventory investment)
   investment tax credit and timing of,
      309–311
   1982–1985 boom in, 318–319
   residential (*see* Residential investment)
   timing of, 317
   uncertain expectations and, 317
Investment subsidy, 162–164
Investment tax credit, 309–311
Involuntary quits, 543
IS curve, goods market and, 114–125
   defined, 114
   derivation of, 118
   excess supply and demand,
      123–124

IS curve, goods market and (*Cont.*):
  interest rate and aggregate demand, 116–119
  investment and the interest rate, 115
  investment demand schedule, 115–116
  position of, 120–123
  positions off, 123–124
  role of the multiplier, 120, 121
  slope of, 119–122
IS-LM model, 112, 173–176
  behavioral equations of (*see* Consumption, *IS-LM* framework and; Demand for money; Investment spending)
  classical case and, 175
  consumption and, 279–284
    dynamics of adjustment, 281–284
    policy implications, 284
    wealth and, 280–281
  defined, 114*n.*
  economic disturbances and, 432–434
  equilibrium income and the interest rate, 173–174
  fiscal policy in, 153–154, 175–176
  fiscal policy multiplier, 174
  interest rates and, 175–176
  liquidity trap and, 176
  monetary policy multiplier, 174–175
  structure of, 113
  (See also *IS* curve, goods market and; *LM* curve, assets markets and)

J curve, 763–765
Jaffe, D., 405*n.*
Jevons, W. S., 339*n.*, 726
Jianakoplos, Nancy, 566*n.*
Johannes, James M., 376*n.*
Johnson, Harry G., 745*n.*
Johnson, Lyndon B., 13, 165
  New Economics and (*see* New Economics)
Joines, Douglas, 644*n.*
Jones, R. W., 204*n.*
Jorgenson, Dale W., 314

Kahuiman, Daniel, 675*n.*
Kareken, John, 442*n.*
Katz, Lawrence, 688*n.*
Kearl, James, 322
Kemp, Jack, 684
Kemp-Roth tax cuts, 598, 663
Kendrick, J. W., 704–706
Kenen, P., 204*n.*
Kennan, J., 481*n.*

Kennedy, John F., 13, 165
  New Economics and (*see* New Economics)
Kennickell, Arthur, 267*n.*
Keynes, John Maynard, 4, 146, 317, 423, 434*n.*, 651, 659
Keynesian economics, 4, 659–660, 680*n.*
  aggregate supply and, 244
    contracts and, 244–245
    coordination and, 245
    efficiency wages and, 245
  aggregate supply curve, 224, 225
  fiscal expansion and, 234–235
  Great Depression and, 423–424
    monetarists and, 424–425
  holding money, motives for, 341
  liquidity trap and, 146
  monetarists vs., 20–21
  New Economics and (*see* New Economics)
  post-, 687–688
  uncertain expectations and, 317
Kindleberger, Charles, 422*n.*
King, Robert, 679*n.*
Klau, Friedrich, 617
Kormendi, Roger, 605*n.*
Kotlikoff, Laurence, 267, 708*n.*, 709*n.*
Kravis, Irving, 699*n.*
Kuznets, Simon, 257, 258*n.*, 259, 266, 704
Kydland, Finn, 455*n.*, 613

Labor:
  full employment of, 11*n.*
  growth in real GNP and, 7
Labor cost, unit, 479–480
Labor demand, 462–463, 494–496
Labor income, 258–259
Labor market (*see* Frictionless neoclassical model of the labor market)
Labor productivity, 429, 477, 701*n.*
Labor supply and supply-side economics, 706–707
Laffer, Arthur, 97*n.*, 600, 684
Laffer curve, 600–601
Lags:
  distributed, 283, 445
  expectations and, 446–448
  long and variable, 668
  monetarism and, 668
  in stabilization policy (*see* Stabilization policy, lags in effects of)
Laidler, David, 355*n.*, 666
Laney, L., 577*n.*
Laspeyres price index, 62
Layoff, 542–543

Leith, J. Clark, 423*n*.
Lessard, Donald, 324*n*.
Life-cycle theory of consumption and
 saving, 258–266
 aggregate consumption and saving, 265
 assets and, 262
 consumption of the elderly, and
  bequests, 267
 defined, 258
 extensions of, 264–265
 implications of, 265–266
 labor income and, 258–259
 lifetime income and, 259–260
 numerical example, 260
 permanent-income hypothesis and,
  272–273
 saving and dissaving, 260–262
 wealth and, 263–264
Lifetime income, 259–260
Limits of growth, 726–727
Lindbeck, Assar, 688*n*.
Liquidity, 336
Liquidity constraints, 274–275, 687
Liquidity effect, 632
Liquidity trap, 146
 crowding out and, 157–158
 IS-LM model and, 176
LM curve, assets markets and, 125–136
 defined, 114*n*.
 demand for money, 129–130
 derivation of, 132
 goods market equilibrium and, 136–139
 money market equilibrium and, 130–133
 position of, 133–134
 positions off, 134–135
 real and nominal variables, 128–129
 slope of, 133
 types of assets, 126–127
 vertical, 146–147
 wealth budget constraint, 127–129
 (See also *IS-LM* model)
Local government spending and financing,
 596
Long-run equilibrium level of
 unemployment (*see* Natural rate of
 unemployment)
Long-term growth and productivity,
 697–732
 growth theory and, 716–728
  capital accumulation and, 719–722
  change in saving rate and, 723–725
  growth process and, 719–723
  limits of growth, 726–727
  population growth and, 725–728

Long-term growth and productivity,
 growth theory and (*Cont.*):
  saving and growth and, 718–719
  steady state and, 717
 measuring potential output (*see*
  Potential output, measuring)
 sources of growth in real income,
  700–706
  decline in growth, 704–706
  economies of scale, 704
  empirical estimates of, 702–706
  production function, 700–702
  technical progress, 701–704
  total factor productivity, 701
 supply-side economics and, 706–710
  budget deficits and growth, 709
  consumption tax and, 708
  government regulation, 709
  growth incentives and, 710
  income effect, 707
  labor supply and, 706–707
  substitution effect, 707
  supply of capital and, 707–709
Los, Cornelis A., 470*n*.
Lovell, Michael, C., 675*n*.
Lucas, Robert E., Jr., 4, 21, 246, 448,
 510, 659, 674, 676–678

M1, 333–337, 341, 363, 369–371
M2, 336–337, 342, 370–371
 speculative demand for money and,
  352–354
McCallum, Bennett T., 399*n*., 666, 674*n*.
McClure, Harold, 684*n*.
McNees, Stephen, 437*n*.
Macroeconomic demand curve (*see*
 Aggregate demand curve)
Macroeconomic models, 437–438
Macroeconomics, 659–696
 aggregate demand and supply, 22–25
 defined, 3–4
 disequilibrium, 687
 the economy, 1969–1986, 660–666
 European unemployment, 690–693
 key concepts of, 5–13
 monetarism, 666–674
 and new directions, 693–694
 policy decisions and, 18–22
 post-Keynesian, 687–688
 rational expectations–equilibrium
  approach, 245–246, 674–683
 recent approaches, 685–690
  disequilibrium, 687
  efficiency wages, 688–689

Macroeconomics, recent approaches
(*Cont.*):
    post-Keynesian, 687–688
    profit sharing, 690
    relative wages, wage contracts, and
        rational expectations, 685–688
    small menu costs, 689–690
  relationships among variables, 13–18
  schools of thought, 4–5
  supply-side economics, 683–685
  (*See also specific theories*)
Maddison, Angus, 699*n.*
Malinvaud, E., 687*n.*
Malthus, Thomas, 726
Mandatory outlays, 593, 594
Mankiw, N. Gregory, 476*n.*, 689*n.*
Marginal product of labor, 494–495
Marginal productivity of capital, 297–300
  Cobb-Douglas production function and,
    299
  defined, 296
  estimating the return to capital,
    299–301
  level of output and capital stock and,
    298–299
  value of, 297
Marginal propensity to consume, 70
  multiplier and, 79–81
Marginal propensity to import, 191–192
Marginal propensity to save, 70
Market clearing approach, 245–246
Market prices, 32–33
  nominal GNP and, 34
Markup, 479–480, 502
Marston, Stephen T., 543*n.*
Martin, J. P., 555*n.*
Materials prices, 486–487
Maurer, Harry, 560*n.*
Mayer, Thomas, 426*n.*, 442*n.*, 666, 672
Measure of economic welfare (MEW), 40
Medium of exchange, 335, 339
Medoff, James, 508*n.*
Meehan, Patricia, 651*n.*
Meek, Paul, 393*n.*
Meltzer, Allan, 241, 407*n.*, 552*n.*, 666
Microeconomics, 3, 4
Minford, Patrick, 557
Minimum reserve requirements, 382
Mishkin, Frederic, 678
Modigliani, Franco, 4, 5, 20, 258, 261*n.*,
    267, 324*n.*, 566*n.*, 672
Moggridge, D. E., 423*n.*
Monetarism, 5, 666–674
  activism and, 20–21

Monetarism (*Cont.*):
  disunity within, 20
  the economy and, 672–674
  Fed's money stock and interest rate
    targets and, 402–403
  Great Depression and, 424–425
    Keynesians and, 425
  importance of fiscal policy, 671
  inherent stability of the private sector,
    671
  long and variable lags, 668
  as modern quantity theory of money,
    241, 243
  monetary rule, 668–669
  money and inflation and (*see* Money
    and inflation)
  rational expectations equilibrium
    approach and, 683
  stock of money and, 667–668
  themes of, 672
  unimportance of interest rates, 669–671
Monetary accommodation, 160, 161
Monetary approach to balance of
    payments, 744–748
  depreciation and, 746–747
  effectiveness of, 746
  IMF and, 745–746
  sterilization and, 744–745
Monetary base (*see* High-powered money)
Monetary base targeting, 407
Monetary Control Act, 372*n.*, 382*n.*
Monetary disturbance, adjustment to,
    210–212
Monetary expansion:
  under classical conditions, 238–240
  effect of, on the aggregate demand
    curve, 232
  perfect capital mobility under fixed
    exchange rates, 202–203
  short- and long-run effects, under
    flexible exchange rates, 748–751
Monetary–fiscal policy mix, 164–172
  capital mobility and (*see* Capital
    mobility and the policy mix)
  defined, 154, 162
  income and interest rates and, 161–162
  investment and, 171–172
  investment subsidy and, 162–164
  1964 tax cut, 165–166
  1969–1970 contraction, 166–168
  1980–1984 policy mix, 168–172
  nominal and real interest rates and,
    170–171
  political economy and, 164–165

Monetary policy, 142–149
  accommodating, 160
  aggregate supply curve and expansion, 482–485
  application of (1979 policy switch), 147–149
  classical case, 146–147
  composition of output and, 161–165
  desired capital stock and, 306
  expected and unexpected changes in, 519–520
  Friedman on, 451
  housing investment and, 323–324
  instruments of, 18
  lags and, 446
  liquidity trap, 146
  open market operations (*see* Open market operations)
  shift of, in 1979, 400–402
  targets for (*see* Money stock and interest rate targets)
  transmission mechanism, 144–145
  uncertainties of, 18
  (*See also* Quantity theory of money)
Monetary policy directive, 393, 395
Monetary policy multiplier, 174–175
Monetary rule, 668–669
Monetizing budget deficits, 160
  Fed's dilemma over, 643–645
Money, 125
  business cycles and, 676–678
  defined, 126, 333, 340
  demand for (*see* Demand for money)
  endogenous money stock, 204
  functions of, 339–340
  high-powered (*see* High-powered money)
  inflation and (*see* Money and inflation)
  as medium of exchange, 335, 339
  neutrality of, 241–242
  nominal (*see* Nominal quantity of money)
  as standard of deferred payment, 340
  as store of value, 340
  as unit of account, 340
Money and inflation, 20, 623–657
  alternative expectations assumptions, 631–632, 634–635
  deficits and, 641–650
    Fed's dilemma, 643–644
    government's budget constraint, 642–643
    hyperinflation and (*see* Hyperinflation)

Money and inflation, deficits and (*Cont.*):
    inflation tax, 645–648
    U.S. evidence, 644–645
    unpleasant arithmetic, 648–650
  empirical evidence, 635–641
    changes in velocity, 637–638
    inflation and interest rates, 639–641
    inflation as monetary phenomenon in the long run, 638–639
    money-inflation link, 635–637
  expectations effect, 632
  Fisher effect, 632
  Fisher equation, 631
  Friedman on, 624–625
  income effect, 632
  increase in money growth, 627–630
  liquidity effect, 632
  model for, 625–627
  rational expectations, 630–631
  real balances, 633–634
Money-financed budget deficits, 584–586, 605–606
Money illusion, 334
Money market deposit accounts (MMDAs), 337, 370
Money market equilibrium, 130–133
  adjustment toward, 139–142
  goods market equilibrium and, 136–139
  money supply, the Fed and, 387–390
    changes in the discount rate and, 389–391
  schedule, 131–133
  (See also *LM* curve, assets markets and)
Money market mutual funds (MMMFs), 337, 370
Money multiplier, 373–377
  adjustment process and, 385–386
  defined, 373
  example of, 374
  graphical analysis of, 374–375
  money stock and, 373–374
  in practice, 375–377
  process, 411–414
Money stock, components of, 333–339, 369–371
  changes in definition of, 335–336
  financial innovation and, 337, 339
  liquidity and, 336
  M1, 333–337
  M2, 336–337
  monetary aggregates, 338–339
  money market deposit accounts, 337
  money market mutual funds, 337

Money stock and interest rate targets, 390–408
  base drift and the fan, 403–406
  choice between, 395–400, 406–408
    broad view, 396–398
    monetary control, 399–400
    short run and long run, 398–399
  credit rationing, 405
  inability to simultaneously hit, 390–393
  intermediate, 406–408
  making monetary policy, 393, 395
  monetarist critique, 402–403
  monetary base, 407
  monetary policy shift of 1979, 400–402
  nominal GNP, 407–408
  open market desk, 392–393
  pegging interest rates, 392
  ultimate, 406–408
  unanticipated increase in the money stock, 394
  weekly money stock announcements, 394–395
Money supply and the Fed, 369–414
  banks' behavior and, 372
  components of (*see* Money stock, components of)
  control of the money stock and interest rates (*see* Money stock and interest rate targets)
  currency-deposit ratio, 371–372, 382, 386
  definitions, 369–371
  equilibrium in the money market, 387–390
    changes in the discount rate and, 389–391
  excess reserves, 383–385
  FDIC and, 385
  federal funds rate, 383
  Fed's behavior and, 372
  high-powered money and (*see* High-powered money)
  instruments of monetary control, 387
  minimum reserve requirements, 382
  money multiplier and (*see* Money multiplier)
  money stock and, 369–371
  money supply function, 386–387
  open market operations (*see* Open market operations)
  public's behavior and, 371–372
  reserve-deposit ratio (*see* Reserve-deposit ratio)
Money supply function, 386–387

Mortgages:
  availability of, 324–325
  floating rate, 323n., 568–569
  interest rates and, 323–324, 567–569
Multilateral exchange rate, 187–188
Multiple expansion of bank deposits, 385–386, 413–414
Multiplier, 78–83
  balanced budget, 97–98, 108–110
  defined, 80
  dynamic, 283–284, 436–437
  econometric models and, 436–437
  fiscal policy, 174
  graphic derivation of, 81–82
  income taxes and, 86
  international, 194
  IS curve and, 120, 121
  marginal propensity to consume and, 79–81
  monetary policy, 174
  money (*see* Money multiplier)
Multiplier uncertainty, 449
Mundell, Robert, 198n., 204, 769n.
Mundell-Fleming model, 204–212
  adjustment to a monetary disturbance, 210–212
  adjustment to a real disturbance, 205–206
  adjustment process, 207, 209
  beggar-thy-neighbor policy and competitive depreciation, 212
  fiscal policy, 208–210
Mussa, Michael, 204n.

National debt:
  burden of, 609–614
  debt management, 508
  deficits and, 587–588
    in the 1980s, 611–612
    optimal, 612–614
  defined, 587
  government assets and, 611
  retiring, 508
  (*See also* Budget deficits)
National income, 42–48
  deriving, from GNP, 43–44
  factor shares in, 44–45
  personal income and, 45–47
  value of output as equal to, 42–43
    qualifications, 43
National income accounting, 29–62
  budget deficits or surpluses and, 93–95
  circular flow of income and spending, 29–30

National income accounting (*Cont.*):
  equilibrium output and, 66–68
  gross national product, 31–33
    real and nominal, 34–40
  national income, 42–48
  outlays and components of demand, 48–52
  price indexes, 41–42
  simple economy, 53–55
    reintroducing government and foreign trade, 55–56
    saving, investment, the government budget, and trade, 56–57
National Recovery Act, 422
Natural rate of unemployment, 549–558
  costs of, 560–561
  defined, 465, 515n., 549
  duration of unemployment and, 549–550
  efficiency wage theory and, 553, 688–689
  estimates of, 551–552
  frequency of unemployment and, 550–551
  Phillips curve and, 466–469
    Friedman-Phelps amendment to, 469–472
  reducing, 553–556
    secondary labor market, 555–556
    targeted programs, 555
  rising, 552–553
  as structural unemployment, 540
  unemployment benefits and (*see* Unemployment benefits)
Negative lag, 441–442
Negative outputs, 38–39
Negotiable order of withdrawal (NOW), 335, 337
Nelson, Charles R., 566n.
Net exports, 51–52
Net national product (NNP), 33, 51
Neutrality of money, 241–242
New classical macroeconomics (*see* Rational expectations–equilibrium approach)
New Deal, 421–422
New Economics, 426–431
  behavior of money wages, 429
  characterization of, 426
  compared to policies in the 1930s, 427
  economy and, 430–431
  full employment budget surplus, 427–428
  growth, 429
  "new," defined, 430
  potential output and the GNP gap, 427

Nixon, Richard M., 13, 659
Nominal exchange rates, 187
Nominal GNP:
  defined, 6, 34
  GNP deflator and, 15n., 41
  income velocity of money and, 361
  inflation and, 7
  real GNP and, 34–35, 38
  targeting, 407–408
Nominal interest rates:
  budget deficit and, 652–653
  defined, 170
  Fisher equation and, 631
  housing investment and, 323–324
  1980–1984 policy mix and, 170–171
Nominal quantity of money, 333
  aggregate demand curve and, 221, 232
  change in the price level and, 226
  under classical conditions, 238–240
  inflation tax and, 645–648
  monetarists and, 241–243
Nonemployment, 547
Noninterest deficit, 597–598
Nordhaus, William, 40

Oil prices, 13, 23
  effects of a favorable shock in, 490–491
Okun, Arthur, 15, 426n., 427, 538n., 674n., 711n.
Okun's law, 15
  costs of cyclical unemployment and, 559–561
  growth in output and changes in unemployment, 573–574, 664n.
Open market operations:
  defined, 142
  high-powered money and, 377–378
  monetary policy directive, 393, 395
  Open Market Committee, 393, 395, 442
  open market desk, 392–393
  purpose of, 143
  workings of. 143–144
Opinion polls, 576
Optimal budget deficits, 612–614
  intergenerational fairness, 613–614
  minimizing intertemporal tax distortions, 613
Orazem, P., 394n.
Output:
  business cycles and, 10–13
  composition of, 161–165
  expected, and capital stock, 300–301
  inflation, unemployment and, 8–9, 512–521
    dynamic adjustment to, 515–521

Output, inflation, unemployment and
(*Cont.*):
in the long run, 514–515
in the short run, 513–514
money stock and interest rate targets
and, 396–398
steady state and, 514–515
wages, prices and, 465–472
(*See also* Real GNP)
Output gap, 10–13
negative, 11
recent history and, 13
Outside lag, 441, 445–446
Overshooting, 518–519
Overtime, 11

Paasche price index, 62
Parkin, Michael, 666
Patinkin, Don, 229*n.*, 423, 687*n.*
Peak, cyclical, 10
Pechman, Joe, 538*n.*, 707*n.*
Peel, David A., 575*n.*
Perfect foresight, 519
Perfect substitutes, 201
Perfectly anticipated inflation, 561–563
Perloff, Jeffrey, 552*n.*
Permanent income, 268
Permanent-income theory of consumption,
266–273
defined, 268
dynamics of consumption and, 270–272
estimating permanent income, 268–269
life-cycle hypothesis and, 272–273
permanent income and, 268
rational expectations and, 269–270
sensitivity to current income, 273–274
liquidity constraints and, 274–275
weighted averaging and, 269
Perpetuity bonds, 139
Perry, George L, 552*n.*, 711*n.*
Personal income, 45
disposable, 47–48
government sector and, 83–85
national income and, 45–47
Phelps, Edmund, 469–472, 502–503,
505–506, 519, 538*n.*, 551*n.*, 704*n.*
Phillips, W. A., 466
Phillips curve, 17–18, 466–469
aggregate supply curve and, 501–507
short- and long-run, 504–507
wage setting and expected inflation,
502–503
defined, 17, 467
equilibrium approach to
macroeconomics and, 676–678

Phillips curve (*Cont.*):
expectations-augmented (*see*
Expectations-augmented Phillips
curve)
extended, 573
Friedman-Phelps amendment to,
469–472, 502–503, 505–506, 519
long-run, 18
policy tradeoff, 469
short-run, 18
skepticism about, 18
sticky wages and, 472–474
typical, 17
Physical output, 34
Pieper, Paul, 611*n.*, 619*n.*
Pindyck, Robert S., 254*n.*, 437*n.*, 449*n.*
Piore, Michael, 555
Planned aggregate demand, 67–68
Planned investment, 73–74, 77
Plosser, Charles, 679*n.*
Policy dilemmas, 738–739
Policy mix (*see* Monetary–fiscal policy mix)
Policy rules, 453–456
Policy synchronization, 769–770
Political business cycles, 575–576
defined, 19–20, 538–539
as economic disturbance, 434
opinion polls and, 576
policy tradeoffs and, 574–575
timing issue and, 576
Political economy, 19
monetary–fiscal policy mix and, 164–165
(*See also* Inflation-unemployment
tradeoffs)
Poole, William, 241, 396*n.*, 666
Population growth, 725–728
Portfolio decisions, 128
Portfolio disequilibrium, 144–145
Post-Keynesian economics, 687–688
Potential output:
BEA on, 13*n.*
defined, 11
establishing the level of, 11–13
GNP gap and, 427
growth rate of, 697–700
(*See also* Long-term growth and
productivity)
measuring, 710–716
high-employment benchmark and, 713
high-employment labor hours and,
711–712
production function approach, 715–716
productivity and, 712–713
traditional approach, 711–715
uncertainty about, 713–715

Potential output (*Cont.*):
   output gap and, 11
   rising level of, 10
Poterba, James, 322*n*., 557, 575*n*., 576*n*.
Precautionary demand for money, 350–352
Prescott, Edward, 455*n*., 613, 674
Present discounted value (PDV), 329–332
Price indexes, 41–42, 61–62
   consumer price index, 41, 42, 61
   GNP deflator, 41, 42
   index of "sensitive materials," 42
   Laspeyres, 62
   Paasche, 62
   producer price index, 42
Prices:
   aggregate demand schedule and changes
      in, 226–227
   aggregate supply theory and, 479–480
   contracts and, 244–245
   coordination and, 245
   role of, in the open economy, 734–735
Primary (noninterest) deficits, 597–598
Private sector, inherent stability of, 671
Producer price index (PPI), 42
Production function, 477, 479
   frictionless neoclassical model and,
      493–494
   measuring potential output and, 715–716
   sources of growth and, 700–701
      derivation of, 731–732
      example of, 701–702
Productivity:
   cyclical behavior of, 478–479
   efficiency improvements and, 8*n*.
   growth and (*see* Long-term growth and
      productivity)
   labor, 429, 477
Productivity shock, 680
Profit sharing, 690
Propagation mechanism, 679–680
Public debt (*see* National debt)
Public's demand for money, 371–372
Purchasing power parity (PPP), 754–757
Pyle, David, 606*n*.

q theory of investment, 322–323
Quality changes, 39–40
Quantity constraint, 687
Quantity equation, 360
Quantity theory of money, 147, 240–243
   defined, 240
      Fisher on, 242
      frictionless neoclassical model and,
         463–465

Quantity theory of money (*Cont.*):
   Friedman on, 242
   income velocity of money and, 360–361
   modern, 241, 243
   neutrality on money and, 241–242

Radecki, Lawrence, 364*n*.
Rasche, Robert H., 376*n*.
Rational expectations–equilibrium
     approach, 245–246, 674–683
   aim of, 675
   described, 21–22, 509–510, 674–675
   equilibrium component of, 676–681
      disturbances, 680–681
      empirical testing, 678
      equilibrium real business cycles,
         678–679
      money and business cycles, 676–678
      Phillips curve and, 676–678
      propagation mechanism, 679–680
   excess sensitivity, liquidity constraints
     and, 273–275
   government sector and, 22
   inflation and, 509–510
      money and, 630–631
   permanent income and, 269–270
   policy making and, 681–683
      credibility and, 681–682
      institutional reform and, 682
      monetarism and, 683
   rational expectations component of, 22,
     675–676
   relative wages, wage contracts and, 685–688
   unemployment and, 21
   (*See also* Expectations-augmented
     Phillips curve)
Rationing, 433*n*.
Reagan, Ronald, 8
   supply-side economics and, 683–685
Reaganomics, 684–685
Real assets, 127
Real balances, 128, 223
   demand for, 333–334
   inflation and, 633–635
Real business cycle theory, 247
Real exchange rate, 188–189, 734
Real GNP:
   business cycles and, 10–13
   defined, 6, 34
   GNP deflator and, 15*n*., 41
   growth and, 7–8
   inflation and, 7
   as measure of economic welfare, 40
   nominal GNP and, 34–35, 38
   trend path of, 10

Real interest rates, 303–304
actual, 304
defined, 170, 303
expected, 303
housing investment and, 323–324
1980–1984 policy mix and, 170–171
Real money balances, 128
Recessions:
business cycles and, 10, 11
disinflation and, 499, 500
Okun's law and, 15
output gap and, 11, 13
Recognition lag, 441–442
Recovery, 10, 11, 15
policy tradeoff over, 574–575
Redistribution of wealth, 565–567
Regulation Q, 325
Relative prices, 762–765
exchange rates and, 762–763
trade balance and, 763–765
Rental cost of capital, 302
defined, 296
deriving the, 296–297
interest rate and, 303–304
stock market and, 305–306
taxes and, 304–305
Repercussion effects, 192–195
Replacement ratio and unemployment
benefits, 557
Reporting effects and unemployment
benefits, 557
Reserve-deposit ratio, 372, 382–385
bank's choice of, 384
defined, 372
excess reserves and, 383–385
FDIC and, 385
federal funds rate and, 383
minimum reserve requirements and, 382
Reserves, 183, 372
Residential investment, 317–326
asset price of housing and, 321
as component of GNP, 291–292
disintermediation and, 324–326
interest rates and, 323–324, 567–569
monetary policy and, 323–324
mortgage availability and, 324–325
during recessions, 319
Regulation Q and, 325
theory of, 320–321
q, 322–323
rate of investment and, 321–322
Resources, 7, 10
Retiring debt, 588
Revaluation, 186
Ricardo, David, 278, 604

Ripley, Duncan M., 764n.
Risk, 352–354
Roberts, Craig, 683
Rockoff, Hugh, 529n.
Roley, V. Vance, 355n., 358n.
Roosevelt, Franklin D., 419–421
Rubinfeld, Daniel L., 254n., 437n., 449n.
Rules versus discretion in activist policy,
453–456
Russek, Frank, 605n.
Russell, Robert, 405, 529n.

Sachs, Jeffrey, 571n.
Sacrifice ratio, 528–529
Samuelson, Paul A., 426n.
Sargent, Thomas, 4, 21, 447n., 510,
609n., 648–650, 674
Saunders, Peter, 617n.
Savings:
change in rate of, 723–725
consumption and, 70–73
interest rates and, 277–278
defined, 70
Denison's Law of, 277
dissaving and, 260–262
growth and, 718–719
household, 279, 280
international differences in rates of, 276–277
inventory-theoretic approach to demand
for money and, 342–346
investment and, 55–57, 77–78
tax cuts, the Barro-Ricardo hypothesis
and, 278–279
(*See also* Life-cycle theory of
consumption and saving)
Sawhill, Isabel, 705n., 706n.
Scadding, Jon, 277n.
Schlozman, Kay L., 560n.
Schwartz, Anna, 241, 385n., 419n., 420n.,
421n., 424–425, 632n., 666, 671
Securities and Exchange Commission, 421
Seigniorage, 645
Self-fulfilling prophecy, 281
Separations, 544
Sharpe, M. E., 687n.
Sheehan, R., 394n.
Shelfrin, Steven, 674n.
Shower, Dennis, 688n.
Shultz, George P., 429n.
Simple economy, 53–57
GNP calculation and, 31, 34–35
reintroducing government and foreign
trade, 55–56
saving, investment, the government
budget, and trade, 56–57

Singuefield, Rex A., 641*n*.
Slow-growth recovery, 574
Small menu costs, 689–690
Smolensky, Eugene, 267
Social Security Administration, 421–422
Solow, Robert, 426*n*., 442*n*., 702
Speculative demand for money, 352–354
Spending, 30
  on domestic goods, 189–190
Sprinkel, Beryl, 241
Square-root formula for money demand,
    346–347
Stabilization policy, 415–458
  activist policy (*see* Activism)
  as countercyclical, 20
  defined, 18
  economic disturbances and, 432–434
  expectations and, 446–448
    econometric policy evaluation
        critique, 448
    policy and, 447
  failures of, 18–19
  Great Depression and (*see* Great
        Depression)
  investment tax credit and, 310
  lags in effects of, 439–446
    action, 442–443
    built-in stabilizers and, 443–445
    decision, 442–443
    discrete, 445
    distributed, 445
    fiscal policy, 446
    inside, 441–443
    monetary policy, 446
    negative, 441–442
    outside, 441, 445–446
    recognition, 441–442
  models for (*see* Econometric models for
        policymaking and forecasting)
  monetarists and activists, 20–21
  New Economics and (*see* New
        Economics)
  political business cycles and, 19–20,
        434
  problem of, 18
  uncertainty and, 449–451
    multiplier, 449, 451
    policy making under, 450–451
  unemployment and, 18–20, 415–417
Stagflation, 517–518
Standard of deferred payment, 340
Standard of living, 8–9
Standardized employment surplus, 99
Startz, Richard, 27

State government spending and financing,
    596
Steady state, 514–515
  growth theory and, 717
    (*See also* Long-term growth and
        productivity, growth theory and)
Stein, Herbert, 430, 445*n*., 575*n*.
Stephenson, James B., 564*n*., 566*n*.
Sterilization, 378, 744–745, 767
Sticky wages, 472–477
  cyclical behavior of productivity and,
        478–479
  defined, 472
  long-term relationships in the labor
        market and, 474–475
  Phillips curve and, 472–474
  questions about, 476
  real disturbances and, 763
  staggered wage-setting dates and,
        475–476
Stiglitz, J., 405*n*.
Stock market and the cost of capital,
    305–306
Stock market crash, 417, 419
    (*See also* Great Depression)
Stockman, David, 684*n*.
Stocks, 126–127
Stone, C., 672*n*.
Strong dollar, 1980–1985, 755
Structural budget deficit, 589–590
Structural surplus, 99
Structural unemployment, 540
  costs of, 560–561
    (*See also* Natural rate of unemployment)
Substitution effect, 707
Summers, Lawrence H., 267, 306*n*.,
    310*n*., 543*n*., 545*n*., 546*n*., 547*n*.,
    552*n*., 557*n*., 568*n*., 641*n*., 693*n*.
Supply shocks, 23, 461, 485–491
  accommodation of, 489–490
  adverse, 487–489
  defined, 486
  effects of a favorable oil shock, 490–
        491
  government spending, 681
  incorporating materials prices in the
        analysis, 486–487
  indexation and, 570
  intertemporal substitution of leisure
        and, 679–680
  money, business cycles and, 676–678
  productivity, 680
Supply-side economics, 4, 22, 683–685
  Laffer curve and, 600–601

Supply-side economics (*Cont.*):
    output growth and (*see* Long-term
        growth and productivity, supply-
        side economics and)
    radical fringe of, 684
    tax rates, deficits and, 598

Targeted programs, 555
Tariffs, 740
Tatom, John, 605*n*.
Taussig, Michael, 267
Tax incentive plans (TIP), 530–531
Taxes:
    as automatic stabilizers, 88
    Barro-Ricardo equivalence proposition
        and, 278–279, 604–605
    bracket creep and, 591–592
    "cruelest," 646*n*.
    disposable income and, 83–85
    effects of a change in, 89–91
        on the budget surplus, 95–98
    fiscal drag and, 591
    government revenue and, 598–601
    government spending and, 601
    hyperinflation and, 652
    indexation of tax brackets, 592
    indirect, 32
    inflation tax, 645–648
        revenue, 648
    investment tax credit, 309–311
    Laffer curve and, 600–601
    multiplier and, 86
    New Economics and, 430–431
    1984 tax cut, 165–166
    rental cost of capital and, 304–305
    supply-side economics and, 598,
        683–685
    tax wedges, 613
    Treasury department's tax and loan
        account and, 380, 381
Taylor, John B., 407*n*., 475*n*., 686*n*.
Technical progress, 701–704, 726
Temin, Peter, 423*n*.
Tobin, James, 4, 5, 20, 40, 125*n*., 343*n*.,
    346, 353, 426*n*., 552*n*., 619*n*.,
    641*n*.
Topel, Robert H., 558*n*.
Total factor productivity, 701
Total incomes system of accounts (TISA),
    39, 50
Trade in goods (*see* Foreign trade)
Trade balance, 181
    (*See also* Balance of payments)
Trade surplus, 56

Transactions demand for money, 341–350
    average cash balance and, 344
    broker's fee and, 343
    defined, 341–342
    demand for real balances, 348
    elasticities, 347–348
    integer constraints, 348–349
    inventory-theoretic approach, 343–346
    payment period, 349
    properties of money demand, 346–347
    square-root formula for, 346–347
    tradeoff involving, 342–343
Transactions velocity, 358*n*.
Transfer payment (transfers), 50
    defined, 45, 46
    effects of increased, 88–89
    as fraction of GNP, 594–595
Transitory budget deficits, 603–604
Transmission mechanism, 144–145
Treasury bills, 587–588
    interest rates on, 111–112, 587*n*.,
        640–641
Treasury Department, U.S.:
    debit-financed deficits and, 583–584
    the Fed and, 380
        financing federal deficits, 381,
            586–587
    money-financed deficits and, 584–586
    national debt and, 587–588
    tax and loan accounts, 380, 381
Trend level of output, 10–11
    deviations from, 11
    (*See also* Potential output)
Trersky, Amos, 675*n*.
Trough, cyclical, 10
Tufte, Edward R., 434*n*., 575*n*.
Turnover in the labor market, 543
Two-tier wage system, 476

Ultimate targets, 406–408
Uncertainty and economic policy, 449–451
    multiplier, 449, 451
    policy making under, 450–451
Underground economy, 36
Unemployment, 539–561
    accessions and, 543–544
    age, race, and sex and, 539–542,
        547–548
    budget deficits and, 590
    characteristics of U.S., 540–542
    classical or Keynesian, 691–693
    costs of, 16, 558–561
        cyclical unemployment, 559

Unemployment, costs of (*Cont.*):
    Okun's law and, 559–561
    other, and benefits, 559–560
    structural unemployment,
        560–561
  cyclical, 540, 559
  defined, 539
  distribution of, 547–549
  duration of, 544–546, 549–550
  European, 690–693
  flows in and out of, 542–544
  frequency of, 550–551
  frictional, 465
  full employment rate of (*see* Natural
    rate of unemployment)
  growth and, 8–9, 13–15
  imperfect information and, 246–247
  inflation and (*see* Inflation and
    unemployment; Inflation-
    unemployment tradeoff)
  involuntary quits, 543
  layoff and, 542
  natural rate of (*see* Natural rate of
    unemployment)
  nonemployment and, 547
  Okun's law and, 15, 559–561, 573–574,
    664n.
  Phillips curve and (*see* Phillips curve)
  potential output and, 11–12
  rate of, 8
    measured, 557
    time unemployed and, 546–547
  rational expectations–equilibrium
    approach and, 21
  reasons for, 545–546
  separations and, 544
  as social and political issue, 9
  spells of, 544–546
    completed, 548n.
  stabilization policy and, 18–20, 415–417
  structural, 540, 560–561
  turnover and, 543
Unemployment benefits, 556–558
  employment stability and, 557–558
  example of, 556
  experience rating and, 558n.
  replacement ratio and, 557
  reporting effects and, 557
Unemployment pool, 542–544
Unintended inventory accumulation,
  67–68
  anticipated versus, 293
Unit of account, 340

Unit labor cost, 479–480
User cost of capital (*see* Rental cost of
  capital)

Value added, 32
Van der Gaag, Jacques, 267
Vault cash, 372
Verba, Sidney, 560n.
Volker, Paul, 644–645

Wachter, Michael, 552
Wage and price controls, 527–530
Wage-price spiral, 762
Wages:
  aggregate supply curve and, 480–481
  behavior of money wages, 429
  contracts and, 244–245
  coordination and, 245
  efficiency theory, 245, 553, 688–689
  expected inflation and, 502–503
  in the frictionless neoclassical model of
    the labor market, 462–465
  imperfect information and, 245–246
  indexation of (*see* Indexation of wages)
  Phillips curve and, 466–469
  prices, and output, 465–472
  relative, 685–688
  sticky (*see* Sticky wages)
  two-tiered, 476
  wage contracts, 685–688
Wakefield, J. C., 100n., 602n.
Wallace, Neil, 21, 447n., 609n., 648–650,
  674
Walsh, Carl, 247n., 679n.
Wealth:
  bonds as, 604–605
  in the consumption function, 280–281
  in the life-cycle theory of consumption
    and saving, 263–264
  portfolios and, 352–353
  redistribution of, 565–567
Wealth budget constraint, 127–128
  demand and, 128–129
Weitzman, Martin, 690
Wenniger, John, 364n.
Whalen, Edward H., 350n.
Willett, Thomas, 577n., 684n.
Wise, David A., 547n.

Yeager, Leland, 651n.
Yellen, Janet, 688n., 689n.

THE U.S. BUDGET DEFICIT AND PUBLIC DEBT

Employment deficit

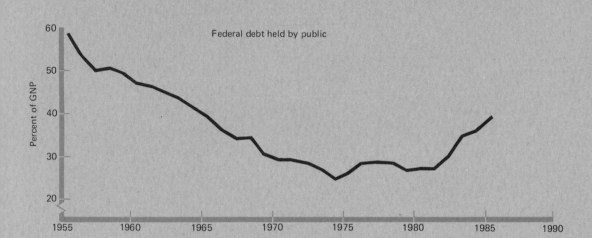

Federal debt held by public

THE U.S. BUDGET AND DEBT
(Percent of GNP)

Year	Budget surplus	H.E. budget surplus	Debt ratio	Year	Budget surplus	H.E. budget surplus	Debt ratio
1955	1.1	1.3	55.8	1971	−2.0	−1.3	28.8
1956	1.4	1.4	51.9	1972	−1.4	−1.3	28.1
1957	0.5	1.6	48.6	1973	−0.4	−1.4	26.7
1958	−2.3	1.5	49.6	1974	−0.8	−0.5	24.4
1959	−0.2	−0.8	47.4	1975	−4.3	−1.1	26.1
1960	0.6	1.7	46.2	1976	−3.0	−1.9	28.3
1961	−0.7	1.8	44.6	1977	−2.3	−1.1	28.5
1962	−0.7	0.4	44.6	1978	−1.3	−1.7	28.1
1963	0.0	0.7	43.2	1979	−0.6	−0.9	26.3
1964	−0.5	0.0	40.9	1980	−2.2	−1.2	26.8
1965	0.1	0.3	38.8	1981	−2.1	−0.5	26.6
1966	−0.2	−0.8	35.7	1982	−4.6	−0.8	29.6
1967	−1.6	−1.4	33.7	1983	−5.3	−2.5	34.4
1968	−0.7	−3.2	34.1	1984	−4.6	−3.2	35.5
1969	0.9	−0.4	30.1	1985	−5.0	−4.1	38.4
1970	−1.2	−0.2	28.8				

Note: The actual and high-employment budget surplus and the debt are expressed as a percent of GNP. From 1973 on, the high-employment budget uses the 6 percent unemployment benchmark. The debt-GNP ratio refers to federal government debt in the hands of the public.